Accounting Reference Desktop

Update Service

BECOME A SUBSCRIBER!

Did you purchase this product from a bookstore?

If you did, it's important for you to become a subscriber. John Wiley & Sons, Inc. may publish, on a periodic basis, supplements and new editions to reflect the latest changes in the subject matter that you *need to know* in order to stay competitive in this ever-changing industry. By contacting the John Wiley & Sons office nearest you, you'll receive any current update at no additional charge. In addition, you'll receive future updates and revised or related volumes on a 30-day examination review.

If you purchased this product directly from John Wiley & Sons, Inc., we have already recorded your subscription for this update service.

To become a subscriber, please call **1-800-225-5945** or send your name, company name (if applicable), address, and the title of the product to:

mailing address: **Supplement Department**
                               John Wiley & Sons, Inc.
                               One Wiley Drive
                               Somerset, NJ 08875

e-mail: **subscriber@wiley.com**
fax: **1-732-302-2300**
on-line: **www.wiley.com**

For customers outside the United States, please contact the John Wiley & Sons office nearest you:

Professional & Reference Division
John Wiley & Sons Canada, Ltd.
22 Worcester Road
Rexdale, Ontario M9W 1L1
CANADA
(416) 675-3580
Phone: 1-800-567-4797
Fax: 1-800-565-6802
canada@jwiley.com

John Wiley & Sons, Ltd.
Baffins Lane
Chichester
West Sussex, PO19 1UD
ENGLAND
Phone: (44) 1243 779777
Fax: (44) 1243 770638
cs-books@wiley.co.uk

Jacaranda Wiley Ltd.
PRT Division
P.O. Box 174
North Ryde, NSW 2113
AUSTRALIA
Phone: (02) 805-1100
Fax: (02) 805-1597
headoffice@jacwiley.com.au

John Wiley & Sons (SEA) Pte. Ltd.
37 Jalan Pemimpin
Block B #05-04
United Industrial Building
SINGAPORE 2057
Phone: (65) 258-1157
Fax: (65) 463-4604
csd_ord@wiley.com.sg

Accounting Reference Desktop

Steven M. Bragg

John Wiley & Sons, Inc.

ISBN: 0-471-39183-2

Printed in the United States of America.

10 9 8 7 6 5 4 3 2 1

To the many adventures still to come with Melissa—
and not all involving children

ABOUT THE AUTHOR

Steven Bragg, CPA, CMA, CIA, CPM, CPIM, has been the chief financial officer or controller of four companies, as well as a consulting manager at Ernst & Young. He received a master's degree in finance from Bentley College, an MBA from Babson College, and a Bachelor's degree in Economics from the University of Maine. Mr. Bragg resides in Englewood, Colorado. He has also written the following books:

Accounting and Finance for Your Small Business (*John Wiley & Sons*)

Accounting Best Practices (*John Wiley & Sons*)

Advanced Accounting Systems

Controllership (*John Wiley & Sons*)

Cost Accounting (*John Wiley & Sons*)

Financial Analysis (*John Wiley & Sons*)

Just-in-Time Accounting (*John Wiley & Sons*)

Managing Explosive Corporate Growth (*John Wiley & Sons*)

Outsourcing (*John Wiley & Sons*)

Sales and Operations for Your Small Business (*John Wiley & Sons*)

The Controller's Function (*John Wiley & Sons*)

ACKNOWLEDGMENTS

A special note of thanks to my managing editor, John DeRemigis, who requests new books faster than I can write them.

PREFACE

The *Accounting Reference Manual* is designed to give the accountant the answers to all of the most important issues that arise during the typical business day. It provides a comprehensive overview of all aspects of the accounting function, including accounting rules and regulations, transactions, control points, and internal and external reports. It also itemizes a wide range of accounting management issues, such as best practices, budgeting, closing the books, control systems, cost accounting, financial analysis, management information systems, accounting for mergers and acquisitions, tax laws, and record keeping. In addition, it covers a number of financial management issues, such as the extension and management of customer credit, financing, cash management, and risk management. The appendices are also rich in detail, describing a sample chart of accounts, itemizing the most common journal entries, displaying interest rate tables, listing the most commonly used business ratios, and finishing with a dictionary of accounting terms. The *Accounting Reference Manual* is a true one-stop source of information for the accountant.

The answers to many of the everyday questions posed to the accountant can be answered with the information provided in this book. One can find within these pages the answers to such questions as:

- What FASB Standards should I be aware of?
- What are the key regulations promulgated by the SEC that apply to my business?
- How are extraordinary income items listed in the income statement?
- How is comprehensive income presented?
- How is the statement of cash flows formatted?
- What types of footnotes should be added to the financial statements?
- How do I convert foreign currency transactions for financial reporting purposes?
- How do I set up a perpetual inventory tracking system?
- How do I account for backflushing transactions?
- What types of inventory valuation methods are available?
- What are the rules related to the recognition of revenue?
- How do I account for stock buybacks, dividends, and convertible securities?
- What best practices are most useful to my business?

- How do I create a budget?

- What techniques can I use to close the books as fast as possible?

- What are the strengths and weaknesses of the various costing systems?

- How do I evaluate a capital project?

- What is my company's cost of capital?

- How do I set up a cash tracking, reporting, and forecasting system?

- What are the key risk management issues to be aware of, and how do I mitigate them?

- What are the current tax laws that address stock options?

- How do I account for a business combination under the purchase method?

- What ratios should I use to monitor corporate cash flows?

- What chart of accounts structure should I use to set up a general ledger?

These and hundreds of other questions are answered in the *Accounting Reference Desktop*. If you have any comments about this book, or would like to see additional chapters added in future editions, please contact the author at *brasto@aol.com*. Thank you!

Steven M. Bragg
Englewood, Colorado
October 2001

CONTENTS

Appendices

Index

Accounting Reference Desktop

Part One

OVERVIEW OF ACCOUNTING AND ITS ROLE IN THE ORGANIZATION

CHAPTER 1

Introduction

The intention of this book is to give the accountant the answers to the largest possible number of accounting issues that are likely to arise. Thus, given the wide-ranging scope of this work, the reader should know about its overall structure in order to locate information more easily.

The *Accounting Reference Desktop* is divided into eight parts, each of which deals with a different aspect of the accounting function. The first part covers the role of accounting within the modern corporation. Chapter 2, The Role of Accounting, describes the primary tasks for which the accountant is responsible, as well as ethical concerns, and lists the job descriptions of the major positions to be found within the accounting department. Chapter 3, The Corporate Structure, describes the organizational layout of the typical corporation, how the transactional systems maintained by the accounting department interact with these other functions, and how the organizational structure can alter the types of accounting systems used.

The second part deals with accounting rules and regulations. Chapter 4, Standard Setting Organizations, describes the origins and responsibilities of the various rule-setting bodies that have created Generally Accepted Accounting Principles (GAAP), not only for United States business entities, but also for government and international organizations. Chapter 5, Accounting Standards, lists all of the various accounting pronouncements, such as FASB Interpretations, FASB Statements, and FASB Technical Bulletins, in summary form; the reader can peruse this list of original source documents in order to determine what additional research may be needed to delve into a particular GAAP issue. Chapter 6, The Securities and Exchange Commission, gives an overview of the Securities and Exchange Commission (SEC), the EDGAR on-line reporting system, and the Acts and SEC regulations that govern the reporting requirements of publicly held corporations.

The third part covers the general format and rules governing the information contained within accounting reports. Chapter 7, The Balance Sheet and Statement of Stockholders' Equity, describes the format of the balance sheet and statement of retained earnings, as well as the definitions of the various categories of assets, liabilities, and equity items that are listed in these reports. Chapter 8, The Income Statement, describes the format of the income statement, as well as the rules governing the presentation of information about discontinued operations, earnings per share, gains and losses, accounting changes, discontinued operations, extraordinary items, other comprehensive income, and prior period adjustments. Chapter 9, The Statement of Cash Flows, describes the format of the statement of cash flows, as well as exemptions from its use and how to handle foreign currency translations when constructing it. Chapter 10, Footnotes, describes a broad range of disclosures that an accountant may be required to attach to the financial statements in the form of footnotes. Chapter 11, Internal Management Reports, departs from the previous chapters in this part, in that it describes reports that are entirely "free form," designed entirely for internal use and not prescribed in format by any accounting pronouncement. These include status, margin, cash, capacity, sales and expense, and payroll reports. The part concludes with Chapter 12, Foreign Currency Translation, which covers the proper treatment of foreign currency translation, including the use of the current rate translation method and the remeasurement method, as well as the proper accounting for foreign exchange sale transactions and the recognition of translation adjustments.

The fourth part departs from the reporting format of the financial statement and delves into the accounting rules and transactions for each of the asset, liability, equity, and revenue categories. Chapter 13, Cash and Investments, defines cash and investments, describes the different types of marketable securities, derivatives, and long-term investments, and how each one is accounted for. Chapter 14, Inventory, describes the types of inventory, how to install an inventory tracking system, the physical inventory counting procedure, and the use of the LIFO, FIFO, average, retail, dollar-value LIFO, and gross margin methods for valuing inventory. The chapter also describes the lower of cost or market rule and the process to follow when allocating overhead costs to inventory. Chapter 15, Accounts Receivable, describes the accounts receivable transaction flow, as well as how to account for factored accounts receivable, sales returns, early payment discounts, long-term accounts receivable, and bad debts. Chapter 16, Fixed Assets, describes the use of a capitalization limit when accounting for newly acquired fixed assets, as well as the proper accounting for newly acquired assets, improvements to existing assets, the disposition of assets, construction in progress, and leasehold improvements. It also covers the various types of depreciation that may be used to account for the gradual reduction in value of fixed assets.

Chapter 17, Current Liabilities, describes the accounts payable transaction flow, and how to account for the period-end cut-off of accounts payable transactions. It also covers the proper accounting for advance payments from customers, accrued expenses, unclaimed wages, interest payable, dividends, termination benefits, estimated product returns, and contingent liabilities. Chapter 18, Debt, describes basic bond transactions and accounting for a bond discount or premium, as well as for non-interest bearing notes payable. It also covers non-cash debt payments, early debt retirement, callable debt, defaulted debt, warrants, sinking funds, bonds converted to equity, and short-term debt that is being refinanced. Chapter 19, Equity, covers the transactions related to common stock, as well as stock options, stock appreciation rights, stock warrants, dividends, stock subscriptions, stock splits, stock retirement, and employee stock ownership plans. Chapter 20, Revenue, covers the multitude of revenue recognition rules, including variations under the accrual method, cash method, installment sales method, completed contract method, percentage of completion method, proportional performance method, production method, and deposit method. It also discusses the special rules related to bill and hold transactions, brokered transactions, appreciation, and initiation fees. Chapter 21, Research and Development, describes the proper accounting for in-house R&D costs, as well as for acquired R&D costs, R&D costs contracted to another party, and the special case of R&D costs in the software industry.

The fifth part of the book covers the crucial area of accounting management. This is the core function for many accountants, who can provide value to the organization through the use of better control systems, financial analysis of key investments, and higher levels of departmental efficiency. Chapter 22, Best Practices, covers several dozen of the most common best practices that can improve a company's performance, including the areas of accounts payable, collections, commissions, filing, finance, financial statements, the general ledger, invoicing, inventory, management, and payroll. For a thorough treatment of this topic, the reader can also consult the author's *Accounting Best Practices,* 2nd Edition (John Wiley & Sons, 2001). Chapter 23, Budgeting, explains the system of interlocking departmental budgets, and presents a sample budget. It also covers a number of budgeting best practices and control systems that assist the accountant in creating a budget in the most efficient manner possible. Chapter 24, Closing the Books, focuses on the various steps required to achieve a fast close, and also describes the steps needed to achieve an instantaneous close. Chapter 25, Control Systems, presents a list of the most essential control points that the accountant should be concerned with. It also discusses the times when it may be appropriate to eliminate controls for efficiency reasons, and covers the various types of fraud that some of these controls are designed to detect and mitigate. Chapter 26, Cost Accounting, focuses on the many types of advanced data collection systems that can be used to compile data for use by cost accounting systems. It also describes the major costing systems that can be used to interpret this data, such as job costing, process costing, standard costing, direct costing, and activity-based costing. It also covers the concepts of throughput accounting, target costing, by-product costing, and cost variances. These topics are covered in more detail in the author's *Cost Accounting* (John Wiley & Sons, 2001). Chapter 27, Financial Analysis, describes how to calculate a company's cost of capital, analyze a capital purchasing decision, discount future cash flows, and conduct both breakeven and risk analyses. These topics and more are described in additional detail in the author's *Financial Analysis* (John Wiley & Sons, 2000). Chapter 28, Management Information Systems, covers information system strategy, how to evaluate and select packaged accounting software, and how to install and test it. The chapter also addresses information system security, data collection and storage tools, electronic data interchange, outsourcing all or portions of the function, and the integration of the accounting system with other computer systems located elsewhere in a company. Finally, Chapter 29, Records Management, deals with the cost of various types of record keeping systems, the policies and procedures required for proper record storage, and the types of tax records that must be kept on hand.

The sixth part of the book deals with financial management, which includes customer credit, cash management, long-term financing, and risk management—all topics that are of particular interest to accountants in smaller organizations that do not have separate finance departments. Chapter 30, Customer Credit, describes the types of selling terms that can be extended, how to conduct a credit investigation, and various techniques for collecting overdue accounts receivable. Chapter 31, Financing, describes how to minimize a company's financing needs through proper management, how to deal with banks, and the pros and cons of delaying payments to suppliers. It also addresses the use of factoring and field warehouse financing, floor planning, inventory reduction, leasing, lines of credit, asset-based loans, bonds, bridge loans, preferred stock, sale and leaseback arrangements, and various types of debt in order to deal with a company's financing requirements. Chapter 32, Cash Management, describes the use of a cash forecasting model and its automation, as well as how to more tightly control cash outflows and how to invest short-term funds. Chapter 33, Risk Management, describes the risk management policies and procedures that can be used to determine and mitigate risks, as well as the types of insurance that are available to reduce any remaining risks. It also describes the claims administration process, claims documentation, and the format of the annual risk management report.

The seventh part of the book deals with two major topics that do not fit easily into any of the preceding categories—mergers and acquisitions, and taxation. In Chapter 34, Mergers and Acquisitions, we cover the accounting required to record a business combination under both the purchase and pooling methods of accounting. The chapter also describes how to record investments in a subsidiary by using the cost method, equity method, or consolidation method. It also delves into inter-company transactions in relation to consolidated financial reporting, contingent payments for a business combination, push-down accounting, leveraged buyouts, spin-off transactions, and the proper treatment of goodwill. Chapter 35, Taxation, covers nearly 50 taxation issues, including the Alternative Minimum Tax, partnership taxation, deferred compensation, stock options, and transfer pricing.

The final part of the *Accounting Reference Desktop* is the appendices, which include additional reference information that the accountant is likely to require on a regular basis. Appendix A describes the different types of account code structures that can be used in a chart of accounts, and gives sample charts of accounts for each structure. Appendix B contains a list of the most common journal entries that an accountant is likely to deal with. Appendix C contains interest rate tables, as well as the formulas used to derive them. These tables cover simple interest, compound interest, the present value of an annuity, and the future amount of an annuity. Appendix D contains more than 40 ratios that can be used to determine a company's financial condition. Finally, Appendix E contains a dictionary of the many accounting terms that are addressed in this book.

In short, the *Accounting Reference Desktop* is a complete source of information for the practicing accountant. By using the table of contents, this introduction, and the index to locate information, one can find the answers to most everyday accounting questions in this book.

CHAPTER 2

The Role of Accounting

2-1 TASKS OF THE ACCOUNTING FUNCTION[1]

The accounting function has had sole responsibility for processing the bulk of a company's transactions for many years. Chief among these transactions has been the processing of customer billings and supplier invoices. Though these two areas comprise the bulk of the transactions, there has also been a long history of delegating asset tracking to the accounting function. This involves all transactions related to the movement of cash, inventory, and fixed assets. Finally, the accounting staff has been responsible for tracking debt, which can involve a continuous tracking of debt levels by debt instrument, as well as the payments made to reduce them. These have been the transaction-based activities of the accounting staff.

A multitude of changes in the business environment have altered the role of the accounting function. One change has been the appearance of the computer services function. In a larger company, this function is managed within its own department and does not fall under the management of the accounting department. However, it is common for the computer services group to fall under the management umbrella of the controller in a smaller company. Likewise, the internal auditing function is sometimes managed by the controller (though this is more commonly managed by the audit committee of the Board of Directors).

Besides adding new functional areas, the accounting staff has other new responsibilities that have arisen due to the increased level of worldwide competition. With worldwide barriers to competition crumbling, every company feels the pinch of lower competitive prices, and now asks its accounting staff to provide analyses of such items as margin reviews on existing or projected product lines, geographic sales regions, or indi-

---

[1] The text in the first three sections is adapted with permission from Willson, Roehl-Anderson, and Bragg, *Controllership,* 6th Edition (John Wiley & Sons, 2000), pp. 3–7.

vidual projects. In addition, the accounting staff may be asked to serve on new product design teams, so that they can determine the projected cost of new products, especially in relation to target costs. Further, the accounting staff must continuously review and report on non-product costs, which can range from advertising to utilities. This level of cost review and reporting calls for a different kind of accounting staff than the traditional one that did nothing but process large volumes of transactions. It now requires highly trained cost accountants and financial analysts with college degrees and professional certifications to conduct the work.

In addition, technology has drastically altered the skill levels required of the accounting staff. For example, employees must know how to implement and operate accounting software, electronic data interchange systems, paperless systems using digitized documents, and Internet transactions. Because most of these elements of technology directly impact the transaction processing staff, it is necessary to raise the level of knowledge of these people. Consequently, the education level of even the lowest accounting positions must be improved to deal with changing circumstances.

The world of business has become more international. Many companies are doing an increasing volume of business with companies and subsidiaries based in other countries. This greatly increases the complexity of accounting, for the accounting staff must now determine currency gains and losses, as well as process customs-related paperwork for individual transactions. There may even be bartering transactions with organizations that do not have ready access to currency. In addition, if there is no separate finance function, the accounting staff may be called upon to handle letters of credit and hedging transactions that are designed to reduce the level of risk that goes with foreign dealings. All of these issues call for a level of skill that was not required in the days of simple transaction processing.

In the face of more intense competition, many companies are also merging or acquiring subsidiaries. This adds a great deal of complexity to the accounting staff's work, for it must now coordinate a multitude of additional tasks in other locations. This includes setting up standard procedures for the processing of receipts, shipments, and cash. Also, closing the financial books at the end of each reporting period becomes much more complex, as the accounting staff must now coordinate the assembly and consolidation of information from multiple subsidiaries. Even if a company decides to consolidate all of its accounting functions into one central processing location to avoid all this trouble, it still requires the management expertise to bring together the disparate accounting systems into a smoothly operating facility.

The tasks of the accounting function are itemized below. The tasks that belong elsewhere, but which are commonly given to the accounting staff in a small company, are noted under a separate heading.

- *Traditional accounting tasks*
    - Accounts payable transaction processing
    - Accounts receivable transaction processing
    - Asset transaction processing
    - Debt transaction processing
- *New accounting tasks*
    - Bartering transactions
    - Coordination and consolidation of accounting at subsidiaries

- Currency translations
- Margin analysis
- Non-product cost analysis
- Selection, implementation, and operation of accounting software and related systems
- Target costing
- *New tasks assigned to the accounting function in smaller companies*
    - Computer services systems installation and maintenance
    - Hedging and letter of credit transactions
    - Internal auditing programs

Given today's highly volatile business environment, the only safe statement to make about the new activities presented in this section is that they will only become more complex over time, requiring even greater skill by the accounting staff to be accomplished in an efficient and effective manner.

2-2 ROLE OF THE ACCOUNTING FUNCTION

Having noted the expanded number of tasks now undertaken by the modern accounting function, it is important to also note how the role of the accounting staff has changed in relation to the rest of the company.

When the number of accounting tasks was more closely defined around transaction processing, it was common for the accounting staff to be housed in an out-of-the-way corner of a business, where it could work without being impeded by other functions. Now, with a much greater number of tasks, the accounting staff finds itself involved in most major decisions. For example, the cost accountant is expected to serve on product design teams and to let other team members know if new designs will have costs that will meet targeted cost goals. An accounting analyst may be asked by the sales manager to evaluate the profitability of a lease deal being extended to a customer. The controller is frequently asked to sit in on executive committee meetings to give opinions on the cash flow issues related to acquisitions or purchases, or to discuss the need for shared services or the outsourcing of some functions. The accounts receivable clerk may work closely with the sales staff to collect overdue invoices from customers. For these reasons and others, the accounting function now finds itself performing a variety of tasks that make it an integral part of the organization.

A particularly important area in which the accounting function has changed is related to processes. When another area of the company changes its operations, the accounting staff must devise alterations to the existing systems for processing transactions that will accommodate those changes. For example, if the manufacturing function switches to just-in-time production or computer-integrated manufacturing, this has a profound impact on the way in which the accounting staff pays its bills, invoices customers, monitors job costs, and creates internal reports. Also, if the materials management staff decides to use material requirements planning or integrated distribution management, these new systems will issue information that is of great use to the accounting staff; it should connect its systems to those of the materials management staff to access that information. To alter its processes, the accounting staff must first be aware of these changes, requiring it to engage in more interaction with other parts of the company to find out what is going on.

The most historically important role that the accounting staff must change is that of being a brake on other activities. Because most accountants are trained in implementing controls to ensure that assets are not lost, the accounting staff tends to shoot down changes proposed by other departments, because the changes will interfere with the controls. The accounting personnel must understand that changes put forward by other functions are not intended to disrupt controls, but rather to improve the company's position in the marketplace or to increase its efficiency. This means that some controls must be modified, replaced, or eliminated. It is very helpful for the accounting personnel to have an open mind about altering systems, even when the new systems interfere with the accounting staff's system of controls.

In today's increasingly competitive environment, it is very important for companies to develop strong relationships with their key suppliers and customers. These business partners will demand extra services, some of which must be fulfilled by the accounting staff. These changes may include using electronic data interchange transactions, providing special billing formats to customers, or paying suppliers by electronic transfer. If these steps are needed to retain key business partners, then the accounting staff must be willing to do its share of the work. Too frequently, the accounting staff resists these sorts of changes, on the grounds that all transactions must be performed in exactly the same manner. The accounting department must realize that altering its way of doing business is sometimes necessary to support ongoing business relationships.

Altering the focus of the accounting staff from an introverted group that processes paper to one that works with other parts of a company and is willing to alter its systems to accommodate the needs of other departments is required in today's business environment. This is in great contrast to the accounting department of the past, which had a minimal role in other company activities, and which was its conservative anchor.

2-3 ETHICS

With the globalization of business, competition has become more intense. It is possible that the ethical foundations to which a company adheres have deteriorated in the face of this pressure. There have been innumerable examples in the press of falsified earnings reports, bribery, kickbacks, and employee thefts. There are vastly more instances of ethical failings that many would consider to be more minimal, such as employee use of company property for personal use, "smoothing" of financial results to keep them in line with investor expectations, or excessively robust sales or earnings forecasts. The accounting staff in general plays a large role in a company's ethical orientation, for they control or have some influence over the primary issues that are most subject to ethical problems—reported earnings, cash usage, and control over assets. This section discusses how the accounting function can modify a company's behavior—for good or bad.

The accounting function can have a serious negative impact on a company's ethical standards through nothing more than indifference. For example, if the accounting staff continually acquiesces to management demands to slightly modify the financial statements, this may eventually lead to larger and larger alterations. Once the accountants have set a standard for allowing changes to reported earnings, how can the controller define where to draw the line? Another example is when the accounting staff does not enforce control over assets; if it conducts a fixed asset audit and finds that a television has been appropriated by an employee for several months, it can indirectly encourage continuing behavior of this kind simply by taking no action. Other employees will see that there is no penalty for removing assets and then will do the same thing. Yet another example is when the accounting staff does not closely review employee expense reports for inappropriate expenditures. Once again, if employees see that the expense report rules are not being enforced, they will gradually include more expenses in their reports that are not legitimate business expenses. Thus, the accounting staff can have a significant negative influence over a company's ethical standards simply by not enforcing the rules.

The previous argument can be turned around for an active accounting department. If the accounting staff rigidly enforces company standards and acquires a reputation for no deviations from them, the rest of the corporation will be dragged into line. It is especially important that the controller adhere closely to the highest standards, for the rest of the accounting staff will follow the controller's lead. Conversely, if the controller does not maintain a high ethical standard, the accounting staff will have no ethical leader, and will lapse into apathy over the issue. Accordingly, the controller can be considered a company's chief ethics officer, given the position's strong influence over ethical behavior.

The accounting staff can play a particularly strong ethics role in the area of systems. If a company does not have a sufficiently well-defined set of computer systems, as well as proper integration with policies and procedures, then employees will make up their own systems to fill in any gaps. These impromptu systems may be easily overridden by anyone desiring to commit fraud, or may be so poorly integrated with formal systems that there are gaping holes in the control structure that would allow someone to remove company assets with little trouble. The accounting staff can shut down these opportunities for ethical problems by paying constant attention to the web of formal systems, as well as how they must be altered to compensate for changes in the way the company does business.

It is not sufficient to state that the accounting staff must uphold high ethical standards if they are not defined. To avoid this problem, there must be a clearly laid out code of ethics. Some illustrative topics to include in the code of ethics are:

- Bidding, negotiating, and performing under government contracts.
- Compliance with antitrust laws.
- Compliance with securities laws and regulations.
- Conflicts of interest.
- Cost consciousness.
- Employee discrimination on any grounds.
- Gifts and monetary payments.
- International boycotts.
- Leave for military or other federal service.
- Meals and entertainment expense submissions.
- Political contributions.

- Preservation of assets.

- Restrictive trade practices.

- Standards of conduct.

- Use of company assets.

In summary, the accounting staff has a large role in enforcing ethical standards throughout a company, since it has such a strong influence over several key areas that require ethical judgments, such as the quality of reported earnings, control over assets, and the use of cash. Accordingly, it is very much in the controller's interest to have a code of ethics that the accounting staff can adhere to in enforcing the appropriate ethical standards.

2-4 ACCOUNTING JOB DESCRIPTIONS[2]

As an accounting department expands, the number of tasks assigned to each position will become more specialized. A larger organization may have specialists in fixed asset accounting, expense reports, or SEC reporting—and these people do nothing else. This section does not attempt to describe the job descriptions of these smaller "niche" positions, but instead provides an overview of the tasks and reporting relationships that one is likely to encounter in an accounting department of moderate size. These descriptions are noted in Exhibits 2-1 through 2-7. These exhibits assume that there is a separate treasurer role that will take cash management functions away from the controller, as well as a CFO who handles the risk management, pension administration, investor relations, and debt/equity planning tasks. Also, the assistant controller job description in Exhibit 2-2 is split into three parts, reflecting the common separation of duties within the department, with one assistant controller being in charge of basic transactions, another of analysis tasks, and a third of financial reporting. These functions may be combined in smaller organizations if there are fewer assistant controllers.

Exhibit 2-1   Controller Job Description

Reports to:	*Chief Financial Officer*
Responsibilities:	Approve the accounting department budget.
	Approve the creation of new report formats and reporting systems.
	Assist in the annual audit as required.
	Attend executive committee meetings as required.
	Authorize accounting capital purchases.
	Discuss financial results with senior management.
	Implement auditor recommendations.
	Manage outsourced functions.
	Manage the accounting staff.
	Provide advice to management regarding the impact of acquisitions.

[2] Some of the line items within the following job descriptions are taken from page 18 of *Controllership,* 6th Edition (John Wiley & Sons, 2000) with permission.

Exhibit 2-2 Assistant Controller Job Description

Reports to:	Controller
Responsibilities: *(Analysis)*	Compile the cash forecast.
	Initiate best practices improvements.
	Issue internal management reports as needed.
	Manage the annual budgeting process.
	Oversee outsourced functions.
	Provide financial analyses as needed.
	Review systems for control weaknesses.
	Supervise cost accounting staff.
	Supervise financial analysis staff.
	Supervise systems analysis staff.
Responsibilities: *(Financial Reporting)*	Initiate best practices improvements.
	Issue timely financial statements.
	Oversee outsourced functions.
	Review capital purchase proposals.
	Supervise general ledger staff.
	Supervise public reporting staff.
	Supervise tax reporting staff.
Responsibilities: *(Transactions)*	Initiate best practices improvements.
	Maintain an orderly accounting filing system.
	Oversee outsourced functions.
	Supervise accounts payable staff.
	Supervise accounts receivable staff.
	Supervise payroll staff.

Exhibit 2-3 Cost Accountant Job Description

Reports to:	Assistant Controller (Analysis)
Systems tasks:	Audit costing systems.
	Review adequacy of activity-based costing system.
	Review adequacy of data collection systems.
	Review system costs and benefits.
Analysis & reporting tasks:	Assist in development of the budget.
	Report on ABC overhead allocations.
	Report on breakeven points by product and division.
	Report on capital budgeting requests.
	Report on margins by product and division.
	Report on periodic variance analyses.
	Report on product target costing.
	Report on special topics as assigned.
Pricing tasks:	Work with marketing staff to update product pricing.

Reprinted with permission from Bragg *Cost Accounting* (John Wiley & Sons, 2000), p. 24.

Exhibit 2-4   Billings and Collections Supervisor Job Description

Reports to:	Assistant Controller (Transactions)
Responsibilities:	Approve invoice write-offs.
	Ensure that accounts receivable are collected promptly.
	Ensure that customer billings are issued promptly.
	Estimate the bad debt reserve.
	Implement best practices to increase efficiency levels.
	Manage the billings and collections staff.
	Project cash requirements from cash receipts.

Exhibit 2-5   Accounts Payable Supervisor Job Description

Reports to:	Assistant Controller (Transactions)
Responsibilities:	Cross-train the accounts payable staff.
	Ensure that accounts payable are not paid early.
	Ensure that all reasonable discounts are taken on payments.
	Handle supplier payment inquiries.
	Implement best practices to increase efficiency levels.
	Manage the accounts payable staff.
	Project cash requirements from accounts payable.

Exhibit 2-6   Payroll Supervisor Job Description

Reports to:	Assistant Controller (Transactions)
Responsibilities:	Convert time cards into payroll system entries.
	Create vacation and pay accruals for the periodic financials.
	Cross-train the payroll clerical staff.
	Implement best practices to increase efficiency levels.
	Manage the payroll clerical staff.
	Monitor vacation and sick time taken and available.
	Process payroll in a timely manner.
	Process termination pay within mandated time periods.
	Update pay changes in a timely manner.

Exhibit 2-7   General Ledger Accountant Job Description

Reports to:	Assistant Controller (Financial Reporting)
Responsibilities:	Consolidate entries from subsidiary organizations.
	Ensure that monthly bank reconciliations are completed.
	Follow the period-end closing schedule in a timely manner.
	Maintain a standard checklist of period journal entries.
	Maintain detailed backup on all account balances.
	Maintain the chart of accounts.

2-5 SUMMARY

This chapter has described the expanded role of the accounting department, as well as how it interacts with other parts of the organization, both from the perspective of providing financial information and of controlling the level of ethical integrity. In the next chapter, we will look in more detail at how transactions flow to and from the accounting department in relation to other parts of the company, and how the corporate structure can influence these transactions.

CHAPTER 3

The Corporate Structure

3-1 INTRODUCTION

Before proceeding to detailed discussions of accounting-specific issues, it is useful to see how the accounting department interacts with the rest of the organization. This chapter discusses the standard organizational structure, and how the primary accounting processes require the involvement of other parts of the company. Only by understanding the role of accounting within the greater structure of the modern corporation can the accountant see how changes in his or her department can cause issues elsewhere in the company, and vice versa.

3-2 THE CORPORATE ORGANIZATIONAL STRUCTURE

The typical corporation is divided into a set of departments, each of which is responsible for a different cluster of tasks. Each department manager reports to a senior-level executive, who in turn reports to the Chief Executive Officer. This structure is shown in Exhibit 3-1. Though there is some variation in the types of departments found in different organizations, the most common ones are:

- *Engineering department.* This department designs new products, modifies existing designs, and fixes design-related problems in existing products. It also has an industrial engineering staff that is responsible for plant layout. It may include a research and development group, though this is sometimes managed separately or contracted out.

- *Production department.* This department manufactures products. It usually includes a maintenance staff that is responsible for equipment and building maintenance, as well as an equipment setup and teardown staff.

16

Exhibit 3-1 The Organizational Structure

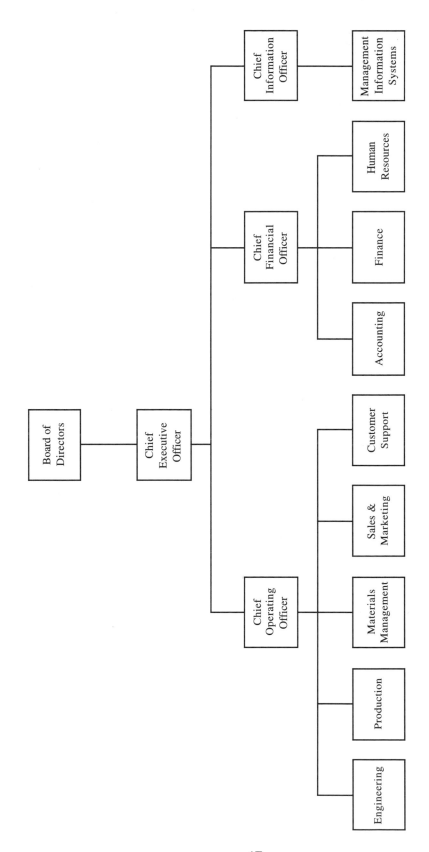

- *Materials management department.* This department is responsible for purchasing, production planning, warehousing, distribution, and materials movement within the facility. Given the wide array of required tasks, it is sometimes split into several smaller departments.

- *Sales and marketing department.* This department is responsible for generating advertising campaigns, creating collateral materials, attending trade shows, merchandising, and selling.

- *Customer support department.* This department is responsible for attending to customer problems, such as tracking down quality issues, verifying order status, and sometimes entering customer orders. It is frequently merged into other departments, with materials management, sales, and accounting being the most common recipients of this function.

- *Accounting department.* This department is responsible for billings, payments, payroll, maintenance of the general ledger, tracking assets, and issuing financial statements.

- *Finance department.* This department is responsible for treasury management, risk management, cash forecasting, and credit analysis. It also frequently conducts financial analysis as requested.

- *Human resources department.* This department is responsible for the maintenance of employee benefit systems, recruiting and terminations, and a wide variety of other employee-related issues.

- *Management information systems department.* This department is responsible for maintaining all computer networks, software, and desktop systems, as well as providing help desk support.

Though many of these departments may seem to have little impact on the accounting department, the discussion in the following four sections will prove that the accountant must be very careful to discuss system changes with all parts of the company, and be aware of changes going on elsewhere, in order to adequately perform his or her job.

3-3 THE CASH DISBURSEMENTS CYCLE

One of the primary functions in which the accounting department is involved is the cash disbursements cycle. This involves the entire process flow that begins with a request for materials, passes through the purchasing department, where an purchase order is placed, and eventually arrives at the accounting department, which is responsible for ensuring that all payments are authorized, and then pays suppliers. The general process flow is shown in Exhibit 3-2.

Initially, it appears that the accounting department is only concerned with the very end of the disbursements process. However, there are several key control points in the process that are of considerable concern to the accountant. For example, the "match documents" step in the exhibit refers to the comparison of purchasing, receiving, and supplier invoicing information to ensure that all payments are authorized and correct in amount. What happens to this step if the receiving department decides to allow the receipt of *all*

Exhibit 3-2 The Cash Disbursements Cycle

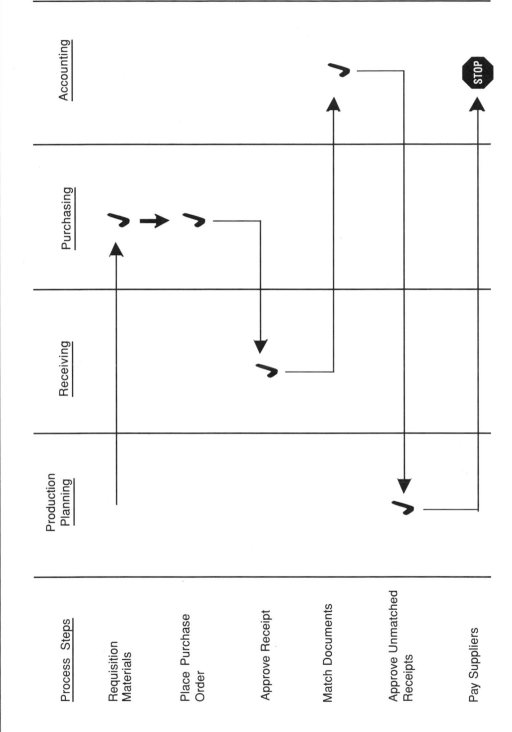

incoming shipments, irrespective of the presence of an authorizing purchasing order? This will result in much more work by the accounting department, since it will have to send out supplier invoices for individual approvals by department managers.

Another area in the cash disbursements cycle that impacts the accounting department is the level of approval required for the issuance of purchase orders. If the purchasing department allows *all* requests for purchases, no matter who makes the request, then there is really no control over the purchasing process. This requires the accounting staff to gather additional approvals from managers prior to making payments to suppliers. Alternatively, if the approval process at the purchasing department were more rigid, the accounting staff could use a signature stamp to sign checks, since the additional control of having a check signer review the checks would then become superfluous.

Yet another impact on the accounting department is the ability of the purchasing software to verify available funding for purchase orders. If the computer system is capable of comparing purchase requests to the amount of budgeted funds available, and requires immediate department manager approval if budgets are exceeded, then the accounting department has no need to issue reports to managers *after* bills are paid, informing them that they have run over their allowable budgetary levels.

An area in which the accounting staff can impose extra work on "upstream" departments is through the use of an advanced accounts payable system. For example, if all purchase orders were to be made available on-line to the receiving staff, these personnel could check off items on purchase orders as soon as they were received, thereby allowing the computer system to automatically make electronic payments to suppliers with no further accounting participation in the process. Such a system would require considerable training of the receiving staff, as well as the design of extra controls.

It is apparent that the accounting department is impacted by many parts of the cash disbursements cycle, and so must coordinate its activities with those of other participants.

3-4 THE SALES CYCLE

The sales cycle begins with the initiation of a customer order with the application for credit, proceeds to order placement, manufacturing and shipment of the order, and finally with the issuance of an invoice to the customer. The general process flow is illustrated in Exhibit 3-3. There are many variations on this process, such as the handling of credit by the accounting department instead of the finance department, shipment from stock instead of having to manufacture a specific product, providing a service instead of a tangible product, and payment by some other format than through an invoice. Nonetheless the process flow shown in the exhibit is indicative of the overall process.

The sales cycle can involve the accounting department only at its termination, when it receives shipping documentation from the warehouse staff, and uses this to create an invoice for the customer to whom a shipment has been made. However, the accountant needs to be concerned about several steps earlier in the process flow that are conducted by other departments. Of primary importance is the shipment itself—if the warehouse ships an order without first consulting a "stop order" report to see if there are any orders on hold, then the collections staff will have a much more difficult time collecting funds from delinquent customers.

Another "upstream" problem in the sales cycle is the credit terms granted to customers. If the finance department grants inordinately large or lengthy terms to a

Exhibit 3-3 The Sales Cycle

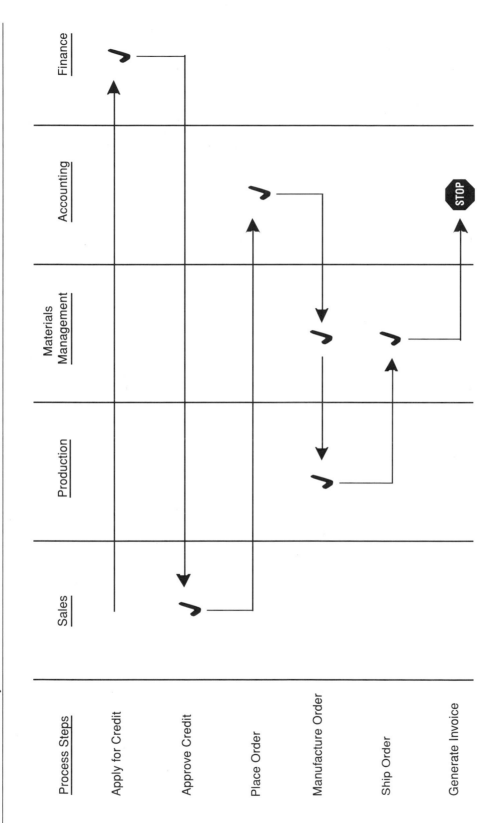

21

customer, then the accounting staff may find itself without enough ready cash to pay for ongoing accounts payable—the company's cash will have been used to fund the customer's order.

Yet another concern is the payment of deposits by customers as part of the order taking process. If orders are being handled by sales personnel, who accept deposits as part of an order, it is entirely possible that they have control over large amounts of funds, which can present a serious control problem. Thus, it is evident that, as was the case for the cash disbursements cycle, the accounting department must be involved in far more than the last step of the process cycle.

3-5 THE ORDER FULFILLMENT CYCLE

The order fulfillment cycle is a subset of the sales cycle, involving the scheduling of production for an order, quality reviews, and shipment of the product to the customer. It is shown in Exhibit 3-4. At first glance, it appears to be entirely concerned with the materials management and production part of the business, which keeps it completely away from the concerns of the accounting department. However, it contains several control issues that impact the accounting department.

One control issue is the movement of materials through the facility. Since the accountant must report on work-in-process inventory levels, it is important that the record keeping system within the manufacturing facility be sufficiently detailed that materials are recorded as being in the production department when they are shifted out of the warehouse, so that they are no longer recorded in the financial statements as being part of raw materials.

Another control issue is that shipped products are removed from the finished goods warehouse records. Otherwise, the period-end inventory levels will be overstated, resulting in an artificially reduced cost of goods sold.

Yet another issue is the proper level of control over materials that are removed from the warehouse as part of the picking process that is used to bring raw materials to the production department. If pick lists are not used, or if unauthorized personnel are allowed into the warehouse to remove items for use by the production staff, then it is very likely that the accuracy of the raw material inventory records will decline in short order, making it necessary for the accounting staff to conduct physical inventory counts to verify the accuracy of the inventory records.

Thus, the order fulfillment cycle has far more impact on the accounting department than at first appears to be the case. The impact is not so much on the paperwork moving from the process to the accounting department, but rather on the accuracy of inventory records that are constantly updated as a result of the fulfillment of customer orders.

3-6 OTHER TOPICAL AREAS

Thus far, we have focused on just a few major processes. Here are several other cases where the accounting department interacts with other departments:

- *Advertising credits.* The marketing staff may issue credits or splits to the distributors of company products if they advertise on behalf of the company. If so, the

Exhibit 3-4 The Order Fulfillment Cycle

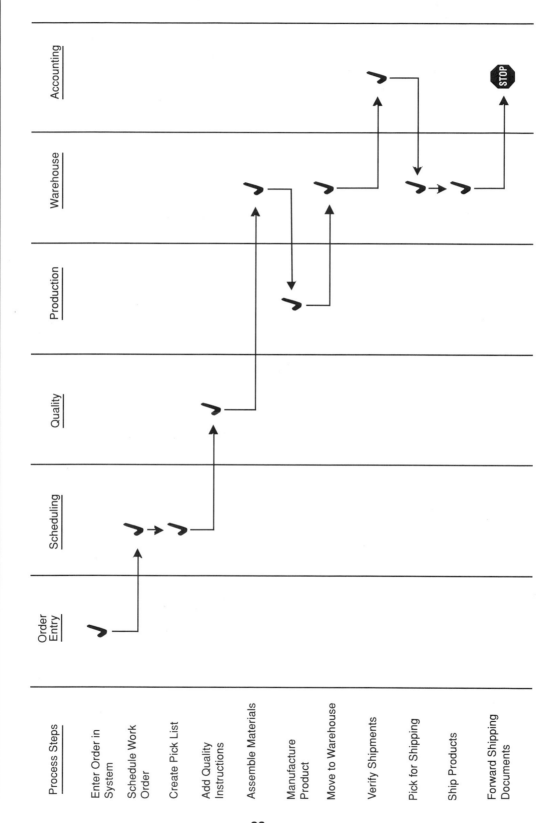

accounting staff can expect to receive requests for payment from distributors, which requires coordination with the marketing staff to verify.

- *Collections.* One of the best ways to collect from customers is to involve the sales staff in the effort. This requires close coordination with individual sales staff, whose assistance is much more forthcoming if sales commissions are based on cash receipts from customers, rather than initial orders.

- *Commissions.* The calculation of commissions can be extremely difficult if the sales manager continually alters the criteria for commissions, such as changing rates, adding commission splits, and changing override levels. Considerable coordination is required to ensure that the accounting staff does not become entangled in a web of continually changing commission calculations.

- *Credit granting.* The accounting department is usually responsible for the granting of credit to customers when there is no finance department to handle this task. If so, a significant potential impediment to its work is sales to new customers before any credit level has been granted. This frequently results in intense pressure by the sales staff (which has a commission riding on the outcome) on the accounting staff to grant the largest possible amount of credit.

- *Credits issued by customer service.* The customer service staff may be empowered to issue credits to customers to compensate them for faulty products or services provided by the company. If so, there must be a feedback loop to the accounting department, so that they can record the credits against customer accounts.

- *Payroll.* If there is a company policy requiring manager approvals of pay rate changes, overtime payments, or shift differentials, then there must be a continual information flow between the accounting department's payroll staff and all department managers.

3-7 SUMMARY

The discussion in this chapter has shown that the accounting department does not conduct its operations in a vacuum. On the contrary, nearly every transaction it processes requires some degree of interaction with another part of the company. When perusing later chapters that cover the use of best practices, control systems, and management information systems, one should keep in mind that a great many of these improvements can only be made with the cooperation of other company managers. Also, the accountant should stay aware of systemic changes elsewhere in the company in order to know in advance when issues will arise that may impact the operations of the accounting department.

Part Two

ACCOUNTING RULES AND REGULATIONS

CHAPTER 4

Standard Setting Organizations

4-1 INTRODUCTION

Who creates the basic rules of accounting that guide the accounting practices of so many accountants? There are several entities that contribute to these basic rules, as will be discussed in this chapter. In addition, the Securities and Exchange Commission (SEC) has a lengthy set of regulations that govern precisely how accounting information is to be presented to the investing public, as discussed in Chapter 6; however, the SEC has chosen to steer clear of the actual accounting rules that govern the profession, choosing instead to strictly focus its attention on the manner of information presentation. The Internal Revenue Service (IRS) also has rules that govern what types of revenue and expense are allowed when compiling an entity's taxable income figure—however, these rules are used in parallel to generally accepted accounting principles (GAAP), and form no part of GAAP. The most common IRS rules are noted in Chapter 35. This chapter focuses strictly on those rule-setting bodies that have gradually compiled the set of rules that we now call GAAP.

4-2 THE COMMITTEE ON ACCOUNTING PROCEDURE

The Committee on Accounting Procedure (CAP) was created in 1939 by the American Institute of Accountants (now known as the American Institute of Public Accountants, or AICPA). It issued a total of 51 Accounting Research Bulletins that responded to specific accounting problems as they arose; this tight focus led to an increasing number of complaints against the CAP over time, because it did not attempt to create an overall accounting framework to which specific accounting pronouncements could then be attached in an orderly manner. Another problem was that it was accused of not conducting a sufficient volume of detailed research to back up the reasoning behind its pronouncements. Yet another issue was the perception that it acted in the interests of the American Institute of Accountants, which was considered a conflict of interest. Furthermore, its pronouncements were not binding on any organizations that issued financial reports. On the plus side, it developed a uniform accounting terminology that was widely used thereafter. Because of the preceding problems, the CAP was eliminated in 1959 in favor of the Accounting Principles Board.

4-3 THE ACCOUNTING PRINCIPLES BOARD

The Accounting Principles Board (APB) was formed in 1958 by the AICPA. Its 18 to 21 member Board and supporting staff was quite active in conducting research on accounting issues and promulgating standards. Even though it was phased out in 1973, its APB bulletin numbers 43, 45, 46, and 51, as well as 19 opinions still form a part of GAAP. The APB gained more regulatory force than its predecessor, because the AICPA required its member CPAs to identify and justify any departures from the APB's opinions and statements, while it also gained support from the Securities and Exchange Commission. Nonetheless, it foundered due to its direct support by the AICPA—a more independent organization was needed, which resulted in the Financial Accounting Foundation.

4-4 THE FINANCIAL ACCOUNTING FOUNDATION

The Financial Accounting Foundation (FAF) was founded in 1972. Its 16-member Board of Trustees is expressly independent from the AICPA, since they come from a number of sponsoring organizations, such as the AICPA, the Financial Executives Institute, the Institute of Management Accountants, the Securities Industry Association, and others. It also has a number of at-large trustees who are not tied to any sponsoring organizations. The FAF does not directly promulgate any accounting standards—rather, it raises funds for the operation of the Financial Accounting Standards Board (FASB) and Government Accounting Standards Board (GASB) that conduct this work, as noted in the following sections. Its fundraising function is enhanced by its being a 501(c)(3) taxable entity, so that contributions to it are tax-deductible. It also exercises general oversight of the FASB and GASB by appointing Board members to them, as well as two advisory councils to those entities. It also approves their annual budgets. The FAF, FASB, and GASB are all located in Norwalk, Connecticut.

4-5 THE FINANCIAL ACCOUNTING STANDARDS BOARD

The successor to the Accounting Principles Board is the Financial Accounting Standards Board (FASB). It was created in 1973. It has a Board of seven members, each of whom has a five-year term, and who can be re-elected once. It has a staff of about 40 personnel. The organization is funded through the FAF. Its mission is to "establish and improve standards of financial accounting and reporting for the guidance and education of the public, including issuers, auditors, and users of financial information." It maintains a web site at *http://accounting.rutgers.edu/raw/fasb/index.html.*

The FASB's authority to issue statements on and interpretations of accounting standards comes from several sources. One is the SEC, which designated it as the source of accounting principles to be used as the basis for financial statements filed with it (as noted in the SEC's Financial Reporting Release No. 1, Section 101). The FASB received similar support from the AICPA through its Rule 203. However, the FASB has no enforcement powers whatsoever—it needs continuing support from the SEC, AICPA, and state boards of accountancy to ensure that its rules are followed.

The FASB works with the Financial Accounting Standards Advisory Council, which is appointed by the FAF. The council's 30 members advise the FASB about technical issues, project priorities, and the selection of task forces to deal with specific accounting issues.

The basic flow of work that the FASB follows when constructing a new accounting pronouncement is:

1. *Admission to agenda.* The FASB's criteria for inclusion of an accounting issue in its work schedule are that there is diverse practice in dealing with it that causes varying financial reporting results that can be misleading. There must also be a technically feasible solution, and an expectation that a solution will be generally accepted.

2. *Early deliberations.* The FASB clarifies the issues and obtains opinions regarding each accounting item on its agenda. If a prospective pronouncement appears to be a major project, it will appoint an advisory task force of outside experts to review it, which tends to involve the services of about 15 people. The FASB staff will then write a discussion memorandum with the assistance of this group.

3. *Public hearing.* The FASB will announce a hearing date that is 60 days in advance. Depending upon the issue, these meetings may be very well attended by interested parties.

4. *Tentative resolution.* Two-thirds of the Board votes in favor of issuing an exposure draft, which includes a proposed effective date and method of transition to the new accounting rule. This document is not the final one, being rather a draft that is made available for public discussion.

5. *Final deliberations and resolution.* Once responses from the public to the exposure draft have been made, the FASB will make minor adjustments to it and take a final vote. The finalized standard, which includes dissenting views, is then published.

6. *Follow-up interpretations.* There may be some issues related to a new standard that do not become apparent until after it has been in use for a short time. If so, the FASB may clarify or elaborate upon the newly issued statement. These interpretations must also be made available for public comment for at least 30 days before being finalized and published.

The process just noted requires a considerable amount of FASB resources, and so cannot be used to address all accounting issues. To provide more rapid resolution to more urgent or minor issues, it may choose to shift them to its Emerging Issues Task Force (EITF). The EITF is a very active group that is mostly composed of public accounting people who are aware of emerging issues before they become widespread. The Chief Accountant of the SEC attends its meetings. If it can reach a rapid consensus on an issue, then its findings are published at once, and become a basis for GAAP. If there is less consensus, then the issue is shifted to the FASB to be resolved through the more tortuous process just described. The EITF has been criticized, because less public discussion is involved in its proceedings than under the more formalized FASB review process.

The FASB also issues technical bulletins when it addresses issues not covered by existing standards, which will not cause a major change in practice, have a minimal perceived implementation cost, and do not result in a unique new accounting practice—in short, technical bulletins address less controversial topics.

A potential problem over the long term is that the SEC, which is a prime sponsor of the FASB, wants it to issue standards that are oriented toward publicly held companies, over which the SEC has reporting control. However, this means that the more onerous reporting requirements intended for larger public companies are also being forced upon smaller private firms that do not have the resources to comply with them. Though there would be great inefficiencies involved in setting up a double accounting standard, one for public and one for private companies, this will be an ongoing cause of tension within the FASB as it continues to churn out pronouncements.

4-6 THE GOVERNMENT ACCOUNTING STANDARDS BOARD

The entity that establishes accounting principles for state and local governments is the Government Accounting Standards Board (GASB), which was created in 1984. It is the successor organization to the National Council on Governmental Accounting, whose standards are still in force unless the GASB has issued specific changes or replacements to them. The GASB's methods of operation (and basic rule-making procedures) are nearly identical to those of the FASB, which is its sister organization. It has seven Board members and a staff of about 10 employees. Like the FASB, it works with an advisory council, this one being called the Government Accounting Standards Advisory Council, which is appointed by the FAF. This council consults with the GASB about technical issues, project priorities, and the selection of task forces to deal with specific issues. An interesting variation from the procedures of the FASB's council is that this one periodically conducts an annual membership survey to identify emerging issues.

Its funding comes from the FAF, as is the case for the FASB. The primary source of funding that goes to the FAF is from state and local governments, as well as the General Accounting Office.

The GASB's pronouncements are recognized as authoritative by the AICPA, but there is no entity like the SEC supporting it (which only deals with publicly held companies), and so it tends to have less overall influence than the FASB. Also, since its funding sources are fewer than for the FASB, it has a substantially smaller staff.

The GASB maintains a general web site at *www.rutgers.edu/accounting/raw/gasb/welcome.htm,* as well as another web site at *www.seagov.org* that is dedicated to the measurement of government performance standards.

4-7 THE INTERNATIONAL ACCOUNTING STANDARDS BOARD

A large number of organizations now do business in multiple countries, and so must deal with different accounting standards within each country where they have subsidiaries. Though a company's headquarters may be located in the United States, which forces the entity as a whole to report under FASB standards, it may be required to make reports, such as loan-related financial statements, at the local level that require different accounting standards. Also, companies that are based abroad but which want to issue securities within the United States must restate their financial results to comply with American accounting rules. In an attempt to standardize the accounting rules of many countries, the International Accounting Standards Board (IASB) was created in April 2001. It is the successor body to the International Accounting Standards Committee (IASC), which in turn was formed in 1973 through an agreement made by the national professional accountancy bodies of Australia, Canada, France, Germany, Japan, Mexico, the Netherlands, the United Kingdom and Ireland, and the United States. The 14 members of its Board serve for a five-year term, which can be renewed once.

The IASB is controlled by a parent organization, which is the IASC Foundation, a Delaware non-profit corporation. Its role is quite similar to that of the FAF in relation to the FASB and GASB—that is, it provides funding and general oversight to the IASB, while also appointing its members. Meanwhile, the IASB is solely responsible for setting international accounting standards, with the support of the Standards Advisory Council and the Standing Interpretations Committee, both of which are funded and supported by the IASC Foundation.

The IASB's staff works on the development of a single set of international accounting standards, coordinating its efforts with the national standard setting bodies, stock exchanges, and securities regulatory agencies in many countries, as well as such international groups as the United Nations and World Bank. Its accounting standards are issued in the form of International Financial Reporting Standards, which are devised through the same process used by the GASB and FASB.

4-8 SUMMARY

The long chain of standard setting organizations that began with the Committee on Accounting Procedure in 1939 and that continues today in the form of the FASB and GASB has produced a prolific volume of pronouncements that form the primary basis for GAAP. We will review some of these pronouncements in the next chapter. In the meantime, it is an open question whether the current FASB and GASB organizations are the final standard setting organizations that we will see, or whether they will begin to mesh their functions with the newly formed International Accounting Standards Board. An additional issue is that a powerful backer of the FASB is the SEC, which pushes it in the direction of primarily creating reporting standards for publicly held companies; the difficulty of complying with these standards for smaller, privately held companies may eventually lead to complaints that could bring about a double standard—one rule for public companies and another for private ones. Only time will tell how these issues will be resolved.

CHAPTER 5

Accounting Standards

5-1 INTRODUCTION

Generally Accepted Accounting Principles come from the pronouncement of the Accounting Procedures Committee of the AICPA (which concluded its operations in 1959), the Accounting Principles Board of the AICPA (which concluded its operations in 1973), and the Financial Accounting Standards Board (FASB), which is now the primary authoritative source of GAAP. Account Research Bulletins (ARB) are the official pronouncements of the Accounting Procedures Committee, while the Accounting Principles Board issued numbered Opinions. The FASB uses a number of pronouncements, including Interpretations, Statements, Statements of Financial Accounting Concepts, and Technical Bulletins. Its Emerging Issues Task Force (EITF) also issues a voluminous number of Abstracts. In addition, the AICPA issues a number of Statements of Position. The identifying numbers, titles, and summaries of all of these GAAP sources, with the exception of EITF abstracts and AICPA Statements of Position, are included in the following sections.

The summaries noted here are not intended to provide the full range of information needed by the accountant to fully research a particular GAAP issue. Instead, one can peruse the list to see which reference sources are most applicable to the problem at hand. At that point, one should refer to the source document to obtain the greatest possible detail. In many cases, source documents also include examples that are invaluable in determining the application of the principles under discussion to actual situations.

There are several sources of GAAP documents. One can go to the FASB web site, located at *http://raw.rutgers.edu/raw/fasb,* to find the complete text of all FASB Statements. A more complete source of nearly all GAAP documents is the excellent three-volume set of *Original Pronouncements,* published by the AICPA. It contains all FASB

Statements, Accounting Research Bulletins, Opinions of the Accounting Principles Board, AICPA Interpretations, FASB Interpretations, FASB Concept Statements, and FASB Technical Bulletins. The documents only show those pronouncements that have not been superseded, and also highlight any text that has been superseded or modified by later pronouncements, thereby eliminating some potential confusion regarding which pronouncements constitute current accounting standards. It can be purchased from the AICPA Web store for $99, which is located at *www.cpa2biz.com.* As of this publication date, the *Original Pronouncements* could only be purchased by AIPCA members—the membership application can be found at the AICPA web site, which is located at *www.aicpa.org.* The information contained within the *Original Pronouncements* is current up until June 1 of each year, and so the most recent year's publication is not usually available until late summer or early fall. Statements of Position can be ordered separately from the AICPA under the title of *AICPA Technical Practice Aids.* They are also available through the AICPA Web store, and can be purchased there at an AICPA member price of $80 and $100 for non-members. Abstracts published by the EITF are available on an annual subscription basis for $338 per year, or may be purchased individually for $44.75 each. They can be ordered by calling the FASB at 800-748-0659, or by ordering on-line by accessing *http://stores/yahoo.com/fasbpubs.*

5-2 ACCOUNTING RESEARCH BULLETINS

The Accounting Research Bulletins listed in the following table are only those that have not been superseded by later accounting standards. Please note that the first one listed, ARB Number 43, is a summary of all preceding ARBs.

Number	Title	Description
43	Restatement of Revision of Previous Bulletins	Represents a revision and summary of the first 42 Accounting Research Bulletins, covering such topics as the form of financial statements, working capital, inventory pricing, intangible assets, contingency reserves, capital accounts, depreciation, taxes, government contracts, pension plans, and pension plan annuity costs.
45	Long-Term Construction-Type Contracts	Describes the use of the percentage-of-completion method and the completed contract method to account for construction contracts.
46	Discontinuance of Dating Earned Surplus	Cancels the dating of an earned surplus following a quasi-reorganization.
51	Consolidated Financial Statements	Discusses the consolidation procedure, the treatment of minority interests, the treatment of stock dividends of subsidiaries, and the uses of both combined and parent company financial statements.

5-3 OPINIONS—ACCOUNTING PRINCIPLES BOARD

The Opinions listed in the following table are only those that have not been superseded by later accounting standards. Several of these Opinions, such as APB Numbers 9, 14, 16, 17, 20–22, and 25, are still the primary source documents for key accounting issues.

Number	Title	Description
2	Accounting for the Investment Credit	Discusses the presentation and recognition of the investment tax credit arising from the Revenue Act of 1962.
4	Accounting for the Investment Credit	Discusses the impact of the Revenue Act of 1964 on the investment tax credit, as well as an additional allowable method for reporting the credit, net of reported federal income taxes.
6	Status of Accounting Research Bulletins	Contains revisions to those sections of ARB 43 relating to treasury stock, current assets and liabilities, stock dividends and splits, and depreciation and appreciation.
9	Reporting the Results of Operations	Concludes that net income should include all profit and loss transactions, with the exception of prior period adjustments. It also specifies the separate treatment of extraordinary items in the income statement.
10	Omnibus Opinion—1966	Covers the allocation of income taxes among different reporting periods, offsetting securities against taxes payable, and denies the use of the installment method of accounting.
12	Omnibus Opinion—1967	Covers the classification and disclosure of allowance accounts, depreciation disclosure, and the reporting of changes in equity; affirms the use of the interest method when amortizing debt discounts and premiums.
14	Accounting for Convertible Debt and Debt Issued with Stock Purchase Warrants	Discusses the applicability of accounting for stock purchase warrants separately from attached debt instruments.
16	Business Combinations	Discusses the purchase and pooling methods of accounting for a business combination, and the circumstances under which each one can be used. It also covers the treatment of acquisition costs, contingent compensation, and the amortization of goodwill.
17	Intangible Assets	Specifies the types of intangibles that may be recorded as assets, how to arrive at their cost, and how they may be amortized.

18	The Equity Method of Accounting for Investments in Common Stock	Specifies the circumstances under which the equity method of accounting can be used, as well as how it should be calculated and then disclosed on the investor's financial statements.
20	Accounting Changes	Discusses the proper treatment of changes in accounting principle, estimate, and reporting entity, as well as of errors in previously issued financial statements, plus how this information is to be disclosed in the financial statements.
21	Interest on Receivables and Payables	Discusses the determination of the proper valuation of a note when it is exchanged for cash, property, or services. It also covers the selection of an appropriate present value discount rate, as well as the disclosure of discounts or premiums from the face value of a note.
22	Disclosure of Accounting Policies	Requires the disclosure of significant accounting policies alongside the financial statements.
23	Accounting for Income Taxes—Special Areas	Discusses the proper accounting for income taxes in relation to the undistributed earnings of subsidiaries, investments in corporate joint ventures, bad debt reserves of savings and loan institutions, and the policyholders' surplus of stock life insurance companies.
25	Accounting for Stock Issued to Employees	Specifies the rules to use when accounting for stock awards. The core principle is that the accounting is based on the intrinsic value of the award, which is the difference between the compensation value of the award, measured as the number of shares multiplied by the fair market value per share, and employee value, measured as the employee price per share multiplied by the number of shares.
26	Early Extinguishment of Debt	Requires that gains or losses from the early extinguishment of debt be recognized in the current period.
28	Interim Financial Reporting	Describes the information that should be contained within interim financial reports, including changes in accounting principles and the disclosure of summarized interim financial data by publicly traded companies.

| 29 | Accounting for Nonmonetary Transactions | Verifies that non-monetary transactions should be valued based on their fair values, except in a limited number of cases in which non-monetary exchanges are not considered to be the culmination of an earnings process. |
| 30 | Reporting the Results of Operations | Discusses the proper disclosure of discontinued operations, as well as the reporting of gains or losses from business disposals. It also defines those transactions that should be categorized as extraordinary items. |

5-4 INTERPRETATIONS—FASB

The Interpretations listed in the following table are intended to clarify or expand upon any accounting pronouncements that have previously been issued, usually addressing very specific topics.

Number	Title	Description
1	Accounting Changes Related to the Cost of Inventory	If there is a change in the costs included in inventory, that is considered an accounting change that must be justified based on some improvement in the level of financial reporting, and not just on favorable income tax results.
4	Applicability of FASB Statement 2 to Purchase Business Combinations	When using the purchase method to account for a business combination, costs should be allocated to assets both resulting from and to be used in research and development activities of the acquired entity. However, assigned R&D costs must then be expensed at the time of the combination if the related assets have no identifiable future use.
6	Applicability of FASB Statement 2 to Computer Software	Specifies that the purchase or development of a process for internal sales or administrative purposes is not classified as research and development costs. The cost associated with the purchase or lease of computer software for use in R&D activities should be charged to expense unless it has an alternative future use. Software development costs through the pre-production phase are considered R&D costs, while programming and testing costs incurred for the improvement of a production model are not considered R&D expenses.

7	Applying FASB Statement 7 in Statements of Established Enterprises	Describes the situations under which a consolidating entity should report the effect of a development stage subsidiary's change in accounting principle, based on the requirements of FASB Statement Number 7.
8	Classification of a Short-Term Obligation Repaid Prior to Being Replaced by a Long-Term Security	Requires the reporting of a short-term debt repayment as a current liability if the repayment occurs prior to the incurrence of long-term debt that was intended to pay for the short-term debt repayment.
9	Applying APB Opinions 16 and 17 When a Savings and Loan or Similar Institution Is Acquired in a Purchase Business Combination	Disallows the use of the "net spread" method for assigning costs to the assets of an acquired company; it also provides guidelines for assigning costs to accounts receivable and payable, as well as intangible assets and savings deposits due on demand.
14	Reasonable Estimation of the Amount of a Loss	Specifies the conditions under which losses can be accrued.
18	Accounting for Income Taxes in Interim Periods	Describes the computation of interim period income taxes and related disclosures, applies the computation to specific situations, and describes special computations that are applicable to multiple jurisdictions.
19	Lessee Guarantee of the Residual Value of Leased Property	Describes the specific situations under which a lease provision can be construed as being a lessee's guarantee of the residual value of leased property, as well as the maximum limitations on the amount of such a guarantee.
20	Reporting Accounting Changes Under AICPA Statements of Position	Notes that any change made to a company's financial statements under an AICPA Statement of Position (SOP) shall do so in accordance with the requirements of the specific SOP.
21	Accounting for Leases in a Business Combination	Notes that a lease's classification as noted in FASB Statement Number 13 shall not be changed because of a business combination, unless the lease's provisions have been specifically modified.
23	Leases of Certain Property Owned by a Governmental Unit or Authority	Narrows the range of leases of government property to be categorized as operating leases, based on the presence of four criteria.
24	Leases Involving Only Part of a Building	Notes that one can reasonably determine the fair value of a partial building lease based on other types of information, if comparable sale data is not available.

26	Accounting for Purchase of a Leased Asset by the Lessee During the Term of the Lease	Specifies that an asset purchase under the terms of a capital lease, and the corresponding lease termination, are covered by a single accounting transaction that may call for an adjustment in the carrying amount of the lease obligation.
27	Accounting for Loss on a Sublease	Allows the recognition of a loss on the difference between a lease and a sublease, and also specifies that this loss is to be included in the overall gain or loss reported on the disposition of a business segment.
28	Accounting for Stock Appreciation Rights and Other Variable Stock Option or Award Plans	Specifies that a company must record a compensation expense at the end of each reporting period for the amount by which the market price of its stock exceeds the option price for any stock appreciation rights or similar plans.
30	Accounting for Involuntary Conversions of Nonmonetary Assets to Monetary Assets	Requires that a gain or loss be recognized when corporate assets are involuntarily converted to cash, even in cases in which the cash is subsequently reinvested in replacement assets.
33	Applying FASB Statement 34 to Oil and Gas Producing Operations	Specifies the conditions under which an oil and gas producing operation whose assets are accounted for under the full cost method may capitalize interest costs.
34	Disclosure of Indirect Guarantees of Indebtedness of Others	Specifies that the disclosure requirements noted in FASB Statement Number 5 for guarantees of indebtedness must also be used for indirect guarantees.
35	Criteria for Applying the Equity Method of Accounting for Investments in Common Stock	Describes the conditions under which the equity method of accounting should be used to account for an investor's stake in an investee's voting stock of 50% or less.
36	Accounting for Exploratory Wells in Progress at the End of a Period	Notes that the costs incurred through the end of a reporting period for an exploratory well that is discovered to be a dry hole prior to the date of statement issuance shall be charged to expense within the period.
37	Accounting for Translation Adjustment Upon Sale of Part of an Investment in a Foreign Entity	Holds that an accumulated foreign currency translation adjustment be recognized upon the sale of part of an investment in a foreign entity in proportion to the amount of the investment being disposed of.

38	Determining the Measurement Date for Stock Option, Purchase, and Award Plans Involving Junior Stock	Specifies that the measurement date for award plans involving junior stock is the date when it is known the exact amount of the common stock for which the junior stock can be exchanged.
39	Offsetting of Amounts Related to Certain Contracts	Defines the right of setoff under which an accountant may net assets and liabilities on the balance sheet, as well as its applicability to conditional or exchange contracts.
40	Applicability of Generally Accepted Accounting Principles to Mutual Life Insurance and Other Enterprises	Requires that mutual life insurance and other enterprises cannot state that they have prepared financial statements in accordance with GAAP in cases where they have actually diverted from GAAP in order to comply with other regulatory accounting practices.
41	Offsetting of Amounts Related to Certain Repurchase and Reverse Repurchase Agreements	Modifies FASB Interpretation Number 39, regarding setoffs of assets and liabilities, to allow this practice in the statement of financial position for receivables and payables that are related to repurchase agreements and reverse repurchase agreements.
43	Real Estate Sales	States that sales of real estate with property improvements or integral equipment that cannot be removed and used separately from the real estate without incurring significant costs should be accounted for under FASB Statement Number 66, "Accounting for Sales of Real Estate."
44	Accounting for Certain Transactions Involving Stock Compensation	Narrows the use of APB Number 25 to just employees, and clarifies the rules for the grant of stock awards to employees of affiliates of the issuer.

5-5 STATEMENTS OF FINANCIAL ACCOUNTING STANDARDS—FASB

The Statements listed in the following table are considered to be the primary source of GAAP to the extent that they supersede any previous pronouncements, either by the FASB or any predecessor organization.

Number	Title	Description
2	Accounting for Research and Development Costs	Requires one to charge research and development costs to expense when they are incurred, and describes the disclosure of R&D information in the financial statements.

3	Reporting Accounting Changes in Interim Financial Statements	Describes the reporting requirements in interim financial statements in relation to changes to LIFO inventory costing, and to cumulative effect types of accounting changes.
4	Reporting Gains and Losses from Extinguishment of Debt	Requires that gains and losses caused by a debt extinguishment shall be reported as an extraordinary item, if material. It also describes the disclosure requirements for such transactions.
5	Accounting for Contingencies	Describes how to account for loss contingencies, including the accrual of a loss contingency if there is a probability of loss and its amount can be reasonably estimated. Alternatively, gain contingencies can only be recognized when they have been realized.
6	Classification of Short-Term Obligations Expected to Be Refinanced	Allows an entity to reclassify its short-term debt as long-term debt, but only if it both intends to complete the required refinancing and has the ability to do so.
7	Accounting and Reporting by Development Stage Enterprises	Describes the types of entities that are considered to be in the development stage, and requires them to use the same accounting methods as those of established companies.
10	Extension of "Grandfather" Provisions for Business Reporting	Extends the grandfather provisions of APB Opinion Number 16 that create an exemption from some criteria used to determine the applicability of the pooling of interests method of accounting for a business combination.
11	Accounting for Contingencies—Transition Method	Requires a company to restate its financial statements for preceding periods in order to comply with FASB Statement Number 5.
13	Accounting for Leases	Describes the proper accounting by both parties to a lease, including the determination and treatment of operating and capital leases by lessees, and the determination and treatment of sales type, direct financing, and leveraged leases by lessors.
15	Accounting by Debtors and Creditors for Troubled Debt Restructurings	Describes the proper accounting by both parties to a troubled debt restructuring, including modifications to the yield of a loan, and the circumstances under which gains or losses can be recognized.
16	Prior Period Adjustments	Allows prior period adjustments only if there are material errors or if there are some income tax benefits associated with pre-acquisition loss carryforwards of a purchased entity.

18	Financial Reporting for Segments of a Business Enterprise—Interim Financial Statements	Stops the FASB Statement Number 14 requirement to report segment information for interim periods.
19	Financial Accounting and Reporting by Oil and Gas Producing Companies	Requires oil and gas producing companies to use the successful efforts method to account for the costs of producing mineral resources, as well as such issues as cost capitalization and amortization, property conveyances, income taxes, and financial statement disclosures.
21	Suspension of the Reporting of Earnings per Share and Segment Information by Nonpublic Enterprises	Suspends the requirement in APB Opinion Number 15 and FASB Statement Number 14 to report segment information, but only for non-public entities.
22	Changes in the Provisions of Lease Agreements	Requires the current recognition of a gain or loss when new debt proceeds are used to retire existing debt, under certain provisions.
23	Inception of the Lease	Alters the lease inception date to the date of lease agreement or any earlier commitment in cases in which the property to be covered by a lease has not yet been purchased or constructed.
24	Reporting Segment Information in Financial Statements that Are Presented in Another Enterprise's Financial Report	Eliminates the requirement to present segment information in some instances where additional entity financial statements are presented alongside consolidated statements.
25	Suspension of Certain Accounting Requirements for Oil and Gas Producing Companies	Suspends the use of some provisions of FASB Statement Number 19 due to some variations between that statement and SEC reporting requirements.
27	Classification of Renewals or Extensions of Existing Sales-Type or Direct Financing Leases	Requires a lessor to classify a lease as a sales-type lease if it is an extension of an existing sales-type or direct financing lease.
28	Accounting for Sales with Leasebacks	Modifies FASB Statement Number 13 to allow the recognition of some profit or loss on sale and leaseback transactions if the seller has minimal usage of the property after the transaction, or if the sale profit exceeds the present value of minimum lease payments due.

29	Determining Contingent Rentals	Defines contingent rentals, as well as what payments should be included in the reporting of minimum lease payments due for this type of rental.
30	Disclosure of Information about Major Customers	Requires that an entity report the amount of sales made to a government entity if those sales are at least 10% of its total revenues.
34	Capitalization of Interest	Describes the rules for capitalizing interest costs in some situations where assets are being acquired, built, or modified, and how the rules will vary if the amount of interest to be capitalized is considered material or not.
35	Accounting and Reporting by Defined Benefit Pension Plans	Describes the rules for the annual financial statements associated with a defined benefit pension plan, requiring the inclusion of such information as net assets available for benefits, changes in these benefits, and the present value of plan benefits.
42	Determining Materiality for Capitalization of Interest Cost	Deletes language from FASB Statement Number 34 that might be construed as allowing one to avoid interest capitalization, and also points out that the same statement does not contain new materiality tests.
43	Accounting for Compensated Absences	Specifies that a liability be accrued for the future absences of employees under certain circumstances.
44	Accounting for Intangible Assets of Motor Carriers	States that the unamortized intangible costs associated with a motor carrier's right to transport goods across state lines should be charged against income.
45	Accounting for Franchise Fee Revenue	Describes the primary accounting concepts for franchisors, including the proper treatment of franchise fee costs and revenues, commingled revenue, agency sales, repossessed franchises, and continuing product sales.
47	Disclosure of Long-Term Obligations	Describes the financial disclosures needed in cases where there are unconditional purchase obligations and future payments on long-term borrowings and redeemable stock.
48	Revenue Recognition When Right of Return Exists	Allows revenue recognition for transactions involving a right of return only if a set of minimum conditions is met.

49	Accounting for Product Financing Arrangements	Defines a product financing arrangement, and requires that it be accounted for as a borrowing transaction, instead of a sale.
50	Financial Reporting in the Record and Music Industry	Describes the accounting practices for both licensors and licensees in the music and recording industry, including revenue recognition for licensing fees, minimum license guarantees, artist compensation, and other costs.
51	Financial Reporting by Cable Television Companies	Describes how to account for the revenues and expenses related to cable television systems, both while under construction, in the prematurity period, and when in operation.
52	Foreign Currency Translation	Describes the treatment of foreign currency translation adjustments in accordance with the operating status of a foreign subsidiary, as well as the treatment of foreign currency transactions with other entities.
54	Financial Reporting and Changing Prices: Investment Companies	Avoids the previous requirements in FASB Statement Number 33 that require investment companies to make disclosures regarding the effects of changing prices.
57	Related-Party Disclosures	Describes the rules to follow when reporting on related party transactions.
58	Capitalization of Interest Cost in Financial Statements that Include Investments Accounted for by the Equity Method	Limits the capitalization of interest costs on an investor's financial statements in a limited number of situations involving the use of the equity method of accounting for an investment in another business entity.
60	Accounting and Reporting by Insurance Companies	Describes the reporting to be used for insurance entities in relation to the treatment of contracts, premiums, claims, and investments.
61	Accounting for Title Plant	Requires that costs incurred to build a title plant be capitalized until activated, and also specifies the treatment of maintenance expenses that are incurred thereafter.
62	Capitalization of Interest Costs in Situations Involving Certain Tax-Exempt Borrowings and Certain Gifts and Grants	Specifies situations in which interest costs are to be capitalized, as well as situations where the capitalization of interest costs is not allowed.
63	Financial Reporting by Broadcasters	Describes the reporting requirements for broadcasters, including treatment of exhibition rights, license agreements, barter transactions, and network affiliation agreements.

64	Extinguishment of Debt Made to Satisfy Sinking Fund Requirements	Specifies that the classification of gains or losses that result from the extinguishment of debt that is required by a sinking fund need not be reported as extraordinary items.
65	Accounting for Certain Mortgage Bank Activities	Specifies that mortgage loans and similar loans be reported at the lower of cost or market. It also notes the treatment of loan origination and commitment fees, loan placement fees, and premiums paid to service loans.
66	Accounting for Sales on Real Estate	Describes the rules for recognizing the profitability of real estate sales. Different standards apply to land sales than to other types of sales, to which the percentage of completion or installment methods may be applied.
67	Accounting for Costs and Initial Rental Operations of Real Estate Projects	Sets forth the rules regarding the types of costs that may be capitalized in relation to real estate projects, as well as the point after which costs may no longer be capitalized.
68	Research and Development Arrangements	Describes the accounting for research and development activities that are performed by a company for other entities. If there is a repayment obligation, its amount must be recorded as a liability.
69	Disclosures about Oil and Gas Producing Activities	Describes the disclosures required by oil and gas producing entities, and reduces or eliminates many of the disclosures by those entities that are not publicly held.
71	Accounting for the Effects of Certain Types of Regulation	Describes the accounting by most types of public utilities for regulation of the variety that allows utilities to set prices that will recover the cost of and capital cost of services provided.
72	Accounting for Certain Acquisitions of Banking or Thrift Institutions	Requires that the fair value of liabilities assumed in the acquisition of a bank or thrift entity over the fair value of acquired assets be amortized by the interest method. Also, any financial assistance obtained from a regulatory agency as part of the combination shall be recorded as an asset if the amount of the receipt can be determined and is likely to be received.
73	Reporting a Change in Accounting for Railroad Track Structures	Requires that railroads change their reporting of depreciation for railroad track structures, including a restatement of this information in prior reporting years.

78	Classification of Obligations that Are Callable by the Creditor	Requires that long-term liabilities callable by creditors be classified as current liabilities on the balance sheet, subject to some qualifications.
79	Elimination of Certain Disclosures for Business Combinations by Nonpublic Enterprises	Eliminates APB Opinion Number 16's requirement for non-public entities to report pro forma results of combinations under the purchase method.
84	Induced Conversions of Convertible Debt	Requires that the debtor recognize an expense equal to the fair value of any extra consideration given to creditors in order to persuade them to convert their convertible debt holdings to equity.
85	Yield Test for Determining Whether a Convertible Security Is a Common Stock Equivalent	Replaces the cash yield test as previously specified in APB Opinion Number 15 with the effective yield test to determine if convertible securities shall be designated common stock equivalents for the purpose of computing primary earnings per share.
86	Accounting for the Costs of Computer Software to Be Sold, Leased, or Otherwise Marketed	States that software development costs shall be expensed as research and development costs prior to the point at which technological feasibility has been proven, after which they may be capitalized and then amortized over the remaining estimated life of the product.
87	Employers' Accounting for Pensions	Establishes new standards for the treatment of pension accounting, superseding previous releases. The primary change is the accounting for a single-employer defined benefit pension plan.
88	Employers' Accounting for Settlements and Curtailments of Defined Pension Benefit Plans and for Termination Benefits	Describes the accounting for the settlement of obligations under a defined benefit pension plan, termination benefits, and the curtailment of such a plan. It also defines settlement and curtailment.
89	Financial Reporting and Changing Prices	Replaces FASB Statement Number 33 and its later amendments. It also specifies that the disclosure of current cost and constant purchasing power information is voluntary.
90	Regulated Enterprises—Accounting for Abandonments and Disallowances of Plant Costs	Describes the accounting for abandonments of utility plants, as well as the disallowance of plant costs by regulators for the calculation of rate changes. Abandoned assets that are to be included in rate making calculations should be included at their present value, while disallowed costs should be recognized as a loss.

91	Accounting for Nonrefundable Fees and Costs Associated with Originating or Acquiring Loans	Describes how to account for the costs related to lending, or buying a loan, as well as costs related to leasing activities.
92	Regulated Enterprises—Accounting for Phase-In Plans	Modifies FASB Statement Number 71 to account for phase-in plans, which are intended to reduce the impact of utility rate increases that are tied to the implementation of expensive new power generation facilities.
93	Recognition of Depreciation by Not-for-Profit Organizations	Requires that not-for-profit organizations disclose depreciation information, though not for some types of art or historical treasures.
94	Consolidation of All Majority-Owned Subsidiaries	Requires that majority-owned subsidiaries be included in the corporate parent's financial statements on a consolidated basis unless there is no control or control is temporary.
95	Statement of Cash Flows	Describes a new format for cash flow reporting that replaces the statement of changes in financial position and which is to be a key part of all financial statements. It categorizes cash flows by operating, investing, and financing activities.
97	Accounting and Reporting by Insurance Enterprises for Certain Long-Duration Contracts and for Realized Gains and Losses from the Sale of Investments	Describes the accounting for universal life-type contracts, as well as for limited-payment long-duration insurance contracts and investment contracts. It also revises the reporting for realized gains and losses that was originally itemized in FASB Statement Number 60.
98	Accounting for Leases: Sale-Leaseback Transactions Involving Real Estate, Sales-Type Leases of Real Estate, Definition of the Lease Term, and Initial Direct Costs of Direct Financing Leases	Itemizes the types of accounting required by the parties to a sale-leaseback transaction, while also modifying a number of issues originally set forth in FASB Statement Number 13.
99	Deferral of Effective Date of Recognition of Depreciation by Not-for-Profit Organizations	Changes the effective date of FASB Statement Number 93 to fiscal years beginning on or after January 1, 1990.

101	Regulated Enterprises—Accounting for Discontinuation of Application of FASB Statement 71	Specifies how a company should report in its financial statements that it is no longer subject to certain types of regulation, including the elimination of any actions by regulators that had been itemized as assets or liabilities in previous financial reports. The profit impact of any such changes should be recorded in the current period as extraordinary items.
102	Statement of Cash Flows—Exemption of Certain Enterprises and Classification of Cash Flows from Certain Securities Acquired for Resale	Allows some employee benefit plans and certain types of investment companies not to follow the dictates of FASB Statement Number 95, regarding the presentation of a statement of cash flows.
104	Statement of Cash Flows—Net Reporting of Certain Cash Receipts and Cash Payments and Classification of Cash Flows from Hedging Transactions	Allows banks and similar entities to report in a statement of cash flows some cash flows related to deposits and loans.
106	Employers' Accounting for Postretirement Benefits Other than Pensions	Requires that post-retirement healthcare benefits be accounted for by accruing the expected cost of future benefits at the time when employees are still working for the company.
107	Disclosures About Fair Value of Financial Instruments	Requires all organizations to itemize the fair value of all financial instruments in the statement of financial position, if this information can be determined.
109	Accounting for Income Taxes	Outlines the bases and resulting rules upon which one should account for income taxes, focusing on an asset and liability approach to the presentation of income tax information.
110	Reporting by Defined Benefit Pension Plans of Investment Contracts	Mandates that an investment contract held by a defined benefit pension plan be stated at its fair value, while only contracts including mortality risk can be recorded at their contract value.
111	Recission of FASB Statement 32 and Technical Corrections	Rescinds FASB Statement Number 32, and also makes technical corrections to several other documents.

112	Employers' Accounting for Postemployment Benefits	Requires that the liability associated with post-employment benefits be recognized if several requirements are met, as well as that the amount of the liability can be reasonably estimated and it is probable that a liability has been incurred.
113	Accounting and Reporting for Reinsurance of Short-Duration and Long-Duration Contracts	Describes how insurance entities should account for the reinsuring of insurance contracts, requiring reinsurance receivables and prepaid reinsurance premiums to be reported as assets.
114	Accounting by Creditors for Impairment of a Loan	Describes the proper accounting for the impairment of some types of loans by creditors, requiring that these loans be recorded at their discounted present values.
115	Accounting for Certain Investments in Debt and Equity Securities	Describes the different types of reporting for debt and equity securities. Debt that is intended to be held to maturity is reported at amortized cost, while both debt and equity securities to be sold in the near term are reported at fair value, with unrealized gains or losses included in current earnings. Finally, debt and equity that falls into neither category is reported at fair value, with any unrealized gains or losses reported in shareholders' equity.
116	Accounting for Contributions Received and Contributions Made	Describes the standards to be used when making or receiving contributions. Essentially, contributions are made and received at their fair value, while conditional contributions are only recognized when all associated conditions have essentially been met.
117	Financial Statements of Not-for-Profit Organizations	Describes the reporting format to be used by not-for-profit organizations.
118	Accounting by Creditors for Impairment of a Loan—Income Recognition and Disclosures	Modifies FASB Statement 114 to allow creditors to use existing methods for recognizing interest income on an impaired loan.
120	Accounting and Reporting by Mutual Life Insurance Enterprises and by Insurance Enterprises for Certain Long-Duration Participating Contracts	Increases the coverage of FASB Statements 60, 97, and 113 to assessment enterprises, fraternal benefit societies, and mutual life insurance organizations.

121	Accounting for the Impairment of Long-Lived Assets and for Long-Lived Assets to Be Disposed Of	Describes how to account for the impairment or disposition of long-lived assets, some identifiable intangibles, and goodwill related to those assets. The basic requirement is to periodically review those assets for impairment by comparing expected future cash flows to their carrying value.
123	Accounting for Stock Compensation	Describes the required reporting for employee compensation plans that include the use of company stock, such as stock appreciation rights, stock options, stock purchase plans, and restricted stock.
124	Accounting for Certain Investments Held by Not-for-Profit Organizations	Describes how not-for-profit organizations must use fair value when reporting on equity securities whose fair values can be determined, as well as all investments in debt securities.
125	Transfers of Financial Assets and Extinguishment of Liabilities	Describes the reporting requirements related to the transfer of financial assets and the extinguishment of liabilities through the recognition of those financial assets under a business's control and derecognizing both those over which control no longer exists and those liabilities that have been extinguished.
126	Exemption from Certain Required Disclosures About Financial Instruments for Certain Nonpublic Entities	Modifies FASB Statement Number 107 to make the reporting requirements in that document optional if the business is non-public, its total assets are less than $100 million, and the business has not been involved with any derivative-related transactions during the reporting period.
127	Deferral of the Effective Date of Certain Provisions of FASB Statement 125	Adds new criteria to those listed in FASB Statement Number 125 for determining whether a sale or a pledge of collateral for debt has occurred when a transfer of assets arises. It also describes how to account for pledged collateral.
128	Earnings Per Share	Describes how to compute and report on earnings per share information, replacing the use of primary earnings per share with basic earnings per share. Requires the use of a dual presentation of basic and diluted earnings per share if a business has a complex capital structure.
129	Disclosures of Information About Capital Structure	Itemizes the standards for reporting a business's capital structure, and spreads this requirement to nonpublic businesses.

130	Reporting Comprehensive Income	Describes how to report comprehensive income, as well as related revenues and expenses in the financial statements.
131	Disclosures About Segments of Enterprise and Related Information	Replaces FASB Statement Number 14; describes reporting requirements about operating segments, products and services, geographic area, and major customers, both in annual and interim financial statements. This is not applicable to not-for-profit and non-public businesses.
132	Employers' Disclosures About Pensions and Other Postretirement Benefits	Describes the types of disclosures required for employers' pension and related retirement plans, which include information about changes in benefit obligations, as well as the fair values of plan assets. It also allows nonpublic companies to have reduced reporting requirements.
133	Accounting for Derivative Instruments and Hedging Activities	Requires that a business entity recognize all derivatives within the statement of financial position, and that they be measured at their fair value. This Statement encompasses the use of derivatives that are embedded in other types of contracts.
134	Accounting for Mortgage-Backed Securities Retained After the Securitization of Mortgage Loans Held for Sale by a Mortgage Banking Enterprise	Modifies paragraphs 4 and 6 of Statement Number 65 (Accounting for Certain Mortgage Bank Activities) and paragraph 12(a) of Statement Number 115 (Accounting for Certain Investments in Debt and Equity Securities).
135	Rescission of FASB Statement 75 and Technical Corrections	Rescinds Statement Number 75 (Deferral of the Effective Date of Certain Accounting Requirements for Pension Plans of State and Local Governmental Entities) in favor of GASB Statement Number 25. It also excludes benefit pension plans sponsored by government entities from the scope of Statement Number 35.
136	Transfers of Assets to a Not-for-Profit Organization or Charitable Trust that Raises or Holds Contributions for Others	Describes the proper accounting for transactions in which a donor contributes assets to a not-for-profit entity that then shifts the assets to a donor-specified third beneficiary.
137	Accounting for Derivative Instruments and Hedging Activities—Deferral of the Effective Date of FASB Statement 133	Amends paragraphs 48 and 50 of Statement Number 133.

138	Accounting for Certain Derivative Instruments and Certain Hedging Activities—An Amendment of FASB Statement 133	As noted in the title. It is effective for all fiscal quarters and years beginning after June 15, 2000.
139	Rescission of FASB Statement 53 and Amendments to FASB Statements 63, 89, and 121	Substitutes Statement of Position Number 00-2 (Accounting by Producers or Distributors of Films) for FASB Statement Number 53. It also revises earlier FASB statements related to accounting by broadcasters, changing prices, and the impairment or disposition of long-lived assets. It should be applied to all fiscal years beginning after December 15, 2000.
140	Accounting for Transfers and Servicing of Financial Assets and Extinguishments of Liabilities	Describes the accounting standards to be used for transactions related to the transfer and servicing of financial assets, as well as the extinguishment of liabilities. It retains most of Statement 125's pronouncements, but revises the rules for accounting for securitizations and related transfers of financial assets.
141	Business Combinations	Describes the use of the purchase method of accounting to account for business combinations; it eliminates the use of the pooling of interests method of accounting.
142	Goodwill and Other Intangible Assets	Describes how to report intangible assets in the financial statements, though not intangible assets acquired through a business combination. It also notes how intangible assets should be accounted for on an ongoing basis.

5-6 STATEMENTS OF FINANCIAL ACCOUNTING CONCEPTS—FASB

The seven Concepts standards that have been issued by the FASB (of which Number 3 has been superseded) are designed to provide the accountant with a background for the understanding of accounting standards.

Number	Title	Description
1	Objectives of Financial Reporting by Business Enterprises	Specifies that financial reporting is designed to allow one to predict cash flows, entity resources and how they are used, and information that the reader can use to make economic decisions.

2	Qualitative Characteristics of Accounting Information	Specifies that accounting information should be comparable and consistent between periods, as well as understandable, reliable, and relevant.
4	Objectives of Financial Reporting by Non-business Organizations	Establishes the objectives of financial reporting by non-business organizations, which are similar to those for business organizations. It defines non-business organizations, identifies transactions common to them that are uncommon for business organizations, and notes that financial reports for these entities should provide additional information about the level of services provided and the quality of stewardship by managers.
5	Recognition and Measurement in Financial Statements of Business Enterprises	Specifies the types of information to include in financial statements, and the timing of their presentation.
6	Elements of Financial Statements	Defines the core elements to be found in financial statements, which are comprehensive income, revenue, expenses, gains, losses, owner investments, owner distributions, assets, liabilities, and equity.
7	Using Cash Flow Information and Present Value in Accounting Measurements	Describes why and when present value, fair value, and the interest rate method for amortization are used to provide valuations, and how future cash flows can be used to determine this information.

5-7 TECHNICAL BULLETINS—FASB

Technical Bulletins are intended to clarify or elaborate upon underlying accounting standards. They typically address narrow subject areas that are not directly addressed by existing accounting standards; part of the resulting discussion may result in some variations from GAAP that are targeted only at the tightly defined areas that are directly addressed by the Technical Bulletins. Any such changes are not expected to create major variations from current GAAP, nor should they be costly to implement.

Number	Title	Description
79-1	Purpose and Scope of FASB Technical Bulletins and Procedures for Issuance	Notes that technical bulletins are intended to provide guidance in applying the opinions, statements, and interpretations previously issued by both the FASB and its predecessors, as well as to address issues not directly covered by those GAAP standards.

79-3	Subjective Acceleration Clauses in Long-Term Debt Agreements	Does not authorize the restatement of long-term debt as short-term debt in situations where there are subjective acceleration clauses in debt agreements, and where there is little likelihood of acceleration.
79-4	Segment Reporting of Puerto Rican Operations	Specifies that a domestic corporation's Puerto Rican operations should be considered part of its domestic operations, and not a foreign entity.
79-5	Meaning of the Term "Customer" as It Applies to Health Care Facilities Under FASB Statement 14	Specifies that an insuring entity is not a customer of a healthcare facility, for the purposes of reporting on customers who represent at least 10% of an entity's business.
79-9	Accounting in Interim Periods for Changes in Income Tax Rates	Specifies the method for determining the reduction in the corporate tax rate resulting from the Revenue Act of 1978 for those entities not using a calendar year as their fiscal year.
79-10	Fiscal Funding Clauses in Lease Agreements	Specifies that the presence of a fiscal funding clause will not result in a lease being considered cancelable if the probability of the clause being invoked is remote.
79-12	Interest Rate Used in Calculating the Present Value of Minimum Lease Payments	Allows a business to use its secured borrowing rate when determining the present value of minimum lease payments, as long as that rate is reasonable and would be representative of the type of financing used for the lease.
79-13	Applicability of FASB Statement 13 to Current Value Financial Statements	Requires that the provisions of FASB Statement Number 13 be applied to financial statements that have been prepared on a current value basis.
79-14	Upward Adjustment of Guaranteed Residual Values	Prohibits the use of upward adjustments of estimated residual values resulting from renegotiations of the guaranteed portions of residual values.
79-15	Accounting for Loss on a Sublease Not Involving the Disposal of a Segment	Describes a loss on a sublease, and specifies that it be recognized as soon as it is expected to be incurred.
79-16	Effect of a Change in Income Tax Rate on the Accounting for Leveraged Leases	Requires that the income effect of a change in the statutory tax rate be recognized in the period immediately after the change becomes law.

79-17	Reporting Cumulative Effect Adjustment from Retroactive Application of FASB 13	States that the cumulative effect of modifying financial statements to comply with the provisions of FASB Statement Number 13 should not be included in the net income of any presented year unless the year prior to the earliest year presented could not be restated.
79-18	Transition Requirements of Certain FASB Amendments and Interpretations of FASB Statement 13	Describes the financial reporting and disclosure requirements associated with the changes required by FASB Statement Number 13.
80-1	Early Extinguishment of Debt Through Exchange for Common or Preferred Stock	Notes that the provisions of APB Opinion Number 26 do apply to the extinguishment of debt through the issuance of common or preferred stock, and also describes its presentation in the financial statements.
80-2	Classification of Debt Restructurings by Debtors and Creditors	Allows different accounting interpretations of the presence of a troubled debt restructuring by debtors and creditors.
81-6	Applicability of Statement 15 to Debtors in Bankruptcy Situations	Specifies that FASB Statement Number 15, which describes troubled debt restructurings, does not apply to bankrupt companies that restructure their debt as part of a general restructuring of all of their liabilities, but does apply if there is not a general restatement of the debtor's liabilities.
82-1	Disclosure of the Sale or Purchase of Tax Benefits Through Tax Leases	Requires that a company engaged in the sale or purchase of tax benefits through tax leases disclose the method of accounting for them, as well as the methods used to recognize revenue and allocate income tax benefits and asset costs to both current and future periods.
84-1	Accounting for Stock Issued to Acquire the Results of a Research and Development Arrangement	Requires that stock exchanged for the results of a research and development arrangement be recorded at either its fair market value or the fair value of the consideration received.
85-1	Accounting for the Receipt of Federal Home Loan Mortgage Corporation Participating Preferred Stock	Requires that the 12 district banks of the Federal Home Loan Banking System record the receipt of participating preferred stock from the Federal Home Loan Mortgage Corporation at its fair value as of the date of receipt, with any resulting income being recorded as an extraordinary item.

85-3	Accounting for Operating Leases with Scheduled Rent Increases	Requires that scheduled rent increases be recognized on a straight-line basis over the lease term unless there is another systematic allocation system available that better represents the time pattern during which the leased property is being used.
85-4	Accounting for Purchases of Life Insurance	Specifies that life insurance be reported as an asset, with the change in cash surrender value during the period being offset against payments made in order to determine the amount of the insurance expense.
85-5	Issues Relating to Accounting for Business Combinations	Specifies that the costs incurred to close duplicate facilities as a result of a business combination shall be charged to expense, and shall not be included in the accounting for the business combination.
85-6	Accounting for a Purchase of Treasury Shares at a Price Significantly in Excess of the Current Market Price of the Shares and the Income Statement Classification of Costs Incurred in Defending Against a Takeover Attempt	Specifies that if treasury stock is acquired at a price significantly higher than its market price, the difference should be accounted for as being consideration for other services provided by the company, unless no other consideration can be identified. Also notes that corporate payments to a shareholder for a standstill agreement be charged to current expense. Also, any costs incurred to defend against a takeover attempt should be charged to operating expenses, not extraordinary expenses.
86-2	Accounting for an Interest in the Residual Value of a Leased Asset	Requires that an unconditional right to own a leased asset at the end of the lease term requires the lessee to account for it as an asset. It also discusses the valuation of the residual value of leased assets for lessees, lessors, and lease brokers.
87-2	Computation of a Loss on an Abandonment	Describes the accounting for deferred income taxes associated with abandonments and the assets remaining thereafter, with separate treatment for regulated entities.
87-3	Accounting for Mortgage Servicing Fees and Rights	Describes the accounting treatment for the impact of estimated future net servicing income from a refinanced loan on the amortization of capitalized costs related to the acquisition of the mortgage servicing rights for the superseded loan.

88-1	Issues Relating to Accounting for Leases	Describes the proper accounting treatment of leasing issues related to incentives in an operating lease, wrap lease transactions, money-over-money lease transactions, the time pattern of the physical use of operating lease property, and the applicability of leveraged lease accounting to a lessor's existing assets.
90-1	Accounting for Separately Priced Extended Warranty and Product Maintenance Contracts	Specifies that income from a separately priced warranty or maintenance agreement be amortized to income on a straight-line basis over the term of the agreement, except in situations where there is historical proof that some other amortization schedule would more accurately reflect the incurrence of related costs, and also describes the proper treatment of losses on such contracts.
94-1	Application of Statement 115 to Debt Securities in a Troubled Debt Restructuring	Specifies that any restructured loans arising from a troubled debt restructuring are subject to the provisions of FASB Statement Number 115 if it meets the definition of a "security" as defined in that Statement.
97-1	Accounting Under Statement 123 for Certain Employee Stock Purchase Plans with a Look-Back Option	Describes the situations in which the fair value measurement technique is used to value awards under various types of employee stock purchase plans with look-back provisions.

5-8 SUMMARY

There is a considerable amount of research involved in tracing the summaries in this chapter back to the source documents. An alternative approach is to consult a summary-level GAAP guide, such as the *GAAP* guide published annually by John Wiley & Sons. The same publishing house also issues a *GAAP for Governments* book, *Not-for-Profit GAAP* book, *GAAP for Governments Field Guide,* and *GAAP for Employee Benefits Plans* book, for those who desire a less comprehensive set of accounting pronouncements. An alternative source is the Topical Index located at the back of the final volume of the AICPA's *Original Pronouncements* book (which was described at the beginning of this chapter). This index provides a handy reference for tracing back from specific subjects to all of the underlying accounting pronouncements.

CHAPTER 6

The Securities and Exchange Commission

6-1 INTRODUCTION

The Securities and Exchange Commission (SEC) exerts a considerable amount of control over the financial reporting activities of publicly held companies, particularly in the areas of new securities issuance and the ongoing release of financial information to the general public (particularly under the new Regulation FD). Though a complete and detailed review of all SEC requirements is beyond the scope of this chapter, we will review the reasons for the SEC's existence, how it is organized, and the laws under which it gains its authority to issue regulations. An overview of many of its key regulations is provided, but their original text is so detailed and in-depth that the reader is advised to peruse the original text of those regulations that are directly applicable to his or her business.

6-2 OVERVIEW OF THE SEC

The SEC was created as a direct result of the stock market crash of October 1929. Given the massive loss of net worth as a result of the plunge in stock market prices at that time, the federal government felt that a considerable degree of regulation over the securities industry was necessary in order to ensure that the resulting increase in public confidence in the stock market would eventually draw the public back to it.

After a series of hearings to determine what specific forms of regulation would meet this goal, Congress passed the Securities Act and the Securities Exchange Act in 1933 and 1934, respectively. As noted in later sections of this chapter, the two Acts were designed to greatly increase the information reported by an entity issuing securities (especially the nature of its business and any associated investment risks), as well as the amount of oversight by the government. The oversight function was centered on the regulation of the markets in which securities were sold, as well as the brokers and investment advisors who worked with investors to buy and sell securities. The reporting of information by securities issuers has blossomed into a key function of the SEC, which requires that timely filings be submitted to it of all material financial information by issuers, which it promptly makes available to the public through its EDGAR on-line database (see later section).

Congress created the SEC as part of the 1934 Act to administer the new Acts. Its powers later increased as other Acts were also passed, eventually giving it regulatory authority over public utility holding companies and mutual funds, too. It has a significant amount of enforcement authority to back up its regulatory oversight function, typically bringing about 500 civil enforcement actions per year against any person or business entity that breaks the securities laws. The remaining sections give an overview of the SEC's structure, as well as the laws under which it issues regulations.

6-3 ORGANIZATION OF THE SEC

The SEC is organized around four divisions and 18 offices, all of which are described below. Its headquarters is located in Washington, D.C. Its staff of 2,900 employees is spread across 11 regional and district offices. It is run by five commissioners (one of whom is appointed Chairman); all are appointed by the President. The term of each commissioner is five years, with the use of staggered appointments to ensure that only one commissioner is approved each year. Only three of the commissioners are allowed to be members of the same political party, thereby bringing a more neutral flavor to the political leanings of the SEC.

The commissioners have regular meetings at which they amend or interpret existing rules, propose new ones within the guidelines set up under existing congressional laws, and enforce existing regulations. These meetings are generally open to the public, except for those related to some enforcement issues.

The creation of new rules is not a simple process, and the commissioners only see proposed rules after a long series of reviews have been completed. It begins with a *concept release,* in which the SEC's staff describes the problem that it is attempting to address, why it feels there is a problem, and lay out a variety of possible regulatory solutions. The public has an opportunity to comment upon these possible solutions. The resulting text is taken into consideration when the SEC then drafts a *rule proposal,* which is a detailed rule in draft form that is presented to the SEC for approval. The public then has 30 to 60 days to comment on the draft rule proposal; the resulting information is then incorporated into the final rule. The rule proposal will sometimes be the start of the rule creation process, rather than the concept release, if the issue under consideration is not thought to be excessively complicated or controversial. The resulting text of the rule is presented to the full commission for approval. If the rule is considered to be a major one, the additional step of seeking congressional approval may also be taken. In either case, the rule then becomes part of the official set of regulations under which the SEC operates.

The responsibilities of the SEC's various divisions and offices are:

- *Division of Corporate Finance.* This Division supervises the corporate disclosure of information to investors. This involves the issuance of information by companies not only when a stock is initially offered to the public, but also on a continuing basis. The basic underlying principle that the Division follows is that corporations must make available a complete set of information regarding positive or negative issues that might be relevant to an investor's decisions regarding corporate securities. The Division also helps companies with any questions they may have regarding submissions. An example of such assistance is advising a company about the need to register a particular type of security with the SEC. At a more advanced level of inquiry, the Division can provide guidance to companies that want to take action in areas that are not clearly governed by existing SEC regulations by writing letters indicating what type of action it would recommend the SEC take if proposed activities were to be taken (a *no-action letter* being an indication that no action would be taken).

  Another task is the review of submitted documents for completeness and compliance with its various rules. The primary documents that it reviews are:

  - Annual (10-K) and quarterly (10-Q) filings of financial results.
  - Annual shareholder reports.
  - Merger and acquisition filings.
  - Proxy materials for annual shareholder meetings.
  - Registration statements for new securities.
  - Tender offer documentation.

The Division also interprets the laws over which it provides jurisdiction, which are primarily the Securities Act of 1933, the Securities Exchange Act of 1934, and the Trust Indenture Act of 1939 (all of which are described in later sections of this chapter), creating regulations that expand upon the specific requirements listed within these Acts. It also provides information and opinions to the Financial Accounting Standards Board, which promulgates accounting principles for professional accountants.

- *Division of Enforcement.* This Division investigates instances where securities laws may have been broken, recommends legal action where necessary, and negotiates settlements with violators. Its investigations include private investigative work by its own staff (including interviews and the examination of brokerage records and trading information, using subpoenas if necessary), as well as the collection of information from other sources, such as the securities industry itself, investors, and the media. A sample of the activities that may bring about an investigation by the division are:

  - Insider trading of securities.
  - Manipulating securities prices.

- Misrepresenting, falsifying, or omitting submitted information about specific securities or a company's financial condition.
- Sale of securities without prior registration with the SEC.
- Theft of customer funds by an investment advisor or broker-dealer.
- Treating customers unfairly.

Legal action is limited to civil cases in federal court or via an administrative law judge, at the discretion of the SEC. If civil action is considered necessary, then the SEC will ask for an injunction from a U.S. District Court to stop whatever activity is violating the law. The court can also authorize penalties or a *disgorgement* (the return of illegally acquired profits). If necessary, the court can prevent an individual from serving as a corporate officer. If an administrative judgment is pursued instead, then the SEC will bring the matter before a judge who works independently from the SEC, and whose decision can be appealed back to the SEC. Penalties can include a censure, monetary payment, disgorgement, disbarment from the securities industry or revocation of one's registration to practice, or a cease-and-desist order. The SEC also provides assistance to various law enforcement agencies if they are working to bring criminal charges in addition to the civil or administrative charges already being brought by the SEC.

- *Division of Market Regulation.* This Division creates standards that result in fair and efficient market activities. It regulates the major participants in the securities markets in order to achieve this goal. Its prime targets for regulation are the stock exchanges, clearing agencies (which facilitate the settlement of trades), the Municipal Securities Rulemaking Board, broker-dealer firms, transfer agents (which maintain securities ownership records), and securities information processors. The Division's primary responsibilities over these market participants is to conduct an ongoing review of market activities, create and update regulations governing securities market operations, and implement the SEC's broker-dealer financial integrity program. It also oversees a private, non-profit company called the Securities Investor Protection Corporation (SPIC), which insures the securities and cash of member brokerages in the event of a bankruptcy of one of the brokerages.

- *Division of Investment Management.* This division regulates investment companies through a variety of federal securities laws, with the twin goals of increasing information disclosure without causing the cost of disclosure to be excessive to issuers. Specifically, it reviews enforcement issues involving investment companies, designs new regulations based on existing laws in order to meet changes in the investment environment, reviews filings by investment companies, and responds to requests regarding the need for specific filings. It conducts similar tasks within the utility industry under the authorization of the Public Utility Holding Company Act of 1935, while also conducting periodic audits of utility holding companies.

- *Office of Administrative and Personnel Management.* This office conducts much of the human resources and general management activities of the SEC. Its tasks include security and safety, publications activities, purchasing, property management, recruitment and pay administration, as well as payroll, employee training, and performance reviews.

- *Office of Administrative Law Judges.* The judges in this office administer non-jury hearings regarding allegations of securities law violations brought by the SEC's staff and issue rulings based on the hearings. Parties involved in the hearings can submit to the judge their proposed findings of fact and conclusions of law for consideration alongside other information revealed during the hearings. Judges can then issue initial decisions, which may be appealed to the SEC.

- *Office of Compliance Inspections and Examinations.* As its name implies, this office is responsible for inspecting those activities of organizations registered with the SEC (such as investment companies, broker-dealers, and transfer agents) to ensure that the applicable securities laws are being complied with. It issues a *deficiency letter* to those organizations whose activities require correction, and then returns to monitor the problem areas until they have achieved compliance with the applicable regulations. Major violations are referred to the Division of Enforcement for more vigorous legal attention.

- *Office of Economic Analysis.* This office investigates the economic impact that results from current and proposed SEC regulatory activities. It also reviews any number of market activities required of it by the SEC, and then reports back to the SEC with its findings and advice.

- *Office of Equal Employment Opportunity.* This office focuses primarily on EEO issues within the SEC, supporting EEO initiatives in the recruitment, training, and compensation of its employees through policy promulgation, audits, and dispute resolutions. It also sponsors diversity and minority forums within the securities industry.

- *Office of Filings and Information Services.* This office is responsible for the receipt, custody, and control of all public records filed with the SEC, as well as the records management system used to track them. It also has a Public Reference Branch, which makes documents available to the public that have previously been submitted to the SEC, such as annual and quarterly financial reports. It makes most of these documents available through the Internet at *www.sec.gov.* The information is also available in a somewhat more readable format through a privately managed site called *www.edgar-online.com.* Paper-based documents are also available through the SEC's public reference room in Washington, D.C.

- *Office of Information Technology.* This office designs, develops, and maintains the SEC's computer systems at both its headquarters and regional locations. It also manages the EDGAR system (see later section), and maintains the SEC's official web site, which is located at *www.sec.gov.*

- *Office of International Affairs.* This office works with foreign governments to share information regarding regulatory enforcement issues, represents the SEC at international organizations, and also provides technical assistance to the governments of other countries that are creating securities markets.

- *Office of Investor Education and Assistance.* This office handles complaints and questions from individual investors; it cannot actively assist investors with their problems, but can offer advice in regard to how they can proceed with specific issues. It also provides an investor education function by setting up Investors' Town Meetings throughout the country in which office representatives lecture about investment and retirement issues.

- *Office of Legislative Affairs.* This office advises the SEC about current federal legislative issues, keeps Congress informed regarding current SEC activities (through testimony and briefings), and advises the SEC regarding the applicability and likely legislative response to its regulatory initiatives. It also keeps other government agencies informed of potential SEC-related legislation that may affect them.

- *Office of Municipal Securities.* This office oversees the municipal securities activities of the SEC, which includes advising it on policy matters, coordinating enforcement issues with the Division of Enforcement, and advising state and local officials about risk management issues and SEC regulations.

- *Office of Public Affairs, Policy Evaluation, and Research.* This office is the public relations arm of the SEC. It reviews media coverage of SEC issues and responds to it, while also providing speech material and planning for special events.

- *Office of the Chief Accountant.* The members of this office work with the various domestic and international standard setting bodies, such as the Financial Accounting Standards Board, The American Institute of Certified Public Accountants, and the International Accounting Standards Committee, and auditors to determine the applicability of existing standards and regulations to specific financial reporting situations. It then advises the SEC regarding possible enforcement issues resulting from this analysis.

- *Office of the Comptroller.* This office manages the budgeting and financial operations of the SEC, including financial system oversight, resource utilization, cash management, collections, and general accounting operations.

- *Office of the Executive Director.* This office oversees the budget process, allocation of SEC resources, control systems, administration, and information systems. In short, it is in charge of management policies within the SEC.

- *Office of the General Counsel.* This is the SEC's chief legal officer. In this capacity, the office represents the SEC in various legal proceedings, while also preparing legal briefs and advising the SEC on legal matters. It sometimes enters into and offers advice on interpretations of securities laws that are part of private appellate litigation.

- *Office of the Inspector General.* This office is the internal audit division of the SEC. As such, it investigates control issues within the SEC's operations, with a specific focus on risk identification and mitigation, as well as making recommendations to improve the efficiency and effectiveness of the SEC's overall operations.

- *Office of the Secretary.* This office schedules SEC meetings, maintains records of SEC actions, publishes official documents in the *SEC Docket, Federal Register,* and SEC web site, tracks documents used in administrative proceedings and similar matters, and tracks the status of financial judgments imposed by the SEC as a result of enforcement rulings.

6-4 EDGAR

EDGAR is an acronym for the Electronic Data Gathering, Analysis, and Retrieval system. It is the SEC's primary on-line tool for automating the collection, validation, indexing, and forwarding of forms filed by companies that are legally required to do so with the SEC. Not only does EDGAR nearly eliminate the paperwork burden on the SEC, but it is also a superior tool for investors and analysts, who have almost immediate on-line access to the forms being filed. The rules and guidelines under which companies are required to make submissions to EDGAR are codified under the SEC's Regulation S-T.

The SEC requires all publicly held companies with more than $10 million in assets and 500 shareholders to file their registration statements and periodic reports through EDGAR. However, Form 144 (Notice of Proposed Sale of Securities), Forms 3, 4, and 5 (which are reports related to security ownership and transaction reports for corporate insiders), and the annual report to shareholders (except for investment companies) only have to be filed through EDGAR at the filer's option. Foreign companies do not have to file forms through EDGAR.

It is not necessary (or allowable) to make electronic submissions for some documents, for which paper-based filings are still necessary. At the moment, these include:

- Applications for deregistration, filed under the Investment Company Act.
- Confidential treatment applications.
- Regulation A filings and any other offering that is exempt from Securities Act registration.
- No-action, exemptive, and interpretive requests.
- Shareholder proposal filings.
- Litigation information filed under the Investment Company Act.

Official submissions to EDGAR must be in either HTML (version 3.2 is the standard as of this writing) or plain text. Anyone who chooses to make a submission in the HTML format is allowed to use hyperlinks between different sections of the same HTML document, and may also include hyperlinks to exhibits that have been included in the same filing. One can also include links to other official filings within the EDGAR database if submissions are made with the new EDGARLink version; however, it is not allowable to include links to documents located outside of the EDGAR database. Hyperlinks are not allowed as a substitute for information that is required to be included in a specific document, even if the required information could be located through a linkage to another document that is also filed through EDGAR.

The SEC does not currently allow video or audio material to be included in submissions to EDGAR, though it is acceptable to include graphic and image material within HTML documents.

It is also possible to make a submission in a PDF (Acrobat) format, but this is considered an unofficial filing that must be accompanied by one of the other two formats. If a PDF file is submitted, only its formatting and graphics may differ from the official filing.

There are two cases in which a company can plead hardship and avoid making an electronic submission of data. In the first instance, Rule 201 of Regulation S-T allows a temporary exemption for an electronic filer that is having unanticipated trouble in submitting a report, such as in cases where the transmitting computer fails. A paper-based filing, using Form TH (Notification of Reliance on Temporary Hardship Exemption), is still required in this instance, and must be followed within six days by an electronic submission. In the second case, Rule 202 of Regulation S-T allows a permanent exemption for a few cases where the information to be filed is so large that the filer would be caused undue hardship to do so. The first case requires no SEC approval, whereas the second case does.

6-5 THE SECURITIES ACT OF 1933

The Securities Act of 1933 requires companies issuing securities for public purchase to issue financial and other significant information to investors, while also prohibiting fraud or misrepresentations of financial information. The issuance of information is accomplished through the registration of information about the securities with the SEC, which will review submitted information to ensure that disclosure requirements under this Act have been met. A key item is that this Act is primarily concerned with the issuance of information related to the initial offering of securities only, rather than with ongoing updates to securities-related information (which is covered by the Securities Exchange Act of 1934).

There are a few instances in which the mandated disclosure requirements do not have to be met. If a securities offering is of a limited size, if it is issued by a municipal, state, or federal government, or if the offering is limited to a small number of investors, then it is exempted from registration with the SEC.

The information sent to the SEC provides essential details about (1) the issuing company's properties and business, (2) securities available for sale, (3) the management team, and (4) audited financial statements.

If the information provided by the issuing company can be proven by an investor to be incomplete or inaccurate, then investors may have the right to recover their invested funds from the company.

6-6 THE SECURITIES EXCHANGE ACT OF 1934

This Act created the SEC, giving it authority to regulate many players in the securities industry, such as stock exchanges (for example, the New York Stock Exchange and National Association of Securities Dealers), clearing agencies, brokerage firms, and transfer agents. The Act requires these market players to register with the SEC, which involves the filing of regularly updated disclosure reports. It prohibits the trading of securities on unregistered exchanges. Also, self-regulatory organizations (such as the National Association of Securities Dealers) are required to set up rules under which they can ensure that investors are adequately protected while conducting transactions with members of the self-regulatory organizations.

The Act requires firms with more than $10 million in assets, and whose securities are held by more than 500 investors, to file both annual reports and a variety of other supplemental reports. The Act also applies to anyone who wishes to acquire more than 5% of a company's securities by tender offer or direct purchase to disclose information to the SEC (this provision was added through a 1970 amendment to the Act).

The Act also creates rules for the types of information included in proxy solicitations that are used to obtain shareholder votes regarding the election of directors and other corporate matters. In brief, the solicitations must disclose all important facts regarding the topics about which the shareholders are being asked to vote. It requires that these solicitations be filed with the SEC prior to their issuance to the shareholders in order to ensure that their content complies with the disclosure rules of the Act.

The Act also gave the Federal Reserve System's Board of Governors the power to determine the allowable credit limits that could be used to purchase securities through margin trading. It also requires broker-dealers to obtain the written permission of investors before lending any securities carried on the investors' accounts. The intention behind these actions was to avoid the massive loss of wealth that occurred during the 1929 stock market crash, when investors who had purchased heavily on margin lost all of their net worth.

It also prohibits insider trading activities, which occur when a person trades a security based on nonpublic information, particularly when that person has a fiduciary duty to refrain from trading. A 1984 amendment to the Act prohibited the officers and directors of a company from short selling the securities issued by their companies. They are also required to report the amount of securities they hold in their companies, and any changes in those holdings, as long as the amount held is more than 10% of the total of registered securities.

The Act specifically prohibits market manipulation through such means as giving a false impression of high levels of trading activity in a stock, issuing false information about possible changes in a stock's price, price fixing, and making false statements in regard to a security.

6-7 THE PUBLIC UTILITY HOLDING COMPANY ACT OF 1935

This Act authorizes the regulation of interstate holding companies that are engaged in the retail distribution of natural gas or in the electric utility business, with particular attention to perceived abuses by this type of business. A holding company is defined as one that owns at least 10% of a public utility company's voting stock. A holding company is exempted from this Act only if it operates within a single state, or is an operating public utility company that operates in a single state or in contiguous ones, is not in the public utility business, is a temporary holding company, or is not a public utility business within the United States.

One intent of the Act is to confine each holding company to a single integrated public utility system that would keep each company contained within a single geographic region. Also, to keep this type of company from expanding outside the boundaries of that single public utility system, the Act provides that only those non-utility businesses can be bought that are "reasonably incidental or economically necessary or appropriate" to its operations.

The Act also provides for the elimination of unnecessary levels of corporate structural complexity, as well as any accumulation of inequitable voting power by certain shareholders. These provisions are designed to keep people with a small number of shares from gaining voting control over a holding company.

The Act clearly identifies the types and amounts of securities that a holding company should issue or acquire. Issued securities must correspond to the earning power and capital structure of the holding company. The SEC can only authorize the issuance of securities for a holding company if the proposed issuance has already cleared all hurdles imposed by applicable local state laws.

Also, the Act requires holding companies to first obtain the approval of the SEC before acquiring any securities, utility assets, or ownership interest in any other business. This restriction includes obtaining SEC approval before becoming an affiliate of another public utility company. These companies are also not allowed to borrow from each other.

The SEC must also be advised before any sale of assets or securities between holding companies occurs, or any transactions at all between affiliates. In addition, any service or construction contracts that holding companies enter into with each other must be fairly priced, so that there is no undue transfer of assets among companies as a result of the contracts.

In short, this Act provides significant restrictions on some types of public utility holding companies in order to forestall the possibility of monopolies being created or an excessive amount of control over this type of company being gathered by a small number of individuals.

6-8 THE TRUST INDENTURE ACT OF 1939

This Act applies to debt securities, such as bonds, debentures, and notes that are made available for public sale. These types of securities cannot be offered for sale to the public if there is a trust indenture agreement already in existence between the bond issuer and the bond holder that follows the rules specified by this Act. The Act also requires that the trustee be a corporation with a minimum amount of capital, that the trustee conforms to high standards of conduct, that the trustee not have conflicting interests that would interfere with its tasks on behalf of the holders of securities, and that the trustee prepare and send reports to security holders.

The Act also requires the trustee to maintain a list of securities holders, which must be issued to them at their request. It also provides that the securities issuer provide to the trustee all necessary evidence of compliance with the terms and conditions of the trust indenture agreement.

6-9 THE INVESTMENT COMPANY ACT OF 1940

This Act is designed to regulate those entities whose primary occupation is investing in and trading securities, especially those whose securities are made available to investors. The Act requires these entities to reveal their investment policies, as well as their financial condition, to investors—both at the initial sale of securities and at regular intervals thereafter. Other information that should be included in these disclosures is the entity's organizational structure, operations, and investment objectives.

The Act does not give the SEC authority to supervise these entities or rate the quality of their investments—only to ensure that they are disclosing the required minimum amount of information to investors.

The Act goes beyond the basic information reporting requirements to also prohibit investment entities from significantly changing their investment policies or entering into management contracts without shareholder approval. Furthermore, anyone guilty of securities fraud is prohibited from becoming an officer of an investment entity, while brokers, underwriters, and investment bankers are prohibited from forming a majority of its Board of Directors. Finally, investment entities are prohibited from cross-ownership of each other's securities.

6-10 THE INVESTMENT ADVISERS ACT OF 1940

The Investment Advisers Act of 1940 defines what constitutes an investment adviser, which (in its amended form) is anyone with at least $25 million of assets under management. The Act then goes on to require these advisers to register with the SEC, as well as conform to a series of rules that are designed to protect investors, such as maintaining their records in accordance with SEC rules, making those records accessible for SEC audits, and clearly identifying any financial interest they may have in transactions that they have executed for their clients.

Violations of the investment adviser rules fall into the general categories of willful violations of the Securities Act of 1933, the Investment Company Act of 1940, or the Securities Exchange Act of 1934. A violation will also be assumed to have occurred if the adviser has "aided, abetted, counseled, commanded, induced, or procured such a violation by any other person," or has failed to properly supervise another person who has committed these acts. It also counts as a violation the misstatement or omission of key facts related to a securities filing. Penalties assessed are primarily monetary in nature, as well as cease-and-desist orders, though the SEC will sometimes deny, suspend, or revoke an adviser's registration if it feels that such action is in the public interest. Beyond these penalties, the SEC can also recommend criminal action to the Justice Department.

6-11 REGULATION FD

The SEC recently released a new regulation, which is the Regulation Fair Disclosure (Regulation FD). The new regulation is designed to curb the disclosure of material information by companies to selected individuals, such as securities analysts, that is not revealed to the general investing public. The regulation will also supposedly reduce a security analyst's incentive not to disclose this information to the general public (on the grounds that the analyst might no longer be given the privileged information). By imposing Regulation FD, this may curb the amount of insider trading that has arisen based on the non-public information.

In essence, the regulation requires that an issuer of material information must do so publicly, either by filing the disclosure with the SEC, or by some other broad, non-exclusionary method, such as an Internet Webcast or press release. If material information is disseminated by mistake, then the issuer must act promptly to publicly disclose the information. The regulation does not apply to issuer communications with the press or rating agencies, and communications during the ordinary course of business with business partners, such as customers and suppliers, nor does it apply to any foreign issuers. It does apply to any communications with anyone who is involved with the securities markets on a professional basis, as well as the holders of any securities issued by the company. Also, to keep a company from having to monitor the communications of its entire staff, the regulation only applies to senior management, its investor relations staff, and anyone else who works for the company and who regularly communicates with holders of company securities or anyone involved with the securities markets.

If an issuer violates the regulation, the SEC can initiate an administrative proceeding resulting in a cease-and-desist order, or can go further to seek an injunction or even civil penalties.

6-12 REGULATION D

This regulation covers the limited offer and sale of securities without having to register under the filing requirements of the Securities Act of 1933. In order to be covered under this regulation, the initial offer and sale of a security must be completed within six months before or after the Regulation D offering, is not sold through any form of advertisement or seminar, and cannot be resold without registration under the Securities Act. The issuer must also exercise reasonable care to ensure that the buyers of its securities are not underwriters. Under Rule 504 of the Regulation, development stage companies (with some exceptions) can issue up to $1 million to an unlimited number of investors within a one-year period. Under Rule 505 of the Regulation, any company (except an investment company) can issue up to $5 million of its securities to an unlimited number of accredited investors or up to 35 non-accredited investors. The offering must be made without advertisement or sale through investment seminars, and must be completed within a one-year period.

This regulation can be overridden by the law of any state in which an issuing company resides, so one should be sure to check local laws before concluding that filing requirements are not required.

6-13 REGULATION M-A

This regulation governs the filing requirements associated with mergers and acquisitions. Information that must be provided to the SEC and securities holders includes:

- *Summary term sheet.* This document itemizes, in bullet point format, the key items of a proposed merger or acquisition transaction, such that securities holders can comprehend its importance and key features.

- *Subject company information.* This includes the acquiree's name and address, types of the acquiree's securities to be bought, their trading price, and amount and timing of dividends paid.

- *Identity and background of filing person.* This includes the name, address, and business background of the filer.

- *Terms of the transaction.* This includes the type of securities to be bought, consideration made, expiration date of the offer, and issues related to the transfer of securities to the buyer. If a merger is contemplated, then the reasons for doing so must be given, the need for a vote by securities holders to approve it (if any), the method of accounting used to record the transaction, and its income tax consequences.

- *Past transactions.* This includes a description of the types and amounts of any material transactions in which the parties were engaged in the past two years, as well as any potential conflicts of interest.

- *Purpose of the transaction.* This includes an itemization of the reason for the transaction, what will happen to any acquired securities, and any plans for the sale of assets, dividend changes, or changes to the subject company's organizational structure that will result from the transaction.

- *Amount and source of funds.* This includes an expected amount of funding that will be required to complete the transaction, as well as where the funds are expected to come from, plus key financing terms.

- *Financial statements.* This includes audited financial statements for the past two years, unaudited statements for the most recent quarter, and pro forma statements for the combined entities.

- *Solicitation or recommendation.* This includes a recommendation to securities holders to either accept or reject the transaction, and any recommended alternatives. If the subject company is filing, it can remain neutral in its recommendation.

6-14 REGULATION S-B

This regulation is similar to Regulation S-K in that it lays out the specific information that issuers must periodically send to the SEC. However, this regulation has a somewhat reduced set of filing requirements that are targeted at small companies that cannot afford the more in-depth filing requirements of S-K. As a qualified small business issuer, a company will file its registration statement under Form SB-2 or Form 10-SB. In order to qualify for these reduced requirements, a company must have revenues of less than $25 million, be an American- or Canadian-based issuer, and not be an investment company. Also, if it is a subsidiary, its corporate parent must also qualify as a small business issuer. Furthermore, its market capitalization must be no more than $25 million, based on the price of its securities within 60 days of its most recent fiscal year end. Finally, the business must meet these requirements for two consecutive years before qualifying as a small business.

6-15 REGULATION S-K

This regulation contains the instructions for filing forms with the SEC under the rules set by the Securities Act of 1933, the Securities Exchange Act of 1934, and the Energy Policy and Conservation Act of 1975. It concentrates primarily upon the content of the non-financial statements that must be filed, dwelling in particular upon the following topics:

- Description of the general development of the business during the past five years.
- Financial information and a narrative description about individual segments of the business for each of the last three years.
- Financial information about geographic areas for each of the last three years.
- The general types of property owned by the company, as well as where it is located.
- Estimates of oil or gas reserves.
- Any legal proceedings currently under way, either at the company's initiation or to which it is subject.
- The primary markets in which each class of the company's common stock is being traded.
- The approximate number of holders of each type of common stock.
- The amount and timing of the cash dividends declared on each class of common stock for the last two years.
- Description of all securities to be offered for sale.
- Key financial information in a columnar format for the last five years.
- Selected quarterly financial information for the last two years.

- Management's discussion of liquidity, capital resources, and the results of operations.

- Material changes during interim reporting periods.

- Any change in the outside auditing firm in the last two years.

- The market risk associated with trading instruments, as well as how these risks are managed.

- Terms and information about derivative financial instruments.

- The name, age, and position of each company director.

- The name, age, and position of each executive officer.

- The compensation of the CEO and the four most highly paid individuals besides the CEO (but only if their total pay exceeds $100,000). This statement shall separately itemize salary, bonus, option, and pension remuneration.

The regulation also sets forth the reporting requirements for a prospectus, and cross-references a series of industry guides that detail additional, and more specific, reporting requirements. The industry guides are for the oil and gas, bank holding company, real estate limited partnership, property-casualty underwriting, and mining businesses. Regulation S-K provides the foundation for much of the information reporting requirements that publicly held companies must file, and so should be perused in detail by those entities.

6-16 REGULATION S-T

This regulation governs the electronic submission of documents to the SEC. Transmissions may be sent to the SEC, either by dial-up modem or directly through the Internet, on any business day except federal holidays and between the hours of 8 A.M. and 10 P.M., Eastern Standard Time. The following types of documents must be filed in an electronic format:

- Registration statements and prospectuses.

- Statements and applications required by the Trust Indenture Act.

- Statements, reports, and schedules required by the Exchange Act.

- Documents required by the Investment Company Act.

- Documents required by the Public Utility Act.

The following documents must be submitted on paper:

- Confidential treatment requests.

- Supplemental information.

- Shareholder proposals and related correspondence.

- No-action and interpretive letter requests.

- Applications for exemptive relief.

- Promotional and sales material.

- Documents in a foreign language.

- Maps submitted by public utility holding companies.

- Applications for exemption from Exchange Act reporting requirements.

- All first electronic filings, which must also be submitted on paper.

If a company is attempting to meet a filing deadline with the SEC, an electronic submission that is filed on or before 5:30 P.M., Eastern Standard Time, will be presumed to have been filed on that business day, whereas any filing submitted after that time will be presumed to have been filed on the next business day. However, this assumption shifts to 10 P.M. for the filing of registration statements.

If the submitting entity makes an electronic submission that contains errors solely due to errors in the transmission, and if the submitter corrects the errors as soon as possible after becoming aware of the difficulty, then there shall be no liability under the antifraud portions of the federal securities laws.

In order to protect itself from computer viruses, the SEC will suspend the filing of any document that appears to contain executable code. If such a document is accepted and the code is discovered at a later date, then it may be deleted from EDGAR and the filer will be required to make a new submission of the required data.

The primary document needed for preparing an electronic document for the SEC is its *EDGAR Filing Manual.* One can download it at *www.sec.gov/info/edgar/filermanual.htm,* or order it from the Public Reference Room, Securities and Exchange Commission, 450 5th Street, N.W., Washington, D.C. 20549-0102.

For more information about Regulation S-T, particularly in relation to hardship filings and the use of HTML documents, please refer to the section in this chapter that describes the SEC's on-line EDGAR filing system.

6-17 REGULATION S-X (REQUIREMENTS FOR FINANCIAL STATEMENT REPORTING)

This regulation is the principal one used by the SEC to oversee the form and content of financial statements submitted by the issuers of securities. This is a very important regulation for a publicly held company; to peruse its entire content, one can access it on the SEC's web site at *www.sec.gov/divisions/corpfin/forms.* The regulation is comprised of the following sections:

- *Article 2: Qualifications and reports of accountants.* The SEC will not recognize as a CPA any person who is not currently registered to practice in the state where his or her home or office is located. It will also not recognize a CPA as being independent if the CPA has a financial interest in the entity being audited, or was a manager or promoter of an auditee at the time of the audit. It requires a CPA's report be dated and manually signed, state that GAAP was followed, state an audit opinion, and clearly itemize any exceptions found.

- *Article 3: General instructions as to financial statements.* Balance sheets must be submitted for the last two year-ends, as well as statements of income and cash flow for the preceding three years. If interim financial statements are provided, then standard year-end accruals should also be made for the shorter periods being reported upon. Changes in stockholders' equity shall be included in a note or a separate statement. The financial statements of related businesses can be presented to the SEC in a single consolidated format if the companies are under common control and management during the period to which the reports apply. There are a number of tests to determine whether or not consolidated results are required, as well as for how many time periods over which the combined financial statements must be reported. If a registrant is inactive (revenues and expenses of less than $100,000, and no material changes in the business or changes in securities) during the period, then its submitted financial statements can be unaudited. There are also special reporting requirements for foreign private issuers, real estate investment trusts, and management investment companies.

- *Article 3a: Consolidated and combined financial statements.* For financial statement reporting purposes, a registrant shall consolidate financial results for business entities that are majority owned, and shall not do so if ownership is in the minority. A consolidated statement is also possible if the year-end dates of the various companies are not more than 93 days apart. Inter-company transactions shall be eliminated from the consolidated reports. If consolidating the results of a foreign subsidiary, then the impact of any exchange restrictions shall be made.

- *Article 4: Rules of general application.* Financial statements not created in accordance with GAAP will be presumed to be misleading or inaccurate. If the submitting entity is foreign-based, it may use some other set of accounting standards than GAAP, but a reconciliation between its financial statements and those produced under GAAP must also be submitted. Footnotes to the statements that duplicate each other may be submitted just once, as long as there are sufficient cross-references to the remaining footnote. The amount of income taxes applicable to foreign governments and the United States government shall be shown separately, unless the foreign component is no more than 5% of the total. There must also be a reconciliation between the reported amount of income tax and the amount as computed by multiplying net income by the statutory tax rate. This article also contains an extensive review of the manner in which oil and gas financial results must be reported.

- *Article 5: Commercial and industrial companies.* This article describes the specific line items and related footnotes that shall appear in the financial statements. *On the balance sheet,* this shall include:
  - Cash.
  - Marketable securities.
  - Accounts and notes receivable.
  - Allowance for doubtful accounts.
  - Unearned income.
  - Inventory.
  - Prepaid expenses.
  - Other current expenses.

- Other investments.
- Fixed assets and associated accumulated depreciation.
- Intangible assets and related amortization.
- Other assets.
- Accounts and notes payable.
- Other current liabilities.
- Long-term debt.
- Minority interests (footnote only).
- Redeemable and non-redeemable preferred stock.
- Common stock.
- Other stockholder's equity.

On the income statement, this shall include:

- Gross revenues.
- Costs applicable to revenue.
- Other operating costs.
- Selling.
- General and administrative expenses.
- Other general expenses.
- Non-operating income.
- Interest.
- Non-operating expenses.
- Income or loss before income taxes.
- Income tax expense.
- Minority interest in income of consolidated subsidiaries.
- Equity in earnings of unconsolidated subsidiaries.
- Income or loss from continuing operations.
- Discontinued operations.
- Income or loss before extraordinary items.
- Extraordinary items.
- Cumulative effect of changes in accounting principles.
- Net income or loss.
- Earnings per share data.

- *Article 6: Registered investment companies.* This type of company is required to file a balance sheet that contains the following line items:
  - Investments in securities of unaffiliated issuers.
  - Investments in and advances to affiliates.

- Investments other than securities.
- Total investments.
- Cash.
- Receivables.
- Deposits for securities sold short and open option contracts.
- Other assets.
- Total assets.
- Accounts payable and accrued liabilities.
- Deposits for securities loaned.
- Other liabilities.
- Notes payable, bonds, and similar debt.
- Total liabilities.
- Commitments and contingent liabilities.
- Units of capital.
- Accumulated undistributed income or loss.
- Other elements of capital.
- Net assets applicable to outstanding units of capital.

The statement of operations for issuers of face-amount certificates shall include the following line items:

- Investment income.
- Investment expenses.
- Interest and amortization of debt discount and expense.
- Provision for certificate reserves.
- Investment income before income tax expense.
- Income tax expense.
- Investment income—net.
- Realized gain or loss on investments—net.
- Net income or loss.

- *Article 6A: Employee stock purchase, savings, and similar plans.* These types of plans must present a statement of financial condition that includes the following line items:
  - Investments in securities of participating employers.
  - Investments in securities of unaffiliated issuers.
  - Investments.
  - Dividends and interest receivable.

- Cash.
- Other assets.
- Liabilities.
- Reserves and other credits.
- Plan equity and close of period.

These plans must include in their statements of income and changes in plan equity the following line items:

- Net investment income.
- Realized gain or loss on investments.
- Unrealized appreciation or depreciation on investments.
- Realized gain or loss on investments.
- Contributions and deposits.
- Plan equity at beginning of period.
- Plan equity at end of period.

- *Article 7: Insurance companies.* An insurance company must present a balance sheet that includes the following line items:
- Investments.
- Cash.
- Securities and indebtedness of related parties.
- Accrued investment income.
- Accounts and notes receivable.
- Reinsurance recoverable on paid losses.
- Deferred policy acquisition costs.
- Property and equipment.
- Title plant.
- Other assets.
- Assets held in separate accounts.
- Total assets.
- Policy liabilities and accruals.
- Other policyholders' funds.
- Other liabilities.
- Notes payable, bonds, mortgages and similar obligations, including capitalized leases.
- Indebtedness to related parties.
- Liabilities related to separate accounts.

- Commitments and contingent liabilities.
- Minority interests in consolidated subsidiaries.
- Redeemable preferred stock.
- Non-redeemable preferred stock.
- Common stock.
- Other stockholders' equity.
- Total liabilities and stockholders' equity.

- *Article 9: Bank holding companies.* A bank holding company must present a balance sheet that includes the following line items:
  - Cash and cash due from banks.
  - Interest-bearing deposits in other banks.
  - Federal funds sold and securities purchased under resale or similar agreements.
  - Trading account assets.
  - Other short-term investments.
  - Investment securities.
  - Loans.
  - Premises and equipment.
  - Due from customers on acceptances.
  - Other assets.
  - Total assets.
  - Deposits.
  - Short-term borrowing.
  - Bank acceptances outstanding.
  - Other liabilities.
  - Long-term debt.
  - Commitments and contingent liabilities.
  - Minority interest in consolidated subsidiaries.
  - Redeemable preferred stock.
  - Non-redeemable preferred stock.
  - Common stock.
  - Other stockholders' equity.
  - Total liabilities and stockholders' equity.

A bank holding company's income statement must include the following line items:
- Interest and fees on loans.
- Interest and dividends on investment securities.

- Trading account interest.
- Other interest income.
- Total interest income.
- Interest on deposits.
- Interest on short-term borrowings.
- Interest on long-term debt.
- Total interest expense.
- Net interest income.
- Provision for loan losses.
- Net interest income after provision for loan losses.
- Other income.
- Other expenses.
- Income or loss before income tax expense.
- Income tax expense.
- Income or loss before extraordinary items and cumulative effects of changes in accounting principles.
- Extraordinary items.
- Cumulative effects of changes in accounting principles.
- Net income or loss.
- Earnings per share data.

- *Article 10: Interim financial statements.* An interim statement does not have to be audited. Only major line items need be included in the balance sheet, with the exception of inventories, which must be itemized by raw materials, work-in-process, and finished goods either in the balance sheet or in the accompanying notes. Any assets comprising less than 10% of total assets, and which have not changed more than 25% since the end of the preceding fiscal year, may be summarized into a different line item. If any major income statement line item is less than 15% of the amount of net income in any of the preceding three years, and if its amount has not varied by more than 20% since the previous year, it can be merged into another line item. Disclosure must also be made in the accompanying footnotes of any material changes in the business since the last fiscal year end.

- *Article 11: Pro forma financial information.* Pro forma information is required in cases where a business entity has engaged in a business combination or roll-up under the equity method of accounting, or under the purchase or pooling methods of accounting, or if a company's securities are to be used to purchase another business. It is also required if there is a reasonable probability of a spin-off, sale, or abandonment of some part or all of a business. The provided information should consist of a pro forma balance sheet, summary-level statement of income, and explanatory notes. The presented statements shall show financial results on the assumption that the triggering transaction occurred at the beginning of the fiscal year, and shall include a net income or loss figure from continuing operations prior to noting the impact of the transaction.

- *Article 12: Form and content of schedules.* This article describes the format in which additional schedules shall be laid out in submitted information, including layouts for valuation and qualifying accounts. It also itemizes formats for the display of information for management investment companies, which include the following formats: investments in securities of unaffiliated issuers, investments in securities sold short, open option contracts written, investments other than securities, investments in and advances to affiliates, summary of investments, supplementary insurance information, reinsurance, and supplemental information.

6-18 FORMS TO BE FILED WITH THE SEC

There are a multitude of forms to be filed with the SEC, depending upon the types of transactions that a publicly held company initiates. Here are brief descriptions of the most commonly used forms:

- *Form 8-K.* This form is used to report on significant events. The form must be filed if an issuer experiences a change in corporate control, the acquisition or disposition of a significant amount of assets, a change in its public accountant, a director's resignation, or a change in its fiscal year.

- *Form 10-K.* This form is used to report annual financial results under the Securities Exchange Act of 1934. It must be filed within 90 days following the end of a fiscal year.

- *Form 10-Q.* This form is used to report quarterly financial results under the Securities Exchange Act of 1934. It must be filed within 45 days following the end of a quarter, though not for the fourth quarter.

- *Form S-1.* This form is used for the registration of securities under the Securities Act of 1933, though not for securities issued by foreign governments.

- *Form TH.* This form is used to allow an electronic filer using the EDGAR system to temporarily file a paper instead of electronic submission under a temporary hardship claim.

6-19 GOING PRIVATE TRANSACTIONS (RULE 13E-3)

If a publicly held company wishes to go private, it must disclose information that is itemized under the SEC's Rule 13e-3. This rule applies to situations in which a company plans to buy back its securities, resulting in any class of equity securities being held by less than 300 individuals, or that the securities will no longer be listed for trade on a national exchange.

The information required under these circumstances must be filed on Schedule 13e-3, to which amendments must be added if there are material changes to the information presented on it. The primary information listed on the schedule includes complete company financial statements and various financial information on a per-share basis. The company must also include information regarding the identity of the persons filing the schedule, terms of the arrangement, future plans, the reason for going private, and the source and financing terms for the funding required to complete the transaction.

6-20 SUMMARY

This chapter gave a brief overview of the mission of the SEC, how it is organized to meet the requirements of that mission, and the specific laws and regulations under which it operates. If one needs a more complete knowledge of the applicable Acts (which are voluminous), one can go to the SEC web site, which is located at *www.sec.gov,* where additional links will direct one to the appropriate information. Please note that the original Acts have been greatly expanded upon by later SEC regulations, so it is best to review the most up-to-date SEC information regarding specific issues.

Part Three

ACCOUNTING REPORTS

CHAPTER 7

The Balance Sheet and Statement of Stockholders' Equity

7-1 INTRODUCTION

The balance sheet presents information about an organization's assets, liabilities, and equity at a specific point in time, rather than for a range of dates (as is the case for the income statement, statement of stockholders' equity, and the statement of cash flows). The statement of stockholders' equity reveals equity-related activities for a specified time period. The balance sheet is the more complex of the two statements, and so is addressed in greater detail in this chapter, both in terms of its contents and the reasons why different types of costs are used for the various line items contained within it.

7-2 USES OF THE BALANCE SHEET AND STATEMENT OF STOCKHOLDERS' EQUITY

The accountant can use the balance sheet to determine a company's level of liquidity, comparing the amount of current assets to current liabilities, as well as the ability of the entity to pay dividends and interest payments. It can also be used to determine a company's valuation, though the presence of historical costs on the balance sheet may mean that the liquidation value of a company varies considerably from its value as listed on the balance sheet. The statement of stockholders' equity is primarily used to determine the types of equity-related transactions that have occurred during the reporting period.

The balance sheet is much more useful when combined with the income statement, since the accountant can then compare activity levels in the income statement to the amount of assets and liabilities needed to support them, thereby yielding information about the overall financial health of the enterprise. For example, one can compare the amount of working capital (located on the balance sheet) invested in the business to the sales volume (located on the income statement) to see if the investment is sufficient to adequately support sales levels—if not, the company may fail in short order. As another example, one can compare sales volume to the amount of accounts receivable, accounts payable, or inventory on the balance sheet to see if the turnover levels for these items are high enough to indicate that they are being managed properly.

7-3 THE BALANCE SHEET FORMAT

There is no specifically mandated format associated with the balance sheet. However, it is customary to divide the report into header, assets, liabilities, and stockholders' equity sections. The header should include the name of the company and its legal status, such as "Premier Steaks, Incorporated" or "Buyer & Son, a Limited Liability Partnership." The header should also include a date, which is the snapshot date on which the balance sheet is based. For example, if the report is dated August 31, 2003, then this is the specific date for which information is being presented. It is common to list the report as of the last day of the fiscal period on which the accompanying income statement is also being reported, so that the reader knows that the information in the two reports addresses the same time frame (an entire reporting period in the case of the income statement, and the last day of that period, in the case of the balance sheet). Finally, if the company conducts its accounting on anything but the accrual basis, this should be noted in the header. A typical header is as follows:

Morgenthau Catering, Inc.
Balance Sheet
As of April 30, 2003

The accountant should list the asset section of the balance sheet immediately below the header. An example is shown in Exhibit 7-1. The presented format is intended for the reporting of a single period, and so uses separate columns for detailed and summary results. If the accountant were to present side-by-side results for multiple periods, the detailed and summary line items could be merged into a single column in order to make room for the results of the extra periods. Current assets are itemized at the top of the assets section, followed by long-term investments, fixed assets (also called "Property, Plant and Equipment") and other assets. The definitions of these categories are described later in the "Asset Definitions" section.

Exhibit 7-1   The Presentation of Assets in the Balance Sheet

Current Assets:		
Cash	$1,500,000	
Investments, short-term	3,850,000	
Accounts receivable	7,425,000	
(Allowance for doubtful accounts)	−205,000	
Other accounts receivable	115,000	
Prepaid expenses	50,000	
Inventory		
Raw materials	3,000,000	
Work-in-process	450,000	
Finished goods	1,850,000	
		$18,035,000
Long-Term Investments:		
Investments available for sale	2,000,000	
Investments held to maturity	500,000	
Cash termination value of life insurance	75,000	
		$ 2,575,000
Fixed Assets:		
Computer equipment	4,050,000	
Leasehold improvements	300,000	
Machinery & equipment	3,955,000	
Buildings	6,900,000	
Land	503,000	
Less: accumulated depreciation	−980,000	
		$14,728,000
Other Assets:		
Organizational costs	200,000	
Copyright and patent costs	325,000	
Goodwill	3,750,000	
		$ 4,275,000
Total Assets:		$39,613,000

Liabilities are listed after the asset section. An example of this continuation of the balance sheet is noted in Exhibit 7-2. As was the case for assets, current items are listed first—in this case as current liabilities. Following this section are long-term liabilities, and then a grand total for all liabilities. The definitions of the line items shown here are described later in the "Liability Definitions" section.

Exhibit 7-2   The Presentation of Liabilities in the Balance Sheet

Current Liabilities:		
Accounts payable	$2,350,000	
Wages payable	450,000	
Taxes payable	175,000	
Current portion of long-term debt	825,000	
Dividends payable	400,000	
Accrued liabilities	265,000	
		$ 4,465,000
Long-Term Liabilities:		
Notes payable	2,575,000	
14% bonds, due in 2025	4,000,000	
Capital lease liabilities	500,000	
Total Long-Term Liabilities:		$ 7,075,000
Total Liabilities:		$11,540,000

The final section of the balance sheet, the stockholders' equity section, is itemized last. An example is shown in Exhibit 7-3. This section is divided into categories for capital stock, additional paid-in capital, retained earnings, and other comprehensive income, followed by a grand total. Descriptions of these line items are provided later in the "Stockholders' Equity Definitions" section.

Exhibit 7-3   The Presentation of Equity in the Balance Sheet

Capital Stock:		
Common stock, $1 par value,	$ 285,000	
1,000,000 shares authorized, 285,000 issued		
10% preferred stock, $10 par value,	3,500,000	
400,000 shares authorized, 350,000 issued		
		$ 3,785,000
Additional Paid-In Capital:		
From common stock	14,000,000	
From 10% preferred stock	4,000,000	
From expired stock options	100,000	
		$18,100,000
Retained Earnings:		$ 6,525,000
Other Comprehensive Income:		
Unrealized foreign currency translation losses	−280,000	
Unrealized available-for-sale security losses	−57,000	
		−$ 337,000
Total Stockholders' Equity:		$28,073,000

If the accountant is presenting balance sheet information for multiple time periods, he or she should restate the numbers for all time periods to conform to the same reporting structure as the most recent one. For example, accounts receivable from employees cannot be itemized under the "accounts receivable" line item for one period and under "other assets" for another period—it must consistently appear under the same line item in all presented reporting periods, so that the information is comparable.

7-4 ASSET DEFINITIONS

To be an asset, a transaction must provide a future economic benefit that will result in cash inflows, the business entity must be able to receive this benefit, and the event that gave the entity the right to the benefit must have already occurred as of the balance sheet date.

In the balance sheet example in Exhibit 7-1, the line items clustered into the current assets section are those assets that the accountant expects to be cash, convertible to cash, or eliminated from the balance sheet within the longer of one year or the company's natural operating cycle. The only exception is any cash that has restrictions on it, such as a borrowing arrangement that requires a company to retain some cash in the lending bank's checking account—in this case, the cash is assumed to be restricted for the term of the loan agreement, and so is classified as a long-term asset until the final year of the loan agreement.

The "cash" line item in the balance sheet can also be entitled "cash and cash equivalents." A cash equivalent is an investment that is highly liquid and within three months of its maturity date. Otherwise, investments are summarized within the "short-term investments" line item, but only for so long as they have maturities of no more than one year, and if the management team is willing to sell them at any time. The accountant can present short-term investments in a single line item, as long as a descriptive footnote describes the types of investments. An alternative is to list the major investment categories in several line items on the balance sheet.

The only accounts receivable that should be contained within the "accounts receivable" line item are those that are acquired during normal business transactions. If there are other accounts receivable, such as from employees or owners, these should be listed in a separate "other accounts receivable" line item. Also, any allowance for doubtful accounts should be shown separately from the accounts receivable as an offset, so that the reader can easily determine the size of the reserve for bad debts.

Prepaid expenses generally involve transactions in which a payment has been made to a supplier, but the related benefit has not yet been obtained. For example, an early rent payment for the following reporting period or a medical insurance payment that applies to the next period would be listed in this account and charged to expense as soon as the related benefit has been incurred.

There are three main types of inventory that should be separately shown on the balance sheet—raw materials, work-in-process, and finished goods. One can also net them into a single line item and present the detail for the three types of inventory in a footnote. Alternatively, if there is very little inventory, then a single line item with no additional disclosure is acceptable.

Long-term investments are usually listed directly after current assets in the balance sheet. These investments are ones that the company intends to retain for more than one year. Examples of such investments are sinking funds for bond payments or pension funds (for which related payouts may be years in the future).

Fixed assets are listed as a separate category, and can be placed on the balance sheet either before or after long-term investments—but certainly after all current assets. They can also be referred to as "property, plant, and equipment." These are tangible assets that are not used as part of the standard operating process, and that are not used within the operating cycle. Fixed assets are usually grouped into several broad categories, which will vary by the types of assets purchased. The following categories are commonly used:

- Buildings
- Computer equipment
- Furniture and fixtures
- Land
- Leasehold improvements
- Machinery and equipment
- Office equipment
- Software

If a fixed asset has been obtained under a capital lease, it should not be separately identified as a capital lease, but rather should be clustered into the asset category that most nearly describes it. Also, the amount of accumulated depreciation thus far recognized should be listed as an offset to the fixed asset line items. Depreciation can be listed as an offset to each fixed asset line item, but is more commonly presented in total and immediately following all of the fixed assets.

Goodwill is typically presented either as a separate line item or within a separate section near the end of the balance sheet assets section that is entitled "Intangible Assets," and which includes such items as goodwill, copyrights, trademarks, and patents. Goodwill can only be shown on the balance sheet if it has been acquired through a business combination. Costs associated with copyrights, trademarks, and patents can only be those directly incurred by the business, unless they have been marked up as a result of having acquired them through a business combination. The amortization of these assets can be either netted against them, or presented on separate line items.

7-5 LIABILITY DEFINITIONS

The format of the liabilities section of the balance sheet was shown earlier in Exhibit 7-2. A liability as recorded on the balance sheet is one that must be settled through the payment of an asset at some point in the future, and where the obligation to make the payment has already occurred as of the balance sheet date. Accrued liabilities involve the recognition of liabilities prior to a related transaction being completed. A liability can expire through no action on the part of an organization; for example, an accrued warranty expense can terminate as soon as the warranty period expires that was associated with any sold products or services.

A liability is listed as a current liability if the accountant expects it to be liquidated within the longer of a company's operating cycle or one year. Current liabilities typically include accounts payable, customer deposits (if the associated deliveries to customers will be made within the operating cycle or one year), accrued taxes, accrued wages and vacation pay, and a variety of other accruals associated with current operations. However, all of these items can also be classified as long-term liabilities if one does not expect them to be liquidated within the later of one year or the operating cycle. There can be a split of the same account type between both current and long-term liabilities. For example, there can be accounts payable that are typically due within 30 days, and which would be categorized as current liabilities; there may also be accounts payable with very long payment terms, and which can therefore be reported under the long-term liabilities section of the balance sheet. Similarly, those capital lease obligations coming due for payment in the short term will be categorized as a current liability, while those portions of the remaining payments coming due at a later date will be listed under the long-term liabilities section of the balance sheet.

Debt is commonly split into short-term and long-term segments in the balance sheet. The portion of debt that is considered to be a current liability is the debt that is expected to be paid off within the longer of one year or the operating cycle. One cannot push debt into the current liabilities section of the balance sheet just because it is the intention of management to pay off the debt in the near term—only the amount of debt specified in the debt agreement for payment in the near term can be itemized as a short-term liability. Also, debt that should clearly be itemized as short term can be shifted into the long-term debt portion of the balance sheet if management intends to refinance it with new debt that is expected to be categorized as long-term debt.

Long-term debt is frequently described in the balance sheet as "Notes Payable" or "Bonds Payable." This is debt that is expected to be paid off in whichever time period is the greater, one year or the operating cycle. This information can be combined with any related discount or premium in a single, summarized line item, or it can be broken out, as in the following example:

Bonds payable	$1,000,000
Plus premium	40,000

If summarized into a single line, the same information would be presented as follows:

Bonds payable, plus premium of $40,000 $1,040,000

A deferred income tax liability is recognized on the balance sheet if the reporting entity has experienced temporary differences between net income that it has reported under GAAP, and net income as reported under IRS regulations.

7-6 STOCKHOLDERS' EQUITY DEFINITIONS

Stockholders' equity is the residual interest in a business that belongs to its owners after all liabilities are subtracted from assets. It is comprised of the initial investment by company shareholders, plus retained earnings, less dividends. An example of the layout of this portion of the balance sheet was shown earlier in Exhibit 7-3. It is comprised of the following categories of equity:

- *Capital stock.* This is the par value of the stock held by shareholders. The balance sheet should enumerate each of the various classes of stock that have been issued, including the par value amount, the number of shares authorized, and the number outstanding. If there is preferred stock outstanding, then additional information for these shares should include their stated interest rate, the callable price point (if any), whether the dividends are cumulative, if the shares give the holder the right to participate in earnings, if they are convertible to common stock, and if so, then at what price they are convertible.

- *Additional paid-in capital.* This is the price at which shares were purchased, less their par value (which was listed in the preceding line item). As was the case for capital stock, additional paid-in capital (APIC) should be listed separately for each type of stock outstanding. There may also be a need for an additional line item to contain cash received from other sources than stock, such as cash from the purchase of warrants that have subsequently expired, from bond conversions at prices greater than the par value of the stock being converted to, or from stock dividends that are recorded at their market price (which is presumably higher than the par value).

- *Treasury stock.* This is any shares that have been repurchased by the corporation, but not canceled.

- *Retained earnings.* This is the cumulative corporate earnings, less any dividends paid out to shareholders.

- *Other comprehensive income.* This is the cumulative change in equity caused by any unrealized gains or losses from foreign currency translation, available-for-sale investments, and the difference between the minimum pension liability and unrecognized previous service costs, if the minimum pension liability is higher.

7-7 THE STATEMENT OF STOCKHOLDERS' EQUITY FORMAT

The statement of stockholders' equity has a relatively undefined format, which gives the accountant a great deal of leeway in designing one that meets her reporting needs. In essence, the report is intended to reveal the beginning and ending stockholders' equity for a specific time period, as well as changes in its subsidiary accounts during the period. An example is shown in Exhibit 7-4; this format lists the main components of equity, as well as those equity transactions that arose during the year. A prior period adjustment is also noted in the exhibit, which requires an accompanying footnote to disclose the type of transaction that occurred. Alternatively, it is acceptable to include explanations directly into the report format, though this can result in a lengthy report. If the accompanying financial statements cover multiple years, the accountant can simply repeat this format for as many additional years as are listed in the other statements.

Exhibit 7-4   The Presentation of the Statement of Stockholders' Equity

Morgenthau Catering, Inc.
Statement of Stockholders' Equity
For the Year Ended December 31, 2003

	Common Stock	Preferred Stock	Additional Paid-In Capital	Retained Earnings
December 31, 2002	$50,000	$15,000	$85,000	$225,000
Prior period adjustment (Note 1)				−35,000
Sale of 2,500 common shares	2,500		7,500	
Net income				42,500
Dividends				−38,000
December 31, 2003	$52,500	$15,000	$92,500	$194,500

Note 1: The prior period adjustment is related to a correction in the depreciation method used for heavy equipment purchases during the preceding year.

7-8 ACCOUNTING TREATMENT OF OFFSETS TO ASSETS AND LIABILITIES

Offsetting refers to the netting of assets and liabilities to yield either no line item at all on the balance sheet (if the assets and liabilities exactly offset each other) or a much smaller residual balance. Offsetting is not allowed, except under the most strictly defined circumstances, since the reader of a balance sheet could be misled by the absence of information about potentially large assets or liabilities. Offsetting is only allowed when *all* of the following conditions are met:

- Two parties owe measurable liabilities to each other.

- At least one party has a legally justifiable right to offset its liability against that of its counterpart.

- The party intends to exercise this right.

- The maturity of the party's obligation arrives prior to that of the other entity (since the party with the earliest liability will likely create an offset prior to the other entity, and therefore controls the outcome of the transaction).

7-9 CRITIQUE OF THE BALANCE SHEET

Many objections have been raised to the structure and underlying basis of information used to formulate the balance sheet. Here are some of the key issues:

- *Use of historical costs.* In most cases, the information presented in the balance sheet is based on the historical cost of assets and liabilities. This is fine in the case of most current assets, whose valuations are unlikely to change much before they are either used up or paid off. However, inventories in volatile industries, such as computer equipment, can drop in value rapidly, which can give an inventory-laden balance sheet a deceptively large amount of current asset valuation. Similarly, a company that has invested heavily in fixed assets can have a misleading balance sheet if the market value of those assets varies significantly from their historical cost.

The alternative to the use of historical costs would be their replacement with current costs. The use of current costs would certainly avoid the above problems, but takes a considerable amount of time to obtain (thereby delaying the release of the financial statements), and are subject to manipulation. Further, adjustments to historical costs with current costs will require the recognition of some gain or loss on the difference between the two values. Finally, the accountant must put a considerable amount of ongoing effort into the updating of current costs for assets— from a maintenance perspective, it is much easier to record an asset or liability just once at its historical cost, and then not have to worry about it again until it is disposed of.

A variation on the use of current costs is the lower of cost or market rule, which is extensively used to reduce the valuation of inventory to its net realizeable value as of the balance sheet date; this approach marks assets *down* to a lower current cost, but does not mark them up to a higher current cost, as would be the case under current costing if the fair market value were higher than the historical cost. Under existing accounting rules, the only circumstance when an asset's cost is increased to reflect its fair market value is when a gain is realized at the point of sale. Thus, the lower of cost or market rule is a half-way measure that reveals the lowest possible current cost.

- *Use of estimates.* The accountant is required to include in the financial statements estimates for bad debts and inventory obsolescence. These reserves are subject to some degree of manipulation, usually so that reported levels of operating income can be changed to suit management's income targets. For example, an accountant could use a standard formula for determining the amount of bad debt to reserve against, but judgmentally elect to recognize some lesser proportion of the result of the calculation if that would result in the achievement of a specific net income figure. Though an auditor could use a firm's recent history of bad debt experiences to impose a different bad debt reserve, this would only apply to those financial statements that are being audited—all intervening statements are still subject to manipulation in this area.

- *No adjustment for present value entries.* There are a few situations in which the accountant is required to record a liability at the present value of all readily discernible cash flows at the time when a transaction initially occurs, which uses a discount rate that makes the most sense at the time of the transaction. Though this is a good, rational entry to make at the time of the transaction, the discount rate will change over time as market conditions vary, resulting in an incorrect discounted present value at a later date.

The obvious solution is to mandate a periodic update of all such transactions with a new discounted present value calculation that is based on the most recent market interest rate. However, this also increases the burden on the accountant, which will also likely delay the release of the financial statements until these calculations can be made.

- *No entry to reflect most intangible assets.* Accounting regulations only require the accountant to record the costs associated with intangible assets, such as the legal fees used to obtain a patent. In some cases, this may grossly understate the actual value of the assets. For example, the Coke formula is worth billions of dollars, but does not appear on that company's balance sheet as a separate line item. Similarly, the market value of many companies, such as Procter & Gamble, Oakley, and Nike are built largely upon the value of the brand names that they have created, but which are not reflected in their balance sheets.

  A possible solution to this dilemma is to have these intangible assets appraised at regular intervals, and noted on the balance sheet, with an adjustment to the equity account to offset the changes in the intangible asset. However, this is also subject to considerable manipulation, because the selection of a tractable appraiser could result in a much higher intangible valuation than a more conservative appraiser might issue.

The primary issue being raised with the information contained in the balance sheet is its use of historical costs. Though certainly a valid point, one must remember that accounting rules are based on the most conservative possible statement of information—that which can be proven through an accounting transaction for which some sort of paperwork exists. Consequently, accounting records tend to be updated only when an asset or liability is procured and later eliminated. If the accounting rules are altered to switch the costs in the balance sheet to the current cost methodology, then the basis of evidence for proving these costs becomes much less solid. Consequently, the legal need to prove where a valuation has come from will probably continue to favor the use of historical costs for most line items in the balance sheet.

7-10 SUMMARY

The content of this chapter focused on the layout of the balance sheet and statement of stockholders' equity. However, there is a great deal of additional information related to this topic. Chapter 10 discusses the footnotes that must accompany the financial statements, while Chapters 13 through 19 cover the proper accounting treatment of every line item in the balance sheet, including cash, investments, inventory, fixed assets, liabilities, and equity.

CHAPTER 8

The Income Statement

8-1 INTRODUCTION

The income statement is perhaps the commonly studied document that the accounting department produces, since it reveals the results of operations and related activities for a business entity. For this reason, the accountant must be careful to create an income statement that reveals the maximum amount of information to the reader without presenting an overwhelming amount of data. To do so, the income statement must be structured to fit the revenue and expense line items that are most crucial within certain industries—for example, development costs are exceedingly important in the software industry, while they are usually an inconsequential item in a consulting business. Thus, there can be an infinite variety of income statement formats that the accountant can create. However, to be acceptable under GAAP, some activities—such as extraordinary items, accounting changes, and discontinued operations—must be accounted for in a particular manner. Thus, this chapter is designed to give the reader the maximum amount of information about those income statement line items that require specific presentation formats.

8-2 FORMAT OF THE INCOME STATEMENT

The basic format of the income statement begins with the name of the business entity, the name of the report, and the period over which its financial performance is being presented. An example of this is shown in Exhibit 8-1. If the cash basis of accounting is used, this

94

should be noted in the report header, since the reader will otherwise assume that the more common accrual method is being used.

The first set of information presented is the revenue from continuing operations, which consists of those revenues from expected or current cash inflows resulting from a company's regular earnings process. The exact format of revenue reporting used is driven more by custom than by GAAP. In Exhibit 8-1, revenues are reported by product line, but they can just as easily be reported by geographic region, individual products, or subsidiary. They may also be lumped together into a single line item.

The cost of goods sold is described in the next block of information in the income statement. This is described more fully in the next section, but it is customarily assumed to be comprised of the materials, labor, and overhead costs included in those products or services that are sold during the reporting period.

The next section of the income statement includes all operating expenses. These are the expenses that are tied to ongoing business transactions and are generally assumed to include the sales and marketing, general and administrative, customer support, and engineering departments. These expenses are usually recognized as soon as they are incurred, but may also be allocated over multiple reporting periods if there is some future benefit associated with them. The exact layout of this section is also subject to considerable variation. Some companies prefer to divide it into specific departments, others (as shown in Exhibit 8-1) prefer to describe it by types of expenses, while others itemize it by business location. It is recommended that not too many expenses be lumped into the "miscellaneous expenses" account, since this provides no information to the reader of the report. As a general rule, shift costs into other, more descriptive line items if the amount in this account reaches or exceeds 10% of the total amount of operating expenses. The full format of the income statement is shown in Exhibit 8-1.

Exhibit 8-1   The Income Statement Format

Lagerfeld & Son Custom Cabinets
Income Statement
For the month ended July 31, 2004

Revenue:		
Product line A	$12,450	
Product line B	9,250	
Product line C	5,000	
Total Revenue		$26,700
Cost of Goods Sold:		
Materials	$ 4,350	
Direct labor	1,000	
Overhead	3,775	
Commissions	1,350	
Total Cost of Goods Sold		$10,475
Gross Margin		$16,225

(continued)

Exhibit 8-1 The Income Statement Format (*cont'd.*)

Operating Expenses:

Advertising	$ 500	
Ban charges	100	
Depreciation	2,000	
Insurance	250	
Legal and accounting	350	
Marketing expenses	600	
Outside services	50	
Payroll taxes	300	
Postage and deliveries	275	
Salaries and wages	3,750	
Supplies	450	
Training	50	
Travel and entertainment	825	
Utilities	435	
Miscellaneous expenses	125	
Total Operating Expenses:		$10,060
Gains (losses) on sale of assets	−425	
Other revenues and expenses	175	
Net Income Before Taxes:		$ 5,915
Taxes		$ 2,250
Net Income:		$ 3,665

As described in the following sections, there are special categories of expense reporting, such as the results from discontinued operations, extraordinary items, and changes in accounting, which must be reported after the results of operations in the income statement. If these items are present, then the "Net Income" line item listed at the bottom of Exhibit 8-1 would be changed to "Net Income before [list additional items to be reported]." A sample format of these extra items is shown in Exhibit 8-2, which is an add-on to Exhibit 8-1.

Exhibit 8-2 Additional Items for the Income Statement

Results from Discontinued Operations:

Income from operations—discontinued operations	−$ 375	
Gain (loss) from disposition of discontinued operations	−450	
Extraordinary items (less related income taxes of $600):	1,300	
Cumulative effect of a change in accounting principle:	−700	
Net income:		−$3,440

In addition to the results of operations and the additional items shown in Exhibit 8-2, the income statement must also translate financial results into earnings per share, which is discussed in Section 8-4. Also, comprehensive income must be added to the statement or reported separately; this information is discussed in Section 8-9.

8-3 EXPENSES LISTED IN THE COST OF GOODS SOLD

The traditional expenses that are reported within the cost of goods sold section are direct materials, direct labor, and manufacturing overhead. These are designated as the cost of goods sold more through tradition than any accounting pronouncement. Consequently, the accountant should actively consider adding several other expenses to the cost of goods sold. The primary criterion for adding expenses to this category is that they should vary directly in proportion to revenues. Stated differently, they should only involve those expenses that are required to manufacture or purchase the items that are being sold. For example, salesperson commissions will only be created if a product is sold—this is therefore a perfect cost of goods sold. Another possibility is any royalty that must be paid as a result of a sale. For example, a publisher should include the royalty associated with a manuscript in its cost of goods sold. A close examination of the operating expenses section of the income statement will likely reveal a few costs that vary directly with revenues, and so can be more precisely grouped within the cost of goods sold category. A good rule to follow to determine if an expense should be included in the cost of goods sold is whether or not the cost will disappear if a sale is not made. If a sale occurs and a specific expense is therefore incurred, then it should be included in the cost of goods sold.

If the accountant chooses to add extra classifications of expenses to the cost of goods sold, she should be sure to revise the financial statements for previous years, so that they are consistently reported within the same expense grouping.

8-4 REPORTING EARNINGS PER SHARE

Basic and diluted earnings per share (EPS) information must be attached to the income statement. *Basic EPS* is the amount of earnings recognized in the reporting period, divided by the average number of shares outstanding during the period. Basic EPS must be shown on the income statement, not only for income from continuing operations, but also for net income.

Diluted earnings per share is also the amount of earnings recognized in the reporting period; however, this is divided not only by the average number of shares outstanding during the period, but also by all potential common shares. Potential shares can include stock options, warrants, convertible securities, employee compensation agreements that involve stock payouts, and vendor agreements that may also involve stock payouts. When calculating diluted EPS, the accountant should add back any interest payments (net of tax effect) made on convertible debt, since the assumption is that all such convertible debt will become common stock for the purposes of the calculation, and so there will be no interest payment made on the debt that presumably no longer exists. An entity with a simple capital structure (that is, one with no additional potential stock) does not need to report diluted EPS on its income statement, since the reported information would be the same as is already shown for basic EPS. However, if there is *any* amount of potential common stock, even if the amount is not material, then diluted EPS must be shown on the income statement.

When determining the number of additional potential shares to include in the diluted EPS calculation, only include those options and warrants for which the average market price for the reporting period is higher than the exercise price—in other words, we assume that the holders of these instruments would have no reason to convert them to common stock unless they had a chance to earn a profit on the transaction during the reporting period.

Similarly, if there are shares that will be issued only if certain contingencies are fulfilled, then they are not included in either basic EPS or diluted EPS until the contingencies have actually been fulfilled; they are included in both forms of EPS at that time, even if the shares are not physically issued before the end date of the reporting period.

The EPS calculation for both basic and diluted EPS requires the use of the average number of common shares outstanding during the period. A good way to determine this amount is shown in Exhibit 8-3, where the calculation is shown for a one-quarter reporting period. In the example, stock is both issued and reduced through a number of transactions. For each transaction, the number of share days outstanding is calculated, and then divided by the number of days in the period in order to determine the average number of total shares outstanding for the entire reporting period.

Exhibit 8-3   Calculation for the Average Number of Common Shares Outstanding

Description	Transaction Date	Number of Shares	Days Outstanding in Period	Number of Share-Days
Beginning shares outstanding	1/1/03	300	90	27,000
Stock bought with options	1/15/03	150	75	11,250
Stock repurchase	2/5/03	−50	55	−2,750
Stock sold to investors	3/1/03	75	30	2,250
Totals	—	575	90	37,750

The exhibit shows a total number of share days of 37,750. When we divide this by the total number of days in the quarter, the average number of shares outstanding becomes:

$$\frac{\text{Total number of share days}}{\text{Number of days in the period}} = \frac{37,750}{90} = 419 \text{ shares}$$

If there is a stock dividend or stock split during the reporting period, the additional shares issued are always assumed to have been issued on the first day of the reporting period. This is done because the total ownership percentages of all shareholders has not changed—it has just been divided into a larger number of shares. Accordingly, a stock split or dividend must be retroactively included in all periods being reported upon, in order to make EPS comparable for all reporting periods.

8-5 TREATMENT OF GAINS AND LOSSES

A gain or loss resulting from a transaction outside of the normal course of operations should be reported as a separate line item in the income statement, as is shown in Exhibit 8-1. Examples of gains and losses of this type are those that result from the sale of assets, a lawsuit judgment, and storm damage to company property. If there is a gain on this type of transaction, then it is only recognized when the related transaction is completed. For example, a gain on sale of machinery is only recognized when the buyer takes possession of the machinery and title is transferred to the new owner. However, a loss is recognized earlier, as soon as the amount of the loss can be reasonably ascertained and it is reasonably certain that the loss will be incurred. Any gain or loss should be reported net of its associated income tax effect.

8-6 TREATMENT OF ACCOUNTING CHANGES

There are several types of accounting changes—in estimate, reporting entity, and principle. Examples of *changes in accounting estimates* can relate to the size of the bad debt reserve, warranty claim reserve, or obsolete inventory reserve, as well as the assumed salvage value of fixed assets and the duration of their useful lives. An example of a *change in reporting entity* is the implementation of a business combination through the pooling of interests method of accounting. Examples of *principle changes* (which is the use of GAAP that is different from the accounting principle previously used, but not for immaterial items) include:

- An accounting change required by a newly promulgated GAAP
- A change from LIFO to the FIFO method of inventory costing
- A change from the full cost method in the minerals extraction industry

An accounting change should be recorded with a cumulative summarization of the change's effect at the beginning of the fiscal year as a line item after extraordinary items on the income statement. This line item should be reported net of the impact of any related income taxes. An example of this reporting structure was shown earlier in Exhibit 8-2. It is also possible to revise earlier income statements with the effect of a change in accounting principle if such a change is specifically mandated by a new accounting principle.

8-7 TREATMENT OF DISCONTINUED OPERATIONS

Discontinued operations refer to a business segment for which there are firm plans for disposition or closure. This would not include a stoppage of production for a single product or ancillary product line, since these are common and ongoing events that represent the incremental changes that businesses regularly make as they modify their operations to meet market demand. Rather, the concept of a discontinued operation refers to a major business division, or the sale of a large interest in another unrelated entity.

If a company plans to discontinue some operations, it must recognize any estimated loss related to the discontinuance in the first accounting period in which the management team commits to a disposition plan, and for which costs can be reasonably estimated. If there is a gain from the transaction, then this is reported later, after the disposition transaction has been completed. The disposition plan should include the timing of the disposition, what types of assets are to be eliminated, the method of disposal, and an estimate of the costs and revenues resulting from the transaction.

Losses expected from discontinued operations can include a reduction in the valuation of assets to be disposed of, down to their net realizeable value. However, it is not allowable to allocate general corporate overhead expenses to a discontinued operation, since this might result in the accelerated recognition of expenses that have nothing to do with the disposition. It is also not allowable to include in the loss the cost of asset disposition, such as brokerage fees—these costs are only recognized when incurred.

It is also possible to allocate interest costs to the cost of discontinued operations, but no more than the amount of the interest on debt assumed by the buyer of the discontinued operations (if any), and a reasonable allocation of interest expense that cannot be specified as being attributed to some other part of the remaining organization.

The financial statements should include information about discontinued operations in a separate set of line items immediately following the net income reported from continuing operations in the income statement (as illustrated in Exhibit 8-2). These line items should separately show the gain or loss from the disposition and the partial year operating results of the discontinued operation leading up to the date on which it was discontinued. This information should be shown net of the impact of any related income taxes. The financial results of discontinued operations can also be revealed through a footnote, though this approach is only recommended if the results are immaterial.

If the management team decides to retain operations that had previously been treated as discontinued, then the accountant should reverse the amount of any loss that had previously been recognized; this reversal should occur in the period when the decision to retain the operations is made. If there was an operating loss in the period of initial loss recognition and this loss was included in the initial write-down, then the accountant should allow the operating loss to continue to be recognized in the period of initial loss recognition.

8-8 TREATMENT OF EXTRAORDINARY ITEMS

An extraordinary item must be reported, net of related taxes, after the results from continuing operations on the income statement, though only if it is material. To qualify as an extraordinary item, something must both occur infrequently and be unusual in nature. A event is considered to occur infrequently if company management does not expect it to happen again, while it is considered to be unusual if it is unrelated to ongoing company operations. Examples of extraordinary items are:

- A gain on a troubled debt restructuring
- A gain or loss on the extinguishment of debt
- Major casualty losses, due to such causes as floods, earthquakes, and fire
- The adjustment of an extraordinary item that was reported in a prior period
- The expropriation of assets
- The write-off of operating rights of a motor carrier

Items that are not categorized as extraordinary items include:

- A write down in the value of assets
- Changes in the valuation of foreign exchange holdings
- Costs related to a plant relocation
- Costs related to a standstill agreement
- Costs related to environmental damages
- Costs related to the defense against a takeover attempt
- Costs related to the settlement of a legal case
- Gains or losses on the sale of assets
- Losses caused by a strike
- The disposal of business segments

8-9 TREATMENT OF OTHER COMPREHENSIVE INCOME

The net income figure that appears on the income statement does not reveal a small number of changes in assets that are instead reported through the balance sheet. These changes are related to adjustments caused by unrealized foreign currency valuation adjustments, minimum pension liability changes, and unrealized gains or losses on some types of investment securities.

An additional reporting category, called Other Comprehensive Income, is added to the bottom of the income statement (in which case the report is called the Statement of Income and Comprehensive Income), presented separately, or included in the Statement of Changes in Stockholders' Equity. This category includes all of the above adjustments that are normally only reported through the balance sheet, so that the reader of the income statement will have a clearer idea of not only the results of company operations, but also of valuation issues that are caused by forces outside of the reporting entity.

Other comprehensive income cannot be reported solely in the footnotes accompanying the financial statements. When reported within the body of the financial statements, the accountant can use any number of formats, since there is no specific format required by GAAP. A possible format is shown in Exhibit 8-4, where each possible adjustment is listed as a separate line item.

Exhibit 8-4   Addition to the Income Statement for Comprehensive Income

Other Comprehensive Income:	
Minimum pension liability adjustments	−$ 35,000
Unrealized gains/losses on securities	120,500
Foreign currency adjustments	−48,250
Comprehensive Income:	−$68,750

8-10 TREATMENT OF PRIOR PERIOD ADJUSTMENTS

There are only two cases where the accountant is allowed to revise the results reported in the income statement of a prior period. The first case is when errors have been discovered in the prior period report that are material enough to require correction. Examples of error corrections include a correction of a computational error, adjustments based on facts that were in existence as of the date of the financial statements being adjusted, and a switch away from an invalid accounting principle to GAAP.

The second case is when material adjustments are required to reflect the realization of income tax benefits caused by the pre-acquisition net operating loss carryforwards of a purchased subsidiary.

In both cases, the impact of the change should be listed both prior to the impact of income taxes and after their effect.

If the accountant is only issuing financial statements that list the results of the current reporting period, then these prior period adjustments can be integrated into the statements simply by modifying the beginning balance of retained earnings. However, if multiple-period results are being reported, then the prior period statements must be restated to reflect these adjustments.

8-11 TREATMENT OF RESTRUCTURING COSTS

If a company decides to restructure itself, it must charge off the costs of doing so within the current period, even if the costs are not to be incurred for some time. This early charge-off is only allowed if the management team has approved an official restructuring plan, communicated the plan to employees, and specified in the plan the approximate number and job categories of workers to be terminated. Also, it must be unlikely that the plan will be altered in its essential structure prior to being completed (though this is a highly subjective criterion).

The SEC requires all publicly held companies to show their restructuring charges as part of continuing operations within the income statements. The FASB has not yet expanded this concept to privately held companies, and so still allows private entities to use their own judgment in determining where this information will be presented within the income statement.

The following categories of costs can all be separately classified as restructuring charges on the income statement:

- Employee severance payments.
- Facility relocation costs.
- Product line elimination costs.
- Product line consolidation costs.
- Employee retraining costs.

8-12 SUMMARY

The basic format of the income statement is quite simple and easy to understand. Complications arise when the accountant must determine whether or not there are extraordinary items, accounting changes, discontinued operations, prior period adjustments, and the like—all of which require separate presentation in the income statement. There can also be some confusion regarding which expenses should be itemized within the cost of goods sold or operating expenses. The accountant should refer to Chapter 10, Footnotes, for more information about the presentation of additional information about these issues, which should be issued alongside the financial statements.

CHAPTER 9

The Statement of Cash Flows

9-1 INTRODUCTION

The statement of cash flows reveals the cash inflows and outflows experienced by an organization during a reporting period. In this respect, it is similar to the income statement, which also covers a specific period of time. The types of cash flows presented are divided into those related to operations, investment activities, and financing activities. This information is intended to give the reader some idea of the ability of an organization to make debt or dividend payments, or to replace needed capital items. It can also be of use in determining whether an organization is issuing more cash in the form of dividends than it is generating from continuing operations, which cannot continue for long. It can also reflect the impact of changes in the management of working capital, since such actions as improved accounts receivable collections or tighter inventory controls will reduce the amount of cash tied up in receivables and inventory (and vice versa, in the case of poor management).

In addition, it presents a clearer picture of cash flows than can be inferred from the income statement or balance sheet, where the use of accruals can make it appear as though an entity is generating large profits, even though it is burning through large quantities of cash. This is of particular concern in rapidly growing companies, where margins from continuing operations may not be sufficient to fund the growth in new sales.

The statement of cash flows is an integral part of the financial statements, and should be presented alongside the balance sheet, income statement, and statement of retained earnings. This is of particular concern if the management team is taking steps to "dress up" the results shown in the statement of cash flows at the expense of a company's long-term financial health, which might be more readily evident through a careful perusal of a complete package of financial statements, rather than just the statement of cash flows. For example, management might not be making a sufficient investment in the replacement of existing fixed assets, thereby making the amount of cash outflows look smaller, even though this will result in more equipment failures and higher maintenance costs that will eventually appear on the income statement.

The following sections itemize the types of cash flows that are to be revealed in each section of the statement of cash flows, as well as its general format, and several special situations. If the reader requires more information about this topic, it is addressed at length in FASB Statement Number 95, with amendments in FASB Statements Number 102 (regarding the exemption of some entities from using it) and 104 (regarding the presentation of deposits and loans in the statement by some types of financial institutions).

9-2 OPERATING ACTIVITIES

The first section of the statement of cash flows contains cash inflows and outflows that are derived from operating activities, which may be defined as any category of cash flows that does not fall into the investing or financing activities in the next two sections of the report. Examples of cash inflows in this category are:

- Collection of interest income or dividends.
- Collection of notes receivable.
- Receipts of sale transactions.

Examples of cash outflows in this category are:

- Interest payments.
- Payments for inventory.
- Payments to suppliers.
- Payroll payments.
- Tax payments.

9-3 INVESTING ACTIVITIES

The second section of the statement of cash flows contains cash inflows and outflows that are derived from investment activities on the part of the organization issuing the report. Examples of cash inflows related to investing activities are:

- Cash received from the sale of assets.
- Loan principal payments by another entity to the reporting entity.
- Sale of another entity's equity securities by the reporting entity.

Examples of cash outflows in this category are:

- Loans made to another entity.
- Purchase of assets.
- Purchases by the reporting entity of another entity's equity securities.

9-4 FINANCING ACTIVITIES

The third section of the statement of cash flows contains cash inflows and outflows that are derived from financing activities on the part of the organization issuing the report. Examples of cash inflows related to financing activities are:

- Proceeds from the sale of the reporting entity's equity securities.
- Proceeds from the issuance of bonds or other types of debt to investors.

Examples of cash outflows in this category are:

- Cash paid for debt issuance costs.
- Debt repayments.
- Dividend payments to the holders of the reporting entity's equity securities.
- Repurchase of the reporting entity's equity securities.

9-5 THE FORMAT OF THE STATEMENT OF CASH FLOWS

The statement of cash flows has no rigidly defined format that the accountant must follow for presentation purposes. Cash flows must be separated into the operating, investing, and financing activities that were just described, but the level of detailed reporting within those categories is up to the accountant's judgment.

The key issue when creating a statement of cash flows is that it contains enough information for the reader to understand where cash flows are occurring, and how they vary from the reported net income. The bottom of the report should include a reconciliation that adjusts the net income figure to the net amount of cash provided by operating activities—this is useful for showing the impact of non-cash items, such as depreciation, amortization, and accruals, on the amount of cash provided from operating activities. An example of the statement of cash flows is shown in Exhibit 9-1.

Exhibit 9-1   Example of the Statement of Cash Flows

Cash flows from operating activities:	
Cash received from customers	4,507
Cash paid to suppliers	−3,016
Cash paid for general & administrative expenses	−1,001
Cash paid for interest	−89
Cash paid for income taxes	−160
Net cash flow from operations:	241

Cash flows from investing activities:

Purchase of securities	−58	
Sale of securities	128	
Purchase of land	−218	
Purchase of fixed assets	−459	
Net cash used in investing activities:		−607

Cash flows from financing activities:

Increase in preferred stock	100	
Decrease in customer deposits	−49	
Dividend payment	−125	
Sale of equity securities	500	
Net cash provided by financing activities:		426
Net increase (decrease) in cash:		−181

Reconciliation of Net Income to Net Cash Provided by Operating Activities:

Net income	206
Reconciling adjustments between net income and net cash from operations:	
Depreciation	39
Change in accounts receivable	200
Change in inventory	138
Change in accounts payable	−275
Change in accrued expenses	−67
Net cash from operations:	241

9-6 EXEMPTIONS FROM THE STATEMENT OF CASH FLOWS

An investment company is not required to present a statement of cash flows, as long as it falls within the following parameters:

- It has minimal debt.
- It issues a statement of changes in net assets.
- Its investments are carried at market value.
- Nearly all of its investments are highly liquid.

Defined benefit plans and certain other types of employee benefit plans are also not required to issue a statement of cash flows, as long as they follow the guidelines of FASB Statement Number 35, "Accounting and Reporting by Defined Benefit Pension Plans." This statement describes the rules for the annual financial statements associated with a defined benefit pension plan, requiring the inclusion of such information as net assets available for benefits, changes in these benefits, and the present value of plan benefits.

9-7 PRESENTATION OF CONSOLIDATED ENTITIES

When constructing the statement of cash flows as part of a consolidated set of financial statements, all other statements must first be consolidated; this is necessary because information is pulled from the other statements in order to complete the statement of cash flows. Then complete the following consolidation steps:

1. Eliminate all non-cash transactions related to the business combination.
2. Eliminate all inter-company operating transactions, such as sales of products between divisions.
3. Eliminate all inter-company investing transactions, such as the purchase of equity securities by different divisions.
4. Eliminate all inter-company financing activities, such as dividend payments between divisions.
5. Add back any income or loss that has been allocated to non-controlling parties, since this is not an actual cash flow.

9-8 TREATMENT OF FOREIGN CURRENCY TRANSACTIONS

When a company is located in a foreign location, or has a subsidiary located there, a separate statement of cash flows should be created for the foreign entity. This statement is then translated into the reporting currency for the parent company (see Chapter 12, Foreign Currency Translation), using the exchange rate that was current at the time when the cash flows occurred. If the cash flows were spread equably over the entire reporting period, then the exchange rate used can be a weighted average, so long as the final reporting result is essentially the same. The resulting statement of cash flows for the foreign entity may then be consolidated into the statement of cash flows for the entire organization.

9-9 SUMMARY

The statement of cash flows is an extremely useful part of the financial statements, because a financial analyst can determine from it the true state of a business entity's cash flows, which can otherwise be hidden under the accrual method of accounting within the income statement and balance sheet. By using this statement, one can spot situations in which a company appears to be reporting healthy profits and revenue growth, and yet suddenly goes bankrupt due to a lack of cash. Given this and other reasons, the statement should be carefully examined in comparison to the information presented in the income statement and balance sheet in order to gain a clearer picture of the financial health of a business.

CHAPTER 10

Footnotes

10-1 INTRODUCTION

There are a great many circumstances under GAAP rules that require the accountant to report additional information in text form alongside the primary set of financial information, such as the nature of accounting policies being used to derive the statements, contingent liabilities, risks related to derivative instruments, discontinued operations, and error corrections. This chapter covers many of the most common footnotes that must be used. In cases where the amount of information is either excessively detailed or only applies to a narrow range of possible situations, the applicable GAAP documents are mentioned, so that the reader can explore the original text related to the issue. In some cases, example footnotes are added in order to clarify the required type of reporting.

10-2 DISCLOSURE OF ACCOUNTING CHANGES

When a company initiates a change in accounting, the accountant must disclose the type of change, and describe why the change is being made. In addition, the footnote should list the dollar impact caused by the change for the current and immediately preceding reporting period, as well as the amount of the change in earnings per share. Further, the cumulative effect of the change on retained earnings should be noted. An example is as follows:

> The company switched from the FIFO to the LIFO inventory valuation method. Its reason for doing so was that a close examination of actual inventory flow practices revealed that the LIFO method more accurately reflected the actual movement of inventory. The net impact of this change in the current period was an increase in the cost of goods sold of $174,000, which resulted in an after-tax reduction in net income of $108,000. This also resulted in a reduction in the reported level of earnings per share of $.02 per share. The same information for the preceding year was a reduction in net income of $42,000 and a reduction in earnings per share of $.01. The cumulative effect of the change on beginning retained earnings for the current period was a reduction of $63,500.

10-3 DISCLOSURE OF ACCOUNTING POLICIES

The financial statements should include a description of the principal accounting policies being followed, such as the method of inventory valuation, the type of depreciation calculation method being followed, and whether or not the lower of cost or market valuation approach is used for inventory costing purposes. Any industry-specific policies should also be disclosed, as well as any unusual variations on the standard GAAP rules. An example is as follows:

> The company calculates the cost of its inventories using the average costing method, and reduces the cost of inventory under the lower of cost or market rule on a regular basis. All fixed assets are depreciated using the sum-of-the-years-digits method of calculation. Since many of the company's boat-building contracts are multi-year in nature and only involve occasional contractually mandated payments from customers, it consistently uses the percentage of completion method to recognize revenues for these contractual arrangements.

10-4 DISCLOSURE OF ASSET IMPAIRMENTS

If a company writes down the value of assets due to the impairment of their value, the accountant should describe the assets, note which segment of the business is impacted by the loss, disclose the amount of the loss, how fair value was determined, where the loss is reported in the income statement, the remaining cost assigned to the assets, and the date by which the company expects to have disposed of them (if it expects to do so). An example is as follows:

The company has written down the value of its server farm, on the grounds that this equipment has a vastly reduced resale value as a result of the introduction of a new generation of microprocessor chips. The services of an appraiser were used to obtain a fair market value, net of selling costs, to which their cost was reduced. The resulting loss of $439,500 was charged to the application service provider segment of the company, and is contained within the "Other Gains and Losses" line item on the income statement. The remaining valuation ascribed to these assets as of the balance sheet date is $2,450,000. There are no immediate expectations to dispose of these assets.

10-5 DISCLOSURE OF BUSINESS COMBINATIONS

If a company enters into a business combination, the accountant should disclose the name of the acquired company, describe its general business operation, the cost of the acquisition, and the number of shares involved in the transaction. If there are contingent payments that are part of the purchase price, then their amount should also be disclosed, as well as the conditions under which the payments will be made. During the accounting period in which the combination is being completed, the accountant should also describe any issues that are still unresolved, as well as the plan for and cost of any major asset dispositions. An example is as follows:

During the reporting period, the company acquired the OvalMax Corporation, which manufactures disposable gaskets. The transaction was completed under the purchase method of accounting, and involved a payment of $52 million in cash, as well as 100,000 shares of common stock. If the OvalMax Corporation can increase its profit level in the upcoming year by 25%, then an additional acquisition payment of $15 million will be paid to its former owners. There are no plans to dispose of any major OvalMax assets, but the majority of its accounting staff will be terminated as part of a plan to merge this function into that of the company. Termination costs associated with this change are expected to be no higher than $2,250,000.

10-6 DISCLOSURE OF CALLABLE OBLIGATIONS

A company may have a long-term liability that can be called if it violates some related covenants. If it has indeed violated some aspect of the covenants, then the accountant must disclose the nature of the violation, how much of the related liability can potentially be called because of the violation, and if a waiver has been obtained from the creditor or if the company has acted to cancel the violation through some action. An example is as follows:

The company has a long-term loan with a consortium of lenders, for which it violated the minimum current ratio covenant during the reporting period. The potential amount callable is one-half of the remaining loan outstanding, which is $5,500,000. However, the consortium granted a waiver of the violation, and also reduced the amount of the current ratio requirement from 2:1 to 1:1 for future periods.

10-7 DISCLOSURE OF COMMITMENTS

There are many types of commitments that may require disclosure. For example, there may be a minimum purchase agreement that extends into future reporting periods, and that obligates a company to make purchases in amounts that are material. Also, a company may have made guarantees to pay for the debts of other entities, such as a subsidiary. If these commitments are material, then their nature must be disclosed in the footnotes. The rules are not specific about identifying the exact cost or probability of occurrence of each commitment, so the accountant has some leeway in presenting this information. An example is as follows:

> The company has entered into a contract to purchase a minimum of 500,000 tons of coal per year for the next 20 years at a fixed price of $20.50 per ton, with no price escalation allowed for the duration of the contract. The company's minimum annual payment obligation under this contract is $10,250,000. The price paid under this contract is $1.75 less than the market rate for anthracite coal as of the date of these statements, and had not significantly changed as of the statement issuance date.

10-8 DISCLOSURE OF COMPENSATING BALANCES

A company may have an arrangement with its bank to keep some minimum portion of its cash in an account at the bank. Since this cash cannot be drawn down without incurring extra fees, it is essentially not usable for other purposes. If this is a significant amount, it should be split away from the cash balance on the balance sheet and either listed as a separate line item in the current assets section (if the related borrowing agreement expires in the current year) or as a long-term asset (if the related borrowing agreement expires in a later year).

10-9 DISCLOSURE OF CONTINGENT LIABILITIES

A contingent liability may require a business entity to pay off a liability, but either the amount of the liability cannot reasonably be determined at the report date, or the requirement to pay is uncertain. The most common contingent liability is a lawsuit whose outcome is still pending. If the contingent amount can be reasonably estimated and the outcome is reasonably certain, then a contingent liability must be accrued. However, in any case where the outcome is not as certain, the accountant should describe the nature of the claim in the footnotes. Also, if a lower limit to the range of possible liabilities has been accrued due to the difficulty of deriving a range of possible estimates, then the upper limit of the range should be included in the footnotes. Finally, if a loss contingency arises after the financial statement date but before the release date, then this information should also be disclosed. An example is as follows:

> The company has one potential contingent liability. The insurance claim related to earthquake damage to the company's California assembly plant. The insurance company is disputing its need to pay for this claim, on the

grounds that the insurance renewal payment was received by it one day after the policy expiration date. Company counsel believes that the insurance company's claim is groundless, and that it will be required to pay the company the full amount of the claim after arbitration is concluded. The total amount of the claim is $1,285,000.

10-10 DISCLOSURE OF CONTINUED EXISTENCE DOUBTS

If there is a significant cause for concern that the business entity being reported upon will not continue in existence, then this information must be included in the footnotes. An example is as follows:

The company has $325,000 of available funds remaining in its line of credit, which it expects to use during the next fiscal year. Thus far, the company has been unable to obtain additional equity or financing to supplement the amount of this line of credit. Given the continuing losses from operations that continue to be caused by a downturn in the chemical production industry, management believes that the company's financing difficulties may result in its having difficulty continuing to exist as an independent business entity.

10-11 DISCLOSURE OF CUSTOMERS

If a company has revenues from individual customers that amount to at least 10% of total revenues, then the accountant must report the amount of revenues from each of these customers, as well as the name of the business segment (if any) with which these customers are doing business. An example is as follows:

The company does a significant amount of its total business with two customers. One customer, comprising 15% of total revenues for the entire company, also comprises 52% of the revenues of the Appliances segment. The second customer, comprising 28% of total revenues for the entire company, also comprises 63% of the revenues of the Government segment.

10-12 DISCLOSURE OF DEBT EXTINGUISHMENT

If a company experiences a gain or loss through a debt extinguishment transaction, the accountant should describe the transaction, the amount of the gain or loss (which must also be recorded as a line item under the "Extraordinary Items" section of the income statement), the impact on income taxes and earnings per share, and the source of funds used to retire the debt. An example is as follows:

The company retired all of its callable Series D bonds during the period. The funds used to retire the bonds were obtained from the issuance of Series A preferred stock during the period. The debt retirement transaction resulted in an extraordinary gain of $595,000, which had after-tax positive impacts on net income of $369,000 and on per share earnings of $.29.

10-13 DISCLOSURE OF DERIVATIVES

The disclosure of derivatives-related information is a complex area with different reporting rules for different types of derivatives. For more detail on this topic, one can consult FASB Statement Numbers 105, 107, 115, 119, and 133. In general, the fair value of a derivative instrument must be disclosed, as well as the assumptions used to calculate the fair value. If the accountant feels that it is not possible to derive a fair value, then one must disclose much of the information that would normally be used to arrive at a fair value— the carrying value, effective interest rate, and maturity date. The risk issues related to derivatives must also be disclosed, such as the maximum amount of any potential loss, collateral that might be lost as a result of derivative transactions, and the transactions for which hedges are used to manage risk. Disclosure should also include the reason for engaging in the use of derivatives.

10-14 DISCLOSURE OF DISCONTINUED OPERATIONS

When some company operations are expected to be discontinued, the accountant should identify the discontinued segment at the earliest possible date, as well as the expected date on which the discontinuation will take place. The disclosure should also note the method of disposal, such as sale to a competitor or complete abandonment. If the discontinuation is occurring in the current reporting period, then the accountant should also itemize both the results of operations for the discontinued operation up until the date of disposal, and any proceeds from sale of the operations. An example is as follows:

The company has elected to discontinue its Carrier Pigeon Quick Delivery Service. No buyer of this business is expected, so the company expects to shut down the operation no later than February of this year. No significant proceeds are expected from the sale of assets, since most of its assets will be absorbed into other operations of the company.

10-15 DISCLOSURE OF EARNINGS PER SHARE

When earnings per share (EPS) data is included in the financial statements, the accountant must also disclose the following information:

- *Omitted securities.* Describe any securities that have been omitted from the diluted earnings per share calculation on the grounds that they are anti-dilutive, but which could have a dilutive effect in the future.

- *Preferred dividends impact.* Note the impact of dividends on preferred stock when calculating the amount of income available for the basic EPS calculation.

- *Reconcile basic and diluted EPS.* The accountant must present a reconciliation of the numerators and denominators for the calculations used to derive basic and diluted EPS for income related to continuing operations.

- *Subsequent events.* The accountant must describe any event that occurs after the date of the financial statements, but before the date of issuance that would have had a material effect on the number of common shares outstanding if it had occurred during the accounting period being reported upon.

10-16 DISCLOSURE OF ERROR CORRECTIONS

When an error correction is made, it is to the financial results of a prior period. The disclosure is primarily contained within the line items on the face of the financial statements. However, the accompanying footnotes should also describe the nature of the error. An example is as follows:

> An error was discovered in the 2002 financial statements, whereby depreciation was incorrectly calculated on the straight line basis for several major plant installations involving the Watertown cement facility. The double declining balance method should have been used, as per company policy for assets of this nature. Correction of the error resulted in a decrease in the reported net income, net of income taxes, of $147,500.

10-17 DISCLOSURE OF GOODWILL

If a company elects to immediately write down some or all of the goodwill recorded on its books, there must be disclosure of the reasons for doing so. The footnote should specify why an impairment of goodwill has occurred, the events that have caused the impairment to take place, those portions of the business to which the impaired goodwill is associated, and how the company measured the amount of the loss. Any calculation assumptions used in determining the amount of the write down should be noted. An example is as follows:

> The company has taken a write down of $1,200,000 in its goodwill account. This write down is specifically tied to the increase in competition expected from the approval of a competing patent, given to Westmoreland Steel Company, which will allow it to produce steel much more efficiently than the company's Arbuthnot Foundry, to which the $1,200,000 in goodwill is associated. This write down is based on the assumption that the Arbuthnot Foundry will not be able to compete with Westmoreland Steel for longer than four years—consequently, the present value of all goodwill that will remain on the company's books four years from the date of these financial statements has been written off.

10-18 DISCLOSURE OF INCOME TAXES

If a company does not recognize a tax liability, then the accountant should disclose the temporary differences, at a summary level, for which no tax liability is recorded, as well as those circumstances under which a liability would be recorded. The accountant should also list any permanent unrecognized tax liabilities related to investments in foreign entities.

The accountant should itemize the amount of any net operating loss carryforwards and related credits, as well as the dates on which they expire. In addition, one should present a reconciliation of the statutory tax rate to the actual rate experienced by the organization during the reporting period, though privately held entities can restrict this reporting to a description of the general types of reconciling items.

The amounts of the following items related to income taxes must be attached to the income statement or reported within it:

- Any investment tax credit.
- Changes in tax assets or liabilities caused by changes in valuation estimates.
- Changes in tax assets or liabilities caused by regulatory changes.
- Net operating loss carryforwards.
- Tax-reducing government grants.
- The current tax expense.
- The deferred tax expense.

10-19 DISCLOSURE OF INTANGIBLES

If a company has a material amount of intangible assets on its books, the accountant should describe the types of intangibles, the amortization period and method used to offset their value, and the amount of accumulated amortization. An example is as follows:

> The company has $1,500,000 of intangible assets on its books that is solely comprised of the estimated fair market value of patents acquired through the company's acquisition of the R.C. Goodnough Company under the purchase method of accounting. This intangible asset is being amortized over 15 years, which is the remaining term of the acquired patents. The accumulated amortization through the reporting period is $300,000.

10-20 DISCLOSURE OF INVENTORY

If a company uses the LIFO valuation method, it should note the financial impact of any liquidation in LIFO inventory layers. Also, if a company uses other methods of valuation in addition to LIFO, then the extent to which each method is used should be described. Irrespective of the type of valuation method used, a company must reveal whether it is using the lower of cost or market adjustment (and the extent of any losses), whether any inventories are recorded at costs above their acquisition costs, whether any inventory is pledged as part of a debt arrangement, and the method of valuation being used. An example is as follows:

> The company uses the LIFO valuation method for approximately 65% of the total dollar value of its inventories, with the FIFO method being used for all remaining inventories. The company experienced a loss of $1.50 per share during the period that was caused by the elimination of LIFO inventory layers. The company also lost $.74 per share during the period as a result of a write down of inventory costs to market. The company records no inventories above their acquisition costs. As of the balance sheet date, the company had pledged $540,000 of its inventory as part of a line of credit arrangement with the First Federal Industrial Credit Bank.

10-21 DISCLOSURE OF INVESTMENTS

If a company holds any investments, the accountant must disclose the existence of any unrealized valuation accounts in the equity section of the balance sheet, as well as any realized gains or losses that have been recognized through the income statement. The classification of any material investments should also be noted (that is, as available for salc or as held to maturity).

If investments are accounted for under the equity method, then the name of the entity in which the investment is made should be noted, as well as the company's percentage of ownership, the total value based on the market price of the shares held, and the total amount of any unrealized appreciation or depreciation, with a discussion of how these amounts are amortized. The amount of any goodwill associated with the investment should be noted, as well as the method and specifications of the related amortization. If this method of accounting is used for an investment in which the company's share of investee ownership is less than 20%, then the reason should be noted; similarly, if the method is not used in cases where the percentage of ownership is greater than 20%, then the reasoning should also be discussed. Finally, the accountant should reveal the existence of any contingent issuances of stock by the investee that could result in a material change in the company's share of the investee's reported earnings.

10-22 DISCLOSURE OF LEASES

If a company is leasing an asset that is recorded as an operating lease, the accountant must disclose the future minimum lease payments for the next five years, as well as the terms of any purchase, escalation, or renewal options. If an asset lease is being recorded as a capital lease, then the accountant should present the same information, as well as the amount of depreciation already recorded for these assets. Capital lease information should also include a summary, by major asset category, of the gross cost of leased assets. An example is as follows:

The company is leasing a number of copiers, which are all recorded as operating leases. There are no escalation or renewal options associated with these leases. There are purchase options at the end of all lease terms that are based on the market price of the copiers at that time. The future minimum lease payments for these leases are:

2003	$195,000
2004	173,000
2005	151,000
2006	145,000
2007	101,000

10-23 DISCLOSURE OF LOANS

If a company has entered into a loan agreement as the creditor, the accountant should describe each debt instrument, as well as all maturity dates associated with principal payments, the interest rate, and any circumstances under which the lender can call the loan (usually involving a description of all related covenants). In addition, the existence of any conversion privileges by the lender and any assets to be used as collateral should be described. Other special disclosures involve the existence of any debt agreements entered into subsequent to the date of the financial statements, related party debt agreements, and the unused amount of any outstanding letters of credit. An example is as follows:

The company has entered into a line of credit arrangement with the First Federal Commercial Bank, which carries a maximum possible balance of $5,000,000. The loan has a variable interest rate that is $\frac{1}{2}$% higher than the bank's prime lending rate. The loan's interest rate as of the date of the financial statements is $8\frac{3}{4}$%. As of the date of the financial statements, the company had drawn down $750,000 of the loan balance. Collateral used to secure the loan is all accounts receivable and fixed assets. The loan must be renegotiated by December 31, 2003; in the meantime, the bank can call the loan if the company's working capital balance falls below $2,000,000, or if its current ratio drops below 1.5 to 1.

10-24 DISCLOSURE OF NON-MONETARY EXCHANGES

If a business engages in the barter of advertising in exchange for goods or services, it must disclose the estimated amount of revenue or expense involved in these transactions. If the fair value of these transactions could not be determined, then the type of advertising used or issued, as well as its volume, must be disclosed. An example is as follows:

The company gives traffic reports to radio stations in exchange for a pre-negotiated amount of advertising time, which it then sells to cover the cost of its traffic reporting function. During the period, it exchanged traffic report information to three radio stations in exchange for 5,412 minutes of advertising time. It sold these blocks for an average of $54 per minute, resulting in $292,248 in revenues.

10-25 DISCLOSURE OF PRIOR PERIOD ADJUSTMENTS

Prior period adjustments should be itemized for all reporting periods that they impact, both at gross and net of income tax effect. This should be done as line items within the financial statements. However, if the accountant wishes to introduce a greater degree of clarity in relation to any such changes, then also including the information in a footnote would be acceptable. An example is as follows:

> The company discovered that the inventory in an outlying warehouse was not counted during the year-end physical inventory count for both of the years reported in the financial statements. The amount of the overlooked inventory in 2001 was $230,000 and in 2002 was $145,000. Retroactive inclusion of these inventory amounts in the financial statements for those years would have resulted in an increase in net income of $142,600 in 2001 and $89,900 in 2002.

10-26 DISCLOSURE OF RELATED PARTY TRANSACTIONS

If there are transactions with related parties, the accountant should disclose the relationship, the degree of control over the company by the related party, the amount and terms of any transactions between the parties, and the nature of any economic dependency between the parties. An example is as follows:

> The company leases its central office location from J.D. Salmouth at a lease rate of $25.80 per square foot, which is $8.10 above the current market rate. Based on the total square footage at this location of 12,500 feet, this represents an excess payment over the market rate of $221,250 per year. The lease expires in three years. Mr. Salmouth is a 20% shareholder in the company, sits on its Board of Directors, and also owns the Salmouth Distributorship, which is a principal supplier of bearings to the company.

10-27 DISCLOSURE OF SEGMENT INFORMATION

If a company is publicly held, the accountant must disclose information about its operating segments in considerable detail, which is described in FASB Statement Number 131. In general, this should include a discussion of the means by which management splits the organization into separate reporting segments. It should also identify the types of products that comprise each segment's revenue, the nature of any inter-company transactions between reporting segments, and the reasons for any differences between reported results by segment and consolidated results. A comprehensive disclosure of segment information can be presented in a grid format that itemizes information for each segment in a separate column, and that summarizes the total for all segments, net of adjustments, into a consolidated company-wide total.

10-28 DISCLOSURE OF SIGNIFICANT RISKS

The accountant must disclose in the footnotes that the creation of any financial statement requires the use of some estimates by management. This notation should be accompanied by a list of any significant items in the financial statements that are based on management estimates, and that could result in material changes if the estimates should prove to be incorrect.

The footnotes should also disclose the existence of any concentrations of revenue with certain customers, as well as concentrations of supplies with certain vendors. In addition, geographic concentrations of business activity should be disclosed, plus the existence of any collective bargaining agreements that cover a significant proportion of the workforce. An example is as follows:

Twenty-three percent of the company's total revenue is to a single customer; there are purchase agreements in place that commit this customer to similar purchase volumes for the next three years. In addition, 10% of company revenues are earned from its Bosnia operation, to which management assigns a high risk of loss if political disturbances in this area continue. Finally, 43% of the company's direct labor force is covered by a collective bargaining agreement with the International Brotherhood of Electrical Workers; the related union agreement is not due to expire for three years.

10-29 DISCLOSURE OF SUBSEQUENT EVENTS

If any event occurs subsequent to the date of the financial statements that may have a material impact on the financial statements, then it should be disclosed in the footnotes. The accountant should consider issuing pro forma statements to include a monetary presentation of this information in cases where the amount of the subsequent event significantly changes the organization's financial position. Some examples of subsequent events that should be disclosed are:

- Gains or losses on foreign exchange transactions of a substantial nature.
- Gains or losses on investments of a substantial nature.
- Loans to related parties.
- Loss contingencies.
- Loss of assets to natural disasters.
- Merger or acquisition.
- Receipt of new funds from debt or equity issuances.
- Sale of major assets.
- Settlement of litigation, including the amount of any prospective payments or receipts.

10-30 SUMMARY

The primary focus of the footnote disclosures in this chapter has been on accounting situations that apply to all industries. In addition to the cases noted here, there are also a number of footnote disclosures required for companies operating within specific industries, such as the banking, broadcasting, insurance, motion picture, and software industries. A review of the GAAP source document summaries in Chapter 5, Accounting Standards, will give the reader some indication of where information about these specialty topics can be found.

CHAPTER 11

Internal Management Reports

11-1 INTRODUCTION

Much of the accountant's work must be translated into a report format that is readily understandable to the layman. Some of these reports are the financial statements, the rules for which are laid down in many other chapters of this book in accordance with GAAP. However, there are no rules for internal management reports. The accountant can use any format that results in the greatest comprehension of accounting information. In this chapter, we focus on specific examples of internal reports that can be adapted to fulfill this comprehension requirement.

11-2 STATUS REPORTS

Though the financial statements are the primary reporting product of the accountant, they are only issued (at most) once a month, which is too long for many managers to go without information about ongoing company performance. Also, much of the financial information contained within a financial statement is of no use to the typical manager, who is more concerned with operational data. A good alternative to the financial statement, both in terms of the frequency of reporting and information presented, is shown in Exhibit 11-1.

This exhibit divides key measurements into three financial areas and three operational areas. The CFO and treasurer are most concerned with the first two blocks of measurements, which describe five separate components of company cash flow. The third block notes financial performance information, while the remaining three blocks of measurements are specifically tailored to the needs of the managers of the sales, production, and warehouse departments.

Exhibit 11-1 Key Company Measurements

		Feb.	Mar.	Apr.	Current Month Week 1	Week 2	Week 3	Week 4	Week 5
Cash	Available Debt (000s)	$1,200	$1,300	$1,400	$1,500				
	Overdue Accounts Receivable (000s)	$269	$312	$315	$388				
	Overdue Accounts Payable (000s)	$401	$312	$276	$114				
Working Capital	Days Accounts Receivable	51	41	43	46				
	Days Total Inventory	46	52	61	49				
Financial	Breakeven, 2 Mo. Rolling (000s)	$1,450	$1,440	$1,430	—	—	—	—	—
	Net Profits Before Tax (000s)	($60)	($33)	$30	—	—	—	—	—
Sales	Backlog for Next Month	$1,651	$1,708	$1,922	$1,724				
	Backlog for Month After Next	$491	$505	$652	$461				
	Backlog for Two Months After Next	$358	$202	$296	$9				
	Backlog, Total (000s)	$2,500	$2,415	$2,870	$2,194				
Production	Machine Utilization	66%	67%	70%	0.8				
	% Order Line Items Shipped on Time	64%	73%	79%	0.83				
	% Actual Labor Hrs over Standard	25%	40%	23%	0.17				
	Scrap Dollars (000s)	$54	$51	$46	—	—		—	—
Warehouse	$$$ of Total Inventory (000s)	$2,273	$2,352	$2,644	$2,604				
	$$$ of Finished Goods (000s)	$668	$454	$496	$536				
	$$$ of Work-in-Process (000s)	$362	$555	$680	$566				
	$$$ of Raw Materials (000s)	$1,243	$1,343	$1,468	$1,502				
	Inventory Accuracy	71%	80%	68%	56%				

Reprinted with permission: Bragg, *Financial Analysis*, John Wiley & Sons, 2000, p. 240.

Another status report is the daily financial statement, which can be issued on paper or converted to HTML format and posted to a company's intranet site for general perusal. The example shown in Exhibit 11-2 contains all of the basic financial statement line items. The main difference is that it contains several extra columns that a reader can use to determine the status of the company in reaching its goals. For example, the two columns farthest to the right itemize the actual year-to-date results through the preceding month, which are then divided by the total number of months in the year thus far to arrive at the average value per month for each line item. This is a useful comparison to the budgeted amount for the current month, which is located in the third column. Yet another source of information is the forecasted result for the month (in the second column), which is the accountant's up-to-the-minute estimate of expected results for the current month. Finally, the first column contains the most recent actual results for the current month, which contains the least complete information until the month is nearly finished. By using four different estimates of financial results for the current month, the reader can draw his or her own conclusions regarding its most likely outcome.

In addition to the monthly information presented in the preceding report, the information in its first few rows details some key accounting measures, such as the volume of invoicing, and the cash and accounts receivable balances. Other measures, such as the total backlog, or the dollar volume of orders completed for the month, can also be added here.

11-3 MARGIN REPORTS

The status reports just described provide a high level of information to the reader. For a more detailed examination of operating results, it is useful to generate several types of margin reports. One option is noted in Exhibit 11-3, which reveals the gross margin of a series of company products, using their standard costs.

This reporting format reveals the gross margin for the sales volumes generated for the year-to-date or month for the listed products. The use of standard costs will reveal accurate margin information, as long as the standard costs are routinely compared to actual costs and adjusted to yield a close approximation to them. By using standards, many computer systems can automatically access all of the listed information and create the report with no human intervention.

Margins can also be presented by customer, as shown in Exhibit 11-4. This format is about the same as the one just shown in Exhibit 11-3, but is summarized by customer. Many accounting systems that are integrated with the production system can automatically provide this information, too. Note, however, that this report does not contain any of the additional sales, packaging, shipping, and customer service costs that are needed to maintain proper relations with customers. These added costs are not normally accessible through a standard costing system, and must be separately derived through an activity-based costing system and then manually added to this report format.

A more complex margin analysis is shown in Exhibit 11-5. This format divides the margins of all customers into high or low margin, with an arbitrary cutoff between the two of 30%. It also splits customers into high or low revenue volume, with an arbitrary cutoff at $100,000 per year. The exact cutoff will vary greatly by company, with the

Exhibit 11-2   Daily Flash Report

May 2002
Daily Flash Report

	Month-to-Date Through 5/3/2002	This Month's Forecast	This Month's Budget	Variance from Budget	Year-to-Date for Prior Months	4 Average for Prior Months
This Month's Invoicing	9,424					
New Business Invoiced	—					
Cash	926,547	—	—	—	—	—
Accounts Receivable	161,311	—	—	—	—	—
Sales, Month-to-Date	62,203	—	—	—	—	—
Sales, Expected This Month	192,697	—	—	—	—	—
Total Projected Sales	254,900	**254,900**	271,454	(16,554)	804,647	201,162
Cost of Sales		13,846	6,770	6,770	43,709	10,927
Commissions		10,661	19,678	19,678	33,655	8,414
Gross Profit	254,900	230,392	245,006	9,894	727,283	181,821
Gross Profit %	100%	90%	90%	—	90%	90%
Expenses:						
Advertising		1,000	2,500	2,500	485	121
Bank Charges		200	185	185	968	242
Copiers		354	700	700	2,468	617
Depreciation	7,223	7,223	7,875	652	24,992	6,248
Dues & Publications		100	400	400	459	115
Insurance		6,869	6,925	6,925	27,477	6,869
Interest Expense	—	—	—	—	4,416	1,104
Legal & Accounting	4,563	4,563	1,500	(3,063)	13,175	3,294
Licenses & Fees		50	150	150	150	38
Marketing		4,500	2,500	2,500	360	90
Meals & Entertainment		1,150	1,500	1,500	4,598	1,150
Outside Services	477	1,055	2,500	2,023	4,221	1,055
Payroll Taxes		10,500	13,119	13,119	39,949	9,987
Postage/Deliveries		550	750	750	2,202	551
Recruiting	1,094	2,000	5,000	3,906	8,469	2,117
Rent	10,788	10,788	10,788	—	43,151	10,788
Reserve for Cancel. Subscr.		6,000	2,032	2,032	21,527	5,382
Salaries		120,000	150,773	150,773	422,280	105,570
Soza/GSA Commissions		350	—	—	1,975	494
Supplies	1,129	4,000	2,500	1,371	39,229	9,807
Telephone	581	2,350	2,800	2,219	7,257	1,814
Training		500	1,250	1,250	5,400	1,350
Trade Shows		1,000	—	—	3,990	998
Travel	41	5,000	6,000	5,959	18,379	4,595
Other Expenses	3,970	4,500	2,265	(1,705)	13,120	3,280
Total Expenses	29,866	194,602	224,012	194,146	710,697	177,674
Profit (Loss)	225,034	35,790	20,994	204,040	16,586	4,147

Exhibit 11-3 Standard Cost of Goods Sold Report by Product

Standard Cost of Goods Sold
Sorted by Margin %

Item No.	Item Description	Qty Sold	Unit Price	Total Revenue	Unit Cost Material	Unit Cost Labor	Total Cost Material	Total Cost Labor	Margin %	Total Margin $
14003.221	Light Diffuser	3,500	0.025	88	0.002	0.032	9	113	−38.5%	−34
12231	Bolster Arm Cover	3,016	0.8	2,413	0.930	—	2,805	—	−16.3%	−392
12350.001	Cradle Rocker	643	15.64	10,057	14.364	1.077	9,236	692	1.3%	128
12200.7	Baby Bath	65,000	0.141	9,165	0.110	0.024	7,119	1,555	5.4%	491
14003.501	Magnet Cover	5,000	0.116	580	0.066	0.027	329	136	19.8%	115
11706	"Pail, 5 Gallon"	96	1.5	144	1.032	0.109	99	10	24.0%	34
14003.201	Key Pad	7,000	0.075	525	0.023	0.032	158	225	26.9%	141
12320.001	Baby Potty	1,710	7.95	13,595	4.304	1.357	7,360	2,321	28.8%	3,914
14039.02	Ruler, 6"	1,741	0.217	378	0.093	0.054	162	95	32.1%	121
14003.352	Terminal Block	20,000	0.1	2,000	0.040	0.026	795	522	34.1%	683
12006	Food Storage Tray	332,640	0.135	44,906	0.067	0.015	22,230	5,064	39.2%	17,612
14037.01	Remote Control Case	1,150	0.317	365	0.104	0.061	120	70	47.9%	175
14026.1	Medicine Spoon	5,000	0.092	460	0.033	0.015	166	72	48.1%	221
14052.021	Water Bottle	20,000	0.105	2,100	0.034	0.017	684	337	51.4%	1,079
14026.07	Key Case	56,000	0.084	4,704	0.014	0.027	790	1,492	51.5%	2,422
14003.64	Battery Holder	2,500	0.123	308	0.018	0.039	44	98	53.7%	165
14001.03	Battery Case	4,320	2.009	8,679	0.722	0.106	3,120	457	58.8%	5,103
14003.76	Light Pipe	21,000	0.145	3,045	0.015	0.037	316	776	64.1%	1,953
14052.01	Water Bottle Cap	22,000	0.093	2,046	0.024	0.008	529	179	65.4%	1,337
14025.046	"Gasket, 23mm"	106	0.179	19	0.017	0.044	2	5	66.0%	13
14010.096	Retaining Strip	3,000	0.412	1,236	0.054	0.057	161	170	73.3%	905
14025.02	Coin Holder	25,872	0.271	7,011	0.041	0.031	1,063	788	73.6%	5,161
14003.28	"Gasket, 35mm"	2,500	0.09	225	0.006	0.017	16	44	73.6%	166
14003.77	LCD Support Bracket	21,000	0.244	5,124	0.023	0.025	481	525	80.4%	4,118
				1,763,913			861,868	231,180	38.0%	670,866

Reprinted with permission: Bragg, *Financial Analysis*, John Wiley & Sons, 2000, p. 253.

Exhibit 11-4   Standard Cost of Goods Sold Report by Customer

Standard Margin by Customer Report

Item No.	Item Description	Customer Name	YTD Units	Unit Price	Std Material Cost	Std Labor Cost	Std Machine Cost	Assembly Overhead Cost	Total Revenue	Total Expense	Total Margin	Direct Std % Margin	Total All Inclusive Margin %
14003	Light Diffuser	Exceptional Child Inc.	2,762	24.830	18.1537	2.0184	3.198	1.457	68,580	68,575	6	19%	0%
12231	Bolster Arm Cover	Exceptional Child Inc.	4,327	25.070	18.1019	2.0184	0.661	1.457	108,478	96,225	12,253	20%	11%
12350	Cradle Rocker	Exceptional Child Inc.	20	0.350	0.0255	0.0435	0.015	0.000	7	2	5	80%	76%
12201	Baby Bath	Exceptional Child Inc.	25	0.250	0.0113	0.0435	0.015	0.000	6	2	4	78%	72%
13250	Mophead	Exceptional Child Inc.	378	56.680	33.2162	5.7876	5.012	4.162	21,425	18,211	3,214	31%	15%
14004	Magnet Cover	Exceptional Child Inc.	17,800	43.600	27.5402	5.7876	5.012	4.162	776,080	756,524	19,556	24%	3%
11706	Pail, 5 Gallon	Anterior Designs	320,869	0.141	0.1095	0.0239	0.052	0.0000	45,243	59,446	(14,203)	5%	-31%
14003	Key Pad	Anterior Designs	45,000	0.230	0.0424	0.0283	0.042	0.0000	10,350	5,074	5,276	69%	51%
12320	Baby Potty	Anterior Designs	53,500	0.250	0.0505	0.0381	0.057	0.0000	13,375	7,769	5,606	65%	42%
13222	Ski Tip	Anterior Designs	3,146	25.670	11.8078	8.1774	2.516	0.202	80,758	71,427	9,331	22%	12%
12300	Diaper Pail	Backman Services	1,022	13.870	7.8078	0.5974	2.516	0.202	14,175	11,369	2,806	39%	20%
14039	Ruler, 6"	Backman Services	3,016	3.970	3.9700	0.0000	—	—	11,974	11,974	—	0%	0%
14003	Terminal Block	Backman Services	3,016	0.800	0.9300	0.0000	—	—	2,413	2,805	(392)	-16%	-16%
13207	Ski Tail	Backman Services	84,090	6.396	3.4643	0.9171	1.769	0.227	537,840	536,270	1,569	31%	0%
12006	Food Storage Tray	Backman Services	10	0.500	0.0671	0.0544	0.019	0.0000	5	1	4	76%	72%
14037	Remote Control Case	Backman Services	127,737	6.019	3.6483	0.6593	1.687	0.328	768,849	807,653	(38,804)	28%	-5%
14026	Medicine Spoon	Diversified Products	7,232	7.290	4.5440	0.6593	1.816	0.328	52,721	53,138	(417)	29%	-1%
14052	Water Bottle	Diversified Products	4,050	7.950	4.3039	1.3573	5.570	0.470	32,199	47,387	(15,188)	29%	-47%
14026	Key Case	Diversified Products	24,614	20.320	13.9105	2.3731	0.947	2.429	500,156	483,908	16,248	20%	3%
14004	Battery Holder	Diversified Products	43,228	6.237	2.5694	0.8685	3.863	0.190	269,591	323,832	(54,241)	45%	-20%
14001	Battery Case	Diversified Products	12	0.200	0.0282	0.0218	0.032	0.0000	2	1	1	75%	59%
14004	Light Pipe	Diversified Products	3,630	15.730	14.3636	1.0766	1.650	0.583	57,100	64,152	(7,052)	2%	-12%
14052	Water Bottle Cap	Diversified Products	25,500	8.915	6.2670	0.4943	0.897	0.291	227,322	202,724	24,599	24%	11%
14025	Gasket, 23mm	Automotive Designs	32,142	7.976	4.6375	0.9292	2.842	0.263	256,365	278,748	(22,383)	30%	-9%
14010	Retaining Strip	Automotive Designs	42,571	5.984	4.4709	0.6200	1.768	0.381	254,753	308,191	(53,438)	15%	-21%
14025	Coin Holder	Automotive Designs	11,881	1.951	0.6697	0.2208	0.431	0.0000	23,180	15,703	7,477	54%	32%
14003	Gasket, 35mm	Automotive Designs	1	13.748	9.3296	1.5807	0.309	0.972	14	12	2	21%	11%
14004	LCD Support	Automotive Designs	3,026	3.017	1.5511	0.3698	0.525	0.0000	9,128	7,400	1,728	36%	19%
									4,142,090	4,238,522	-96,432		-2%

Reprinted with permission: Bragg, *Financial Analysis*, John Wiley & Sons, 2000, p. 256.

Exhibit 11-5 Customer Margin Analysis

	Low Revenue	High Revenue
High Margin	**No. Customers = 30** **Percent of Sales = 5%** **Annual Sales = $531K** **Annual Margin = 47%** AMG Industries Audobon Park Boulder Technology Brindle Corporation Bucktooth Inc. Bushmaster Weaponry Chemical Devices Corp. Convertible Devices Corp. Dutch-Made Devices Englewood Instruments Great Peaks & Sons On Top Gourmet Foods SMC Corp. Huntington Brickworks Initial Response Units International Clearance Co. Mann's Cutlery Material Upgrade Company Newco Pottery Oliphaunt Fencing Peak Industries Quorum Software	**No. Customers = 10** **Percent of Sales = 42%** **Annual Sales = $4,313K** **Annual Margin = 37%** _Margin % / Annual Dollars_ Acme — 33% — $607,600 Best Western — 39% — $134,200 Champion — 43% — $154,900 Estes Door Frames — 38% — $340,400 Gates and Fencing Int'l — 39% — $129,800 Hudson River Upholstery — 35% — $1,586,200 Killer Kitchen Products — 39% — $964,400 Monster Equipment — 32% — $423,300 Sudden Coffee — 41% — $440,100 Venture Home Foods — 41% — $139,500 Total — $4,312,800
Low Margin	**No. Customers = 19** **Percent of Sales = 5%** **Annual Sales = $493K** **Annual Margin = 11%** Aston Davidson Aerospace Backup Services Brush Logic Defensive Innovations Entirely Upscale Renderings Fashionable Furniture Gecko Lawn Furnishings Halston Oil & Gas Immediate Response Co. Jervis Book Binders Poly Cracker Bird Supply Primary Rescue Services Rocky Mountain Oil Scott Primary Services Sun Tanning Oil Co. Tofu Deluxe	**No. Customers = 9** **Percent of Sales = 48%** **Annual Sales = $4,871K** **Annual Margin = 22%** _Margin % / Annual Dollars_ Anterior Designs — 29% — $204,000 Bombproof Draperies — 14% — $130,900 Early Research Corp. — 24% — $925,000 Engineered Solutions — 25% — $256,400 Highland Scots — 26% — $146,500 Kanberra Koala — 19% — $1,559,500 Optimum Energy — 22% — $904,500 Terrible Trouble Kid Stores — 16% — $548,300 Vertical Drapery Company — 24% — $196,000 Total — $4,871,100

Vertical axis threshold: 30%
Horizontal axis threshold: $100K

intention being to give management a good feel for which customers provide a combination of the highest margins and volumes (located in the upper right corner) and which are the least profitable ones (in the lower left corner). Also, all of the customers shown in the high volume categories on the right side of the exhibit have their individual margin percentages listed next to them, for easy reference. Each of the four segments also contains a small block of information that lists the number of customers located within it, the total proportion and dollar amount of sales that they represent, and their combined gross margin. Though this is a labor-intensive report to create, it presents a great deal of information to management regarding which customers to cultivate, which ones to drop, which ones require a price increase, and which ones require additional sales efforts.

Many managers do not know the sales level at which their companies will reach a profitability breakeven point. This point will vary somewhat every month, as margins and fixed costs change. The report shown in Exhibit 11-6 can keep this information squarely in front of managers by itemizing the current gross margin level (second column) and the current level of fixed costs (fourth column) to arrive at an expected level of loss or profit, depending upon the exact revenue level reached. In the example, a wide array of revenue levels are itemized in $50,000 increments, which happens to be useful for the small business for which this analysis was constructed. Businesses of other sizes would use revenue ranges that more appropriately fit their high-low range of possible revenue levels.

11-4 CASH REPORTS

The standard cash forecast report is discussed in detail in Chapter 13. However, the accountant may wish to obtain additional cash-related information beyond the standard forecasting model. One possibility is to determine the accuracy level of the forecast on a weekly basis, in order to see if the assumptions or data used in the forecast must be changed to make it more accurate. An example of this reporting format is shown in Exhibit 11-7. This report lists the actual cash balance at the end of each week for the last few months, showing alongside each item the cash forecast that had been made one month prior to each actual cash balance. The dollar and percentage amount of each variance are then listed, as well as an explanation of any especially large variances. This can be a most instructive exercise, as the accountant will initially find significant variances between forecasted and actual cash balances; continual examination of the underlying problems that caused the variances is needed in order to eventually arrive at a more accurate cash forecasting system.

The most likely source of large changes in cash requirements tends to come from working capital, simply because of the large investment that is typically required in this area. To see how the main categories of working capital will vary over time, one can set up a combination of numerical and graphical information, as shown in Exhibit 11-8, that not only shows monthly totals for accounts receivable, accounts payable, and inventory, but also the trend line for working capital levels. This is a most useful tool for determining the existence of any problems related to a company's investment in working capital.

Exhibit 11-6 Breakeven Analysis

		Breakeven Analysis (2 Month Average)		
Revenue	Margin	Gross Margin	Fixed Cost	Net Profit (Loss)
950,000	34.0%	323,124	545,000	−221,877
1,000,000	34.0%	340,130	545,000	−204,870
1,050,000	34.0%	357,137	545,000	−187,864
1,100,000	34.0%	374,143	545,000	−170,857
1,150,000	34.0%	391,150	545,000	−153,851
1,200,000	34.0%	408,156	545,000	−136,844
1,250,000	34.0%	425,163	545,000	−119,838
1,300,000	34.0%	442,169	545,000	−102,831
1,350,000	34.0%	459,176	545,000	−85,825
1,400,000	34.0%	476,182	545,000	−68,818
1,450,000	34.0%	493,189	545,000	−51,812
1,500,000	34.0%	510,195	545,000	−34,805
1,550,000	34.0%	527,202	545,000	−17,799
1,600,000	34.0%	544,208	545,000	−792
1,650,000	34.0%	561,215	545,000	16,215
1,700,000	34.0%	578,221	545,000	33,221
1,750,000	34.0%	595,228	545,000	50,228
1,800,000	34.0%	612,234	545,000	67,234
1,850,000	34.0%	629,241	545,000	84,241
1,900,000	34.0%	646,247	545,000	101,247
1,950,000	34.0%	663,254	545,000	118,254
2,000,000	34.0%	680,260	545,000	135,260
2,050,000	34.0%	697,267	545,000	152,267
2,100,000	34.0%	714,273	545,000	169,273
2,150,000	34.0%	731,280	545,000	186,280
2,200,000	34.0%	748,286	545,000	203,286
2,250,000	34.0%	765,293	545,000	220,293
2,300,000	34.0%	782,299	545,000	237,299
2,350,000	34.0%	799,306	545,000	254,306
2,400,000	34.0%	816,312	545,000	271,312

Reprinted with permission: Bragg, *Financial Analysis,* John Wiley & Sons, 2000, p. 266.

Exhibit 11-7   Cash Forecasting Accuracy Report

Cash Forecasting Accuracy Report

[Explanatory Notes Included If Variance Greater than 5%]

Week	Actual Cash Balance	Forecast 1 Mo. Ago	Variance	Percentage Variance	Explanatory Notes
7-Jan	2,275	2,075	200	9%	DEF customer paid early
14-Jan	2,150	2,109	41	2%	
21-Jan	2,425	2,581	−156	−6%	ABC customer paid late
28-Jan	2,725	2,843	−118	−4%	
4-Feb	3,125	3,000	125	4%	
11-Feb	3,225	3,305	−80	−2%	
18-Feb	3,495	3,450	45	1%	
25-Feb	3,445	2,942	503	15%	Bank error in recording check
4-Mar	3,645	3,751	−106	−3%	
11-Mar	3,555	3,500	55	2%	
18-Mar	3,604	3,209	395	11%	Paid for capital expenditures
25-Mar	3,704	3,589	115	3%	
1-Apr	3,754	3,604	150	4%	
8-Apr	3,879	3,802	77	2%	
15-Apr	3,939	3,921	18	0%	
22-Apr	3,864	3,900	−36	−1%	
29-Apr	4,264	3,781	483	11%	Customers took 2% early payment discount
6-May	4,464	4,351	113	3%	
13-May	4,434	4,031	403	9%	Customers took 2% early payment discount
20-May	4,188	4,000	188	4%	
27-May	4,339	4,503	−164	−4%	

Exhibit 11-8   Working Capital Trend Line

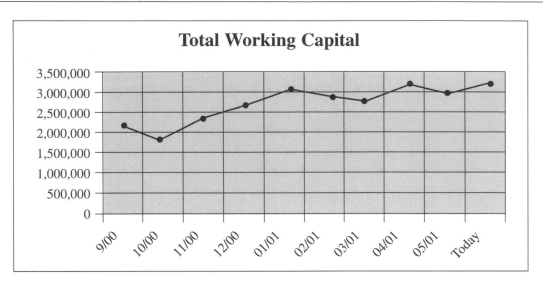

	Accounts Receivable		Inventory		Accounts Payable		Total Working Capital
9/00	2,028,000	9/00	1,839,000	9/00	1,604,000	9/00	2,263,000
10/00	1,663,000	10/00	1,614,000	10/00	1,423,000	10/00	1,854,000
11/00	1,498,000	11/00	1,784,000	11/00	933,000	11/00	2,349,000
12/00	1,664,000	12/00	1,932,000	12/00	942,000	12/00	2,654,000
01/01	2,234,000	01/01	2,007,000	01/01	1,152,000	01/01	3,089,000
02/01	2,450,000	02/01	2,273,000	02/01	1,862,000	02/01	2,861,000
03/01	2,042,000	03/01	2,419,000	03/01	1,671,000	03/01	2,790,000
04/01	3,036,000	04/01	2,715,000	04/01	2,575,000	04/01	3,176,000
05/01	2,998,000	05/01	2,588,000	05/01	2,585,000	05/01	3,001,000
Today	2,875,000	Today	2,976,000	Today	2,606,000	Today	3,245,000

Reprinted with permission: Bragg, *Financial Analysis,* John Wiley & Sons, 2000, p. 262.

11-5 CAPACITY REPORTS

The extent to which a company is utilizing its assets tends to be one of the least reported by the accountant, even though it represents one of a company's core drivers of overall profitability. There may not be any systems in place that track the time during which a machine is being used, but some simplified measure can usually be derived, even if one must back into the number by calculating backward from production volumes the amount of machine time that must have been used to conduct the required manufacturing operations. The result can be plotted graphically, as shown in Exhibit 11-9. This exhibit shows the percentage of utilization for a series of plastic injection molding machines. The calculation of capacity should include a notation regarding the number of hours per day that are used for the measurement—otherwise, management may feel compelled to purchase more equipment if the calculation is based on an eight-hour shift, rather than a 24-hour day.

The capacity planning report can also be used in the service industry, with the chargeable hours of individual employees or departments being substituted for machines.

Another way to present capacity utilization measurements is to focus solely upon the key bottleneck operation that drives the overall level of production of an entire manufacturing line or facility. Since even minor fluctuations in the production level at this point can have a major impact on the volume of units produced, such an analysis should delve into the specific causes of even the smallest production variances from the maximum theoretical production level, so that they can be addressed and eliminated.

11-6 SALES AND EXPENSE REPORTS

When actual sales differ from expectations, the accountant needs a report format that reveals exactly where the variance arose. The format shown in Exhibit 11-10 is a good way to show, customer by customer, the cause of the variance. This report shows both the monthly and year-to-date variance by customer. However, many organizations do not budget their sales by specific customer, unless there are ongoing orders from each one that are easy to predict. If so, this format can be reduced to a smaller number of line items that reveal variances only for specific market segments or groups of customers.

A similar type of format can be used for expense control. Exhibit 11-11 contains an expense control report that is sorted by responsible party within each department. By using this approach, the report can be distributed to department managers, who can then issue it to the individuals within their departments who are responsible for specific expense line items. Of particular interest in this report is the last column, which notes the full-year budget for each expense line item. This number is placed next to the year-to-date actual expense and variance numbers, so that managers can see exactly how much allocated funding is still available to them for the rest of the year.

11-7 PAYROLL REPORTS

The largest expense item in many organizations is payroll, which exceeds even the cost of materials. Proper control of this cost requires a detailed report that lists the salary or wage cost of each employee in comparison to the original budget. Such a format is shown in Exhibit 11-12. In the exhibit, employees are grouped by department, with the budgeted salary or wage level for each person noted in bold. Actual pay on an annualized basis is then shown for each successive month of the year. This format gives an extremely detailed view of exactly where a company is investing its payroll dollars. If there are too many employees to make the report easily readable, they can also be summarized by job title within departments, or simply by department, though some of the effectiveness of the report will be lost with the higher degree of summarization.

Exhibit 11-9 Capacity Utilization by Machine

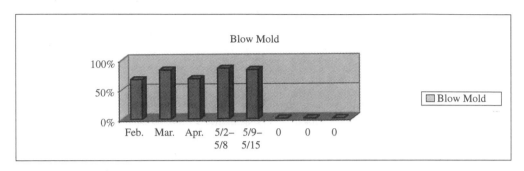

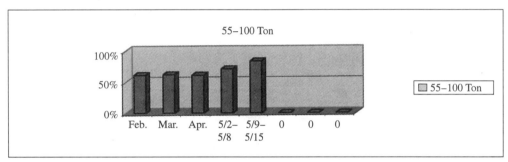

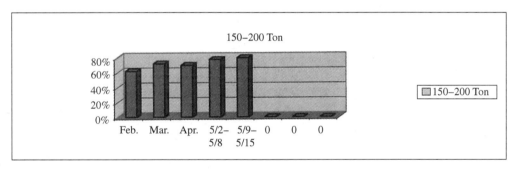

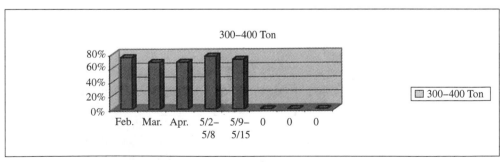

Reprinted with permission: Bragg, *Financial Analysis,* John Wiley & Sons, 2000, p. 268.

Exhibit 11-10   Forecasted Sales vs. Actual Sales Report

Customer Name	YTD Forecast	YTD Actual	Variance	Month Forecast	Month Actual	Variance
AC Dingo	58,000	73,506	15,506	21,000	8,417	−12,583
Admedix	285,000	738,205	453,205	85,000	178,489	93,489
Best Eastern	32,000	45,886	13,886	15,000	13,041	−1,959
BonaLisa	48,000	44,453	−3,547	8,000	10,868	2,868
Case Western	26,000	74,513	48,513	8,000	13,147	5,147
Champion Systems	24,000	24,493	493	0	11,480	11,480
Easy Go Services	45,000	45,589	589	15,000	17,548	2,548
EMC	1,779,396	2,488,239	708,843	723,878	1,094,675	370,797
Engineered Skating Products	47,000	58,800	11,800	25,000	18,074	−6,926
Estep Industries	26,000	83,858	57,858	12,000	26,539	14,539
Gates Plastics	40,000	42,630	2,630	14,000	12,395	−1,605
Great Plains Software	6,600	2,854	−3,746	2,200		−2,200
Great Deal Foods	0	25,678	25,678	0	25,678	25,678
Hudson & Sons	525,000	409,968	−115,032	300,000	91,459	−208,541
Hunter Stevenson	9,000	38,139	29,139	3,000	6,983	3,983
Innovative Boulder Tech.	22,000	44,970	22,970	14,000	15,001	1,001
Inovonics	9,000	30,173	21,173	3,000	8,386	5,386
Intermediate Diverse Foods	72,000	83,417	11,417	24,000	13,920	−10,080
Kountry Kitchen	350,265	371,051	20,786	138,795	66,964	−71,831
Magma Volcanic Gear	0	4,620	4,620	0	4,620	4,620
Martin Stevenson	9,000	11,647	2,647	3,000	3,975	975
Mile High Sun Systems	80,000	116,002	36,002	30,000	36,457	6,457
Miscellaneous	75,000	2,160	−72,840	25,000		−25,000
Optimus Stoves	390,000	423,465	33,465	120,000	100,274	−19,726
Polyseasonal Designs	27,000	28,063	1,063	5,000	7,244	2,244
Prime Target Company	3,600	1,000	−2,600	1,200	1,000	−200
Product Design Assoc.	5,000	12,348	7,348	5,000	4,020	−980
Progressive Ancillary Co.	25,000	6,402	−18,598	0	5,561	5,561
Ryco Boxes	0	7,387	7,387	0	3,381	3,381
Scott Paper Company	30,000	58,475	28,475	0	36,468	36,468
Sensory Deprivation Co.	0	810	810	0	810	810
Superior Furnishings	210,000	183,743	−26,257	60,000	49,493	−10,507
T. Rex Eatery	8,000	17,197	9,197	0	3,839	3,839
T-Pastry Company	0	2,500	2,500	0	2,500	2,500
Tenerific Kid Toys	0	431	431	0	431	431
Toxonomical Products	4,000	8,348	4,348	0		0
Tranway	9,000		−9,000	3,000		−3,000
Tristar Airways	60,000	10,831	−49,169	20,000	8,244	−11,756
Vendomatic Machinery	41,000	177,399	136,399	20,000	99,641	79,641
Volway Distribution	46,000	118,023	72,023	14,000	27,947	13,947
Westway Oil & Gas	0	2,889	2,889	0	1,445	1,445
Totals	4,426,861	5,920,162	1,493,301	1,718,073	2,030,414	312,341

Reprinted with permission: Bragg, *Financial Analysis,* John Wiley & Sons, 2000, p. 243.

Exhibit 11-11 Expense Control Report

Department	Description	Responsible	April Expense	April Budget	April Variance	YTD Expense	YTD Budget	YTD Variance	Full Year Budget
					ADMINISTRATION				
Admin	Accounting & Tax	Underhill, David	2,500	2,500	—	11,832	10,000	(1,832)	30,000
Admin	Advertising	Morris, William	1,680	833	(847)	4,959	3,332	(1,627)	9,996
Admin	Auto Expense	Morris, William	1,435	4,316	2,881	7,823	17,264	9,441	51,792
Admin	Bad Debt	Underhill, David	3,000	1,000	(2,000)	6,849	4,000	(2,849)	12,000
Admin	Charitable	Morris, William	—	1,250	1,250	179	5,000	4,821	15,000
Admin	Consultants	Underhill, David	6,363	2,000	(4,363)	17,415	8,000	(9,415)	24,000
Admin	Keyman Insurance	Morris, William	1,337	1,333	(4)	4,659	5,332	673	15,996
Admin	Legal	Morris, William	688	666	(22)	982	2,664	1,682	7,992
Admin	Liability Insurance	Underhill, David	3,500	3,500	—	13,001	14,000	999	42,000
Admin	Maintenance	Underhill, David	256	2,812	2,556	5,406	11,248	5,842	33,744
Admin	Other Expense	Underhill, David	161	1,500	1,339	3,881	6,000	2,119	18,000
Admin	Phones	Underhill, David	6,341	4,750	(1,591)	25,854	19,000	(6,854)	57,000
Admin	Postage	Underhill, David	740	1,270	530	3,719	5,080	1,361	15,240
Admin	Salaries	Underhill, David	48,803	39,215	(9,588)	151,656	156,860	5,204	470,580
Admin	Supplies	Underhill, David	1,668	3,541	1,873	1,749	7,082	5,333	42,492
Admin	Taxes	Underhill, David	(465)	166	631	(1,399)	664	2,063	1,992
Admin	Training	Underhill, David	1,437	291	(1,146)	6,215	1,164	(5,051)	3,492
Admin	Travel	Morris, William	259	3,750	3,491	5,205	15,000	9,795	45,000
	Grand Total		**79,703**	**74,693**	**(5,010)**	**269,985**	**291,690**	**21,705**	**896,316**

136

MANUFACTURING

Assembly	Building Maintenance	2,434	—	(2,434)	5,284	—	(5,284)	—
Assembly	Building Rent	17,100	17,100	—	57,670	57,000	(670)	205,200
Assembly	Liability Insurance	500	500	—	2,000	2,000	—	6,000
Assembly	Maintenance	1,235	1,200	(35)	3,122	4,400	1,278	14,400
Assembly	Other Expenses	144	—	(144)	402	—	(402)	—
Assembly	Rentals	1,767	1,400	(367)	7,430	4,600	(2,830)	16,800
Assembly	Salaries	33,445	23,197	(10,248)	97,245	92,788	(4,457)	278,364
Assembly	Supplies	2,303	200	(2,103)	9,182	5,700	(3,482)	2,400
Assembly	Training	—	116	116	—	116	116	1,392
Assembly	Travel	3,117	200	(2,917)	4,261	800	(3,461)	2,400
	Grand Total	**62,045**	**43,913**	**(18,132)**	**186,596**	**167,404**	**(19,192)**	**526,956**

Reprinted with permission: Bragg, *Financial Analysis*, John Wiley & Sons, 2000, p. 259.

Exhibit 11-12   Annualized Pay Levels Report Compared to Budget

Name	Department	Budget	Jan	Feb	Mar	Apr	May	Jun
Bowery, Dan	Assembly	**28,752**	19,524	19,524	19,524	20,267	20,267	20,216
Johnson, Gregory	Assembly	**28,752**	33,052	33,052	33,052	34,944	32,968	32,272
Monfort, Pat	Assembly	**43,260**	46,521	46,521	46,521	47,060	47,060	47,060
Zwonter, Steve	Assembly	**39,996**	47,788	47,788	47,788	47,788	45,019	36,078
Mayes, Dennis	Engineering	**48,456**	36,504	36,504	36,504	36,504	36,504	38,000
Open	Engineering	**48,456**	0	0	0	0	0	0
Linger, Lowell	Logistics	**25,392**	39,750	39,250	39,500	39,000	36,595	41,550
Rose, Jim	Logistics	**55,116**	53,200	54,990	54,990	54,990	54,990	55,000
Stewart, Thomas	Logistics	**25,392**	33,058	31,954	32,058	34,359	30,888	29,571
Wallace, Loretha	Logistics	**25,392**	30,966	30,966	30,966	30,966	24,115	23,870
Delany, Eric	Maintenance	**35,880**	29,500	29,500	34,320	33,839	34,320	32,020
Henderson, Alex	Maintenance	**35,880**	49,321	50,721	49,384	51,155	49,348	29,264
Norris, Aaron	Maintenance	**35,880**	50,960	50,960	50,960	50,960	54,379	67,227
Allen, Mark	Process Tech	**40,992**	38,972	39,067	38,555	41,574	33,618	44,630
Phorest, Michael	Process Tech	**40,992**	30,555	30,706	30,541	29,185	31,434	30,145
Short, Bob	Process Tech	**None**	30,000	32,000	32,000	32,877	32,071	26,018
Anderson, Carl	Production Mgmt	**110,000**	110,000	110,000	110,000	110,006	110,006	110,000
Graham, Lee	Production Mgmt	**42,996**	32,000	32,000	34,996	34,996	34,996	35,000
Honest, Darrell	Production Mgmt	**70,800**	70,798	70,798	70,798	70,798	70,798	70,799
Lawrence, Michael	Production Mgmt	**42,996**	47,996	47,996	47,996	47,996	47,996	48,000
Summers, Theresa	Production Mgmt	**42,996**	36,010	36,010	36,010	36,010	36,010	36,000
Bella, Donna	Quality Assurance	**24,996**	24,031	24,258	24,258	23,465	24,258	22,381
McDonald, Robert	Quality Assurance	**24,996**	25,386	25,971	25,069	24,063	30,069	27,585
Mills, Alan	Quality Assurance	**50,004**	49,998	49,998	49,998	49,998	49,998	50,000
Smith, George	Quality Assurance	**24,996**	18,538	18,538	18,538	18,538	18,528	18,538
Walmsley-Dunnet, Al	Quality Assurance	**None**	26,000	26,000	26,000	26,000	26,000	26,000
Bossy, Frank	S, G & A	**84,456**	82,004	82,004	82,004	82,004	82,004	82,000
Gainer, George	S, G & A	**124,992**	125,008	125,008	125,008	125,008	125,008	125,000
Hammit, Robert	S, G & A	**46,056**	45,240	45,240	45,240	45,240	45,916	46,000
Spudsit, Jeffrey	S, G & A	**75,000**	82,550	82,550	82,550	82,550	82,550	89,196
		1,323,872	1,345,230	1,349,874	1,355,128	1,362,140	1,347,713	1,339,420

Reprinted with permission: Bragg, *Financial Analysis*, John Wiley & Sons, 2000, p. 250.

The report shown in Exhibit 11-12 may not include the overtime pay for non-exempt employees, since this information could skew the annualized payroll information shown. If overtime is a significant proportion of payroll, then it can be shown separately, as in the report format noted in Exhibit 11-13. This report assumes that payrolls are completed once every two weeks, and itemizes the percentage of overtime paid by person within each department. This is most useful if issued to department managers immediately following each payroll, so that they can see who consistently works excessive amounts of overtime.

11-8 GRAPHICAL REPORT LAYOUTS

Many of the preceding reports can be modified to fit into a more easily readable graph format, of which there are many varieties. Six possible graph types are shown in Exhibit 11-14. The formats presented in the exhibit are:

- *Pie chart.* This graph is shown in a three-dimensional format, and can also be presented in a two-dimensional layout (especially when there is more information to pack into the chart). It is best used to show the proportion of parts to the whole amount, and cannot be used to show more than a half-dozen items without severely cluttering the graph.

- *Bar chart.* Immediately below the pie chart is a bar chart, also in three-dimensional format. It can be used to compare the amount of a similar item for different entities (in the exhibit, it compares the travel cost for different corporate facilities), and can also be used for a limited amount of trend line analysis. However, similar to the pie chart, it can easily become overloaded if too much data is presented.

- *Scattergraph.* The scattergraph is shown at the bottom of the first page of graphs. It is very useful for pattern analysis, since a large number of data points can be entered into the graph, and then fitted with a trend line that is a "best fit" based on the positions of all data items. As shown in the graph, the slope formula for the line can also be shown.

- *Trend line.* This graph is shown at the top of the second page of graphs. It is heavily used to reveal patterns that occur over time, such as expense levels over multiple periods. It is best not to clutter this graph with too many lines; rather, create a separate graph for each trend in order to more clearly present the data.

- *Bubble chart.* The bubble chart is shown immediately below the trend line graph. This format is more rarely used, since it is designed specifically to reveal market share information.

- *Area chart.* This graph is located at the bottom of the second page of graphs. It resembles a bar chart, in that data can be stacked on top of each other, while also presenting the stacked information over a series of time periods, as is done by a trend line. It is useful for seeing changes in the proportions of revenues or expenses over time. However, it is easily cluttered if too many data items are stacked on top of each other, and so should be used with care.

Exhibit 11-13   Overtime Report by Employee

	1/4	1/18	2/1	2/15	3/01	3/15	3/29	4/12	4/26
Engineering									
Nelson, Mark	23%	6%	15%	10%	18%	15%	0%	6%	18%
Maintenance									
Delatore, Alex	31%	15%	13%	24%	16%	26%	8%	15%	36%
Hansen, Erik	0%	11%	16%	41%	39%	32%	31%	28%	41%
Lage, Laurence	15%	19%	13%	26%	39%	21%	24%	4%	
Mold Shop									
Davidson, Raymond	0%	5%	0%	5%	13%	6%	10%	8%	18%
Miller, Jerry	11%	31%	10%	9%	20%	25%	16%	25%	11%
Stallsworth, Delbert	25%	23%	19%	34%	14%	30%	28%	26%	30%
Process Technicians									
Allen, Aaron	8%	13%	28%	21%	40%	30%	0%	21%	11%
Barron, Alejandro					14%	54%	44%	0%	15%
Estrada, Steve	15%	15%	11%	11%	8%	11%	10%	9%	11%
Michels, Shayne					36%	25%	33%	11%	34%
Reynolds, Mike	0%	0%	11%	0%	11%	34%	11%	14%	10%
Sherman, William					11%	11%	5%	0%	11%
Quality Assurance									
McDonald, Theresa	11%	0%	14%	0%	25%	6%	13%	0%	10%
Reidenbach, Donna	10%	14%	8%	28%	30%	9%	19%	25%	24%
Smith, Jacqueline	0%	13%	13%	13%	13%	13%	13%	0%	13%
Logistics									
Chhoeung, Lin					0%	0%	0%	0%	13%
Gage, Clarence							39%	9%	41%
Jacques, Kum	10%	0%	33%	45%	20%	23%	51%	29%	30%
Stewart, Loretha							26%	53%	46%
Webber, Ricky							0%	1%	0%
SG&A									
Courtney, Debbie	8%	9%	6%	13%	5%	13%	6%	13%	8%
Martin, Beverly	3%	1%	14%	6%	4%	0%	3%	0%	0%
Newby, Ginger	4%	9%	6%	9%	11%	10%	9%	9%	15%
Assembly									
Bowden, Greg				13%	5%	3%	23%	29%	40%
Jackson, Mike				18%	16%	8%	21%	6%	33%
Williams, Rosa				8%	3%	11%	20%	0%	74%
Average of all Overtime	10%	11%	13%	17%	17%	17%	17%	13%	23%

Reprinted with permission: Bragg, *Financial Analysis,* John Wiley & Sons, 2000, p. 250.

Exhibit 11-14   Examples of Graphical Report Formats

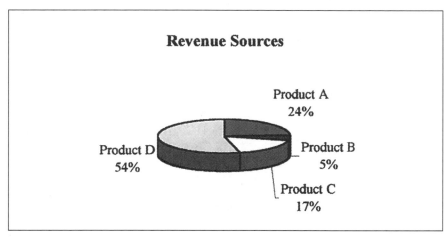

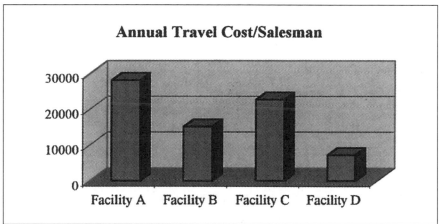

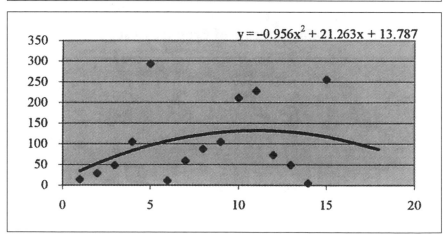

(continued)

Exhibit 11-14   Examples of Graphical Report Formats *(cont'd.)*

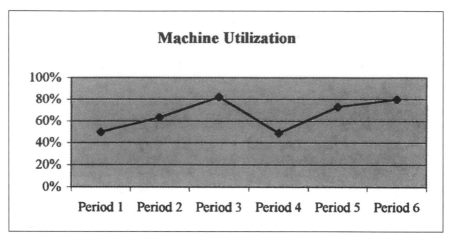

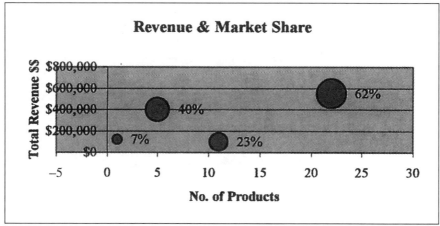

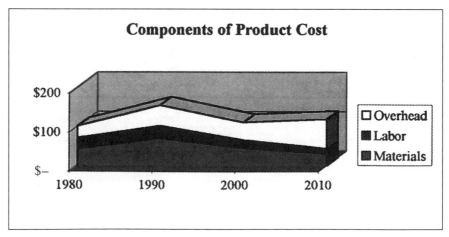

Reprinted with permission: Bragg, *Cost Accounting,* John Wiley & Sons, 2001, pp. 304–305.

11-9 SUMMARY

It is evident from the wide array of internal reports presented here that the types and formats of reports available to the accountant are limited only by his or her imagination. None of the reports shown here will precisely fit every organization's needs—on the contrary, the accountant is expected not only to custom-design reports that meet a company's specific informational requirements, but also to continuously modify them as circumstances change over time.

CHAPTER 12

Foreign Currency Translation

12-1 INTRODUCTION

In today's world of multi-national business transactions, even the smallest company may find that it deals with partners in other countries to a large extent. If so, there are a number of transactions, such as accounts receivable and accounts payable, as well as loans and forward exchange contracts, that may be denominated in foreign currencies. Larger organizations may also have foreign subsidiaries that deal primarily in foreign currency transactions. In either case, generally accepted accounting principles state that the transactions must be converted back into U.S. dollars when they are accounted for in a company's financial statements. Since there is some exchange rate risk associated with conducting business in other currencies, this conversion will likely result in the recognition of some gains or losses associated with transactions that are denominated in foreign currencies. In this chapter, we will review how foreign currency translation is accomplished in order to meet the objectives of GAAP.

The key consideration when making foreign currency translations is that when the conversion is complete, we will see an accurate translation of accounting performance in a foreign currency into precisely the same performance in U.S. dollars. In other words, a foreign subsidiary whose financial statements have specific current ratios, gross margins, and net profits will see the same results when translated into a report presentation in U.S. dollars.

12-2 THE CURRENT RATE TRANSLATION METHOD

The *current rate translation method* is used when a currency besides the U.S. dollar is determined to be the primary currency used by a subsidiary. This approach is usually selected when a subsidiary's operations are not integrated into those of its U.S.-based parent, if its financing is primarily in that of the local currency, or if the subsidiary conducts most of its transactions in the local currency. However, one cannot use this method if the country in which the subsidiary is located suffers from a high rate of inflation, which is defined as a cumulative rate of 100% or more over the most recent three years. In this case, the *remeasurement method* must be used (as described in a later section).

To complete the current rate translation method, the first order of business is to determine the functional currency of the subsidiary. In some locations, a subsidiary may deal with a variety of currencies, which makes this a less-than-obvious decision. The functional currency should be the currency that is used in the bulk of the subsidiary's transactions and financing. Next, convert all of the subsidiary's transactions to this functional currency. One must continue to use the same functional currency from year to year in order to provide a reasonable basis of comparison when multiple years of financial results are included in the corporate parent's financial results.

The next step is to convert all assets and liabilities of the subsidiary to U.S. dollars at the current rate of exchange as of the date of the financial statements. The stockholder's equity accounts are converted at the historical rate of exchange, while revenues and expenses that have occurred throughout the current fiscal year should be converted at a weighted-average rate of exchange for the entire year. Any resulting translation adjustments should be stored in the equity section of the corporate parent's consolidated balance sheet.

12-3 EXAMPLE OF THE CURRENT RATE METHOD

An extremely simplified example of a corporate subsidiary's (located in Mexico) balance sheet is shown in Exhibit 12-1. The peso exchange rate at the beginning of the year is assumed to be .08 to the dollar, while the rate at the end of the year is assumed to be .10 to the dollar. A highly abbreviated income statement is also shown in Exhibit 12-2. For the purposes of this exhibit, the blended full-year rate of exchange for the peso is assumed to be .09 to the dollar. Note that the net income figure derived from Exhibit 12-2 is incorporated into the retained earnings statement at the bottom of the exhibit, and is incorporated from there into the retained earnings line item in Exhibit 12-1. For simplicity, the beginning retained earnings figure in Exhibit 12-2 is assumed to be zero, implying that the company is in its first year of existence.

12-4 THE REMEASUREMENT METHOD

The remeasurement method is used when the U.S. dollar is designated as the primary currency in which transactions are recorded at a foreign location. Another clear indicator of when this method is used is when the subsidiary has close operational integration with its U.S. parent, and has most of its financing denominated into dollars.

Under this method, we translate not only cash, but also any transactions that will be settled in cash (mostly accounts receivable and payable, as well as loans) at the cur-

Exhibit 12-1   Balance Sheet Conversion Under the Current Rate Method

	Pesos	Exchange Rate	U.S. Dollars
Assets			
Cash	427	.08	34
Accounts Receivable	1,500	.08	120
Inventory	2,078	.08	166
Fixed Assets	3,790	.08	303
Total Assets	7,795		623
Liabilities & Equity			
Accounts Payable	1,003	.08	80
Notes Payable	4,250	.08	340
Common Stock	2,100	.10	210
Additional Paid-In Capital	428	.10	43
Retained Earnings	14	Note 1	0
Translation Adjustments	—	—	−50
Total Liabilities & Equity	7,795		623

Note 1: As noted in the income statement.

Exhibit 12-2   Income Statement Conversion Under the Current Rate Method

	Pesos	Exchange Rate	U.S. Dollars
Revenue	6,750	.09	608
Expenses	6,736	.09	607
Net Income	14		1
Beginning Retained Earnings	0		0
Add: Net Income	14	.09	0
Ending Retained Earnings	14		0

rent exchange rate as of the date of the financial statements. All other assets and liabilities (such as inventory, prepaid items, fixed assets, trademarks, goodwill, and equity) will be settled at the historical exchange rate on the date when these transactions occurred.

There are a few cases where the income statement is affected by the items on the balance sheet that have been translated using historical interest rates. For example, the cost of goods sold will be affected when inventory that has been translated at a historical exchange rate is liquidated. When this happens, the inventory valuation at the historical exchange rate is charged through the income statement. The same approach is used for the depreciation of fixed assets and the amortization of intangible items.

Other income statement items primarily involve transactions that arise throughout the reporting year of the subsidiary. For these items, it would be too labor intensive to determine the exact exchange rate for each item at the time it occurred. Instead, one can determine the weighted average exchange rate for the entire reporting period, and apply this average to the income statement items that have occurred during that period.

12-5 EXAMPLE OF THE REMEASUREMENT METHOD

An extremely simplified example of a corporate subsidiary's (located in Mexico) balance sheet is shown in Exhibit 12-3 (which is the same balance sheet shown in Exhibit 12-1). The peso exchange rate at the beginning of the year is assumed to be .08 to the dollar, while the rate at the end of the year is assumed to be .10 to the dollar. The primary difference in calculation from the current rate method shown in Exhibit 12-1 is that the exchange rate for the inventory and fixed assets accounts have changed from the year-end rate to the rate at which they are assumed to have been originated at an earlier date. Also, there is no translation adjustment account in the equity section, as was the case under the current rate method.

A highly abbreviated income statement is shown in Exhibit 12-4. For the purposes of this exhibit, the blended full-year rate of exchange for the peso is assumed to be .09 to the dollar. Note that the net income figure derived from Exhibit 12-4 is incorporated into the retained earnings statement at the bottom of the exhibit, and is incorporated from there into the retained earnings line item in Exhibit 12-3.

Exhibit 12-3   Balance Sheet Conversion Under the Remeasurement Method

	Pesos	*Exchange Rate*	*U.S. Dollars*
Assets			
Cash	427	.08	34
Accounts Receivable	1,500	.08	120
Inventory	2,078	.10	208
Fixed Assets	3,790	.10	379
Total Assets	7,795		741
Liabilities & Equity			
Accounts Payable	1,003	.08	80
Notes Payable	4,250	.08	340
Common Stock	2,100	.10	210
Additional Paid-In Capital	428	.10	43
Retained Earnings	14	Note 1	68
Total Liabilities & Equity	7,795		741

Note 1: As noted in the income statement.

A major issue is that, under the current rate translation method, there was a translation *loss* of $50, while the remeasurement approach resulted in a translation gain of $61. This was caused by a difference in the assumptions used in deriving the exchange rate that in turn was used to convert the inventory and fixed asset accounts from pesos into dollars. Consequently, the choice of conversion methods used will have a direct impact on the reported level of profitability.

Exhibit 12-4   Income Statement Conversion Under the Remeasurement Method

	Pesos	*Exchange Rate*	*U.S. Dollars*
Revenue	6,750	.09	608
Goodwill Amortization	500	.08	40
Other Expenses	6,236	.09	561
Remeasurement Gain	—		**61**
Net Income	14		68
Beginning Retained Earnings	0		0
Add: Net Income	14		68
Ending Retained Earnings	14		68

12-6   FOREIGN EXCHANGE SALE TRANSACTIONS

For smaller companies that only rarely deal with foreign exchange transactions, there is no need to formally recall the details of either of the preceding translation methods. Instead, if they only participate in an occasional sale transaction, they can simply record the initial sale and related account receivable based on the spot exchange rate on the date when the transaction is initially completed. From that point forward, the amount of the recorded sale will not change—only the related receivable will be altered based on the spot exchange rate as of the date of the balance sheet on which it is reported, adjusting it up or down to reflect the existence of a potential gain or loss at the time of the eventual collection of the receivable. The final gain or loss will be recorded when the receivable is settled, using the spot rate on that date. This procedure will cover the most common transactions that a small business will encounter.

12-7   RECOGNITION OF TRANSLATION ADJUSTMENTS

The gains and losses resulting from various translation adjustments are treated in different ways, with some initially being stored in the balance sheet and others being recorded at once in the income statement. Here are the key rules to remember:

- If a company is directly engaged in foreign exchange transactions that are denominated in foreign currencies, then any translation adjustments to U.S. dollars that result in gains or losses should be immediately recognized in the income statement. The company can continue to make these adjustments for changes between the last reporting date and the date of the current financial statements, and may continue to do so until the underlying transactions have been concluded.

- If a company has a subsidiary whose results must be translated into U.S. dollars, then any translation gains or losses should be recorded in equity until such time as the subsidiary is sold or liquidated. However, if any portions of the subsidiary's financial statements will have an impact on the reported cash flows of the corporate parent, then any gains or losses on those portions of the subsidiary's financial statements must be recognized at once in the income statement of the corporate parent.

- If a company is including translated foreign results in its financial statements, and wishes to include its financial results for other years in the same statements, then it must restate the results of the other years to conform to the same foreign exchange calculations and procedures.

- If there has been a material change in an exchange rate in which a company's obligations or subsidiary results are enumerated, and the change has occurred subsequent to the date of financial statements that are being included in a company's audited results, then the change and its impact on the financial statements should be itemized in a footnote that accompanies the audited results.

- If there are inter-company long-term investment transactions between a U.S.-based parent and a foreign subsidiary, any transaction gains or losses resulting from foreign exchange considerations should not be recognized in the income statement.

12-8 EXCHANGE RATES USED FOR CALCULATIONS

There can be some confusion regarding the precise exchange rate to be used when conducting foreign currency translations. Here are some guidelines:

- If there is no published foreign exchange rate available on the specific date when a transaction occurred that requires translation, one should use the rate for the date that most immediately follows the date of the transaction.

- If the date of a financial statement that is to be converted from a foreign currency is different from the date of the financial statements into which they are to be converted into U.S. dollars, then use the date of the foreign currency financial statements as the date for which the proper exchange rate shall be used as the basis for translation.

- If there is more than one published exchange rate available that can be used as the basis for a translation, use the rate that could have been used as the basis for the exchange of funds that could then be used to remit dividends to shareholders. Alternatively, use the rate at which a settlement of the entire related transaction could have been completed.

12-9 SUMMARY

This chapter has described several approaches for converting transactions and financial statements that are denominated in foreign currencies into U.S. dollars. A good knowledge of the rules upon which these conversions are based is essential for determining the correct method of translation. This can have an impact on the recognition or non-recognition of translation gains and losses.

Part Four

ELEMENTS OF THE BALANCE SHEET AND INCOME STATEMENT

CHAPTER 13

Cash and Investments

13-1 INTRODUCTION

The reporting of cash and investments is generally considered to be one of the easiest parts of the balance sheet to complete. However, as noted in the following section, there are a number of instances where the reporting of these categories will be altered, depending upon the existence of such factors as restrictions on the use of cash, the reasons for purchasing and holding short-term investments, and the level of equity investment attained in another business entity. The footnote disclosures required for these line items are covered in Chapter 10.

13-2 CASH

Cash is defined as all petty cash, currency, held checks, certificates of deposit, traveler's checks, money orders, letters of credit, bank drafts, cashier's checks, and demand deposits that are held by a company without restriction, and that are readily available on demand. If there is a short-term restriction on the cash, such as a requirement that it be held in a sinking fund in anticipation of the payment of a corresponding debt within a year, then it should still be itemized as a current asset, but as a separate line item. If there is a long-term restriction on the cash, such as a compensating balance agreement that is linked to debt that will not be paid off within the current year, then the cash must be itemized as a long-term asset. Alternatively, if a compensating balance agreement is tied to a loan that matures within the current period, then it may be recorded separately as a current asset.

If a company issues checks for which there are not sufficient funds on hand, it will find itself in a negative cash situation as reported on its balance sheet. Rather than show a negative cash balance there, it is better to shift the amount of the excess checks back into the accounts payable liability account, thereby leaving the reported cash balance at or near zcro.

Cash held in foreign currencies should be included in the cash account on the balance sheet, subject to two restrictions. First, it must be converted to U.S. dollars at the prevailing exchange rate as of the balance sheet date. Second, the funds must be readily convertible into U.S. dollars; if not, perhaps due to currency restrictions by the foreign government, the cash cannot properly be classified as a current asset, and instead must be classified as a long-term asset. This later item is a key issue for those organizations that want to report the highest possible current ratio by shifting foreign currency holdings into the cash account.

Marketable securities may be included in the cash account if their maturity dates are so close that there is essentially no risk of changes in valuation prior to actual maturity. For practical purposes, this essentially limits one to overnight repurchase agreements, for which the amount of interest earned overnight is contractually identifiable in advance, or treasury bills, commercial paper, and money market funds for which the company commits to no more than a three-month term to maturity at the time the investment is bought. In other words, a company cannot shift funds from a long-term investment representation on the balance sheet into a cash representation, just because its term to maturity has dropped to less than three months; this option is only available if the entire term to maturity from the date of acquisition is three months or less.

Given the preceding points, the following line item descriptions can be used to represent a company's cash in the balance sheet:

1. Current assets: Cash and cash equivalents $1,000,000
   [covers the bulk of cash reporting situations]

2. Current assets: Restricted cash—compensating balances $250,000
   [describes the additional amount of cash held for loan
   compensating balance agreements]

3. Current assets: Restricted cash—sinking fund $225,000
   [describes the cash set aside to pay off a short-term debt]

4. Long-term assets: Restricted cash—sinking fund $445,000
   [describes the cash set aside to pay off a long-term debt]

5. Long-term assets: Restricted cash—foreign currency $105,000
   [describes foreign currencies that cannot be readily
   converted to dollars in the short term]

13-3 MARKETABLE SECURITIES

Marketable securities are investments that can be easily liquidated through an organized exchange, such as the New York Stock Exchange. If a company also holds securities that are intended for the control of another entity, then these securities should be separately segregated as a long-term investment (see the "Long-Term Investments" section).

Marketable securities are recorded in different ways, depending upon how they are categorized. They must be grouped into one of the following three categories at the time of purchase, and re-evaluated periodically to see if they still belong in the designated categories:

1. *Available for sale.* This category can include both debt and equity securities. It contains those securities that do not readily fall into either of the following two categories. It can include investments in other companies that comprise less than 20% of total ownership. These securities are reported on the balance sheet at their fair value, while unrealized gains and losses are charged to an equity account, from which they are later shifted to earnings upon sale of the securities. If a permanent reduction in value occurs, then the unrealized loss is charged against earnings, resulting in a new and lower cost basis in the remaining investment. Any subsequent increase in the value of such an investment above the new cost basis cannot be formally recognized in earnings until the related security is sold, and so the interim gains will be temporarily "parked" in the unrealized gains account in the equity section of the balance sheet.

   All interest, realized gains or losses, and debt amortization are recognized within the continuing operations section of the income statement. The listing of these securities on the balance sheet under either current or long-term assets is dependent upon their ability to be liquidated in the short term and to be available for disposition within that time frame, unencumbered by any obligations.

2. *Held to maturity.* This category only includes debt securities for which the company has both the intent and ability to hold them until their time of maturity. Their amortized cost is recorded on the balance sheet. These securities are likely to be listed on the balance sheet as long-term assets.

   If marketable securities are shifted into the held-to-maturity category from debt securities in the available-for-sale category, their unrealized holding gain or loss should continue to be stored in the equity section, while being gradually amortized down to zero over the remaining life of each security.

3. *Trading.* This category includes both debt and equity securities that the company intends to sell in the short term. It can include investments in other companies that comprise less than 20% of total ownership. They are recorded on the balance sheet at their fair value. This type of marketable security is always positioned in the balance sheet as a current asset.

   All interest and dividends resulting from these securities are recorded within the continuing operations section of the income statement. If the fair market value of any individual trading securities changes, either up or down, then the changes must be noted at once on the income statement as an unrealized gain or loss. One may also store unrealized gains and losses in a contra account, which is used to offset the investment account, thereby revealing the extent of changes in the trading securities from their purchased cost.

   If marketable securities are shifted into the trading category from another category, then they should be recorded at fair value at the time of transfer, with any resulting gain or loss being recognized in income.

In most cases, the recording of gains or losses on securities that have not yet been sold means that the company is making an assumption that the securities could be sold at the current market rates, which will result in associated income taxes. Accordingly, the related deferred income taxes should also be recorded on the balance sheet, either as assets or liabilities (depending upon the presence of investment losses or gains, respectively). These tax entries will vary over time, both in proportion to changes in the level of investment gains or losses, and any changes in the statutory tax rates related to the investments.

When the sale of a security occurs, both the net amount of its original cost and the amount in the unrealized loss account that has gradually built up over time must be eliminated.

Whenever financial statements are generated, the net amount of earnings generated by a debt security in the form of interest earned must be calculated and recognized as accrued interest income.

13-4 DERIVATIVES

A *derivative* is a financial instrument or contract whose value is based on a financial measurement, such as an interest rate or exchange rate, and which results in a payout based on the amount of the related financial measurement. It does not require an initial investment equal to the notional amount of the underlying contract, since its intent is for the participant to participate in a rate or price change with a corresponding reduced investment. Though derivatives can be used for speculative purposes, most organizations use them to manage risk (mostly those associated with variations in interest and currency rates). One type of derivative is the forward contract, which is settled at any time prior to or on the delivery date, usually by cash payment rather than delivery of the goods noted in the contract. Other types of derivatives are futures, swaps, option contracts, and interest rate caps and floors.

Derivatives must be reported on the balance sheet as assets and liabilities that accurately reflect their fair value as of the balance sheet date. Any gains or losses on derivatives from their acquired cost must be recognized in income. Some companies will attempt to avoid this requirement by merging derivatives into other types of contracts. If so, and if the derivative is not *clearly and closely* related to the contract into which it has been merged, then it must still be separated out and reported in a different line item in the balance sheet. Probable merged derivatives would be leveraged inflation-indexed payments and interest payments based on an equity index or commodity index. For example, if there is an underlying linkage to an interest rate or rate index that has the potential for altering the interest rate payments in a contract, then the fair value of the embedded derivative must be separately accounted for if the merged derivative could result in the investor's doubling of the initial rate of return, and could result in at least a doubling of the market rate of return.

13-5 LONG-TERM INVESTMENTS

If a company has a long-term investment in another business entity that totals less than 20% ownership in that entity, then it can record the investment value on its books at fair market value. As noted earlier under the "Marketable Securities" section, this investment can be recorded in either the "trading" or "available for sale" categories of securities.

If the investing company is considered to have significant influence over the company whose securities it has acquired, then it must instead use the equity method of accounting to record the value of its securities in that entity. Any ownership in the range of 20% to 50% is considered to involve significant ownership. Under the equity method, the securities holder must increase the recorded value of its holdings by its pro rata share of any net income reported by the subject entity, as well as its pro rata share of any issued dividends. It must also reduce its cost basis by its pro rata share of any losses recorded by the subject entity. If the subject entity has extraordinary items or prior period adjustments on its financial statements, then the investing company must separately record its pro rata share of these items under the same headings in its own financial statements (if material in relation to its own financial statements).

If one owns more than 50% of another entity, then full control is considered to have been achieved (even if this is not actually the case), and consolidated financial statements must then be created.

13-6 SUMMARY

The accounting for cash is more complex than one would initially suppose, since any restrictions on the use of cash, such as offsetting borrowing arrangements, can shift it into a long-term asset category, thereby reducing an organization's reported total amount of current assets. Likewise, marketable securities require careful attention to the purpose for which they are intended, with the exact categorization resulting in a change in both reported totals on the balance sheet and the treatment of realized and unrealized gains and losses. Derivatives are the most difficult of the investment categories to itemize on the balance sheet, since they must first be identified and then valued (a difficult chore, given the complexity of many derivatives contracts). Finally, long-term investments have different reporting requirements, depending on the level of investment that a company has achieved in the securities of other entities. Thus, though the cash and investments category initially seems like one of the easiest parts of the balance sheet to report upon, there are a number of rules to be aware of that can alter both the amount and location of presented financial information.

CHAPTER 14[1]

Inventory

14-1 INTRODUCTION

This chapter could also be called "cost flow assumptions," because that is the essence of its content. Cost flows describe the order in which costs are incurred. The reason why cost flows are important is that the cost incurred for an item may change over time, so that different costs will appear in the accounting records for the same item. If so, how does the cost accountant handle these costs? Are the earliest costs charged off first, or the later ones? Or is there an alternative approach that avoids the issue? In this chapter, we will look at the last-in first-out (LIFO), first-in first-out (FIFO), retail, and average costing systems, and how each one is used under a different assumption of cost flows. In addition, we will review how to create an inventory tracking system, how to conduct a physical inventory, how to identify and allocate overhead costs, and how the lower of cost or market rule is to be used.

14-2 TYPES OF INVENTORY

Items that may be included in inventory are those that are held for sale, are being produced prior to sale, or are consumed in the production of such items. The main categories of inventory are:

---

[1] The sections of this chapter dealing with LIFO, FIFO, and average costing were taken from pages 165–173 of Bragg, *Cost Accounting,* John Wiley & Sons, 2001 with permission. The sections dealing with physical inventory counts and tracking systems were taken from pages 209–216 of Bragg and Roehl-Anderson, *The Controller's Function,* John Wiley & Sons, 2000 with permission.

- *Raw materials.* Any materials that are to be used in the production process, and that will become part of a salable product, fall into this category.

- *Work-in-process.* Any materials, labor, and related overhead costs used during the production process fall into this category. Raw materials are shifted into this category as soon as they are physically moved to the production process, and the finished goods account is the recipient of all products leaving this category.

- *Finished goods.* Any goods that have passed through the production process, or which have been purchased for resale, fall into this category.

- *Supplies.* Incidental items that are consumed during the production process may be included in this category. Many organizations choose to charge all supplies to expense in the current period, rather than track them through an inventory account.

- *Consignment inventory.* Goods held at another location for sale by another party (such as through a distributor agreement) fall into this category. Consigned inventory is not owned by the secondary party, and should not be listed on its books.

- *Spare parts.* A company may keep a significant quantity of spare parts on hand, which it then sells to its customers as replacements for worn-out components within the products that it has sold to them in the past. This category can also be rolled into the finished goods category.

14-3 THE INVENTORY TRACKING SYSTEM

A physical inventory count can be eliminated if accurate perpetual inventory records are available. Many steps are needed to implement such a system, requiring considerable effort. The accountant should evaluate a company's resources prior to embarking on this process to ensure that they are sufficient to set up and maintain this system. The 17 steps needed to implement an accurate inventory tracking system are:

1. *Select and install inventory tracking software.* The primary requirements for this software are:
   - *Track transactions.* The software should list the frequency of product usage, which allows the materials manager to determine what inventory quantities should be changed, as well as to determine which items are obsolete.
   - *Update records immediately.* The inventory data must always be up-to-date, because production planners must know what is in stock, while cycle counters require access to accurate data. Batch updating of the system is not acceptable.
   - *Report inventory records by location.* Cycle counters need inventory records that are sorted by location in order to more efficiently locate and count the inventory.

2. *Test inventory tracking software.* Create a set of typical records in the new software, and perform a series of transactions to ensure that the software functions properly. In addition, create a large number of records and perform the transactions again, to see if the response time of the system drops significantly. If the software appears to function properly, continue to the next step. Otherwise, fix the problems with the software supplier's assistance, or acquire a different software package.

3. *Train the warehouse staff.* The warehouse staff should receive software training immediately before using the system, so that they do not forget how to operate the software. Enter a set of test records into the software, and have the staff simulate all common inventory transactions, such as receipts, picks, and cycle count adjustments.

4. *Revise the rack layout.* It is much easier to move racks prior to installing a perpetual inventory system, because no inventory locations must be changed in the computer system. Create aisles that are wide enough for forklift operation, and cluster small parts racks together for easier parts picking.

5. *Create rack locations.* A typical rack location is, for example, A-01-B-01. This means that this location code is located in Aisle A, Rack 1. Within Rack 1, it is located on Level B (numbered from the bottom to the top). Within Level B, it is located in Partition 1. Many companies skip the use of partitions, on the grounds that an aisle-rack-level numbering system will get a stock picker to within a few feet of an inventory item.

   As one progresses down an aisle, the rack numbers should progress in ascending sequence, with the odd rack numbers on the left and the even numbers on the right. This layout allows a stock picker to move down the center of the aisle, efficiently pulling items from stock based on sequential location codes.

6. *Lock the warehouse.* One of the main causes of record inaccuracy is removal of items from the warehouse by outside staff. To stop this removal, all entrances to the warehouse must be locked. Only warehouse personnel should be allowed access to it. All other personnel entering the warehouse should be accompanied by a member of the warehouse staff to prevent the removal of inventory.

7. *Consolidate parts.* To reduce the labor of counting the same item in multiple locations, group common parts into one place.

8. *Assign part numbers.* Have several experienced personnel verify all part numbers. A mislabeled part is as useless as a missing part, since the computer database will not show that it exists. Mislabeled parts also affect the inventory cost; for example, a mislabeled engine is more expensive than the item represented by its incorrect part number, which may identify it as (for example) a spark plug.

9. *Verify units of measure.* Have several experienced people verify all units of measure. Unless the software allows multiple units of measure to be used, the entire organization must adhere to one unit of measure for each item. For example, the warehouse may desire tape to be counted in rolls, but the engineering department had rather create bills of material with tape measured in inches instead of fractions of rolls.

10. *Pack the parts.* Pack parts into containers, seal the containers, and label them with the part number, unit of measure, and total quantity stored inside. Leave a few parts free for ready use. Only open containers when additional stock is needed. This method allows cycle counters to rapidly verify inventory balances.

11. *Count items.* Count items when there is no significant activity in the warehouse, such as during a weekend. Elaborate cross-checking of the counts, as would be done during a year-end physical inventory count, is not necessary. It is more

important to have the perpetual inventory system operational before the warehouse activity increases again; any errors in the data will quickly be detected during cycle counts and flushed out of the database. The initial counts must include a review of the part number, location, and quantity.

12. *Enter data into the computer.* Have an experienced data entry person input the location, part number, and quantity into the computer. Once the data has been input, another person should cross-check the entered data against the original data for errors.

13. *Quick-check the data.* Scan the data for errors. If all part numbers have the same number of digits, then look for items that are too long or short. Review location codes to see if inventory is stored in nonexistent racks. Look for units of measure that do not match the part being described. For example, is it logical to have a pint of steel in stock? Also, if item costs are available, print a list of extended costs. Excessive costs typically point to incorrect units of measure. For example, a cost of $1 per box of nails will become $500 in the inventory report if nails are incorrectly listed as individual units.

14. *Initiate cycle counts.* Print out a portion of the inventory list, sorted by location. Using this report, have the warehouse staff count blocks of the inventory on a continuous basis. They should look for accurate part numbers, units of measure, locations, and quantities. The counts should concentrate on high-value or high-use items, though the entire stock should be reviewed regularly. The most important part of this step is to examine why mistakes occur. If a cycle counter finds an error, its cause must be investigated and then corrected, so that the mistake will not occur again.

15. *Initiate inventory audits.* The inventory should be audited frequently, perhaps as often as once a week. This allows the accountant to track changes in the inventory accuracy level and initiate changes if the accuracy drops below acceptable levels. In addition, frequent audits are an indirect means of telling the staff that inventory accuracy is important, and must be maintained. The minimum acceptable accuracy level is 95%, with an error being a mistaken part number, unit of measure, quantity, or location. This accuracy level is needed to ensure accurate inventory costing, as well as to assist the materials department in planning future inventory purchases. In addition, establish a tolerance level when calculating the inventory accuracy. For example, if the computer record of a box of screws yields a quantity of 100 and the actual count results in 105 screws, then the record is accurate if the tolerance is at least 5%, but inaccurate if the tolerance is reduced to 1%. The maximum allowable tolerance should be no higher than 5%, with tighter tolerances being used for high-value or high-use items.

16. *Post results.* Inventory accuracy is a team project, and the warehouse staff feels more involved if the audit results are posted against the results of previous audits.

17. *Reward the staff.* Accurate inventories save a company thousands of dollars in many ways. This makes it cost-effective to encourage the staff to maintain and improve the accuracy level with periodic bonuses that are based on the attainment of higher levels of accuracy with tighter tolerances.

14-4 THE PHYSICAL INVENTORY PROCEDURE

The physical inventory is a manual count of all inventory on hand, and is used to obtain an inventory valuation for the period-end financial statements. Physical inventories are still used by many companies; even those that have converted to perpetual systems may find that sections of the inventory located outside of the warehouse, such as work-in-process, require a periodic physical count. Companies using such advanced systems as manufacturing cells may still require a physical count of work-in-process, unless all production is allowed to flow through the manufacturing process and into finished goods prior to conducting the count.

Preplanning the physical inventory is critical. The following points will ease the counting process:

- *Use trained personnel.* The inventory counters should all be experienced warehouse personnel, because they are familiar with the parts, as well as their related part numbers and units of measure. The front-office staff has no place in the counting process, because they have no knowledge of these items.

- *Use "dead time."* It is difficult to count while production operations are occurring. Consequently, using weekend or evening time will hasten the counting process.

- *Clean up in advance.* A messy counting area means that the counting team must find the stock before counting it. Save time by organizing the inventory in advance, clearly labeling part numbers and units of measure, and cleaning the counting areas.

- *Train the staff.* The physical inventory teams must be trained in counting procedures, as well as proper cutoff procedures and the completion of forms. The training may require detailed written instructions.

- *Assign the staff.* Allocate inventory locations to specific counting areas.

- *Create an inventory tag form.* This tag is used to record the inventory count for each item, and should include fields for the part number, description, location, unit of measure, counter's signature, and last job performed (if it is a work-in-process item). The tags must be pre-numbered.

The actual counting process should include the following eight steps:

1. *Notify the auditors.* The auditors must be notified of the time and place of the physical inventory. An audit team will conduct test counts, observe the procedure generally, and trace the counts to the inventory summary.

2. *Assign counting teams to areas.* The following areas should be counted:
   - Central warehouse
   - Receiving inspection
   - Staging areas
   - Finished goods area
   - Work-in-process area
   - Shipping area

- Outside storage (for example, in trailer storage or company-owned inventory located at other companies)
- Rework areas
- Packaging materials

The following items should *not* be counted:

- Consignment inventory
- Maintenance equipment
- Material handling containers
- Office supplies
- Tools and equipment
- Written-off inventory

3. *Count all areas.* Attach a pre-numbered inventory tag to each area that has been counted, in order to prove that the count was completed. The tag should be a two-part form, so that one copy can be removed and used to summarize the inventory. The count is usually conducted by two-person teams, with one counting and the other recording the information.

4. *Review counted areas.* Review the counted areas for missing or duplicate counts, and spot-check counts for correct quantities, part numbers, and units of measure. High dollar-value items should be 100% checked.

5. *Control tags.* Collect all tags and look for missing or duplicate tag numbers; resolve any problems before summarizing the information in the next step.

6. *Summarize tags.* Input the tag information into the computer, or record it manually on a summary sheet. This sheet should include all of the information contained on the tags. Whether an automated or manual report, the summary should include sufficient space to mark down the market value of each item, so that the cost of each one can be marked to the lower of cost or market for financial statement reporting purposes.

7. *Look for discrepancies.* Problems can be unearthed with any of the following techniques:

   - Compare the physical inventory records to perpetual records.
   - Review the extended costs for excessively large dollar amounts. Frequently, incorrect units of measure are the root cause of these problems.
   - Review the unit counts for excessively high counts. Once again, incorrect units of measure may be the culprit.
   - Compare expensive items in the inventory to the summary, to ensure that the correct quantities are recorded, and that their costs appear reasonable.

8. *Review the cutoff.* Even with an excellent inventory count, the inventory can be severely misstated if inventory is included or excluded without a corresponding sale or liability entry in the accounting records. Review the receiving and shipping records for several days before and after the inventory count, and ensure that an accounting entry exists for each transaction.

14-5 THE LAST-IN FIRST-OUT (LIFO) METHOD

In a supermarket, the shelves are stocked several rows deep with products. A shopper will walk by and pick products from the front row. If the stocking person is lazy, he will then add products to the front row locations from which products were just taken, rather than shifting the oldest products to the front row and putting new ones in the back. This concept of always taking the newest products first is called last-in first-out, or LIFO. It is illustrated numerically in Exhibit 14-1, where we list a number of inventory purchases and usages down the left side, and note various calculations across the top.

In the exhibit, we purchase 500 units of a product with part number BK0043 on May 3, 2000 (as noted in the first row of data), and use 450 units during that month, leaving us with 50 units. These 50 units were all purchased at a cost of $10.00 each, so we itemize them in Column 6 as our first layer of inventory costs for this product. In the next row of data, we see that an additional 1,000 units were bought on June 4, 2000, of which only 350 units were used. This leaves us with an additional 650 units at a purchase price of $9.58, which we place in the second inventory layer, as noted on Column 7. In the third row, we have a net decrease in the amount of inventory, so this reduction comes out of the second (or last) inventory layer in Column 7; the earliest layer, as described in Column 6, remains untouched, since it was the first layer of costs added, and will not be used until all other inventory has been eliminated. The exhibit continues through seven more transactions, at one point increasing to four layers of inventory costs.

There are several factors to consider before implementing a LIFO system. They are:

- *Has many layers.* The LIFO cost flow approach can result in a large number of inventory layers, as shown in the exhibit. Though this is not important when a computerized accounting system is used that will automatically track a large number of such layers, it can be burdensome if the cost layers are manually tracked.

- *Alters the inventory valuation.* If there are significant changes in product costs over time, the earliest inventory layers may contain costs that are wildly different from market conditions in the current period, which could result in the recognition of unusually high or low costs if these cost layers are ever accessed.

- *Reduces taxes payable in periods of rising costs.* In an inflationary environment, costs that are charged off to the cost of goods sold as soon as they are incurred will result in a higher cost of goods sold and a lower level of profitability, which in turn results in a lower tax liability. This is the principal reason why LIFO is used by most companies.

- *Requires consistent usage for all reporting.* Under IRS rules, if a company uses LIFO to value its inventory for tax reporting purposes, then it must do the same for its external financial reports. The result of this rule is that a company cannot report lower earnings for tax purposes and higher earnings for all other purposes by using an alternative inventory valuation method. However, it is still possible to mention what profits would have been if some other method have been used, but only in the form of a footnote appended to the financial statements. If financial reports are only generated for internal management consumption, then any valuation method may be used.

Exhibit 14-1 LIFO Valuation Example

LIFO Costing
Part Number BK0043

Column 1	Column 2	Column 3	Column 4	Column 5	Column 6	Column 7	Column 8	Column 9	Column 10
Date Purchased	Quantity Purchased	Cost per Unit	Monthly Usage	Net Inventory Remaining	Cost of 1st Inventory Layer	Cost of 2nd Inventory Layer	Cost of 3rd Inventory Layer	Cost of 4th Inventory Layer	Extended Inventory Cost
5/3/00	500	$10.00	450	50	(50 × $10.00)	—	—	—	$500
6/4/00	1,000	$9.58	350	700	(50 × $10.00)	(650 × $9.58)	—	—	$6,727
7/11/00	250	$10.65	400	550	(50 × $10.00)	(500 × $9.58)	—	—	$5,290
8/1/00	475	$10.25	350	675	(50 × $10.00)	(500 × $9.58)	(125 × $10.25)	—	$6,571
8/30/00	375	$10.40	400	650	(50 × $10.00)	(500 × $9.58)	(100 × $10.25)	—	$6,315
9/9/00	850	$9.50	700	800	(50 × $10.00)	(500 × $9.58)	(100 × $10.25)	(150 × $9.50)	$7,740
12/12/00	700	$9.75	900	600	(50 × $10.00)	(500 × $9.58)	(50 × $9.58)	—	$5,769
2/8/01	650	$9.85	800	450	(50 × $10.00)	(400 × $9.58)	—	—	$4,332
5/7/01	200	$10.80	0	650	(50 × $10.00)	(400 × $9.58)	(200 × $10.80)	—	$6,492
9/23/01	600	$9.85	750	500	(50 × $10.00)	(400 × $9.58)	(50 × $9.85)	—	$4,825

- *Interferes with the implementation of just-in-time systems.* As noted in the last bullet point, clearing out the final cost layers of a LIFO system can result in unusual cost of goods sold figures. If these results will cause a significant skewing of reported profitability, company management may be put in the unusual position of opposing the implementation of advanced manufacturing concepts, such as just-in-time, that reduce or eliminate inventory levels (with an attendant, and highly favorable, improvement in the amount of working capital requirements).

In short, LIFO is used primarily for reducing a company's income tax liability. This single focus can cause problems, such as too many cost layers, an excessively low inventory valuation, and a fear of inventory reductions due to the recognition of inventory cost layers that may contain very low per-unit costs, which will result in high levels of recognized profit and therefore a higher tax liability. Given these issues, one should carefully consider the utility of tax avoidance before implementing a LIFO cost layering system.

14-6 THE FIRST-IN FIRST-OUT (FIFO) METHOD

A computer manufacturer knows that the component parts it purchases are subject to extremely rapid rates of obsolescence, sometimes rendering a part worthless in a month or two. Accordingly, it will be sure to use up the oldest items in stock first, rather than running the risk of scrapping them just after entering the future. For this type of environment, the first-in first-out (FIFO) method is the ideal way to deal with the flow of costs. This method assumes that the oldest parts in stock are always used first, which means that their associated old costs are used first, as well.

The concept is best illustrated with an example, which we show in Exhibit 14-2. In the exhibit, we list the same data previously used for parts purchases and usage in Exhibit 14-1, but now we account for the costs using FIFO, instead of LIFO. In the first row, we create a single layer of inventory that results in 50 units of inventory, at a per-unit cost of $10.00. So far, the extended cost of the inventory is the same as we saw under the LIFO, but that will change as we proceed to the second row of data. In this row, we have monthly inventory usage of 350 units, which FIFO assumes will use the entire stock of 50 inventory units that were left over at the end of the preceding month, as well as 300 units that were purchased in the current month. This wipes out the first layer of inventory, leaving us with a single new layer that is composed of 700 units at a cost of $9.58 per unit. In the third row, there is 400 units of usage, which again comes from the first inventory layer, shrinking it down to just 300 units. However, since extra stock was purchased in the same period, we now have an extra inventory layer that is comprised of 250 units, at a cost of $10.65 per unit. The rest of the exhibit proceeds using the same FIFO layering assumptions.

There are several factors to consider before implementing a FIFO costing system. They are:

- *Has fewer inventory layers.* The FIFO system generally results in fewer layers of inventory costs in the inventory database. For example, the LIFO model shown in Exhibit 14-1 contained four layers of costing data, whereas the FIFO model shown in Exhibit 14-2, which used exactly the same data, resulted in no more than two inventory layers. This conclusion generally holds true, because a LIFO system will

Exhibit 14-2 FIFO Valuation Example

FIFO Costing
Part Number BK0043

Column 1	Column 2	Column 3	Column 4	Column 5	Column 6	Column 7	Column 8	Column 9
Date Purchased	Quantity Purchased	Cost per Unit	Monthly Usage	Net Inventory Remaining	Cost of 1st Inventory Layer	Cost of 2nd Inventory Layer	Cost of 3rd Inventory Layer	Extended Inventory Cost
5/3/00	500	$10.00	450	50	(50 × $10.00)	—	—	$500
6/4/00	1,000	$9.58	350	700	(700 × $9.58)	—	—	$6,706
7/11/00	250	$10.65	400	550	(300 × $9.58)	(250 × $10.65)	—	$5,537
8/1/00	475	$10.25	350	675	(200 × $10.65)	(475 × $10.25)	—	$6,999
8/30/00	375	$10.40	400	650	(275 × $10.40)	(375 × $10.40)	—	$6,760
9/9/00	850	$9.50	700	800	(800 × $9.50)	—	—	$7,600
12/12/00	700	$9.75	900	600	(600 × $9.75)	—	—	$5,850
2/8/01	650	$9.85	800	450	(450 × $9.85)	—	—	$4,433
5/7/01	200	$10.80	0	650	(450 × $9.85)	(200 × $10.80)	—	$6,593
9/23/01	600	$9.85	750	500	(500 × $9.85)	—	—	$4,925

leave some layers of costs completely untouched for long time periods, if inventory levels do not drop, whereas a FIFO system will continually clear out old layers of costs, so that multiple costing layers do not have a chance to accumulate.

- *Reduces taxes payable in periods of declining costs.* Though it is very unusual to see declining inventory costs, it sometimes occurs in industries where there is either ferocious price competition among suppliers, or else extremely high rates of innovation that in turn lead to cost reductions. In such cases, using the earliest costs first will result in the immediate recognition of the highest possible expense, which reduces the reported profit level, and therefore reduces taxes payable.

- *Shows higher profits in periods of rising costs.* Since it charges off the earliest costs first, any very recent increase in costs will be stored in inventory, rather than being immediately recognized. This will result in higher levels of reported profits, though the attendant income tax liability will also be higher.

- *Offers less risk of outdated costs in inventory.* Because old costs are used first in a FIFO system, there is no way for old and outdated costs to accumulate in inventory. This prevents the management group from having to worry about the adverse impact of inventory reductions on reported levels of profit, either with excessively high or low charges to the cost of goods sold. This avoids the dilemma noted earlier for LIFO, where just-in-time systems may not be implemented if the result will be a dramatically different cost of goods sold.

In short, the FIFO cost layering system tends to result in the storage of the most recently incurred costs in inventory and higher levels of reported profits. It is most useful for those companies whose main concern is reporting high profits rather reducing income taxes.

14-7 THE AVERAGE COSTING METHOD

The average costing method is calculated exactly in accordance with its name—it is a weighted average of the costs in inventory. It has the singular advantage of not requiring a database that itemizes the many potential layers of inventory at the different costs at which they were acquired. Instead, the weighted average of all units in stock is determined, at which point *all* of the units in stock are accorded that weighted-average value. When parts are used from stock, they are all issued at the same weighted-average cost. If new units are added to stock, then the cost of the additions is added to the weighted average of all existing items in stock, which will result in a new, slightly modified weighted-average for *all* of the parts in inventory (both old and new ones).

This system has no particular advantage in relation to income taxes, since it does not skew the recognition of income based on trends in either increasing or declining costs. This makes it a good choice for those organizations that do not want to deal with tax planning. It is also useful for very small inventory valuations, where there would not be any significant change in the reported level of income even if the LIFO or FIFO methods were to be used.

Exhibit 14-3 illustrates the weighted-average calculation for inventory valuations, using a series of 10 purchases of inventory. There is a maximum of one purchase per month, with usage (reductions from stock) also occurring in most months. Each of the columns in the exhibit show how the average cost is calculated after each purchase and usage transaction.

Exhibit 14-3 Average Costing Valuation Example

Average Costing
Part Number BK0043

Column 1	Column 2	Column 3	Column 4	Column 5	Column 6	Column 7	Column 8	Column 9
Date Purchased	Quantity Purchased	Cost per Unit	Monthly Usage	Net Inventory Remaining	Net Change in Inventory During Period	Extended Cost of New Inventory Layer	Extended Inventory Cost	Average Inventory Cost/Unit
5/3/00	500	$10.00	450	50	50	$500	$500	$10.00
6/4/00	1,000	$9.58	350	700	650	$6,227	$6,727	$9.61
7/11/00	250	$10.65	400	550	−150	$0	$5,286	$9.61
8/1/00	475	$10.25	350	675	125	$1,281	$6,567	$9.73
8/30/00	375	$10.40	400	650	−25	$0	$6,324	$9.73
9/9/00	850	$9.50	700	800	150	$1,425	$7,749	$9.69
12/12/00	700	$9.75	900	600	−200	$0	$5,811	$9.69
2/8/01	650	$9.85	800	450	−150	$0	$4,359	$9.69
5/7/01	200	$10.80	0	650	200	$2,160	$6,519	$10.03
9/23/01	600	$9.85	750	500	−150	$0	$5,014	$10.03

169

We begin the illustration with a purchase of 500 units of item BK0043 on May 3, 2000. These units cost $10.00 per unit. During the month in which the units were purchased, 450 units were sent to production, leaving 50 units in stock. Since there has only been one purchase thus far, we can easily calculate, as shown in column 7, that the total inventory valuation is $500, by multiplying the unit cost of $10.00 (in column 3) by the number of units left in stock (in column 5). So far, we have a per-unit valuation of $10.00.

Next we proceed to the second row of the exhibit, where we have purchased another 1,000 units of BK0043 on June 4, 2000. This purchase was less expensive, since the purchasing volume was larger, so the per-unit cost for this purchase is only $9.58. Only 350 units are sent to production during the month, so we now have 700 units in stock, of which 650 are added from the most recent purchase. To determine the new weighted average cost of the total inventory, we first determine the extended cost of this newest addition to the inventory. As noted in column 7, we arrive at $6,227 by multiplying the value in column 3 by the value in column 6. We then add this amount to the existing total inventory valuation ($6,227 plus $500) to arrive at the new extended inventory cost of $6,727, as noted in column 8. Finally, we divide this new extended cost in column 8 by the total number of units now in stock, as shown in column 5, to arrive at our new per-unit cost of $9.61.

The third row reveals an additional inventory purchase of 250 units on July 11, 2000, but more units are sent to production during that month than were bought, so the total number of units in inventory drops to 550 (column 5). This inventory reduction requires no review of inventory layers, as was the case for the LIFO and FIFO calculations. Instead, we simply charge off the 150 unit reduction at the average per-unit cost of $9.61. As a result, the ending inventory valuation drops to $5,286, with the same per-unit cost of $9.61. Thus, reductions in inventory quantities under the average costing method require little calculation—just charge off the requisite number of units at the current average cost.

The remaining rows of the exhibit repeat the concepts just noted, alternatively adding units to and deleting them from stock. Though there are a number of columns noted in this exhibit that one must examine, it is really a simple concept to understand and work with. The typical computerized accounting system will perform all of these calculations automatically.

14-8 RETAIL METHOD

The retail method is used by resellers, such as department stores. It provides them with a simple approach for determining the valuation of inventory on hand without compiling a database of invoices that provide evidence for specific items purchased in the past. It also avoids the need for any inventory layering concepts, such as LIFO or FIFO.

To implement the retail method, a company should conduct a period-end count of all inventory on hand, storing the data separately for each department from which inventory is sold. The extended retail price of these inventory items should then be compiled by multiplying the standard price of each item (not the price based on any markdowns) by the number of units on hand.

It must then reduce this total inventory value at retail prices by multiplying it by the *cost ratio*. This is the ratio of the cost of goods available for sale to the retail price of the same goods. This ratio can be derived using the FIFO, average costing, or LIFO assumptions, but is only calculated using aggregate numbers, rather than for each individual item in inventory. If one is using the FIFO costing method, the calculation shown in Exhibit 14-4 should be used to determine the cost ratio. Under this calculation, we assume that the beginning inventory was used first, and therefore is no longer on hand at the end of the period for inclusion in the cost ratio calculation. Accordingly, we only include in the cost ratio the purchases during the period.

Exhibit 14-4   Cost Ratio Calculation Using FIFO Costing

	Actual Inventory Cost	*Actual Retail Price*
Beginning inventory	$400,000	$650,000
Purchases during the period	200,000	300,000
Total inventory	600,000	950,000
Sales during the period		700,000
Ending inventory		250,000
Cost ratio		(200,000/300,000) = 67%
Ending inventory	(250,000 × 67%) = **167,500**	

The cost ratio calculation using average costing is shown in Exhibit 14-5. In this case, we assume that all inventory that was available during the period is to be included in the cost ratio calculation. Consequently, the total inventory line is used as the basis for the calculation, rather than just the purchases during the period.

Exhibit 14-5   Cost Ratio Calculation Using Average Costing

	Actual Inventory Cost	*Actual Retail Price*
Beginning inventory	$400,000	$650,000
Purchases during the period	200,000	300,000
Total inventory	600,000	950,000
Sales during the period		700,000
Ending inventory		250,000
Cost ratio		(600,000/950,000) = 63%
Ending inventory	(250,000 × 63%) = **157,500**	

The cost ratio calculation using LIFO costing is shown in Exhibit 14-6. The example assumes that this is the first year in which the calculation is made, so that there is no LIFO inventory layer from a preceding period. Even if there had been a beginning inventory, it would not be included in the calculation for the LIFO-based cost ratio. Also, the calculation should include the cost of any markups or markdowns, which are added to this exhibit.

Though an ending inventory figure was derived in Exhibit 14-6, this represents only the first LIFO layer, to which additional layers can be added if the inventory level increases from year to year. To determine the amount of any additional layers in later years, we first determine the price index of product prices in the current year in comparison to those of the base year (see the next section for two ways to determine this index). We then calculate the ending inventory using the same approach shown in Exhibit 14-6.

If the new inventory level is less than the amount in the base year, then there is no new LIFO inventory layer. However, if it is higher than the amount in the preceding year, then the incremental increase becomes a new layer. If a new layer is being added, it must first be multiplied by the price index for the current year in order to convert its costs back to current costs. If inventory levels subsequently drop, then the newest layer will be the first one to be reduced to reflect the amount of the drop.

Exhibit 14-6   Cost Ratio Calculation Using LIFO Costing

	Actual Inventory Cost	*Actual Retail Price*
Beginning inventory	$0	$0
Purchases during the period	200,000	300,000
Markups		42,000
Markdowns		−16,000
Total inventory	200,000	326,000
Sales during the period		250,000
Ending inventory		76,000
Cost ratio		(200,000/326,000) = 61%
Ending inventory	(76,000 × 63%) = **47,880**	

14-9 DOLLAR-VALUE LIFO METHOD

The cost ratio calculation that we just completed for the LIFO retail method is essentially the same calculation used for the dollar-value LIFO method. This approach is specifically designed for those companies that do not wish to store the large quantity of inventory records needed to track the layered LIFO costs of each individual item in the company inventory. Instead, inventory costs are summarized into inventory pools, with changes in the cost of each pool being measured in comparison to the total base-year cost of the pool.

The number of pools used to accumulate inventory costs is largely driven by the amount of effort the accountant wishes to expend in segregating and tracking costs by pool. An additional consideration is that, if inventory is aggregated into a smaller number of pools, it is less likely that there will be a reduction in the LIFO layers associated with each one, whereas segregation into a larger number of pools will probably result in more cases in which some pools will experience layer reductions, simply because there is more variability in inventory levels on an individual basis than on a group basis. This later situation can mean that using a larger number of pools will result in greater changes in the cost of goods sold, since it is more likely that old LIFO layers will be tapped that contain cost levels that vary from current costs.

The simplest way to determine the contents of an inventory pool is to base it on a natural business unit, which means that all of the supplies, raw materials, work-in-process, and finished goods inventory associated with a specific product line should be clustered into the same pool. The natural business unit can also be defined by the presence of separate manufacturing facilities for each business unit, or by separately reported income statements for each one. Alternatives to the use of the natural business unit to define inventory pools are the clustering together of all inventory items that are substantially similar, or clustering for wholesalers, retailers, jobbers, and distributors based on IRS regulation 1.472-8(c).

Following the formation of inventory pools, the remaining step is to calculate their LIFO value. Either of the following two approaches can be used to do so:

1. *Double-extension method.* This method converts pool costs for the current year directly into the base-year costs of the pool to see if another LIFO layer exists for the current year. One can run the calculation based on a representative sample of inventory items, but the base-year price records must be maintained for *all* inventory items. Also, IRS regulations can construe the size of the representative sample to be as large as 70% of the total inventory. A further problem is that the accountant is required to convert newly acquired inventory items to their base year costs, which can be a significant chore if the base year is many years in the past (requiring considerable historical research), if the product has been substantially modified over time (requiring reverse engineering to derive a cost), or if the product simply did not exist during the base year (in which case the most recent cost can be used). Consequently, the record keeping for this method is considerable, making it the least desirable method for calculating dollar-value LIFO.

    This method gets its name from the need to calculate the extended year-end inventory value twice: first at current year costs and again at base year costs. By doing so, we can divide the current-cost total by the base-year cost total to derive the index of current to base year costs. We then use the index to convert the beginning and ending inventory costs for the current period to base year costs. If there is a net gain in the inventory value at the end of the year over the beginning of the year, then we must create a new LIFO layer (which is converted back to current-year costs using the same index). If the reverse occurs, then we reduce the inventory by eliminating the most recent LIFO layers.

2. *Link-chain method.* This method converts current-year pool costs into base-year costs by calculating a current-year index based on cost increases in the current year, and multiplying this new index by the cumulative index that was calculated through the end of the preceding year. More specifically, we take a large sample of the inventory (50% to 75% of the total dollar value) and extend this sample at the costs existing at the beginning and end of the year. Comparing the two values yields a cost index for the current year. We then multiply this index by the cumulative index through the end of the previous year, which yields a new cumulative cost index through the end of the current year. We then divide the extended year-end inventory value by the cumulative index to determine its base year cost. If this extended base year cost is greater than the original base year cost, then the difference becomes a new LIFO layer, which must be multiplied by the cumulative index to return its value to that of current year costs.

    This is a much simpler technique to use than the double extension method, primarily because there is no need to retain actual unit costs earlier than for the current year. However, its use is greatly limited by IRS regulations, which only permit it in organizations that can demonstrate a high degree of change in their product lines over time, and where the double extension and indexing methods can be proven to be clearly impractical. It can still be used by most companies for financial reporting purposes, but this would, in most cases, require a separate calculation of inventory valuation for tax purposes.

14-10 GROSS MARGIN METHOD

The gross margin method is a simple calculation that is used to approximately determine the amount of ending inventory without going through the period-end inventory counting process. Given its approximate nature, it is not acceptable for year-end reporting or tax reporting, but can be used for interim financial reporting, where it is not possible to more accurately derive the ending inventory. To calculate it, add beginning inventory to purchases during the period to obtain the total amount of inventory available for sale. Then subtract out the estimated cost of goods sold (actual sales dollars during the period, multiplied by one minus the estimated gross margin), which yields the estimated ending inventory figure. Clearly, the weak link in this calculation is the estimated gross margin percentage, which is typically based on historical performance. However, historical rates may no longer be valid, or there may be an unusual number of markups or markdowns in the current period that skew the historical gross margin percentage, or the mix of products sold in the current period may be so different from historical results that their associated gross margins result in a substantially different actual gross margin percentage. For these reasons, the gross margin method should be used in only a limited number of situations.

14-11 THE LOWER OF COST OR MARKET RULE

The accountant should regularly review the contents of the inventory to see if there are any items whose fair market value (assumed to be replacement cost) has fallen below their cost as recorded in the accounting books. If so, each item should be marked down to its fair market value. However, there are some restrictions on the use of this rule. First, there can be no mark up to fair market value if the market value is currently higher than the recorded cost of the inventory item. Second, inventory that has been marked down as per this rule cannot subsequently be marked back up to its initial cost if the fair market value subsequently increases to that point. Third, if an inventory item must have additional costs added to it before it can be prepared for sale, then the lower of cost or market comparison should be between the completed cost and the fair market value, unless a fair market value can reasonably be determined for the uncompleted inventory item. Finally, the lowest amount to which an inventory item can be written down is its net realizable value, less its profit percentage; this last rule is used to prevent a company from being forced to record a loss on inventory items, even when it has a ready market for them at a higher price.

If a small loss is recognized based on this rule, it is typically recorded within the cost of goods sold category. If the loss is significant, it should be itemized separately.

14-12 OVERHEAD IDENTIFICATION AND ALLOCATION TO INVENTORY

Some overhead costs can be charged off to inventory, rather than being recognized in the cost of goods sold or some other expense category within the current period. Since the proper allocation of these costs can have a large impact on the level of reported income in any given period, it is important for the accountant to fully understand which costs can be shifted to a cost pool for eventual allocation, and how this allocation is to be accomplished. The first question is answered by Exhibit 14-7, which itemizes precisely which costs can be shifted into a cost pool. The only cost category about which there is some uncertainty is rework labor, scrap, and spoilage. The exhibit shows that this cost can be charged in either direction. The rule in this case is that any rework, scrap, or spoilage that falls within a normally expected level can be charged to a cost pool for allocation, whereas unusual amounts must be charged off at once. This is clearly a highly subjective area, where some historical records should be maintained that will reveal the trend of these costs, and which can be used as the basis for proving the charging of costs to either category.

With Exhibit 14-7 in hand, one can easily construct a cost pool into which the correct costs can be accumulated for later distribution to inventory as allocated overhead costs. The next problem is how to go about making the allocation. This problem is comprised of four issues, which are:

Exhibit 14-7   Allocation of Costs Between Cost Pool and Expense Accounts

Description	Cost Pool	Expense
Advertising expenses		XXX
Costs related to strikes		XXX
Depreciation and cost depletion	XXX	
Factory administration expenses	XXX	
General and administrative expenses related to overall operations		XXX
Income taxes		XXX
Indirect labor and production supervisory wages	XXX	
Indirect materials and supplies	XXX	
Interest		XXX
Maintenance	XXX	
Marketing expenses		XXX
Officers' salaries related to production services	XXX	
Other distribution expenses		XXX
Pension contribution related to past service costs		XXX
Production employees' benefits	XXX	
Quality control and inspection	XXX	
Rent	XXX	
Repair expenses	XXX	
Research and experimental expenses		XXX
Rework labor, scrap, and spoilage	XXX	XXX
Salaries of officers related to overall operations		XXX
Selling expenses		XXX
Taxes other than income taxes related to production assets	XXX	
Tools and equipment not capitalized	XXX	
Utilities	XXX	

Adapted with permission: Bragg, *The Controller's Function,* John Wiley & Sons, 2000, p. 147.

1. *How to smooth out sudden changes in the cost pool.* It is quite common to see an unusual expenditure cause a large jump or drop in the costs accumulated in the cost pool, resulting in a significant difference between periods in the amount of per-unit costs that are allocated out. This can cause large changes in overhead costs from period to period. Though perfectly acceptable from the perspective of generally accepted accounting principles, one may desire a more smoothed-out set of costs from period to period. If so, it is allowable to average the costs in the cost pool over several months, as long as the underlying inventory is actually in stock for a similar period of time. For example, if the inventory turns over four times a year, then it is acceptable to allocate overhead costs each month based on a rolling average of the costs for the preceding three months.

2. *What basis to use when allocating costs.* The accounting literature has bemoaned the allocation of costs based on direct labor for many years. The reason for this judgment is that direct labor makes up such a small component of total product cost that small swings in the direct labor component can result in a large corresponding swing in the amount of allocated overhead. To avoid this issue, some other unit of activity can be used as the basis for allocation that not only comprises a larger share of total product cost, but that also relates to the incurrence of overhead costs. Another criterion that is frequently overlooked is that the accounting or manufacturing system must have a means of accumulating information about this activity measure, so that the accountant does not have to spend additional time manually compiling the underlying data. An example of an activity measure that generally fulfills these three criteria is machine hours, since standard machine hours are readily available in the bill of materials or labor routing for each product, many overhead costs are related to machine usage, and the proportion of machine time used per product is commonly greater than the proportion of direct labor.

   An even better alternative than the use of machine hours (or some similar single measure) as the basis for allocation is the use of multiple cost pools that are allocated with multiple activity measures. This allows a company to (for example) allocate building costs based on the square footage taken up by each product, machine costs based on machine time used, labor costs based on direct labor hours used, and so on. The main issue to be aware of when using this approach is that the financial statements must still be produced in a timely manner, so one should not go overboard with the use of too many cost pools that will require an inordinate amount of time to allocate.

3. *How to calculate the overhead allocation.* When allocating overhead costs, they are not simply charged off in total to the on-hand inventory at the end of the month, since the result would be an ever-increasing overhead balance stored in the on-hand inventory that would never be drawn down. On the contrary, much of the overhead is also related to the cost of goods sold. In order to make a proper allocation of costs between the inventory and cost of goods sold, the accountant must determine the total amount of each basis of activity that occurred during the reporting period, and divide this amount into the total amount of overhead in the cost pool, yielding an overhead cost per unit of activity. This cost per unit should then be multiplied by the total amount of the basis of activity related to the period-end inventory to determine the total amount of overhead that should be charged to inventory. This is then compared to the amount of overhead already charged to inventory in the previous report-

ing period to see if any additional overhead costs should be added or subtracted to arrive at the new allocated overhead figure. All other overhead costs, by default, are charged to the cost of goods sold. For example, if there is a cost pool of $100,000 to be allocated, and a total of 25,000 machine hours were used in the period, then the overhead cost per hour of machine time is $4. According to the standard labor routings for all inventory items in stock, it required 17,250 hours of machine time to create the items currently stored in inventory. Using the current cost per machine hour of $4, this means that $69,000 (17,250 hours $\times$ $4/hour) can be charged to inventory. However, the inventory overhead account already contains $52,000 of overhead that was charged to it in the preceding month, so the new entry is to debit the inventory overhead account for $17,000 ($69,000 – $52,000), and to debit the cost of goods sold for the remaining amount of overhead, which is $83,000, while the cost pool is credited for $100,000.

4. *How to adjust for any unallocated or over-allocated costs.* It was recommended earlier in this section that one could smooth out the cost totals in a company's overhead cost pools by averaging the costs on a rolling basis over several months. The only problem with this approach is that the amount of costs allocated each month will differ somewhat from the actual costs stored in the cost pools. How do we reconcile this difference? The annual financial statements should not include any differences between actual and allocated overhead costs, so the variance should be allocated between inventory and the cost of goods sold at that time, using the usual bases of allocation. If shareholder reporting occurs more frequently than that (such as quarterly), then the accountant should consider making the same adjustment on a more frequent basis. However, if the amount in question will not have a material impact on the financial statement results, the adjustment can be completed just once, at the end of the fiscal year.

14-13 SUMMARY

An examination of a company's flow of costs will result in the decision to value its inventories based on the LIFO, FIFO, retail, dollar-value LIFO, or average costing concepts. The LIFO method is the most complex, results in reduced profit recognition and a lower income tax liability in periods of rising inventory costs. The FIFO method is almost as complex, but tends to result in fewer inventory cost layers; it reports higher profits in periods of rising inventory costs, and so has higher attendant tax liabilities. The retail and dollar-value LIFO methods are useful for avoiding the detailed tracking of individual costs for inventory items. The average costing concept avoids the entire layering issue by creating a rolling average of costs without the use of any cost layers; it tends to provide reported profit figures that are between those that would be described using either the LIFO or FIFO methods. As more companies reduce their inventory levels with advanced manufacturing techniques such as material requirements planning and just-in-time, they will find that the reduced amount of inventory left on hand will make the choice of cost flow concept less relevant.

CHAPTER 15

Accounts Receivable

15-1 INTRODUCTION

The accounting for accounts receivable appears to be quite straightforward—just convert credit sales into accounts receivable and then cancel them when the corresponding cash is collected. Actually, in a number of instances where this simple process becomes more complicated—credit card transactions, factoring of receivables, sales returns, early payment discounts, long-term receivables, and bad debts. The following sections discuss the proper accounting steps to take when dealing with these special situations.

15-2 DEFINITION OF ACCOUNTS RECEIVABLE

The accounts receivable account tends to accumulate a number of transactions that are not strictly accounts receivable, so it is useful to define what should be stored in this account. An account receivable is a claim that is payable in cash, and that is in exchange for the services or goods provided by the company. This definition excludes a note payable, which is essentially a return of loaned funds, and for which a signed note is usually available as documentary evidence. A note payable should be itemized in the financial statements under a separate account. It also excludes any short-term funds loaned to employees (such as employee advances), or employee loans of any type that may be payable over a longer term. These items may more appropriately be stored in an Other Accounts Receivable or Accounts Receivable from Employees account. Also, an accountant should not create an accrued account receivable to offset an accrued sale transaction (as may occur under the percentage of completion method of recognizing revenue from long-term construction projects); on the contrary, the accounts receivable account should only contain transactions for which there is a clear, short-term expectation of cash receipt from a customer.

15-3 THE ACCOUNTS RECEIVABLE TRANSACTION FLOW

The typical flow into and out of accounts receivable is quite simple. If there is a sale on credit terms, then the accountant credits the sales account and debits accounts receivable. When cash is received in payment from a customer, the cash account is debited and accounts receivable are credited. Also, there is usually some type of sales tax involved in the transaction, in which case the account receivable is debited for the additional amount of the sales tax and a sales tax liability account is credited for the same amount. There may be several sales tax liability accounts involved, since the typical sales tax can be broken down into liabilities to city, county, and state governments. These liability accounts are later emptied when sales taxes are remitted to the various government tax collection agencies. Though these steps appear quite simple, they can be complicated by a variety of additional transactions, many of which occur frequently. The following sections outline their treatment.

15-4 CREDIT CARD ACCOUNTS RECEIVABLE

When recording an account receivable that is based on a credit card payment, the accountant may record the receipt of cash at the same time as the credit card transaction; however, the receipt of cash from the credit card provider will actually be several days later, so this results in an inaccurate representation of cash receipts. This is a particular problem if the credit card transaction is recorded at month-end, since the bank reconciliation will show the cash receipt as an unreconciled item that has not really appeared at the bank yet.

A better treatment of credit card accounts receivable is to batch the credit card slips for each credit card provider for each day, and record a single credit to sales and debit to accounts receivable at the time of the credit card transaction for each batch of credit card slips. If the accountant is aware of the credit card processing fee charged by the credit card provider, this should be recorded at once as an offsetting expense. If there is some uncertainty regarding the amount of the fee, then the accountant should expense an estimated amount to a reserve at the time the account receivable is set up, and adjust the reserve when the transaction is settled.

15-5 ACCOUNTING FOR FACTORED ACCOUNTS RECEIVABLE

If a company uses its accounts receivable as collateral for a loan, then no accounting entry is required. However, if it directly sells the receivables with no continuing involvement in their collection, and with no right to pay back the factor in case a customer defaults on payment of a receivable, then a sale transaction must be recorded. Typically, this involves a credit to the accounts receivable account, a debit to the cash account for the amount of the buyer's payment, and a gain or loss entry to reflect any gain or loss on the transaction. The amount of cash received from the factor will also be reduced by an interest charge that is based on the amount of cash issued to the company for the period when the factor has not yet received cash from the factored accounts receivable; this results in a debit to the interest expense account and a credit to the accounts receivable account.

A variation on this transaction is if the company only draws down cash from the factor when needed, rather than at the time when the accounts receivable are sold to the factor. This arrangement results in a smaller interest charge by the factor for the period when it is awaiting payment on the accounts receivable. In this instance, a new receivable is created that can be labeled "Due from Factoring Arrangement."

Another variation is when the factor holds back payment on some portion of the accounts receivable, on the grounds that there may be inventory returns from customers that can be charged back to the company. In this case, the proper entry is to offset the account receivable being transferred to the factor with a holdback receivable account. Once all receipt transactions have been cleared by the factor, any amounts left in the holdback account are eliminated with a debit to cash (from the factor) and a credit to the holdback account.

A sample journal entry that includes all of the preceding factoring issues is shown in Exhibit 15-1. In this case, the company has sold $100,000 of accounts receivable to a factor, which requires a 10% holdback provision. The factor also expects to lose $4,800 in bad debts that it must absorb as a result of the transaction, and so pays the company $4,800 less than the face value of the accounts receivable, which forces the company to recognize a loss of $4,800 on the transaction. Also, the company does not elect to take delivery of all funds allowed by the factor, in order to save interest costs; accordingly, it only takes delivery of $15,000 to meet immediate cash needs. Finally, the factor charges 18% interest for the 30 day period that it is expected to take to collect the factored accounts receivable, which results in an interest charge of $200 on the $15,000 of delivered funds.

Exhibit 15-1   Sample Factoring Journal Entry

Account	Debit	Credit
Cash	$15,000	
Accounts Receivable—Factoring Holdback	10,000	
Loss on Factoring	4,800	
Interest Expense	200	
Due from Factoring Arrangement	70,000	
Accounts Receivable		$100,000

If the company factors its accounts receivable, but the factor has recourse against the company for uncollectible amounts or if the company agrees to service the receivables subsequent to the factoring arrangement, then the company still can be construed as having retained control over the receivables. In this case, the factoring arrangement is considered to be a loan, rather than a sale of receivables, resulting in the retention of the accounts receivable on the company's balance sheet, as well as the addition of a loan liability.

15-6 ACCOUNTING FOR SALES RETURNS

When a customer returns goods to a company, the accountant should set up an offsetting sales contra account, rather than backing out the original sale transaction. The resulting transaction would be a credit to the account receivable account and a debit to the contra account. There are two reasons for using this approach. First, a direct reduction of the original sale would impact the financial reporting in a prior period, if the sale originated in a prior period. Second, a large number of sales returns charged directly against the sales account would essentially be invisible on the financial statements, with management only seeing a reduced sales volume. Only by using (and reporting) an offsetting contra account can management gain some knowledge of the extent of any sales returns.

15-7 ACCOUNTING FOR EARLY PAYMENT DISCOUNTS

Unless a company offers an exceedingly large early payment discount, it is unlikely that the total amount of this discount taken will have a material impact on the financial statements. Consequently, some variation in the allowable treatment of this transaction can be used. The most theoretically accurate approach is to initially record the account receivable at its discounted value, which assumes that all customers will take the early payment discount. Any cash discounts that are not taken will then be recorded as additional revenue. This results in a properly conservative view of the amount of funds that one can expect to receive from the accounts receivable. An alternative that results in a slightly higher initial revenue figure is to record the full, undiscounted amount of each sale in the accounts receivable, and then record any discounts taken in a sales contra account. One objection to this second approach is that the discount taken will only be recognized in an accounting period that is later than the one in which the sale was initially recorded (given the time delay usually associated with accounts receivable payments), which is an inappropriate revenue recognition technique. An alternative approach that avoids this problem is to set up a reserve for cash discounts taken in the period in which the sales occur, and offset actual discounts against it as they occur.

Given the relatively small size of early payment discounts, the accountant may be more concerned with finding the most cost-effective approach for handling them, rather than the most technically correct one that will yield slightly greater accuracy at a cost of increased accounting labor.

15-8 ACCOUNTING FOR LONG-TERM ACCOUNTS RECEIVABLE

If an account receivable is not due to be collected for more than one year, then it should be discounted at an interest rate that fairly reflects the rate that would have been charged to the debtor under a normal lending situation. An alternative is to use any interest rate that may be noted in the sale agreement. Under no circumstances should the interest rate be one that is less than the prevailing market rate at the time when the receivable was originated. The result of this calculation will be a smaller receivable than is indicated by its face amount. The difference should be gradually accrued as interest income over the life of the receivable.

15-9 ACCOUNTING FOR BAD DEBTS

The accountant must recognize a bad debt as soon as it is reasonably certain that a loss is likely to occur, and the amount in question can be estimated with some degree of accuracy. For financial reporting purposes, the only allowable method for recognizing bad debts is to set up a bad debt reserve as a contra account to the accounts receivable account. Under this approach, one estimates a long-term average amount of bad debt, debits the bad debt expense (which is most commonly kept in the operating expenses section of the income statement) for this percentage of the period-end accounts receivable balance, and credits the bad debt reserve contra account. When an actual bad debt is recognized, the accountant credits the accounts receivable account and debits the reserve. No offset is made to the sales account. If there is an unusually large bad debt to be recognized that will more than offset the existing bad debt reserve, then the reserve should be sufficiently increased to ensure that the remaining balance in the reserve is not negative.

There are several ways to determine the long-term estimated amount of bad debt for the preceding calculation. One is to determine the historical average bad debt as a proportion of the total credit sales for the past 12 months. Another option that results in a more accurate estimate is to calculate a different historical bad debt percentage based on the relative age of the accounts receivable at the end of the reporting period. For example, accounts aged greater than 90 days may have a historical bad debt experience of 50%, whereas those over 25% have a percentage of 20%, and those below 30 days are at only 4%. This type of experience percentage is more difficult to calculate, but can result in a considerable degree of precision in the size of the bad debt allowance. It is also possible to estimate the bad debt level based on the type of customer. Though rarely used, one could historically prove that, for example, government entities never go out of business, and so have a much lower bad debt rate than other types of customers. Whatever approach is used must be backed up quantitatively, so that an auditor can trace through the calculations to ensure that a sufficient bad debt reserve has been provided for.

15-10 SUMMARY

This section covered a number of special situations in which the accountant must depart from the standard conversion of sales to accounts receivable to cash. Though some transactions, such as factoring, are relatively uncommon, others (such as bad debt accruals and early payment discounts) occur quite frequently, and can have some impact on the reported level of profitability if not handled correctly. Thus, a careful review of these issues is recommended.

CHAPTER 16

Fixed Assets

16-1 INTRODUCTION

This chapter covers a wide range of topics related to the types of costs that should be recorded as fixed assets and how they should be depreciated and disposed of. The chapter also covers the treatment of special types of fixed assets, such as construction-in-progress, leasehold improvements, and intangible assets. There is additional treatment of the tax implications of fixed assets, such as Section 179 deductions and IRS-allowable depreciation schedules, which can be found in Chapter 35, Taxation.

16-2 THE CAPITALIZATION LIMIT

A company must set a minimum level of investment in any asset, below which it will record the asset as a current-period expense, rather than a long-term asset. This is called the *capitalization limit*. It is imposed from a practicality perspective, since there are a number of potential long-term assets (such as a computer mouse, whose utility will extend over many years) whose costs are so low that they will clutter up a company's asset listings to a great extent. If all potential long-term assets are indeed recorded in the fixed asset register as assets, a company can easily find that its asset tracking and depreciation calculation chore is increased tenfold.

To avoid these problems, a company should have the Board of Directors approve a capitalization limit, below which nothing is capitalized. There are several ways to determine what this limit should be. For example, common usage in the industry may suggest an amount. A company's auditors may suggest an amount based upon what they have seen at other clients' businesses. A good alternative is to simply review all transactions for the past few months to see what level of capitalization could potentially be used in order to avoid an excessive amount of record keeping. If this latter approach is used, one can use the 80/20 pareto rule, selecting a capitalization limit that capitalizes only those 20% of all potential assets that comprise 80% of the dollar volume of all potential assets. A fourth option is to set the capitalization limit at the point where IRS rules recommend items to be capitalized. For example, there are IRS depreciation rules for personal computers; since personal computers cost somewhat more than $1,000, one could set the limit at $1,000 in order to ensure that these items are included in fixed assets.

16-3 FIXED ASSET ACQUISITION

When a company purchases a fixed asset, there are a number of expenditures that it is allowed to include in the capitalized cost of the asset. These costs include the sales tax and ownership registration fees (if any). Also, the cost of all freight, insurance, and duties required to bring the asset to the company can be included in the capitalized cost. Further, the cost required to install the asset can be included. Installation costs include the cost to test and break in the asset, which can include the cost of test materials.

If a fixed asset is acquired for nothing but cash, then its recorded cost is the amount of cash paid. However, if the asset is acquired by taking on a payable, such as a stream of debt payments (or taking over the payments that were initially to be made by the seller of the asset), then the present value of all future payments yet to be made must also be rolled into the recorded asset cost. If the stream of future payments contains no stated interest rate, then one must be imputed based on market rates when making the present value calculation. If the amount of the payable is not clearly evident at the time of purchase, then it is also admissible to record the asset at its fair market value.

If an asset is donated to the company (only common in the case of a not-for-profit corporation), it can record the asset at its fair market value.

If an asset is purchased with company stock, the most readily determinable cost is the fair market value of the asset (especially through the use of an appraisal), and so is the preferred cost at which the asset should be recorded. If the fair market value is not readily determined, then the fair market value of the stock may also be used. The latter cost is more readily acceptable if the shares are publicly traded, since the fair market value at the time of sale is much more easily determined.

If a company obtains an asset through an exchange, it should record the incoming asset at the fair market value of the asset for which it was exchanged. However, if this fair value is not readily apparent, the fair value of the incoming asset can be used instead. If no fair market value is readily obtainable for either asset, then the net book value of the relinquished asset can be used.

If a company exchanges an asset for a similar asset (such as through a trade-in of old equipment for new equipment of the same general type), and there is a loss on the transaction, then the fair market value of the asset given up should be used as the cost basis for the transaction. However, if there is a gain on the transaction and a cash payment is made as part of the transaction, then one values the transaction at the book value of the asset given up.

If a group of assets is acquired through a single purchase transaction, the cost should be allocated among the assets in the group based on their proportional share of their total fair market values. The fair market value may be difficult to ascertain in many instances, in which case an appraisal value or tax assessment value can be used. It may also be possible to use the present value of estimated cash flows for each asset as the basis for the allocation, though this measure can be subject to considerable variability in the foundation data, and also requires a great deal of analysis to obtain.

16-4 IMPROVEMENTS TO EXISTING ASSETS

A company will frequently continue to make expenditures related to assets after the assets have been acquired and recorded on the books as capital items. How should these additional expenditures be recorded? They should be capitalized if they act to prolong the life of the asset, increase its productive capacity, or increase its operating efficiency—all being attributes that will impact the asset in future time periods. Thus, the key consideration in the capitalization decision is whether or not each additional expenditure has an incremental impact on the asset in future periods, rather than solely in the current period.

An example of current-period expenditures is routine machine maintenance, such as the replacement of worn-out parts. This expenditure will not change the ability of an asset to perform in a future period, and so should be charged to expense within the current period. If repairs are effected in order to repair damage to an asset, this is also a current-period expense. Also, even if an expenditure can be proven to impact future periods, it may still be charged to expense if it is too small to meet the corporate capitalization limit. If a repair cost can be proven to have an impact covering more than one accounting period, but not many additional periods into the future, a company can spread the cost over a few months or all months of a single year by recording the expense in an allowance account that is gradually charged off over the course of the year. In this last case, there may be an ongoing expense accrual throughout the year that will be charged off, even in the absence of any major expenses in the early part of the year—the intention being that the company knows that expenses will be incurred later in the year, and chooses to smooth out its expense recognition by recognizing some of the expense prior to it actually being incurred.

Expenses may sometimes be incurred in order to move equipment into a different arrangement that may yield operating efficiencies for a company. If the cost of this rearrangement can be broken out, then the cost may be capitalized. If not, it should be charged to current expense. However, if there is not a defensible future benefit to the rearrangement, then its cost should always be charged to current expense.

If an expenditure essentially rehabilitates old equipment, thereby prolonging its useful life, then this cost should be capitalized. This type of expenditure tends to be characterized by expensive equipment overhauls that occur at infrequent intervals.

If a company incurs costs to avoid or mitigate environmental contamination (usually in response to government regulations), these costs must generally be charged to expense in the current period. The only case in which capitalization is an alternative is when the costs incurred can be demonstrated to reduce or prevent future environmental contamination, as well as improve the underlying asset. If so, the asset life associated with these costs should be the period over which environmental contamination is expected to be reduced.

16-5 FIXED ASSET DISPOSITION

When a company disposes of a fixed asset, it should completely eliminate all record of it from the fixed asset and related accumulated depreciation accounts. In addition, it should recognize a gain or loss on the difference between the net book value of the asset and the price at which it was sold. For example, Company ABC is selling a machine, which was originally purchased for $10,000, and against which $9,000 of depreciation has been recorded. The sale price of the used machine is $1,500. The proper journal entry is to credit the fixed asset account for $10,000 (thereby removing the machine from the fixed asset journal), debit the accumulated depreciation account for $9,000 (thereby removing all related depreciation from the accumulated depreciation account), debit the cash account for $1,500 (to reflect the receipt of cash from the asset sale), and credit the "gain on sale of assets" account for $500.

16-6 CONSTRUCTION IN PROGRESS

If a company constructs its own assets, it should compile all costs associated with it into an account or journal, commonly known as the construction-in-progress (CIP) account. There should be a separate account or journal for each project that is currently under way, so that there is no risk of commingling expenses among multiple projects. The costs that can be included in the CIP account include all costs normally associated with the purchase of a fixed asset, as well as the direct materials and direct labor used to construct the asset. In addition, all overhead costs that are reasonably apportioned to the project may be charged to it, as well as the depreciation expense associated with any other assets that are used during the construction process.

One may also charge to the CIP account the interest cost of any funds that have been loaned to the company for the express purpose of completing the project. If this approach is used, one can either use the interest rate associated with a specific loan that was procured to fund the project, or the weighted-average rate for a number of company loans, all of which are being used for this purpose. The amount of interest charged in any period should be based on the cumulative amount of expenditures thus far incurred for the project. The amount of interest charged to the project should not exceed the amount of interest actually incurred for all associated loans through the same time period.

Once the project has been completed, all costs should be carried over from the CIP account into one of the established fixed asset accounts, where the new asset is recorded on a summary basis. All of the detail-level costs should be stored for future review. The asset should be depreciated beginning on the day when it is officially completed. Under no circumstances should depreciation begin prior to this point.

16-7 LAND

Land cannot be depreciated, and so companies tend to avoid charging expenses to this account. Nonetheless, those costs reasonably associated with the procurement of land, such as real estate commissions, title examination fees, escrow fees, and accrued property taxes paid by the purchaser, should all be charged to the fixed asset account for land. This should also include the cost of an option to purchase land. In addition, all subsequent costs associated with the improvement of the land, such as draining, clearing, and grading, should also be added to the land account. The cost of interest that is associated with the development of land should also be capitalized. Property taxes incurred during the land development process should also be charged to the asset account, but should be charged to current expenses once the development process has been completed.

16-8 LEASEHOLD IMPROVEMENTS

When a lessee makes improvements to a property that is being leased from another entity, it can still capitalize the cost of the improvements (subject to the amount of the capitalization limit), but the time period over which these costs can be amortized must be limited to the lesser of the useful life of the improvements or the length of the lease.

If the lease has an extension option that would allow the lessee to increase the time period over which it can potentially lease the property, the total period over which the leasehold improvements can be depreciated must still be limited to the initial lease term, on the grounds that there is no certainty that the lessee will accept the lease extension option. This limitation is waived for depreciation purposes only if there is either a bargain renewal option or extensive penalties in the lease contract that would make it highly likely that the lessee would renew the lease.

16-9 DEPRECIATION BASE

The basis used for an asset when conducting a depreciation calculation should be its capitalized cost less any salvage value that the company expects to receive at the time when the asset is expected to be taken out of active use. The salvage value can be difficult to determine, for several reasons. First, there may be a removal cost associated with the asset, which will reduce the net salvage value that will be realized. If the equipment is especially large (such as a printing press) or involves environmental hazards (such as any equipment involving the use of radioactive substances), then the removal cost may exceed the salvage value. In this latter instance, the salvage value may be negative, in which case it should be ignored for depreciation purposes.

A second reason why salvage value is difficult to determine is that asset obsolescence is so rapid in some industries (especially in relation to computer equipment) that a reasonable appraisal of salvage value at the time an asset is put into service may require drastic revision shortly thereafter. A third reason is that there is no ready market for the sale of used assets in many instances. A fourth reason is that the cost of conducting an appraisal in order to determine a net salvage value may be excessive in relation to the cost of the equipment being appraised. For all these reasons, a company should certainly attempt to set a net salvage value in order to arrive at a cost base for depreciation purposes, but it will probably be necessary to make regular revisions to its salvage value estimates in a cost-effective manner in order to reflect the ongoing realities of asset resale values.

In the case of low-cost assets, it is rarely worth the effort to derive salvage values for depreciation purposes; as a result, these items are typically fully depreciated on the assumption that they have no salvage value.

16-10 DEPRECIATION

Depreciation is designed to spread an asset's cost over its entire useful service life. Its service life is the period over which it is worn out for any reason, at the end of which it is no longer usable, or not usable without extensive overhaul. Its useful life can also be considered terminated at the point when it no longer has a sufficient productive capacity for ongoing company production needs, rendering it essentially obsolete.

Anything can be depreciated that has a business purpose, has a productive life of more than one year, gradually wears out over time, and whose cost exceeds the corporate capitalization limit. Since land does not wear out, it cannot be depreciated.

There are a variety of depreciation methods, as outlined in the following sections. Straight-line depreciation provides for a depreciation rate that is the same amount in every year of an asset's life, whereas various accelerated depreciation methods (such as sum of the years digits and double declining balance) are oriented toward the more rapid recognition of depreciation expenses, on the grounds that an asset is used most intensively when it is first acquired. Perhaps the most accurate depreciation methods are those that are tied to actual asset usage (such as the units of production method), though they require much more extensive record keeping in relation to units of usage. There are also depreciation methods based on compound interest factors, resulting in delayed depreciation recognition; since these methods are rarely used, they are not presented here.

The term over which an asset should be depreciated is its useful life. Since this is subject to a great deal of interpretation, many companies instead use the recommended depreciation rates of the Internal Revenue Service, which are required for tax calculation purposes, but not for financial reporting purposes. These taxable asset lives are described in Chapter 35. If a periodic review of assets reveals that an asset's useful life has been shortened, then its associated depreciation calculation should be altered to reflect the shorter useful life.

If an asset is present but is temporarily idle, then its depreciation should be continued using the existing assumptions for the usable life of the asset. Only if it is permanently idled should the accountant review the need to recognize impairment of the asset (see the later section discussing impairment).

An asset is rarely purchased or sold precisely on the first or last day of the fiscal year, which brings up the issue of how depreciation is to be calculated in these first and last partial years of use. There are a number of alternatives available, all of which are valid as long as they are consistently applied. One option is to record a full year of depreciation in the year of acquisition and no depreciation in the year of sale. Another option is to record a half-year of depreciation in the first year and a half-year of depreciation in the last year. One can also prorate the depreciation more precisely, making it accurate to within the nearest month (or even the nearest day) of when an acquisition or sale transaction occurs.

A curious issue regarding depreciation is that, when the depreciation for a specific asset is included in a cost pool for further allocation of overhead elsewhere in a company, the expense can be rolled into the capitalized cost of another asset to which the overhead is being allocated. The net impact of this transaction is that the recognition of the expense is delayed until depreciation commences on the new asset to which the overhead cost has been charged.

16-11 STRAIGHT-LINE DEPRECIATION

The straight-line depreciation method is the simplest method available, and is the most popular one when a company has no particular need to recognize depreciation costs at an accelerated rate (as would be the case when it wants to match the book value of its depreciation to the accelerated depreciation used for income tax calculation purposes). It is also used for all amortization calculations.

It is calculated by subtracting an asset's expected salvage value from its capitalized cost, and then dividing this amount by the estimated life of the asset. For example, a candy wrapper machine has a cost of $40,000 and an expected salvage value of $8,000. It is expected to be in service for eight years. Given these assumptions, its annual depreciation expense is:

= (Cost − salvage value)/number of years in service

= ($40,000 − $8,000)/8 years

= $32,000/8 years

= $4,000 depreciation per year

16-12 DOUBLE DECLINING BALANCE DEPRECIATION

The double declining balance method (DDB) is the most aggressive depreciation method for recognizing the bulk of the expense toward the beginning of an asset's useful life. To calculate it, determine the straight-line depreciation for an asset for its first year (see the last section for the straight-line calculation). Then double this amount, which yields the depreciation for the first year. Then subtract the first-year depreciation from the asset cost (using no salvage value deduction), and run the same calculation again for the next year. Continue to use this methodology for the useful life of the asset.

For example, a dry cleaning machine costing $20,000 is estimated to have a useful life of six years. Under the straight-line method, it would have depreciation of $3,333 per year. Consequently, the first year of depreciation under the 200% DDB method would be double that amount, or $6,667. The calculation for all six years of depreciation is noted in Exhibit 16-1.

Exhibit 16-1   Double Declining Balance Method

Year	Beginning Cost Basis	Straight-Line Depreciation	200% DDB Depreciation	Ending Cost Basis
1	$24,000	$3,333	$6,667	$17,333
2	17,333	2,889	5,778	11,555
3	11,555	1,926	3,852	7,703
4	7,703	1,284	2,568	5,135
5	5,135	856	1,712	3,423
6	3,423	571	1,142	2,281

Note that there is still some cost left at the end of the sixth year that has not been depreciated. This is usually handled by converting over from the DDB method to the straight-line method in the year in which the straight-line method would result in a higher amount of depreciation; the straight-line method is then used until all of the available depreciation has been recognized.

16-13 SUM OF THE YEARS DIGITS DEPRECIATION

This depreciation method is designed to recognize the bulk of all depreciation within the first few years of an asset's depreciable period, but does not do so quite as rapidly as the double declining balance method that was described in the last section. Its calculation can be surmised from its name. For the first year of depreciation, one adds up the number of years over which an asset is scheduled to be depreciated, and then divides this into the total number of years remaining. The resulting percentage is used as the depreciation rate. In succeeding years, simply divide the reduced number of years left into the same total number of years remaining.

For example, a punch press costing $24,000 is scheduled to be depreciated over five years. The sum of the years digits is 15 (Year 1 + Year 2 + Year 3 + Year 4 + Year 5). The depreciation calculation in each of the five years is:

$$\text{Year } 1 = (5/15) \times \$24,000 = \$8,000$$
$$\text{Year } 2 = (4/15) \times \$24,000 = \$6,400$$
$$\text{Year } 3 = (3/15) \times \$24,000 = \$4,800$$
$$\text{Year } 4 = (2/15) \times \$24,000 = \$3,200$$
$$\text{Year } 5 = (1/15) \times \$24,000 = \underline{\$1,600}$$
$$\$24,000$$

16-14 UNITS OF PRODUCTION DEPRECIATION METHOD

The units of production depreciation method can result in the most accurate matching of actual asset usage to the related amount of depreciation that is recognized in the accounting records. Its use is limited to those assets to which some estimate of production can be attached. It is a particular favorite of those who use activity-based costing systems, since it closely relates asset cost to actual activity.

To calculate it, one should first estimate the total number of units of production that are likely to result from the use of an asset. Then divide the total capitalized asset cost (less salvage value, if this is known) by the total estimated production to arrive at the depreciation cost per unit of production. Then the depreciation recognized is derived by multiplying the number of units of actual production during the period by the depreciation cost per unit. If there is a significant divergence of actual production activity from the original estimate, the depreciation cost per unit of production can be altered from time to time to reflect the realities of actual production volumes.

As an example of this method's use, an oil derrick is constructed at a cost of $350,000. It is expected to be used in the extraction of 1,000,000 barrels of oil, which results in an anticipated depreciation rate of $0.35 per barrel. During the first month, 23,500 barrels of oil are extracted. Under this method, the resulting depreciation cost is:

= (cost per unit of production) $\times$ (number of units of production)

= ($0.35 per barrel) $\times$ (23,500 barrels)

= $8,225

This calculation can also be used with service hours as its basis, rather than units of production. When used in this manner, the method can be applied to a larger number of assets for which production volumes would not otherwise be available.

16-15 ASSET IMPAIRMENT

A company is allowed to write down its remaining investment in an asset if it can be proven that the asset is impaired. Impairment can be proven if the asset results in a continuing stream of negative cash flows that can be expected into the future, thereby giving rise to the supposition that the asset's use may shortly be discontinued. Another evidence of impairment is when new government regulations have been imposed that are likely to significantly reduce a company's ability to use the asset (such as may be the case for a coal-fired electricity generating facility that is subject to pollution controls). A final possibility is a large reduction in the market value of the asset; this last case is not usually used as a valid reason for an asset write-down, since the asset may still have considerable utility within the company, no matter what its market value may be.

To calculate an impairment loss, estimate the stream of cash flows (both positive and negative) to be expected from an asset, and compare the present value of these flows to the fair market value of the asset. If the fair market value is higher than the net present value of the cash flows, then the difference should be written off, thereby reducing the remaining book value of the asset (and also reducing the remaining depreciation expense that can be recognized at a later date). A key issue is the assumptions used to derive cash flows, since they can result in wide swings in cash flow estimates. One should derive a set of guidelines in estimating cash flows that is consistently followed for all asset impairment reviews, so that all write-offs can be reasonably defended.

16-16 INTANGIBLE ASSETS

An intangible asset is an economic resource having no physical existence. Examples of intangible assets are patents, trademarks, copyrights, franchise rights, goodwill, and airport landing rights.

When an intangible asset is purchased, it should be capitalized on the company books at the amount of cash for which it was paid. If some other asset was used in exchange for the intangible, then the cost should be set at the fair market value of the asset given up. A third alternative for costing is the present value of any liability that is assumed in exchange for the intangible asset. It is also possible to create an intangible asset internally (such as the creation of a customer list), as long as the detail for all costs incurred in the creation of the intangible asset is adequately tracked and summarized (much as would be the case for construction in progress—see the previous section discussing that topic).

The amortization of intangible assets is limited to any legally imposed maximum (such as 17 years for a patent). If there is no legal maximum, then current accounting rules limit the maximum period of amortization to 40 years. However, the amortization term should be limited to the terms of any associated contractual documents. For example, the costs associated with a franchise fee should be amortized over the term of the franchise, as stated in the franchise agreement. Similarly, the costs associated with a trademark should be amortized over its legal term, while the costs associated with any trademark renewals should be amortized over the renewal period. Goodwill is amortized over no more than 40 years. Under no circumstances should the amortization period for an intangible asset exceed its expected useful life. The only allowable type of amortization for an intangible asset is the straight-line calculation method.

New rules being contemplated by the Financial Accounting Standards Board at the time of this writing will limit the maximum number of years for all intangibles (to be overridden only in very specific instances) to 20 years. The new rules may also include a provision that allows some intangible assets with no clear diminution of future value to not be amortized at all (though an annual impairment review would be required that would force the accountant to write down such an asset if value impairment is present).

If any intangible asset's usefulness is declining or evidently impaired, then its remaining value should be written down to no lower than the present value of its remaining future cash flows.

16-17 SUMMARY

This chapter has presented a number of rules regarding the proper costing of incoming assets, the recognition of gains or losses on their disposition, how to calculate the proper depreciable basis for a new asset, what types of costs may be added to the capitalized cost of an existing asset, and what types of depreciation calculation can be applied to an asset. The key factor to consider when using this information is that one should establish a firm set of guidelines for the consistent treatment of all assets, so that there is no long-term inconsistency in the method of recording asset-related transactions.

CHAPTER 17

Current Liabilities

17-1 INTRODUCTION

The treatment of accounts payable is somewhat more complicated than the treatment of its counterpart on the balance sheet, accounts receivable. This is because the underlying transaction is more complex, and also due to the wide range of accruals that may potentially be required for the accountant to fairly represent the state of current liabilities on the balance sheet. This chapter describes a wide range of current liabilities, and how they should be accounted for.

17-2 DEFINITION OF CURRENT LIABILITIES

A *trade account payable* is one for which there is a clear commitment to pay, and that generally involves an obligation related to goods or services. Typically, it also involves a payment that is due within one year, and is considered to include anything for which an invoice is received.

An *accrued liability* is one for which there is also a clear commitment to pay, but for which an invoice has not yet been received. Typical accrued liabilities are wages payable, payroll taxes payable, and interest payable.

A *contingent liability* is one that will occur if a future event comes to pass, and that is based on a current situation.

17-3 THE ACCOUNTS PAYABLE TRANSACTION FLOW

The typical transaction flow for the accounts payable process is for the purchasing department to release a purchase order to a supplier, after which the supplier ships to the company whatever was ordered. The shipping manifest delivered with the product contains the purchase order number that authorizes the transaction. The receiving staff compares the delivery to the referenced purchase order, and accepts the delivery if it matches the purchase order. The receiving staff then sends a copy of the receiving documentation to the accounts payable department. Meanwhile, the supplier issues an invoice to the company's accounting department. Once the accounting staff receive the invoice, they match it to the initiating purchase order as well as the receiving documentation, thereby establishing proof that the invoice was both authorized and received. If everything cross-checks properly, then the invoice is entered into the accounting system for payment, with a debit going to either an expense account or an asset account, and a credit going to the accounts payable account. Once the invoice is due for payment, a check is printed, and a credit is made to the cash account and a debit to the accounts payable account.

A variation on this transaction is for the accounting staff to initially record an account payable at an amount net of its early payment discount. However, this requires one to apportion the amount of the discount over all line items being billed on the supplier invoice. Also, since taking or avoiding the early payment discount can also be viewed as an unrelated financing decision, this would lead one to record each invoice at its gross amount and then to record the discount separately if the decision is made to take it.

The accounts payable transaction flow is one requiring a number of types of paperwork to be assembled from three different departments, which tends to lead to a great deal of confusion and missing paperwork. Frequently, the delay is so excessive that the accounting staff cannot process the paperwork in time to meet the deadlines by which early payment discounts can be taken. Accordingly, there are several alternatives to the basic process flow that can alleviate its poor level of efficiency:

- *Pay without approval.* Invoices may be entered into the system immediately upon receipt and paid, irrespective of where they may stand in the approval process. This approach ensures that all early payment discounts are taken, but tends to result in some payments for unauthorized shipments.

- *Pay from the purchase order.* A much simpler approach than the traditional one just described is to require that all deliveries be authorized by a purchase order, and that the receiving staff have access to this information on-line at the receiving dock, so that it can check off receipts as soon as they appear. The computer system then automatically schedules payment to the supplier, based on the price per unit listed in the purchase order and the quantity recorded at the receiving dock. This approach requires considerable interaction with suppliers to ensure that the resulting payments are acceptable.

- *Pay from completed production.* The most streamlined approach to the payment of accounts payable is that used by just-in-time manufacturing systems, under which suppliers are pre-certified as to the quality of their products, which therefore require no inspection by a company's receiving staff at all. Instead, they deliver directly to the production workstations where they are immediately needed, avoiding all receiving paperwork. Once the company completes its production process, it determines the number of finished goods completed, and the number of units of parts from each supplier that were included in those completed finished goods. It then pays the suppliers based on this standard number of parts. This system requires a high degree of accuracy in production tracking, as well as a separate scrap tracking system that accumulates all parts thrown out or destroyed during the production process (because suppliers must also be reimbursed for these parts).

Many invoices are also received that have nothing to do with the production process, such as utility, subscription, and rent billings. These should first be entered in the accounts payable system for processing, and then routed to the applicable managers for approval. In many cases, the accounts payable staff is authorized to approve these invoices up to the amount of the periodic budget, with further inspection required if the budget is exceeded.

17-4 ACCOUNTING FOR THE PERIOD-END CUTOFF

If an accountant were to issue financial statements immediately after the end of a reporting period, it is quite likely that the resulting financial statements would underreport the amount of accounts payable. The reason is that the company may have received inventory items prior to period-end and recorded them as an increase in the level of inventory (thereby reducing the cost of goods sold), without having recorded the corresponding supplier invoice, which may have been delayed by the postal service until a few days following the end of the period.

Proper attention to the period-end cutoff issue can resolve this problem. The key activity for the accountant is to compare the receiving department's receiving log for the few days near period-end to the supplier invoices logged into that period, to see if there are any receipts for which there are no supplier invoices. If not, the accountant can accrue the missing invoice at the per-unit rate shown on the originating purchase order, or else used the cost noted on an earlier invoice for the same item.

Similarly, there will be a number of other types of invoices that will arrive several days after the end of the period, such as maintenance billings and telephone bills. The accountant can anticipate their arrival by accruing for them based on a checklist of invoices that are typically late in arriving, and for which an estimate can be made that is based on invoices from previous reporting periods.

Proper attention to the cutoff issue is extremely important, since ignoring it can lead to wide gyrations in reported income from period to period, as invoices are continually recorded in the wrong period.

17-5 ACCOUNTING FOR ADVANCE PAYMENTS FROM CUSTOMERS

If a customer makes a payment for which the company has not made a corresponding delivery of goods or services, then the accountant must record the cash receipt as a customer advance, which is a liability. This situation commonly arises when a customer order is so large or specialized that the company is justified in demanding cash in advance of the order. Another common situation is when customers are required to make a deposit, such as when a property rental company requires one month's rent as a damage deposit.

This may be recorded as a current liability if the corresponding delivery of goods or services is expected to be within the next year. However, if the offset is expected to be further in the future, then it should be recorded as a long-term liability.

17-6 ACCOUNTING FOR ACCRUED EXPENSES

One of the primary tasks of the accountant during the period-end closing process is the calculation of expense accruals, of which there are potentially a great number. Here are the most common ones:

- *Accrued bonuses.* Rather than waiting until bonuses are fully earned and payable to recognize them, the accountant should accrue some proportion of bonuses in each reporting period if there is a reasonable expectation that they will be earned and that the eventual amount of the bonuses can be approximately determined.

- *Accrued commissions.* The amount of commissions due to the sales staff may not be precisely ascertainable at the end of the reporting period, since they may be subject to later changes based on the precise terms of the commission agreement with the sales staff, such as subsequent reductions if customers do not pay for their delivered goods or services. In this case, commissions should be accrued based on the maximum possible commission payment, minus a reduction for later eventualities; the reduction can reasonably be based on historical experience with actual commission rates paid.

- *Accrued property taxes.* The accounting staff is usually notified well in advance by the local government authorities of the exact amount of property tax that will be payable on a later date. However, there is no reason to record the entire amount of this tax at the point of notification; since property taxes do not vary much from year to year, the accountant can easily record a monthly property tax accrual, and adjust it slightly when the exact amount payable becomes known.

- *Accrued royalties.* A royalty expense accrual should be treated in the same manner as a commission—if there is any uncertainty in regard to the amount due, record the maximum amount, less a reduction for future eventualities that is based on historical results.

- *Accrued sick time.* The amount of sick time allowed to employees is usually so small that there is no discernible impact on the financial statements if they are accrued or not. This is particularly true if unused sick time cannot be carried forward into future years as an ongoing residual employee benefit that may be paid out at some future date. If these restrictions are not the case, then the accounting treatment of sick time is the same as for vacation time, which is noted in the next bullet point.

- *Accrued vacations.* The accountant should accrue for vacation hours earned, but only if they are already earned as of the end of the reporting period. For example, if a company awards vacation hours to its employees at a constant hourly rate that adds up to two weeks per year, then it should accrue the difference between the amount accrued to date and the amount taken in actual vacation hours. However, if there is a "use it or lose it" limitation that restricts the number of vacation hours that can be carried forward into future periods, then the accrual is limited to the maximum of this carry forward amount.

- *Accrued wages.* Even if a company times its payroll period-end dates to correspond with the end of each reporting period, this will only ensure that no accrual is needed for those employees who receive salaries (because they are usually paid through the payroll period ending date). The same is not usually true for those who receive an hourly wage. In their case, the pay period may end as much as a week prior to the actual payment date. Consequently, the accountant must accrue the wage expense for the period between the pay period end date and the end of the reporting period. This can be estimated on a person-by-person basis, but an easier approach is to accrue based on a historical hourly rate that includes average overtime percentages. One must also include the company's share of all payroll taxes in this accrual.

- *Accrued warranty claims.* The accountant should accrue an expense for warranty claims, based on the company's past history with claims for similar types of products or product lines. It may also use industry information if in-house data is not available.

17-7 ACCOUNTING FOR UNCLAIMED WAGES

There are a small number of cases in which employees do not cash their payroll checks. This most commonly arises when an employee has left the company and moved away, so that the company cannot track down the person's whereabouts. In this case, the funds can be deposited to an unclaimed wages account in the current liabilities section of the balance sheet. Under some state laws, these funds must be forwarded to the state government after they have gone unclaimed for a certain period of time. If so, the accountant should be very careful in regard to the record keeping for these transactions. If there is no such state law, the company should reverse the original payroll transaction, crediting the salaries and wages account for the amount of the unclaimed check.

17-8 ACCOUNTING FOR INTEREST PAYABLE

If a company has an obligation to pay back a loan, it should accrue the interest payable under the terms of that note for the current reporting period, and store this information in the current liabilities section of the balance sheet. The required calculation is to multiply the average loan balance outstanding per day by the interest rate stated on the loan document. However, if the stated interest rate is substantially lower than the market rate at the time the loan document was initiated, then the interest rate should be an imputed one, based on the market rate at the time of loan initiation. In this later case, the loan should have been recorded on the company's books at its net present value, using the market interest rate as the discount rate. The resulting interest expense will be debited to the interest expense account and credited to the accrued interest liability account.

17-9 ACCOUNTING FOR DIVIDENDS

If the Board of Directors authorizes a stock dividend to shareholders, there is no change to any current liability account. The reason is that stock dividends only impact the number of shares outstanding, and so are accounted for within the equity section of the balance sheet. However, if the Board authorizes a cash dividend, then this must be recorded as a current asset for the unpaid amount. The balance in this account will be eliminated at the time the cash dividends are paid to shareholders.

17-10 ACCOUNTING FOR TERMINATION BENEFITS

If company management has formally approved of a termination plan that is designed to reduce headcount, the expenses associated with the plan should be recognized at once, under certain circumstances that will allow the accountant to reasonably estimate the associated costs. The first requirement after plan approval is that the plan clearly outline the benefits to be granted. This information usually specifies a fixed dollar payout based on the amount of time that an employee has been with the company. Though there is typically a lack of knowledge regarding precisely which employees will be terminated at the time the plan is approved, the accountant can use the fixed benefit payment amounts and general estimates of which groups of employees are likely to be terminated to arrive at a reasonably accurate accrual of benefit expenses.

The second requirement is that the plan must specify the general categories and numbers of employees to be let go, since the accountant needs this information to extend the per-person benefit costs specified in the first requirement. The remaining requirements are that employees be informed about the plan, and that further significant changes to the plan be unlikely; these requirements lock in the range of possible costs that are likely to occur as a result of the plan, rendering the benefit cost accrual more accurate.

17-11 ACCOUNTING FOR ESTIMATED PRODUCT RETURNS

Manufacturing companies will occasionally experience product returns from their customers. This may involve an amount too small to register on the financial statements, or such large ones that they have a major impact on the reported level of profitability. Recent examples of the latter case include tires, automobiles, and even infant car seats. If there is some reasonable expectation of product returns, then a reserve must be estimated and recorded within the current liabilities section of the balance sheet. This estimate may be based on a company's past history with similar products, or industry experience in general.

If there are no reasonable grounds for calculating an estimate, but there is an expectation of product returns, then the company cannot recognize revenue from the underlying product sales until either there are better grounds for making an estimate or the time period during which returns are allowed from customers has expired. This situation may arise if few products have been sold, if each product is customized to some degree, if there is no returns experience with the product (usually because it is a new product line), if there is a long period during which returns are allowed, or if rapid obsolescence is a possibility. Given that few companies wish to delay the recognition of revenue for a potentially long period, the accountant will be under some pressure to calculate a reasonably justifiable product return percentage.

17-12 ACCOUNTING FOR CONTINGENT LIABILITIES

A *contingent liability* is one that will occur if a future event comes to pass, and that is based on a current situation. For example, a company may be engaged in a lawsuit; if it loses the suit, it will be liable for damages. Other situations that may give rise to a contingent liability are a standby letter of credit (if the primary creditor cannot pay a liability, then the company's standby letter of credit will be accessed by the creditor), a guarantee of indebtedness, an expropriation threat, a risk of damage to company property, or any potential obligations associated with product warranties or defects.

If any of these potential events exists, then the accountant is under no obligation to accrue for any potential loss until the associated events come to pass, but should disclose them in a footnote. However, if the conditional events are probable, then the accountant must accrue a loss against current income. The amount of the contingent liability must be reasonably determinable, or at least be stated within a high-low range of likely outcomes. If the liability can only be stated within a probable range, then the accountant should accrue for the most likely outcome. If there is no most likely outcome, then the minimum amount in the range should be accrued.

An interesting variation pertaining to litigation is that many companies are unwilling to accrue for a contingent liability even after there has been a finding against them in a lower court. Instead, they prefer to disclose this information without an associated accrual, until such time as the ruling is confirmed by a court of appeals.

17-13 ACCOUNTING FOR LONG-TERM PAYABLES NEARING PAYMENT DATES

If a company has a long-term payable that is approaching its termination date, then any amount due under its payment provisions within the next year must be recorded as a current liability. If only a portion of total payments due under the liability is expected to fall within that time frame, then only that portion of the liability should be reported as a current liability. A common situation in which this issue arises is for a copier leasing arrangement, where the most recent payments due under the agreement are split away from the other copier lease payments that are not due until after one year. This situation commonly arises for many types of long-term equipment and property rentals.

17-14 SUMMARY

There are a number of situations applying to current liabilities that require differing accounting treatment—unclaimed payroll checks, warranties, contingent liabilities, and the like. In addition, there are a number of ways to handle the accounts payable process flow that will result in varying degrees of efficiency and accuracy. Best practices related to the accounts payable function can be explored in greater detail in Chapter 22, Best Practices, as well as in Bragg, *Best Practices,* 2nd Edition (John Wiley & Sons, 2001).

CHAPTER 18

Debt

18-1 INTRODUCTION

There are a number of issues related to debt that the accountant is likely to face. For example, how should one account for the early retirement of debt, a change in the terms of a debt agreement, the presence of a discount or premium on the sale of bonds, or the use of warrants? These common issues, as well as others related to defaulted debt, callable debt, sinking funds, debt that has been converted to equity, debt refinancings, and non-cash debt payments, are all addressed in this chapter.

18-2 BONDS DEFINED

The typical bond is a long-term (1 to 30 year) obligation to pay a creditor, and which may be secured by company assets. A traditional bond agreement calls for a semi-annual interest payment, while the principal amount is paid in a lump sum at the termination date of the bond. The issuing company may issue periodic interest payments directly to bond holders, though only if they are registered; another alternative is to send the entire amount of interest payable to a trustee, who exchanges bond coupons from bond holders for money from the deposited funds.

The issuing company frequently creates a sinking fund well in advance of the bond pay-off date, so that it will have sufficient funds available to make the final balloon payment (or buy back bonds on an ongoing basis). The bond agreement may contain a number of restrictive covenants that the company must observe, or else the bond holders will be allowed a greater degree of control over the company or allowed to accelerate the payment date of their bonds.

A bond will be issued at a stated face value interest rate. If this rate does not equate to the market rate on the date of issuance, then investors will either bid up the price of the bond (if its stated rate is higher than the market rate) or bid down the price (if its stated rate is lower than the market rate). The after-market price of a bond may subsequently vary considerably if the market rate of interest varies substantially from the stated rate of the bond.

Some bonds are issued with no interest rate at all. These *zero-coupon bonds* are sold at a deep discount and are redeemed at their face value at the termination date of the bond. They are of particular interest to those companies that do not want to be under the obligation of making fixed interest payments during the term of a bond.

The interest earned on a bond is subject to income taxes, except for those bonds issued by government entities. Theses bonds, known as *municipal bonds,* pay tax-free interest. For this reason, they can be competitively sold at lower actual interest rates than the bonds offered by commercial companies.

The *serial bond* does not have a fixed termination date for the entire issuance of bonds. Instead, the company is entitled to buy back a certain number of bonds at regular intervals, so that the total number of outstanding bonds declines over time.

The *convertible bond* contains a feature that allows the holder to turn in the bond in exchange for stock when a pre-set strike price for the stock is reached. An alternative is the use of attached warrants, which allow the bond holder to buy shares of company stock at a pre-specified price. If the warrants are publicly traded, then their value can be separated from that of the bond, so that each portion of the package is recognized separately in a company's balance sheet.

18-3 BASIC BOND TRANSACTIONS

Though some corporations issue their own bonds directly to investors, it is much more common to engage the services of an investment banker, who not only lines up investors for the company, but who may also invest a substantial amount of its own funds in the company's bonds. In either case, the Board of Directors must approve any new bonds, after which a trustee is appointed to control the bond issuance, certificates are printed and signed, and delivery is made to either the investment banking firm or directly to investors in exchange for cash.

When bonds are initially sold, the entry is a debit to cash and a credit to bonds (or notes) payable. If the bonds are sold at a discount (see next section), then the entry will include a debit to a discount on bonds payable account. For example, if $10,000 of bonds are sold at a discount of $1,500, the entry would be:

Cash	$8,500	
Discount on bonds payable	1,500	
Bonds payable		$10,000

If the same transaction were to occur, with the exception that a premium (see next section) on sale of the bonds were to occur, then the entry would be:

Cash	$11,500	
Premium on bonds payable		$ 1,500
Bonds payable		10,000

The costs associated with issuing bonds can be substantial. These include the legal costs of creating the bond documents, printing the bond certificates, and (especially) the underwriting costs of the investment banker. Since these costs are directly associated with the procurement of funds that the company can be expected to use for a number of years (until the bonds are paid off), the related bond issuance costs should be recorded as an asset and then written off on a straight-line basis over the period during which the bonds are expected to be used by the company. This entry is a debit to a bond issuance asset account and a credit to cash. However, if the bonds associated with these costs are subsequently paid off earlier than anticipated, one can reasonably argue that the associated remaining bond issuance costs should be charged to expense at the same time.

18-4 ACCOUNTING FOR BOND PREMIUM OR DISCOUNT

As noted in the last section, investors may purchase bonds at a reduced price if the market interest rate is greater than the stated rate on the bonds, or at an increased price if the reverse is true. The following example is used to illustrate how this discount or premium is calculated:

The Arabian Knights Security Company issues $1,000,000 of bonds at a stated rate of 8% in a market where similar issuances are being bought at 11%. The bonds pay interest once a year, and are to be paid off in 10 years. Investors purchase these bonds at a discount in order to earn an effective yield on their investment of 11%. The discount calculation requires one to determine the present value of 10 interest payments at 11% interest, as well as the present value of $1,000,000, discounted at 11% for 10 years. The result is:

Present value of 10 payments of $80,000 = $	80,000 × 5.8892 = $	471,136
Present value of $1,000,000 =	$1,000,000 × .3522 = $	352,200
		$ 823,336
	Less: stated bond price	$1,000,000
	Discount on bond	$ 176,664

(The present value multipliers shown in this example can be found in the interest rate tables located in Appendix C.)

In this example, the entry would be a debit to Cash for $823,336, a credit to Bonds Payable for $1,000,000, and a debit to Discount on Bonds Payable for $176,664. If the calculation had resulted in a premium (which would only have occurred if the market rate of interest was less than the stated interest rate on the bonds), then a credit to Premium on Bonds Payable would be in order.

The amount of a discount should be gradually written off to the interest expense account over the life of the bond, while the amount of a premium should be written off in a similar manner to the interest income account. The only acceptable method for writing off these accounts is through the *interest method,* which allows one to charge off the difference between the market and stated rate of interest to the existing discount or premium account. To continue with our example, the interest method holds that, in the first year of interest payments, the Arabian Knights Security Company's accountant would determine that the market interest expense for the first year would be $90,567 (bond stated price of $1,000,000 minus discount of $176,664, multiplied by the market interest rate of 11%). The resulting journal entry would be:

	Debit	*Credit*
Interest expense	$90,567	
Discount on bonds payable		$10,567
Interest payable		$80,000

The reason why only $80,000 is listed as interest payable is that the company only has an obligation to pay an 8% interest rate on the $1,000,000 face value of the bonds, which is $80,000. The difference is netted against the existing Discount on Bonds Payable account.

When reporting this information in the financial statements, the amount of the discount or premium should be combined with the face value of bonds outstanding, though it is also acceptable to note the amount of the discount or premium in an attached footnote.

18-5 ACCOUNTING FOR NON-INTEREST BEARING NOTE PAYABLE

If a company issues debt that has no stated rate of interest, then the accountant must create an interest rate for it that approximates the rate that the company would likely obtain, given its credit rating, on the open market on the date when the debt was issued. The accountant then uses this rate to discount the face amount of the debt down to its present value, and then records this present value as the loan balance. For example, if a company issued debt with a face amount of $1,000,000, payable in five years and at no stated interest rate, and the market rate for interest at the time of issuance was 9%, then the discount factor to be applied to the debt would be .6499 (see Appendix C). This would give the debt a present value of $649,900, at which it should be recorded. The difference between the face amount of $1,000,000 and the present value of $649,900 should be recorded as interest expense payable, with that portion of the expense due within the next year being recorded as a current liability and the remainder as a long-term liability.

18-6 ACCOUNTING FOR NON-CASH DEBT PAYMENT

In some cases where the issuing company is unable to pay bond holders, it gives them other company assets in exchange for the interest or principal payments owed to them.

When this occurs, the issuing company records a gain or loss on the transaction if there is a difference between the carrying value of the debt being paid off and the fair market value of the asset being transferred to the bond holder.

18-7 ACCOUNTING FOR EARLY DEBT RETIREMENT

A company may find it advisable to repurchase its bonds prior to their maturity date, perhaps because market interest rates have dropped so far below the stated rate on the bonds that the company can profitably refinance at a lower interest rate. Whatever the reason may be, the resulting transaction should recognize any gain or loss on the transaction, as well as recognize the transactional cost of the retirement, and any proportion of the outstanding discount, premium, or bond issuance costs relating to the original bond issuance. To return to our earlier example, if the Arabian Knights Security Company were to buy back $200,000 of its $1,000,000 bond issuance at a premium of 5%, and does so with $125,000 of the original bond discount still on its books, it would record a loss of $10,000 on the bond retirement ($200,000 × 5%), while also recognizing one fifth of the remaining discount, which is $25,000 ($125,000 × $\frac{1}{5}$). The entry would be:

Bonds payable	$200,000	
Loss on bond retirement	10,000	
Discount on bonds payable		$ 25,000
Cash		185,000

Any gain or loss resulting from this early retirement must be recorded in current income. If the amount is material, it should be recorded as an extraordinary item, net of any related income tax effect. Accompanying this information should be a notation in the financial statements that describes the sources of funds used to purchase the debt, as well as the related income tax effect and the per-share impact of the transaction.

18-8 ACCOUNTING FOR CALLABLE DEBT

If a debt can be called by the creditor, then it must be classified as a current liability. However, if the period during which the creditor can call the debt is at some point subsequent to one year, then it may still be classified as a long-term debt. Also, if the call option only applies if the company defaults on some performance measure related to the debt, then the debt only needs to be classified as a current liability if the company cannot cure the performance measure within whatever period is specified under the terms of the debt. Further, if a debt agreement contains a call provision that is likely to be activated under the circumstances present as of the balance sheet date, then the debt should be classified as a current liability; conversely, if the probability of the call provision being invoked is remote, then the debt does not have to be so classified. Finally, if only a portion of the debt can be called, then only that portion need be classified as a current liability.

18-9 ACCOUNTING FOR DEFAULTED DEBT

If the issuing company finds itself in the position of being unable to pay either interest or principal to its bond holders, there are two directions the accountant can take in reflecting the problem in the accounting records. In the first case, the company may only temporarily be in default, and is attempting to work out a payment solution with the bond holders. Under this scenario, the amortization of discounts or premiums, as well as of bond issuance costs and interest expense, should continue as they have in the past. However, if there is no chance of payment, then the amortization of discounts or premiums, as well as of bond issuance costs, should be accelerated, being recognized in full in the current period. This action is taken on the grounds that the underlying accounting transaction that specified the period over which the amortizations occurred has now disappeared, requiring the accountant to recognize all remaining expenses.

If the issuing company has not defaulted on a debt, but rather has restructured its terms, then the accountant must determine the present value of the new stream of cash flows and compare it to the original carrying value of the debt arrangement. In the likely event that the new present value of the debt is less than the original present value, the difference should be recognized in the current period as an extraordinary gain.

Alternatively, if the present value of the restructured debt agreement is *more* than the carrying value of the original agreement, then a loss is *not* recognized on the difference — instead, the effective interest rate on the new stream of debt payments is reduced to the point where the resulting present value of the restructured debt matches the carrying value of the original agreement. This will result in a reduced amount of interest expense being accrued for all future periods during which the debt is outstanding.

18-10 ACCOUNTING FOR SHORT-TERM DEBT BEING REFINANCED

It is generally not allowable to reclassify a debt that is coming due in the short term as a long-term liability on the grounds that it is about to be refinanced as a long-term debt. This treatment would likely result in no debt ever appearing in the current liabilities portion of the balance sheet. This treatment is only allowable if the company intends to refinance the debt on a long-term basis, rather than simply rolling over the debt into another short-term debt instrument that will, in turn, become due and payable in the next accounting year. Also, there must be firm evidence of this roll-over into a long-term debt instrument, such as the presence of a debt agreement or an actual conversion to long-term debt subsequent to the balance sheet date.

18-11 ACCOUNTING FOR WARRANTS SOLD WITH BONDS

A company may attach warrants to its bonds in order to sell the bonds to investors more easily. A warrant gives an investor the right to buy a specific number of shares of company stock at a set price for a given time interval.

To account for the presence of a warrant, the accountant must determine its value if it were sold separately from the bond, determine the proportion of the total bond price to allocate to it, and then credit this proportional amount into the additional paid-in capital account. For example, a bond/warrant combination is purchased by an investor at its stated value of $1,000. The investment banker handling the transaction estimates that the value of the warrant is $50, and that the bond would have sold for $980 if the warrant had not been attached to it. Accordingly, the value the accountant assigns to the warrant is $48.54, which is calculated as follows:

$$\frac{\text{Warrant value}}{\text{Bond value} + \text{Warrant value}} \times \text{Purchase price} = \text{Price assigned to warrant}$$

$$\frac{\$50}{\$980 + \$50} \times \$1,000 = \$48.54$$

The accountant then credits the $48.54 assigned to the warrant value to the additional paid-in capital account, since this is a form of equity funding, rather than debt funding, for which the investor has paid.

18-12 ACCOUNTING FOR BOND CONVERSION TO EQUITY

If a company issues bonds that are convertible to stock, then bond holders may either convert the bonds to stock on specific dates or (more commonly) at any date, but only at a specific conversion price per share, which is typically set at a point that makes the transaction uneconomical unless the share price rises at some point in the future.

To account for this transaction, the principal amount of the bond is moved to an equity account, with a portion being allocated to the capital account at par value and the remainder going to the additional paid-in capital account. A portion of the discount or premium associated with the bond issuance is also retired, based on the proportion of bonds converted to equity. For example, a bond holder owns $50,000 of bonds and wishes to convert them to 1,000 shares of company stock that has a par value of $5. The total amount of the premium associated with the original bond issuance was $42,000, and the amount of bonds to be converted to stock represents 18% of the total amount of bonds outstanding. In this case, the amount of premium to be recognized will be $7,560 ($42,000 × 18%), while the amount of funds shifted to the Capital Stock at Par Value account will be $5,000 (1,000 shares × $5). The entry is:

Bonds payable	$50,000	
Premium on bonds payable	7,560	
Capital stock at par value		$ 5,000
Additional paid-in capital		52,560

18-13 ACCOUNTING FOR SINKING FUNDS

A bond agreement may contain specific requirements to either create a sinking fund that is used at the maturity date to buy back all bonds, or to gradually buy back bonds on a regular schedule, usually through a trustee. In either case, the intention is to ensure that the company is not suddenly faced with a large repayment requirement at the maturity date.

In this situation, the company usually forwards funds, at regular intervals, to a trustee who in turn uses the funds to buy back bonds. The resulting accounting is identical to that noted under the "Accounting for Early Debt Retirement" section. In addition, if the company forwards interest payments to the trustee for bonds that the trustee now has in its possession, these payments are used to purchase additional bonds (since there is no one to whom the interest can be paid). In this case, the journal entry that would normally record this transaction as interest expense is converted into an entry that reduces the principal balance of the bonds outstanding.

18-14 SUMMARY

Among all the preceding topics, a few key issues arise. First, debt must always be recorded at the market interest rate, which may involve the use of present value discounting or the use of discounts or premiums from the stated face value of a bond; this principle is designed to give the reader of a financial statement a clear idea of the true cost of a company's debt. Second, any debt origination costs associated with a debt should be amortized over the life of the debt, so that the cost is matched to the underlying benefit—that of having obtained the debt. Third, if there is a reasonable expectation that a debt may be due and payable within one year, then it must be listed as a current liability—this clearly identifies the risk that debt may be payable in the short term, which may potentially result in a cash flow problem. Finally, any change in the terms of a debt agreement that results in a gain or loss should be recognized at once, either through monetary recognition or footnotes, so that one can readily see its long-term financial impact. Thus, the key issues involving debt are the clear presentation of the cost and timing of debt liabilities.

CHAPTER 19

Equity

19-1 INTRODUCTION

A small company will start with nothing more than the issuance of common stock to create its equity. However, as the organization grows and its funding and compensation needs proliferate, a wide range of additional equity-related stratagems will arise—stock splits, stock subscriptions, warrants, options, and stock appreciation rights are some of the topics that one should address. In this chapter, we review all of these items and more, with particular attention to the journal entries required to record each transaction.

19-2 COMMON STOCK

The owners of common stock are the true owners of the corporation. Through their share ownership, they have the right to dividend distributions, vote on various issues presented to them by the Board of Directors, elect members of the Board of Directors, and share in any residual funds left if the corporation is liquidated. If the company is liquidated, they will not receive any distribution from its proceeds until all creditor claims have been satisfied, as well as the claims of holders of all other classes of stock. There may be several classes of common stock, which typically have different voting rights attached to them; the presence of multiple types of common stock generally indicates that some shareholders are attempting some degree of preferential control over a company through their type of common stock.

Most types of stock contain a par value, which is a minimum price below which the stock cannot be sold. The original intent for using par value was to ensure that a residual amount of funding was contributed to the company, and that could not be removed from it until dissolution of the corporate entity. In reality, most common stock now has a par value that is so low (typically anywhere from a penny to a dollar) that its original intent no longer works. Thus, even though the accountant still tracks par value separately in the accounting records, it has little meaning.

If an investor purchases a share of stock at a price that is greater than its par value, the difference is credited to an additional paid-in capital account. For example, if an investor buys one share of common stock at a price of $82, and the stock's par value is $1, then the entry would be:

	Debit	Credit
Cash	$82	
Common stock—par value		$ 1
Common stock—additional paid-in capital		81

When a company initially issues stock, there will be a number of costs associated with it, such as the printing of stock certificates, legal fees, investment banker fees, and security registration fees. These costs can be deferred and written off over time, rather than be recognized as expenses within the current period.

If a company accepts property or services in exchange for stock, the amount listed on the books as the value of stock issued should be based on the fair market value of the property or services received. If this cannot easily be determined, then the current market price of the shares issued should be used. If neither is available, then the value assigned by the Board of Directors at the time of issuance will be assumed to be the fair market value.

19-3 PREFERRED STOCK

Preferred stock comes in many flavors, but essentially is stock that has fewer (or none) of the rights conferred upon common stock, but that offers a variety of incentives, such as guaranteed dividend payments and preferential distributions over common stock, to convince investors to buy them. The dividends can also be pre-configured to increase to a higher level at a later date, which is called *increasing rate preferred stock*. This is an expensive form of funds for a company, since the dividends paid to investors are not tax deductible as interest expense.

The dividends provided for in a preferred stock agreement can only be distributed after the approval of the Board of Directors (as is the case for dividends from common stock), and so may be withheld. If the preferred stock has a cumulative provision, then any dividends that were not paid to the holders of preferred shares in preceding years must be paid prior to dividend payments for any other types of shares. Also, some preferred stock will give its owners voting rights in the event of one or more missed dividend payments.

Because this stock is so expensive, many companies issue it with a call feature that states the price at which the company will buy back the shares. The call price must be high enough to give investors a reasonable return over their purchase price, or else no one will initially invest in the shares.

Preferred stock may also be converted by the shareholder into common stock at a preset ratio, if the preferred stock agreement specifies that this option is available. If this conversion occurs, the accountant must reduce the par value and additional paid-in capital accounts for the preferred stock by the amount at which the preferred stock was purchased, and then shift these funds into the same common stock funds. For example, if a shareholder of preferred stock were to convert one share of the Grinch Toy Removal Company's preferred stock into five shares of its common stock, the journal entry would be as follows, on the assumption that the preferred stock was bought for $145, and that the par value of the preferred stock is $50 and the par value of the common stock is $1:

	Debit	Credit
Preferred stock—par value	$50	
Preferred stock—additional paid-in capital	95	
Common stock—par value		$ 5
Common stock—additional paid-in capital		140

In the journal entry, the par value account for the common stock reflects the purchase of five shares, since the par value of five individual shares (that is, $5) has been recorded, with the remaining excess funds from the preferred stock being recorded in the additional paid-in capital account. However, if the par value of the common stock were to be greater than the entire purchase price of the preferred stock, the journal entry would change to bring in extra funds from the retained earnings account in order to make up the difference. If this were to occur with the previous assumptions, except with a common stock par value of $200, the journal entry would be:

	Debit	Credit
Preferred stock—par value	$50	
Preferred stock—additional paid-in capital	95	
Retained earnings	55	
Common stock—par value		$200

19-4 RETAINED EARNINGS

Retained earnings is that portion of equity that is not encompassed by the various par value or additional paid-in capital accounts. It is increased by profits and decreased by distributions to shareholders and several types of stock transactions.

Retained earnings can be affected if the accountant makes a prior period adjustment that results from an error in the prior financial statements; the offset to this adjustment will be the retained earnings account, and will appear as an adjustment to the opening balance in the retained earnings account. A financial statement error would be one that involved a mathematical error or the incorrect application of accounting rules to accounting entries. A change in accounting *estimate* is not an accounting error, and so should not be charged against retained earnings.

Retained earnings can be restricted through the terms of lending agreements. For example, a lender may require the company to keep some portion of its retained earnings through the term of the loan, thereby giving the lender some assurance that funds will be available to pay off the loan. Such a restriction would keep the company from issuing dividends in amounts that cut into the restricted retained earnings.

19-5 STOCK OPTIONS

Stock options are dealt with in detail in Chapter 35, Section 42 in relation to their tax consequences to the recipients. In this section, we will only deal with how options are recorded in the accounting records.

An option is an agreement between a company and another entity (frequently an employee), that allows the entity to purchase shares in the company at a specific price within a specified date range. The assumption is that the options will only be exercised if the fixed purchase price is lower than the market price, so that the buyer can turn around and sell the stock on the open market for a profit.

If stock options are issued at a strike price that is the same as the current market price, then there is no journal entry to record. However, if the strike price at the time of the issuance is lower than the market price, then the difference must be recorded in a deferred compensation account. For example, if 5,000 options are issued at a price of $25 each to the president of the Long Walk Shoe Company on a date when the market price is $40, then Long Walk's accountant must charge a deferred compensation account for $75,000 ($40 market price minus $25 option price, times 5,000 options) with the following entry:

	Debit	Credit
Deferred compensation	$75,000	
Options—additional paid-in capital		$75,000

In this example, the options cannot be exercised for a period of three years from the date of grant, so the accountant regularly charges off the deferred compensation account to expense over the next three years.

If Long Walk's president elects to use all of the stock options to buy stock at the end of the three-year period, and the par value of the stock is $1, then the entry would be:

	Debit	Credit
Cash	$125,000	
Options—additional paid-in capital	75,000	
Common stock—par value		$ 5,000
Common stock—additional paid-in capital		195,000

If, during the period between the option grant date and the purchase of stock with the options, the market price of the stock were to vary from the $40 price at which the deferred compensation liability was initially recorded, the accountant would not be required to make any entry, since subsequent changes in the stock price are beyond the control of the company, and so should not be recorded as a change in the deferred compensation account.

The Financial Accounting Standards Board has also issued Statement of Financial Accounting Standards (SFAS) number 123, which requires a minimum of footnote reporting using a different valuation approach; or a company may use it exclusively for both financial and footnote reporting (though few have chosen to do so, since it results in higher expenses being reported). If a company chooses to use the SFAS 123 approach for its normal financial reporting of stock option transactions (as opposed to just using it in footnotes), then the decision cannot be rescinded, and the company must continue to use this method in the future.

Under the SFAS 123 approach, compensation expense must be recognized for options granted, even if there is no difference between the current market price of the stock and the price at which the recipient can purchase the stock under the terms of the option. The compensation expense is calculated by estimating the expected term of the option (that is, the time period extending to the point when one would reasonably expect them to be used), and then using the current risk-free market interest rate to create a discounted present value of what the buyer is really paying for the option. The difference between the discounted price of the stock and the purchase price as listed in the option agreement is then recognized as compensation expense. For example, if the current interest rate on 90-day treasury bills is 7% (assumed to be the risk-free interest rate), the expectation for purchase of stock is three years in the future, and the option price of the stock is $25, then its present value is $20.41 ($25 $\times$ .8163). (Present value discount rates can be found in Appendix C.) The difference between $25 and $20.41 is $4.59, which must be itemized in the footnotes as an accrued compensation liability.

Under SFAS 123, the present value of the stock that is to be purchased at some point in the future under an options agreement must also be reduced by the present value of any stream of dividend payments that the stock might be expected to yield during the interval between the present time and the point when the stock is expected to be purchased, since this is income forgone by the buyer.

The use of present value calculations under SFAS 123 means that financial estimates are being used to determine the most likely scenario that will eventually occur. One of the key estimates to consider is that not all stock options will eventually be exercised—some may lapse due to employees leaving the company, for example. One should include these estimates when calculating the total amount of accrued compensation expense, so that actual results do not depart significantly from the initial estimates. However, despite the best possible estimates, the accountant will find that actual option use will inevitably vary from original estimates. When these estimates change, one should account for them in the current period as a change of accounting estimate. However, if estimates are not changed and the accountant simply waits to see how many options are actually exercised, then any variances from the accounting estimate will be made on the date when options either lapse or are exercised. Either of these methods is acceptable and will eventually result in the same compensation expense, but the first approach is technically better, because it attempts to recognize changes as soon as possible, and so results in an earlier representation of changes in a company's compensation expenses.

19-6 STOCK APPRECIATION RIGHTS

Sometimes the management team chooses not to issue stock options to employees, perhaps because employees do not have the funds to purchase shares, or because no stock is available for an option plan. If so, an alternative is the stock appreciation right (SAR). Under this approach, the company essentially grants an employee a fake stock option, and issues compensation to the employee at a future date if the price of company stock has risen from the date of grant to the date at which the compensation is calculated. The amount of compensation paid is the difference between the two stock prices.

To account for an SAR, the accountant must determine the amount of any change in company stock during the reporting period, and charge the amount to an accrued compensation expense account. If there is a decline in the stock price, then the accrued expense account can be reduced. If an employee cancels the SAR agreement (perhaps by leaving the company), then the entire amount of accrued compensation expense related to that individual should be reversed in the current period.

The company pays the recipients of SAR compensation in stock, and then it usually grants shares on the payment date based on the number of shares at their fair market value that will eliminate the amount of the accrued compensation expense. The journal entry required is a debit to the accrued compensation liability account, and credits to the stock par value and stock additional paid-in capital accounts.

To illustrate the SAR transaction flow, the Big Fat Pen Company decides to grant 2,500 SARs to its chief pen designer. The stock price at the grant date is $10. After one year, the stock price has increased to $12. After the second year, the stock price has dropped to $11. After the third year, the price increases to $15, at which point the chief pen designer chooses to cash in his SARs and receive payment. The related transactions would be:

	Debit	Credit
End of Year 1:		
Compensation expense ($2 net gain × 2,500 shares)	$ 5,000	
SAR liability		$ 5,000
End of Year 2:		
SAR liability	$ 2,500	
Compensation expense ($1 net loss × 2,500 shares)		$ 2,500
End of Year 3:		
Compensation expense ($4 net gain × 2,500 shares)	$10,000	
SAR liability		$10,000
SAR liability (payment of employee)	$12,500	
Cash		$12,500

19-7 STOCK WARRANTS

A stock warrant is a legal document that gives the holder the right to buy a company's shares at a specific price, and usually for a specific time period, after which it becomes invalid. It is used as a form of compensation instead of cash for services performed by other entities to the company, and may also be attached to debt instruments in order to make them appear to be more attractive investments to buyers.

If the warrant attached to a debt instrument cannot be detached and sold separately from the debt, then it should not be separately accounted for. However, if it can be sold separately by the debt holder, then the fair market value of each item (the warrant and the debt instrument) should be determined, and then the accountant should apportion the price at which the combined items were sold among the two, based on their fair market values. For example, if the fair market value of a warrant is $63.50 and the fair market value of a bond to which it was attached is $950, and the price at which the two items were sold was $1,005, then an entry should be made to an outstanding warrants account for $62.97 to account for the warrants, while the remaining $942.03 is accounted for as debt. The apportionment of the actual sale price of $1,005 to warrants is calculated as follows:

$$\frac{\text{Fair market value of warrant}}{\text{Fair market value of warrant} + \text{Fair market value of bond}} \times \text{Price of combined instruments}$$

Or,

$$\frac{\$63.50}{(\$63.50 + \$950.00)} \times \$1,005 = \$62.97$$

If a warrant expires, then the funds are shifted from the outstanding warrants account to an additional paid-in capital account. To continue with the last example, this would require the following entry:

	Debit	Credit
Outstanding warrants	$62.97	
Common stock—additional paid-in capital		$62.97

If a warrant is subsequently used to purchase a share of stock, then the value allocated to the warrant in the accounting records should be shifted to the common stock accounts. To use the preceding example, if the warrant valued at $62.97 is used to purchase a share of common stock at a price of $10.00, and the common stock has a par value of $25, then the par value account is credited with $25 (since it is mandatory that the par value be recorded), and the remainder of the funds are recorded in the additional paid-in capital account. The entry is:

	Debit	Credit
Cash	$10.00	
Outstanding warrants	62.97	
Common stock—par value		$25.00
Common stock—additional paid-in capital		47.97

19-8 DIVIDENDS

Dividends must be authorized for distribution by the Board of Directors. The Board is not allowed to make such a distribution if the company is or would become insolvent as a result of the transaction.

The date when the Board of Directors votes to issue dividends is the *declaration date*. At this time, by the Board's action, the company has incurred a liability to issue a dividend. Unless the dividend is a stock dividend, the accountant must record a dividend payable at this time, and debit the retained earnings account to indicate the eventual source of the dividend payment.

The dividend will be paid as of a *record date*. This date is of considerable importance to share holders, since the entity holding the share on that date will be entitled to receive the dividend. If a share is sold the day before the record date, then the old shareholder forgoes the dividend and the new one receives it. As of the payment date, the company issues dividends, thereby debiting the dividends payable account and crediting the cash account (or the account of whatever asset is distributed as a dividend).

A dividend may also take the form of a *stock dividend*. This allows a company to shift funds out of the retained earnings account and into the par value and additional paid-in capital accounts, which reduces the amount of funding that the Internal Revenue Service would see when reviewing the company for an excessive amount of retained earnings (which can be taxed). These distributions are also not taxable to the recipient. If the amount of a stock dividend represents less than one quarter of the total number of shares currently outstanding, then this is considered to be a distribution that will not greatly impact the price of existing shares through dilution; accordingly, the accountant records the *fair market value* of these shares in the par value and additional paid-in capital accounts, and takes the offsetting funds out of the retained earnings account. For example, if the Bobber Fishing Equipment Company wishes to issue a stock dividend of 10,000 shares and their fair market value is $32 per share, with a par value of $1, then the entry would be:

	Debit	*Credit*
Retained earnings	$320,000	
Common stock—par value		$ 32,000
Common stock—additional paid-in capital		288,000

If more than one quarter of the total amount of outstanding shares is to be distributed through a stock dividend, then we assume that the value of the shares will be watered down through such a large distribution. In this case, funds are shifted from retained earnings only to cover the amount of the par value for the shares to be distributed. Using the preceding example (and assuming that 10,000 shares were more than 25% of the total outstanding), the entry would change to:

	Debit	*Credit*
Retained earnings	$32,000	
Common stock—par value		$32,000

If there are not sufficient funds in the retained earnings account to make these entries, then the number of shares issued through the stock dividend must be reduced.

However, given the small size of the par values that many companies have elected to use for their stock, the amount of retained earnings required may actually be less for a very large stock dividend than for a small one, since only the par value of the stock must be covered in the event of a large distribution.

On rare occasions, a company will choose to issue a *property dividend* to its shareholders. Under this scenario, the assets being distributed must be recorded at their fair market value, which usually triggers the recognition of either a gain or loss in the current income statement. For example, the Burly Book Binders Company issues to its shareholders a rare set of books, which have a fair market value of $500 each. The 75 shareholders receive one book each, which represents a total fair market value of $37,500. The books were originally obtained by the company at a cost of $200 each, or $15,000 in total. Consequently, a gain of $22,500 ($37,500 – $15,000) must be recognized. To do so, the accountant credits the gain—investments account for $22,500, credits its book inventory account for $15,000 to clear out the original cost of the books, and debits the retained earnings account for $37,500.

A *liquidating dividend* is used to return capital to investors; thus, it is not strictly a dividend, which is intended to be a distribution of earnings. This transaction is afffected by the laws of the state of incorporation for each organization, and so cannot be readily summarized here. However, the general entry in most cases is to credit cash and debit the additional paid-in capital account.

19-9 STOCK SUBSCRIPTIONS

Stock subscriptions allow investors or employees to pay in a consistent amount over time and receive shares of stock in exchange. When such an arrangement occurs, a receivable is set up for the full amount expected, with an offset to a common stock subscription account. When the cash is collected and the stock is issued, the funds are deducted from these accounts and shifted to the standard common stock accounts. For example, if the Slo-Mo Molasses Company sets up a stock subscription system for its employees and they choose to purchase $50,000 of stock, the entry would be:

	Debit	Credit
Accounts Receivable—Stock Subscriptions	$50,000	
Common Stock Subscriptions		$50,000

When cash is received, the account receivable will be reduced, but funds located in the common stock subscriptions account will be the same until stock is actually issued to employees. For example, if $48,000 of common stock, comprised of 3,000 shares at a par value of $10, were to be issued toward the end of the subscription program, the entry would be:

	Debit	Credit
Common Stock Subscriptions	$48,000	
Common Stock—Par Value		$30,000
Common Stock—Additional Paid-In Capital		18,000

19-10 STOCK SPLITS

A stock split involves the issuance of a multiple of the current number of shares outstanding to current shareholders. For example, a one-for-two split of shares when there are currently 125,000 shares outstanding will result in a new amount outstanding of 250,000. This is done to reduce the market price on a per-share basis. In addition, by dropping the price into a lower range, it can have the effect of making it more affordable to small investors, who may then bid up the price to a point where the split stock is cumulatively more valuable than the un-split stock.

A stock split is typically accompanied by a proportional reduction in the par value of the stock. For example, if a share with a par value of $20 were to be split on a two-for-one basis, then the par value of the split stock would be $10 per share. This transaction requires no entry on a company's books. However, if the split occurs without a change in the par value, then funds must be shifted from the additional paid-in capital account to the par value account. For example, if 250,000 shares were to be split on a one-for-three basis, creating a new pool of 750,000 shares, and the existing par value per share of $2 were not changed, then the accountant would have to transfer $1,000,000 (the number of newly-created shares times the par value of $2) from the additional paid-in capital account to the par value account to ensure that the legally mandated amount of par value per share was stored there.

A reverse split may also be accomplished if a company wishes to proportionally increase the market price of its stock. For example, if a company's common stock sells for $2.35 per share and management wishes to see the price trade above the $20 price point, then it can conduct a 10-for-1 reverse split, which will raise the market price to $23.50 per share while reducing the number of outstanding shares by 90%. In this case, the par value per share would be increased proportionally, so that no funds were ever removed from the par value account.

19-11 THE RETIREMENT OF STOCK

If the Board of Directors elects to have the company buy back shares from shareholders, the stock that is brought in-house is called *treasury stock*. A corporation's purchase of its own stock is normally accounted for under the *cost method*. Under this approach, the cost at which shares are bought back is listed in a treasury stock account. When the shares are subsequently sold again, the cost is removed from the treasury stock account and any adjustments in price are made to the additional paid-in capital account. These purchase and sale transactions should be accounted for on the specific identification or first-in, first-out (FIFO) inventory method, so that the cost associated with specific shares are charged in and out of the treasury account. For example, if a company chooses to buy back 500 shares at $60 per share, the transaction would be:

	Debit	*Credit*
Treasury stock	$30,000	
Cash		$30,000

If the company subsequently chooses to sell the shares back to investors at a price of $80 per share, the transaction is:

	Debit	Credit
Cash	$40,000	
Treasury stock		$30,000
Additional paid-in capital		10,000

If treasury stock is subsequently sold for more than it was originally purchased, the excess amount may also be recorded in an additional paid-in capital account that is specifically used for treasury stock transactions; the reason for this segregation is that any subsequent sales of treasury stock that are for less than the original buy-back price require the accountant to make up the difference from any gains that are recorded in this account. If the account is emptied and there is still a difference, then the shortage is made up from the additional paid-in capital account for the same class of stock, and then from retained earnings.

In the less common case where there is no intention of ever reselling treasury stock, it is accounted for at the point of purchase from shareholders under the *par value method*. Under this approach, the stock is assumed to be retired, and so the original common stock and additional paid-in capital accounts will be reversed, with any loss on the purchase being charged to the retained earnings account, and any gain being credited to the additional paid-in capital account. To use the same example, if a company were to buy back 500 shares at $60 per share under the par value method, and the original issuance price was $52 (par value of $1), then the transaction would be:

	Debit	Credit
Common stock—par value	$ 500	
Additional paid-in capital	25,500	
Retained earnings	4,000	
Cash		$30,000

19-12 EMPLOYEE STOCK OWNERSHIP PLANS

An employee stock ownership plan (ESOP) is one in which employees receive additional compensation in the form of stock that is purchased by the ESOP from the corporation. Since the company usually has a legal obligation to provide shares or contributions to the ESOP (which are then used to buy its stock), the ESOP should be considered an extension of the company for accounting purposes. This means that if the ESOP obligates itself to a bank loan in order to buy shares from the company, the company should record this liability on its books if the company is a guarantor of the loan. The entry would be a debit to cash and a credit to loans payable. However, a loan from the company to the ESOP does not require an accounting entry, since the company is essentially making a loan to itself.

In addition, if the company has obligated itself to a series of future contributions of stock or cash to the ESOP, it should recognize this obligation by recording a journal entry that debits the full amount of the obligation to a common stock—unearned ESOP obligation account (this is reported as a contra-equity account) and crediting the common stock account.

When the company makes a contribution to the plan, it debits a compensation expense account and credits the common stock—unearned ESOP obligation account.

19-13 SUMMARY

Many of the topics addressed in this chapter are designed to assist a company in bringing in more funds or acquiring funds at a lower cost. These include stock splits (which can increase a firm's overall capitalization by making individual shares of stock more affordable), stock subscriptions (which bring in a steady stream of new capital), and warrants (which reduce the cost of any debt instruments to which they are attached). Other topics are more oriented toward innovative ways to compensate employees, such as stock options, stock appreciation rights, and employee stock ownership plans. Though it is a rare organization that will make use of all these concepts, one should be aware of the information presented here for each item, in order to understand which ones would work best for an organization. Several of the topics covered, such as options, stock appreciation rights, and ESOPs, involve highly technical accounting and legal rules that call for the active participation of specialists to ensure that they are set up and administered properly.

CHAPTER 20

Revenue

20-1 INTRODUCTION

When considering revenue, the accountant typically assumes that there is only one point at which revenue is recognized, which is when the completed product or service is delivered to the customer. However, this chapter will cover 10 revenue recognition methods, all of which can be used under specific circumstances, and few of which precisely conform to this accounting rule. Consequently, the accountant should be aware of which of the revenue recognition scenarios presented in this chapter are most applicable to his or her situation, and report revenues accordingly.

20-2 REVENUE PRESENTATION

Revenue is the inflow of funds or related accounts receivable or other assets from other business entities in exchange for the provision of products or services by a company. It may also include incidental revenues from financing activities, such as dividends, interest income, or rent, or through the sale of assets. However, gains and losses that have little to do with the ongoing activities of the corporation (such as through an asset sale) should not be combined with revenues garnered from standard operations, because this would improperly show revenues that do not reveal the scale of ongoing operations.

A gain or loss on a transaction that is essentially unrelated to a company's ongoing operations should not be recorded as revenue at the top of the income statement, but rather as a separate line item below the results of continuing operations. See Chapter 8, The Income Statement, for more information about the presentation of this information. However, if the amount of the gain or loss is not material, it can be offset against other operating expenses and lumped into the results from continuing operations.

The "Other Income" category on the income statement typically includes all revenues not directly associated with operations, and that do not include gains or losses on other transactions, as just noted. This category includes income from financing activities, such as dividends or interest income (unless this is a primary activity of the business, such as would be the case for a mutual fund or insurance company). It can also include any profits earned on the sale of those assets not normally offered for sale (typically fixed asset sales).

20-3 REVENUE RECOGNITION RULES

The accountant should not recognize revenue until it has been earned. There are a number of rules regarding exactly when revenue can be recognized, but the key point is that revenue occurs at the point when substantially all services and deliveries related to the sale transaction have been completed. Within this broad requirement, here are a number of more precise rules regarding revenue recognition:

- *Recognition at point of delivery.* One should recognize revenue when the product is delivered to the customer. For example, revenue is recognized in a retail store when a customer pays for a product and walks out of the store with it in hand. Alternatively, a manufacturer recognizes revenue when its products are placed onboard a conveyance owned by a common carrier for delivery to a customer; however, this point of delivery can change if the company owns the method of conveyance, since the product is still under company control until it reaches the customer's receiving dock.

- *Recognition when customer acceptance is secured.* The Securities and Exchange Commission has become increasingly disturbed by the amount of abuse in the area of revenue recognition by public companies, and accordingly issued Staff Accounting Bulletin Number 101 in 1999 to tighten the rules under which revenues may be recognized. For example, if there is any uncertainty about customer acceptance after a product or service has been delivered, then revenue should not be recognized until acceptance occurs. This is quite a draconian ruling, for the SEC specifies that customer acceptance is assumed not to have been secured at the point of delivery if the sales contract allows the customer to subsequently test the product, force the seller to make any additional post-delivery services, or specify any other work that is required before accepting the product. If customer acceptance cannot be secured (that is, documented), then revenue cannot be recognized until the time period during which the contractual acceptance provisions are in effect has lapsed.

The SEC's bulletin applies only to publicly held companies, but the SEC also has a great deal of input into formal pronouncements made by the AICPA (see Chapter 4, Standard Setting Organizations), so we should expect that this 1999 bulletin may eventually find its way into an AICPA pronouncement that will make it standard practice for *all* companies at some point in the future.

- *Recognition at time of payment.* If payment by the customer is not assured, even after delivery of the product or service has been completed, then the most appropriate time to recognize revenue is upon receipt of cash. For example, if a book publisher issues new editions of books to the buyers of the last edition without any indication that they will accept the new shipments, then waiting for the receipt of cash is the most prudent approach to the recognition of revenue.

- *Other rules.* In addition to the above rules, there are a few others that should be applicable in all instances. The first is that the seller should have no obligation to assist the buyer in reselling the product to a third party; if this were the case, then the seller would have an outstanding obligation to assist in further sales, which would imply that the initial sale had not yet been completed. The second is that any damage to the product subsequent to the point of sale will have no impact on the buyer's obligation to pay the seller for the full price of the product; if this were the case, one would reasonably assume that at least some portion of the sale price either includes a paid warranty that should be separated from the initial sale price and recognized at some later date, or that the sale cannot be recognized until the implied warranty period has been completed. The third rule is that the buying and selling entities cannot be the same entity, or so closely related that the transaction might be construed as an inter-company sale; if this were the case, the inter-company sale would have to be eliminated from the financial statements of both the buyer and the seller for reporting purposes, since the presumption would be that the sale had not really occurred.

20-4 REVENUE RECOGNITION UNDER THE ACCRUAL METHOD

The most common revenue recognition system is based on the accrual method. Under this approach, if the revenue recognition rules presented in the last section have been met, then revenue may be recognized in full. In addition, expenses related to that revenue, even if supplier invoices have not yet been received, should be recognized and matched against the revenue. The name of this method does not imply that the revenue should be accrued—the name of this approach only applies to the accrual of *expenses.*

For example, if the High Pressure Dive Company sells a set of face masks for $500 and recognizes the revenue at the point of shipment, then it must also recognize at the same time the $325 cost of those masks, even if it has not yet received a billing from the supplier that sold it the masks. In the absence of the billing, the cost can be accrued based on a purchase order value, market value, or supplier price list.

20-5 REVENUE RECOGNITION UNDER THE CASH METHOD

Revenue recognition under the cash method simply means that revenues are recognized at the point when cash is received from a customer that is in payment of a sale to that customer.

There is no difference between the accrual and cash methods if sales are over-the-counter, but there can be a significant difference if the majority of sales are billed to customers, for which payment is received at some later date. The cash basis of revenue recognition is not recognized as an acceptable reporting method by GAAP, since it does not match revenues to related expenses. Instead, the matching of revenues and expenses is entirely dependent upon the timing of cash receipts and expenses, which are subject to manipulation.

This method is acceptable to the Internal Revenue Service for tax reporting purposes, but only in a limited number of cases and for smaller companies. This subject is covered in greater detail in the taxation chapter (Chapter 35).

20-6 REVENUE RECOGNITION UNDER THE INSTALLMENT SALES METHOD

The installment method is used when there is a long string of expected payments from a customer that are related to a sale, and for which the level of collectibility of individual payments cannot be reasonably estimated. This approach is particularly applicable in the case of multi-year payments by a customer. Under this approach, revenue is recognized only in the amount of each cash receipt, and for as long as cash is received. Expenses can be proportionally recognized to match the amount of each cash receipt, creating a small profit or loss at the time of each receipt.

An alternative approach, called the *cost recovery method,* uses the same revenue recognition criterion as the installment sales method, but the amount of revenue recognized is exactly offset by the cost of the product or service until all related costs have been recognized; all remaining revenues then have no offsetting cost, which effectively pushes all profit recognition out until near the end of the installment sale contract.

20-7 REVENUE RECOGNITION UNDER THE COMPLETED CONTRACT METHOD

In the construction industry, one option for revenue recognition is to wait until a construction project has been completed in all respects before recognizing any related revenue. This method makes the most sense when the costs and revenues associated with a project cannot be reasonably tracked, or when there is some uncertainty regarding either the addition of costs to the project or the receipt of payments from the customer. However, this approach does not reveal the earning of any revenue on the financial statements of a construction company until its projects are substantially complete, which gives the reader of its financial statements very poor information about its ability to generate a continuing stream of revenues. Consequently, the percentage of completion method (see next section) is to be preferred when costs and revenues can be reasonably estimated.

20-8 REVENUE RECOGNITION UNDER THE PERCENTAGE OF COMPLETION METHOD

This method is most commonly used in the construction industry, where very long-term construction projects would otherwise keep a company from revealing any revenues or expenses on its financial statements until its projects are completed, which might occur only at long intervals. Under this approach, the accountant develops a percentage of project completion based on the total costs incurred as a percentage of the estimated total cost of the project, and multiplies this percentage by the total revenue to be earned under the contract (even if the revenue has not yet been billed to the customer). The resulting amount is recognized as revenue. The gross profit associated with the project is proportionally recognized at the same time that revenue is recognized.

The trouble with this method is that one must have good cost tracking and project planning systems in order to ensure that all related costs are being properly accumulated for each project, and that cost overruns are accounted for when deriving the percentage of completion. For example, if poor management results in a doubling of the costs incurred at the half-way point of a construction project, from $5,000 up to $10,000, this means that the total estimated cost for the entire project (of $10,000) would already have been reached when half of the project had not yet been completed. In such a case, one should review the remaining costs left to be incurred and change this estimate to ensure that the resulting percentage of completion is accurate.

If the percentage of completion calculation appears to be suspect when based on costs incurred, one can also use a percentage of completion that is based on a Gantt chart or some other planning tool that reveals how much of the project has actually been completed. For example, if a Microsoft Project plan reveals that a construction project has reached the 60% milestone, then one can reasonably assume that 60% of the project has been completed, even if the proportion of costs incurred may result in a different calculation.

If the estimate of costs left to be incurred, plus actual costs already incurred, exceeds the total revenue to be expected from a contract, then the full amount of the difference should be recognized in the current period as a loss, and presented on the balance sheet as a current liability.

20-9 REVENUE RECOGNITION UNDER THE PROPORTIONAL PERFORMANCE METHOD

This method is only applicable to service sales. It is used when a number of specific and clearly identifiable actions are taken as part of an overall service to a customer. Rather than waiting until all services have been performed to recognize any revenue, this approach allows one to proportionally recognize revenue as each individual action is completed. The amount of revenue recognized is based on the proportional amount of direct costs incurred for each action to the estimated total amount of direct costs required to complete the entire service. For example, if a service contract for $100,000 involved the completion of a single step that required $8,000 of direct costs to complete, and the total direct cost estimate for the entire job were $52,000, then the amount of revenue that could be recognized at the completion of that one action would be $15,385 (($8,000/$52,000) × $100,000).

20-10 REVENUE RECOGNITION UNDER THE PRODUCTION METHOD

It is generally not allowable to record inventory at market prices at the time when production has been completed. However, this is allowed in the few cases where the item produced is a commodity, has a ready market, and can be easily sold at the market price. Examples of such items are gold, silver, and wheat. In these cases, the producer can mark up the cost of the item to the market rate at the point when production has been completed. However, this amount must then be reduced by the estimated amount of any remaining selling costs, such as would be required to transport the commodity to market. In practice, most companies prefer to record the cost of commodities at cost, and recognize revenue at the point of sale. Consequently, this practice tends to be limited to those companies that produce commodities, but which have difficulty in calculating an internal cost at which they can record the cost of their production (and so are forced to use the market price instead).

20-11 REVENUE RECOGNITION UNDER THE DEPOSIT METHOD

When property is sold on a conditional basis, whereby the buyer has the right to cancel the contract and receive a refund up until a pre-specified date, the seller cannot recognize any revenue until the date when cancellation is no longer allowed. Until that time, all funds are recorded as a deposit liability. If only portions of the contract can be canceled by the buyer, then revenue can be recognized at once by the seller for just those portions that are not subject to cancellation.

20-12 REVENUE RECOGNITION UNDER BILL AND HOLD TRANSACTIONS

When a company is striving to reach difficult revenue goals, it will sometimes resort to bill and hold transactions, under which it completes a product and bills the customer, but then stores the product rather than sending it to the customer (who may not want it yet). Though there are a limited number of situations in which this treatment is legitimate (perhaps the customer has no storage space available), there have also been a number of cases in which bill and hold transactions have subsequently been proven to be a fraudulent method for recognizing revenue. Consequently, the following rules must now be met before a bill and hold transaction will be considered valid:

- *Completion.* The product that is being stored under the agreement must be ready for shipment. This means that the seller cannot have production staff in the storage area, making changes to the product subsequent to the billing date.

- *Delivery schedule.* The products cannot be stored indefinitely. Instead, there must be a schedule in place for the eventual delivery of the goods to the customer.

- *Documentation.* The buyer must have signed a document in advance that clearly states that it is buying the products being stored by the seller.

- *Origination.* The *buyer* must have requested that the bill and hold transaction be completed, and have a good reason for doing so.

- *Ownership.* The buyer must have taken on all risks of ownership, so that the seller is now simply the provider of storage space.

- *Performance.* The terms of the sales agreement must not state that there are any unfulfilled obligations on the part of the seller at the time when revenue is recognized.

- *Segregation.* The products involved in the transaction must have been split away from all other inventory and stored separately. They must also not be made available for the filling of orders from other customers.

20-13 REVENUE RECOGNITION FOR BROKERED TRANSACTIONS

Some companies that act as brokers will over-report their revenue by recognizing not just the commission they earn on brokered sales, but also the revenue earned by their clients. For example, if a brokered transaction for an airline ticket involves a $1,000 ticket and a $20 brokerage fee, the company will claim that it has earned revenue of $1,000, rather than the $20 commission. This results in the appearance of enormous revenue (albeit with very small gross margins), which can be quite misleading. Consequently, one should apply the following rules to see if the full amount of brokered sales can be recognized as revenue:

- *Principal.* The broker must act as the principal who is originating the transaction.

- *Risks.* The broker must take on the risks of ownership, such as bearing the risk of loss on product delivery, returns, and bad debts from customers.

- *Title.* The broker must obtain title to the product being sold at some point during the sale transaction.

20-14 REVENUE RECOGNITION FOR ACCRETION AND APPRECIATION

Some company assets will grow in quantity over time, such as the timber stands owned by a lumber company. A case could be made that this accretion is a form of revenue, against which some company costs can be charged that are related to the accretion. However, this accretion in value is *not* one that can be recognized in a company's financial reports. The reason is that no sale transaction has occurred that shifts ownership in the asset to a buyer.

Some company assets, such as property or investments, will appreciate in value over time. Once again, a case could be made that the financial statements should reflect this increase in value. However, as was the case with accretion, accounting rules do not allow one to record revenue from appreciation in advance of a sale transaction that shifts the asset to a buyer.

For both accretion and appreciation, it is not allowable to record an unrealized gain in the financial statements; instead, the gain can only appear at the time of a sale transaction. The current accounting treatment tends to understate a company's assets, since it restricts the recorded valuation to the original purchase price; however, the use of estimates to reflect increases in asset value could be so easily skewed by corporate officers striving to improve reported level of profitability or company valuation that there would not necessarily be any improvement in the accuracy of reported information if the accretion or appreciation methods were to be used.

20-15 REVENUE RECOGNITION FOR INITIATION FEES

A company may charge an initiation fee as part of a service contract, such as the up-front fee that many health clubs charge to new members. This fee should only be recognized immediately as revenue if there is a discernible value associated with it that can be separated from the services provided from ongoing fees that may be charged at a later date. For example, if a health club initiation fee allowed a new member access to the swimming pool area, which would not otherwise be available to another member who did not pay the fee, then this could be recognized as revenue. However, if the initiation fee does not yield any specific value to the purchaser, then revenue from it can only be recognized over the term of the agreement to which the fee is attached. For example, if a health club membership agreement were to last for two years, then the revenue associated with the initiation fee should be spread over two years.

20-16 SUMMARY

Despite the large number of revenue recognition scenarios presented in this chapter, the accountant will probably only use the accrual method in most situations. The other revenue recognition methods noted here are designed to fit into niche situations in which the circumstances of an industry require other solutions to be found. There are also very specific revenue recognition rules that apply to some industries, such as the broadcasting, software development, motion picture, and oil and gas industries; for more detailed information about revenue recognition in these cases, please refer to the specialized industry GAAP section in the most recent annual edition of *GAAP,* which is written by Delaney, Epstein, Nach, and Budak, and published by John Wiley & Sons.

CHAPTER 21

Research and Development

21-1 INTRODUCTION

Research and development (R&D) costs are a growing portion of the expenses recognized by companies. Given their growing size, accountants are increasingly concerned with their impact on the financial statements. In this chapter, we will review the definition of R&D, how it is reported if conducted in-house or if purchased, and from the perspective of a contract R&D organization. We conclude with a discussion of R&D costs as they relate to software development.

21-2 DEFINITION OF RESEARCH AND DEVELOPMENT

The definition of R&D is broken into two parts. *Research* is the planned search for the discovery of new knowledge. Obviously, the intent of research is that it will result in either an improvement in an existing product or process, or the creation of a new one. However, there is no assurance that this will happen, so the primary definition of research is the *search* for new knowledge.

Development is the enhancement of existing products or processes, or the creation of entirely new ones. This process does not have to be the direct outgrowth of in-house research efforts, for the knowledge gained from new research can be acquired from any source. Paragraph 8 of SFAS No. 2 states that development "includes the conceptual formulation, design, and testing of product alternatives, construction of prototypes, and operation of pilot plants. It does not include routine or periodic alterations to existing products, production lines, manufacturing processes, and other on-going operations even though these operations may represent improvements and it does not include market research or market testing activities." Thus, development is essentially the application of knowledge for specific business purposes.

Both research and development activities can be conducted by an in-house department, or they can be bought from another company, perhaps as part of an ongoing research contract or through the outright purchase of another business. It is also possible for a company to be formed for the sole purpose of conducting research and development activities, followed by the transference of any new knowledge, products, or processes to another entity that has sponsored the work.

21-3 ACCOUNTING FOR IN-HOUSE R&D COSTS

Any R&D costs incurred by a company must be charged to expense in the current period, unless they have alternative future uses (such as fixed assets). R&D costs cannot be included in an overhead cost pool, since these costs might then be deferred into a future period. The total amount of R&D expense must be reported in the financial statements. The following list includes the R&D costs that must be expensed:

- *Contract services.* R&D work performed by an outside entity on behalf of the company, and for which the company pays, must be charged to expense as an R&D cost.

- *Indirect costs.* Any costs that can be reasonably allocated to R&D activities through a consistently applied cost allocation system shall be charged to R&D expense.

- *Intangibles purchased from others.* See the next section.

- *Materials, equipment, and facilities.* Any of these costs that are acquired for R&D work, and which have no alternative future value, must be expensed. If they do have an alternative future value, then they must be capitalized and depreciated over time as a cost of R&D.

- *Personnel.* Any personnel costs, such as salaries, wages, benefits, and payroll taxes that are associated with personnel engaged in R&D work, shall be charged as an R&D expense.

This rule covers all research, plus testing and modification of product alternatives, prototypes and models, the design of new tools and dies, pilot plants not commercially feasible, or any engineering work conducted prior to being ready for manufacture.

There are also a number of costs that are not to be included in the R&D expense category. They are nearly always costs that must be expensed as incurred, rather than capitalized, and so are not different from R&D costs in terms of their treatment. However, companies would artificially increase their reported R&D expense (which is a separate line item in the financial statements) if they were to include these items in the R&D category, which might give investors an artificial impression of the size of funding being directed toward R&D activities. The costs not to be included in R&D are:

- *Engineering costs.* These include efforts to make minor incremental enhancements to existing products, or to make minor customized adjustments to products for existing customers, as well as the design of tools and dies on a routine basis.

- *Facility costs.* These include the start-up cost of new facilities that are not intended for use as R&D facilities.

- *Legal costs.* These include the cost of patent applications, the cost of litigation to support them, and the costs associated with their licensing to or from other parties.

- *Production costs.* These include industrial engineering, quality, and troubleshooting work engaged in during the commercial production of a product.

21-4 ACCOUNTING FOR ACQUIRED R&D COSTS

If a company purchases its R&D work from some other entity, then the cost of this work to the company must be expensed in the period incurred. However, if a company acquires intangibles that may be used in R&D activities (such as through a corporate acquisition), and which have alternative future uses, the intangibles must be amortized over time. For example, if a company were to purchase another entity, then under the purchase method of accounting, it could assign intangible costs to identifiable assets that are related to R&D, such as patents, formulas, and new product designs, as well as to more concrete items, such as equipment used in R&D experiments.

This latter case has given rise to inconsistent accounting treatment, because acquiring companies sometimes make the assumption that some acquired intangibles are directly associated with R&D costs (rather than being capitalized under the assumption that they have alternative future uses), and are using this assumption as the basis for writing them off at once, rather than amortizing their cost over a number of years. Under this scenario, if there is any doubt regarding the proper treatment of intangibles associated with R&D, it is best to amortize the cost.

21-5 ACCOUNTING FOR R&D COSTS CONTRACTED TO ANOTHER PARTY

If a company specializes in the provision of R&D to other businesses, the accounting for these costs will essentially be determined by the contents of each R&D contract signed. For example, if a contract states that R&D work will be billed to a client on a time and materials basis, then the expense can easily be recorded in conjunction with any associated billings. A more common case is that the R&D organization receives a large amount of initial funding; if there is no obligation to return the funds, they may be recorded at once as revenue. However, if there is a requirement that the funds be used for specific R&D work or else be returned, then the funds must be recorded as a liability that will gradually be drawn down as offsetting R&D costs are incurred.

21-6 R&D COSTS IN THE SOFTWARE INDUSTRY

The basic rule regarding the recognition of R&D expenses for software development (for software to be sold to customers, as opposed to software developed strictly for in-house use) is that development is considered to be R&D (and therefore to be expensed at once) until the point is reached when technological feasibility has been demonstrated. All costs incurred from the point when that demonstration occurs to the time when commercial products are delivered can be capitalized and amortized over time (which is the period over which some economic benefit is expected from the sale of the software).

This is a somewhat more liberal treatment than under the traditional R&D rules, since there is a short time period during which some costs can be deferred through capitalization. However, the point at which technological feasibility is most easily demonstrated is the release of a beta test version of the software, which may be so close to the commercial release date (usually a matter of months) that the amount of costs that can be capitalized during this short period is relatively small. A more aggressive approach is available if a company uses detailed program designs, which allows it to prove technological feasibility at an earlier point in the software development process. Under this approach, feasibility occurs when the product design is complete, when the design has been traced back to initial product specifications, *and* when it can be proved that all high-risk elements in the product design have been investigated and resolved through coding and testing.

If a company is developing software strictly for internal use, a different set of rules applies. In this case, all costs associated with the development work can be capitalized. However, it must not be the intention of management at the time of development to externally market the software (in which case the preceding rule applies). If management subsequently decides to market software that was originally intended solely for internal use, then any profits received will first be offset against the carrying value of the software; once the carrying value is reduced to zero, subsequent profits may be recognized as such.

The only costs that cannot be capitalized under this approach are those associated with the conceptual formulation of the software, the review and testing of alternative systems, and any overhead and training costs associated with the project. In particular, if the total price of a purchased software package includes the cost of training and maintenance, then the training cost must be split out and expensed as training is incurred, while the maintenance fee must be spread equably over the period to which it applies.

Costs that can be capitalized for internal software projects are all those incurred during the coding and system implementation phases of the project; these costs typically include the salaries of all personnel involved in the project, as well as their related payroll tax and benefit costs, plus the cost of outside services required to assist with the project (such as consultants). This capitalization rule also applies to the internal cost required to modify purchased software that is intended for internal use. Amortization of these costs must begin at the point when essentially all testing has been completed, even if there is no one currently using the system. If an internal development project appears to be in danger of not being completed (as defined by lack of completion funding, significant programming difficulties, major cost overruns, or lack of profits within the sponsoring business unit), then all related costs that have thus far been capitalized must be expensed in the current period.

21-7 SUMMARY

In brief, R&D costs must be expensed in the current period unless there is some future alternative use to which they can be put, which then relegates the R&D costs to a lifetime of amortization. Of some concern to the accountant is which costs are to be included in the R&D category for financial statement reporting purposes, since this line item can be greatly increased by incorrectly including a number of ongoing expenses that are more properly related to commercial production activities (and which would artificially reduce the cost of goods sold at the same time). There are some limited cases in which R&D costs for software firms can be capitalized, thereby increasing their short-term reported level of income, but the restrictions placed on this option do not allow for a large amount of capitalization, except for software that is developed strictly for internal use.

Part Five

ACCOUNTING MANAGEMENT

CHAPTER 22

Best Practices

22-1 INTRODUCTION

All accounting processes can be improved in some manner in order to increase the overall efficiency and effectiveness of the accounting department. Such improvements are known as best practices. They can range from such simple expedients as the creation of a signature stamp to increase the speed of check signing to the installation of advanced document management systems that allow one to avoid most records management issues. The full range of best practices would encompass an entire book (and does: for a full treatment of this topic, please refer to Bragg, *Accounting Best Practices,* Second Edition, John Wiley & Sons, 2001). This chapter contains a number of the more common best practices, listed in alphabetical order by functional area, as well as a graphical representation of the approximate cost and implementation time needed to install each one. Any best practice that requires a high cost has a notation of three stacks of money, while those best practices requiring fewer funds have a correspondingly smaller number of stacks. Similarly, a best practice requiring a lengthy installation time has a notation containing three alarm clocks, while those with shorter installation times have a smaller number of clocks.

22-2 BEST PRACTICES

- *Accounts payable: accept electronic data interchange invoices.* Many larger companies with advanced operational capabilities prefer to issue invoices to their customers by electronic data interchange (EDI), rather than with a paper invoice, because of the increased transaction speed and reduced cost of this approach. A company can alter its internal systems to accept these invoices by creating an interface between its accounting system and its packaged EDI acceptance software, so that an incoming EDI transaction will be sent directly to the accounting system in the correct format without the need for any manual re-entry by a keypunching staff.

Though a very efficient approach to the entry of supplier invoices, the creation of a customized interface is both lengthy and expensive.

Cost:

Installation time:

- *Accounts payable: audit expense reports.* Rather than review every line item on every expense report submitted, the accounting manager can schedule a random audit of a small number of expense reports, which will be indicative of any problems that may be present in other, unaudited reports. If so, either the scope of the audit can be expanded, or else the accounting staff can focus on just those issues that are uncovered in a broader sample of expense reports. Also, if the audits of certain employees continue to reveal ongoing problems, those individuals can be scheduled for full reviews of all expense reports submitted. By taking this approach, a company can still spot the majority of expense report exceptions, while expending much less effort in finding them.

Cost:

Installation time:

- *Accounts payable: automate recurring payments.* A few payments, such as space rental, copier lease, and subscription billings, are the same every month, and are likely to last for some time into the future. To avoid the repetitive entry of these items into the accounts payable database, many off-the-shelf accounting packages allow one to set up automatically recurring payments that must only be entered in the system one time. This option should only be used if it allows for a termination date, since automated payments may otherwise inadvertently pass well beyond their actual termination dates.

Cost:

Installation time:

- *Accounts payable: automate supplier query responses.* The accounts payable staff can spend a large part of its time answering queries from suppliers who want to know when they will be paid. The staff time devoted to this activity can be sharply reduced by installing a computerized phone linkage system that steps suppliers through a menu of queries, so that they can find out the status of payments directly from the computer system. It is also possible to do this through an Internet site. Some employee interaction with suppliers will still be necessary, since there will be cases where invoices are not recorded in the system at all, and so will require manual intervention to fix.

Cost:

Installation time:

- *Accounts payable: automate three-way matching.* The most labor-intensive effort by the accounts payable staff is to manually compare receiving documents to supplier invoices and internal purchase orders to ensure that all payments made to suppliers are both authorized and received in full. To avoid much of this work, a number of high-end computerized accounting systems will conduct the comparison automatically, and warn the staff when they find inconsistencies. However, this means that the purchasing staff must enter its purchase orders into the same system, as well as the receiving staff, which requires extra coordination with these departments.

  Cost:

  Installation time:

- *Accounts payable: create an on-line purchasing catalog.* Employee purchases of office supplies and maintenance items comprise a large part of the purchases made by most companies, as well as a correspondingly large part of the accounts payable transactions that it must handle. To avoid this payable work, an on-line purchasing catalog can be created that itemizes all company-approved items; employees can select items directly from this catalog, and place an on-line order. These orders will be batched by the computer system and automatically sent to suppliers, who will ship directly to the ordering personnel. Suppliers will then issue summarized invoices to the company, which greatly reduces the paperwork of the accounting staff. It will also reduce a large part of the work of the purchasing staff. However, setting up the system and coordinating its installation with suppliers results in a very lengthy installation interval.

  Cost:

  Installation time:

- *Accounts payable: eliminate manual check payments.* There are some instances when checks are needed on such short notice that they cannot be included in the scheduled check runs of the accounting staff. Instead, someone must obtain approval on short notice, cut a manual check, have it signed, and log it into the computer system. To avoid these time-consuming steps, one can promulgate a general prohibition on issuing this sort of payment, and can increase the use of petty cash if this will allow the accounting staff to replace manual check payments with cash payments.

  Cost:

  Installation time:

- *Accounts payable: issue payments based on purchase order approval only.* The typical company payment requires multiple approvals: on the purchase requisition, the purchase order, supplier invoice, and check. A much simpler approach is to require a single approval on the purchase order and ignore all other required

approvals. By doing so, the amount of time required to complete accounting transactions can be substantially reduced, since documents must no longer be sent to
managers for approval and sit in their "in" boxes. However, this means that the controls over purchase order approvals must be iron-clad, so that there is no chance of
a supplier payment being sent out without some sort of authorized approval.

Cost:

Installation time: 🕐 🕐

- *Accounts payable: issue payments based on receipts only.* As previously noted in
  a preceding best practice, one of the most time-consuming aspects of the accounts
  payable function is the matching of receiving documents to purchase orders and
  supplier invoices. To avoid this entire approach, a company can have the receiving
  staff access purchase orders through a computer terminal, and approve received
  items on the spot through the terminal. The company then issues payments to suppliers based on the prices listed on the purchase orders, rather than waiting for a
  supplier invoice to arrive. This completely eliminates the matching process.
  However, this approach requires a great deal of computer software customization,
  the integration of sales tax tables into the software, and the cooperation of suppliers
  in accepting payments from the system. This should be considered an advanced best
  practice that requires great expertise to install.

Cost: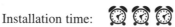

Installation time: 🕐 🕐 🕐

- *Accounts payable: pay via automated clearing house transactions.* The check payment transaction involves printing checks, attaching backup materials to the
  checks, sending them out for signatures, then attaching check stubs to supporting
  documents and filing them away, while the checks are mailed. A much simpler
  approach that avoids all of these steps is to obtain the bank routing numbers and
  account numbers from all suppliers, and then send payments directly to these
  accounts with automated clearing house transactions. This can be accomplished
  with customized accounting software, but is much easier if the software already
  contains this feature; it is normally only found on more expensive packages.

Cost: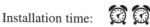

Installation time: 🕐 🕐

- *Accounts payable: pay with purchasing cards.* The bulk of all paperwork dealt
  with by the accounts payable staff is for small-dollar items. Many of these purchases can be consolidated by distributing purchasing cards (for example, credit
  cards) to those employees who most frequently make purchases. By doing so, a
  company can reduce the amount of paperwork to a single supplier statement each
  month. Furthermore, some cards can be set to only allow a certain dollar amount of
  purchases per day, purchases from only certain types of stores, and even to show

daily purchases on an Internet site, where a supervisor can immediately restrict purchasing levels if spending habits appear to be a problem. On the downside, it can be difficult to report use taxes based on purchasing card receipts, which may lead to slightly higher use tax remittances.

Cost:

Installation time:

- *Accounts payable: send supplier invoices to an EDI data entry shop.* When a company creates the capability to accept on-line invoices from suppliers via EDI transmissions, it will find that it must still maintain a clerical staff in order to conduct data entry on those paper invoices still being mailed to the company by some suppliers. It can avoid this expense by re-mailing the invoices to a data entry outsourcing shop that will re-enter the invoices into an EDI format and transmit them to the company, thereby ensuring that 100% of all invoices will be received in the EDI format. A good way to avoid the time delay associated with re-mailing invoices to the data entry supplier is to have all suppliers (those not using EDI) send their invoices to a lockbox that is accessed directly by the supplier. It may also be possible to charge suppliers a small fee if they do not use EDI, thereby covering the cost of the data entry work.

Cost:

Installation time:

- *Accounts payable: sign checks with a signature stamp.* One of the slowest parts of the check creation process is finding an authorized check signer and waiting for that person to sign the checks (which could be days if the person is busy). A better approach is to purchase a signature stamp and have someone on the accounting staff stamp the checks. However, the stamp must be kept locked up in a secure location, so that no unauthorized check signing occurs. Also, since there will no longer be a review of checks before they are sent out, there must be a strong control over payments earlier in the process, by requiring purchase order authorizations before any goods or services are ordered from suppliers.

Cost:

Installation time:

- *Collections: approve customer credit prior to sales.* The accounting or finance staff will sometimes find that it is put under considerable pressure by the sales staff to give credit approval to sales already made to prospective customers. Since the sales staff will earn a commission on these sales, the pressure to approve credit can be quite intense, even if the customer does not have a sufficient credit history to deserve it. This can result in an excessive amount of bad debt write-offs. To avoid this situation, the sales and accounting departments can work together to create a list of sales prospects and determine credit levels for them, based on publicly available credit information, before the prospects are ever contacted. However, this is not a cost-effective solution if new customers are of the walk-in variety or if average per-customer sales are so low that the cost of conducting credit checks makes this best practice too expensive to implement.

Cost:

Installation time:

- *Collections: authorize small balance write offs with no management approval.* Customers will occasionally pay for slightly less than the amount of an account receivable, leaving a small balance cluttering up the accounts receivable database. It can be quite time-consuming to create a permission form for signature by an accounting manager that will lead to the elimination of these small balances. A better approach is to create a policy that allows the collections staff to write off small balances without any permission from management personnel.

Cost:

Installation time:

- *Collections: automate fax delivery of dunning letters.* A computer can be attached to the accounting computer system that is dedicated to sending faxes. This machine is quite useful if it is linked to the collections database, so that reminder faxes can be sent to those customers whose payments are overdue. The severity of the wording on these faxes can increase over time as the number of days late increases. Faxes can even be sent slightly prior to payment due dates, to jog the memory of customers in regard to payment. However, this can be a very expensive option if a customized software linkage must be created between the collections database and the automated faxing system.

Cost:

Installation time:

- *Collections: automate fax delivery of overdue invoices.* The preceding best practice for faxing dunning letters can be expanded to also send customers copies of their overdue invoices. In addition, it can be used by the collections staff to only send invoices to those customers to whom collection calls have been made, and who do not have the invoice in hand already. The same software customization issues apply to this best practice as the last one.

Cost: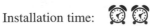

Installation time:

- *Collections: freeze pending customer orders.* If a customer is not paying its overdue invoices, then it certainly makes no sense to send more goods to it, so that even more accounts receivable can become overdue. Consequently, the collections staff should have access to the database of pending customer orders, with authority to halt any further shipments until payment is received for prior shipments. This process can be automated through many accounting systems by setting up maximum credit levels for each customer and allowing the system to automatically freeze shipments once those credit limits are reached. However, some recurring manual review of frozen shipments should be made in order to keep from reducing relations with key customers.

Cost:

Installation time:

- *Collections: receive bankruptcy notices from collection agency.* A company may not realize that a customer has declared bankruptcy, and so will not assert its rights in regard to unpaid invoices, while also continuing to ship to the customer (thereby putting even more accounts receivable at risk of not being paid). To avoid this problem, the Dun & Bradstreet credit agency has an automated bankruptcy notification service that will fax bankruptcy notices to a company for selected customers as soon as a bankruptcy filing becomes public knowledge.

Cost:

Installation time:

- *Collections: print separate invoices for each line item billed.* Sometimes, customers will take issue with one line item on an invoice and refuse to pay the entire invoice until the pricing on that one line item has been resolved, which lengthens the overall interval for collections. To avoid this problem, a company can consider issuing a separate invoice for each line item, rather than clustering them onto a single invoice. This will reduce the average collection period, but may not be cost-effective if the average price for each line item is quite small. It can be a very effective approach, however, for large-dollar line items.

Cost:

Installation time:

- *Collections: send out repeating invoices before the scheduled date.* If a company has a database of prices that it knows it will charge customers on set dates, such as for subscriptions or ongoing standard maintenance fees, it can create and mail the invoices a few days prior to the dates on which they are scheduled to be sent. By creating invoices early, the receiving companies have more time to route the invoices through their internal approval processes, resulting in slightly earlier payments to the issuing company. This is a very inexpensive way to improve the speed of cash flow.

Cost:

Installation time:

- *Collections: stratify required collection calls.* There can be an overwhelming number of potential collection calls to make, and not enough employees to make the calls. In these situations, one should sort the overdue invoices by dollar size, and target the largest ones for the bulk of all calls. This means that the collections staff will focus its efforts on those invoices with the greatest potential dollar return in exchange for the effort put into the calls. This does not mean that small dollar invoices will be ignored, but the related calls may be delayed or fewer in number.

Cost:

Installation time:

- *Commissions: automate commission calculations.* The calculation of commissions can be a painful process of ascertaining the latest commission deals struck by the sales manager, combing through all of the invoices from the latest month to calculate the preliminary calculation, sending the resulting commission reports to the sales staff, and then dealing with irate sales personnel who think that they have not been fully compensated. A better approach is to first standardize the commission calculation system so that it can be automated through the accounting computer system. By doing so, there will be far fewer complaints from the sales staff about supposedly incorrect commission calculations, no chance of the accounting staff making calculation errors (since the computer is now doing it for them), as well as a much faster completion of this key step in the month-end closing process.

Cost:

Installation time:

- *Commissions: calculate commissions based on cash received.* The sales staff is most concerned with completing a sale to a customer, which it usually defines as the moment when the customer signs a purchase order. However, this ignores the ability of the customer to pay for what it has ordered, which can result in a high level of bad debts. To avoid this problem, the sales staff should be compensated based on cash received from customers. By doing so, the sales staff will be more likely to verify the creditworthiness of customers before selling to them, and will also be more likely to assist in collection efforts.

Cost:

Installation time:

- *Commissions: simplify and standardize the commission payment structure.* As noted earlier in the "automate commission calculations" best practice, a company's commission structure can be an extremely complex one that is difficult to calculate, and that can take a considerable amount of practice to calculate properly. Even if automation of the process is considered too difficult, one can still work with the sales manager to improve the simplicity of calculations. This results in much less review time for the calculations, as well as a more understandable system about which the sales staff will be less likely to make inquiries.

Cost:

Installation time: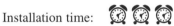

- *Filing: create a document archiving and destruction system.* The operations of the accounting department can be significantly slowed if there is either some difficulty with finding documents, or if there are so many stored in the department that it is difficult to rapidly locate the correct items amid the proliferation of paper. As noted in Chapter 29, the accounting department can set up and follow a detailed set of policies and procedures that are designed to codify and streamline the storage of documents. Such a system can also ensure that stored documents are tagged with destruction dates, as per a standard document retention policy, so that they can be removed from storage on the predetermined dates, thereby creating more room for the accounting department. Please refer to Chapter 29 for more details about this best practice.

Cost:

Installation time:

- *Filing: install a document imaging system.* The problems that a company experiences with missing documents, excessive amounts of space devoted to document storage, and attendant filing costs can largely be eliminated by installing a document imaging system. This involves digitizing documents through a scanner and storing them in a high-capacity storage device on a computer network, so that employees can call up images of the documents on-line. This eliminates the risk of lost documents, and vastly reduces the amount of required document storage space. However, there may still be a need for off-site storage of some documents if there is a legal requirement for their retention. Also, this system can be very expensive, especially if employees requiring access to it do not already have computer terminals for access to the image database, and must be so equipped.

Cost:

Installation time:

- *Filing: stop attaching payment information to checks.* The review of payment information associated with checks by an authorized check signer is considered a key control over the proper disbursement of funds. However, many check signers sign checks with no review at all, considering this step to be a nuisance. If so, an alternative that streamlines the check creation process is to require approval of expenditures earlier in the process, thereby eliminating the need for a check signer (see the previous best practice related to the use of a signature stamp). If there is no check signer, then there is no need to attach related paperwork to checks. An alternative is to have check signers request additional paperwork for only those checks that they wish to inquire more closely about, which relieves the accounts payable staff of the chore of attaching paperwork to the vast majority of all checks.

Cost:

Installation time:

- *Filing: stop storing computer reports.* It is common practice to store paper copies of all computer reports, even when the information is still available either in the computer system or on archiving tapes. One can greatly reduce the amount of required document storage space by only printing out reports for archiving purposes when the related computer files are about to be deleted. Also, there should be a standardized list of reports whose paper copies must be archived—by doing so, a number of unnecessary reports will be kept out of the archives. To make this best practice work properly, there must be sufficient control over the deletion of computer files to ensure that information is not deleted before related reports that are required for archiving have been printed.

Cost:

Installation time:

- *Filing: store canceled checks on CD-ROM.* Canceled checks that are returned by the bank are stored with the bank statement by the month in which the checks cleared the bank, rather than the month in which the checks were created. This can make it difficult to quickly locate checks. A number of national and regional banks are now offering to store check images on CD-ROMs, which makes it much easier to find canceled check information. It also eliminates the need to store the actual checks. Further, the information on the CD-ROMs can be sorted with a variety of indexes, which makes it very easy to look up information.

Cost:

Installation time:

- *Filing: store records for more time periods in the computer system.* The typical packaged accounting computer system allows for the on-line storage of information for the current and immediately preceding years. The detailed information pertaining to all years prior to these dates will be eliminated, which means that this information must be converted to a paper format and archived. To avoid the associated cost of storing these files, some accounting packages are now offering the option to store records for more accounting periods on-line. Though there can be a considerable additional storage cost associated with this activity, plus a slower computer access speed, this can greatly reduce the need to store archived paper documents. An additional benefit is that accounting reports can be created that will automatically generate comparison reports from many years of on-line data, which eliminates the need to do so manually with information gleaned from paper documents.

Cost:

Installation time:

- *Finance: collect invoice payments through a lock box.* A company with a large quantity of accounts receivable will lose a day or two of interest income on funds that cannot be invested, because the checks from customers are slowly wending their way through the check posting process in the accounting department. A better approach is to have customers send their checks directly to a lock box that is opened by the company's bank, which will cash the checks and then forward the related materials to the company, from which it can post cash payments to the accounting system at its leisure. This process can be quite sophisticated, for a company can operate multiple lock boxes, setting them up in those regions where customers are most densely concentrated. This reduces the lag time caused by mail deliveries. There is some consulting cost associated with determining the correct configuration of lock boxes, as well as the cost of notifying customers that they must change the addresses to which they have been sending payments.

Cost:

Installation time:

- *Finance: consolidate bank accounts.* Bank accounts tend to increase in number over time, especially if a company has many stores or subsidiaries. If so, each account will accumulate bank service charges, which can add up if there are many accounts. Also, stray funds may reside in low-interest or no-interest bank accounts for long periods. To avoid these problems, a company should periodically schedule a review of all open accounts and eliminate those that are no longer needed.

Cost:

Installation time:

- *Finance: pay through automated clearing house transactions.* There is a significant cost associated with creating checks, such as buying the check stock and a printer on which to print them, staff time to conduct printing, envelope stuffing, and mailing. All of these costs can be eliminated if payments are instead made through ACH (Automated Clearing House) transactions, which sends funds straight from the company's bank account to the accounts of its suppliers. This can be difficult to set up unless a company's accounting system is already pre-configured to issue payment transactions to its bank. This best practice works best if there are a small number of suppliers, since it can take a considerable amount of effort to collect bank account information from many suppliers and set them up for ACH payments.

Cost:

Installation time:

- *Finance: set up a zero balance account.* In order to invest the maximum amount of excess funds, a company must clear the cash out of all of its checking accounts every day and shift the funds into some sort of interest-bearing account. This is a very labor-intensive task, and also is likely to be forgotten from time to time, resulting in less income from invested funds as well as a high cost associated with the transaction. A better approach is to have the bank set up a zero balance account, which parks all funds in an interest-bearing account that is tied back to the corporate checking account. Only enough funds are automatically shifted into the checking account to ensure that those checks being presented for payment each day will be cleared. By using this automated approach, a company can avoid the cost of manually shifting funds between accounts, and also benefit from increased investment income.

Cost:

Installation time:

- *Financial statements: automate recurring journal entries.* Some journal entries that are created each month as part of the financial statement production process are unlikely to change from month to month. For example, a standard amortization or depreciation expense will not change from period to period unless the underlying amount of assets is altered. Rather than manually re-entering these journal entries in each accounting period, one can use a common feature in most accounting software packages that provides for the repetitive automatic creation of selected journal entries for as far into the future as specified. This reduces the labor associated with the closing process, and also ensures that recurring entries will not accidentally be skipped.

Cost:

Installation time:

- *Financial statements: conduct an on-line bank reconciliation.* Some of the larger national and super-regional banks have created either dial-up or Internet access to detailed bank account information for their customers. This is a considerable benefit from the perspective of completing the monthly bank reconciliation, since the accounting staff can now review the bank's detailed records as frequently as each day, and conduct an ongoing bank reconciliation. This will not only ensure that company records exactly match bank records at all times, but also eliminates the need to wait for the formal bank statement to be mailed to the company at the end of the month before the closing process is completed, thereby speeding up the production of accurate financial statements.

Cost:

Installation time: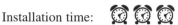

- *Financial statements: create a closing itinerary.* The production of financial statements in an orderly manner requires a tightly scheduled process that interlinks the activities of a number of people. It is very difficult to manage this process without a formal document that itemizes each step in the process, who is responsible for each step, and when each step should be completed. The steps required for the closing process are described in Chapter 24. One should also regularly revise the closing itinerary to reflect ongoing changes in the closing process that are improving its speed and accuracy.

Cost:

Installation time:

- *Financial statements: reduce the number of accruals.* An accounting staff that is excessively focused on achieving perfect accuracy in its financial statements can create a large number of accruals. However, accruals can take a great deal of research to prepare, and interfere with the timely closing of the accounting records. It is better to ignore those smaller accruals that will have only a minimal impact on the financial statements, and concentrate on completing a smaller number of key accruals, thereby improving the overall speed of closing.

Cost:

Installation time:

- *Financial statements: reduce the number of variances investigated.* Whenever a preliminary version of the financial statements is completed, there will be a large number of possible variances from the budget or historical records that the accounting staff could investigate before closing the accounting books. Such investigation takes a great deal of time, so pursuing all possible variance analyses will interfere with the timely closing of the books. To avoid this trouble, the accounting manager should create a rule that forbids all variance analysis if variances fall below a standard dollar or percentage amount. If there still appears to be reason for further review of smaller variances, this can be done *after* the financial statements have been produced, with any resulting changes being recorded in the next accounting period.

Cost:

Installation time:

- *Financial statements: use standardized journal entries.* The majority of journal entries that are made each month are similar in format to those made in previous months; they involve the same account numbers, and may even use the same debits and credits, though the dollar figures may change. Re-creating these entries every month requires time and runs the risk of making an error. To avoid these problems, one can create either automated or paper-based standard journal entry forms that are cross-referenced in the closing checklist. By doing so, the accounting staff can verify that all required journal entries have been completed, and that the same journal entry format is used during every closing process.

  Cost:

  Installation time:

- *General ledger: copy the chart of accounts for all subsidiaries.* The consolidation of accounting results for all corporate subsidiaries can be quite a chore if each one uses a different chart of accounts. A mapping table is needed to convert each subsidiary's results into the format used by the corporate parent. Though the mapping table can be incorporated into a reasonably advanced computerized general ledger, it is much simpler to require all subsidiaries to use the same chart of accounts. However, this best practice requires a considerable amount of time to implement, since all subsidiaries must have input into the account structure used; just because the corporate parent prefers to use a particular format does not mean that the businesses it owns can easily dovetail the results of their operations into the same format.

  Cost:

  Installation time: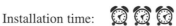

- *General ledger: eliminate small-balance accounts.* Over time, there is a tendency to add accounts to the general ledger in order to track special types of expenses. However, many of these expenses are so small in amount that the resulting information does not justify the added cost of tracking the additional account. Consequently, it is best to periodically review the amount of funds being stored in all accounts, and eliminate those that are too small.

  Cost:

  Installation time: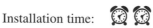

- *General ledger: reduce the number of line items in the chart of accounts.* As noted in the preceding best practice, one can regularly eliminate accounts that experience excessively small amounts of activity. This process can be taken a step further by merging larger accounts together if there is no good reason for separating the information contained within the accounts. For example, there may be a dozen different types of work-in-process inventory that are recorded in different accounts, but the separated information is not used by anyone. Consequently, a general ongoing best practice is to continually examine the chart of accounts with the objective of shrinking it down to only those accounts that are necessary for significant reporting purposes.

Cost:

Installation time:

- *General ledger: store operating data in the general ledger.* When financial statements are produced, they frequently contain operating data, such as headcount, sales backlog dollars, and production capacity. To ensure that this information is reliably stored and readily accessible, extra fields can be created in many general ledger software packages that allow for the storage of alphanumeric information. One can then store operating data in these fields. This is an inexpensive form of data warehouse.

Cost:

Installation time:

- *Inventory: institute cycle counting.* When inventory balances are continually inaccurate, the accounting manager may be uncomfortable with the concept of reporting financial results without first conducting a complete inventory count. This is a very time-consuming and expensive approach that also does not yield completely accurate information. It also slows down the production of financial statements. A better approach is to authorize the warehouse manager to send a counting person through the warehouse on a continual basis to compare perpetual inventory records to what is physically on hand, and to delve into the reasons why there are differences between the two types of data. By doing so, the level of inventory accuracy will always be sufficiently high to avoid the need for a physical inventory count, while there will also be much more attention paid to the reasons why inventory accuracy errors are occurring.

Cost:

Installation time: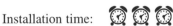

- *Inventory: measure inventory accuracy.* The accounting staff will never be sure of the extent to which the inventory is accurate unless it conducts periodic measurements. To do so, someone must select a random sample of inventory items in the warehouse and trace them back to the perpetual inventory database, and vice versa. Any errors in quantity, location, unit of measure, or description should be counted as an incorrect inventory record. By calculating this measurement at a minimum of once a month, the accounting staff will know if the accuracy level has fallen to the point where a physical inventory count will be needed in order to ensure accurate financial results.

Cost:

Installation time:

- *Inventory: move inventory to floor stock.* Counting the entire inventory in the warehouse is a substantial chore. The most difficult items to count tend to be the smallest and least expensive, such as fittings and fasteners. To avoid counting these items, one can expense them when purchased and shift them to inventory storage bins near the manufacturing area. By doing so, the production staff will also have much better access to the parts, and will no longer waste time requisitioning them from the warehouse. Offsetting these advantages is the added cost of some pilferage of the items (since they are no longer protected within the confines of the warehouse), as well as some increased tracking difficulty by the purchasing staff, which can no longer rely on perpetual inventory records to determine when additional fittings and fasteners must be purchased.

Cost:

Installation time:

- *Inventory: report on part usage levels.* The most common way to determine inventory obsolescence is to query the warehouse staff about which inventory items appear to be the oldest. This is a decidedly non-scientific approach. A better method is to create several computerized reports that are linked to the perpetual inventory records and the bills of material. These reports will reveal the time period since the last inventory item was requisitioned from stock, as well as the parts that are not used on any bills of material. Both reports clearly indicate which inventory items are at risk of obsolescence, and are also excellent tools for determining which items are candidates for returns to suppliers.

Cost:

Installation time:

- *Inventory: restrict access to the warehouse.* When the warehouse is open to all employees, it is essentially impossible to maintain an accurate inventory. The reason is that employees with no responsibility for inventory accuracy will take parts without removing them from the inventory database. Consequently, a fence must be constructed around the entire warehouse area, with access being strictly limited to warehouse personnel at all times of the day or night. This is an essential requirement for inventory accuracy.

Cost:

Installation time: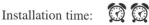

- *Inventory: segregate customer-owned inventory.* The total inventory valuation can be overstated if customer-owned inventory is mixed into it. This occurs when a company manufactures products that require attachments that are provided by customers. To avoid the problem, it is best to create a fenced-off area within the warehouse whose only use is to store customer-owned inventory. Another option is to create a different set of inventory identification codes for this inventory, so that all inventory valuation reports will automatically set the valuation for these items at zero.

Cost:

Installation time:

- *Inventory: update bill of material records based on extra warehouse issuances and returns.* Bills of material are commonly used as the basis for issuing parts from the warehouse to the production floor. For example, if 10 units of a product are to be created, then the warehouse multiplies all of the parts listed on that product's bill of materials by 10 and issues that many items to the production department. However, this can cause problems for the production staff if the bills of material are inaccurate. A good way to correct the bills is to carefully track the number of special requisitions made by the production staff for additional parts, as well as returns from them, since this is a clear indicator of inaccuracies in the bill of material records. By doing so, a company can also eliminate production delays due to parts shortages, while also avoiding rush delivery costs to bring in additional parts on short notice.

Cost:

Installation time:

- *Invoicing: computerize the shipping log.* There can be a delay of one or more days in invoicing customers because of the time required for the shipping staff to complete its shipping documentation and deliver it to the accounting department. There is also a risk that some of the paperwork will be lost in transit. To avoid these problems, the shipping staff should be equipped with a computer terminal that allows them to directly enter shipping information into the accounting database. Armed with this data, the accounting staff can issue invoices much more quickly.

Cost:

Installation time:

- *Invoicing: delivery person creates the invoice.* Invoices sent to customers may require subsequent correction with credits if the customer disagrees with the quantity delivered, or rejects some items based on quality issues. Since it takes a great deal of time for the accounting staff to complete these corrections, a better approach is to have the delivery person create an invoice at the point of delivery that contains the quantities to which the customer has already agreed. This eliminates the need for subsequent adjustments. However, this best practice requires a company to have its own employees make deliveries, and also calls for a portable computer and printer for the use of each delivery person. There can also be control problems, since the delivery person may collude with the recipient to bill for a smaller quantity than is actually delivered.

Cost:

Installation time:

- *Invoicing: issue electronic data interchange invoices.* Sending a paper invoice requires that it be sent through the mail, which introduces a time lag before it reaches the recipient. In addition, it may be lost in the mail, mis-routed once it arrives at the target company, or some data on it may be incorrectly keyed into the customer's accounts payable system. To avoid all of these problems, one can issue invoices by electronic data interchange, which involves filling out a standardized transaction form and e-mailing it either directly to the customer or to a third party organization that maintains an electronic mailbox on behalf of the customer. This approach ensures that invoices will reach customers at once, and can be verified by the return transmission of an acknowledgment of receipt. This method works best when EDI transmission software is directly linked to the billing system, so that invoices will be issued automatically.

Cost:

Installation time:

- *Invoicing: issue single-period invoices.* When a company sells products at very low prices, such as nuts and bolts, the cost of the invoice to the customer may be more than the cost of the products. In these instances, it makes more sense to only issue a single invoice at the end of each month, rather than a series of small invoices. Though this saves on invoicing costs, it will shift cash flows from accounts receivable farther into the future, due to the delay in billings. To avoid this problem, one should also look into shortening the payment terms listed on the invoices.

Cost:

Installation time:

- *Invoicing: reduce the number of invoice parts printed.* When invoices are printed, there may be several copies that go to the customer, another that is filed alphabetically, another that is filed numerically, and yet another that is sent to the collections staff. This requires an expensive multi-part form, as well as greater filing costs and a virtual blizzard of paperwork within the accounting department. It is better to reduce the number of invoice parts to the absolute minimum required. This may include sending just one invoice copy to the customer, and retaining one other copy for internal reference purposes.

Cost:

Installation time:

- *Management: create a policies and procedures manual.* Though a highly experienced accounting staff may know its tasks by heart and require no written manual, this is not the case when new employees are added to the department or tasks are swapped within the existing staff. When this happens, there is no documentation available that can be used as a basis for training, resulting in slow improvements in knowledge and lots of mistakes in the interim. A policies and procedures manual also improves the level of transactional consistency between the accounting operations of multiple subsidiaries, since their procedures would otherwise tend to diverge over time. It is also possible to issue the manual over the company intranet, which greatly reduces the cost of distribution and the frequency of updates.

  Cost: 💵💵

  Installation time: ⏰⏰⏰

- *Management: create a staff training schedule.* When new employees are hired into the accounting department, they are typically given enough training to perform their jobs, and nothing more. Instead, a training schedule should be tailored to the needs of each employee, so that each is cross-trained in the tasks of other employees, and also learns about process improvement to constantly enhance the transactions for which they are already responsible. This does not mean that all employees require extensive funding to take college courses, but rather that a company develop a mix of seminars, readings, and outside courses that will meet its own particular training needs.

  Cost: 💵💵

  Installation time: ⏰⏰

- *Management: issue a monthly schedule of activities.* The accounting staff is driven by a specific schedule of activities to an extent greater than that of any other department—it must pay taxes on certain dates, process payroll on other dates, issue financial statements on still other dates, and so on. It is a rare case when all of these dates can be memorized, and so some items will occasionally not be completed on time. To avoid this situation, there should be a standard calendar of activities that is updated at the end of each month and issued to the entire accounting staff, with the due dates of each recipient highlighted on it. This requires constant updating as requirements change.

  Cost: 💵

  Installation time: ⏰⏰

- *Management: measure key departmental performance items.* The accounting manager does not have any idea whether the performance of the accounting department is improving or degrading over time unless there is a set of measurements that can be used to create a trend line of performance. This may involve meeting due dates earlier, such as issuing financial statements in two days instead of three, or creating fewer transactional errors. The measurement list should be relatively short, so that attention can be focused on just those few issues that are most crucial to departmental performance. Other measures can be added over time, as original measurement targets are met or exceeded. This can also be a useful tool for setting up performance-based pay changes for employees.

Cost:

Installation time: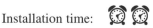

- *Management: outsource selected functions.* Some accounting functions are of such a technical nature, or are so prone to error, that it may be easier to let an experienced supplier handle them instead. A commonly outsourced function is payroll, which can be shifted to a supplier that will not only calculate payroll and issue checks, but also issue management reports related to payroll, as well as pay various governing authorities all associated payroll taxes. Other functions that can be outsourced include collections, accounts payable, the production of financial statements, and local, state, and federal taxes. The downside to these services is that they cost more than they would if they were handled internally, and they require some oversight by the accounting manager to ensure that they are handled properly.

Cost:

Installation time: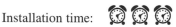

- *Management: review process flows.* Most processes are altered over time as variations occur in the way a company does business. The result is a patchwork of inefficient steps that increase both the time and cost of doing business. This can be avoided by flowcharting the process behind each accounting transaction and then reviewing it over time to see if it can be streamlined. Though this requires some skill in examining process flows, the result can be significant reductions in the cost of transaction processing.

Cost:

Installation time: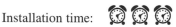

- *Payroll: automate vacation accruals.* Accruing and tracking vacation time for employees can be full of errors, for each employee may have been awarded a different vacation period, become employed at a different date during the year, or have some vacation carry-forward from the previous year. To avoid these problems, some payroll outsourcing companies and most high-end payroll software packages contain features that allow one to set up standard vacation accruals for each employee. They can factor in vacation carry-forwards as well as individual employee start dates. The only trouble with this best practice is that a company must still manually accumulate and deduct vacation time taken, so that employees can see their net vacation time available. This information will typically be added to their pay stubs.

Cost:

Installation time:

- *Payroll: collect time worked data through an automated time clock.* The collection of hours worked by hourly employees for the purposes of paying them and tracking hours charged to specific jobs is among the most time-consuming and error-filled transactions in the accounting profession. These problems are caused by the manual timecard entries that must be interpreted by payroll clerks into hours worked for each employee—frequently involving missing, false, or unreadable entries. To avoid these problems, a company can invest in electronic time clocks. Under this system, employees are issued bar coded or magnetic stripe cards, which they slide through a slot on the clock when they are clocking in or out. This action triggers a time entry that is sent to a central payroll computer, where the time entries are stored. Missing scans are noted on management reports, so that they can be fixed before the payroll processing date. By using this approach, there is only a minimal need for data correction, thereby eliminating much of the work by payroll clerks. However, these clocks can cost $2,000 each, and so can only be justified if there are currently many payroll errors or a large staff of payroll clerks that can be eliminated.

Cost:

Installation time:

- *Payroll: eliminate deductions from paychecks for employee purchases.* Employees sometimes buy products for themselves through the company's purchasing department in order to take advantage of the lower prices offered to the company. When this happens, they may ask that the cost of the purchased items be gradually deducted from their paychecks. This means that the accounting staff must determine the amount of periodic deductions, as well as when the deductions must stop—all of which takes up valuable accounting time. It is better to create a policy that no employee purchases will be allowed (or at least that employees must pay for all purchases themselves, without deductions), thereby keeping extra deduction-related work away from the payroll staff.

Cost:

Installation time:

- *Payroll: integrate the 401(k) plan into the payroll system.* The typical 401(k) plan is operated separately from the payroll system, so either the accounting or human resources staff must manually compile payroll and 401(k) participation information, summarize this data into a separate spreadsheet, and send it to the 401(k) administration firm. To avoid this task, some payroll outsourcing companies now offer 401(k) plans that are integrated into their payroll systems. This means that all data collection tasks for 401(k) reporting are fully automated and handled directly by the supplier, rather than the accounting department. However, switching this task to the payroll supplier can be expensive, since it will charge a setup fee as well as ongoing administration fees.

Cost:

Installation time: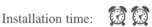

- *Payroll: pay employees with direct deposit.* There is no significant difference in efficiencies when a company pays its employees with a check or direct deposit, since the company must still deliver to each employee either a paper check or a deposit advice. Direct deposit may even be slightly more expensive, since there may be a small ACH transfer fee associated with each deposit. Nonetheless, the use of direct deposit is generally welcomed by employees, who appreciate not having to physically travel to a bank to deposit payments. It is particularly useful for employees who travel, since they may not be in a position to cash their checks until well after pay dates, and no longer have to worry about cash shortages when direct deposits are used.

Cost:

Installation time:

- *Payroll: reduce the number of payrolls per year.* Every time that a payroll cycle is processed, the payroll staff must accumulate all hours worked, deduction information, and other payroll data, summarize it into either an in-house payroll system or send it to a supplier, and then issue checks to employees. This effort can be reduced by shrinking the number of payrolls that are processed each year. The best alternatives are to process either 24 or 26 payrolls per year. Twenty-six payrolls tend to work better if there are a number of hourly employees, since payrolls will correspond to their weekly timekeeping system. If there are mostly salaried employees, then 24 payrolls can be used, since processing dates will correspond to the end of each month, making it unnecessary to create a salary accrual for hours worked but not paid at the end of each month.

Cost:

Installation time: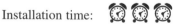

- *Payroll: restrict prepayments.* Some employees who travel will request an advance on their paychecks prior to taking trips, so that they will have enough funds to pay for travel costs. This requires that the accounting staff track the amount of all advances, as well as their later deduction from expense reports. It is a system that is highly subject to abuse, since employee advances may never be deducted from expense reports or employees may leave without reimbursing the company. The same problem arises when employees request advances on their paychecks for personal reasons. To avoid these problems, a policy can be created that forbids the use of prepayments. Instead, company purchasing cards can be issued to employees who travel, so that all travel charges are paid directly by the company. If employees want advances on their pay, the company can direct them to a local finance company.

Cost:

Installation time:

22-3 SUMMARY

There are thousands of best practices that a company can use to enhance its accounting operations. The best practices noted here are only some of the more common ones currently in use. To acquire information about additional best practices, one can attend seminars that deal specifically with this issue. Another source of information is accounting periodicals, which sometimes contain articles about how other companies have implemented improvements to their systems. This source is particularly useful, because the articles may include information about how to reach the author, so that additional information can be gleaned about specific best practices. Also, local accounting organizations may sometimes sponsor presentations from members at other companies who have installed system enhancements. Finally, a multi-division company may contain a number of accounting departments, any of which may have unique best practices that would be useful. Thus, one must tap into a number of data resources in order to obtain information about additional best practices.

CHAPTER 23

Budgeting

23-1 INTRODUCTION

Budgeting is one of the most important activities that an accountant can engage in, for it provides the basis for the orderly management of activities within a company. A properly created budget will funnel funding into those activities that a company has determined to be most essential, as defined in its strategic plan. Furthermore, it provides a bridge between strategy and tactics by itemizing the precise tactical events that will be funded, such as the hiring of personnel or acquisition of equipment in a key department. Once the budget has been approved, it also acts as the primary control point over expenditures, since it should be compared to purchase requisitions prior to purchases being made, so that the level of allowed funding can be ascertained. In addition, the results of specific departments can be compared to their budgets, which is an excellent tool for determining the performance of department managers. For all of these reasons, a comprehensive knowledge of the budgeting process is crucial for the accountant.

In this chapter, we will look at the system of budgets and how they are linked together, review a sample budget, cover the key elements of flex budgeting, address the processes required to construct a budget, and finish with coverage of the control systems that can be used if a budget is available.

23-2 THE SYSTEM OF INTERLOCKING BUDGETS

A properly designed budget is a complex web of spreadsheets that account for the activities of virtually all areas within a company. As noted in Exhibit 23-1, the budget begins in two places, with both the revenue budget and research and development budget. The revenue budget contains the revenue figures that the company believes it can achieve for each upcoming reporting period. These estimates come partially from the sales staff, which is responsible for estimates of sales levels for existing products within their current territo-

Exhibit 23-1 The System of Budgets

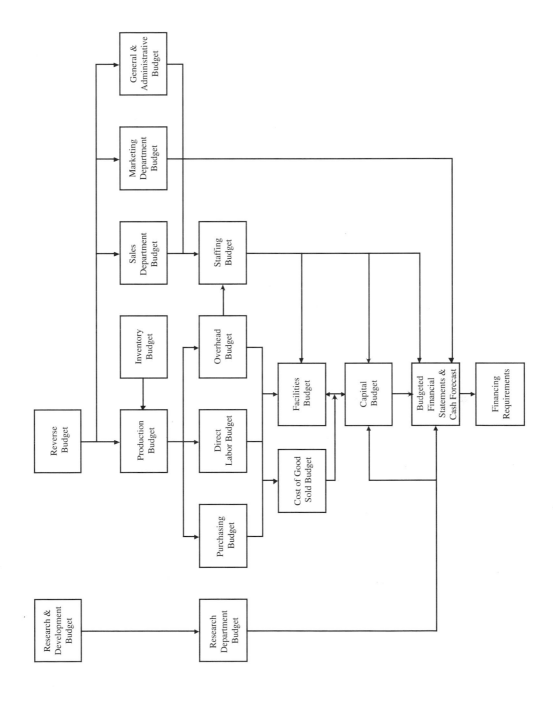

ries. Estimates for the sales of new products that have not yet been released and for existing products in new markets will come from a combination of the sales and marketing staffs, who will use their experience with related product sales to derive estimates. The greatest fallacy in any budget is to impose a revenue budget from the top management level without any input from the sales staff, since this can result in a company-wide budget that is geared toward a sales level that is most unlikely to be reached.

A revenue budget requires prior consideration of a number of issues. For example, a general market share target will drive several other items within the budget, since greater market share may come at the cost of lower unit prices or higher credit costs. Another issue is the compensation strategy for the sales staff, since a shift to higher or lower commissions for specific products or regions will be a strong incentive for the sales staff to alter their selling behavior, resulting in some changes in estimated sales levels. Yet another consideration is which sales territories are to be entered during the budget period—those with high target populations may yield very high sales per hour of sales effort, while the reverse will be true if the remaining untapped regions have smaller target populations. It is also necessary to review the price points that will be offered during the budget period, especially in relation to the pricing strategies that are anticipated from competitors. If there is a strategy to increase market share as well as to raise unit prices, then the budget may fail due to conflicting activities. Another major factor is the terms of sale, which can be extended, along with easy credit, to attract more marginal customers; conversely, they can be retracted in order to reduce credit costs and focus company resources on a few key customers. A final point is that the budget should address any changes in the type of customer to whom sales will be made. If an entirely new type of customer will be added to the range of sales targets during the budget period, then the revenue budget should reflect a gradual ramp-up that will be required for the sales staff to work through the sales cycle of the new customers.

Once all of these factors have been ruminated upon and combined to create a preliminary budget, the sales staff should also compare the budgeted sales level per person to the actual sales level that has been experienced in the recent past to see if the company has the existing capability to make the budgeted sales. If not, the revenue budget should be ramped up to reflect the time it will take to hire and train additional sales staff. The same cross-check can be conducted for the amount of sales budgeted per customer, to see if historical experience validates the sales levels noted in the new budget.

Another budget that initiates other activities within the system of budgets is the research and development budget. This is not related to the sales level at all (as opposed to most other budgets), but instead is a discretionary budget that is based on the company's strategy to derive new or improved products. The decision to fund a certain amount of project-related activity in this area will drive a departmental staffing and capital budget that is, for the most part, completely unrelated to the activity conducted by the rest of the company. However, there can be a feedback loop between this budget and the cash budget, since financing limitations may require management to prune some projects from this area. If so, the management team must work with the research and development manager to determine the correct mix of projects with both short-range and long-range payoffs that will still be funded. This is as much an art as a science, though the process can be helped along by a capital budgeting evaluation, as described in Chapter 27, Financial Analysis.

The production budget is largely driven by the sales estimates contained within the revenue budget. However, it is also driven by the inventory-level assumptions in the inventory budget. The inventory budget contains estimates by the materials management supervisor regarding the inventory levels that will be required for the upcoming budget period. For example, a new goal may be to reduce the level of finished goods inventory from 10 turns per year to 15. If so, some of the products required by the revenue budget can be bled off from the existing finished goods inventory stock, requiring smaller production requirements during the budget period. Alternatively, if there is a strong focus on improving the level of customer service, then it may be necessary to keep more finished goods in stock, which will require more production than is strictly called for by the revenue budget. This concept can also be extended to work-in-process (WIP) inventory, where the installation of advanced production planning systems, such as manufacturing resources planning or just-in-time, can be used to reduce the level of required inventory. Also, just-in-time purchasing techniques can be used to reduce the amount of raw materials inventory that is kept on hand. All of these assumptions should be clearly delineated in the inventory budget, so that the management team is clear about what systemic changes will be required in order to effect altered inventory turnover levels. Also, one should be aware that any advanced production planning system takes a considerable amount of time to install and tune, so it is best if the inventory budget contains a gradual ramp-up to different planned levels of inventory.

Given this input from the inventory budget, the production budget is used to derive the unit quantity of required products that must be manufactured in order to meet revenue targets for each budget period. This involves a number of inter-related factors, such as the availability of sufficient capacity for production needs. Of particular concern should be the amount of capacity at the bottleneck operation. Since this tends to be the most expensive capital item, it is important to budget a sufficient quantity of funding to ensure that this operation includes enough equipment to meet the targeted production goals. If the bottleneck operation involves skilled labor, rather than equipment, then the human resources staff should be consulted regarding its ability to bring in the necessary personnel in time to improve the bottleneck capacity in a timely manner.

Another factor that drives the budgeted costs contained within the production budget is the anticipated size of production batches. If the batch size is expected to decrease, then more overhead costs should be budgeted in the production scheduling, materials handling, and machine setup staffing areas. If longer batch sizes are planned, then there may be a possibility of proportionally reducing overhead costs in these areas. This is a key consideration that is frequently overlooked, but which can have an outsized impact on overhead costs. If management attempts to contain overhead costs in this area while still using smaller batch sizes, then it will likely run into larger scrap quantities and quality issues that are caused by rushed batch setups and the allocation of incorrect materials to production jobs.

Step costing is also an important consideration when creating the production budget. Costs will increase in large increments when certain capacity levels are reached. The management team should be fully aware of when these capacity levels will be reached, so that it can plan appropriately for the incurrence of added costs. For example, the addition of a second shift to the production area will call for added costs in the areas of supervisory staff, an increased pay rate, and higher maintenance costs. The inverse of this condition can also occur, where step costs can decline suddenly if capacity levels fall below a specific point.

Production levels may also be affected by any lengthy tooling setups or changeovers to replacement equipment. These changes may halt all production for extended periods, and so must be carefully planned for. This is the responsibility of the industrial engineering staff. The accountant would do well to review the company's history of actual equipment setup times to see if the current engineering estimates are sufficiently lengthy, based on past history.

The expense items included in the production budget should be driven by a set of subsidiary budgets, which are the purchasing, direct labor, and overhead budgets. These budgets can simply be included in the production budget, but they typically involve such a large proportion of company costs that it is best to lay them out separately in greater detail in separate budgets. Specific comments on these budgets are:

- *Purchasing budget.* The purchasing budget is driven by several factors, first of which is the bill of materials that comprises the products that are planned for production during the budget period. These bills must be accurate, or else the purchasing budget can include seriously incorrect information. In addition, there should be a plan for controlling material costs, perhaps through the use of concentrated buying through few suppliers, or perhaps through the use of long-term contracts. If materials are highly subject to market pressures, comprise a large proportion of total product costs, and have a history of sharp price swings, then a best case and worst case costing scenario should be added to the budget, so that managers can review the impact of costing issues in this area. If a just-in-time delivery system from suppliers is contemplated, then the purchasing budget should reflect a possible increase in material costs caused by the increased number of deliveries from suppliers. It is also worthwhile to budget for a raw material scrap and obsolescence expense; there should be a history of costs in these areas that can be extrapolated based on projected purchasing volumes.

- *Direct labor budget.* One should not make the mistake of budgeting for direct labor as a fully variable cost. The production volume from day to day tends to be relatively fixed, and requires a set number of direct labor personnel on a continuing basis to operate production equipment and manually assemble products. Further, the production manager will realize much greater production efficiencies by holding onto an experienced production staff, rather than letting them go as soon as production volumes make small incremental drops. Accordingly, it is better to budget based on reality, which is that direct labor personnel are usually retained, even if there are ongoing fluctuations in the level of production. Thus, direct labor should be shown in the budget as a fixed cost of production, within certain production volume parameters.

  Also, this budget should describe staffing levels by type of direct labor position; this is driven by labor routings, which are documents that describe the exact type and quantity of staffing needed to produce a product. When multiplied by the unit volumes located in the production budget, this results in an expected level of staffing by direct labor position. This information is most useful for the human resources staff, which is responsible for staffing the positions.

  The direct labor budget should also account for any contractually mandated changes in hourly rates, which may be itemized in a union agreement. Such an agreement may also have restrictions on layoffs, which should be accounted for in the budget if this will keep labor levels from dropping in proportion budgeted reductions in production levels. Such an agreement may also require that layoffs be conducted in order of seniority, which may force higher-paid employees into positions that would normally be budgeted for less expensive laborers. Thus, the presence of a union contract can result in a much more complex direct labor budget than would normally be the case.

The direct labor budget may also contain features related to changes in the efficiency of employees, and any resulting changes in pay. For example, one possible pay arrangement is to pay employees based on a piece rate, which directly ties their performance to the level of production achieved. If so, this will probably only apply to portions of the workforce, so the direct labor budget may involve pay rates based on both piece rates and hourly pay. Another issue is that any drastic increases in the budgeted level of direct labor personnel will likely result in some initial declines in labor efficiency, since it takes time for new employees to learn their tasks. If this is the case, the budget should reflect a low level of initial efficiency, with a ramp-up over time to higher levels that will result in greater initial direct labor costs. Finally, efficiency improvements may be rewarded with staff bonuses from time to time; if so, these bonuses should be included in the budget.

- *Overhead budget.* The overhead budget can be a simple one to create if there are no significant changes in production volume from the preceding year, because this involves a large quantity of static costs that will not vary much over time. Included in this category are machine maintenance, utilities, supervisory salaries, wages for the materials management, production scheduling, and quality assurance personnel, facilities maintenance, and depreciation expenses. Under the no-change scenario, the most likely budgetary alterations will be to machinery or facilities maintenance, which is dependent on the condition and level of usage of company property.

   If there is a significant change in the expected level of production volume, or if new production lines are to be added, then one should examine this budget in great detail, for the underlying production volumes may cause a ripple effect that results in wholesale changes to many areas of the overhead budget. Of particular concern is the number of overhead-related personnel who must be either laid off or added when capacity levels reach certain critical points, such as the addition or subtraction of extra work shifts. Costs also tend to rise substantially when a facility is operating at very close to 100% capacity, because maintaining a high level of capacity on an ongoing basis tends to call for an inordinate amount of effort.

The purchasing, direct labor, and overhead budgets can then be summarized into a cost of goods sold budget. This budget should incorporate, as a single line item, the total amount of revenue, so that all manufacturing costs can be deducted from it to yield a gross profit margin on the same document. This budget is referred to constantly during the budget creation process, since it tells management whether its budgeting assumptions are yielding an acceptable gross margin result. Since it is a summary-level budget for the production side of the budgeting process, this is also a good place to itemize any production-related statistics, such as the average hourly cost of direct labor, inventory turnover rates, and the amount of revenue dollars per production person.

Thus far, we have reviewed the series of budgets that descend in turn from the revenue budget and then through the production budget. However, there are other expenses that are unrelated to production. These are categories in a separate set of budgets. The first is the sales department budget. This includes the expenses that the sales staff must incur in order to achieve the revenue budget, such as travel and entertainment, as well as sales training. Of particular concern in this budget is the amount of budgeted headcount that is required to meet the sales target. It is essential that the actual sales per salesperson from the most recent completed year of operations be compared to the same calculation in the budget to ensure that there is a sufficiently large budget available for an adequate number of sales personnel. This is a common problem, for companies will make the false assumption that the existing sales staff can make heroic efforts to wildly exceed its previous-year sales efforts. Furthermore, the budget must account for a sufficient time period in which new sales personnel can be trained and form an adequate base of customer contacts to create a meaningful stream of revenue for the company. In some industries, this learning curve may be only a few days, but it can be the better part of a year if considerable technical knowledge is required to make a sale. If the latter situation is the case, it is likely that the procurement and retention of qualified sales staff is the key element of success for a company, which makes the sales department budget one of the most important elements of the entire budget.

The marketing budget is also closely tied to the revenue budget, for it contains all of the funding required to roll out new products, merchandise them properly, advertise for them, test new products, and so on. A key issue here is to ensure that the marketing budget is fully funded to support any increases in sales noted in the revenue budget. It may be necessary to increase this budget by a disproportionate amount if one is trying to create a new brand, issue a new product, or distribute an existing product in a new market. These costs can easily exceed any associated revenues for some time. A common budgeting problem is not to provide sufficient funding in these instances, leading to a significant drop in expected revenues.

Another non-production budget that is integral to the success of the corporation is the general and administrative budget. This contains the cost of the corporate management staff, plus all accounting, finance, and human resources personnel. Since this is a cost center, the general inclination is to reduce these costs to the bare minimum. However, in order to do so, there must be a significant investment in technology to achieve reductions in the manual labor usually required to process transactions; thus, there must be some provision in the capital budget for this area.

There is a feedback loop between the staffing and direct labor budgets and the general and administrative budget, because the human resources department must staff itself based on the amount of hiring or layoffs that are anticipated elsewhere in the company. Similarly, a major change in the revenue volume will alter the budget for the accounting department, since many of the activities in this area are driven by the volume of sales transactions. Furthermore, a major increase in the capital budget, especially for items requiring prolonged construction activities, will require an investment in additional cost accounting personnel, who will track these expenditures. Thus, the general and administrative budget generally requires a number of iterations in response to changes in many other parts of the budget.

Though salaries and wages should be listed in each of the departmental budgets, it is useful to list the total headcount for each position through all budget periods in a separate staffing budget. By doing so, the human resources staff can tell when specific positions must be filled, so that they can time their recruiting efforts most appropriately. This budget also provides good information for the person responsible for the facilities budget, since he or she can use it to determine the timing and amount of square footage requirements for office space. Rather than being a standalone budget, the staffing budget tends to be one whose formulas are closely intertwined with those of all other departmental budgets, so that a change in headcount information on this budget will automatically translate into a change in the salaries expense on other budgets. It is also a good place to store the average pay rates, overtime percentages, and average benefit costs for all positions. By centralizing this cost information, the human resources staff can more easily update budget information. Since salary-related costs tend to comprise the highest proportion of costs in a company (excluding materials costs), this tends to be a heavily used budget.

The facilities budget is based on the level of activity that is estimated in many of the budgets just described. For this reason, it is one of the last budgets to be completed. This budget is closely linked to the capital budget, since expenditures for additional facilities will require more maintenance expenses in the facilities budget. This budget typically contains expense line items for building insurance, maintenance, repairs, janitorial services, utilities, and the salaries of the maintenance personnel employed in this function. It is crucial to estimate the need for any upcoming major repairs to facilities when constructing this budget, since these can greatly amplify the total budgeted expense.

Another budget that includes input from virtually all areas of a company is the capital budget. This should comprise either a summary listing of all main fixed asset categories for which purchases are anticipated, or else a detailed listing of the same information; the latter case is only recommended if there are comparatively few items to be purchased. The capital budget is of great importance to the calculation of corporate financing requirements, since it can involve the expenditure of sums far beyond those that are normally encountered through daily cash flows. The contents of the capital budget should be carefully examined to determine if it has an impact on a company's bottleneck operation. All too often, expenditures are made that make other operations more efficient, but that do not increase its ability to produce more product by increasing the capacity of the bottleneck operation. For more information about this topic, please refer to the throughput accounting chapter in Bragg, *Cost Accounting,* John Wiley & Sons, 2001. It is also necessary to ensure that capital items are scheduled for procurement sufficiently far in advance of related projects that they will be fully installed and operational before the scheduled first activity date of the project. For example, a budget should not itemize revenue from a printing press for the same month in which the press is scheduled to be purchased, for it may take months to set up the press. A final item is that capital purchases may be tied to the pet projects of senior managers, rather than to the strategic or tactical goals of the company. Consequently, it may be useful to review all capital items in the budget to ensure that they are all needed in order to meet these goals.

The end result of all budgets just described is a set of financial statements that reflect the impact on the company of the upcoming budget. At a minimum, these statements should include the income statement and cash flow statement, since these are the best evidence of fiscal health during the budget period. The balance sheet is less necessary, since the key factors upon which it reports are related to cash, and that information is already contained within the cash flow statement. These reports should be directly linked to all the other budgets, so that any changes to the budgets will immediately appear in the financial statements. The management team will closely examine these statements and make numerous adjustments to the budgets in order to arrive at a satisfactory financial result.

The budget-linked financial statements are also a good place to store related operational and financial ratios, so that the management team can review this information and revise the budgets in order to alter the ratios to match benchmarking or industry standards that may have been set as goals. Typical measurements in this area can include revenue and income per person, inventory turnover ratios, and gross margin percentages. This type of information is also useful for lenders, who may have required minimum financial performance results as part of loan agreements, such as a minimum current ratio or debt-to-equity ratio.

The cash forecast is of exceptional importance, for it tells company managers whether the proposed budget model will be feasible. If cash projects result in major cash needs that cannot be met by any possible financing, then the model must be changed. The assumptions that go into the cash forecast should be based on strictly historical fact, rather than the wishes of managers. This stricture is particularly important in the case of cash receipts from accounts receivable. If the assumptions are changed in the model to reflect an advanced rate of cash receipts that exceeds anything that the company has heretofore experienced, then it is very unlikely that it will be achieved during the budget period. Instead, it is better to use proven collection periods as assumptions and alter other parts of the budget to ensure that cash flows remain positive.

The cash forecast is a particularly good area in which to spot the impact of changes in credit policy. For example, if a company wishes to expand its share of the market by allowing easy credit to marginal customers, then it should lengthen the assumed collection period in the cash forecast to see if there is a significant downgrading of the resulting cash flows.

The other key factor in the cash forecast is the use of delays in budgeted accounts payable payments. It is common for managers to budget for extended payment terms in order to fund other cash flow needs, but several problems can result from this policy. One is the possible loss of key suppliers who will not tolerate late payments. Another is the risk of being charged interest on late payments to suppliers. A third problem is that suppliers may relegate a company to a lower level on their lists of shipment priorities, since they are being paid late. Finally, suppliers may simply raise their prices in order to absorb the cost of the late payments. Consequently, the late payment strategy must be followed with great care, only using it on those suppliers who do not appear to notice, and otherwise only doing it after prior negotiation with targeted suppliers to make the changed terms part of the standard buying agreement.

The last document in the system of budgets is the discussion of financing alternatives. This is not strictly a budget, though it will contain a single line item, derived from the cash forecast, which itemizes funding needs during each period itemized in the budget. In all other respects, it is simply a discussion of financing alternatives, which can be quite varied. This may involve a mix of debt, supplier financing, preferred stock, common stock, or some other, more innovative approach. The document should contain a discussion of the cost of each form of financing, the ability of the company to obtain it, and when it can be obtained. Managers may find that there are so few financing alternatives available, or that the cost of financing is so high, that the entire budget must be restructured in order to avoid the negative cash flow that calls for the financing. There may also be a need for feedback from this document back into the budgeted financial statements in order to account for the cost of obtaining the funding, as well as any related interest costs.

In the next section, we will review an example of the budgets that have just been described, to see how they are formatted and link together to result in a cohesive set of budgets that can be used to conduct a business's future operations.

23-3 A SAMPLE BUDGET

In this section, we will review several variations on how a budget can be constructed, using a number of examples. The first budget covered is the revenue budget, which is shown in Exhibit 23-2. The exhibit uses quarterly revenue figures for a budget year rather than monthly, in order to conserve space. It contains revenue estimates for three different product lines that are designated as Alpha, Beta, and Charlie.

The Alpha product line uses a budgeting format that identifies the specific quantities that are expected to be sold in each quarter, as well as the average price per unit sold. This format is most useful when there are not so many products that such a detailed delineation would create an excessively lengthy budget. It is a very useful format, for the sales staff can go into the budget model and alter unit volumes and prices quite easily. An alter-

Exhibit 23-2   The Revenue Budget

Revenue Budget for the Fiscal Year Ended xx/xx/02					
	Quarter 1	*Quarter 2*	*Quarter 3*	*Quarter 4*	*Totals*
Product Line Alpha:					
Unit price	$ 15.00	$ 14.85	$ 14.80	$ 14.75	—
Unit volume	14,000	21,000	25,000	31,000	91,000
Revenue subtotal	$ 210,000	$ 311,850	$ 370,000	$ 457,250	$1,349,100
Product Line Beta:					
Revenue subtotal	$1,048,000	$1,057,000	$1,061,000	$1,053,000	$4,219,000
Product Line Charlie:					
Region 1	$ 123,000	$ 95,000	$ 82,000	$ 70,000	$ 370,000
Region 2	$ 80,000	$ 89,000	$ 95,000	$ 101,000	$ 365,000
Region 3	$ 95,000	$ 95,000	$ 65,000	$ 16,000	$ 271,000
Region 4	$ 265,000	$ 265,000	$ 320,000	$ 375,000	$1,225,000
Revenue subtotal	$ 563,000	$ 544,000	$ 562,000	$ 562,000	$2,231,000
Revenue grand total	$1,821,000	$1,912,850	$1,993,000	$2,072,250	$7,799,100
Quarterly revenue proportion	23%	24.5%	25.6%	26.6%	100.0%
Statistics:					
Product line proportion:					
Alpha	11.5%	16.3%	18.6%	22.1%	17.3%
Beta	57.6%	55.3%	53.2%	50.8%	54.1%
Charlie	30.9%	28.4%	28.2%	27.1%	28.6%
Product line total	100.0%	100.0%	100.0%	100.0%	100.0%

native format is to only reveal this level of detail for the most important products, and to lump the revenue from other products into a single line item, as is the case for the Beta product line.

The most common budgeting format is used for the Beta product line, where we avoid the use of detailed unit volumes and prices in favor of a single lump-sum revenue total for each reporting period. This format is used when there are multiple products within each product line, making it cumbersome to create a detailed list of individual products. However, this format is the least informative and gives no easy way to update the supporting information.

Yet another budgeting format is shown for the Charlie product line, where projected sales are grouped by region. This format is most useful when there are many sales personnel, each of whom has been assigned a specific territory in which to operate. This budget can then be used to judge the ongoing performance of each salesperson.

These revenue reporting formats can also be combined, so that the product line detail for the Alpha product can be used as underlying detail for the sales regions used for the Charlie product line—though this will result in a very lengthy budget document.

There is also a statistics section at the bottom of the revenue budget that itemizes the proportion of total sales that occurs in each quarter, plus the proportion of product line sales within each quarter. Though it is not necessary to use these exact measurements, it is useful to include some type of measure that informs the reader of any variations in sales from period to period.

Both the production and inventory budgets are shown in Exhibit 23-3. The inventory budget is itemized at the top of the exhibit, where we itemize the amount of planned inventory turnover in all three inventory categories. There is a considerable ramp-up in work-in-process inventory turnover, indicating the planned installation of a manufacturing planning system of some kind that will control the flow of materials through the facility.

The production budget for just the Alpha product line is shown directly below the inventory goals. This budget is not concerned with the cost of production, but rather with the number of units that will be produced. In this instance, we begin with an on-hand inventory of 15,000 units, and try to keep enough units on hand through the remainder of the budget year to meet both the finished goods inventory goal at the top of the exhibit and the number of required units to be sold, which is referenced from the revenue budget. The main problem is that the maximum capacity of the bottleneck operation is 20,000 units per quarter. In order to meet the revenue target, we must run that operation at full bore through the first three quarters, irrespective of the inventory turnover target. This is especially important because the budget indicates a jump in bottleneck capacity in the fourth quarter from 20,000 to 40,000 units—this will occur when the bottleneck operation is stopped for a short time while additional equipment is added to it. During this stoppage, there must be enough excess inventory on hand to cover any sales that will arise. Consequently, production is planned for 20,000 units per quarter for the first three quarters, followed by a more precisely derived figure in the fourth quarter that will result in inventory turns of 9.0 at the end of the year, exactly as planned.

The production budget can be enhanced with the incorporation of planned machine downtime for maintenance, as well as for the planned loss of production units to scrap. It is also useful to plan for the capacity needs of non-bottleneck work centers, since these areas will require varying levels of staffing, depending upon the number of production shifts needed.

Exhibit 23-3   The Production and Inventory Budget

	Production and Inventory Budget for the Fiscal Year Ended xx/xx/02				
	Quarter 1	*Quarter 2*	*Quarter 3*	*Quarter 4*	*Totals*
Inventory Turnover Goals:					
Raw Materials Turnover	4.0	4.5	5.0	5.5	4.8
W-I-P Turnover	12.0	15.0	18.0	21.0	16.5
Finished Goods Turnover	6.0	6.0	9.0	9.0	7.5
Product Line Alpha Production:					
Beginning Inventory Units	15,000	21,000	20,000	15,000	—
Unit Sales Budget	14,000	21,000	25,000	31,000	91,000
Planned Production	20,000	20,000	20,000	27,375	87,375
Ending Inventory Units	21,000	20,000	15,000	11,375	
Bottleneck Unit Capacity	20,000	20,000	20,000	40,000	
Bottleneck Utilization	100%	100%	100%	68%	
Planned Finished Goods Turnover	15,167	15,167	11,375	11,375	

The purchasing budget is shown in Exhibit 23-4. It contains several different formats for planning budgeted purchases for the Alpha product line. The first option summarizes the planned production for each quarter; this information is brought forward from the production budget. We then multiply this by the standard unit cost of materials to arrive at the total amount of purchases that must be made in order to adequately support sales. The second option identifies the specific cost of each component of the product, so that management can see where cost increases are expected to occur. Though this version provides more information, it occupies a great deal of space on the budget if there are many components in each product, or many products. A third option shown at the bottom of the exhibit summarizes all purchases by commodity type. This format is most useful for the company's buyers, who usually specialize in certain commodity types.

The purchasing budget can be enhanced by adding a scrap factor for budgeted production, which will result in slightly higher quantities to buy, thereby leaving less chance of running out of raw materials. Another upgrade to the exhibit would be to schedule purchases for planned production some time in advance of the actual manufacturing date, so that the purchasing staff will be assured of having the parts on hand when manufacturing begins. A third enhancement is to round off the purchasing volumes for each item into the actual buying volumes that can be obtained on the open market. For example, it may only be possible to buy the required labels in volumes of 100,000 at a time, which would result in a planned purchase at the beginning of the year that would be large enough to cover all production needs through the end of the year.

The direct labor budget is shown in Exhibit 23-5. This budget assumes that only one labor category will vary directly with revenue volume—that category is the final assembly department, where a percentage in the far right column indicates that the cost in this area will be budgeted at a fixed 3.5% of total revenues. In all other cases, there are assumptions for a fixed number of personnel in each position within each production department. All of the wage figures for each department (except for final assembly) are derived from the planned hourly rates and headcount figures noted at the bottom of the page. This budget can be enhanced with the addition of separate line items for payroll tax percentages, benefits, shift differential payments, and overtime expenses. The cost of the final assembly department can also be adjusted to account for worker efficiency, which will be lower during production ramp-up periods when new, untrained employees are added to the workforce.

Exhibit 23-4   The Purchasing Budget

Purchasing Budget for the Fiscal Year Ended xx/xx/02					
	Quarter 1	*Quarter 2*	*Quarter 3*	*Quarter 4*	*Totals*
Inventory Turnover Goals:					
Raw Materials Turnover	4.0	4.5	5.0	5.5	4.8
Product Line Alpha Purchasing (Option 1):					
Planned Production	20,000	20,000	20,000	27,375	
Standard Material Cost/Unit	$ 5.42	$ 5.42	$ 5.67	$ 5.67	
Total Material Cost	$108,400	$108,400	$113,400	$155,216	$485,416
Product Line Alpha Purchasing (Option 2):					
Planned Production	20,000	20,000	20,000	27,375	
Molded Part	$ 4.62	$ 4.62	$ 4.85	$ 4.85	
Labels	$ 0.42	$ 0.42	$ 0.42	$ 0.42	
Fittings & Fasteners	$ 0.38	$ 0.38	$ 0.40	$ 0.40	
Total Cost of Components	$ 5.42	$ 5.42	$ 5.67	$ 5.67	
Product Line Alpha Purchasing (Option 3):					
Plastic Commodities					
Molded Part Units	20,000	20,000	20,000	27,375	
Molded Part Cost	$ 4.62	$ 4.62	$ 4.85	$ 4.85	
Adhesives Commodity					
Labels Units	20,000	20,000	20,000	27,375	
Labels Cost	$ 0.42	$ 0.42	$ 0.42	$ 0.42	
Fasteners Commodity					
Fasteners Units	20,000	20,000	20,000	27,375	
Fasteners Cost	$ 0.38	$ 0.38	$ 0.40	$ 0.40	
Statistics:					
Materials as Percent of Revenue	36%	36%	38%	38%	

Exhibit 23-5   The Direct Labor Budget

	Quarter 1	Quarter 2	Quarter 3	Quarter 4	Totals	Notes
Direct Labor Budget						
for the Fiscal Year Ended xx/xx/02						
Machining Department:						
Sr. Machine Operator	$15,120	$ 15,372	$ 23,058	$ 23,058	$ 76,608	
Machining Apprentice	$ 4,914	$ 4,964	$ 9,929	$ 9,929	$ 29,736	
Expense subtotal	$20,034	$ 20,336	$ 32,987	$ 32,987	$106,344	
Paint Department:						
Sr. Paint Shop Staff	$ 15,876	$ 16,128	$ 16,128	$ 16,128	$ 64,260	
Painter Apprentice	$ 5,065	$ 5,216	$ 5,216	$ 5,216	$ 20,714	
Expense subtotal	$ 20,941	$ 21,344	$ 21,344	$ 21,344	$ 84,974	
Polishing Department:						
Sr. Polishing Staff	$ 16,632	$ 11,844	$ 11,844	$ 11,844	$ 52,164	
Polishing Apprentice	$ 4,360	$ 4,511	$ 4,511	$ 4,511	$ 17,892	
Expense subtotal	$ 20,992	$ 16,355	$ 16,355	$ 16,355	$ 70,056	
Final Assembly Department:						
General Laborer	$ 63,735	$ 66,950	$ 69,755	$ 72,529	$272,968	3.5%
Expense subtotal	$ 63,735	$ 66,950	$ 69,755	$ 72,529	$272,968	
Expense grand total	$125,702	$124,985	$140,441	$143,215	$534,343	
Statistics:						
Union Hourly Rates:						
Sr. Machine Operator	$15.00	$15.25	$15.25	$15.25		
Machining Apprentice	$ 9.75	$ 9.85	$ 9.85	$ 9.85		
Sr. Paint Shop Staff	$15.75	$16.00	$16.00	$16.00		
Painter Apprentice	$10.05	$10.35	$10.35	$10.35		
Sr. Polishing Staff	$11.00	$11.75	$11.75	$11.75		
Polishing Apprentice	$ 8.65	$ 8.95	$ 8.95	$ 8.95		
Headcount by Position:						
Sr. Machine Operator	2	2	3	3		
Machining Apprentice	1	1	2	2		
Sr. Paint Shop Staff	2	2	2	2		
Painter Apprentice	1	1	1	1		
Sr. Polishing Staff	3	2	2	2		
Polishing Apprentice	1	1	1	1		

A sample of the overhead budget is shown in Exhibit 23-6. In this exhibit, we see that the overhead budget is really made up of a number of subsidiary departments, such as maintenance, materials management, and quality assurance. If the budgets of any of these departments are large enough, it makes a great deal of sense to split them off into a separate budget, so that the managers of those departments can see their budgeted expectations more clearly. Of particular interest in this exhibit is the valid capacity range noted on the far right side of the exhibit. This signifies the production activity level within which the budgeted overhead costs are accurate. If the actual capacity utilization were to fall outside of this range, either high or low, a separate overhead budget should be constructed with costs that are expected to be incurred within those ranges.

A sample cost of goods sold budget is shown in Exhibit 23-7. This format splits out each of the product lines noted in the revenue budget for reporting purposes, and subtracts from each one the materials costs that are noted in the purchases budget. This results in a contribution margin for each product line that is the clearest representation of the impact of direct costs (that is, material costs) on each one. We then summarize these individual contribution margins into a summary-level contribution margin, and then subtract the total direct labor and overhead costs (as referenced from the direct labor and overhead budgets) to arrive at a total gross margin. The statistics section also notes the number of production personnel budgeted for each quarterly reporting period, plus the average annual revenue per production employee—these statistics can be replaced with any operational information that management wants to see at a summary level for the production function, such as efficiency levels, capacity utilization, or inventory turnover.

The sales department budget is shown in Exhibit 23-8. This budget shows several different ways in which to organize the budget information. At the top of the budget is a block of line items that lists the expenses for those overhead costs within the department that cannot be specifically linked to a salesperson or region. In cases where the number of sales staff is quite small, *all* of the department's costs may be listed in this area.

Another alternative is shown in the second block of expense line items in the middle of the sales department budget, where all of the sales costs for an entire product line are lumped together into a single line item. If each person on the sales staff is exclusively assigned to a single product line, then it may make sense to break down the budget into separate budget pages for each product line, and list all of the expenses associated with each product line on a separate page.

A third alternative is shown next in Exhibit 23-8, where we list a summary of expenses for each salesperson. This format works well when combined with the departmental overhead expenses at the top of the budget, since this accounts for all of the departmental costs. However, this format brings up a confidentiality issue, since the compensation of each salesperson can be inferred from the report. Also, this format would include the commission expense paid to each salesperson—since commissions are a variable cost that is directly associated with each incremental dollar of sales, they should be itemized as a separate line item within the cost of goods sold.

A final option listed at the bottom of the example is to itemize expenses by sales region. This format works best when there are a number of sales personnel within the department who are clustered into a number of clearly identifiable regions. If there were no obvious regions or if there were only one salesperson per region, then the better format would be to list expenses by salesperson.

Exhibit 23-6 The Overhead Budget

Overhead Budget
for the Fiscal Year Ended xx/xx/02

	Quarter 1	Quarter 2	Quarter 3	Quarter 4	Totals	Valid Capacity Range
Supervision:						
Production Manager Salary	$ 16,250	$ 16,250	$ 16,250	$ 16,250	$ 65,000	—
Shift Manager Salaries	$ 22,000	$ 22,000	$ 23,500	$ 23,500	$ 91,000	40%–70%
Expense subtotal	$ 38,250	$ 38,250	$ 39,750	$ 39,750	$ 156,000	40%–70%
Maintenance Department:						
Equipment Maint. Staff	$ 54,000	$ 56,500	$ 58,000	$ 60,250	$ 228,750	40%–70%
Facilities Maint. Staff	$ 8,250	$ 8,250	$ 8,500	$ 8,500	$ 33,500	40%–70%
Equipment Repairs	$225,000	$225,000	$275,000	$225,000	$950,000	40%–70%
Facility Repairs	$ 78,000	$ 29,000	$ 12,000	$ 54,000	$ 173,000	40%–70%
Expense subtotal	$365,250	$318,750	$353,500	$347,750	$1,385,250	
Materials Management Department:						
Manager Salary	$ 18,750	$ 18,750	$ 18,750	$ 18,750	$ 75,000	—
Purchasing Staff	$ 28,125	$ 18,750	$ 18,750	$ 18,750	$ 84,375	40%–70%
Materials Mgmt Staff	$ 28,000	$ 35,000	$ 35,000	$ 35,000	$ 133,000	40%–70%
Production Control Staff	$ 11,250	$ 11,250	$ 11,250	$ 11,250	$ 45,000	40%–70%
Expense subtotal	$ 86,125	$ 83,750	$ 83,750	$ 83,750	$ 337,375	
Quality Department:						
Manager Salary	$ 13,750	$ 13,750	$ 13,750	$ 13,750	$ 55,000	—
Quality Staff	$ 16,250	$ 16,250	$ 16,250	$ 24,375	$ 73,125	40%–70%
Lab Testing Supplies	$ 5,000	$ 4,500	$ 4,500	$ 4,500	$ 18,500	40%–70%
Expense subtotal	$ 35,000	$ 34,500	$ 34,500	$ 42,625	$ 146,625	
Other Expenses:						
Depreciation	$ 14,000	$ 15,750	$ 15,750	$ 15,750	$ 61,250	—
Utilities	$ 60,000	$ 55,000	$ 55,000	$ 60,000	$ 230,000	40%–70%
Boiler Insurance	$ 3,200	$ 3,200	$ 3,200	$ 3,200	$ 12,800	—
Expense Subtotal	$ 77,200	$ 73,950	$ 73,950	$ 78,950	$ 304,050	
Expense Grand Total	$601,825	$549,200	$585,450	$592,825	$2,329,300	

273

At the bottom of the budget is the usual statistics section. The sales department budget is only concerned with making sales, so it should be no surprise that revenue per salesperson is the first item listed. Also, since the primary sales cost associated with this department is usually travel costs, the other statistical item is the travel and entertainment cost per person.

Exhibit 23-7   The Cost of Goods Sold Budget

Cost of Goods Sold Budget for the Fiscal Year Ended xx/xx/02					
	Quarter 1	*Quarter 2*	*Quarter 3*	*Quarter 4*	*Totals*
Product Line Alpha:					
Revenue	$ 210,000	$ 311,850	$ 370,000	$ 457,250	$1,349,100
Materials expense	$ 108,400	$ 108,400	$ 113,400	$ 155,216	$ 485,416
Contribution Margin $$	$ 101,600	$ 203,450	$ 256,600	$ 302,034	$ 863,684
Contribution Margin %	48%	65%	69%	66%	64%
Product Line Beta:					
Revenue	$1,048,000	$1,057,000	$1,061,000	$1,053,000	$4,219,000
Materials expense	$ 12,000	$ 14,000	$ 15,000	$ 13,250	$ 54,250
Contribution Margin $$	$1,036,000	$1,043,000	$1,046,000	$1,039,750	$4,164,750
Contribution Margin %	99%	99%	99%	99%	99%
Revenue—Product Line Charlie:					
Revenue	$ 563,000	$ 544,000	$ 562,000	$ 562,000	$2,231,000
Materials expense	$ 268,000	$ 200,000	$ 220,000	$ 230,000	$ 918,000
Contribution Margin $$	$ 295,000	$ 344,000	$ 342,000	$ 332,000	$1,313,000
Contribution Margin %	52%	63%	61%	59%	59%
Total Contribution Margin $$	$1,432,600	$1,590,450	$1,644,600	$1,673,784	$6,341,434
Total Contribution Margin %	79%	83%	83%	81%	81%
Direct Labor Expense:	$ 125,702	$ 124,985	$ 140,441	$ 143,215	$ 534,343
Overhead Expense:	$ 601,825	$ 549,200	$ 585,450	$ 592,825	$2,329,300
Total Gross Margin $$	$ 705,073	$ 916,265	$ 918,709	$ 937,744	$3,477,791
Total Gross Margin %	39%	48%	46%	45%	44%
Statistics:					
No. of Production Staff*	23	22	22	23	
Avg. Annual Revenue per Production Employee	$ 316,696	$ 347,791	$ 362,364	$ 360,391	

* Not including general assembly staff.

Exhibit 23-8   The Sales Department Budget

Sales Department Budget for the Fiscal Year Ended xx/xx/02					
	Quarter 1	*Quarter 2*	*Quarter 3*	*Quarter 4*	*Totals*
Departmental Overhead:					
Depreciation	$ 500	$ 500	$ 500	$ 500	$ 2,000
Office supplies	$ 750	$ 600	$ 650	$ 600	$ 2,600
Payroll taxes	$ 2,945	$ 5,240	$ 5,240	$ 8,186	$ 21,611
Salaries	$ 38,500	$ 68,500	$ 68,500	$107,000	$ 282,500
Travel & entertainment	$ 1,500	$ 1,500	$ 1,500	$ 2,000	$ 6,500
Expense subtotal	$ 44,195	$ 76,340	$ 76,390	$118,286	$ 315,211
Product Line Alpha:	$ 32,000	$ 18,000	$ 0	$ 21,000	$ 71,000
Expenses by Salesperson:					
Jones, Milbert	$ 14,000	$ 16,500	$ 17,000	$ 12,000	$ 59,500
Smidley, Jefferson	$ 1,000	$ 9,000	$ 8,000	$ 12,000	$ 30,000
Verity, Jonas	$ 7,000	$ 9,000	$ 14,000	$ 12,000	$ 42,000
Expense subtotal	$ 22,000	$ 34,500	$ 39,000	$ 36,000	$ 131,500
Expenses by Region:					
East Coast	$ 52,000	$ 71,000	$ 15,000	$ 0	$ 138,000
Midwest Coast	$ 8,000	$ 14,000	$ 6,000	$ 12,000	$ 40,000
West Coast	$ 11,000	$ 10,000	$ 12,000	$ 24,000	$ 57,000
Expense subtotal	$ 71,000	$ 95,000	$ 33,000	$ 36,000	$ 235,000
Expense grand total	$137,195	$205,840	$148,390	$190,286	$ 681,711
Statistics:					
Revenue per salesperson	$607,000	$637,617	$664,333	$690,750	$2,599,700
T&E per salesperson	$ 500	$ 500	$ 500	$ 667	$ 2,167

Exhibit 23-9 shows a sample marketing budget. As was the case for the sales department, this one also itemizes departmental overhead costs at the top, which leaves space in the middle for the itemization of campaign-specific costs. The campaign-specific costs can be lumped together for individual product lines, as is the case for product lines Alpha and Beta in the exhibit, or with subsidiary line items, as is shown for product line Charlie. A third possible format, which is to itemize marketing costs by marketing tool (for example, advertising, promotional tour, coupon redemption, etc.) is generally not recommended if there is more than one product line, since there is no way for an analyst to determine the impact of individual marketing costs on specific product lines. The statistics at the bottom of the page attempt to compare marketing costs to sales; however, this should only be treated as an approximation, since marketing efforts will usually not result

Exhibit 23-9 The Marketing Department Budget

	Quarter 1	Quarter 2	Quarter 3	Quarter 4	Totals
	Marketing Budget for the Fiscal Year Ended xx/xx/02				
Departmental Overhead:					
Depreciation	$ 650	$ 750	$ 850	$ 1,000	$ 3,250
Office supplies	$ 200	$ 200	$ 200	$ 200	$ 800
Payroll taxes	$ 4,265	$ 4,265	$ 4,265	$ 4,265	$ 17,060
Salaries	$ 55,750	$ 55,750	$ 55,750	$55,750	$223,000
Travel & entertainment	$ 5,000	$ 6,500	$ 7,250	$ 7,250	$ 26,000
Expense subtotal	$ 65,865	$ 67,465	$ 68,315	$68,465	$270,110
Campaign-Specific Expenses:					
Product Line Alpha	$ 14,000	$ 26,000	$ 30,000	$ 0	$ 70,000
Product Line Beta	$ 18,000	$ 0	$ 0	$24,000	$ 42,000
Product Line Charlie					$ 0
Advertising	$ 10,000	$ 0	$ 20,000	$ 0	$ 30,000
Promotional Tour	$ 5,000	$ 25,000	$ 2,000	$ 0	$ 32,000
Coupon Redemption	$ 2,000	$ 4,000	$ 4,500	$ 1,200	$ 11,700
Product Samples	$ 2,750	$ 5,250	$ 1,250	$ 0	$ 9,250
Expense subtotal	$ 51,750	$ 60,250	$ 57,750	$25,200	$194,950
Expense grand total	$117,615	$127,715	$126,065	$93,665	$465,060
Statistics:					
Expense as percent of total sales	6.5%	6.7%	6.3%	4.5%	6.0%
Expense proportion by quarter	25.3%	27.5%	27.1%	20.1%	100.0%

in immediate sales, but rather will result in sales that build over time. Thus, there is a time lag after incurring a marketing cost that makes it difficult to determine the efficacy of marketing activities.

A sample general and administrative budget is shown in Exhibit 23-10. This budget can be quite lengthy, including such additional line items as postage, copier leases, and office repair. Many of these extra expenses have been pruned from the exhibit in order to provide a compressed view of the general format to be used. The exhibit does not lump together the costs of the various departments that are typically included in this budget, but rather identifies each one in separate blocks; this format is most useful when there are separate managers for the accounting and human resources functions, so that they will have a better understanding of their budgets. The statistics section at the bottom of the page itemizes a benchmark target of the total general and administrative cost as a proportion of revenue. This is a particularly useful statistic to track, since the general and administrative function is a cost center, and requires such a comparison in order to inform management that these costs are being held in check.

Exhibit 23-10   The General and Administrative Budget

	General and Administrative Budget for the Fiscal Year Ended xx/xx/02					
	Quarter 1	*Quarter 2*	*Quarter 3*	*Quarter 4*	*Totals*	*Notes*
Accounting Department:						
Depreciation	$ 4,000	$ 4,000	$ 4,250	$ 4,250	$ 16,500	
Office supplies	$ 650	$ 650	$ 750	$ 750	$ 2,800	
Payroll taxes	$ 4,973	$ 4,973	$ 4,973	$ · 4,973	$ 19,890	
Salaries	$ 65,000	$ 65,000	$ 65,000	$ 65,000	$260,000	
Training	$ 500	$ 2,500	$ 7,500	$ 0	$ 10,500	
Travel & entertainment	$ 0	$ 750	$ 4,500	$ 500	$ 5,750	
Expense subtotal	$ 75,123	$ 77,873	$ 86,973	$ 75,473	$315,440	
Corporate Expenses:						
Depreciation	$ 450	$ 500	$ 550	$ 600	$ 2,100	
Office supplies	$ 1,000	$ 850	$ 750	$ 1,250	$ 3,850	
Payroll taxes	$ 6,598	$ 6,598	$ 6,598	$ 6,598	$ 26,392	
Salaries	$ 86,250	$ 86,250	$ 86,250	$ 86,250	$345,000	
Insurance, business	$ 4,500	$ 4,500	$ 4,500	$ 4,500	$ 18,000	
Training	$ 5,000	$ 0	$ 0	$ 0	$ 5,000	
Travel & entertainment	$ 2,000	$ 500	$ 500	$ 0	$ 3,000	
Expense subtotal	$105,798	$ 99,198	$ 99,148	$ 99,198	$403,342	
Human Resources Department:						
Benefits programs	$ 7,284	$ 7,651	$ 7,972	$ 8,289	$ 31,196	**0.4%**
Depreciation	$ 500	$ 500	$ 500	$ 500	$ 2,000	
Office supplies	$ 450	$ 8,000	$ 450	$ 450	$ 9,350	
Payroll taxes	$ 2,869	$ 2,869	$ 2,869	$ 2,869	$ 11,475	
Salaries	$ 37,500	$ 37,500	$ 37,500	$ 37,500	$150,000	
Training	$ 5,000	$ 0	$ 7,500	$ 0	$ 12,500	
Travel & entertainment	$ 2,000	$ 1,000	$ 3,500	$ 1,000	$ 7,500	
Expense subtotal	$ 55,603	$ 57,520	$ 60,291	$ 50,608	$224,021	
Expense grand total	$236,523	$234,591	$246,411	$225,278	$942,804	
Statistics:						
Expense as proportion of revenue	13.0%	12.3%	12.4%	10.9%	12.1%	
Benchmark comparison	11.5%	11.5%	11.5%	11.5%	11.5%	

A staffing budget is shown in Exhibit 23-11. This itemizes the expected headcount in every department by major job category. It does not attempt to identify individual positions, since that can lead to an excessively lengthy list. Also, because there may be multiple positions identified within each job category, the *average* salary for each cluster of jobs is identified. If a position is subject to overtime pay, its expected overtime percentage is identified on the right side of the budget. Many sections of the budget should have linkages to this page, so that any changes in headcount here will be automatically reflected in the other sections. This budget may have to be restricted from general access, since it contains salary information that may be considered confidential information.

Exhibit 23-11   The Staffing Budget

Staffing Budget
for the Fiscal Year Ended xx/xx/02

	Quarter 1	Quarter 2	Quarter 3	Quarter 4	Average Salary	Overtime Percent
Sales Department:						
Regional Sales Manager	1	2	2	3	$120,000	0%
Salesperson	2	4	4	6	$ 65,000	0%
Sales Support Staff	1	1	1	2	$ 34,000	6%
Marketing Department:						
Marketing Manager	1	1	1	1	$ 85,000	0%
Marketing Researcher	2	2	2	2	$ 52,000	0%
Secretary	1	1	1	1	$ 34,000	6%
General & Administrative:						
President	1	1	1	1	$175,000	0%
Chief Operating Officer	1	1	1	1	$125,000	0%
Chief Financial Officer	1	1	1	1	$100,000	0%
Human Resources Mgr.	1	1	1	1	$ 80,000	0%
Accounting Staff	4	4	4	4	$ 40,000	10%
Human Resources Staff	2	2	2	2	$ 35,000	8%
Executive Secretary	1	1	1	1	$ 45,000	6%
Research Department:						
Chief Scientist	1	1	1	1	$100,000	0%
Senior Engineer Staff	3	3	3	4	$ 80,000	0%
Junior Engineer Staff	3	3	3	3	$ 60,000	0%
Overhead Budget:						
Production Manager	1	1	1	1	$ 65,000	0%
Quality Manager	1	1	1	1	$ 55,000	0%
Materials Manager	1	1	1	1	$ 75,000	0%
Production Scheduler	1	1	1	1	$ 45,000	0%
Quality Assurance Staff	2	2	2	3	$ 32,500	8%
Purchasing Staff	3	2	2	2	$ 37,500	8%
Materials Mgmt Staff	4	5	5	5	$ 28,000	8%
Total Headcount	39	42	42	48		

The facilities budget tends to have the largest number of expense line items. A sample of this format is shown in Exhibit 23-12. These expenses may be offset by some rental or sub-lease revenues if a portion of the company facilities is rented out to other organizations. However, this revenue is only shown in this budget if the revenue amount is small; otherwise, it is more commonly found as an "other revenue" line item on the revenue budget. A statistics section is found at the bottom of this budget; it refers to the total amount of square feet occupied by the facility. A very effective statistic is the amount of unused square footage, which can be used to conduct an ongoing program of selling off, renting, or consolidating company facilities.

The research department's budget is shown in Exhibit 23-13. It is most common to segregate the department-specific overhead that cannot be attributed to a specific project at the top of the budget, and then cluster costs by project below that. By doing so, the management team can see precisely how much money is being allocated to each project. This may be of use in determining which projects must be canceled or delayed as part of the budget review process. The statistics section at the bottom of the budget notes the pro-

Exhibit 23-12   The Facilities Budget

<table>
<tr><td colspan="6" align="center">Facilities Budget
for the Fiscal Year Ended xx/xx/02</td></tr>
<tr><td></td><td>Quarter 1</td><td>Quarter 2</td><td>Quarter 3</td><td>Quarter 4</td><td>Totals</td></tr>
<tr><td>Facilty Expenses:</td><td></td><td></td><td></td><td></td><td></td></tr>
<tr><td>Contracted Services</td><td>$ 5,500</td><td>$ 5,400</td><td>$ 5,000</td><td>$ 4,500</td><td>$ 20,400</td></tr>
<tr><td>Depreciation</td><td>$29,000</td><td>$29,000</td><td>$28,000</td><td>$28,000</td><td>$114,000</td></tr>
<tr><td>Electricity Charges</td><td>$ 4,500</td><td>$ 3,500</td><td>$ 3,500</td><td>$ 4,500</td><td>$ 16,000</td></tr>
<tr><td>Inspection Fees</td><td>$ 500</td><td>$ 0</td><td>$ 0</td><td>$ 500</td><td>$ 1,000</td></tr>
<tr><td>Insurance</td><td>$ 8,000</td><td>$ 0</td><td>$ 0</td><td>$ 0</td><td>$ 8,000</td></tr>
<tr><td>Maintenance Supplies</td><td>$ 3,000</td><td>$ 3,000</td><td>$ 3,000</td><td>$ 3,000</td><td>$ 12,000</td></tr>
<tr><td>Payroll Taxes</td><td>$ 1,148</td><td>$ 1,148</td><td>$ 1,148</td><td>$ 1,186</td><td>$ 4,628</td></tr>
<tr><td>Property Taxes</td><td>$ 0</td><td>$ 5,000</td><td>$ 0</td><td>$ 0</td><td>$ 5,000</td></tr>
<tr><td>Repairs</td><td>$15,000</td><td>$ 0</td><td>$29,000</td><td>$ 0</td><td>$ 44,000</td></tr>
<tr><td>Sewage Charges</td><td>$ 250</td><td>$ 250</td><td>$ 250</td><td>$ 250</td><td>$ 1,000</td></tr>
<tr><td>Trash Disposal</td><td>$ 3,000</td><td>$ 3,000</td><td>$ 3,000</td><td>$ 3,000</td><td>$ 12,000</td></tr>
<tr><td>Wages—Janitorial</td><td>$ 5,000</td><td>$ 5,000</td><td>$ 5,000</td><td>$ 5,500</td><td>$ 20,500</td></tr>
<tr><td>Wages—Maintenance</td><td>$10,000</td><td>$10,000</td><td>$10,000</td><td>$10,000</td><td>$ 40,000</td></tr>
<tr><td>Water Charges</td><td>$ 1,000</td><td>$ 1,000</td><td>$ 1,000</td><td>$ 1,000</td><td>$ 4,000</td></tr>
<tr><td>**Expense grand total**</td><td>$85,898</td><td>$66,298</td><td>$88,898</td><td>$61,436</td><td>$302,528</td></tr>
<tr><td>Statistics:</td><td></td><td></td><td></td><td></td><td></td></tr>
<tr><td>Total Square Feet</td><td>52,000</td><td>52,000</td><td>78,000</td><td>78,000</td><td></td></tr>
<tr><td>Square Feet/Employee</td><td>839</td><td>813</td><td>1,219</td><td>1,099</td><td></td></tr>
<tr><td>Unused Square Footage</td><td>1,200</td><td>1,200</td><td>12,500</td><td>12,500</td><td></td></tr>
</table>

portion of planned expenses in the categories of overhead, research, and development. These proportions can be examined to see if the company is allocating funds to the right balance of projects that most effectively meets its product development goals.

Exhibit 23-13 The Research Department Budget

	Quarter 1	Quarter 2	Quarter 3	Quarter 4	Totals
Research Department Budget for the Fiscal Year Ended xx/xx/02					
Departmental Overhead:					
Depreciation	$ 500	$ 500	$ 400	$ 400	$ 1,800
Office supplies	$ 750	$ 2,000	$ 1,500	$ 1,250	$ 5,500
Payroll taxes	$ 9,945	$ 9,945	$ 9,945	$ 11,475	$ 41,310
Salaries	$130,000	$130,000	$130,000	$150,000	$ 540,000
Travel & entertainment	$ 0	$ 0	$ 0	$ 0	$ 0
Expense subtotal	$141,195	$142,445	$141,845	$163,125	$ 588,610
Research-Specific Expenses:					
Gamma Project	$ 20,000	$ 43,500	$ 35,000	$ 12,500	$ 111,000
Omega Project	$ 5,000	$ 6,000	$ 7,500	$ 9,000	$ 27,500
Pi Project	$ 14,000	$ 7,000	$ 7,500	$ 4,500	$ 33,000
Upsilon Project	$ 500	$ 2,500	$ 5,000	$ 0	$ 8,000
Expense subtotal	$ 39,500	$ 59,000	$ 55,000	$ 26,000	$ 179,500
Development-Specific Expenses:					
Latin Project	$ 28,000	$ 29,000	$ 30,000	$ 15,000	$ 102,000
Greek Project	$ 14,000	$ 14,500	$ 15,000	$ 7,500	$ 51,000
Mabinogian Project	$ 20,000	$ 25,000	$ 15,000	$ 10,000	$ 70,000
Old English Project	$ 6,250	$ 12,500	$ 25,000	$ 50,000	$ 93,750
Expense subtotal	$ 68,250	$ 81,000	$ 85,000	$ 82,500	$ 316,750
Expense grand total	$248,945	$282,445	$281,845	$271,625	$1,084,860
Statistics:					
Budgeted number of patent applications filed	2	0	1	1	4
Proportion of expenses:					
Overhead	56.7%	50.4%	50.3%	60.1%	217.5%
Research	15.9%	20.9%	19.5%	9.6%	65.8%
Development	27.4%	28.7%	30.2%	30.4%	116.5%
Total Expenses	100.0%	100.0%	100.0%	100.0%	400.0%

The capital budget is shown in Exhibit 23-14. This format clusters capital expenditures by a number of categories. For example, the first category, entitled "bottleneck-related expenditures," clearly focuses attention on those outgoing payments that will increase the company's key productive capacity. The payments in the third quarter under this heading are directly related to the increase in bottleneck capacity that was shown the production budget (Exhibit 23-3) for the fourth quarter. The budget also contains an automatic assumption of $7,000 in capital expenditures for any net increase in non-direct labor headcount, which encompasses the cost of computer equipment and office furniture for each person. If the company's capitalization limit is set too high to list these expenditures on the capital budget, then a similar line item should be inserted into the general and administrative budget, so that the expense can be recognized under the office supplies or some similar account.

The capital budget also includes a category for profit-related expenditures. Any projects listed in this category should be subject to an intensive expenditure review, using cash flow discounting techniques (as described in Chapter 27, Financial Analysis) to ensure that they return a sufficient cash flow to make their acquisition profitable to the

Exhibit 23-14   The Capital Budget

Capital Budget for the Fiscal Year Ended xx/xx/02					
	Quarter 1	*Quarter 2*	*Quarter 3*	*Quarter 4*	*Totals*
Bottleneck-Related Expeditures:					
Stamping Machine			$150,000		$150,000
Facility for Machine			$ 72,000		$ 72,000
Headcount-Related Expenditures:					
Headcount Change ×					
$7,000 Added Staff	$ 0	$21,000	$ 0	$ 42,000	$ 63,000
Profit-Related Expenditures:					
Blending Machine		$50,000			$ 50,000
Polishing Machine		$27,000			$ 27,000
Safety-Related Expenditures:					
Machine Shielding		$ 3,000	$ 3,000		$ 6,000
Handicapped Walkways	$8,000	$ 5,000			$ 13,000
Required Expenditures:					
Clean Air Scrubber			$ 42,000		$ 42,000
Other Expenditures:					
Tool Crib Expansion				$ 18,500	$ 18,500
Total expenditures	$ 8,000	$106,000	$267,000	$ 60,500	$441,500

company. Other categories in the budget cover expenditures for safety or required items, which tend to be purchased with no cash flow discounting review. An alternative to this grouping system is to only list the sum total of all capital expenditures in each category, which is most frequently used when there are far too many separate purchases to list on the budget. Another variation is to only list the largest expenditures on separate budget lines, and cluster together all smaller ones. The level of capital purchasing activity will determine the type of format used.

All of the preceding budgets roll up into the budgeted income and cash flow statement, which is noted in Exhibit 23-15. This format lists the grand totals from each of the preceding pages of the budget in order to arrive at a profit or loss for each budget quarter. In the example, we see that a large initial loss in the first quarter is gradually offset by smaller gains in later quarters to arrive at a small profit for the year. However, the presentation continues with a cash flow statement that has less positive results. It begins with the net profit figure for each quarter, adds back the depreciation expense for all departments, and subtracts out all planned capital expenditures from the capital budget to arrive at cash flow needs for the year. This tells us that the company will experience a maximum cash shortfall in the third quarter. This format can be made more precise by adding in time lag factors for the payment of accounts payable and the collection of accounts receivable.

The final document in the budget is an itemization of the finances needed to ensure that the rest of the budget can be achieved. An example is shown in Exhibit 23-16, which carries forward the final cash position at the end of each quarter that was the product of the preceding cash flow statement. This line shows that there will be a maximum shortfall of $223,727 by the end of the third quarter. The next section of the budget outlines several possible options for obtaining the required funds (which are rounded up to $225,000)—debt, preferred stock, or common stock. The financing cost of each one is noted in the far right column, where we see that the interest cost on debt is 9.5%, the dividend on preferred stock is 8%, and the expected return by common stockholders is 18%.

The third section on the page lists the existing capital structure, its cost, and the net cost of capital. This is quite important, for anyone reviewing this document can see what impact the financing options will have on the capital structure if any of them are selected. For example, the management team may prefer the low cost of debt, but can also use the existing capital structure presentation to see that this will result in a very high proportion of debt to equity, which increases the risk that the company would not be able to repay the debt to the lender.

The fourth and final part of the budget calculates any changes in the cost of capital that will arise if any of the three financing options are selected. A footnote points out the incremental corporate tax rate—this is of importance to the calculation of the cost of capital, because the interest cost of debt can be deducted as an expense, thereby reducing its net cost. In the exhibit, selecting additional debt as the preferred form of financing will result in a reduction in the cost of capital to 10.7%, whereas a selection of high-cost common stock will result in an increase in the cost of capital, to 12.9%. These changes can have an impact on what types of capital projects are accepted in the future, for the cash flows associated with them must be discounted by the cost of capital in order to see if they result in positive cash flows. Accordingly, a reduction in the cost of capital will mean that projects with marginal cash flows will become more acceptable, while the reverse will be true for a higher cost of capital.

Exhibit 23-15   The Budgeted Income and Cash Flow Statement

	Budgeted Income and Cash Flow Statement for the Fiscal Year Ended xx/xx/02				
	Quarter 1	*Quarter 2*	*Quarter 3*	*Quarter 4*	*Totals*
Revenue:	$1,821,000	$1,912,850	$1,993,000	$2,072,250	$7,799,100
Cost of Goods Sold:					
Materials	$ 388,400	$ 322,400	$ 348,400	$ 398,466	$1,457,666
Direct Labor	$ 125,702	$ 124,985	$ 140,441	$ 143,215	$ 534,343
Overhead					
Supervision	$ 38,250	$ 38,250	$ 39,750	$ 39,750	$ 156,000
Maintenance Department	$ 365,250	$ 318,750	$ 353,500	$ 347,750	$1,385,250
Materials Management	$ 86,125	$ 83,750	$ 83,750	$ 83,750	$ 337,375
Quality Department	$ 35,000	$ 34,500	$ 34,500	$ 42,625	$ 146,625
Other Expenses	$ 77,200	$ 73,950	$ 73,950	$ 78,950	$ 304,050
Total Cost of Goods Sold	$1,115,927	$ 996,585	$1,074,291	$1,134,506	$4,321,309
Gross Margin	$ 705,073	$ 916,265	$ 918,709	$ 937,744	$3,477,791
Operating Expenses					
Sales Department	$ 137,195	$ 205,840	$ 148,390	$ 190,286	$ 681,711
General & Admin. Dept.					
Accounting	$ 75,123	$ 77,873	$ 86,973	$ 75,473	$ 315,440
Corporate	$ 105,798	$ 99,198	$ 99,148	$ 99,198	$ 403,343
Human Resources	$ 55,603	$ 57,520	$ 60,291	$ 50,608	$ 224,021
Marketing Department	$ 117,615	$ 127,715	$ 126,065	$ 93,665	$ 465,060
Facilities Department	$ 85,898	$ 66,298	$ 88,898	$ 61,436	$ 302,528
Research Department	$ 248,945	$ 282,445	$ 281,845	$ 271,625	$1,084,860
Total Operating Expenses	$ 826,176	$ 916,888	$ 891,609	$ 842,290	$3,476,963
Net Profit (Loss)	–$ 121,103	–$ 624	$ 27,100	$ 95,455	$ 828
	Quarter 1	*Quarter 2*	*Quarter 3*	*Quarter 4*	*Totals*
Cash Flow:					
Beginning Cash	$ 100,000	$ 20,497	–$ 34,627	–$ 223,727	
Net Profit (Loss)	–$ 121,103	–$ 624	$ 27,100	$ 95,455	$ 828
Add Depreciation	$49,600	$ 51,500	$ 50,800	$ 51,000	$ 202,900
Minus Capital Purchases	–$8,000	–$ 106,000	–$ 267,000	–$ 60,500	–$ 441,500
Ending Cash	$20,497	–$ 34,627	–$ 223,727	–$ 137,772	

Exhibit 23-16 The Financing Budget

Financing Budget for the Fiscal Year Ended xx/xx/02					
	Quarter 1	*Quarter 2*	*Quarter 3*	*Quarter 4*	*Financing Cost*
Cash Position:	$ 20,497	–$ 34,627	–$223,727	–$137,772	
Financing Option One:					
Additional Debt		$225,000			9.5%
Financing Option Two:					
Additional Preferred Stock	$225,000				8.0%
Financing Option Three:					
Additional Common Stock	$225,000				18.0%
Existing Capital Structure:					
Debt	$400,000				9.0%
Preferred Stock	$150,000				7.5%
Common Stock	$500,000				18.0%
Existing Cost of Capital	11.8%				
Revised Cost of Capital:					
Financing Option One	10.7%				
Financing Option Two	11.2%				
Financing Option Three	12.9%				

Note: Tax rate equals 38%.

The budgeting examples shown here can be used as the format for a real-life corporate budget. However, it must be adjusted to include a company's chart of accounts and departmental structure, so that it more accurately reflects actual operations. Also, it should include a detailed benefits and payroll tax calculation page, which will itemize the cost of social security taxes, Medicare, unemployment insurance, workers' compensation insurance, medical insurance, and so on. These costs are a substantial part of a company's budget, and yet are commonly lumped together into a simplistic budget model that does not accurately reflect their true cost.

Though the budget model presented here may seem excessively large, it is necessary to provide detailed coverage of all aspects of the corporation, so that prospective changes to it can be accurately modeled through the budget. Thus, a detailed format is strongly recommended over a simple, summarized model.

23-4 THE FLEX BUDGET

One problem with the budget model shown in the last section is that many of the expenses listed in it are directly tied to the revenue level. If the actual revenue incurred is significantly different from the budgeted figure, then so many expenses will also shift in association with the revenue that the comparison of budgeted to actual expenses will not be valid. For example, if budgeted revenues are $1 million and budgeted material costs are $450,000, one would expect a corresponding drop in the actual cost of materials incurred if actual revenues drop to $800,000. A budget-to-actual comparison would then show a significant difference in the cost of materials, which would in turn cause a difference in the gross margin and net profit. This issue also arises for a number of other variable or semi-variable expenses, such as salesperson commissions, production supplies, and main-tenance costs. Also, if there are really large differences between actual and budgeted rev-enue levels, other costs that are more fixed in nature will also change, such as the salaries, office supplies, and even facilities maintenance (because facilities may be sold off or added to, depending on which direction actual revenues have gone). These represent large step cost changes that will skew actual expenses so far away from the budget that it is dif-ficult to conduct any meaningful comparison between the two.

A good way to resolve this problem is to create a flexible budget, or "flex" budget, that itemizes different expense levels depending upon changes in the amount of actual rev-enue. In its simplest form, the flex budget will use percentages of revenue for certain expenses, rather than the usual fixed numbers. This allows for an infinite series of changes in budgeted expenses that are directly tied to revenue volume. However, this approach ignores changes to other costs that do not change in accordance with small revenue vari-ations. Consequently, a more sophisticated format will also incorporate changes to many additional expenses when certain larger revenue changes occur, thereby accounting for step costs. By making these changes to the budget, a company will have a tool for com-paring actual to budgeted performance at many levels of activity.

Though the flex budget is a good tool, it can be difficult to formulate and adminis-ter. One problem with its formulation is that many costs are not fully variable, instead having a fixed cost component that must be included in the flex budget formula. Another issue is that a great deal of time can be spent developing step costs, which is more time than the typical accounting staff has available, especially when in the midst of creating the standard budget. Consequently, the flex budget tends to include only a small number of step costs, as well as variable costs whose fixed cost components are not fully recognized.

Implementation of the flex budget is also a problem, for very few accounting soft-ware packages incorporate any features that allow one to load in multiple versions of a budget that can be used at different revenue levels. Instead, some include the option to store a few additional budgets, which the user can then incorporate into the standard budget-to-actual comparison reports. This option does not yield the full benefits of a flex budget, since it only allows for a few changes in expenses based on a small number of rev-enue changes, rather than a set of expenses that will automatically change in proportion to actual revenue levels incurred. Furthermore, the option to enter several different budg-ets means that someone must enter this additional information into the accounting soft-ware, which can be a considerable chore if the number of budget line items is large. For these reasons, it is more common to see a flex budget incorporated into an electronic spreadsheet, with actual results being manually posted to it from other accounting reports.

23-5 THE BUDGETING PROCESS

The budgeting process is usually rife with delays, which are caused by several factors. One is that information must be input to the budget model from all parts of the company—some of which may not put a high priority on the submission of budgeting information.

Another reason is that the budgeting process is highly iterative, sometimes requiring dozens of budget recalculations and changes in assumptions before the desired results are achieved. The typical budgeting process is represented in Exhibit 23-17, where we see that there is a sequential process that requires the completion of the revenue plan before the production plan can be completed, which in turn must be finished before the departmental expense budgets can be finished, which then yields a financing plan. If the results do not meet expectations, then the process starts over again at the top of the exhibit. This process is so time-consuming that the budget may not be completed before the budget period has already begun.

There are a number of best practices that can be used to create a more streamlined budgeting process. Here are some of the more common ones:

- *Reduce the number of accounts.* The number of accounts included in the budget should be reduced, thereby greatly reducing the amount of time needed to enter and update data in the budget model.

- *Reduce the number of reporting periods.* One can consolidate the 12 months shown in the typical budget into quarterly information, thereby eliminating two-thirds of the information in the budget. If the budget must later be re-entered into the accounting system in order to provide budget-to-actual comparisons, then a simple formula can be used to divide the quarterly budget back into its monthly components—which is still much less work than maintaining 12 full months of budget information.

- *Use percentages for variable cost updates.* When key activities, such as revenues, are changed in the budget model, one must peruse the entire budget in order to determine what related expenses must change in concert with the key activities. A much easier approach is to use percentage-based calculations for variable costs in the budget model, so that these expenses will be updated automatically. They should also be color-coded in the budget model, so that they will not be mistaken for items that are manually changed.

- *Report on variables in one place.* A number of key variables will impact the typical budget model, such as the assumed rate of inflation in wages or purchased parts, tax rates for income, payroll, and workers' compensation, medical insurance rates, and so on. These variables are much easier to find if they are set up in a cluster within the budget, so that one can easily reference and alter them. Under this arrangement, it is also useful to show key results (such as net profits) on the same page with the variables, so that one can make alterations to the variables and immediately see their impact without having to search through the budget model to find the information.

- *Use a budget procedure and timetable.* The budget process is plagued by many iterations, since the first results will nearly always yield profits or losses that do not meet a company's expectations. Furthermore, it requires input from all parts of a company, some of which may lag in sending in information in a timely manner. Accordingly, it is best to construct a budgeting procedure that specifically identifies what job positions must send budgeting information to the budget coordinator, what information is required of each person, and when that information is due. Furthermore, there should be a clear timetable of events that is carefully adhered to, so that plenty of time is left at the end of the budgeting process for the calculation of multiple iterations of the budget.

Exhibit 23-17   Traditional Budgeting Process

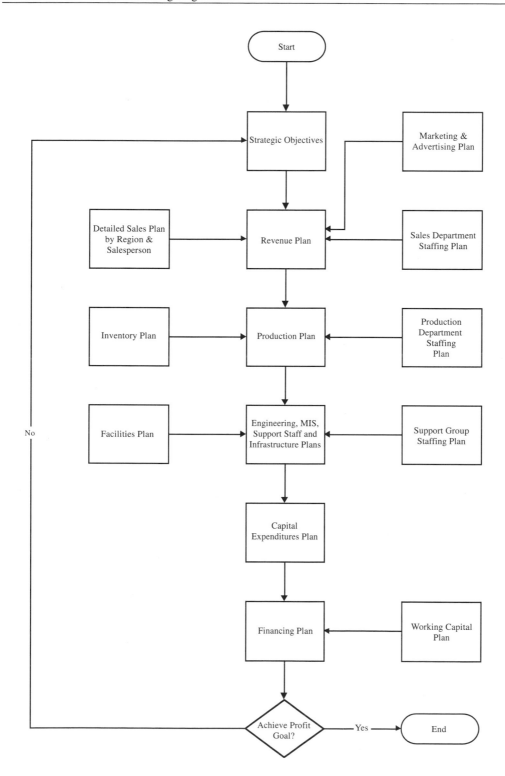

In addition to these efficiency-improvement issues, there are other ways to modify the budgeting process so that it can be completed much more quickly. The following changes should be considered:

- *Itemize the corporate strategy.* The strategy and related tactical goals that the company is trying to achieve should be listed at the beginning of the budget model. All too frequently, management loses sight of its predetermined strategy when going through the many iterations that are needed to develop a realistic budget. By itemizing the corporate strategy in the budget document, it is much less likely that the final budget model will deviate significantly from the company's strategic direction.

- *Identify step-costing change points.* The budget model should have notations incorporated into it that specify the capacity levels at which expenses are valid. For example, if the production level for Product A exceeds 100,000 per year, then a warning flag should be generated by the budget model that informs the budget manager of the need to add an extra shift to accommodate the increased production requirements. Another example is to have the model generate a warning flag when the average revenue per salesperson exceeds $1,000,000, since this may be the maximum expectation for sales productivity, and will require the addition of more sales personnel to the budget. These flags can be clustered at the front of the budget model, so that problems will be readily apparent to the reader.

- *Specify maximum amounts of available funding.* One of the warning flags just noted should include the maximum level of funding that the company can obtain. If an iteration of the budget model results in excessively high cash requirements, then the flag will immediately point out the problem. It may be useful to note next to the warning flag the amount by which the maximum funding has been exceeded, so that this information is readily available for the next budget iteration.

- *Base expense changes on cost drivers.* Many expenses in the budget will vary in accordance with changes in various activities within the firm. As noted earlier in this section, expenses can be listed in the budget model as formulas, so that they vary in direct proportion to changes in budgeted revenue. This same concept can be taken a step further by listing other types of activities that drive cost behavior, and linking still other expenses to them with formulas. For example, the amount of telephone expense is directly related to the number of employees, so it can be linked to the total number of employees on the staffing budget. Another example is the number of machine setup personnel, which will change based on the planned number of production batches to be run during the year. This level of automation requires a significant degree of knowledge of how selected expenses interact with various activities within the company.

- *Budget by groups of staff positions.* A budget can rapidly become unwieldy if every position in the company is individually identified—especially if the names of all employees are listed. This format requires constant updating as the budget progresses through multiple iterations. A better approach is to itemize by job title, which allows one to vastly reduce the number of job positions listed in the budget.

- *Rank projects.* A more complex budget model can incorporate a ranking of all capital projects, so that any projects with a low ranking will be automatically eliminated by the model if the available amount of cash drops below the point where they could be funded. However, this variation requires that great attention be paid to the ranking of projects, since there may be some interrelationship between projects—if one is dropped but others are retained, then the ones retained may not be functional without the missing project.

- *Issue a summary-level model for use by senior management.* The senior management team is primarily concerned with the summary results of each department, product line, or operating division, and does not have time to wade through the details of individual revenue and expense accounts. Further, it may require an increased level of explanation from the budgeting staff if they do choose to examine these details. Accordingly, the speed of the iteration process can be enhanced by producing a summary-level budget that is directly linked to the main budget, so that all fields in it are updated automatically. The senior management team can more easily review this document, yielding faster updates to the model.

- *Link budget results to employee goal and reward system.* The budgeting process does not end with the final approval of the budget model. Instead, it then passes to the human resources department, which uses it as the foundation for an employee goal and reward system. The trouble is that if budget approval is delayed, the human resources department will have very little time in which to create its goal and reward system. Accordingly, this add-on project should be incorporated directly into the budget model, so that it is approved alongside the rest of the budget. For example, a goals and rewards statement added to the budget can specify a bonus payment to the manager of the production department if he or she can create the number of units of product specified in the production budget. Similarly, the sales manager can receive a bonus based on reaching the sales goals noted in the revenue budget. By inserting the bonus amounts in this page of the budget, the model can automatically link them to the final targets itemized in the plan, requiring minimal further adjustments by the human resources staff.

As a result of these improvements, the budgeting process will change to the format shown in Exhibit 23-18, where the emphasis changes away from many modeling iterations toward the incorporation of a considerable level of automation and streamlining into the structure of the budget model. By following this approach, the budget will require much less manual updating, and will allow it to sail through the smaller number of required iterations with much greater speed.

23-6 BUDGETARY CONTROL SYSTEMS

There are several ways in which a budget can be used to enhance a company's control systems, so that objectives are met more easily and it is more difficult for costs to stray from approved levels.

One of the best methods for controlling costs is to link the budget for each expense within each department to the purchasing system. By doing so, the computer system will automatically accumulate the total amount of purchase orders that have been issued thus

Exhibit 23-18   Streamlined Budgeting Process

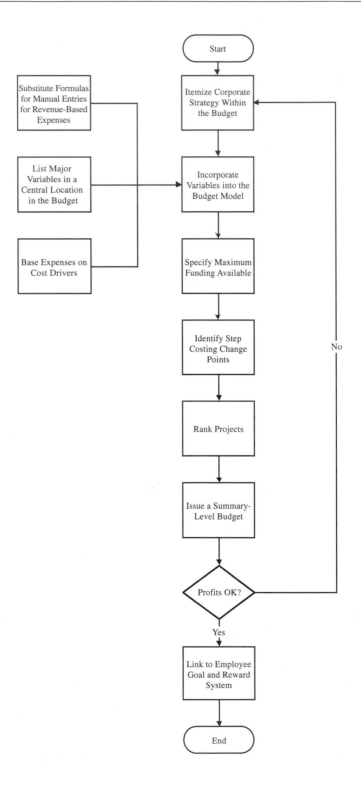

far against a specific account, and will refuse any further purchase orders when the budgeted expense total has been reached. This approach can involve the comparison of the monthly budget to monthly costs, or compare costs to annual budgeted totals. The latter approach can cause difficulty for the inattentive manager, since actual expenses may be running well ahead of the budget for most of the year, but the system will not automatically flag the problem until the entire year's budget has been depleted. Alternatively, a comparison to monthly budgeted figures may result in so many warning flags on so many accounts that the purchasing staff is unable to purchase many items. One workaround for this problem is to use a fixed overage percentage by which purchases are allowed to exceed the budget; another possibility is to only compare cumulative expenses to quarterly budget totals, which reduces the total number of system warning flags.

Another budgetary control system is to compare actual to budgeted results for the specific purpose of evaluating the performance of employees. For example, the warehouse manager may be judged based on actual inventory turnover of 12x, which compares unfavorably to a budgeted turnover rate of 15x. Similarly, the manager of a cost center may receive a favorable review if the total monthly cost of her cost center averages no more than $152,000. This also works for the sales staff, who can be assigned sales quotas that match the budgeted sales levels for their sales territories. In this manner, a large number of employees can have their compensation levels directly tied to the achievement of budgeted goals. This is a highly effective way to ensure that the budget becomes a fixture in the lives of employees.

Yet another budgetary control system is to use it as a feedback loop to employees. This can be done by issuing a series of reports at the end of each reporting period that are specifically designed to match the responsibilities of each employee. For example, Exhibit 23-19 shows a single revenue line item that is reported to a salesperson for a single territory. The salesperson does not need to see any other detailed comparison to the budget, because he is not responsible for anything besides the specific line item that is reported to him. This reporting approach focuses the attention of many employees on just those segments of the budget that they have control over. Though this approach can result in the creation of dozens or even hundreds of reports by the accounting department, they can be automated on most packaged accounting software systems, so that only the initial report creation will take up much accounting time.

Exhibit 23-19 Line Item Budget Reporting for Specific Employees

Account No.	Description	Actual Results	Budgeted Results	Variance
4500-010	Arizona Revenue	$43,529	$51,000	–$7,471

An additional control use for the budget is to detect fraud. The budget is usually based upon several years of actual operating results, so unless there are major changes in activity levels, actual expense results should be fairly close to budgeted expectations. If not, variance analysis is frequently used to find out what happened. This process is an excellent means for discovering fraud, since this activity will usually result in a sudden surge in expense levels, which the resulting variance analysis will detect. The two instances in which this control will not work is when the fraud has been in existence for a long time (and so is incorporated into the budgeted expense numbers already) or the amount of fraud is so low that it will not create a variance large enough to warrant investigation.

23-7 SUMMARY

The budget should not be treated as a chore that must be completed at the end of each fiscal year and then ignored, but rather as the foundation for all activities to be completed during the upcoming budget period. It drives the planning for capital expenditures, sales efforts, hiring, marketing campaigns, and research efforts. Due to its comprehensive nature, the accountant should use the budget as both a planning tool and a subsequent control over activities throughout the organization. The budget explanations, examples, and processes shown in this chapter will assist the accountant in achieving these goals.

CHAPTER 24

Closing the Books

24-1 INTRODUCTION

One of the primary tasks faced by any accountant is either some participation in, or the management of, the periodic delivery of financial statements. When poorly managed, this can result in the late delivery of the statements, as well as inconsistent treatment of recurring accounting issues from period to period, incorrect information, and minimal supporting commentary. In this chapter, we will cover the steps needed not only to properly organize the financial statement production process, but also how to close the books quite rapidly.

Speed of closure is an important goal, for it shifts the focus of the accounting department away from the production of the statements for a large part of the following month, which leaves more time for other activities, such as process improvement of accounting transactions, creating new data collection systems, or providing better financial analysis to the management team. This also results in better morale within the department, since the accounting staff can take pride in knowing that they are part of an efficient and effective process that results in a quality deliverable. Also, a key element in the organization of the financial statement production process is the ongoing and in-depth review of all accounting transactions that feed into the statements, so that errors can be eliminated from them before they reach the financial statements. This ongoing review process leads to considerable efficiencies in operations throughout the accounting department. Consequently, rapidly producing accurate financial statements should be considered an important goal for the accounting department.

24-2 INTERIM REPORTS

One of the best ways to satisfy financial report recipients with information is to query them about what types of information they need to see as soon as possible, and then report

293

on this information apart from the financial statements. For example, if they need to see revenue figures for the full month as soon as possible, it may make sense to issue daily or weekly summaries instead, as well as an estimated revenue figure just before the end of the reporting period. By taking this approach, the management team gets to see what it wants at regular intervals, and has less need to see the full set of financial statements, which the accounting staff can then complete and issue a few days later, with no pressure being exerted by anyone because they want to see the information. Other examples of the types of information that report recipients might want to see in advance of the financial statements are both revenue and margins by salesperson, product, or region; cash flow; capital expenditures; and specific performance measurements, such as the days of accounts receivable on hand.

If this approach is taken, then it is very important to build especially strong control systems around the information that is reported early. The main reason for doing this is that the recipients have already established that this is the most important information that they want to see, so it has to be as accurate as possible when issued. Since the time of issuance will be prior to the release of the full financial statements, there will be little time to cross check the underlying data for accuracy. Consequently, the control systems used to collect and summarize the data must be good enough to spot any errors at once and warn the accounting staff that there is a problem.

The use of interim reports is an effective way to issue only the most crucial information as early and frequently as possible, resulting in better information for recipients and less pressure on the accounting staff to complete the financial statements in short order.

24-3 GENERAL IMPROVEMENTS FOR CLOSING THE BOOKS

There are several general activities that will contribute to the speedy and orderly closing of the financial records. One of the most important is to create an expectation with the management team that it will take some time before the speed of closure will improve. The process described in the next few sections is a highly iterative one that can drive the closing process down to as little as one day, but it may be a year or more before this goal is attained. By pointing out the gradual nature of this process, there will be no expectation that a sudden leap in closure speed will occur.

Another general improvement is to place rigid controls over the types of preclosure information being released by the accounting department. When information is handed out before it has been checked for accuracy, the accounting staff will find itself in the uncomfortable position later on of having to waste time issuing revised reports and explaining why the original information was incorrect. These activities will take place right in the middle of the closing process, and so contribute to a much slower release of financial statements. However, management may insist on receiving some types of information as soon as possible; if so, the best approach is to create extra controls over the data that goes into the reported information, so that there is little risk of its inaccuracy. Thus, it is crucial to avoid releasing inaccurate information prior to the issuance of the financial statements.

Another general activity is to document the existing process that is used to create financial statements. This should include a listing of which employees perform certain tasks, the dates on which those tasks are to be completed, and their sequential order. This information forms the basis upon which changes will be made. Writing down the process will likely increase the speed of closure, since the accounting manager can then use it as a checklist to monitor the progress of the closing process.

The standardization of the chart of accounts throughout the organization is a very useful activity, for it reduces the work required to consolidate the financial statements. With a common account structure, there is no need to create a detailed system for mapping accounts from various subsidiaries into a master chart of accounts. Though this can be a difficult and prolonged task to accomplish, the result will be a much smoother closing process.

Yet another general activity is to organize the resources of the department so that it is fully staffed during the periods when financial statements are being compiled. This means that vacations should not be allowed for those employees who are expected to work on the statements during the days when the closing process is under way. If there will be periods when the workload is expected to exceed the available capacity of the staff, then overtime hours should be scheduled well in advance. It also means that any other activities within the accounting area, such as meetings, the preparation of other reports, or training sessions, should be routinely shifted to some other dates that will not conflict with the closing process.

A final general activity is to include a class on the closing process in the mix of departmental training activities. By doing so, the accounting staff can learn about the entire process, so that they will realize how their individual activities affect it. They can also learn about the various techniques available for documenting and analyzing process flows, with a particular focus on reducing cycle times. This knowledge is of great value when the accounting department works on the reduction of time needed to close the books. This training can be extended to include additional personnel, so that the department is fully cross-trained in all of the tasks associated with producing financial statements; by doing so, the department will still be able to complete financial statements on time, even if a few employees are not available to work on them during the closing period.

24-4 CLOSING ACTIVITIES PRIOR TO PERIOD-END

The days prior to the end of the accounting period can be used to complete a large quantity of activities related to the close. This is a prime area for improvements, since many accounting organizations seem to think that the closing process does not begin until the accounting period is complete. In reality, a properly managed closing process will have very few tasks to complete *after* the end of the accounting period. In this section, we will review many of these activities.

In terms of slowing down the production of financial statements, one of the worst offenders is the bank reconciliation. It does not usually arrive from the bank until a week after the account period has closed, and then requires a rush effort to complete. To avoid this problem, several of the larger national and super-regional banks now offer on-line access to detailed banking records, which allows one to conduct an ongoing bank reconciliation throughout the month. As a result, all adjusting entries for the bank reconciliation will have been made well before the end of the accounting period, so that there is no further work to be done in this area after the period-end.

Another activity is the ongoing review of key account balances during the accounting period, or at least a single review several days prior to the period-end. By doing so, the accounting staff can see if there are any unusually high or low account balances that require investigation. This review may involve a comparison to budgeted levels or a trend line of balances from previous periods. By checking balances a few days early, the accounting staff can spot and correct problems that would otherwise require examination during the "crunch period" immediately following the end of the accounting period, when there are few resources available for such activities.

It is also possible to complete all depreciation and amortization calculations prior to period-end. Though it is quite likely that a few assets arriving close to the period-end will not be recorded in these calculations, they will be picked up for the following period's financial statements, and so will have a minimal impact on reported results. If this method is used, there should be an additional waiting period at the end of the fiscal year, so that *all* assets can be recorded for auditing purposes.

Another possibility is to create a bad debt reserve in advance of the period-end that is based on a historical trend line of bad debt experiences. This accrual can be adjusted every quarter or so in order to reflect actual bad debt experience. As long as there is a reasonably well-founded history of bad debts upon which to rely, there is no reason to conduct a painstaking review of this reserve at the end of each reporting period.

One can also reduce the time needed to produce the written financial statements by creating boilerplate footnotes in advance to accompany the statements. The footnotes can have blank spots in the few areas that require adjustments based on the period-end figures, while the remaining verbiage is reviewed in advance to verify that it is still applicable to the financial situation.

Another report-related activity is to review the format and content of the previous period's financial statements with the management team to see if they need all of the information that was presented. If not, then these items can be eliminated, which reduces the amount of data gathering and summarization that would otherwise be required.

Cost allocations are a prime target for advance work. The bases upon which overhead allocations are typically made are carefully recalculated after every period-end, even though the percentage changes in the bases tend to be quite small. A better approach is to allocate costs using bases that are developed from the financial and operational results of the last few reporting periods, which ignores the results of the current period. By doing so, the allocation bases can be developed at any time during the current accounting period, and can then be quickly multiplied by period-end costs to determine actual allocations.

Another possibility is to create and partially populate journal entry forms in advance. For example, forms can be created in advance for all of the following entries, including account numbers and descriptions:

- Amortization
- Audit fee
- Bad debt
- Depreciation
- Insurance
- Interest income
- Interest expense
- Property taxes

- Royalties
- Salaries and wages accrual
- Vacation accrual
- Bank reconciliation

Some accruals, such as for salaries and wages, can also be completed in advance using estimations. For example, the accounting staff can approximate the number of people who will be working during the period between the last pay day and the end of the accounting period, and create an accrual for this amount. These entries tend to be slightly inaccurate, but can be improved upon by diligent reviews of variances between estimates and actual results.

A small number of accruals will involve the exact same amount of money in every accounting period. If so, these can be converted into automatically recurring entries (assuming that the accounting software will allow this), and so can be entered once and then avoided, save for an occasional review to see if the entry is still valid.

The number of possible activities that one can engage in prior to the period-end makes it clear that the closing process is one that can be conducted in a continuous manner, rather than in a rush, and so is more conducive to smooth scheduling of accounting staff time.

24-5 CLOSING ACTIVITIES SUBSEQUENT TO PERIOD-END

Once the accounting period has ended, the primary focus should be on the remaining activities needed to complete the close that are bottleneck operations. In other words, all management attention should focus on those few items that require the largest amount of staff time to complete. There are only a few items in this category. The worst one used to be the bank reconciliation, but in the last section we learned how to shift the bulk of the work associated with that activity into the prior period. One of the other bottlenecks is the completion of invoicing from activities at the end of the prior period. The completion of this activity is dependent upon the forwarding of shipping documentation by the shipping staff, so it is helpful to send the accounting staff to that area to assist in the completion of paperwork, which they can then hand-carry back to the accounting department. This activity can also be automated, as noted in the next section.

Another bottleneck operation is the completion of accounts payable. One could wait a week for all supplier invoices to arrive in the mail and then enter them into the computer system, but this introduces a one-week delay into the closing process. A better approach is to compile a list of recurring invoices that always arrive late, and accrue an estimated balance for each one, rather than wait for the actual invoice to arrive. Also, if purchase orders are used, any open ones can be compared to the receiving log to see if the associated purchases have arrived, even if the supplier invoice has not, and then accrue for the amount of the purchase order. This process can also be automated, as noted in the next section.

Another bottleneck operation is the investigation and resolution of variances. This step tends to occur last, after the financial statements have been produced, but are clearly not showing accurate results. As noted in the last section, some variance analysis can be conducted in the prior period, based on partial results. However, some variances will still arise. One way to reduce the workload is to only review items that exceed a minimum variance threshold percentage, and leave all other variances for investigation after the statements have been released. Though this defers some likely transactional corrections, they will be so small that they would not have made a significant alteration in the reported financial results.

A final bottleneck is the accumulation of quantity and costing information for the period-end inventory. If a manual inventory count is conducted at the end of each period, then several days and many hours of staff time must be devoted to this activity, resulting in significant delays in the closing. To combat this, the inventory system should be shifted to a perpetual one, where ongoing inventory balances are constantly updated. This allows one to avoid period-end inventory counts and focus instead on cycle counts, which are small ongoing counts that constantly review different parts of the inventory area. These steps avoid all period-end activities related to inventory.

Even with the bottleneck-related problems being systematically addressed and reduced in size, there are a number of other activities that can be improved upon, though their impact will not be as great. One is to avoid the creation of small accruals. In too many instances, an overly zealous accounting manager requires the staff to calculate and create accruals for every conceivable expense, even though their net impact is minimal. This results in a barely discernible impact on the financial statements, but a considerable workload on the staff. To avoid the problem, there should be a minimum accrual size below which accruals will not be created.

There can also be a problem with an overabundance of journal entries that are made during this period, possibly conflicting with each other. The problem arises because multiple employees have the ability to enter journal entries. A better approach is to funnel all journal entries through a small group of authorized personnel, so that these employees can track what entries are made, compare them to a standard set of entries, and verify that the correct entries are made, in the correct amounts, and to the correct accounts.

It is also possible to analyze the post period-end processing flow and revise it so that activities are accomplished in parallel, rather than serially. For example, a processing flow may be arranged so that the first task must be completed before the next task is addressed, which in turn feeds into yet another task. This process flow incorporates a great deal of wait time between activities, and therefore tends to greatly extend the time required to complete the final task at the end of the chain of activities. It is better to split apart these processes into smaller groups, so that the number of dependencies is reduced. This allows one to complete the closing much more quickly.

A final item is related to management of the process—the accounting manager should schedule a daily meeting with the accounting staff to go over the tasks that need to be completed in order to close the books. These meetings should always include a handout that specifies the exact tasks required of each person on the team, when the tasks must be completed, and whether or not they have been done. If the closing process is a highly accelerated one, it may even be necessary to hold more than one meeting per day to ensure that tasks are being properly completed. This task cannot be overemphasized—proper management has a major positive impact on the efficiency and effectiveness of the closing process.

24-6 CLOSING ACTIVITIES SUBSEQUENT TO STATEMENT ISSUANCE

During the issuance of financial statements, it is quite likely that several problems will be encountered, such as errors in a few transactions that required manual correction by the accounting staff, or perhaps a failure in the closing schedule that resulted in some wasted time and delayed issuance of the statements. If these problems crop up once, they will very likely do so again, unless prompt action is taken to resolve them before the next set of financial statements must be issued. Consequently, it is important to call a meeting immediately after the financial statements have been completed, so that all participants in the process can categorize the problems encountered and prioritize them for resolution. Responsibility for completion of the most critical items can then be handed out, with follow-up meetings scheduled by the accounting manager to ensure that progress is made in resolving the issues.

These meetings do not have to focus on just the problems that were encountered. Another major topic of discussion can be streamlining methods that further reduce the time period needed before the statements can be issued. This may involve changes in who does some portions of the work, or perhaps the reduced use of some accounting controls that are interfering with the processing time. This may also include an ongoing analysis of the critical path used by the accounting team, with particular attention being paid to the time required for the completion of certain processing steps, as well as wait times for key activities. The number of potential topics is quite large, and should keep an accounting team busy on an ongoing basis with a continual stream of prospective improvements to be considered.

Another valuable activity is to utilize the services of the internal audit department in arriving at solutions to systemic problems that are interfering with the production of financial statements. Specifically, if the accounting staff finds recurring transactional problems that are originating outside of the accounting department, then it should call for an audit to ascertain the root cause of the problem, as well as recommendations for how to resolve it. The only problem is that the internal audit staff may have a long backlog of requested audits, and cannot address the requested issues for some time. Consequently, it is important to list all issues to be handed over to the internal audit staff as soon as they are discovered, rather than burying them in a long list of problems to be addressed at a later date.

24-7 THE INSTANTANEOUS CLOSE

A few companies are now touting their achievement of an instantaneous close. In its ultimate form, this means that one can request a financial statement from the computer system at the stroke of midnight on the last day of the accounting period, and expect to see an accurate set of financial statements.

To achieve this extraordinary level of promptness and accuracy requires a correspondingly extraordinary attention to all of the systems that feed into the financial statements. There should be minimal manual data entry or intervention of any sort, as well as such a small number of transactional errors that their incurrence results in no discernible difference in the accuracy of the financial statements. Here are some of the areas in which significant changes must be made in order to achieve the instantaneous close:

- *Accurate perpetual inventory system.* There can be no problems with the perpetual inventory system in terms of inventory identification, location codes, quantities, or units of measure. To achieve such a high degree of accuracy calls for a very highly trained warehouse staff, as well as constant cycle counts of the inventory and immediate follow-up of any issues found during the counts. Furthermore, the perpetual inventory records must be linked to the accounting database, so that the data can be immediately pulled into the financial statements.

- *Automated bank reconciliations.* To avoid the lengthy delays typically associated with bank reconciliations, a company must arrange with its bank for a direct electronic linkage to its banking records, so that it can electronically compare its book records to the bank records. The result will be a small number of reconciling items that can be quickly reviewed and fixed by the accounting staff.

- *Automatic accrual calculations.* Accruals can be automated if there are linkages to supporting databases. For example, the payroll database should contain a record of how many hours have been reported by all hourly employees, right up to the last day of the accounting period; a program can multiply these hours worked by employee pay rates, including shift differentials and overtime, to arrive at quite an accurate wage accrual. The salary accrual calculation can also be automated by linking it to the payroll database, which allows a program to determine a salary accrual in a similar manner. This approach will also work for the vacation accrual (by a linkage to the payroll database), and the bad debt accrual (by a linkage to the collections history database, along with some collection assumptions).

- *Automatic commission calculations.* There is no time to manually review all invoices completed during the past accounting period, calculate commission splits, overrides, and bonuses, and still meet the financial statement issuance deadline. Instead, the commission structure must be converted into a comprehensible and standardized structure that can be programmed into the accounting system, resulting in the automatic calculation of commissions. It is even better to post commissions for the sales staff to review over the course of the accounting period, so that they can talk to the accounting staff if they see any errors in the calculations.

- *Automatic depreciation calculations and posting.* When an account payable that is coded for a fixed asset is entered, the computer system must be able to automatically pull the entered data into a fixed asset program that will calculate depreciation and post the information to the accounting records. This will require some programming work to allow for additional data entry up front that will sufficiently identify each asset, as well as the asset class in which it should be recorded.

- *Automatic invoice generation.* A common delay in the financial statement completion process is the transfer of shipping data from the shipping department to the accounting staff, which bills it to customers. This is a highly manual process. To get around it, the receiving staff must create bills of lading through a computer that is linked to product price tables, which in turn can be used to automatically create invoices. Even better, the invoices can be replaced by electronic data interchange transactions that are automatically sent to customers. This process is more difficult for services companies, since they must collect information from employees regarding hours worked during the period, as well as the tasks on which they worked. This issue can be alleviated by having employees enter their information through a company Internet site, which in turn is linked to an invoicing program within the accounting system. This tends to be a lengthy process to accomplish.

- *Automatic payables posting.* Financial statements can be seriously delayed if a company is waiting for a few remaining supplier invoices to arrive—which may take one or two extra weeks. To avoid this, a company can revert to the use of purchase orders for all purchases of any significant size; if a product has been received from a supplier by the end of the accounting period, but not its associated invoice, then the company can use the underlying purchase order information to accrue for the cost of the received item, thereby avoiding the need for the supplier invoice to create an accurate set of financial statements. In addition, there can be a considerable delay associated with the comparison of purchase orders to supplier invoices and receiving documentation before accounts payable will be entered into the accounting database. To avoid this trouble, the receiving staff can check off receipts at a computer terminal in the receiving area that are authorized through a purchase order, which in turn triggers an automatic payment to the supplier. This avoids the entire document matching process, thereby eliminating a hindrance to the creation of instantaneous financial statements.

Though the word "automatic" occurs a great deal in the preceding list of capabilities, it is not really necessary to have a fully automated system in order to achieve an instantaneous close. Any activity that can be completed before the end of an accounting period, such as estimated accruals or on-line bank reconciliations, can still be performed manually, since it will have no impact on the release date for the financial statements.

It is also possible to take the concept of the instantaneous close a step further and close the books at any time during the reporting period, so that one can see an accurate picture of the company's financial results. This capability requires somewhat more work to become perfectly accurate, since the system must incorporate incremental journal entries that itemize costs for a partial period that would normally only be entered at the end of the period. The most common issues here are accrued salaries and wages, as well as depreciation. For example, salaries are normally paid just a few times per month, and are only recorded in the accounting records at those intervals. This means that anyone trying to create financial statements just prior to the date when salary information is entered into the system will see financial results that are deficient in the amount of salary expense. A reasonable way to avoid this problem for salary expenses is to link the accounting database to the human resources database, so that a computer program can make a reasonable estimate of the daily salary expense based on the number of employees, and create an entry in the general ledger that reflects this estimate. The computer system must also be able to reverse out these daily entries whenever actual salary costs are entered, in order to avoid double counting of salary expenses. This level of sophistication calls for a great deal of programming expertise, as well as a more cluttered general ledger that will contain many daily accruals and related accrual reversals.

An alternative approach to the use of automated daily accruals is to have the accounting staff manually determine the amount of the daily accruals in advance, set them up into a single journal entry, and make the journal entry every morning, so that anyone accessing the company's financial information after that time will be able to see reasonably accurate daily financial information. This is a much less expensive way to handle daily accruals. However, the accounting staff must frequently update its standard daily journal entry to ensure that the accrual is as close to actual results as possible.

The instantaneous close, as well as its more advanced cousin, the daily close, require extraordinarily accurate underlying accounting information in order to yield accurate results. This means that the accounting staff must labor to clean up the processes for all of the transactions that flow into the financial statements, which can take a very long time to achieve. In addition, the accounting computer systems must be modified to achieve higher levels of automation than is normally found in a standard off-the-shelf accounting package. Accordingly, this level of achievement is only found in companies with a great devotion to transactional excellence and a large budget for computer system customizations.

24-8 SUMMARY

This chapter has pointed out a number of activities that can be of great assistance in reducing the time frame needed to close the accounting books and issue financial statements. Doing so properly requires three key elements: an intense focus on the improvement of all processes that feed into the production of financial statements, an accounting supervisor who can effectively manage the entire process, and (for those companies looking to achieve an extremely fast close) the transfer of nearly all manual accounting functions to a computer system that automatically completes all but the most complicated transactions. With all of these components in place, a company can achieve not only very fast closing times, but also an exceptionally efficient accounting department.

CHAPTER 25

Control Systems

25-1 INTRODUCTION

One of the chief roles of the accountant is to examine each process that involves financial transactions to see where there is a risk of losing assets, and installing control points that will prevent those losses from occurring. For example, a major potential weakness in the billing process is that the shipping department may never inform the accounting staff of a shipment, resulting in no invoice being sent to a customer. In this chapter, we review the need for control systems, the types of fraudulent activities that make the use of controls particularly important, and describe over 60 controls that can be added to the typical accounting system.

Since controls frequently have a cost associated with them, it is also possible to take them *out of* an accounting system in order to save money; we will discuss the process of spotting these controls, and evaluating their usefulness prior to removing them.

25-2 THE NEED FOR CONTROL SYSTEMS

The most common situation in which a control point is needed is when an innocent error is made in the processing of a transaction. For example, an accounts payable clerk neglects to compare the price on a supplier's invoice to the price listed on the authorizing purchase order, which results in the company paying more than it should. Similarly, the warehouse staff decides to accept a supplier shipment, despite a lack of approving purchasing documentation, resulting in the company being obligated to pay for something that it does not need. These types of actions may occur because of poor employee training, inattention, or the combination of a special set of circumstances that were unforeseen when the accounting processes were originally constructed. There can be an extraordinary number of reasons why a transactional error arises, which can result in errors that are not caught, and which in turn lead to the loss of corporate assets.

Controls act as review points at those places in a process where these types of errors have a habit of arising. The potential for some errors will be evident when a process flow expert reviews a flowchart that describes a process, simply based on his or her knowledge of where errors in similar processes have a habit of arising. Other errors will be specific to a certain industry—for example, the casino industry deals with enormous quantities of cash, and so has a potential for much higher monetary loss through its cash handling processes than do similar processes in other industries. Also, highly specific circumstances within a company may generate errors in unlikely places. For example, a manufacturing company that employs mostly foreign workers who do not speak English will experience extra errors in any processes where these people are required to fill out paperwork, simply due to a reduced level of comprehension of what they are writing. Consequently, the typical process can be laced with areas in which a company has the potential for loss of assets.

Many potential areas of asset loss will involve such minor or infrequent errors that accountants can safely ignore them, and avoid the construction of any offsetting controls. Others have the potential for very high risk of loss, and so are shored up with not only one control point, but a whole series of multi-layered cross-checks that are designed to keep all but the most unusual problems from arising or being spotted at once.

The need for controls is also driven by the impact of their cost and interference in the smooth functioning of a process. If a control requires the hiring of an extra person, then a careful analysis of the resulting risk mitigation is likely to occur. Similarly, if a highly efficient process is about to have a large and labor-intensive control point plunked down into the middle of it, it is quite likely that an alternative approach should be found that provides a similar level of control, but from outside the process.

The controls installed can be of the preventive variety, which are designed to spot problems as they are occurring (such as on-line pricing verification for the customer order data entry staff), or of the detective variety, which spot problems after they occur, so that the accounting staff can research the associated problems and fix them after the fact (such as a bank reconciliation). The former type of control is the best, since it prevents errors from ever being completed, whereas the second type results in much more labor by the accounting staff to research each error and correct it. Consequently, the type of control point installed should be evaluated based on its cost of subsequent error correction.

All of these factors—perceived risk, cost, and efficiency—will have an impact on a company's need for control systems, as well as the preventive or detective type of each control that is contemplated.

25-3 TYPES OF FRAUD

The vast majority of transactional problems that controls guard against are innocent errors that are caused by employee mistakes. These tend to be easy to spot and correct, when the proper control points are in place. However, the most feared potential loss of assets is not through these mistakes, but through deliberate fraud on the part of employees, since these transactions are deliberately masked, making it much more difficult to spot them. Here are the most common types of fraud that are perpetrated:

- *Cash and investment theft.* The theft of cash is the most publicized type of fraud, and yet the amount stolen is usually quite small, when compared to the byzantine layers of controls that are typically installed to prevent such an occurrence. The real problem in this area is the theft of investments, when someone sidesteps existing controls to clean out a company's entire investment account. Accordingly, the accountant should spend the most time designing controls over the movement of invested funds.

- *Expense account abuse.* Employees can use fake expense receipts, apply for reimbursement of unapproved items, or apply multiple times for reimbursement through their expense reports. Many of these items are so small that they are barely worth the cost of detecting, while others, such as the duplicate billing to the company of airline tickets, can add up to very large amounts. Controls in this area tend to be costly and time-consuming.

- *Financial reporting misrepresentation.* Though no assets appear to be stolen, the deliberate falsification of financial information is still fraud, because it impacts a company's stock price by misleading investors about financial results. Controls in this area should involve internal audits to ensure that processes are set up correctly, as well as full audits (not reviews or compilations) by external auditors.

- *Fixed assets theft.* Though the fixed assets name implies that every asset is big enough to be immovable, many items—particularly computers—can be easily stolen and then resold by employees. In many instances, there is simply no way to prevent the loss of assets without the use of security guards and surveillance equipment. Given that many organizations do not want to go that far, the most common control is the purchase of insurance with a minimal deductible, so that losses can be readily reimbursed.

- *Inventory and supplies theft.* The easiest theft for an employee is to remove inventory or supplies from a storage shelf and walk away with them. Inventory controls can be enhanced through the use of fencing and limited access to the warehouse, but employees can still hand inventory out through the shipping and receiving gates. The level of controls installed in this area will depend upon the existing level of pilferage, and the value of inventory and supplies.

- *Nonpayment of advances.* The employees who need advances, either on their pay or for travel, are typically those who have few financial resources. Consequently, they may not pay back advances unless specifically requested to do so. This requires detailed tracking of all outstanding advances.

- *Purchases for personal use.* Employees with access to company credit cards can make purchases of items that are diverted to their homes. Controls are needed that require one to have detailed records of all credit card purchases, rather than relying on a cursory scan and approval of an incoming credit card statement.

- *Supplier kickbacks.* Members of the purchasing staff can arrange with suppliers to source purchases through them in exchange for kickback payments directly to the purchasing staff. This usually results in a company paying more than the market rate for those items. This is a difficult type of fraud to detect, since it requires an ongoing review of prices paid as compared to a survey of market rates.

Fraud problems are heightened in some organizations, because the environment is such that fraud is easier to commit. For example, a rigorous emphasis on increasing profits by top management may lead to false financial reporting in order to "make the numbers." Problems can also arise if the management team is unwilling to pay for controls or for a sufficient number of supervisory personnel, if it is dominated by one or two people who can override existing controls, or if it has high turnover, so that new managers have a poor grasp of existing controls. Fraud is also common when the organizational structure is very complex or the company is growing quite rapidly, since both situations tend to result in fewer controls that create opportunities to remove assets. Consequently, fraud is much more likely if there are unrealistic growth objectives, if there are problems within the management ranks, or if controls are not keeping pace with changes in the organizational structure.

25-4 KEY CONTROLS

There are thousands of possible controls that can be used to ensure that a company maintains proper control over its assets. The following list, which is an expanded version of the controls listed on pages 132–134 of Willson, Roehl-Anderson, and Bragg, *Controllership,* John Wiley & Sons, 1999, represents the most common controls found in most organizations. These can be supplemented by additional controls in cases where the potential for loss of assets is considered to be exceptionally high, with the reverse being true in other instances. The 14 controls are:

1. *Cash.* The handling of cash is considered to be rife with control issues, resulting in perhaps an excessive use of controls. Though many potential controls are listed below, one should attempt to create a mix of controls that balances their cost against incremental gains in the level of control achieved. They are as follows:

   - *Compare check register to actual check number sequence.* The computer's list of checks printed should exactly match the checks that have actually been used. If not, this can be evidence that someone has removed a check from the check stock in hopes that it will not be noticed. This irregularity is most common for laser check stock, since these checks are stored as separate sheets, rather than as a continuous roll of check stock, and so can be more easily pilfered.

   - *Conduct spot audits of petty cash.* It is possible to misrepresent the contents of a petty cash box through the use of miscellaneous receipts and IOU vouchers. By making unscheduled audits, one can sometimes spot these irregularities.

   - *Control check stock.* The check stock cannot be stored in the supply closet along with the pencils and paper, because anyone can remove a check from the stack, and then is only a forged signature away from stealing funds from the company. Instead, the check stock should locked in a secure cabinet, to which only authorized personnel have access.

   - *Control signature plates.* If anyone can access the company's signature plates, then it is not only possible to forge checks, but also to stamp authorized signatures on all sorts of legal documents. Accordingly, these plates should always be kept in the company safe.

- *Create a check list in the mail room.* If there is any chance that someone in the accounting department is removing customer checks before they are included in the daily deposit records, then the mail room staff can be asked to create a separate list, which can later be compared to the deposit slip list to see if there are any differences.

- *Deposit all checks daily.* If checks are kept on hand for several days, there is an increased likelihood that someone will gain access to them and cash them into his or her own account. Consequently, bank deposits should be made every day.

- *Divert incoming cash to a lockbox.* If cash or checks from customers never reach a company, then a host of control problems related to the potential misuse of that cash goes away. To do this, a lockbox can be set up that is controlled by the company's bank, and customers can be asked to send their payments to the lockbox address.

- *Fill in empty spaces on checks.* If the line on a check that lists the amount of cash to be paid is left partially blank, a forger can insert extra numbers on words that will result in a much larger check payment. This can be avoided by having the software that prints checks insert a line or series of characters in the spaces.

- *Fill out petty cash vouchers in ink.* Petty cash receipts can be modified to make it appear that they are larger than was really the case, with the perpetrator removing the difference from the cash box. This issue can be resolved by requiring that all vouchers be filled out in ink.

- *Limit petty cash reserves.* If there is little money in a petty cash box, then there is less incentive for anyone to steal the box. If there is a large amount of cash volume flowing through the box, then a useful alternative is procurement cards.

- *Mutilate voided checks.* A voided check can be retrieved and cashed. To keep this from happening, a stamping device that cuts the word "void" into the surface of the check should be used, thereby sufficiently mutilating it that it cannot be used again.

- *Perform bank reconciliations.* This is one of the most important controls anywhere in a company, for it reveals all possible cash inflows and outflows. The bank statement's list of checks cashed should be carefully compared to the company's internal records to ensure that checks have not been altered once they leave the company, or that the books have not been altered to disguise the amount of the checks. It is also necessary to compare the bank's deposit records to the books to see if there are discrepancies that may be caused by someone taking checks or cash out of the batched bank deposits. Further, one should compare the records of all company bank accounts to see if any check kiting is taking place. In addition, it is absolutely fundamental that the bank reconciliation be completed by someone who is completely unassociated with the accounts payable, accounts receivable, or cash receipts functions, so that there is no way for anyone to conceal the wrongdoings by altering the bank reconciliation. Finally, it is now possible to call up on-line bank records through the Internet, so that a reconciliation can be conducted every day. This is a useful approach, since irregularities can be spotted and corrected much more quickly.

- *Review uncashed checks.* If checks have not been cashed, it is possible that they were created through some flaw in the accounts payable system that sent a check to a non-existent supplier. An attempt should be made to contact these suppliers to see if there is a problem.

- *Update signature cards.* A company's bank will have on file a list of check signatories that the company has authorized to sign checks. If one of these people leaves the company for any reason, he or she still has the ability to sign company checks. To void this control problem, the bank's signature card should be updated as soon as a check signer leaves the company.

- *Stamp incoming checks with "deposit to account number . . ."* It is possible that employees with access to customer checks will try to cash them, as might anyone with access to the mail once it has left the company. This can be made more difficult by stamping the back of the check with "deposit to account number xxxxx," so that someone would have to deface this stamp in order to cash the check.

2. *Investments.* The shifting of investment funds is the area in which a person has the best chance for stealing large quantities of company funds, or of placing them in inappropriate investments that have a high risk of loss. The following controls are designed to contain these risks:

- *Impose investment limits.* When investing its excess funds, a company should have a policy that requires it to only invest certain amounts in particular investment categories or vehicles. For example, only the first $100,000 of funds are insured through a bank account, so excess funding beyond this amount can be shifted elsewhere. As another example, the Board of Directors may feel that there is too much risk in junk bond investments, and so will place a general prohibition on this type of investment. These sorts of policies can be programmed into a treasury workstation, so that the system will automatically flag investments that fall outside a company's pre-set investment parameters.

- *Require authorizations to shift funds among accounts.* A person who is attempting to fraudulently shift funds out of a company's accounts must have approval authorization on file with one of the company's investment banks to transfer money out to a non-company account. This type of authorization can be strictly controlled through signatory agreements with the banks. It is also possible to impose strict controls over the transfer of funds *between* company accounts, since a fraudulent person may uncover a loophole in the control system whereby a particular bank has not been warned *not* to allow fund transfers outside of a pre-set range of company accounts, and then shift all funds to that account and thence to an outside account.

3. *Accounts Receivable.* Controls are needed in the accounts receivable area to ensure that employees do not take payments from customers and then hide the malfeasance by altering customer receivable records. Here are the most common controls:

- *Compare checks received to applications made against accounts receivable.* It is possible for an accounts receivable clerk with the dual responsibility of cash application to cash a check to his or her personal account, and then hide evidence of the stolen funds by continually applying subsequent cash received against the oldest accounts receivable. This can be spotted by conducting an occasional comparison of checks listed on the deposit slip for a given day to the accounts against which the funds were credited.

- *Confirm receivables balances.* If an employee is falsely applying cash from customers to different accounts in order to hide the loss of some cash that he or she has extracted from the company, it is possible to detect this problem by periodically sending out a confirmation form to customers to verify what they say they have paid to the company.

- *Require approval of bad debt expenses.* A manager should approve any bad debt write-offs from the accounts receivable listing. Otherwise, it is possible for someone to receive a check from a customer, cash it into their own account, and write off the corresponding account receivable as a bad debt. This control can be greatly enhanced by splitting the cash receipts function away from the collections function, so that it would require collusion to make this type of fraud work.

- *Require approval of credits.* It is possible for someone in the accounts receivable area to grant a credit to a customer in exchange for a kickback from the customer. This can be prevented through the use of approval forms for all credits granted, as well as a periodic comparison of credits granted to related approval forms. It is acceptable to allow the accounting staff to grant very small credits in order to clean up miscellaneous amounts on the accounts receivable listing, but these should be watched periodically to see if particular customers are accumulating large numbers of small credits.

4. *Inventory.* A company's inventory can be so large and complex that extensive controls are needed simply to give it any degree of accuracy at all. Consequently, virtually all of the following controls are recommended to achieve a high level of inventory record accuracy:

- *Conduct inventory audits.* If no one ever checks the accuracy of the inventory, it will gradually vary from the book inventory, as an accumulation of errors builds up over time. To counteract this problem, one can either schedule a complete re-count of the inventory from time to time, or else an ongoing cycle count of small portions of the inventory each day. Whichever method is used, it is important to conduct research in regard to why errors are occurring, and attempt to fix the underlying problems.

- *Control access to bill of material and inventory records.* The security levels assigned to the files containing bill of material and inventory records should allow access to only a very small number of well-trained employees. By doing so, the risk of inadvertent or deliberate changes to these valuable records will be minimized. The security system should also store the keystrokes and user access codes for anyone who has accessed these records, in case evidence is needed to prove that fraudulent activities have occurred.

- *Keep bill of material accuracy levels at a minimum of 98%.* The bills of material are critical for determining the value of inventory as it moves through the work-in-process stages of production and eventually arrives in the finished goods area, since they itemize every possible component that comprises each product. These records should be regularly compared to actual product components to verify that they are correct, and their accuracy should be tracked.

- *Require approval to sign out inventory beyond amounts on pick list.* If there is a standard pick list used to take raw materials from the warehouse for production purposes, then this should be the standard authorization for inventory removal. If the production staff requires any additional inventory, they should go to the warehouse gate and request it, and the resulting distribution should be logged out of the warehouse. Furthermore, any inventory that is left over after production is completed should be sent back to the warehouse and logged in. By using this approach, the cost accountant can tell if there are errors in the bills of material that are used to create pick lists, since any extra inventory requisitions or warehouse returns probably represent errors in the bills.

- *Require transaction forms for scrap and rework transactions.* A startling amount of materials and associated direct labor can be lost through the scrapping of production or its occasional rework. This tends to be a difficult item to control, since scrap and rework can occur at many points in the production process. Nonetheless, the manufacturing staff should be well trained in the use of transaction forms that record these actions, so that the inventory records will remain accurate.

- *Restrict warehouse access to designated personnel.* Without access restrictions, the company warehouse is like a large store with no prices—just take all you want. This does not necessarily mean that employees are taking items from stock for personal use, but they may be removing excessive inventory quantities for production purposes, which leads to a cluttered production floor. Also, this leaves the purchasing staff with the almost impossible chore of trying to determine what is in stock and what needs to be bought for immediate manufacturing needs. Consequently, a mandatory control over inventory is to fence it in and closely restrict access to it.

- *Segregate customer-owned inventory.* If customers supply a company with some parts that are used when constructing products for them, it becomes very easy for this inventory to be mingled with the company's own inventory, resulting in a false increase in its inventory valuation. Though it is certainly possible to assign customer-specific inventory codes to these inventory items in order to clearly identify them, a more easily discernible control is to physically segregate these goods in a different part of the warehouse.

5. *Employee Advances.* Employees may ask for advances on their next paycheck, or to cover the cost of their next trip on the company's behalf. In either case, it is easy to lose track of the advance. The following controls are needed to ensure that an advance is eventually paid back.

- *Continually review all outstanding advances.* When advances are paid to employees, it is necessary to continually review and follow up on the status of these advances. Employees who require advances are sometimes in a precarious financial position, and must be issued constant reminders to ensure that the funds are paid back in a timely manner. A simple control point is to have a policy that requires the company to automatically deduct all advances from the next employee paycheck, thereby greatly reducing the work of tracking advances.

- *Require approval of all advance payments to employees.* When employees request an advance for any reason—as a draw on the next paycheck or as funding for a company trip—this should always require formal signed approval from their immediate supervisors. The reason is that an advance is essentially a small short-term loan, which would also require management approval. The accounts payable supervisor or staff should only be allowed to authorize advances when they are in very small amounts.

6. *Fixed Assets.* The purchase and sale of fixed assets require special controls to ensure that proper authorization has been obtained to conduct either transaction, and also to ensure that the funds associated with fixed assets are properly accounted for. All of the following controls should be implemented to ensure that these goals are achieved.

- *Ensure that fixed asset purchases have appropriate prior authorization.* A company with a capital-intensive infrastructure may find that its most important controls are over the authorization of funds for new or replacement capital projects. Depending upon the potential amount of funding involved, these controls may include a complete net present value (NPV) review of the cash flows associated with each prospective investment, as well as multi-layered approvals that reach all the way up to the Board of Directors. A truly comprehensive control system will also include a post-completion review that compares the original cash flow estimates to those actually achieved, not only to see if a better estimation process can be used in the future, but also to see if any deliberate misrepresentation of estimates was initially made.

- *Verify that correct depreciation calculations are being made.* Though there is no potential loss of assets if incorrect depreciation calculations are being made, it can result in an embarrassing adjustment to the previously reported financial results at some point in the future. This control should include a comparison of capitalized items to the official corporate capitalization limit, in order to ensure that items are not being inappropriately capitalized and depreciated. The control should also include a review of the asset categories in which each individual asset has been recorded, in order to ensure that an asset has not been mis-classified, and therefore incorrectly depreciated.

- *Verify that fixed asset disposals are properly authorized.* A company does not want to have a fire sale of its assets taking place without any member of the management team knowing about it. Consequently, the sale of assets should be properly authorized prior to any sale transaction being initiated, if only to ensure that the eventual price paid by the buyer is verified as being a reasonable one.

- *Verify that cash receipts from asset sales are properly handled.* Employees may sell a company's assets, pocket the proceeds, and report to the company that the asset was actually scrapped. This control issue can be reduced by requiring that a bill of sale or receipt from a scrapping company accompany the file for every asset that has been disposed of.

- *Verify that fixed assets are being utilized.* Many fixed assets are parked in a corner and neglected, with no thought to their being profitably sold off. To see if this problem is occurring, the accounting staff should conduct a periodic review of all fixed assets, which should include a visual inspection and discussion with employees to see if assets are no longer in use.

7. *Accounts Payable.* This is one of the most common areas in which the misuse of assets will arise, as well as the one where transactional errors are most likely to occur. Nonetheless, an excessive use of controls in this area can result in a significant downgrading in the performance of the accounts payable staff, so a judiciously applied blend of controls should be used.

   - *Audit credit card statements.* When employees are issued company credit cards, there will be some risk that the cards will be used for non-company expenses. To avoid this, one can spot-check a few line items on every credit card statement, if not conduct a complete review of every statement received. For those employees who have a history of making inappropriate purchases, but for whom a credit card is still supplied, it is also possible to review their purchases on-line (depending upon what services are offered by the supplying bank) on the same day that purchases are made, and alter credit limits at the same time, thereby keeping tighter control over credit card usage.

   - *Compare payments made to the receiving log.* With the exception of payments for services or recurring payments, all payments made through the accounts payable system should have a corresponding record of receipt in the receiving log. If not, there should be grounds for investigation into why a payment was made. This can be a difficult control to implement if there is not an automated three-way matching system already in place, since a great deal of manual cross-checking will otherwise be needed.

   - *Compare the invoice numbers of supplier invoices received.* When suppliers are not paid promptly, they will probably send another copy of an invoice to the company, on the grounds that the first one must have been lost. If the first invoice is just being processed for payment, there is a good chance that the company will pay for both the original invoice and its copy. Consequently, the accounting software should automatically compare the invoice numbers of all invoices received, to see if there are duplications.

   - *Impose limitations on credit card purchases.* When credit cards are issued to employees, a company has a number of possible restrictions it can place on the cards that will help to keep employee spending within certain pre-defined limits. For example, if the card is issued by a specific store, then purchases can be limited to that entity. However, since this can result in a large number of credit card types, a more popular alternative is the procurement (or purchasing) card. This is a credit card for which a number of additional limits are imposed. This can include a maximum dollar amount for individual transactions, or maximum amounts per day, or be restricted to stores that have a certain SIC code. Depending on the level of service offered through the procurement card, the monthly charge statement can also list the general category of product purchased.

- *Require approval of all invoices that lack an associated purchase order.* If the purchasing department has not given its approval to an invoice, then the accounting staff must send it to the supervisor of the department to whom it will be charged, so that this person can review and approve it.

- *Require supervisory review and approval of credit card statements.* Even with the restrictions just noted for procurement cards, it is still possible for purchases to be made that are not authorized. If it seems necessary to verify employee spending habits, then copies of credit card statements can be sent to employee supervisors for review. This does not have to be for payment approval, but at least to ensure that supervisors are aware of the types of charges being made.

- *Verify authorizations with a three-way match.* Though extremely labor-intensive, it is important to compare a supplier's invoice to the authorizing purchase order to ensure that the details of each one match, while also matching the billed amount to the receiving documentation to ensure that the company is only paying for the amount received. Some computer systems can automate this matching process. An alternative is to have the receiving staff approve the amounts received from suppliers by comparing them to purchase orders, which then allows the accounting staff to pay suppliers from the authorizing purchase order, rather than the supplier invoice.

8. *Notes Payable.* The acquisition of new debt is usually a major event that is closely watched by the CFO, and so requires few controls. Nonetheless, the following control points are recommended as general corporate policies.

   - *Require approval of the terms of all new borrowing agreements.* A senior corporate manager should be assigned the task of reviewing all prospective debt instruments to verify that their interest rate, collateral, and other requirements are not excessively onerous or conflict with the terms of existing debt agreements. It may also be useful from time to time to see if a lending institution has inappropriate ties to the company, such as partial or full ownership in its stock by the person responsible for obtaining debt agreements.

   - *Require supervisory approval of all borrowings and repayments.* As was the case with the preceding control point, high-level supervisory approval is required for all debt instruments—except this time it is for final approval of each debt commitment. If the debt to be acquired is extremely large, it may be useful to have a policy requiring approval by the Board of Directors, just to be sure that there is full agreement at all levels of the organization regarding the nature of the debt commitment. To be a more useful control, this signing requirement should be communicated to the lender, so that it does not inadvertently accept a debt agreement that has not been signed by the proper person.

9. *Revenues.* The key controls concern related to revenues is that all shipments be invoiced in a timely manner. A controls failure in this area can lead to a major revenue shortfall and threaten overall company liquidity.

   - *Compare all billings to the shipping log.* There should be a continual comparison of billings to the shipment log, not only to ensure that everything shipped is billed, but also to guard against illicit shipments that involve collusion between outside parties and the shipping staff. Someone who is handing out products at the shipping dock will rarely be obliging enough to record this transaction in the shipping log, so the additional step of carefully comparing finished goods inventory levels to physical inventory counts and reviewing all transactions for each item must be used to determine where inventory shrinkage appears to be occurring.

- *Compare discounts taken to return authorizations granted.* Customers will sometimes take deductions when paying company invoices, on the grounds that they have returned some products to the company. The problem is that the company may never have authorized the returns, much less received them. A comparison of the returns authorization log to the list of discounts taken in the cash receipts journal will provide evidence that a customer is not paying for its obligations.

- *Identify shipments of product samples in the shipping log.* A product that is shipped with no intention of being billed is probably a product sample being sent to a prospective customer, marketing agency, and so on. These should be noted as product samples in the shipping log, and the internal audit staff should verify that each of them was properly authorized, preferably with a signed document.

10. *Cost of Goods Sold.* There are many ways in which a company can lose control over its costs in the cost of goods sold area, since it involves many personnel and the largest proportion of company costs. The application of the following suggested controls to a production environment will rely heavily on the perceived gain that will be experienced from using them, versus the extent to which they will interfere with the smooth functioning of the production department.

- *Compare the cost of all completed jobs to budgeted costs.* A company can suffer from major drops in its gross margin if it does not keep an eagle eye on the costs incurred to complete jobs. To do so, the cost accountant should compare a complete list of all costs incurred for a job to the initial budget or quote, and determine exactly which actual costs are higher than expected. This review should result in a list of problems that caused the cost overruns, which in turn can be addressed by the management team so that they do not arise again. This process should also be performed while jobs are in process (especially if the jobs are of long duration) so that these problems can be found and fixed before job completion.

- *Compare projected manning needs to actual direct labor staffing.* The production manager will have a tendency to overstaff the production area if this person is solely responsible for meeting the requirements of the production plan, since an excess of labor will help to ensure that products are completed on time. This tendency can be spotted and quantified by using labor routings to determine the amount of labor that should have been used, and then comparing this standard to the actual labor cost incurred.

- *Pick from stock based on bills of material.* An excellent control over material costs is to require the use of bills of material for each item manufactured, and then require that parts be picked from the raw materials stock for the production of these items based on the quantities listed in the bills of material. By doing so, a reviewer can hone in on those warehouse issuances that were *not* authorized through a bill of material, since there is no objective reason why these issuances should have taken place.

- *Purchase based on blanket purchase orders and related releases.* The purchasing staff is already doing its job if all purchases are authorized through purchase orders. However, they will be doing this work more efficiently if repeating purchase orders can be summarized into blanket purchase orders, against which releases are authorized from time to time. The internal audit staff should periodically determine if there are opportunities for the use of additional blanket purchase orders, if current ones are being used properly, and if the minimum quantity commitments listed on existing blanket orders are being met, thereby keeping the company from paying penalties for missing minimum order totals.

- *Reject all purchases that are not preapproved.* A major flaw in the purchasing systems of many companies is that all supplier deliveries are accepted at the receiving dock, irrespective of the presence of authorizing paperwork. Many of these deliveries are verbally authorized orders from employees throughout the company, many of whom are not authorized to make such purchases, or are not aware that they are buying items at high prices. This problem can be eliminated by enforcing a rule that all items received must have a corresponding purchase order on file that has been authorized by the purchasing department. By doing so, the purchasing staff can verify that there is a need for each item requisitioned, and that it is bought at a reasonable price from a certified supplier.

11. *Travel and Entertainment Expenses.* Employee expense reports can involve dozens of line items of requested expense reimbursements, a few of which may conflict with a company's stated reimbursement policies. In order to ensure that these "gray area" expense line items are caught, many accountants will apply a disproportionate amount of clerical time to the minute examination of expense reports. The need for this level of control will depend upon the accountant's perception of the amount of expenses that will be reduced through its use. In reality, some lesser form of control, such as expense report audits, are generally sufficient to keep expense reports "honest."

- *Audit expense reports at random.* Employees may be more inclined to pass through expense items on their expense reports if they think that the company is not reviewing their expenses. This issue can be resolved fairly inexpensively by conducting a few random audits of expense reports, and following up with offending employees regarding any unauthorized expense submissions. Word of these activities will get around, resulting in better employee self-monitoring of their expense reports. Also, if there is evidence of repeat offenders, the random audits can be made less random by requiring recurring audits for specific employees.

- *Issue policies concerning allowable expenses.* Employees may submit inappropriate expenses for reimbursement simply because they have not been told that the expenses are inappropriate. This problem can be resolved by issuing a detailed set of policies and procedures regarding travel. The concept can be made more available to employees by posting the information on a corporate intranet site. Also, if there is an on-line expense report submission system in place, these rules can be incorporated directly into the underlying software, so that the system will warn employees regarding inappropriate reimbursement submissions.

- *Require supervisory approval of all expense reports.* If there are continuing problems with expense reimbursement submissions from employees, it may be necessary to require supervisory approval of all expense reports. This has the advantage of involving someone who presumably knows why an employee is submitting a reimbursement form, and who can tell if the company should pay for it. The downside is that expense reports tend to sit on managers' desks for a long time, which increases the time period needed before an employee will receive payment.

12. *Payroll Expenses.* The controls used for payroll cover two areas—the avoidance of excessive amounts of pay to employees, and the avoidance of fraud related to the creation of paychecks for non-existent employees. Both types of controls are addressed here.

- *Require approval of all overtime hours worked by hourly personnel.* One of the simplest forms of fraud is to come back to the company after hours and clock out at a later time, or have another employee do it on one's behalf, thereby creating false overtime hours. This can be resolved by requiring supervisory approval of all overtime hours worked. A more advanced approach is to use a computerized time clock that categorizes each employee by a specific work period, so that any hours worked after his or her standard time period will be automatically flagged by the computer for supervisory approval. They may not even allow an employee to clock out after a specific time of day without a supervisory code first being entered into the computer.

- *Require approval of all pay changes.* Pay changes can be made quite easily through the payroll system if there is collusion between a payroll clerk and any other employee. This can be spotted through regular comparisons of pay rates *paid* to the approved pay rates *stored* in employee folders. It is best to require the approval of a high-level manager for all pay changes, which should include that person's signature on a standard pay change form. It is also useful to audit the deductions taken from employee paychecks, since these can be altered downward to effectively yield an increased rate of pay. This audit should include a review of the amount and timing of garnishment payments, to ensure that these deductions are being made as required by court orders.

- *Issue checks directly to recipients.* A common type of fraud is for the payroll staff to either create employees in the payroll system, or to carry on the pay of employees who have left the company, and then pocket the resulting paychecks. This practice can be stopped by ensuring that every paycheck is handed to an employee who can prove his or her identity.

- *Issue lists of paychecks issued to department supervisors.* It is quite useful to give supervisors a list of paychecks issued to everyone in their departments from time to time, because they may be able to spot payments being made to employees who are no longer working there. This is a particular problem in larger companies, where any delay in processing termination paperwork can result in continuing payments to ex-employees. It is also a good control over any payroll clerk who may be trying to defraud the company by delaying termination paperwork and then pocketing the paychecks produced in the interim.

- *Compare the addresses on employee paychecks.* If the payroll staff is creating additional fake employees and having the resulting paychecks mailed to their home addresses, then a simple comparison of addresses for all check recipients will reveal duplicate addresses (though employees can get around this problem by having checks sent to post office boxes — this control issue can be stopped by creating a policy to prohibit payments to post office boxes).

13. *Occupancy Expenses.* Though a relatively minor item, the following control is intended to ensure that employees are prudent in their acquisition of furnishings for company offices.

    - *Compare the cost of employee furnishings to company policy.* Employees may obtain furnishings at a cost that is well beyond what would be obtained by a prudent manager. This issue can be addressed by promulgating a policy that outlines the maximum cost of furnishings per employee, and by enforcing it with occasional internal audits of costs incurred. Another means of enforcement is to authorize a standard set of furnishings for the purchasing staff to procure, with any furnishings outside this list requiring special approval.

14. *General.* A few continuing payments to suppliers are based on long-term contracts. Most of the following controls are associated with having a complete knowledge of the terms of these contracts, so that a company does not make incorrect payment amounts.

    - *Monitor changes in contractual costs.* This is a large source of potential expense reductions. Suppliers may alter the prices charged to the company on their invoices from the rates specified on purchase orders, blanket purchase orders, or long-term contracts, in hopes that no one at the receiving company will notice the change in prices. Of particular concern should be prices that the supplier can contractually change in accordance with some underlying cost basis, such as the price of oil, or the consumer price index — suppliers will promptly increase prices based on these escalator clauses, but will be much less prompt in reducing prices in accordance with the same underlying factors. The internal audit team can review these prices from time to time, or the accounting computer system can automatically compare invoice prices to a database of contract terms. Another alternative is to only pay suppliers based on the price listed in the purchase order, which entirely negates the need for this control.

    - *Monitor when contracts are due for renewal.* A company may find itself temporarily paying much higher prices to a supplier if it inadvertently lets expire a long-term contract containing advantageous price terms. To avoid this difficulty, a good control is to set up a master file of all contracts that includes the contract expiration date, so that there will be fair warning of when contract renegotiations must be initiated.

- *Require approval for various levels of contractually based monetary commitment.* There should be a company policy that itemizes the levels of monetary commitment at which additional levels of management approval are required. Though this may not help the company to disavow signed contracts, it is a useful prevention tool for keeping managers from signing off on contracts that represent large or long-term monetary commitments.

- *Obtain bonds for employees in financially sensitive positions.* If there is some residual risk that, despite all the foregoing controls, corporate assets will still be lost due to the activities of employees, it is useful to obtain bonds on either specific employees or for entire departments, so that the company can be reimbursed in the event of fraudulent activities.

The preceding set of recommended controls only encompasses the most common ones. These should be supplemented by reviewing the process flows used by a company to see if there is a need for additional (or fewer) controls, depending upon how the processes are structured. Controls will vary considerably by industry, as well—for example, the casino industry imposes multi-layered controls over cash collection, since it is a cash business. Thus, these controls should only be considered the foundation for a comprehensive set of controls that must be tailored to each company's specific needs.

25-5 WHEN TO ELIMINATE CONTROLS

Despite the lengthy list of controls noted in the last section, there are times when one can safely take controls away. By doing so, one can frequently eliminate extra clerical costs, or at least streamline the various accounting processes. To see if a control is eligible for removal, the following five steps should be used:

1. *Flowchart the process.* The first step is to create a picture of every step in the entire process in which a control fits by creating a flowchart. This is needed in order to determine where other controls are located in the process flow. With a knowledge of redundant control points or evidence that there are no other controls available, one can then make a rational decision regarding the need for a specific control.

2. *Determine the cost of a control point.* Having used a flowchart to find controls that may no longer be needed, we must then determine their cost. This can be a complex calculation, for it may not just involve a certain amount of labor, material, or overhead costs that will be reduced. It is also possible that the control is situated in the midst of a bottleneck operation, so that the presence of the control is directly decreasing the capacity of the process, thereby resulting in reduced profits. In this instance, the incremental drop in profits must be added to the incremental cost of operating the control in order to determine its total cost.

3. *Determine the criticality of the control.* If a control point is merely a supporting one that backs up another control, then taking it away may not have a significant impact on the ability of the company to retain control over its assets. However, if its removal can only be counteracted by a number of weaker controls, it may be better to keep it in operation.

4. *Calculate the control's cost/benefit.* The preceding two points can be compared to see if a control point's cost is outweighed by its criticality, or if the current mix of controls will allow it to be eliminated with no significant change in risk, while stopping the incurrence of its cost.

5. *Verify the use of controls targeted for elimination.* Even when there is a clear-cut case for the elimination of a control point, it is useful to notify everyone who is involved with the process in which it is embedded, in order to ascertain if there is some other use for which it is being used. For example, a control that measures the cycle time of a manufacturing machine may no longer be needed as a control point, but may be an excellent source of information for someone who is tracking the percentage utilization of the equipment. In these cases, it is best to determine the value of the control to the alternate user of the control before eliminating it. It may be necessary to work around the alternate use before the control point can be removed.

This control evaluation process should be repeated whenever there is a significant change to a process flow. Even if there has not been a clear change for some time, it is likely that a large number of small changes have been made to a process, whose cumulative impact will necessitate a controls review. The period of time between these reviews will vary by industry, since some have seen little process change in many years, while others are constantly shifting their business models, which inherently requires changes to their supporting processes.

If there are any significant changes to a business model, such as the addition of any kind of technology, entry into new markets, or the addition of new product lines, a complete review of all associated process flows should be conducted both prior to and immediately after the changes, so that unneeded controls can be promptly removed or weak controls enhanced.

25-6 SUMMARY

The main focus of this chapter has been on the specific control points that can be attached to an accounting system in order to reduce the risk of loss. The selection of these controls should be contingent upon an evaluation of the risks to which an accounting system is subject, as well as the cost of each control point and its impact on the overall efficiency of each accounting process. In a large organization, the continuing examination, selection, and installation of control points can easily become a full-time job for a highly trained process expert. Smaller organizations that cannot afford the services of such a person will likely call upon the in-house accounting staff to provide such control reviews, which should be conducted on a fixed schedule in order to ensure that ongoing incremental changes to processes are adequately supported by the correct controls.

CHAPTER 26

Cost Accounting

26-1 INTRODUCTION

Cost accounting is one of the most crucial aspects of the accounting profession, for it is the primary means by which the accounting department transmits company-related performance information to the management team. A properly organized cost accounting function can give valuable feedback regarding the impact of product pricing, cost trends, the performance of cost and profit centers, and production and personnel capacity, and can even contribute to some degree to the formulation of company strategy. Despite this wide array of uses, many accountants rarely give due consideration to the multitude of uses to which cost accounting can be put. Instead, they only think of how cost accounting will feed information into the financial statements. This orientation comes from a strong tendency in business schools to train students in generally accepted accounting principles (GAAP) and how they are used to create financial statements.

In this chapter, we will depart from the strong orientation toward GAAP that is observed in much of the remainder of this book, and instead focus on how one can collect data, summarize it, and report it to management with the goal of helping the management team to run the business. For this function, we care much less about the proper reporting of accounting information and more about how information can be presented in a format that yields the greatest possible level of utility to the recipient. For issues regarding the proper valuation of inventory in accordance with GAAP, please refer to Chapter 14.

26-2 THE PURPOSE OF COST ACCOUNTING INFORMATION

The purpose of cost accounting differs from that of many other topics discussed in this book. It is primarily concerned with helping the management team to understand the company's operations. This is in opposition to many other accounting topics, which are more concerned with the proper observance of very precise accounting rules and regulations, as laid down by various accounting oversight entities, to ensure that reported results meet certain standards.

The cost accounting function works best without any oversight rules and regulations, because, in accordance with its stated purpose of assisting management, it tends to result in hybrid systems that are custom-designed to meet specific company needs. For example, a company may find that a major requirement is to determine the incremental cost that it incurs for each additional unit of production, so that it can make accurate decisions regarding the price of incremental units sold (possibly at prices very close to the direct cost). If it were to use accounting standards, it would be constrained to use only a costing system that allocated a portion of overhead costs to product costs—even though these are not incremental costs. Accordingly, the cost accounting system used for this specific purpose will operate in contravention of GAAP, because following GAAP would yield results that do not assist management.

Because there are many different management decisions for which the cost accounting profession can provide valuable information, it is quite common to have several costing systems in place, each of which may use different costing guidelines. To extend the previous example, the incremental costing system used for incremental pricing decisions may not be adequate for a different problem, which is creating profit centers that are used to judge the performance of individual managers. For this purpose, a second costing system must be devised that allocates costs from internal service centers to the various profit centers; in this instance, we are adding an allocation function to the incremental costing system that was already in place. Even more systems may be required for other applications, such as transfer pricing between company divisions and the costing of inventory for external financial reporting purposes (which does require attention to GAAP guidelines). Consequently, cost accounting frequently results in a multitude of costing systems, which may only follow GAAP guidelines by accident. The cost accountant's primary concern is whether or not the information resulting from each system adequately meets the needs of the recipients.

Any cost accounting system is comprised of three functional areas: the collection of raw data, the processing of this data in accordance with a costing methodology, and the reporting of the resulting information to management in the most understandable format. The remainder of this chapter is split into sections that address each of these three functional areas. The area that receives the most coverage is the processing function, for there are a number of different methodologies available, each of which applies to different situations. For example, job costing is used for situations where specifically identifiable goods are produced in batches, while direct costing is most applicable in situations in which management does not want to see any overhead allocation attached to the directly identifiable costs of a product. The large number of processing methodologies presented here is indicative of the broad range of options available to the cost accountant for processing raw data into various types of reports for management use.

26-3 INPUT: DATA COLLECTION SYSTEMS

The first step in setting up a data collection system is to determine what *types* of data to gather. One can simply collect every conceivable type of data available, but this will result in immensely detailed and cumbersome collection systems that are expensive and require a great deal of employee time to collect and record. A better approach is to determine what types of outputs are required, which can then be used to ascertain the specific data items needed to create those outputs. This allows the cost accountant to ignore many types of data, simply because no one needs them. However, the process of determining data requirements from projected outputs must be revisited on a regular basis, for changes in the business will require changes in the required cost accounting reports, and therefore changes in the types of data collected.

The process of backtracking from a required output to a set of required data elements is best illustrated with an example. If a company is manufacturing a set of products whose components and assembly are entirely outsourced, then it is logical to create management reports that focus on the prices being charged to the company by its suppliers, rather than to create an elaborate time recording system for the small number of quality inspectors who are responsible for reviewing completed goods before they are shipped out to customers. In this case, the bulk of the data used by the costing system will come out of the accounts payable and purchasing records. Another example is a software company, where the costing focus is on the labor time charged to specific development projects and the ability of project managers to meet their deadlines, rather than on the minor cost of purchasing compact disks, packaging, and training materials that are shipped to customers. In this case, most of the cost accounting data will come from the timekeeping and project tracking databases. Thus, the nature of the business will drive the decision to collect certain types of data.

Once the cost accountant knows what data to collect, there is still the issue of creating a data accumulation system. There are several factors that will influence this decision. One is *cost;* if there are many employees who will be recording information continuously, then the unit cost of the data collection device cannot be too expensive, or else its total cost will exceed the utility of the collected data. Another issue is *data accuracy;* if the data collected absolutely, positively must be correct, then a more elaborate solution, such as bar code scanning, which is designed to yield super-accurate results, should be the preferred solution. However, if the level of required accuracy is lower, then perhaps manual keypunch entry or handwritten data sheets would be acceptable. Another factor is the *employees* who will use the data collection systems; if they are highly trained, then they can be relied upon to use complex keypunching systems, whereas a poorly trained workforce that has no idea of what data it is collecting, or why it is being used, should only be allowed to collect data that will be heavily cross-checked for errors. Of additional concern is the *timeliness* of the data collected. If there is a need for up-to-the-minute transmission of data to managers, then the only solution will be some form of automated data gathering. On the other hand, only an occasional report to management may require a slower manual data gathering approach. Another factor to consider is the *existing level of automation* within the company. For example, if there is a clear production path for all products that sends every completed item down a specific conveyor belt, then the installation of a fixed bar code scanner on that conveyor is a reasonable approach for recording data about production quantities. However, this would be a poor solution if products were being hand carried away from a multitude of production processes to the warehouse, since many of the items created would never pass by the bar code scanner. A final consideration is the *production methodology* currently in use. If it is a lean manufacturing system, such as just-in-time, there will be a strong orientation away from requiring employees to conduct any data entry work, since extremely focused and efficient workflows are the key to success in this environment—which is interrupted if data entry tasks are included. In these cases, one should avoid any type of manual data entry, focusing instead on more automated approaches.

Given the above parameters, it is clear that the cost accountant must devise a wide array of data collection tools in order to collect data in the most appropriate manner. The following bullet points describe a number of the more common (and upcoming) data collection tools:

- *Punch clocks.* A data collection tool that is proving to have a great deal of longevity is the punch clock. This is used by hourly employees to record the times when they arrive for work and leave at the end of the day. The process is a simple one; take your time card from a storage rack, insert it into the top of the clock, which stamps the time on it, and return your card to the storage rack. The payroll staff then uses these cards to calculate payroll. The greatest advantage of this approach is that a time clock is very inexpensive. However, it requires conversion of the time card data by the payroll staff into another format before it can be used, which introduces the likelihood of computational errors. Also, it is difficult to use for recording time worked on specific jobs.

- *Electronic time clocks.* This type of clock allows employees to swipe a badge through a reader on the side or top of the clock. This results in a computer entry for the time of the scan, which is also associated with the employee code that is embedded in the card, either through the use of a bar code or a magnetic stripe. A more advanced version uses the biometric measurement of the outlines of one's hand to determine the identity of the employee (thereby eliminating the need for an employee badge, which might otherwise be lost or used to make a scan for someone who is not on the premises). This represents a significant advance over the punch clock, because there is no need for secondary calculations that might result in an error. It also yields greater control over the time recording process, since it gives immediate feedback to supervisors regarding missed or late scans. An additional benefit is that employees can enter job numbers as part of the scanning process, so that time is charged to specific jobs. However, the electronic time clock costs up to $2,000 each, and so is usually restricted to high-volume applications where there are many employees—punch clocks are therefore still used in low-volume locations where they are more cost-effective.

- *Bar code scanners.* A bar code scanner is a device that reads bar code labels with either a fixed or rapidly rotating laser beam, and converts the bar code symbology into a character-based format that is then stored in the computer system. These scanners come in many shapes and sizes, ranging from a $100 fixed-beam scanner that looks like a pen (but which may require a number of scans to read a bar code) to a $10,000 fixed position scanner that is bolted to a conveyor belt, and that emits 30 scans per second as bar coded packages move past it. There are also portable scanners, which are heavily used in warehousing operations, that can either stored scanned information in local RAM memory for later uploading to a computer, or that contain direct radio frequency access to the company computer, and can therefore transmit the data immediately. The type of scanner purchased will depend on the level of automation required, and the budget available for this purpose. Bar code scanning is highly recommended for repetitive data entry situations in which the *same* data is collected many times. On the other hand, it is of less use where the data collected changes constantly, or involves a large quantity of text that would require an extremely large bar code. Nonetheless, some portion of most data entry applications can involve the use of bar code scanning.

- *Terminal data entry.* An increasingly common form of data entry does not involve the use of any new data collection devices—instead, just buy lots more computer terminals and make them available to users throughout the company. Employees can then be given direct access to the computer screens that require input from them, and can enter information directly into the computer system. This avoids the middleman data entry person, as well as the risk that the data entry staff might misinterpret the data on an employee's form and type in the wrong information. The process can be facilitated by the use of error-checking protocols within the computer software, so that users will be flagged if they make entries that are clearly outside of a narrow band of expected responses. Also, computer screens can be devised for individual users that are designed to assist them in entering only the data they have access to, and in the most efficient manner. However, it can be expensive to rig all locations in a company with computer terminals and all the linking wiring. Moreover, some employees may move around so much that having them use a fixed terminal is not a viable option. Consequently, this approach may have limited applicability, depending upon the situation.

- *Paper-based data entry.* Despite all of the other forms of advanced data entry noted here, the most common method for collecting data is still from a paper document. This approach is inexpensive, requires no web of interlinked electronic devices throughout a facility, and is familiar to all employees as a method of data capture. However, it does not result in a fast flow of data through an organization, since it may be days or weeks before the information contained on a form is re-keyed into the computer system. Also, it is easy to lose forms, especially when they are being used throughout a facility and there is no rigid tracking of individual forms to ensure that none is lost. Furthermore, this approach requires the services of an expensive data entry person to interpret the data on the forms (sometimes incorrectly) and type the results into the computer system. Given these problems, it is no surprise that the proportion of data gathering that uses this approach is shrinking—nonetheless, it still comprises the majority of all data gathering techniques in most organizations.

- *Electronic pen data entry.* A very new data gathering approach is the electronic pen. This is a pen that not only marks in ink on paper, but also tracks its exact position on a pad of "smart" paper (that has a built-in identifying grid that tells the pen where it is touching the paper). The pen transmits its position via the new Bluetooth data transmission protocol to any nearby receiver that is tuned to the pen's transmission frequency. This results in a digital copy of the writer's penmanship that can then be converted into text, which in turn can be stored in the company database. Though this is a nascent technology, it may become an important form of data collection in the years to come.

Thus, there are a wide range of data entry systems available. In most instances, the cost accountant who is designing a data collection system will need to use a mix of these options to ensure that the correct mix of high data accuracy and low collection cost is achieved.

26-4 PROCESSING: DATA SUMMARIZATION SYSTEMS

Having covered the data collection portion of cost accounting, we now move to the various costing methodologies that are available for processing the raw data into a format that is most useful for management consumption. Here are the primary advantages and disadvantages of the systems whose functions are noted in the following sections:

- *Job costing.* This is a commonly used system that is primarily targeted at production situations where customized goods are produced for specific customers. It is very useful for tracking the exact cost of individual products, and is the only valid technique for accumulating costs for cost-plus contractual arrangements. It can also yield accurate results about the ongoing costs of a current job, which is useful for monitoring purposes. However, this system requires a large quantity of detailed data collection and data entry, which is expensive. It also runs the risk of including some inaccurate data, which requires expensive control systems to minimize. Furthermore, there may be a significant allocation of overhead costs to each job, which may be inaccurately applied.

- *Process costing.* This is also a heavily used system, and is most common in situations in which large quantities of exactly the same product are created. Costs are collected in bulk for entire time periods, and then allocated out to the volume of entire production runs during that period. This results in a fair degree of accuracy when costs are averaged out and assigned to individual units. However, some degree of estimation is required when determining total production quantities completed, since some units may be only partially completed at the end of the production period. Consequently, there is some room for variation in final production costs. This method requires much less data collection than job costing, but the level of information accuracy is correspondingly less.

- *Standard costing.* This methodology has been installed in many companies as an adjunct to both the job costing and process costing systems. It is designed to set standard costs for all material and labor costs incurred by a company, against which actual results can be compared through variance analysis. This can result in excellent control over company costs, but only if the accounting staff is diligent in uncovering the reasons for variances from costing standards, and the management team is helpful in correcting the discovered problems. It is also useful for budgeting, setting prices, and closing the financial books in a rapid manner. However, it is also time-consuming to set and maintain standards; in environments where this maintenance function is not performed, standards can be so far away from actual results that variance analysis is no longer useful for management purposes. Also, a company that has adopted continuous process improvement principles will find that any standards adopted will almost immediately become obsolete, requiring constant correction. Furthermore, most standards are set at the product level, rather than at the batch level, so there is no basis of comparison when using this method for cost control over production batches. Another problem is that comparisons to actual costs tend to focus management attention on labor variances, which have historically been a large part of the cost accounting report package, even though these costs comprise only a small proportion of total production costs in most manufacturing environments. Finally, it tends to perpetuate inefficiencies if personnel use the current standard cost as a baseline for behavior; they will have no incentive to improve costs to a point that is substantially better than the pre-set standard, resulting in languishing efficiency levels. For these reasons, standard costing is now used in a more limited role that in previous years.

- *Direct costing.* This is a favorite methodology for those managers who are constantly confronted with incremental costing and pricing decisions where the inclusion of overhead costs in a product's total cost will yield inaccurate information. Thus, direct costing is an ideal approach for determining the lowest possible price at which to sell incremental units. However, it yields inaccurate results when used for long-term pricing, since it takes no account of overhead costs that must be included in a company's standard prices if it is to assure itself of long-term profitability. It is also not allowed for inventory valuation purposes by GAAP, which requires the inclusion of allocated overhead costs.

- *Throughput accounting.* A variation on direct costing is throughput costing. This methodology holds that the only direct cost is direct materials, with even direct labor costs being thrown out when making most cost-related management decisions. The main tenet of throughput accounting is that a company must carefully manage the bottleneck operation in its production facility, so that the largest possible contribution margin is created. The main advantage of throughput accounting is that it yields the best short-term incremental profits if it is religiously followed when making production decisions. However, this can result in production mixes that seriously delay the completion of jobs for some customers, which is not good for customer relations.

- *Activity-based costing (ABC).* The ABC methodology is a much more accurate way to associate overhead costs with specific activities, which in turn can be assigned to product costs. Its main advantage is that it builds a direct correlation between the occurrence of an activity and related overhead costs, so that changes in the activity can reliably be expected to result in corresponding changes in the overhead costs. This results in valuable information for the management team, which uses it not only to gain some measure of control over its overhead costs, but also to gain an understanding of which products use more activities (and therefore overhead costs) than others. The downside of this methodology is that it requires a great deal of costing knowledge, time, and management commitment before an ABC system becomes operational, and henceforth require considerable upkeep to maintain. It also requires the construction of an ABC database that is separate from the general ledger, which can be an expensive proposition to both create and maintain. It is not really necessary in situations in which there are few products, obvious process flows, and minimal machine setups, because a less complex cost accumulation system will still result in reasonably accurate product costs.

- *Target costing.* This costing methodology is the most proactive of all the methodologies, for it involves the direct intervention of the cost accounting staff in the product design process, with the express intent of creating products that meet pre-set cost and gross margin goals. This is opposed to the usual practice of accumulating costs after products have been designed and manufactured, so that managers will find out what a product costs after it is too late to make any changes to the design. This costing system is highly recommended to any company that designs its own products, since it can result in significant reductions in product costs before they are "locked in" when the design is completed. This technique usually requires a great deal of cost accounting staff time, and can lengthen the product development process, but is well worth the effort.

- *By-product and joint product costing.* This type of costing involves using some rational means for allocating costs to products for which there is no clearly attributable cost. The various methods for conducting these allocations are primarily used for valuing inventory for external reporting purposes. It is generally unwise to use this information for any management purpose, since decisions based on allocated costs, with the intention of changing those costs, will usually fail. Consequently, by-product and joint product costing is not recommended for anything other than inventory valuation.

This brief review of the advantages and disadvantages of each costing methodology should make it clear that they are not only wildly different from each other in concept, but also that they are all designed to deal with different situations, several of which may be found within the same company. Accordingly, a cost accountant must become accustomed to slipping in and out of a methodology when the circumstances warrant the change, and will very likely use a combination of these systems at the same time, if demanded by the circumstances.

In the following sections, we will review the workings of each of these costing methodologies.

26-5 PROCESSING: JOB COSTING

Job costing involves a series of transactions that accumulate the cost of materials, labor, and overhead (of which there are two different calculations) to a specific job. For each of these costing categories, costs are accumulated through a series of transactions before they are finally charged to a specific job. In this section, we will trace the journal entries used for all of these costs.

The basic flow of journal entries required for direct materials is noted in Exhibit 26-1, which itemizes the general format of each sequential transaction. When raw materials are purchased, they are rarely charged to a particular job upon receipt. Instead, they are stored in the warehouse, so there is a debit to the raw materials inventory and a credit to accounts payable. Once production is scheduled, the raw materials will be sent to the production floor, which triggers another transaction, to be created by the warehouse staff—a debit to the work-in-process inventory account and a credit to the raw materials inventory account.

Exhibit 26-1   Job Costing Transactions for Direct Materials

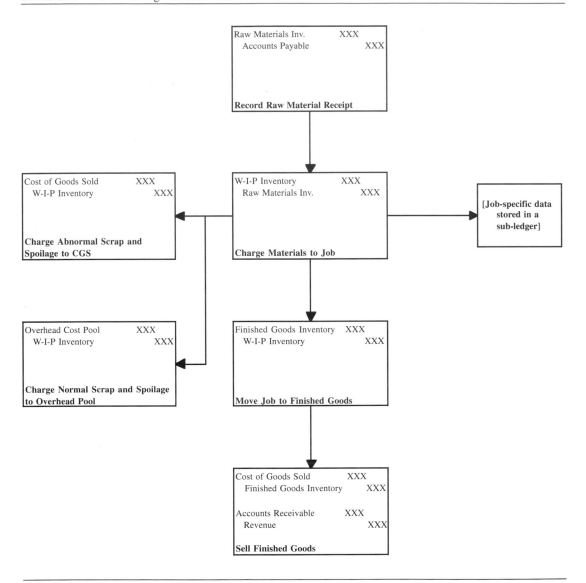

Reprinted with permission: Bragg, *Cost Accounting: A Comprehensive Guide,* John Wiley & Sons, 2001, Chapter 10.

During the production process, it is quite likely that some portion of the materials will be destroyed as part of the normal production process; if so, another entry will be required that creates a debit to the overhead cost pool, and a credit to remove the cost from the work-in-process inventory account. This normal amount of scrap will then be allocated through the overhead cost pool back to product costs—we will deal with this issue shortly, when we talk about the cost flow for overhead costs. If there are excessive amounts of scrap, then these will instead be charged directly to the cost of goods sold with a debit, while the work-in-process account is reduced with a credit.

Once the production process has been completed (which may be a few moments for simple products, and months for complex ones), it is shifted back to the warehouse in the form of finished goods. To record this transaction, we use a debit to the finished goods inventory account and a credit to work-in-process inventory. Once the goods are sold from stock, a final entry relieves the finished goods inventory account with a credit, and charges the cost to the cost of goods sold with a debit.

One of the numerous benefits of a just-in-time system is that materials are in the production process for such a short period of time that there is no point in creating transactions that move their cost in and out of work-in-process inventory. Instead, a single transaction shifts raw material costs from the raw materials inventory account to cost of goods sold (though there may be an extra entry to record the cost in finished goods inventory if completed products are not immediately sold). This greatly reduces the number of potential problems that can arise with the recording of transactions.

The recording of labor costs follows a slightly different path than what is typically seen for materials costs. Instead of taking a direct route into the work-in-process inventory account, labor costs can either be charged at once to the overhead cost pool or go into work-in-process inventory. The charge to an overhead cost pool is done if there is no direct relationship between the incurrence of the labor cost and the creation of a product — this results in a debit to the overhead cost pool and a credit to the wages expense account. However, if there is a direct tie between the incurrence of labor costs and the production of specific products, then the debit is instead to the work-in-process inventory (or a separate labor) account. These cost flows are shown in Exhibit 26-2.

If the wages have flowed into an overhead cost pool, these costs will be summarized at the end of the accounting period and charged to specific products based on any number of allocation methodologies. The allocation calculation will result in another transaction that shifts the overhead costs to product costs, which can occur both at the work-in-process and finished goods stages of production. Meanwhile, labor costs that have been charged directly to work-in-process inventory will then be shifted to finished goods inventory and later to the cost of goods sold in the same manner as for materials costs.

As was the case for materials costs, a large number of labor transactions are required to track the flow of labor costs through the production process under the job costing methodology. There is a high risk that transactional errors will arise, just because of the large number of transactions, so control systems must be created that keep errors from occurring, and verify that completed transactions are correct.

The final job costing process under the job costing system is the allocation of costs to products. There are two ways to do this—either with the actual costs incurred during the production process, or else with standard costs that are later adjusted to match actual costing experience. The first of these approaches is called actual cost overhead allocation, while the latter is called normal cost overhead allocation. We will address the actual cost overhead allocation first.

Under actual costing, there are several sources of costs that will flow into an overhead cost pool. As shown in Exhibit 26-3, all production supplies that cannot be traced to a specific product will be debited to the overhead account and credited to accounts payable (the credit may also be charged to raw materials inventory or supplies expense, if supplies were first charged to either of these accounts). As already noted, some labor costs will also be charged to the overhead account. Also, and as previously noted under the materials costing flow, normal amounts of production scrap and spoilage will be charged to overhead. Indirect wages and other indirect costs will also flow into the overhead cost

Exhibit 26-2 Job Costing Transactions for Labor

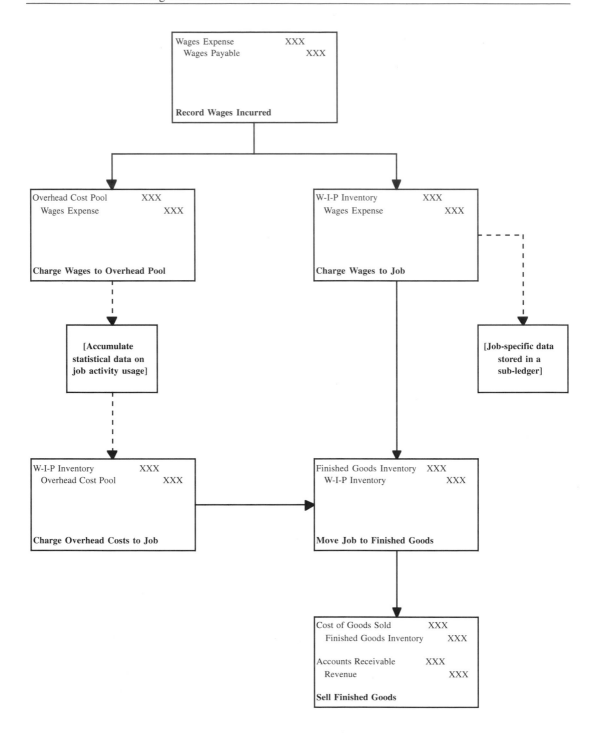

Reprinted with permission: Bragg, *Cost Accounting: A Comprehensive Guide,* John Wiley & Sons, 2001, Chapter 10.

Exhibit 26-3   Job Costing Transactions for Actual Overhead Allocations

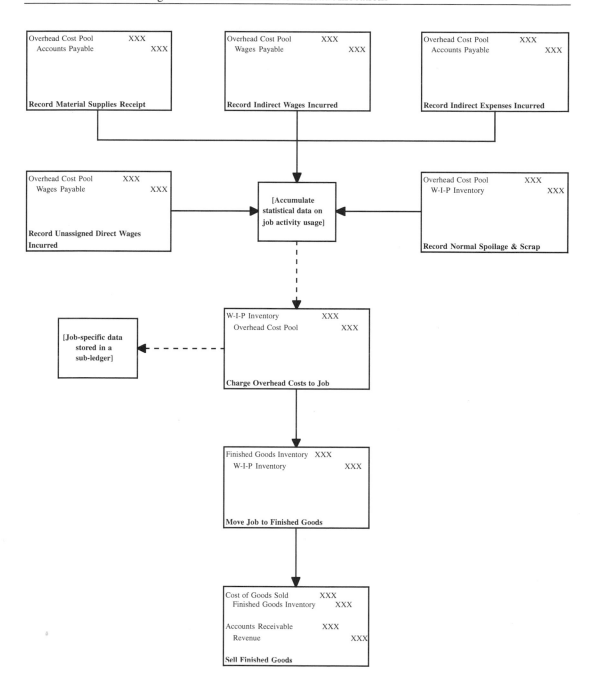

Reprinted with permission: Bragg, *Cost Accounting: A Comprehensive Guide,* John Wiley & Sons, 2001, Chapter 10.

Exhibit 26-4 Job Costing Transactions for Normal Overhead Cost Allocations

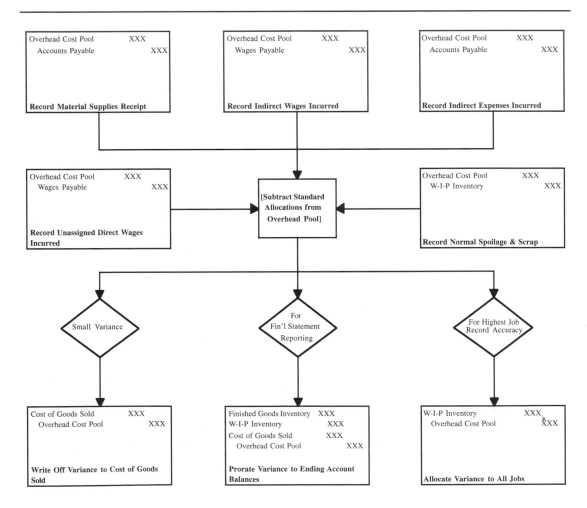

Reprinted with permission: Bragg, *Cost Accounting: A Comprehensive Guide,* John Wiley & Sons, 2001, Chapter 10.

pool. At the end of the accounting period, the cost pool is charged out to various products based on a variety of possible allocation calculations, which are addressed in the activity-based costing section later in this chapter. Once overhead costs have been assigned to specific products, they follow the usual pattern of being moved to the finished goods inventory while their associated completed products are held in storage, and from there to the cost of goods sold upon sale of the product.

The allocation of costs to specific jobs can be delayed for some time under the actual cost overhead allocation method, because some costs can only be compiled at the end of the month, or perhaps not until several weeks thereafter. This is a problem for those companies that want more immediate costing information. We use normal overhead cost allocations to resolve this problem. Normal costing means that a company charges out costs in the short-term using a historical average for its overhead costs, rather than actual costs. This process is shown in Exhibit 26-4. This allows costs to be charged to jobs at once. To ensure that the historical average being used for allocations does not stray too far from actual results, it is periodically compared to actual costs (which must still be accumulated), and adjusted as necessary.

When actual and normal costs are compared, there should be a small variance, which can be disposed of in several ways. One approach is to charge off the entire variance to the cost of goods sold, though this can create an unusually high or low cost of goods sold. Another approach is to spread the variance among the cost of goods sold, work-in-process inventory, and finished goods inventory, based on the total balances remaining in each account at the end of the reporting period. A final approach is to retroactively charge the variance to every job. These three options require an increasing amount of work to accomplish, in the order described. For that reason, the first option is the most commonly used, while allocation to individual jobs is a rarity.

The very large number of transactions required in a job costing system makes it a very inefficient costing methodology from the perspective of the accounting department, which must verify that all of the transactions entered are correct. It can also call for the purchase of large quantities of data collection equipment, such as automated time clocks and bar code scanners, which can be quite expensive. Furthermore, this system requires some participation by production personnel in the data collection process, which detracts from their primary mission of manufacturing products. However, given the need for job costing information, a company may find that there is no reasonable alternative to using this system. If so, the cost accountant should carefully review the need for each type of data that can potentially be produced by the system, and only collect those that will result in valuable information—this will create a more efficient data collection environment that only focuses on the key cost elements.

26-6 PROCESSING: PROCESS COSTING

Process costing is used in those situations in which it is impossible to clearly differentiate the cost of individual units of production. For example, it is a prime candidate for use in an oil refinery, where it is impossible to track the cost of an individual gallon of diesel fuel.

The most common method for calculating process costs on a per-unit basis is to accumulate all production-related costs during the accounting period and calculate a weighted average per-unit cost based on these totals and the amount of production that was completed during the period, or which is currently still in process. An example of this calculation is shown in Exhibit 26-5.

Exhibit 26-5   Weighted Average Process Costing Calculation

Units Summary	Direct Material Units	Conversion Factor	Conversion Cost Units
Completed Units	1,000		1,000
Ending Units in Process	350	60%	210
Unit Totals	1,350		1,210

Unit Cost Calculation	Direct Materials		Conversion Costs	Totals
Beginning Work-in-Process Cost	$20,000		$15,000	$35,000
Current Period Costs	$28,000		$21,500	$49,500
Total Costs	$48,000		$36,500	$84,500
Unit Totals (see above)	1,350		1,210	
Cost per Unit	$35.556		$30.165	

Unit Cost Allocation	Direct Materials		Conversion Costs	Totals
Cost of Completed Units	$35,556		$30,165	$65,721
Cost of Ending WIP Units	$12,444		$ 6,335	$18,779
Totals	$48,000		$36,500	$84,500

Reprinted with permission: Bragg, *Cost Accounting: A Comprehensive Guide,* John Wiley & Sons, 2001, Chapter 11.

In the exhibit, there are three blocks of calculations, each one segregated by a horizontal line. The top block contains a conversion calculation, which converts the amount of completed and work-in-process units into units to which materials and other costs can be allocated. The first column of numbers contains the calculation for the allocation of direct materials costs, while the final column of numbers calculates the allocation of all other production costs. For the purposes of this calculation, we assume that there are two types of costs—direct materials, which are typically added at the beginning of the production process, and all other costs, which can be added at a multitude of other points during the manufacturing sequence.

Since materials costs are assumed to occur at the earliest stage of production, the calculation of equivalent units for direct material cost allocation is quite easy—just use the number of finished goods completed (1,000) and the number of units in work-in-process inventory (350). However, for the purposes of allocating all other production costs, we must reduce the amount of work-in-process inventory by an estimate of their aggregate level of completion, which in the example is 60%. This results in total converted units of production of 1,210.

In the middle block of calculations, we accumulate the total cost of production and divide it by the equivalent number of units of production to determine the cost per unit. This calculation includes the costs that had been carried over in the work-in-process inventory from the preceding accounting reporting period, totaling $35,000. We add to this the current cost of production, which is $49,500, to yield a total cost of $84,500 that must be allocated to units of production. When divided by the slightly different units of production being used for direct material costs and all other production costs, we arrive at a direct material cost per unit of $35.556, and all other costs per unit of $30.165.

The lowermost block of calculations requires us to multiply the cost per unit (as determined in the middle block) by the total number of units (as determined in the top block). The calculation is identified with arrows. The result is $48,000 in direct material costs, of which $35,556 is charged to completed units and the remainder to work-in-process units. Total other production costs are $36,500, of which $30,165 is charged to completed units and the remainder to work-in-process. As a cross-check, we can see that the total allocated is $84,500, which matches the total amount of funds that were to be allocated, as noted on the far right side of the middle block.

This method is a simple one that requires very little data collection. However, some companies like to make the task even easier by avoiding the collection and interpretation of actual costs at the end of each accounting period. Instead, they prefer to use standard unit costs for their calculations, which allows them to calculate total costs more frequently and with no related data collection costs. This type of calculation is shown in Exhibit 26-6.

In the exhibit, the first block of calculations does not change—we still assume that a conversion factor must be applied to the ending work-in-process inventory for the purposes of assigning other production costs than direct materials. The difference arises in the

Exhibit 26-6   Process Costing Calculation Using Standard Costs

Units Summary	Direct Material Units	Conversion Factor	Conversion Cost Units	
Completed Units	1,000		1,000	
Ending Units in Process	350	60%	210	
Unit Totals	1,350		1,210	
Unit Cost Calculation	Direct Materials		Conversion Costs	
Standard Unit Cost	$32.000		$31.500	
Unit Cost Allocation	Direct Materials		Conversion Costs	Totals
Standard Cost of Completed Units	$32,000		$31,500	$63,500
Standard Cost of Ending WIP Units	$11,200		$ 6,615	$17,815
Standard Cost Totals	$43,200		$38,115	$81,315
Period Variance				
Beginning Standard Work-in-Process Cost	$20,000		$15,000	$35,000
Current Period Actual Costs	$28,000		$21,500	$49,500
Total Period Costs	$48,000		$36,500	$84,500
Standard Cost Totals	$43,200		$38,115	$81,315
Cost Variance	$ 4,800		$(1,615)	$ 3,185

Reprinted with permission: Bragg, *Cost Accounting: A Comprehensive Guide,* John Wiley & Sons, 2001, Chapter 11.

second block, where we only use a standard cost per unit, rather than a summarization of actual costs. This cost is then carried forward into the third block of calculations, where we see that a total of $81,315 has been allocated to the ending finished goods and work-in-process inventory. However, this ending figure varies from the $84,500 that resulted from the preceding actual costing calculation in Exhibit 26-5. The difference of $3,185 was caused by a slight variance between the pre-set standard cost and the actual cost. The presence of this variance causes us to add a fourth block of calculations at the bottom of the exhibit, in which we compare the actual costs incurred during the period to the standard costs, which shows that more costs than expected were incurred in the direct materials column, while fewer costs were incurred under the other production costs column.

The main issue for the cost accountant is what to do with this variance. If negligible, it can be charged off to the cost of goods sold. If it is so large that expensing the difference will result in an appreciable impact on reported earnings, then a more accurate approach is to apportion the variance among the cost of goods sold, work-in-process inventory, and finished goods inventory.

The data collection and calculations required for a process costing system are substantially simpler than what is required for a job costing system, and so is a favorite approach for those who wish to pare their data collection costs or who produce such large volumes of similar products that there is no point in attempting to track the costs of individual products.

26-7 PROCESSING: STANDARD COSTING

The first step in the creation of a standard costing system is to create a set of standard costs in a variety of different areas. The industrial engineering staff is assigned the task of creating direct labor standard costs, while the purchasing staff is most typically assigned the chore of creating standard costs for purchased goods, and the cost accountant is called upon to coordinate the development of a set of standard overhead costs. If there are subproducts created during the production process that may be valued at the end of each accounting reporting period, then the industrial engineering staff will calculate these standards. It is also possible to reduce the areas in which standard costs are used, with actual costs being accumulated in other areas. This mix of costing types can arise when there is some concern that reasonably accurate standard costs cannot be constructed, or if existing actual costing systems already produce reasonably accurate results.

Another issue to settle as soon in the standard cost development process as possible is the timing of changes to these standards. This can be done quite infrequently, perhaps once every few years, or as rapidly as once a month (which results in standard costs that are nearly indistinguishable from actual costs). The key determinant influencing the pace of change is the perceived pace at which actual costs are changing. If there are minimal changes to a manufacturing process, then there is certainly no reason to constantly review the process and set new standards. Conversely, a company that has installed an aggressive continuous improvement strategy will find that its standard costs are constantly falling behind changes in actual costs, which requires constant revisions to standards.

The assumptions used to create standard costs must also be addressed. For example, an industrial engineer must make some assumptions about the speed of efficiency improvements being realized by the production staff (known as the learning curve) in order to determine the future standard cost that roughly matches these expected changes in efficiency. Similarly, a standard cost must be matched to the expected production equipment configuration to be used, since this has a considerable impact on the overhead costs that can be assigned to a product. Another key assumption is the volume of production, since a large assumed production run will spread its setup cost over many units, whereas a short production run will result in higher setup costs on a per-unit basis. Yet another factor is the assumed condition of the equipment to be used in the manufacturing process, since poorly maintained or old equipment will be in operation for fewer hours than would otherwise be the case. The production system being used, such as just-in-time or manufacturing resource planning, will also have a significant impact on standard costs, since different systems result in the accumulation of different types of costs in such areas as machine setup time, equipment depreciation, materials handling costs, and inventory investment costs. An issue that is particular to direct labor is the anticipated result of union negotiations, since these directly and immediately impact hourly wage rates. A final issue to consider is the presence and quality of work instructions for the production staff; the absence of detailed and accurate instructions can have a profound and deleterious impact on costs incurred. Given the large number of issues involved in the setting of accurate standard costs, it is no surprise that this task can require the ongoing services of an experienced group of professionals, the cost of which must be considered when making the decision to use a standard costing system.

A final factor to consider when creating standard costs is the level of attainability of the costs. One option is to devise an *attainable standard,* which is a cost that does not depart very much from the existing actual cost. This results in reasonable cost targets that employees know they can probably meet. Another alternative is to use *historical costs* as the basis for a standard cost. This is generally not recommended, for the resulting costs are no different from a company's existing actual cost structure, and so give employees no incentive to attempt to reduce costs. The diametrically opposite approach is to create a set of *theoretical standards,* which are based on costs that can only be achieved if the manufacturing process runs absolutely perfectly. Since employees cannot possibly meet these cost goals for anything but very short periods of time, it tends to result in lower employee morale. Thus, regarding the potential range of standard costs that can be set, the best approach is to set moderate stretch goals that are achievable.

Finally, we are ready to begin using standard costs. But for what purpose do we use them? One common usage is in budgeting. By creating detailed standard costs for all budgeting line items, company managers can be presented with financial statements that compare actual results to standard costs, so that they can see where actual results are falling behind expectations. However, this is a simple approach that requires little real attention to the setting of standards at the product level.

Another reason for using standards is to create benchmarks for inclusion in a manufacturing resources planning (MRP II) production system. This commonly used system multiplies a production forecast by a detailed set of product labor, materials, and capacity requirements to determine how many direct labor personnel, what specific materials, and how much machine capacity will be needed. This system requires extremely detailed and accurate standards to be successful. The standards needed by MRP II are for units of labor, materials, and capacity, rather than their costs. In other words, a direct labor standard for an MRP II system may be 12 minutes of labor, rather than its cost for those 12 minutes of $4.58.

Yet another use for standards is in product pricing. The company sales staff frequently asks the engineering staff to provide it with cost estimates for new product configurations, many of which are only slightly different from existing products. However, the engineering staff may take days or weeks to provide the sales personnel with this information—which may be too long to satisfy an impatient customer. By using standard costs, the sales staff can compile product costs very quickly with only a brief approval review from the engineering staff. Or, if the engineering staff are still in charge of creating new product cost estimates, then they can also use standard costs to more rapidly arrive at their estimates. In either case, the customer will receive reliable price quotes much more rapidly than was previously the case.

A very common use for standard costs is for the valuation of inventory. Many companies do not want to be bothered with the time-consuming accumulation of actual inventory costs at the end of each accounting period, and so they create standard costs for valuation purposes, which they occasionally compare to actual costs to ensure that the inventory valuation is accurate. It is not worth the effort to create standard costs for this purpose if a company's inventory levels are extremely low, or if a just-in-time manufacturing system is in use, since the amount of time that will be saved in valuing inventory is small, given the minor quantities of stock that will be kept in the warehouse. However, manufacturers with large inventory balances will find that this is still an effective way to rapidly determine the value of inventory.

Unfortunately, the use of standard costs for inventory valuation is also subject to control problems, for deliberate manipulation of standards can result in large changes in the value of inventory, which in turn impacts the reported level of company profits. For example, the standard cost for a finished goods item can include an assumption for the amount of production setup costs allocated to each item, which is heavily influenced by the assumed number of units produced in a manufacturing run. By shifting the assumed length of the production run downward, the amount of cost allocated to each unit goes up. This type of interference with standard costs can result in wildly inaccurate reported financial results.

If standard costs are used for inventory valuation, the accounting staff will periodically compare standard to actual costs to ensure that there are not excessively large differences between the two. If a company is audited at year-end, then the auditors will require a comparison to actual costs, and a write-off of the difference to the cost of goods sold (if standard costs are higher than actual costs) or an increase in the inventory balance (if actual costs are higher than standard costs). Since a significant difference between the two types of costs can result in a startling change in the reported level of income during the period when this adjustment is made, it is wise to review some of the large-cost items on a regular basis in order to ensure that there will be no surprises at the time of reconciliation to actual costs.

Consequently, we can see that there are still several areas in which standard costs can be used to create greater efficiencies in selected areas of activity. However, the number of viable applications has fallen with the advent of new computer systems and production methodologies, so one should carefully review the proposed applications for standard costs before conducting an implementation.

26-8 PROCESSING: DIRECT COSTING

A direct cost is a cost that is directly associated with changes in production volume. This usually restricts the definition of direct costs to direct materials and direct labor (and a strong case can be made for *not* using direct labor, since this cost tends to be present even when production volumes vary). For example, the materials used to create a product are a direct cost, whereas the machine used to convert the materials into a finished product is not a direct cost, because it is still going to be sitting on the factory floor, irrespective of any changes in production volume. The use of direct costing results in a slightly different income statement, as shown in Exhibit 26-7.

Exhibit 26-7   Income Statement Formatted for Direct Costing

Revenue		$1,000,000
Cost of Goods Sold		
Direct Materials	$320,000	
Direct Labor	$170,000	
Total Direct Costs		$ 490,000
Gross Margin		
Operating Expenses		
Production Department	$325,000	
General & Administrative	$115,000	
Total Operating Expenses		$ 440,000
Net Profit		$ 50,000

The only difference between the income statement shown in Exhibit 26-7 and a more traditional format is that all non-direct costs have been shifted below the gross margin line and into the production department's costs. Though this seems like a subtle change, it focuses the attention of the management team on the incremental changes in the cost of goods sold that are usually masked by a large and relatively fixed amount of overhead costs.

By focusing solely on the direct cost of a product or activity, a cost accountant can provide valuable information to management regarding prospective changes in costs that will arise as a result of some management action. For example, if a change to a more efficient type of processing equipment is contemplated, then the direct cost of a product may be lowered if this will result in less material usage. This may also result in less direct labor cost if the machine takes over some tasks previously performed by employees—this will cut direct costs, but may increase overhead costs if the cost of the machine is higher than that of the machine that it is replacing. Yet another example is when a customer wants the lowest possible price for a product, and the company has some free capacity available for producing what the customer needs; the use of direct costing will reveal the lowest possible cost that must be covered by the price charged to the customer in order to break even. Direct costing can also be used to determine which customers are the most profitable, by subtracting the direct cost of their purchases from the prices paid, which yields the amount they are contributing toward the company's coverage of overhead costs and profit. Another very good use for direct costing is to include the concept in the budgeting system, where it is used to change budgeted variable costs to match the actual sales volumes achieved; this approach achieves a much closer match between the budgeted and actual cost of goods sold, because the budget now flexes with the actual volume level experienced. For all of these reasons, direct costing is a highly recommended costing system.

However, there are a number of situations in which direct costing should *not* be used, and in which it will yield incorrect information. Its single largest problem is that it completely ignores all indirect costs, which make up the bulk of all costs incurred by today's companies. This is a real problem when dealing with long-term costing and pricing decisions, since direct costing will likely yield results that do not achieve long-term profitability. For example, a direct costing system may calculate a minimum product price of $10.00 for a widget that is indeed higher than all direct costs, but which is lower than the additional overhead costs that are associated with the product line. If the company continues to use the $10.00 price for all product sales for well into the future, then the company will experience losses because overhead costs are not being covered by the price. The best way to address this problem is to build strict boundaries around the circumstances where incremental prices derived from a direct costing system are used.

Another problem with direct costing is that it assumes a steady level of unit costs for the incremental costing and pricing decisions for which it is most often used. For example, a company receives an offer from a customer to buy 5,000 units of Product ABC at a fixed price. The cost accounting staff may determine that the proposed price will indeed yield a profit, based on the direct cost per unit, and so recommends that the deal be approved. However, because the staff has only focused on direct costs, it has missed the fact that the company is operating at near full-capacity levels, and that to process the entire 5,000-unit order will require the addition of some costly machinery, the acquisition of which will make the proposed deal a very expensive one indeed. To avoid this problem, anyone using a direct costing system must have access to company capacity information, and should coordinate with the production scheduling staff to ensure that capacity levels will permit their incremental pricing and costing scenarios to be achieved.

A subtle issue that many users of direct costing systems miss is that the types of costs that fall within the direct costing definition will increase as the volume of units in a direct costing decision go up. For example, the only direct cost involved with a single unit of production is the direct materials used to build it, whereas a larger production volume will likely involve some change in the related number of manufacturing employees needed on the production line; these are well-accepted concepts. However, cost accountants frequently forget that additional direct costs will be included when the production volume rises to even higher levels. For example, if the direct costing decision involves an entire production line, then all of the equipment and supervisory costs that are tied to that production line are now also influenced by the decision to produce or not produce, and so should be included in the direct costing system. At an even higher level, the decision to use the production of an entire facility should include every cost needed to run that facility, which may include utilities, rent, and insurance—costs that are not normally included in smaller-volume production decisions. Consequently, direct costing analysis must be conducted within narrowly defined volume ranges, with careful attention to what costs are likely to vary with the volumes that are under review.

Direct costing cannot be used for inventory valuation, because it is disallowed by GAAP. The reason for this is that, under a direct costing system, all costs besides direct costs are charged to the current period. There is no provision for capitalizing overhead costs and associating them with inventory that will be sold off in future periods. This results in an imbalance between the reported level of profitability in each period and the amount of production that occurred. For example, a manufacturer of Christmas ornaments with a direct costing system may sell all of its output in one month of the year, but be forced to recognize all of its non-direct production costs in every month of the year, which will result in reported losses for 11 months of the year. Under GAAP, these non-direct costs would be capitalized into inventory and recognized only when the inventory is sold, thereby more closely matching reported revenues and expenses. Given the wide disparity between the reported results, it is no surprise that GAAP bans the use of direct costing for inventory valuation.

26-9 PROCESSING: THROUGHPUT COSTING

A costing methodology that focuses on capacity utilization is called throughput accounting. It assumes that there is always one bottleneck operation in a production process that governs the speed with which products or services can be completed. This operation becomes the defining issue in determining what products should be manufactured first, since this in turn results in differing levels of profitability.

The basic calculation used for throughput accounting is shown in Exhibit 26-8. This format is a simplified version of the layout used by Thomas Corbett on page 44 of *Throughput Accounting* (Great Barrington, MA: The North River Press, 1998), though all of the numbers contained within the example have been changed.

The exhibit shows a series of electronic devices that a company can choose from for its near-term production requirements. The second column describes the amount of throughput that each of the products generates per minute in the bottleneck operation; "throughput" is the amount of margin left after all direct material costs have been subtracted from revenue. For example, the 19″ color television produces $81.10 of throughput, but requires 10 minutes of processing time in the bottleneck operation, resulting in throughput per minute of $8.11. The various electronic devices are sorted in the exhibit

Exhibit 26-8   The Throughput Accounting Model

		Maximum Constraint Time:	**62,200**		
Product	*Throughput $$/minute of Constraint*	*Required Constraint Usage (min.)*	*Unit Demand/ Actual Production*	*Cumulative Constraint Utilization*	*Cumulative Throughput Product*
19″ Color Television	$8.11	10	1,000/1,000	10,000	$ 81,100
100 Watt Stereo	$7.50	8	2,800/2,800	22,400	$168,000
5″ LCD Television	$6.21	12	500/500	6,000	$ 37,260
50″ High Definition TV	$5.00	14	3,800/1,700	23,800	$119,000
			Throughput Total		$405,360
			Operating Expense Total		$375,000
			Profit		$ 30,360
			Profit Percentage		7.5%
			Investment		$500,000
			Return on Investment		6.1%

from top to bottom in order of largest throughput per minute. This ordering tells the user how much of the most profitable products can be produced before the total amount of available time in the bottleneck (which is 62,200 minutes, as noted at the top of the exhibit) is used up. The calculation for bottleneck utilization is shown in the "Unit Demand/Actual Production" column. In that column, the 19″ color television has a current demand for 1,000 units, which requires 10,000 minutes of bottleneck time (as shown in the following column). This allocation of bottleneck time progresses downward through the various products until we come to the 50″ High Definition TV at the bottom of the list, for which there is only enough bottleneck time left to manufacture 1,700 units.

By multiplying the dollars of throughput per minute times the number of minutes of production time, we arrive at the cumulative throughput dollars resulting from the manufacture (and presumed sale) of each product, which yields a total throughput of $405,360. We then add up all other expenses, totaling $375,000, and subtract them from the total throughput, which gives us a profit of $30,360. These calculations comprise the basic throughput accounting analysis model.

Now let's re-examine the model based on a re-juggling of the priority of orders. If the cost accounting manager were to examine each of the products based on the addition of allocated overhead and direct labor costs to the direct materials that were used as the foundation for the throughput dollar calculation, she may arrive at the conclusion that, when fully burdened, the 50″ High Definition TV is actually the most profitable, while the 19″ Color Television is the least profitable. Accordingly, she recommends that the order of production be changed to reflect these "realities," which gives us the new throughput report shown in Exhibit 26-9.

The result is a significant loss, rather than the increase in profits that had been expected. Why the change? The trouble is that allocated overhead costs have no bearing on throughput, because allocated costs will not change in accordance with incremental

Exhibit 26-9   A Revised Throughput Analysis Based on Allocated Costs

			Maximum Constraint Time:	62,200	
Product	Throughput $$/minute of Constraint	Required Constraint Usage (min.)	Unit Demand/ Actual Production	Cumulative Constraint Utilization	Cumulative Throughput Product
50″ High Definition TV	$5.00	14	3,800/3,800	53,200	$266,000
100 Watt Stereo	$7.50	8	2,800/1,125	9,000	$ 67,500
5″ LCD Television	$6.21	12	500/0	0	$ 0
19″ Color Television	$8.11	10	1,000/0	0	$ 0
			Throughput Total		$333,500
			Operating Expense Total		$375,000
			Profit		—$ 41,500
			Profit Percentage		−12.4%
			Investment		$500,000
			Return on Investment		−8.3%

production decisions, such as which product will be manufactured first. Instead, the over-head cost pool will exist, irrespective of any modest changes in activity levels. Consequently, it makes no sense to apply allocated costs to the production scheduling decision, when the only issue that matters is how much throughput per minute a product can generate.

Capital budgeting is an area in which throughput costing analysis can be applied with excellent results. The trouble with most corporate capital budgeting systems is that they do not take into consideration the fact that the only valid investment is one that will have a positive impact on the amount of throughput that can be pushed through a bottleneck operation. Any other investment will result in greater production capacity in other areas of the company that still cannot produce any additional quantities, since the bottleneck operation controls the total amount of completed production. For example, the throughput model in Exhibit 26-10 shows the result of an investment of $28,500 in new equipment that is added later in the production process than the bottleneck operation. The result is an increase in the total investment, to $528,500, and absolutely no impact on profitability, which yields a reduced return on investment of 5.7%.

A more profitable solution would have been to invest in anything that would increase the productivity of the bottleneck operation, which could be either a direct invest-ment in that operation, or an investment in an upstream operation that would reduce the amount of processing required for a product by the bottleneck operation.

As another example, the cost accounting staff has conducted a lengthy activity-based costing analysis, which has determined that a much larger amount of overhead cost must be allocated to the high definition television, which results in a loss on that product. Accordingly, the product is removed from the list of viable products,

Exhibit 26-10   A Revised Throughput Analysis Based on Additional Investment

Product	Throughput $$/minute of Constraint	Required Constraint Usage (min.)	Unit Demand/ Actual Production	Cumulative Constraint Utilization	Cumulative Throughput Product
	Maximum Constraint Time:	**62,200**			
19" Color Television	$8.11	10	1,000/1,000	10,000	$ 81,100
100 Watt Stereo	$7.50	8	2,800/2,800	22,400	$168,000
5" LCD Television	$6.21	12	500/500	6,000	$ 37,260
50" High Definition TV	$5.00	14	3,800/1,700	23,800	$119,000
			Throughput Total		$405,360
			Operating Expense Total		$375,000
			Profit		$ 30,360
			Profit Percentage		7.5%
			Investment		$528,500
			Return on Investment		5.7%

Reprinted with permission: Bragg, *Cost Accounting: A Comprehensive Guide,* John Wiley & Sons, 2001, Chapter 15.

Exhibit 26-11 A Revised Throughput Analysis with One Less Product

			Maximum Constraint Time:	**62,200**	
Product	Throughput $$/minute of Constraint	Required Constraint Usage (min.)	Unit Demand/ Actual Production	Cumulative Constraint Utilization	Cumulative Throughput Product
19" Color Television	$8.11	10	1,000/1,000	10,000	$ 81,100
100 Watt Stereo	$7.50	8	2,800/2,800	22,400	$168,000
5" LCD Television	$6.21	12	500/500	6,000	$ 37,260
			Throughput Total		$286,360
			Operating Expense Total		$375,000
			Profit		−$ 88,640
			Profit Percentage		−30.9%
			Investment		$500,000
			Return on Investment		−17.7%

which reduces the number of products in the mix of production activity, as shown in Exhibit 26-11.

The result is a reduction in profits. The reason is that the cost accounting staff has made the incorrect assumption that, by eliminating a product, all of the associated overhead cost will be eliminated, too. Though a small amount of overhead might be eliminated when the production of a single product is stopped, the bulk of it will still be incurred.

Throughput accounting does a very good job of tightly focusing attention on the priority of production in situations where there is a choice of products that can be manufactured. It can also have an impact on a number of other decisions, such as whether to grant volume discounts, outsource manufacturing, stop the creation of a product, or invest in new capital items. Given this wide range of activities, it should find a place in the mix of costing methodologies at many companies. We now shift to a discussion of activity-based costing (ABC), whose emphasis is the complete reverse of throughput accounting—it focuses on the proper allocation of overhead.

26-10 PROCESSING: ACTIVITY-BASED COSTING

An ABC system is designed to match overhead costs as closely as possible with company activities. By doing so, overhead costs can be reasonably associated with products, departments, customers, or other users of activities, which tells managers where overhead costs are being used within a company. This results in much better control over overhead costs.

There are several ways to allocate overhead costs. Some overhead costs, such as utilities, are associated with specific machines. For example, a machine may require 10 cents of electricity per minute. If so, this overhead cost can be charged out to those products that are run through the machine, based on the time spent being worked upon it. Other overhead costs are associated with a specific product line, and can reasonably be allocated to the activities performed within that product line. For example, there is typically a supervisor who is assigned to a single product line. If so, the fully burdened salary of this person can be charged to such related activities as production and maintenance scheduling. Still other overhead costs may be grouped by commodity used in the production process. For example, each member of the purchasing staff may be responsible for the procurement of a specific commodity. If so, this overhead cost can be distributed to individual products based on their usage of the commodity. Clearly, there are many valid ways to allocate overhead costs to various activities, and from there to users of those costs. An ABC system creates a structured approach to the accumulation, storage, and allocation of overhead costs using many of these activity measures.

An ABC system is a difficult and complex one to create, because of the wide variety of costs that must be accumulated, tracked in relation to different types of activities, and charged off. Here are the eight primary steps involved in creating such a system:

1. *Determine the scope of the system.* A fully developed ABC system that encompasses all costs throughout a company is a massive undertaking that may not yield any results for several years. A better approach is to conduct a gradual rollout of the system that produces results more quickly. Accordingly, a key factor is limiting each incremental rollout of the system to a carefully defined segment of the business. The determination of scope should also include a review of the level of detailed analysis that the system is to produce, since an excessive focus on detail may result in a system that is too expensive in relation to the utility of the information produced.

2. *Set aside direct costs.* There will be several direct costs that can be clearly and indisputably traced to specific products. These costs should be identified early in the design phase, so that they will not be erroneously added to the ABC allocation system.

3. *Locate costs in the general ledger.* The next step is to identify each of the overhead costs in the general ledger that will be allocated by the ABC system. This can be a difficult undertaking, for the required costs may be lumped together in the ledger, and must be segregated through a new data collection system that involves the creation of a new general ledger account number. Alternatively, the split may be achieved less accurately by allocating a percentage of the cost in a single general ledger account to several overhead cost items that will then be allocated.

4. *Store costs in cost pools.* All of the costs that have been identified within the general ledger must now be stored in a series of cost pools. Each cost pool accumulates costs that are similar to each other. For example, a building cost pool will include the costs of insurance and maintenance for a building, whereas a product line cost pool may include the marketing and supervisory costs that can be traced to a specific product line. A third type of cost pool is one that is related to a specific production batch, and can include such costs as production control labor, tooling, materials handling, and quality control. The total number of cost pools used will have a direct impact on the maintenance costs of an ABC system, so the design team must balance the increased allocation accuracy associated with more cost pools with the extra labor needed to maintain them.

5. *Determine activity drivers.* Having summarized overhead costs into a set of cost pools, we must now allocate them, which we do with an activity driver —this is a

variable that reasonably explains the consumption of costs from a cost pool. For example, some accounts payable costs are closely associated with the number of checks printed and mailed, while some engineering costs vary directly with the number of design changes added to a product. Examples of other activity drivers are the number of machine setups, the number of maintenance work orders, the number of purchase orders, and the number of customer orders processed. Whichever activity driver is chosen as the basis for cost pool allocation should be easy to calculate, require minimal data collection, and have a reasonably close cause-and-effect relationship with a cost pool.

6. *Spread costs from secondary to primary cost pools.* Some of the cost pools include costs that are, in turn, distributed to other cost pools. These costs are usually for internal company services, such as management information systems services that are provided to other departments. These secondary cost pools must be allocated to primary cost pools.

7. *Calculate the overhead cost per activity unit.* We then divide the total number of occurrences of each activity driver into the total amount of costs in the primary cost pools for the accounting period, which results in a dollar figure per unit of activity.

8. *Assign activity costs to cost objects.* The final step is to calculate the usage of each activity driver by a cost object (which is anything that uses activities, such as products or customers). For example, if a product requires the creation of two purchase orders (which are activity drivers) and the ABC system has determined that each purchase order requires $32.15 to create, then the amount of overhead charged to the product will be $64.30.

In brief, the ABC process involves taking costs out of the general ledger and assigning them to either secondary or primary cost pools, which are then distributed to cost objects through the use of activity drivers. The overall process is shown in Exhibit 26-12.

26-11 PROCESSING: TARGET COSTING

Most of the costing methodologies described in this chapter are primarily concerned with the interpretation of costing data after it has already been incurred. Target costing differs from them in that it describes the costs that are expected to be incurred, and how this will impact product profitability levels. By describing costs in a proactive and future-oriented manner, managers can determine how they should alter product designs before they enter the manufacturing process in order to ensure that the company earns a reasonable profit on all new products.

To use this methodology, a cost accountant is assigned to a new product design team, and asked to continually compile the projected cost of a product as it moves through the design process. Managers will use this information not only to make product alterations, but also to drop a product design if it cannot meet its cost targets.

There are four basic steps involved in target costing. First, the design team conducts market research to determine the price points that a company is most likely to achieve if it creates a product with a certain set of features. The research should include information about the perceived value of certain features on a product, so that the design team can add or subtract features from the design with a full knowledge of what these changes will

Exhibit 26-12   The ABC Process Flow

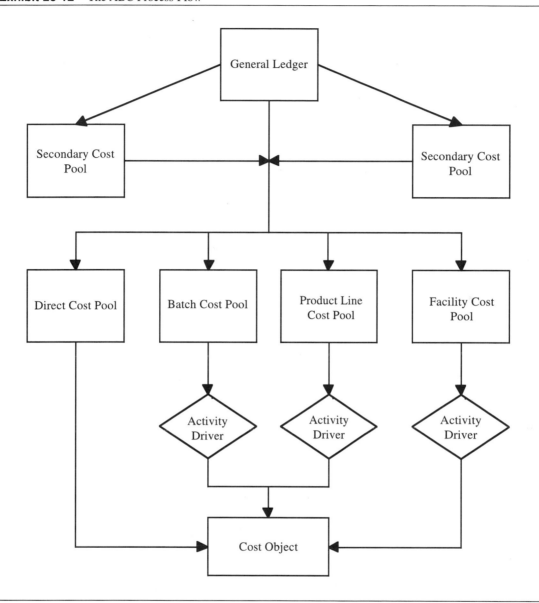

Reprinted with permission: Bragg, *Cost Accounting: A Comprehensive Guide,* John Wiley & Sons, 2001, Chapter 17.

probably do to the final price at which the product will be sold. The second step is to subtract from the prospective product price a gross margin that must be earned on the product; this can be a standard company-wide margin that must be earned on all new products, or perhaps a more specific one that management has imposed based on the perceived risk of the project. By subtracting the required margin from the expected price, we arrive at the maximum amount that the product can cost. This total cost figure drives the next step.

The design team then uses value engineering to drive down the cost of the product until it meets its overall cost target. Value engineering requires considerable attention to the elimination of production functions, a product design that is cheaper to manufacture, a planned reduction of product durability in order to cut costs, a reduced number of product features, less expensive component parts, and so on—in short, any activity that will lead to a reduced product cost. This process also requires the team to confirm costs with the suppliers of raw materials and outsourced parts, as well as the processing costs that will be incurred internally. The cost accountant plays a key role at this stage, regularly summarizing costing information and relaying it not only to the team members, but to the managers who are reviewing the team's progress. A standard procedure at this point is to force the team to come within a set percentage of its cost target at various milestones (such as being within 12% of the target after three months of design work, 6% after four months, and on target after five months); if the team cannot meet increasingly tighter costing targets, then the project will be canceled.

Once these design steps have been completed and a product has met its targeted cost level, the target costing effort is shifted into a different activity, which involves follow-on activities that will reduce costs even further after the product has entered its production phase. This final step is used to create some excess gross margin over time, which allows the company to reduce the price of the product to respond to presumed increases in the level of competition. The sources of these cost reductions can be either through planned supplier cost reductions or through waste reductions in the production process (known as kaizen costing). The concepts of value engineering and kaizen costing can be used repeatedly to gradually reduce the cost of a product over time, as shown in Exhibit 26-13. In the exhibit, we see that the market price of a product follows a steady downward trend, which is caused by ongoing competitive pressure as the market for the product matures. To meet this pricing pressure with corresponding reductions in costs, the company initially creates Product A, and uses value engineering to design a pre-set cost into the product. Once the design is released for production, kaizen costing is used to further reduce costs in multiple stages until there are few additional reductions left to squeeze out of the original design. At this point, the design team uses value engineering to create a replacement Product B that incorporates additional cost savings (likely including the cost reduction experience gleaned from the kaizen costing stages used for Product A) that result in an even lower initial cost. Kaizen costing is then used once again to further reduce the cost of Product B, thereby keeping the cost reduction process moving in an ever-downward direction.

The entire target costing process, incorporating all of the preceding steps, is shown in Exhibit 26-14.

26-12 PROCESSING: BY-PRODUCT AND JOINT PRODUCT COSTING

There are a few situations in which multiple salable products are created as part of a production process, and for which there are no demonstrably clear-cut costs beyond those incurred for the main production process. When this happens, the cost accountant must determine a reasonable method for allocating these costs.

The first step in this allocation process is to determine the "split off" point, which is the last point in the production process where one still cannot determine the final product. For example, a batch of sugar, water, and corn syrup can be converted into any of a number of hard candy products, up until the point where the slurry is shifted to a slicing

Exhibit 26-13   Stages in the Cost Reduction Process

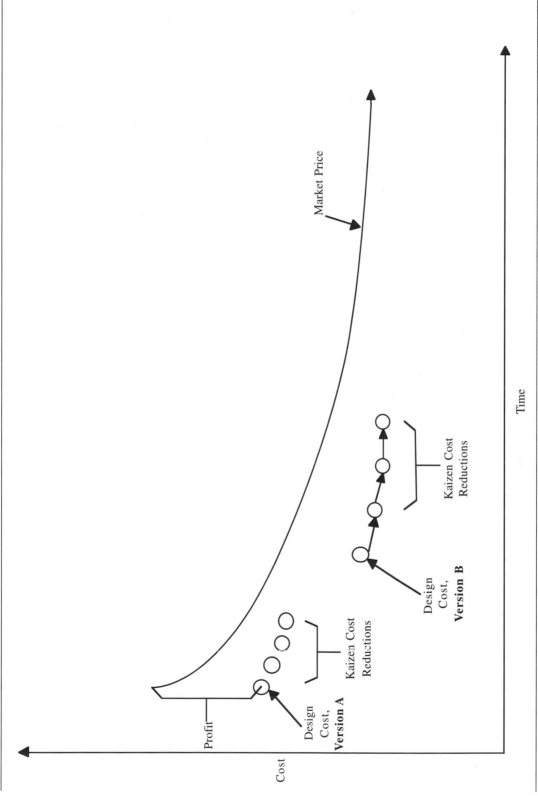

Exhibit 26-14   The Target Costing Process

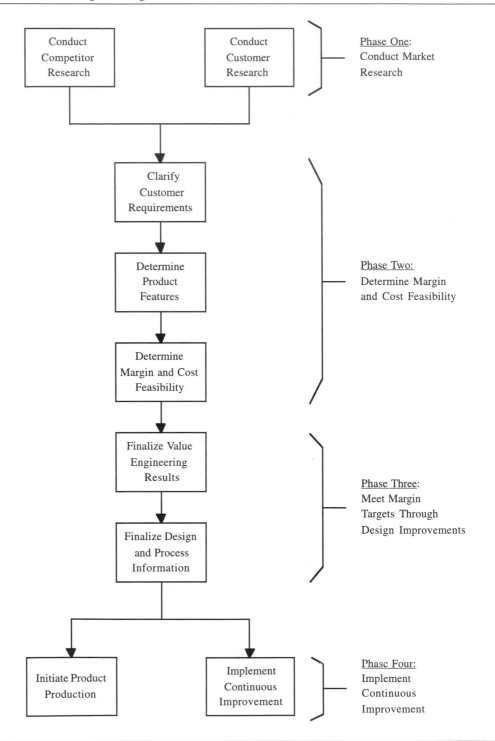

Reprinted with permission: Bragg, *Cost Accounting: A Comprehensive Guide,* John Wiley & Sons, 2001, Chapter 18.

machine that cuts up the work-in-process into a final and clearly identifiable product. From this point onward in the production process, we can either have a main product and an incidental side product (known as a "by-product"), or several major products (which are known as "joint" products). The accounting for these different types of final products is somewhat different.

The simplest cost allocation method is to determine the proportion of total revenue that each product coming from a joint production process will generate, and then apportion all joint costs based on the relative proportions of revenue that are to be earned by each product. For example, if Product A earns $10 and Product B earns $5, then two thirds of the total joint cost will be allocated to Product A and one third of the total joint cost will be allocated to Product B. By-products are assumed to have such a minor incidental impact on revenues that it is simpler to apportion no costs to them at all; instead, any revenues gained from the sale of by-products will be credited to the cost of goods sold.

This assumption that by-products have minimal value can be flawed in some circumstances. For example, the metal scrap that arises from a stamping operation may be accumulated for several months, at which point enough has been accumulated that a reasonable amount of revenue is realized. Because no cost has been assigned to the metal scrap, there is no cost to offset this modest surge in revenues, which therefore creates an unexpected jump in gross margins in the period when the sale of scrap occurs. This can be a particular problem if a company designates a by-product as being anything resulting in a moderately large proportion of total production, such as 5 to 10%; the revenue to be gained from such a large quantity of by-product, against which no costs are charged, can cause quite a dramatic change in the reported gross margin level. To avoid this problem, it is best to charge some cost to *all* products coming from a joint manufacturing process, even if they are by-products.

An alternative calculation for joint costs is to estimate the final gross margin of each joint product, which is based on the final sale price less the amount of costs incurred by each product between the split-off point and the point of sale. This is a more complicated approach to the allocation problem, and can be especially difficult to calculate if the costs incurred after the split-off point are so variable that they are difficult to estimate in advance. Consequently, the simpler method of basing joint cost allocations only on revenues earned by each joint product is the preferred approach.

An example of the two joint cost allocation methods is shown in Exhibit 26-15. The calculation that is based solely on revenues is shown on the left side of the exhibit. For this calculation, we see that $250.00 of production costs have been incurred up to the split-off point; this cost is split based on the final revenues to be gained from the sale of Product A and Product B. There is no allocation to Product C, since it is not estimated to have any revenue. The result is an allocation of $148.15 in costs to Product A and $101.85 to Product B. The greater complexity of the second allocation method is shown on the right side of the exhibit. This calculation requires us to not only determine the final per-unit revenues expected from each product, but also to summarize the costs that will accrue to each product after the split-off point. The calculation then subtracts these incremental costs from the final revenues for each product to arrive at a gross margin figure. The allocated cost of $250.00 is then allocated to each product based on the proportional size of each product's gross margin. The result is substantially different from the first calculation. Thus, we can see that a shift from one allocation calculation to another can have a substantial impact on the reported profitability of each product that comes out of a joint production process.

Exhibit 26-15   Example of Different Joint Cost Allocation Methodologies

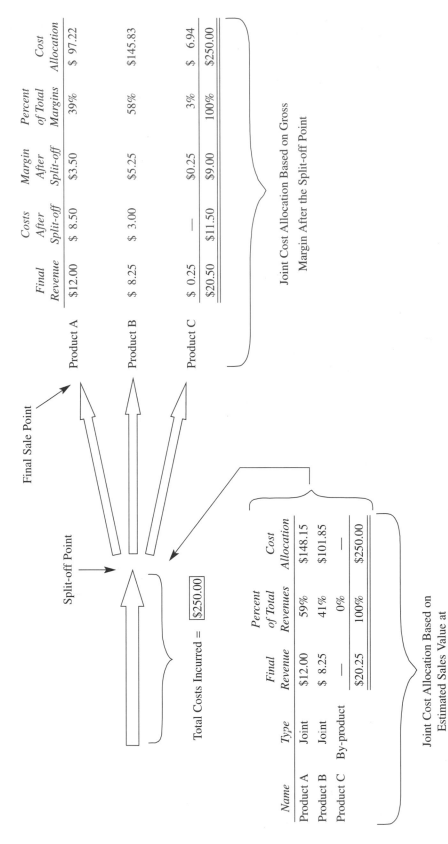

	Final Revenue	Costs After Split-off	Margin After Split-off	Percent of Total Margins	Cost Allocation
Product A	$12.00	$ 8.50	$3.50	39%	$ 97.22
Product B	$ 8.25	$ 3.00	$5.25	58%	$145.83
Product C	$ 0.25	—	$0.25	3%	$ 6.94
	$20.50	$11.50	$9.00	100%	$250.00

Joint Cost Allocation Based on Gross

Margin After the Split-off Point

Final Sale Point

Split-off Point

Total Costs Incurred = $250.00

Name	Type	Final Revenue	Percent of Total Revenues	Cost Allocation
Product A	Joint	$12.00	59%	$148.15
Product B	Joint	$ 8.25	41%	$101.85
Product C	By-product	—	0%	—
		$20.25	100%	$250.00

Joint Cost Allocation Based on
Estimated Sales Value at
the Split-off Point

352

Reprinted with permission: Bragg, *Cost Accounting: A Comprehensive Guide*, John Wiley & Sons, 2001, Chapter 16.

A key issue related to joint and by-product pricing is how to set prices for products that contain some allocated joint costs. The main point is not to base prices on allocated costs at all, since these costs have no direct bearing on the incremental cost of each product. For example, if one were to alter the method of allocation for Product A in the last exhibit from the revenue-based model to the gross-margin based model, the allocated cost would change from $148.15 to $97.22—the price should not change to match the cost decrease, just because someone inside the company has decided to alter the allocation calculation. A better approach is to determine the cost of each product after the split-off point, since these costs are directly associated with individual products; the total of these costs should constitute the minimum acceptable price at which a company is willing to sell its products, since this price would allow it to cover the clearly identifiable costs associated with each of its products. Of course, this minimum price does not allow for a profit, so the actual price should be at a higher level that will cover all joint costs when the sale of all resulting joint products occurs.

26-13 OUTPUTS: COST VARIANCES

A costing methodology of any type is not of much use if there is no output from it that gives valuable information to the management team. One of the primary outputs that is expected is a listing of costing variances, which are actual costs that depart from expectations. There are a number of standard variance calculations that can be summarized into a report, and which we will cover in this section.

Variances fall into three categories. The first is a price variance, and is the difference between the standard purchase cost of an item and the actual cost at which it was purchased, multiplied by the actual number of units purchased. It can be used to describe the variances in the general cost categories of purchased parts, direct labor, and overhead, and so is seen in three different places on cost variance reports.

The second type of variance is the efficiency variance. This is the difference between the actual quantity of resources needed to manufacture something less the standard quantity, multiplied by its standard cost. This variance can also be broken down into three sub-variances: a direct labor efficiency variance, a yield variance that relates to materials usage, and a variable overhead efficiency variance. There is no efficiency variance related to fixed overhead costs, since they are not expected to change with volume, and so have no targeted level of efficiency against which to compare.

The final variance is the volume variance. It applies to only one cost type, as opposed to the other variances; this is fixed overhead costs. Fixed overhead costs are charged to the cost of goods sold, or other parts of the income statement, as a fixed amount per accounting period, rather than as a percentage of the volume of production. Because of this difference in the method of cost allocation, a change in the actual production volume from the level that was expected when the allocation was set will result in a volume variance. It is calculated by multiplying the fixed overhead portion of the overhead rate by the number of units produced, and then subtracting this amount from the total fixed overhead cost pool.

An example of these variances, and the calculations used to derive them, is shown in Exhibit 26-16. In the upper left corner of the variance report, we see that there is a total variance of $61,725. The block of costs immediately below this shows the cost categories in which the variance arose, which sum to $61,725. Below and to the side of these vari-

Exhibit 26-16   Cost Variance Report

Product Line 400GL3
Cost Variance Report

	Actual	Budget	Variance
Cost of Goods Sold	265,000	203,275	(61,725)

Account					
Number	Account Name	Actual	Budget	Variance	
4000-020	Direct Materials	102,500	76,500	(26,000)	
4000-030	Direct Labor	34,000	29,450	(4,550)	
4000-040	Variable Overhead	50,000	36,550	(13,450)	
4000-050	Fixed Overhead	78,500	60,775	(17,725)	
		265,000	203,275	(61,725)	

Material Price Variance:

Total actual price/unit paid	10.25
− Total std price/unit paid	9.00
= Variance per unit	1.25
× No. of units consumed	10,000
= Material price variance	**12,500**

Material Yield Variance:

Total actual units consumed	10,000
− Total std units consumed	8,500
= Unit variance	1,500
× Std price per unit	9
= Material yield variance	**13,500**

Fixed Overhead Price Variance:

Total actual price/unit pd	7.85
− Total std price/unit paid	7.15
= Variance per unit	0.7
× No. of units consumed	10,000
= Fixed overhead price variance	**7,000**

Fixed Overhead Volume Variance:

Std overhead rate per unit	7.15
× No. of units consumed	10,000
= Total overhead charged to exp.	71,500
− Actual overhead cost pool	60,775
= Volume variance	**10,725**

Labor Price Variance:

Total actual price/hour paid	8.00
− Total std price/hour paid	7.75
= Variance per hour	0.25
× No. of units consumed	4,250
= Labor price variance	**1,062**

Labor Efficiency Variance:

Total actual units consumed	4,250
− Total std units consumed	3,800
= Unit variance	450
× Std price per unit	7.75
= Labor efficiency variance	**3,488**

Variable O/H Price Variance:

Total actual rate/unit paid	5.00
− Total std rate/unit paid	4.30
= Variance per unit	0.70
× No. of units consumed	10,000
= Variable O/H price variance	**7,000**

Variable O/H Efficiency Variance:

Total actual units consumed	10,000
− Total std units consumed	8,500
= Unit variance	1,500
× Std price per unit	4.3
= Variable O/H eff. variance	**6,450**

Reprinted with permission: Bragg, *Cost Accounting: A Comprehensive Guide,* John Wiley & Sons, 2001, Chapter 16.

ances are subsidiary variances that are linked back to the four major cost categories. For instance, the materials price variance in the upper right corner reveals that the price paid for materials is $1.25 higher than expected, while the material yield variance located directly below it shows that 1,500 more units of materials were used for production than had been anticipated. The total variance from these two calculations is $26,000, which traces back to the total direct materials variance on the left side of the report. All of the various variances trace back through the report in a similar manner. This is a good format for showing how variance calculations are derived, and how they flow through the accounting reporting system.

A company may not choose to report on all of these variances, since the detailed investigation of each one can be extremely time consuming. Thus, the variance for the direct labor price variance may not be reported, on the grounds that management has little control over it when pricing is ruled by a formal agreement with a labor union. Similarly, the fixed overhead volume variance may not be reported, because it relates more to ongoing production volumes than to management's ability to control the size of the overhead cost pool. Variances that are more commonly reported on are the material price variance and all types of efficiency variances; the material price variance is used to monitor the performance of the purchasing staff, while efficiency variances are used to oversee the entire manufacturing process.

Some variances are not worthy of regular reporting, because they require an inordinate amount of data collection work in exchange for information that is not of much use to management. For example, a detailed scrap variance that itemizes every item that was thrown out during a reporting period, alongside the reasons for each disposal, calls for a very large amount of investigative effort. The resulting report will contain information that may result in some long-term savings, but probably not enough to justify the work required to create the report. Thus, report compilation work should be considered when reporting on variances.

Once the cost variance report has been completed, the accounting staff will either be asked to conduct an investigation into the causes of specific variances, or should do so on its own. If so, it is useful to know in advance what types of problems are most likely to cause variances, so that investigative work can first be targeted at these items. Here are the most common causes of each major variance:

- *Fixed overhead spending variance.*
  - Suppliers have increased their prices for products and services that fall into this expense category. Review related supplier contracts for scheduled price increases.
  - The company has increased its usage of the products or services recorded in this category. If so, the costs may actually be variable, and should be shifted to a variable overhead account.

- *Labor price variance.*
  - The standard rate has not been altered to match changes in the union's labor contract.
  - The standard does not include extra charges, such as shift premiums, bonuses, or overtime.

- The people actually conducting work are at different pay rates than those who were assumed to be doing the work when the labor standards were created.

- *Material price variance.*
  - The actual price paid is based on a different purchasing volume than what was assumed when the price standard was originally set.
  - The standard price was erroneously copied from a similar product that has a significantly different price.
  - The purchasing staff is now buying replacement parts that have a different price than the parts that were the basis for the standard.

- *Selling price variance.*
  - Products were sold with different options than the products used to set selling price standards.
  - Customers have ordered in different unit volumes than those used to determine the standard price.
  - Customers have paid prices different from the invoiced prices (which will require investigation to resolve).
  - Customers were given promotional discounts on prices paid.

- *Variable overhead spending variance.*
  - The supplier has changed its per-unit pricing. Look for a contractually mandated change in the per-unit price.
  - The company is purchasing in different volumes, which alters the per-unit price paid.
  - There are mis-classifications in costs between the variable overhead and other accounts.

Though there are certainly other causes for variances, these are among the most common ones, and so should be investigated first. Also, the accounting staff will find that the same causes are likely to crop up over and over again, so it is useful to develop and continually update a list of variances caused during previous reporting periods. This becomes the accounting staff's "short list" of variance causes that can be used to track down similar problems in the future.

26-14 SUMMARY

This chapter has covered the variety of methods that can be used for data collection purposes, what types of costing methodologies can be utilized to process this incoming data, and how the results can be reported to management. Of the three areas covered, the most important is the proper use of the correct costing methodology, for this has a major impact on the type of information reported to management. There are many ways to reshuffle the incoming data, using systems as diverse as activity-based costing and throughput accounting (which emphasize entirely different information), so the cost accountant must have an excellent knowledge of what each system does and how it can be used. A key issue to remember is that a single costing system will not meet all of a company's reporting needs. The result should be a mix of systems that are selected for specific purposes, and that can be changed to meet different information reporting requirements.

CHAPTER 27

Financial Analysis

27-1 INTRODUCTION

The accountant must be concerned with more than the proper handling and reporting of transactions. It is becoming increasingly common for the accounting staff to be asked to review the data behind key financial decisions, and to make recommendations to management. In this chapter, we cover the topics that are most commonly seen by the accountant—the cost of capital, capital budgeting, breakeven, risk analysis, and business cycle forecasting. A basic grounding in these topics is becoming a necessary skill for the accountant.

27-2 THE COST OF CAPITAL

The accountant is sometimes called upon to render an opinion about the wisdom of investing in new assets. The basis for any such opinion is a knowledge of a firm's cost of capital. If the return from any asset investment will be less than the cost of capital, then the accountant's opinion should be to forgo the investment. Consequently, it is crucial to know the amount of a company's cost of capital, and under what circumstances it may vary.

The cost of capital is composed of three forms of funding—debt, preferred stock, and common stock. There are other forms of funding, such as convertible stock, but these are all variations on one of the three primary types of funding. Descriptions of each type of funding are:

- *Debt.* This includes any arrangement by a company to accept cash in exchange for a future return of principal as well as interest. It is the least expensive form of funding, because the interest charged by lenders can be deducted as a business expense for tax purposes, which can result in an extremely low net cost of funds.

- *Preferred stock.* This includes any stock issuance in which shareholders are entitled to some form of dividend, while the company has no obligation to return the underlying funds contributed by the shareholders. Because these payments take the form of dividends, rather than interest, they are not tax deductible, and so result in a higher cost of funds. It can be difficult to place a value on the exact cost of preferred stock, because the company may have the right to delay dividend payments (which reduces their cost) and preferred shareholders may have the right to convert their shares to common stock (which increases the cost of funds).

- *Common stock.* This type of stock carries with it no direct requirement by the company to pay back shareholders in any way, though the Board of Directors can authorize dividend distributions to them. Investors rely instead on stock appreciation and the eventual sale of their stock to realize a return. Because of the greater risk of this type of investment, common stock will have the greatest assumed return to the investor, and so has the highest cost of funds.

A few calculations will show how these three types of funding can be combined to create a cost of capital. We will calculate the cost of each funding type in turn, and then combine them into a weighted average. To calculate the cost of debt, we first determine the after-tax cost of the interest expense, which is one minus the tax rate, multiplied by the interest expense; we then multiply this by the total amount of debt outstanding, which results in the total interest expense. We then divide this by the total amount of debt, which is decreased by any discount or increased by any premium that occurred on the initial issuance of the debt to buyers. For example, if we issued $1,000,000 of debt at a discount of 5%, had an incremental corporate income tax rate of 38%, and paid an interest rate of 8%, the formula for the cost of debt would look like this:

$$\text{After-tax cost of debt} = \frac{((\text{Interest percentage}) \times (1 - \text{incremental tax rate})) \times \text{total debt}}{(\text{Total debt}) - (\text{discount on sale of debt})}$$

$$\text{After-tax cost of debt} = \frac{((8\%) \times (1 - 38\%)) \times \$1,000,000}{(\$1,000,000) - (\$50,000)}$$

After-tax cost of debt = 5.221%

Determining the cost of preferred stock is much simpler than was the case for debt, since the interest paid on this type of "mixed" equity is not tax deductible. Consequently, if the stated interest rate for preferred stock is 12%, then that is its actual cost to the company—the impact of income taxes does enter into the equation. However, there may be instances where the holder of a preferred share is allowed the option to convert the share to common stock (which has a higher cost to the company, as we shall discuss shortly). If so, should the cost of capital incorporate the potential conversion to common stock, or use the cost of the existing share? The answer depends upon the exact terms under which the preferred shareholder will convert to common stock. Usually, there is a conversion ratio or strike price at which the conversion can take place, and that will only be cost-beneficial to the holder of the preferred stock under certain circumstances. For example, a preferred share may be convertible to common stock once the price of the common stock on the open market reaches $18.00; or it may have a fixed conversion ratio of one share of preferred stock for $\frac{1}{2}$ share of common stock. Given these conversion options, it will be apparent to the preferred stock shareholder when it becomes economically viable to convert the share to common stock. It will be equally apparent to the person who is deriving the cost of capital; this person should include in the cost of capital the cost of preferred stock until such time as conditions make it feasible for preferred shareholders to switch to common stock, and then alter the cost of capital calculation accordingly. This is in opposition to the view that one should convert all preferred stock to common stock under the terms of any conversion formula, on the grounds that it yields the most expensive cost of capital. On the contrary, the cost of capital should reflect all funding costs at the current time, which should include preferred stock that will not be converted to common stock.

The cost of common stock is more difficult to determine. To calculate it, we start with the rate of return that investors are historically achieving with similar stocks, which requires the assembly of a market basket of similar stocks and then taking an average of the group. This calculation is subject to some interpretation, both in terms of which stocks to include in the market basket and what historical period to use to determine the average rate of return. Then we subtract from this average the standard rate of return that one can achieve by purchasing any risk-free security, such as United States government securities. The difference is an incremental amount that investors expect to earn above the risk-free rate of return. In addition, the specific common stock under examination may vary more or less than the average market rate of variance, depending upon the cyclicality of its industry, the degree of financial leverage that it uses, and other factors. This variability, known as its "beta," is calculated by many stock monitoring services. The beta should be multiplied by the incremental rate of return above the risk-free return, with the result being added back to the risk-free return in order to derive the cost of capital for common stock. The formula is:

Cost of capital
for common   = Risk-free return + (beta $\times$ (average return minus risk-free return))
stock

For example, a company with a beta of .85 would have a cost of common stock of 12.9625% if the risk-free rate of return, as evidenced by U.S. Treasuries, was 4.25% and a market basket of similar stocks yielded an average return of 14.5%. The calculation is:

Cost of capital
for common   = 4.25% + (.85 $\times$ (14.5% minus 4.25%))
stock

Though we have reviewed the costing calculations for each component of the cost of capital, we must still combine them into a blended rate. This is done using a weighted average, based on the amount of funding obtained from each source. If we were to use the $1,000,000 of debt (less a discount of $50,000) that was used as an example earlier in this section, plus $500,000 of preferred stock and $2,500,000 of common stock at the costing levels just noted, we would arrive at the weighted average cost of capital noted in Exhibit 27-1.

Exhibit 27-1   Weighted Average Cost of Capital

Funding Source	Total Funding	×	Percentage Cost of Funding	Dollar Cost of Funding
Debt	$ 950,000	×	5.221%	$ 49,600
Preferred stock	500,000	×	12.000	60,000
Common stock	2,500,000	×	12.963	324,075
Totals	$3,950,000	×	**10.979%**	$433,675

In the exhibit, there is a large proportion of high-cost common stock to debt and preferred stock, which gives the company a minimal risk of not meeting its fixed interest payments. If a company's management were inclined to reduce the cost of capital, it could do so by obtaining more debt and using it to buy back common stock. This would certainly eliminate some high-cost common stock, but at the price of increasing the size of interest payments, which in turn would increase the amount of fixed costs, and therefore raise the breakeven point for the company, which can be risky if it is already operating at close to the breakeven level. Thus, there is an increased risk of business failure for those companies that attempt to reduce their cost of capital by transferring their sources of funding from equity to debt.

Though we have just reviewed the calculations for determining a company's existing cost of capital, this does not necessarily mean that it is the cost that should be applied to the valuation of all prospective capital projects. There are two issues that may require one to use a different cost of capital. The first is that the company may have to alter its capital structure in order to obtain any additional funding. For example, lenders may have informed the company that no more debt will be available unless more equity is added to its capital base. In this instance, the cost of capital to be applied to a new capital purchase should be the incremental cost of funds that will specifically apply to the next investment. The second issue is that the cost of capital just calculated was for the existing blend of debt and equity, whose costs may very well have changed on the open market since the date when it was obtained. Debt costs will vary on the open market, as will investor expectations for returns on stock. Consequently, it may be advisable to periodically recalculate the cost of capital not only to reflect current market conditions for new funding, but also on an incremental basis, which can then be applied to a review of new capital investments. The only case where these strictures would not apply is when the amount of new capital investments is so small that there is little likelihood that obtaining funds for them will require a significant change in the existing capital structure.

If there are too many possible capital investments for the amount of funding available, one can keep increasing the cost of capital that is used to discount the cash flows from each project (as noted in the next section) in order to see which projects have the highest discounted cash flows. However, capital investments that are only based on discounted cash flow will ignore other issues that should have a bearing on the investment decision. One such factor is the risk of the project; it will be higher if the investment is in a new market, as opposed to one that is an extension of an existing market. Also, if there is a history of good returns on investment in a particular area, then there is a lower risk of loss on future investments in the same area. Further, the risk of heightened competition in some areas should be factored into the investment decision. Consequently, it is better to

use the cost of capital to throw out only those capital investments that are clearly inca-
pable of achieving a minimum return, and then further narrow the field of potential investment candidates by carefully reviewing other strategic and tactical factors related to each
project.

One must also be aware of changes in the cost of capital that may arise in various
subsidiaries of a conglomerate, where there may be significantly different levels of business risk in each one. One of the reasons why conglomerates are assembled is to combine
the varying levels of business risk in each component business, so that the average level
of risk, as defined by the probability of achieving an even stream of cash flows, is maximized. The problem with using a blended cost of capital that is based on a multitude of
disparate businesses is that the rate may be applied to individual businesses whose levels
of risk would normally involve a much higher cost of capital, while other businesses operating in mature industries with predictable results may be constrained by the use of a cost
of capital that is too high. One way to avoid this problem is to derive a cost of capital that
is based on the debt and equity structure of other companies that are located solely in the
industries within which specific subsidiaries operate. This yields a cost of capital for the
subsidiary, which may be a more accurate measure for determining the discounted return
on various capital projects. However, there may be some companies within the industry
that have excessively aggressive or conservative capital structures, which may result in a
range of possible costs of capital.

27-3 CAPITAL PURCHASE EVALUATIONS

When evaluating whether or not one should invest a considerable amount of funds in capital projects, the accountant has a number of tools available, such as the hurdle rate, payback period, net present value, and internal rate of return—all of which are covered in this
section.

The hurdle rate, with some variations, is a company's cost of capital, which we
covered in the last section. Most capital projects must generate a stream of cash flows that,
when discounted at the hurdle rate, will generate a positive cash balance. If this were not
the case, then a company would be investing funds at a rate of return less than the cost of
the capital it would be using to pay for the project. However, there are cases where the
hurdle rate will diverge from the cost of capital. For instance, if a project is perceived to
have an extremely high level of risk (such as investments in unproven technology), then
the rate may be increased substantially. Another example is a government-mandated
enhancement to the air "scrubbers" in a coal-fired electrical generating plant, which must
be installed irrespective of the hurdle rate. Thus, there can be justifiable variations
between the hurdle rate and the cost of capital.

The hurdle rate is used to discount the stream of cash flows spun off by a capital
project, so that the cash flows are translated into their current-period value. To do so, we
use a discounting factor that is listed in the "Compound Interest (Present Value of 1 Due
in N Periods)" table in Appendix C to discount a cash flow estimated to occur in a future
period back to the present period, using the hurdle rate as the discount rate. For example,
if we have a cash flow of $100,000 occurring in Year Four, and assume a hurdle rate of
9%, then we will use a discount rate of .7084 to determine that the current value of this

cash flow is $70,840. In case one's assumptions fall outside of the table in Appendix C, the formula to use is:

$$\frac{1}{(1 + \text{discount rate})^{\text{number of years}}}$$

If one is using Microsoft Excel to derive the calculation, then the formula in that electronic spreadsheet is:

$$=1/((1+[\text{enter the discount rate}])\verb|^|[\text{enter the number of years}])$$

Virtually all cash flows caused by a capital project should be subject to cash discounting. For example, Exhibit 27-2 shows a stream of cash flows for a capital project that are spread over a five-year period. They relate to the initial capital and working capital cost, ongoing maintenance costs, annual gross margin on sale of products created by the capital item (net of income taxes), and the sale of equipment and release of working capital at the end of the project. Each cash flow is assigned a discounting factor that is based on the year in which it occurs, based on an assigned hurdle rate of 7%.

The exhibit shows a stream of cash flows that results in a slight positive cash flow, and so should be approved. A more comprehensive review would also include the positive tax impact of depreciation costs on the cash flows, and any personnel or other overhead costs associated with the project. This summation of all discounted cash flows is called the "net present value" method (NPV), and is a commonly used technique for evaluating capital investments.

Exhibit 27-2   Discounted Cash Flows from a Capital Project

Year	Description	Cash Flow	Discount Factor	Present Value
0	Initial capital purchase	−$250,000	1.000	−$250,000
0	Working capital requirement	−175,000	1.000	−175,000
1	Gross margin on product sales	+45,000	.9346	+42,057
1	Project maintenance costs	−10,000	.9346	−9,346
2	Gross margin on product sales	+85,000	.8734	+74,239
2	Project maintenance costs	−15,000	.8734	−13,101
3	Gross margin on product sales	+120,000	.8163	+97,956
3	Project maintenance costs	−20,000	.8163	−16,326
4	Gross margin on product sales	+120,000	.7629	+91,548
4	Project maintenance costs	−25,000	.7629	−19,073
5	Gross margin on product sales	+60,000	.7130	+42,780
5	Project maintenance costs	−27,500	.7130	−19,608
5	Release of working capital	+175,000	.7130	+124,775
5	Sale of capital equipment	+60,000	.7130	+42,780
	Present value of cash flows	—	—	13,681

Another evaluation method that relies on discounting is the "internal rate of return" method (IRR). This approach alters the discount rate until the stream of discounted cash flows equals zero. By doing so, one can see if the adjusted discount rate is relatively close to the standard corporate hurdle rate, and so may require only minor changes to the cash flow estimates to bring them up to or in excess of the hurdle rate. It is also useful when the management team wants to compare the rates of return on different projects, usually when there is only limited funding available and it wants to invest in those projects with the highest possible rate of return. It is determined manually with a "high-low" approach of calculating discounted cash flows that gradually brings the accountant to the correct IRR value. It is more easily calculated with an electronic spreadsheet, such as Microsoft Excel. If that software is used, the calculation would be:

= ([range of values],[guess as to the value of the IRR])

The NPV and IRR methods are quantitatively valid ways to either justify or cancel proposed capital investments. However, they involve estimates of cash flows that may be well into the future, and calculations using discount rates that may also be subject to some degree of dispute. In cases where these issues make the use of NPV or IRR somewhat questionable, one can fall back on the old technique of "payback." Under the payback approach, we ignore the time value of money and instead create a simple calculation that estimates the earliest date on which the initial investment in a capital project is paid back to the company. If the payback period is quite short, then the company's risk of loss on investment is minimal. Unfortunately, this technique does not focus on the potential for substantial cash flows from a project some years into the future, and may result in investments only in projects with rapid returns, which is not a way to run a business with a long-range view of its prospects.

To calculate a project's payback, one can divide the total investment in it by its average annual cash flows. For example, a project with an initial investment of $500,000 and average annual returns of $175,000 would have a payback period of 2.86 years ($500,000/$175,000). However, this approach may yield flawed results if the cash flows vary widely from year to year. This concept is illustrated in Exhibit 27-3, where we see that the cash flows resulting from the $500,000 investment are skewed well into the future, even though their average annual cash flow is $175,000, resulting in a payback that does not actually occur until 4.0 years have passed. Consequently, it is safer to calculate payback on a year-by-year basis.

Exhibit 27-3   Payback Calculation on a Year-By-Year Basis

Year	Net Cash Flow	Net Unreturned Investment
0	−$500,000	−$500,000
1	0	−500,000
2	0	−500,000
3	200,000	−300,000
4	300,000	0
5	375,000	+375,000

The accountant is likely to not only evaluate capital proposals with the preceding evaluation methods, but also to handle much of the application paperwork associated with them. A sample of a capital request form is shown in Exhibit 27-4. This form contains the fields needed to conduct a discounted cash flow analysis, for it requires a detailed list of expected cash flows by year, by using a number of key revenue and expense categories. The "type of project" section is also of importance, for it tells the reviewer if a project is subject to a different hurdle rate. For example, a project that is being implemented to resolve a safety issue will probably be approved, irrespective of the hurdle rate or the presence of any positive cash flows at all. The bottom section of the form is crucial for the approval process. It notes the range of approval signatures that must be obtained before the proposal will be completed, with the number of approvals rising with the level of proposed investment in the project. This form should be issued to the sponsors of capital projects with a sample form and instructions, so they can easily see how it is to be filled out.

After a capital proposal has been approved, the accountant should continue to track actual cash flows and compare them to budgeted levels, so that the management team can see if some project sponsors have a history of incorrectly estimating cash flows in order to obtain project approvals. The post-approval review will also spot any control issues that may arise with the capital approval process, so that the process can subsequently be enhanced for future capital investments.

27-4 BREAKEVEN ANALYSIS

Every accountant should be aware of a company's breakeven point, for this tells management what revenue level it must maintain in order to achieve a profit. The formula for breakeven is simple enough—just add up all fixed costs for the period, divide by the gross margin percentage, and the result will be the total revenue level to be achieved in order to yield a profit of exactly zero. For example, a company with fixed costs of $3,700,000 and gross margins of 33% must sell more than $11,212,121 to earn a profit.

It can be of use to translate the breakeven formula into a graphical representation, such as the one noted in Exhibit 27-5. This graph contains a horizontal line that represents the level of fixed costs, such as salaries, rent, and leases, that will be incurred irrespective of the revenue level. The slanted line that connects at the x-intercept with the fixed cost line represents variable costs, such as the materials used to manufacture products. The slanted line beginning at the x-y intercept represents the revenue to be recognized at various levels of production volume. According to the exhibit, the company will begin to generate a profit at an approximate capacity utilization level of 40%. Above the noted breakeven point, income taxes will be subtracted from profits, which are shown in the upper right corner of the graph.

The breakeven chart shown in Exhibit 27-5 is a very simple one, because it assumes that there are no changes in costs at any volume level. In reality, additional fixed costs must be incurred as production volumes increase. For example, there will come a point where production capacity for one eight-hour shift cannot be expanded; only by hiring additional supervisors, production planners, maintenance staff, and materials management personnel for the second and third shifts can capacity be increased. All of these costs are shown in Exhibit 27-6, where there is a large jump in the level of fixed costs at about the time when production capacity reaches the 70% level. Because of this significant increase,

Exhibit 27-4 Capital Request Form

Capital Investment Proposal Form

Name of Project Sponsor: *H. Henderson*

Submission Date: *09/09/01*

Investment Description:

Additional press for newsprint.

Cash Flows:

Year	Equipment	Working Capital	Maintenance	Tax Effect of Annual Depreciation	Salvage Value	Revenue	Taxes	Total
0	−5,000,000	−400,000						−5,400,000
1			−100000	320,000		1,650,000	−700,000	1,170,000
2			−100,000	320,000		1,650,000	−700,000	1,1700,00
3			−100,000	320,000		1,650,000	−700,000	1,170,000
4			−100,000	320,000		1,650,000	−700,000	1,170,000
5		400,000	−100,000	320,000	1,000,000	1,650,000	−700,000	2,570,000
Totals	−5,000,000	0	−500,000	2,400,000	1,000,000	8,250,000		1,850,000

(Boxed value in Tax Effect of Annual Depreciation column: 800,000)

Tax Rate:	**40%**
Hurdle Rate:	**10%**
Payback Period:	4.28
Net Present Value:	(86,809)
Internal Rate of Return:	9.4%

Type of Project (check one):

Legal requirement _____

New product-related _____

Old product extension ___Yes___

Repair/replacement _____

Safety issue _____

Approvals:

Amount	Approver	Signature
<$5,000	Supervisor	_____
$5–19,999	General Mgr	_____
$20–49,999	President	_____
$50,000+	Board	_____

Reproduced with permission: Bragg, *Financial Analysis: A Controller's Guide*, John Wiley & Sons, 2000, p. 24.

367

Exhibit 27-5   Simplified Breakeven Chart

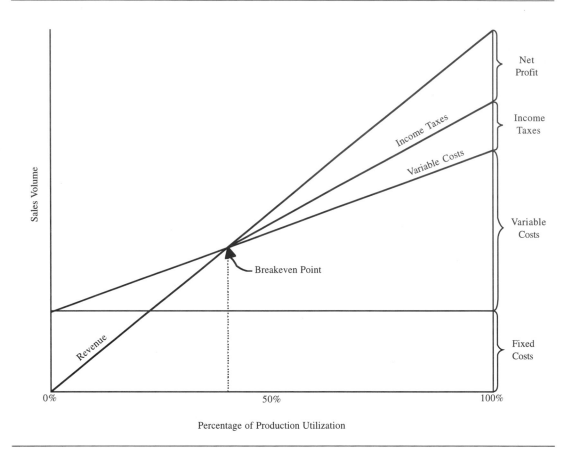

Percentage of Production Utilization

Reproduced with permission: Bragg, *Financial Analysis: A Controller's Guide,* John Wiley & Sons, 2000, p. 118.

the exhibit shows that the point at which profits are maximized is just prior to the jump in fixed costs. The accountant should be aware of the points where costs will step up in this manner, and advise management of the resulting changes in profits.

The breakeven graph is of particular use in determining the inherent risk in a business forecast. A well-designed forecast will contain high, median, and low revenue and cost levels that bracket the full range of expected company performance for the upcoming year. By adding the full range of these estimates to a breakeven graph, as shown in Exhibit 27-7, one can see if there is any risk of loss during the forecasted period. In the exhibit, the lowest level of projected revenue will result in a loss; this issue should be communicated back to management as part of the forecasting process, so that it can alter its budget to avoid the potential loss.

Other situations in which the breakeven graph can be used are to determine the impact of a changed product mix on overall profits, changes in per-unit selling prices, the range of potential profits to be expected, production volumes needed to offset various per-unit prices, and the level of revenue needed to cover the cost of a capital acquisition. Thus, breakeven analysis is an essential tool for financial analysis.

Exhibit 27-6   Breakeven Chart Including Impact of Step Costing

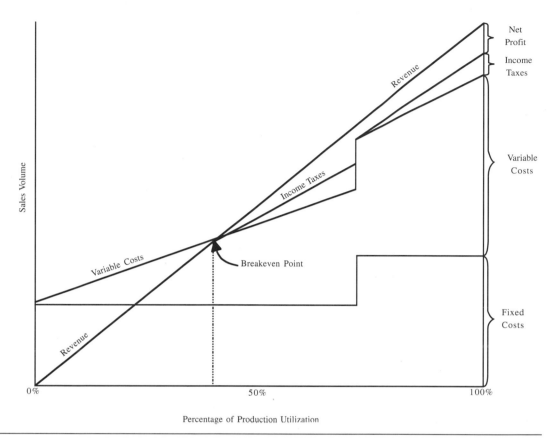

Reproduced with permission: Bragg, *Financial Analysis: A Controller's Guide,* John Wiley & Sons, 2000, p. 120.

27-5 RISK ANALYSIS

The preceding forms of analysis all assume that the data being used as input to the various calculations is accurate. If not, then the results of each analysis may be incorrect, and lead to bad business decisions. There are several ways to improve the accuracy of data used, as well as quantify the level of risk associated with it.

The primary area in which there is a high risk of inaccuracy is in forecasts of any kind. The information used for a forecast is frequently based on the opinions of a small number of people, who may have biases that skew their forecasts away from actual results. The accuracy of forecasts can be improved by a number of means, such as calling upon outside experts for independent analysis and review, using an internal review board that discusses the data and recommends changes where needed, or calling upon the sales staff (those with the best knowledge of market conditions) for an opinion. It is also useful to compare actual results against forecasts by person, to see who is consistently making the best (and worst) forecasts.

Once all estimates have been received, the accountant should determine their range of values. If they are broadly dispersed, then there is a strong likelihood that using the

Exhibit 27-7   Risk Analysis of a Business Forecast

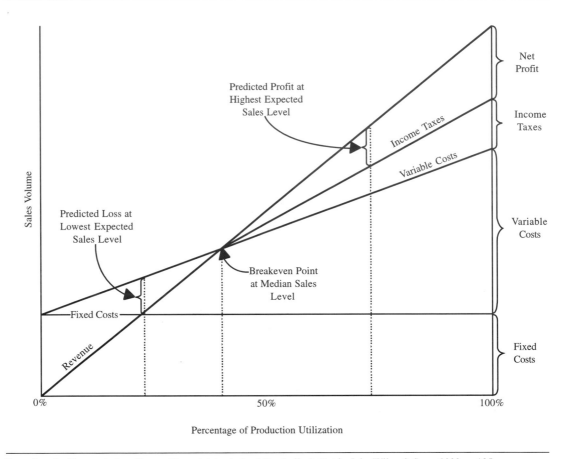

Reproduced with permission: Bragg, *Financial Analysis: A Controller's Guide,* John Wiley & Sons, 2000, p. 125.

median of all estimates as the basis for financial analysis will not include many of the estimates, which may be far higher or lower than the median. When there is a great deal of dispersion in the data, it is best to calculate its amount, and report this information alongside any resulting financial analysis, so that the reader can form an opinion regarding the level of risk for which the resulting analysis is not accurate. Dispersion can be determined with the standard deviation calculation. This measures the average scatter of data about the mean by arriving at a figure that represents the average distance of every data item from the midpoint. A large standard deviation means that the range of data is quite varied. In such cases, one should be wary of any resulting summarization of the data, since there are many possible outcomes that vary substantially from each other.

The standard deviation can be converted into the coefficient of variation by dividing the standard deviation by the mean of the data. The coefficient of variation is a more useful number, because it restates the standard deviation in terms of a percentage. For example, a standard deviation may be 152.7, but one cannot tell if this is good or bad until it is converted into the coefficient of variation, where one then finds out that it represents only a 5% standard deviation from the mean, which therefore gives one good reliance on the underlying data.

There is always a chance that the data used to make financial projections will be incorrect. This risk can be related to the reader of a financial report in terms of a quantification, such as the coefficient of variation, or in relation to the relative level of inaccuracy that has occurred in projections in the past, or in a narrative format; in this last case, it is up to the reader of the report to judge how much risk is included in the presented information.

27-6 BUSINESS CYCLE FORECASTING

Business cycles tend to be of very long duration, involving gradual expansions and contractions of the national and international economies. They are influenced by an enormous array of issues—raw material availability, wars, earthquakes, monetary policy, and so on. At this level, the typical corporation will rely upon large banks, investment houses, or forecasting specialists to give it information about expected changes in the economy, for it simply does not have the time, money, expertise, or inclination to undertake such a task by itself.

However, every company operates within one or more much smaller niches within the national economy, and these niches may be influenced by a sufficiently small number of variables that it is worthwhile for a company to maintain its own forecasting function that addresses those variables. For example, United Airlines operates within the air travel segment of the economy, while the Ford Motor Company operates within the motor vehicles segment. The level of business activity that United will experience within its niche is heavily influenced by the cost of jet fuel, since this cost is typically passed along to the consumer through ticket prices. Similarly, Ford is also influenced by the cost of fuel, because demand for its fuel-efficient cars will rise and demand for its "gas hog" cars will fall in association with long-term gas price increases.

If the accountant becomes involved in business cycle forecasting, there are a number of forecasting models that may be of use. One is the anticipation survey. This approach holds that the best determinant of future conditions is to poll the most experienced and knowledgeable people in the industry and summarize their opinions regarding future conditions. Another approach is to construct a time series model that extends historical trend lines into the future; this approach can be reasonably accurate in the very short term, but is similar to driving a car by peering closely into the rearview mirror. A third alternative is to use econometric models, which are complex formulations that depend upon the interaction of hundreds of variables; these are too expensive for a single company to maintain, but can be managed by well-funded industry trade groups or more commonly by specialist forecasting firms. A fourth approach is to use leading indicators to forecast economic changes. These are activities that have a history of changing prior to changes in the economy, such as the number of new business formations, unemployment insurance claims, and capacity utilization. If a small number of leading indicators are tracked that have a specific bearing upon the conditions within one's industry, it is possible to obtain a general idea of near-term economic conditions.

What approach should the accountant use in creating forecasts? One alternative is to use the national forecasts that are published in the major business magazines on a regular basis. However, these apply to the economy as a whole, and may have little applicability to a specific market niche. A more accurate, but more expensive, approach is to hire a forecasting firm that can develop a forecast for a specific subset of the economy. Finally, one can develop an in-house forecasting capability. Under this scenario, it is best to work with the management team to develop a small set of key variables that they believe has the largest impact on the business cycle within the company's industry. Then collect data about these variables for as many years in the past as possible, and compare them to actual business conditions over time to see if they are correlated. If so, initiate a system for collecting the variables on a regular basis, and then develop a simplified spreadsheet model into which they can be loaded for forecasting purposes. Before sharing the results of this model with the management team, be sure to summarize the variables and key assumptions used in the development of the model, so that management will have a general understanding of its formulation. Finally, the actual business cycle results should be compared to predicted results to see if the model works properly, and adjusted as necessary to bring it into closer alignment with actual results. This last approach to forecasting is clearly the most time-consuming one to implement, but can result in the best information, especially if a great deal of time goes into its creation, data collection, and ongoing maintenance.

27-7 SUMMARY

The accountant will be called upon to provide financial analyses on nearly any topic imaginable—whether to buy capital equipment, invest in different types of securities, select a price point for a new product, replace manual labor with automation, and so on. There is no way to prepare the accountant for every possible situation that may arise, so this chapter has focused solely on those key concepts that are most likely to arise on the most frequent basis. These are the cost of capital, capital budgeting, breakeven analysis, risk analysis, and business cycle forecasting. The concepts included within them can be combined and built upon to derive financial analyses for more topics than those presented here.

CHAPTER 28

Management Information Systems

28-1 INTRODUCTION

The accountant can no longer be skilled in just the management and technical aspects of accounting. The continuing need to improve the efficiency and effectiveness of the accounting function has driven organizations to install the most technologically advanced accounting software systems, which allows them to automate some functions, pull in data from other departments that was not previously available, and issue timely and specially formatted reports on an ongoing basis that are of great use in running the modern business. In order to use these systems properly, the accountant must understand how to create a management information systems strategy, select software, and install and test it. There are other technology-related issued to be aware of as well, such as information security, automated data collection and storage systems, electronic data interchange, and the shifting of selected computer functions to suppliers. This chapter addresses the key issues behind each of these topics.

28-2 THE MANAGEMENT INFORMATION SYSTEMS STRATEGY

The adoption of new management information systems can be an extraordinarily expensive commitment that can channel a great deal of management effort into its installation and away from other projects. If the installation is not directly associated with a company's overall strategic direction, then an excessive amount of both funding and management time will be redirected away from the organization's primary focus.

To keep management information systems closely aligned with overall corporate strategy, it is very important to determine their place within the overall strategy. To do this, one should document all of the technologies currently being used, including the various methods of data capture, software applications, and abilities of the staff that runs those systems. Then compare this information to the data that the company needs to collect, the types of software applications needed to collect and manage this data, and the technical platform needed to support the software. The comparison should reveal several very specific shortfalls that must be corrected in order to align the company's management information systems with the overall corporate strategy.

With this list of specific issues in hand, it is then much easier to create a plan for rolling out the changes, which should include a budget for all monetary and human resources needed to implement the changes.

A final issue is that one should create a procedure that calls for the regular review of the company's strategic plan to ensure that the revised management information systems are continuing to support it. By taking these steps, a company will focus its resources most effectively on the support of its overall strategy, and not channel an excessive amount of funds and effort into the wrong management information systems.

28-3 SOFTWARE EVALUATION AND SELECTION

The accountant is likely to become deeply involved in the evaluation and selection of an accounting software package at some point during his or her career. When this happens, the chief issue to consider during the process is what features are needed for the software to be acceptable to the buyer. The following list of features is grouped by the type of accounting module most likely to be found in the software, and covers the most important accounting features:

1. *Accounts payable.* This module includes those transactions that require the most time by accounting clerks, and so should be designed for the highest level of accountant efficiency, including "hot keys" to shift quickly between screens, a simple user interface, and an automated three-way matching process. The key features it should contain are:

   - *1099 reporting.* All companies are required to issue 1099 forms following the end of each calendar year to non-corporate entities for payments made by the company to them during the year. The software should allow one to flag these entities for easy identification, as well as to print out the necessary 1099 form. Since the 1099 format can change from year to year, the system should also allow for minor adjustments to the format of the report.

   - *Allow for purchasing approval at the receiving dock.* An advanced feature is to allow open purchase orders to suppliers to be accessed at a computer terminal at the receiving dock, so that the receiving staff can check off those purchase order line items that have been received as soon as they arrive at the dock. This is a crucial means for reducing the effort involved in three-way matching.

   - *Automated clearing house (ACH) payments.* An advanced feature is to transmit a set of electronic payment requests directly to the company's bank from the software, requesting the electronic transfer of funds straight to the accounts of suppliers. This avoids the need for a time-consuming check run.

- *Bank reconciliation.* The software should list all checks that have not yet cleared the bank, so that the person performing the bank reconciliation can check them off on the computer, based on their presence in a bank statement. The bank reconciliation function may be listed elsewhere in the software, but it is largely based on this activity.

- *Cash forecast.* The software should determine the amounts of cash that will be required to pay for accounts payable that are already stored in the accounting database, based on the dates when they are due for payment.

- *Identification of discount payments.* The software should flag any payments for which the company will earn a discount if it pays early. In addition, there should be a user-defined field that represents the minimum discount percentage that will be flagged, on the grounds that a very small discount will not be worth the associated cost of funds if the associated invoice is paid early.

- *Linkage to electronic data interchange (EDI).* The data entry of supplier invoices is a very time-consuming and error-prone task that can be avoided if the software contains an EDI interface that will automatically translate incoming electronic invoices into the proper format and enter them into the accounting database—without any manual intervention.

- *Pay based on receipt, rather than supplier invoice.* An advanced feature is to pay suppliers upon the approval of the receiving personnel, who verify that incoming goods are noted in company purchase orders. This feature entirely avoids the use of supplier invoices as the basis for payment. For it to work appropriately, the system must include sales tax tables for all of the jurisdictions from which suppliers are sending goods, in order to ensure that sales taxes are paid. An alternative is to calculate use taxes and remit them directly to government authorities, but this will still require the use of tax tables.

- *Print supplier checks.* The software should support the printing of check-based payments to suppliers. The software should allow for adjustments to the layout of the check form, so that any type of form can be used. An advanced form of this feature is to transmit a file containing all prospective payments to the company's bank, which will print and mail the checks on its behalf.

- *Select payments by due date.* The software should automatically determine which payments are due as of a date that is manually input by the user, and allow the user to manually exclude any items that will be paid at a later date.

- *Simple entry of data from supplier invoices.* The software should allow one to set up default information for each supplier, such as a default expense account, payment term, and discount rate, at the time when it is initially entered into the system, so that this information will not have to be entered again in the future.

- *Simplified payments to one-time suppliers.* The software should allow the user to avoid the entry of detailed payment information (such as address, default account number, and 1099 flag) for suppliers who are only paid one time. Instead, a simplified data entry process should be available for these payments.

- *Three-way matching.* An advanced feature is for the software to automatically cross-check the existence of a purchase order, a supplier invoice, and receiving information for each item to be paid, and warn the user of any discrepancies among these three sources of information. This level of automation greatly reduces the workload of the accounts payable staff, which must otherwise conduct this research manually.

- *Void checks.* The software should provide for a simple check-off function that allows one to quickly void a check, so that the related expense account is automatically credited and the cash account is debited.

2. *Accounts receivable.* This module focuses on two primary functions, which are the creation of customer billings and the receipt of cash. The most essential features of this kind of software are:

- *Aging reports.* The software must create a report that itemizes when payments are due from suppliers. The on-line report should also include some degree of interactivity, so that clicking on a listed invoice number will switch the user to a screen that lists the details of each invoice.

- *Bank reconciliation.* Part of the bank reconciliation process is to have the software present a list of all cash receipts that have been received in the past month, so that one can check them off as having been received, as per the bank statement. The other portion of the bank reconciliation process is checking off cashed checks, which is noted under the listing of accounts payable functions.

- *Billings by job.* An advanced function is that the software should summarize the labor and materials costs charged to a specific job and carry this information forward into an invoice for billing purposes. The billing should include default hourly rates for each person billed, as well as a default price for each part or product billed.

- *Cash application.* The software should allow one to easily apply cash to either specific invoices or to expense accounts, as well as allow for partial payments, the use of discounts by customers, and immediate write-offs of remaining balances by the person applying cash through the software.

- *Cash forecast.* The software should automatically determine the dates when cash is expected to be received from each customer, based on the origination dates or due dates of the invoices sent to them, which can then be used as part of a cash forecasting function. A more advanced feature is for the software to more precisely determine the dates when invoices are most likely to be received from customers, based on the individual payment history of each customer.

- *Collection notes.* The software should allow the collections staff to store their collection notes on-line, alongside each invoice being collected. An advanced feature is for the system to automatically issue reminders to the collection personnel regarding when they are supposed to contact customers to follow up on payment issues.

- *Collection statistics.* An advanced feature is for the software to automatically determine the collection statistics for the collections person assigned to each invoice, such as the average time required for collection.

- *Credit hold flag.* The software must have a feature that allows the collections staff to flag a customer's account, indicating that no further shipments will be made to it until pending credit issues are resolved. A key issue is that the software should not just issue a warning regarding these customers, but must completely shut down any processing of related orders, so that the company does not waste time processing orders that may never be shipped.

- *Customer statements.* The software should be capable of creating a periodic report for customers that itemizes all outstanding invoices, as well as when they are due for payment. A more advanced feature is to render this information into an e-mail format for automatic delivery to customers, thereby avoiding the cost of mailing the statements.

- *Dunning e-mails.* An advanced feature is for the software to issue warning e-mails to customers that notify them when payments have not been received on a timely basis. The timing, repetitiveness, and content of these messages should be controllable by the user.

- *Dunning letters.* The software should be able to print out a series of pre-formatted dunning letters that vary based on the time that has passed since an invoice became overdue. The content of these letters should be adjustable by the user.

- *Electronic data interchange billings.* An advanced feature is for the software to automatically reformat invoices into a standard EDI transaction and send them to customers. This will also require the use of a flag that tells the software which billings are to printed and which are to be sent out electronically.

- *Finance charge processing.* The software should notify the user of any invoices that are so overdue that they qualify for an additional billing of finance charges, and create the invoice containing this charge, if so approved by the user.

- *Multiple bill-to and ship-to addresses.* The software should at least contain space for multiple ship-to addresses, and preferably for a number of bill-to addresses as well. This is crucial in some industries, such as retail stores, whose shipments may be sent to hundreds of different locations. Be sure to ascertain the maximum number of addresses allowed by the system, and compare this to the expected number of addresses per customer.

- *Web linkage to on-line credit reports.* An advanced feature is to include an icon in the software that allows collections personnel to quickly jump from the in-house accounting software to an external credit reporting service, such as Dun & Bradstreet, so that they can verify credit information about new or existing customers.

3. *General ledger.* This module requires a number of key capabilities, such as consolidations, financial reporting, account setup, and drill down for researching transactions. Here are some of the most crucial capabilities to look for:

- *Account format copying.* The software should allow one to quickly replicate a pre-determined set of accounts for other uses. For example, one should be able to create a set of accounts for one company, and then copy the codes in their entirety to another company or subsidiary. This can be a great time saver when setting up the chart of accounts for multiple entities.

- *Account formatting.* The software should allow one to create any possible format for account codes, including coding for companies, departments, product lines, and so on. The number of allowable digits in the account code should be at least a dozen. There should also be a feature that allows one to link subsidiary-level accounts to master accounts, so that results reported in the subsidiary accounts will roll up into the master accounts.

- *Cost allocations.* If a company expects to charge out costs to various functions or activities from cost pools, then the accounts designated as cost pools should have a feature that allocates a pre-set percentage of costs to pre-determined accounts. An advanced feature is for the allocation percentages to be automatically changed in each period based on the amount of costs or other activities that have occurred in other accounts.

- *Create financial statements.* The software should contain a boilerplate version of the financial statements that is already available for use. There should also be a report writer that allows one to make adjustments to the basic layout of these reports. Further, the report writer should allow one to create specialized reports based on specific accounts and multiple years of data.

- *Drill down capability.* A key feature for research purposes is for the software to allow the user to access a transaction at a summary level, and then "drill down" through many layers of detail to find the root cause for the transaction. For example, an excessively high cost of goods sold total might require one to access the variance accounts within the cost of goods sold, then scan through the detail for the key variance, then access the line item within that variance that caused the problem, and then go all the way down to the original transaction to determine the root cause of the problem. This represents an enormous labor savings for the accountant.

- *Entity consolidations.* If a company has a number of subsidiaries, then the software must be able to consolidate the results of all these entities into a single set of financial statements, which must include the capability to automatically eliminate any inter-company transactions.

- *Multiple budget versions.* A company may use one budget for calculating manager performance, another to report performance against a different target for shareholder reporting purposes, and perhaps other budgets for other reasons. Accordingly, the software should allow for the entry of multiple budgets that can then be used during financial reporting to create different comparisons to actual financial results.

- *Recurring journal entries.* The software should allow one to create a journal entry and then set it up so that it automatically repeats for a pre-set number of future accounting periods. This eliminates the need for anyone to manually enter transactions that are not expected to change. A key feature is that the software should offer the option to update future recurring entries if the accountant decides to change the entry in the current period, since this eliminates the work associated with manually updating the transactions in all future periods.

- *Reversing journal entries.* The software should be able to automatically reverse a journal entry in the following accounting period. This keeps an accountant from having to re-enter the system and manually reverse the journal entry. For example, a wage accrual must be reversed in the following period, and this can be completed most easily if the user simply checks off a reversing entry box in the journal entry screen.

- *Standard journal entries.* The software should allow one to devise a series of standard journal entry formats, with pre-set description fields, that can be called up for use in each reporting period. This makes it easier for the accountant to quickly run through a standard set of transactions in order to close the books. Examples of such transactions are accruals for interest expense or income, wages, and property taxes.

- *Statistical data fields.* The general ledger can be used as a data warehouse by allowing for the entry of non-accounting information in some fields. The user should be able to enter alphanumeric information in them, so that the operating or statistical data related to a reporting period can be permanently stored alongside the accounting data for that period.

- *Unbalanced entry warning.* A very basic function is for the software to warn the user whenever a journal entry is made that does not contain the same dollar value of debits and credits (for example, does not sum to zero). Otherwise, the balance sheet will not have a matching amount of debits and credits.

4. *Inventory/Cost costing.* The job costing functionality within the accounting software tends to be spread across several other modules, rather than concentrated in a separate module. Here are the most essential features to look for:

- *Backflushing capability.* An advanced feature is for the system to skip the use of all picking transactions for moving inventory out to the shop floor, and instead to have the user enter the completed amount of production at the end of the production process, which the system then multiplies by the bill of materials for each item to determine what inventory was used, and then subtracts this total from the inventory records.

- *Bill of materials.* The presence of a bill of materials should be considered a crucial feature for cost accounting purposes, for it is used to define the exact contents of each product, which can then be used as a point of comparison to determine what should have been used during an accounting period. The software should allow one to include the expected scrap rate for each component, as well as the use of sub-assemblies that can roll up into a master bill of materials.

- *Comparison to purchase order upon receipt.* As was also noted under the accounts payable module, the software should allow the receiving staff to compare the detail on purchase orders to what is actually received, and check off those items on-line, thereby eliminating much of the three-way matching work performed by the accounts payable staff.

- *Cycle counting report generation.* The software should allow the user to enter a range of inventory locations and print out a report that lists the contents of those bins. This information is then used by a cycle counter to compare actual quantities to what is sitting on the shelf.

- *Direct and step-down allocation capability.* If a company likes to allocate costs to various production functions, then its software should include the capability not only to directly allocate costs from a cost pool, but also to allocate costs from a service center into a cost pool, and thence to the final costing target.

- *Inventory disposition tracking.* It is most useful for a cost accountant to know how each item of inventory is disposed of that is not consumed through its inclusion in a product. There should be a number of available codes in the system that users can enter to describe how they are eliminating various inventory items from stock, which the cost accountant can later compile and report upon.

- *Inventory location tracking.* The software absolutely must allow for the precise definition of inventory locations within the warehouse. Otherwise, it is impossible to determine where items can be found for cycle counting purposes. The ideal location format should allow space for row, rack, and bin designations.

- *Inventory usage report.* This report should itemize those units of stock that are being used most heavily, and should also offer the option of sorting in the reverse order, so that the warehouse manager can determine which inventory items are being used the least.

- *Labor routings.* A labor routing is most useful in organizations in which there is a large labor content in its manufactured goods, or where it can use this information to schedule labor for upcoming production activities. The labor routing contains the exact types of labor categories and time required to manufacture a product.

- *Linkage to bar code scanning capability.* The warehouse is one of the primary areas for efficiency improvements through the use of bar coding technology. Accordingly, the software should allow one to create bar codes for both inventory location codes as well as identification codes for each item in stock, as well as provide an interface for bar code scanning equipment that will send scanned data back into the accounting system.

- *Multiple storage location capability.* An essential item is the capability to store multiple location codes for a single inventory part number. Less expensive software packages will force one to always store an inventory item in a single preset inventory location, while more advanced systems will allow for storage in any location at all.

- *Multiple types of cost layering.* The software should at least allow one to create inventory layers using first-in first-out, last-in first out, and average costing. This is mandatory for external financial reporting purposes.

- *Multiple units of measure.* There should be a table in the module that allows one to set up multiple types of units of measure that are valid for each inventory item. For example, the purchasing staff may buy tape in rolls, and so prefers to measure it in rolls, while the engineering staff prefers to measure it in terms of inches for its bills of material. This table will itemize the quantities associated with each type of measure, so that any designated unit of measure can be used without destroying the integrity of the underlying data.

- *Obsolete inventory warning report.* This report should itemize those inventory items that have not been used within a user-specified time period. It is also useful for this report to list the quantity and valuation of inventory on hand for each item, so that the purchasing staff can see if there is a possibility of returning inventory items to suppliers for credit.

- *Rework tracking.* The system should have a field available that identifies any jobs that are comprised of products that are being reworked. The accountant needs to determine the stage of completion for each of these jobs and determine the labor and other costs charged to them, in order to calculate the cost of rework.

- *Scrap tracking.* The system should have a disposition code available that can be used to describe inventory that is thrown away. This is a particularly important feature if a company wants to use backflushing, since any excess scrap will otherwise not be recorded in the system, and will result in incorrect raw material inventory balances.

- *Transfer pricing accumulations.* Though only an issue for those companies that transfer goods between subsidiaries, this function is useful for separately compiling the variable and fixed costs associated with each product as it moves through a series of companies. This information is quite useful for determining a product's minimum allowable price, based on the cumulative variable costs assigned to it. Without this costing split, a company would be forced to price its transferred products based on their total cost, which may include irrelevant allocated overhead costs.

- *Unit cost database at different volume levels.* An advanced function is to have a separate database that stores costing data for all component parts that a company uses, noting specifically how much each one costs if production volumes change to different levels (that is, typically higher costs if volumes are lower, and the reverse if volumes rise). This information is most valuable for budgeting product costs for various production levels, as well as for target costing activities in which the accountant assists in the determination of expected new product margins.

5. *Payroll.* Though many organizations outsource their payroll function to a supplier, many still use the full functionality of this application within their accounting software. The following functions should still be considered even if outsourcing is currently used, in case a company wants to have the option to switch to an in-house solution at some later date. The key payroll functions are:

   - *Accepts input from automated time clocks.* If a company has invested in automated time clocks, then the pre-formatted time keeping data generated by these miniature computers should be readily accepted by the accounting software and automatically converted into payroll records with minimal review needed by a staff person. The worst possible software functionality would be to re-key all of this data into the payroll software, since it would negate the value having purchased the time clocks.

   - *Allows for user formatting of check layout.* A different type of check format is generally created through the payroll software than what is normally generated through the accounts payable function. This format should include space to identify the gross pay earned, all deductions, net pay, and perhaps a notation regarding accrued and unused vacation and sick time. Generally, the more information allowed on the check, the less contact employees will need to have with the payroll staff, since they are being presented with all the information they need through this document.

- *Allows for user-defined deduction types.* There are a large number of potential deductions that can be taken from a paycheck, such as garnishments, health club fees, or dental insurance deductions. The software should allow for an unlimited number of user-defined deductions, which will cover all possible deduction contingencies.

- *Blocks mandatory tax deductions.* There are a few cases involving the use of foreign employees where mandatory tax deductions, such as social security taxes, do not have to be deducted from their pay. If a company has these employees, the software must be able to block these deductions from the standard payroll calculation.

- *Calculates time worked from time cards.* Rather than forcing a staff person to manually calculate all hours worked from a time card, the software should allow one to enter each employee's start and ending times for each day, from which it will calculate hours worked. Depending upon company pay policy, there may also be a need for the software to round off these times. For example, a person may clock in at 7:55 A.M., but that person's work shift does not start until 8:00 A.M.; accordingly, the software can automatically round the start time up to 8:00 A.M. Further, it may be necessary for the software to automatically deduct the standard time period allowed for lunch or other types of breaks. It is also useful for the software to generate a report that itemizes those employees who have punched in but not out, or vice versa, so that the payroll staff can resolve these discrepancies.

- *Linkage to direct deposit function.* If the company provides direct deposit of payroll funds to employee bank accounts, then the software should provide either a tape of these transactions to the company bank for direct deposit processing, or else generate an electronic transmittal containing this information.

- *Payment reversal function.* There are times when paychecks must be backed out of the system. This can be a painful process, involving the reversal of the multitude of possible accounts that are used to distribute expenses on a paycheck. The software can ease this process by providing a simple check-off field that will automatically reverse the function.

- *Records different types of hours worked.* There should be fields available that will describe every type of time that a company uses. For example, employees may categorize their time as sick time, vacation time, jury duty, military leave, overtime, or regular hours.

- *Records time worked by job.* In many industries, billings to customers are primarily based on jobs completed, rather than products shipped. If so, the software must allow for the creation of job numbers and the subsequent application of hours worked against those jobs. The software should also allow one to split hours worked between multiple jobs and transfer time worked from one job to another, and allow for the closure of jobs, so that no additional time can be charged to them.

- *Regularly updates tax tables.* The software provider should issue tax tables as part of the maintenance agreement that updates the software. Any problem in this area can result in significant potential liability to a company, and so should be grounds for the immediate transfer of the payroll function to some other software or to an outsourcing firm.

- *Transfers existing employees among departments.* Employees will sometimes change the departments in which they work. If so, the software should track this change, keeping a record of both the old department and the new one. It is not acceptable to store just a single department in the software, since this means that all payroll costs for an employee for all dates prior to the transfer will also show the employee as working in the new department, which will unfairly record the person's pay in the new department for as far back in time as the payroll system stores payroll data.

- *W-2 form preparation.* The software should automatically generate W-2 tax reporting forms for all employees, as well as allow for changes in the W-2 report format, so that it can easily be matched to any changes in the form that the federal government may make from year to year.

6. *Purchasing.* Though the purchasing function is generally considered to be separate from the most common accounting activities, a purchasing package that is closely meshed with the accounting software results in significant efficiencies in the processing of accounts payable. Here are the key functions to look for in a purchasing software package:

- *Automated requisition processing.* Employees should be able to log onto an electronic requisition form and enter the items they need. This information is immediately transferred to the screens of the purchasing staff, who use it to create purchase orders.

- *On-line supplies catalog.* An advanced feature is to have an on-line supplies catalog available to employees. They can scan through the various items for which the purchasing staff has already negotiated bulk purchasing deals with suppliers, enter their ship-to addresses, and the system will automatically bypass the purchasing department and issue orders directly to suppliers, who in turn will send the supplies straight to the ordering employees.

- *Blanket purchase order tracking.* The system should automatically compile a list of all receipts that were ordered under a blanket purchase order, so that the purchasing staff can see how much of an ordering commitment it has still remaining under the blanket order.

- *Commodity volume tracking.* The system should categorize each item purchased by commodity code, and regularly summarize the quantity of commodities purchased, both in terms of units and dollars ordered. This is most useful for re-shuffling the workload of the purchasing staff, each of whom is usually assigned a specific commodity code for purchasing activities.

- *Electronic data interchange transactions.* The software should allow one to issue an EDI transaction to a supplier. The software should automatically convert a purchase order into EDI format and transmit the transaction to the supplier. This may call for a custom interface to a separate EDI transmission package.

- *Linkage to material requirements planning (MRP) system.* The purchasing staff can plan for purchases much more easily if the purchasing software is linked to an MRP system. An MRP system determines the exact amount and timing of all purchases related to the upcoming production plan, based on material quantities listed in the bill of materials and on-hand raw material inventories. A high-end MRP system will even create purchase orders for review by the purchasing staff, or bypass the manual review stage and place orders directly with suppliers.

- *Purchase order transfer to three-way match processing.* The purchasing software should be linked to the accounts payable software, so that the accounts payable system can automatically reference issued purchase orders during the three-way matching process in order to ensure that received items were properly ordered by the company.

- *Supplier performance tracking.* An advanced feature is for the software to automatically compile performance statistics on each supplier. This may include the time variance between when items are supposed to be delivered and when they are actually received, or the percentage of items that are rejected based on poor quality. The system can even compile reports and automatically issue them as a periodic "report card" to suppliers.

- *Track receipts against due dates.* The software should notify the purchasing staff when there are shipment due dates coming up in the near term that may call for a verification phone call to the supplier to ensure that the shipment is indeed on its way. Alternatively, the software can warn the purchasing staff when expected receipts have already passed their expected due dates.

7. *Report Writer.* Though the report writer is not usually treated as a separate module within an accounting system, it is an extremely important part of the overall system, for it allows one to group and summarize data in ways that cannot be anticipated by the pre-formatted reports that were created by the software supplier. Here are key functions to look for:

- *Download to multiple formats.* Any report format created should download with minimal keystrokes into any of several popular formats, such as *.wks, *.wk1, *.doc, or ASCII. The main point is that the downloadable format available should be the one most used by the company—there should be no need to convert all other electronic spreadsheets, databases, and word processing packages throughout the organization to the format used by the accounting software.

- *Linkages to multiple tables.* There are dozens of different data tables in which accounting information is stored. The most primitive type of report writer will only allow reports to be created from a single table, which greatly restricts the types of reports that can be created. A much better approach is for the report writer to link a number of tables together, so that data can be pulled together from multiple sources.

- *Pre-formatted reports.* There should be a formatting template integrated into the report writer that allows the user to specify different margin and header settings, as well as the proper formatting of rows, columns, subtotals, and totals.

- *Conversion of reports to HTML.* The report writer should allow the user to convert a completed report into hypertext markup language with a single keystroke and then paste the resulting report into a Web page, so that the report can be viewed by anyone with access to the company intranet site.

- *Automatic report content updating.* If the preceding HTML conversion capability is available, the report writer should also have the capability to automatically update the data on the report, so that users can view data in real time, rather than as of the date when the original report was created.

- *Query capability.* Beyond the basic capabilities of the report writer lies the query language. This is a search engine that should allow a user to input a short string of characters related to a search for data that is sufficiently precise for the computer system to return the desired information. The query language can be in free-form text, or in a more rigid format with specific data entry fields. The first format is more powerful but more difficult to learn, while the latter format has the reverse attributes.

8. *General.* The following issues should also be considered when purchasing accounting software, but cross over the functionality of any single software module.

   - *Hot keys for rapid screen switching.* An expert user will not want to work her way through a series of windows to reach the required one, but would rather enter a few keystrokes that are specifically related to the screen in question. These "hot keys" may either be pre-set by the software designer or designated by the user.

   - *Linkage to Internet help site.* A useful feature is for the software provider to maintain a web site that lists crucial responses to problems that other users have discovered with the software. This may include patches to bugs, lists of frequently asked questions (FAQs), or a complete index of help files. Such sites can be much more informative than the help screen typically provided with the software, and is certainly more up-to-date. This feature works best when there is an access button on the screen that takes the user straight to the Web site.

   - *On-line help screens.* The software should always have a complete set of help screens that itemize the various accounting functions and how they are to be used. This should include a table of contents or index that allows the user to enter the first few letters of the topic about which help is needed, which will bring up a list of close matches.

   - *On-line software tutorial.* Though the accounting staff may be sent off to training classes prior to using a new accounting system, refresher training is still required for those functions that are rarely used, as well as new training for employees who are hired after the initial training took place. A good solution to these issues is computer-based training (CBT). The software provider should have training modules available for all aspects of its software, preferably including module quizzes that can be used to test the comprehension of the staff.

   - *Pull-down menu options.* Though this may seem obvious, some older character-based software does not contain any pull-down menu system that allows new users to more easily navigate their way through the maze of screens. Instead, they must work their way up and down through a hierarchy of screens to reach a small number of master lists of screens; this is much less efficient than pull-down menus.

- *Security at multiple levels.* The type of security needed for the computer system will vary with the structure of the business using the accounting software. For example, a single computer that houses the entire accounting system will only need security to access the entire computer, since only one person will be using the machine—all others are locked out. However, multi-user systems will require more specific types of security. The most common security system is to set up a permissions profile for each user that allows him or her access to specific applications within the accounting system. More detailed (but less common) security systems can also restrict access to specific screens or fields within screens. It is also possible to specially format screens that only reveal certain fields, which is an alternative approach for providing field-specific security.

- *Windowing capability.* There are a few instances when the accountant may need to flip rapidly between screens of information, or at least set up screen information side-by-side on the computer terminal. If so, it can be useful to have a windowing capability that allows one to maintain multiple windows on the computer screen at the same time.

In addition to the items just noted, one should investigate the level of customer support provided by the software supplier. Some of this information can be obtained simply by visiting the supplier's web site, since it is increasingly common for them to maintain extensive on-line help files. In addition, it may be possible to obtain copies of their documentation, to see how complete it is. Also, the supplier should offer a complete set of courses designed to educate users in the basics of operating the software, as well as advanced topical areas, such as report writer usage and the construction of queries. Further, one can see if there are any active user groups for the software in the local area, and contact their members to obtain unbiased commentary regarding the level of support provided by the supplier. The importance of this topic will increase with the price of the software, since a software package that cost a great deal, but that no one can use, will not enhance the rest of a company's opinion of the accounting department.

One should also determine the size and location of the supplier's support staff. If it is too small, it may not be able to handle large incoming call volumes, nor provide answers at any time of the day or night. If it is concentrated in a central location, it is likely to only be accessible during the business hours of the time zone in which it is located.

Another issue is its financial condition; any organization without sufficient funding is unlikely to invest enough resources in the continual upgrading of its software, while its customers are also at risk of losing key customer support services if the supplier goes into bankruptcy.

Yet another factor is the number of other customers that are using the supplier's software. If there are few customers, this will impact the amount of maintenance fees collected by the supplier, and therefore its financial condition. Also, a small number of customers does not give a company much of a selection when making reference calls during the software selection process. If there are few customers, it may mean that the software has only just been rolled out, which may indicate the presence of an excessive quantity of software bugs that have not yet been found by customers. A final issue for more advanced computer systems is that the supplier should be able to test one's software through the use of remote diagnostics, so that its customer service personnel can see exactly what problems are occurring.

Another issue related to software selection is its cost. There are several factors to consider besides the initial purchase price. There will usually be a maintenance fee charged each year that can be as high as 18% of the original purchase price. If the purchase price was heavily discounted, the supplier will probably calculate the maintenance fee as a percentage of the original price, rather than the discounted price. Also, the supplier may offer on-site training classes, though the company must pay for the travel cost of the trainer. This is usually a less expensive option than sending employees to the supplier's location if there are so many employees to be trained that their travel cost will exceed that of the trainer. Also, it is generally not acceptable to use a "train the trainer" approach, since there will be a loss of knowledge when the supplier only trains a few people and then relies on these employees to turn around and train other staff.

Another cost issue is the programming related to adjustments that the company makes to the software. If this programming is conducted by the supplier, the time required may be somewhat less than if other programmers are used, since they have a better knowledge of the underlying software code. However, the entire concept of modifying software should be discouraged, since it prevents a company from taking advantage of future upgrades to the software package that are routinely issued by the supplier, since an upgrade would wipe out custom programming that had previously been added to the software.

Of all the preceding factors to consider when purchasing new software, the accountant will probably feel that only a small proportion are truly essential to company operations. If so, these key items should be used to judge the worth of each software package under consideration. It may be useful to assign a priority weighting to each factor, so that a numeric score can be constructed for each package, with the winning package being the one with the highest score.

Even though a software package may have received a high score, this does not automatically qualify it for purchase. The buying company should also make reference calls to other current users of the software, using a standard checklist of its own devising that focuses on the issues that are most important to it. It is quite important to call customers of the supplier that have not been recommended by it, in order to gain access to customers who may have had problems with the software. To obtain the names of these customers, one can go to local support group meetings, or call the customers recommended by the software supplier and ask them if they know of other customers who are not on the supplier's official reference list.

It is also useful to have the supplier conduct an on-site demonstration of the software. If this is done, the company's evaluation team should construct a set of questions to ask prior to the demonstration that focus on the most crucial functions. Otherwise, the salesperson demonstrating the software will tend to channel the discussion toward the nifty "bells and whistles" that make the software look good.

A final way to review the software is to conduct site visits that take the company's review team to the locations of other companies that have previously installed the software. It is important to only visit sites where the software has been completely installed, since the point of the visit is to determine the level of implementation difficulty for *all* software modules, as well as how it has been integrated into the manual systems that surround the software. Once again, the team should construct a standard list of questions to ask before making any site visits, so that the responses to a standard set of questions can be compared, as well as to ensure that all key issues are addressed during the visits.

Once the software has been selected based on the preceding reviews, it must be installed, as is described in the next section.

28-4 SOFTWARE INSTALLATION

Only under the most limited circumstances can one simply buy an accounting software package over the phone, shove the resulting CD delivery into the computer's CD drive, and install the software in a few minutes. This is not possible if there are many computers that must access the software, since a more complex installation must be made through the central file server. It is even more difficult to install if the software has been designed for very high transaction volumes and large numbers of users, for these are installed on complex systems that may require weeks or even months of customized installation effort. It is also a problem when there is a pre-existing system in place, since the data from the old system must be converted over to the format used by the new system, and checked to ensure that it is correct. If there is a need to run portions of both systems at the same time while the conversion takes place, then a team of programmers must construct interfaces between the old and new systems for use during the transition period, so that data can be exchanged between the two systems. For these reasons, it is important to plan carefully for the installation of accounting software.

On the assumption that the system installation will be a complex one, the accountant should be prepared to develop a comprehensive infrastructure to deal with it. The first step is to obtain approval of the funding for the software and all accompanying installation costs (which can be as much as five times the cost of the software itself) from the senior management group. However, this is not the last action taken by senior management, for someone from this group must also agree to be the champion for the project. Since the more complex installations can require several years of effort and the active assistance of virtually all departments, this person must be willing to support the installation effort even over the objections of some parts of the company.

Once this groundwork has been laid, a competent manager must be re-assigned to the full-time task of managing the installation. This person will in turn obtain the full-time services of an experienced project team. The words "full time" recur in this discussion, because the people being shifted to this project already have full-time jobs doing something else, and will likely continue to spend much of their time on those other activities, to the detriment of the software installation. Accordingly, they must be loaned to the installation project full time and for the duration of the installation, with no work obligations to their original departments.

Though this group may be highly experienced in the inner workings of the company, they may have little experience in the area of software installation. Accordingly, it may be useful to hire a small group of consultants whose experience is centered on the proper installation of the specific type of software that the company has purchased. Though consultants are very expensive, their advice can greatly reduce the time period required to complete a successful installation, as well as help to avoid unnecessary expenditures on system modifications.

With the proper team in place, the next step is to develop a work plan. This document should itemize the milestones, due dates, and resources required for each of the hundreds of steps involved in a proper software installation. Particular attention should be paid to the interrelationships of the various modules that comprise the accounting software, since it is very likely that they can only be installed in a certain order, or in specific groups, due to the interactive nature of the data that they use. If some modules will be installed without other supporting modules, then the plan must also allow sufficient time to design, program, and test interfaces between the new modules and the old software that will eventually be replaced. The planning process can be so complex that a full-time planner is needed just to maintain the work plan.

Management tools will be needed to assist the planner. This should certainly include a computerized project tracking tool, such as Microsoft Project, and be supported by a complete set of status reports from each team leader. There should also be an issues log that lists all problems that have arisen during the installation process. These issues should be brought to the attention of the project team at daily meetings, with responsibilities handed out for the fixing of each item. It is also important to maintain a log of software change requests, which should include an estimate of the time and resources required to complete each one. This is a valuable tool in identifying the specific changes that will cause due dates to slip and budgeted costs to be exceeded.

The project team must also analyze the risks associated with the installation. These will vary greatly by company, but here are some of the most common that should be addressed:

- *Software failure.* If the software has been installed in few locations, is a new release, or has not be installed on the hardware platform that the company intends to use it on, then there is considerable risk that the software will not function as planned. Though one way to resolve the issue is not to buy the software, the installation team may have been presented with a signed purchasing agreement and have no input into the issue. If so, there are several ways to mitigate this risk. If the risk is related to the type of hardware platform used, then part of the project plan can be to conduct a test installation on the hardware and run a series of transactions through it to see if there are problems. If there are, then the team can request a switch to a more acceptable type of hardware early in the project before too many resources have been committed, or at least arrange to have the software supplier directly assist in the installation. If the software itself runs a high risk of containing bugs that may halt the processing of key transactions, then the software should be tested early on with a series of sample transactions, so that the bugs can be identified and evaluated.

- *Employee resistance.* The installation of new software involves a number of departments, and is likely to cause changes in the work routines of some employees in each department. If so, it is quite common to meet with resistance from some employees. Given past experiences with the staff, it is possible to identify who these employees are likely to be, so that the project team can arrange to have them personally review the software and suggest some changes that may increase their feeling of buy-in to the installation. If this does not work, then the team should make arrangements early in the project to have these employees removed from any positions in which they can influence the installation in a negative way.

- *Lack of management support.* A key item is that the team may lose its key sponsor within the management team. This issue is crucial, and so should be mitigated con-

> tinually by working with the current project sponsor to increase the number of management supporters, as well as to identify any back-up sponsors in the event of the main sponsor's departure from that position.
>
> - *Lack of funding.* A major software installation can require several years of effort, and so is subject to the vagaries of company finances and the need for funding by competing projects. To reduce this risk, the team should schedule the least necessary software installations or custom programming work toward the end of the project, so that the key functions will be covered by the current budget.

Even though the purchased software may have been tested extensively by the supplier, and already be installed in hundreds of other locations, there are still good reasons to test it. One is that custom interfaces may have been created between the packaged software and other legacy systems maintained by the company—these should certainly be tested. Another reason is that the hardware platform or network configuration may be a unique one for which the software was not originally created—this too must be tested. Yet another reason is that the volume and type of transactions may be unique, and so should also be tested. Without proper testing, the result may be a software installation that is theoretically installed, but which is barely operational. This topic is covered in more detail in the next section.

As just noted, there may be a need for interfaces between the packaged software and other programs. For example, there may be a custom-designed inventory tracking database in place that should be connected to the accounting software, so that inventory valuations can be compiled from it. Similarly, there may be an electronic data interchange system that must be linked to the accounting package in order to automate the transfer of transactions through the EDI system. Further, it is quite common to install packaged software in a series of discrete steps, so that only one module at a time will become operational. When this approach is used, a custom interface must be written between the module to be installed and the other software that it must access, so that the module functions properly. For example, if the fixed assets module is installed without any accompanying modules, then an interface must be written between it and the pre-existing accounts payable module, so that newly purchased assets can be entered once into the accounts payable module and then transferred automatically to the fixed assets module. The design, programming, and testing of interfaces can be a major activity for larger software installations.

For all but the smallest organizations, there will be a large accounting database already in existence that must be entered into the new accounting system. This can be done manually, but is not recommended for several reasons. First, the incidence of keystroke errors will almost certainly result in a considerable number of inaccuracies that must later be reconciled. Second, the time period required to re-enter information is so long that the conversion to the new system may require months of concentrated effort. Third, the amount of labor required to convert the data will result in a considerable expense. For these reasons, it is better to work with the programming staff to create programs that will automatically convert the old formats used to store data in the old system to the revised formats used for the new system. The resulting programs should be carefully tested to ensure that data will be transferred in a reliable manner. There cannot be enough testing in this area, since an improperly handled data conversion will immediately shut down a newly installed accounting system.

The operation of any new software will probably vary in some respects from the software that it is replacing. If so, this may call for different procedures within the accounting department, not only for using the software, but also for any manual procedures that are linked in some way to it, and that must therefore be altered to reflect the changes in the software. The project team should review the need for procedural changes as early as possible, in order to estimate the probable extent of work required in this area. If the required changes are extensive, a separate team should be assigned to work on changes in the process flow, while an experienced procedure-writing team updates any existing manuals or creates new ones.

The accounting staff will require training in the use of the new system. Though this can be provided either by the software supplier or a local training provider, it is also important to develop in-house training for those transactions considered to be critical to company operations, so that a carefully defined training class can be offered to new employees on an as-needed basis. Some software suppliers also offer computer-based training that is available either on compact disk or via the Internet.

A key training issue is its timing. People receiving training will rapidly lose their newly acquired knowledge if they cannot put it to use immediately. Consequently, training should be scheduled for a period within just a few days of the cut-over to the new software.

The project team must also plan for the cut-over from any existing accounting systems to the new software. This includes not just the time period when many of the just-described activities are taking place, but also the first month of operations on the new system, since this is the period when software glitches and additional training issues are most likely to arise. The cut-over phase should include a great deal of fine-tuning of system performance, to ensure that response times fall within previously defined parameters. Planning during this period should certainly include the use of a greatly enlarged help desk, staffed by senior team personnel, that can quickly address problems as soon as they arise. Careful planning in this area is crucial to the successful installation and acceptance of a new accounting system.

It is evident from the previous discussion that a great deal of coordinated work by many specialists is required to ensure that a software installation is successful. One can therefore equate the presence of a properly supported, fully staffed project team with the success of any new accounting software.

28-5 SOFTWARE TESTING

The type of software testing required for new accounting software will vary greatly, depending upon the type of software, the amount of required customization, the type of software rollout used to replace the existing software, the transaction volumes that are likely to be run through it, the type of hardware and network platform upon which it will run, and the set of manual procedures with which it is expected to mesh. For example, a software package that has already been installed thousands of times by other companies on all kinds of hardware and network platforms will probably not require much testing of any kind. However, if a number of changes must be made to it to fit it into the existing environment, then all changes must be carefully tested. Also, if the software will only be rolled out in pieces, with software interfaces being used to connect each newly installed piece to existing software, then each interface will require heavy testing. Further, a software package that is to be installed on a hardware platform on which it has never been installed before will certainly require testing to see if it will function properly in that environment. In addition, if very large transaction volumes are expected, then these volumes should certainly be run through the new system in a test environment to ensure that it can handle the load. And if the software is completely custom-designed, then nearly every possible type of test must be conducted on it to ensure that it is fully functional and meets user requirements.

There are many types of software tests, which can be mixed and matched to fit the needs of any type of software. Here are some of the most common ones:

- *Delivered package test.* This is a comparison of the functionality within a software package to the requirements defined by prospective software users. The result is a list of missing functionality that must be custom designed and added to the software.

- *Acceptance test.* The eventual users of a software package (or custom-built software) are asked to test the new software to ensure that it meets their needs. To avoid an excessively lengthy testing period, the testing should be restricted to only the most critical functions.

- *Unit test.* When software has been modified, this test is used to check its functionality within the specific software module within which the change was made.

- *Volume test.* A large quantity of test transactions can be run through the software to see how response times will be reduced. This is very useful for "tuning" the system to ensure that maximum permissible response times are not exceeded.

- *Integration test.* After software changes have been made to specific software modules and have passed a unit test, an integration test should be completed to ensure that the modified software module will still interact properly with other software modules.

- *Installation test.* This test ensures that the software works in a production environment, which simulates the actual computing environment of the company. This review is a comprehensive one that includes the use of data that have been converted from the old system that the new one is replacing. If the company is installing the software in many locations throughout the company, and there is a mix of hardware platforms on which it is to be installed, then the installation test should be conducted separately for each of the platforms.

Software testing can involve a number of personnel over a long period of time, and will probably result in a number of possible changes. Due to the investment in time and personnel at this stage of a software installation, it is important to have a control system in place that will efficiently deal with the flow of resources for each test, to ensure that tests are conducted efficiently, and that software-related problems are addressed in a methodical manner.

The software testing plan should begin with an overview of the entire process, followed by an itemization of the entire set of resources needed to conduct the tests: people, hardware, software, and testing facilities. All remaining portions of the plan should be referenced back to this resources section, so that all testing objectives are supported by a sufficient amount of resources. Here are the remaining subjects that should be addressed by the plan:

- *Testing roles.* For larger projects, there will be so much testing that some employees will do nothing but a particular kind of test. If so, job descriptions should be outlined for each type of tester.

- *Test reporting.* There should be a standard format for reporting on the status of each test being conducted. This may include the number of test transactions completed, the number or proportion of unresolved defects, and particularly the number or proportion of unresolved *major* issues that will keep the system from becoming operational.

- *Defect tracking and correction.* This is a key procedure, for it involves the precise method for identifying software defects, logging them into a database, prioritizing them, assigning them for resolution, and testing the resulting fixes. The data logged into the defects database should include a unique identifier code, a status code or description, a severity ranking, a defect's priority for resolution, a description of the issue, and the dates when it was detected, assigned for correction, targeted for completion, and closed out.

The discussion in this section should make it clear that a great deal of time and effort is required to thoroughly test new or modified software. With that in mind, the accountant should have a strong preference for purchasing off-the-shelf software and then modifying it as little as possible, thereby avoiding the bulk of the testing noted here.

28-6 INFORMATION SYSTEM SECURITY

The accounting system contains some of the most critical information in the entire company. If key information, such as the outstanding accounts receivable, were to be lost, a company could find itself in a crisis situation, not knowing who owed it money. It is also important to restrict access to some information, either because it is crucial to corporate competitiveness, or because it is employee-specific (such as payroll data) and should not become public knowledge. There are a variety of ways to ensure the security of the accounting system that will mitigate the risk of having these problems arise.

The physical protection of computer hardware is one element of system security. The data storage systems should have a multi-layered backup system in place, which should include off-site data storage, in order to keep hardware damage from ruining key data. Also, if data is stored on stand-alone devices, such as laptop computers, then users must be given some provision for either backup of their systems, perhaps through a mass storage system like a Zip drive, or else through a central backup system that periodically polls and backs up any data, as long as the devices are linked to a network through a docking station.

If a company has made a major investment in mainframes or minicomputers, it should also consider a carefully controlled environment with multi-layered security systems that prevent intrusion from unauthorized personnel, and that also automatically start fire suppression systems as well as protect the equipment against natural hazards.

Virus protection is an increasing concern to the accountant, since viruses can destroy one's data, requiring time-consuming data restorations from backups. One way to protect against viruses is to have a policy of not allowing employees to load their own software onto company computers, which keeps viruses that may be resident on employee-owned diskettes from entering the company computer system by that means. Another approach is to remove the diskette drives from all company computers, which is a highly effective way to keep viruses from entering through a diskette. A third approach is to install virus detection software on all computers. This software screens all programs within the computer on a regular basis, while also checking the code of all new software being introduced into the system; however, it must be updated regularly, so that it can detect and nullify the most recently constructed viruses. A final option is to add a firewall to the company network, which acts like the virus program on a single computer, except that it is a barrier between the entire network and any on-line data sources, such as the Internet.

It is also necessary to deny access to various parts of the computer system, if only because the information contained therein is considered confidential. There are a variety of ways to keep an unauthorized user out of a computer system, as well as to track that person's activities if access occurs, so that one can determine what information has been accessed or damage caused. They are:

- *Issue and regularly change system access passwords.* There should be a password required at the network level. This should force one to use a minimum number of digits, and the system should force the user to change it at regular intervals. If password alterations do not occur regularly, a determined hacker has a greater chance to find one, simply through making a high volume of repeated guesses at it.

- *Install biometric scanners.* There are retinal and fingerprint scanners available that can be used to screen and deny access to computer facilities. Due to their cost, they are usually only used to prevent access to the most expensive equipment. However, recent advances have resulted in the incorporation of fingerprint scanners on a computer mouse, which can be used to deny access to specific directories or programs within computers.

- *Password protection at the program level.* Many computer programs, especially accounting packages, include password protection. This can be for access to the entire package, but higher-end software allows one to be more selective in denying access through the use of passwords at the module, screen, and even field level within a screen. It is also possible to permit full access to information, but only in "read only" mode, so that no alterations to the underlying data can be made. The basic rule for access to specific information is that it be on a "need to know" basis, which generally results in a significant limitation on access rights to all but a few employees.

- *Protect the password file.* If passwords are used to protect any part of the computer system, then a hacker who has gained access to the system will go straight to the password file to read it and gain access to the passwords of those employees with "God rights" that allow access to all parts of the system. This can be prevented by encrypting the password file, though the hacker can (and probably will) download the password file and then try to break the encryption at his or her leisure.

- *Call tracing on call-in modems.* A likely means of entrance into a computer system for a hacker is through a call-in modem. The computer system should have a caller identification and storage feature on all call-in modems, so that one can determine from this record who is trying to gain entrance to the system.

- *Use a keystroke monitor.* Some areas of the computer system should only rarely be accessed by authorized personnel, so any changes to them will have a high probability of being made by a hacker. To track the activities of such people, a keystroke monitor can be installed that traces the exact keystrokes of anyone accessing specific system areas. This approach is not recommended for the entire computer system, since the volume of keystrokes by all authorized computer users would result in a massive file of keystrokes. Targeted usage of this technique is more efficient.

- *Employ intrusion detection.* The classic sign of a hacker is repeated and prolonged attempts to gain access to a system by repetitively trying different password keystroke combinations. A computer system can detect and track these multiple-attempt situations, and deny access after a small number of access attempts have been made. In addition, the system can record a log of activities by anyone who makes multiple access attempts, so that the system administrator will be aware that the system is under attack.

To be more certain of improving a system's security features, the accountant should also insist that the company's internal audit department be regularly involved in the design of any new systems, so that they can spot control weaknesses that may lead to security breaches at a later date, and require improvements in these areas. The internal audit staff should also schedule regular reviews of the computer system to ascertain if any security problems have arisen as a result of ongoing software or hardware updates to the system.

Despite all of the security enhancement techniques just noted, there may still be some open security issues left that the company feels are either too insignificant or expensive to address. If so, they should be carefully documented, so that the internal audit team can continue to address them over time to see if corrective action is needed at some point in the future. Also, this document can be used by the corporate risk management group as the basis for purchasing insurance as an alternative means of covering the risk.

28-7 AUTOMATED DATA COLLECTION TOOLS

The basic accounting system calls for the services of a large number of clerks, who are responsible for entering accounts payable, billing, payroll, inventory, and cash receipts information into it. The volume of data entry generally calls for the services of most of the employees in the accounting department, not only to initially enter the data, but also to track down and correct any entry errors. Consequently, much of the accounting department budget is used for data collection activities.

Fortunately, there are some ways to avoid data entry. One of the best is through the use of bar coding. For example, employees can be issued badges that contain a bar code. They swipe the card through a computerized time clock that automatically notes their employee number (which is recorded on the bar code), plus the time when the swipe occurs. The clock then compares this to the next swipe by the same employee to determine the number of hours worked, and sends this information straight to the accounting system so that it can be used as the basis for the next paycheck issued to the employee. At no point in this process is there any need for data entry.

Bar codes can also be used to process inventory transactions. For example, a company can require its suppliers to add an identifying bar code to all shipments, so that the receiving staff can scan the bar code and have the related purchase order number appear on the computer screen. They then check off the quantity received on the computer terminal, and the receiving transaction is completed. They then create a bar code that represents the quantity received, attach this to the inventory item, and put it in an empty bin in the warehouse. They scan the quantity and bin location into a portable scanner, which transmits this information to a central computer, thereby updating the inventory database. The same process can be used to shift goods to the production area, and from workstation to work station within the production process, thereby giving the accounting staff perfect information about where all inventory items are positioned within the production process.

Bar codes can also be used for fixed asset audits. To do so, an identifying bar code is attached to each fixed asset. Periodically, a company auditor walks through the facility, scanning all bar codes into a portable scanning device. At its most sophisticated level, the scanner will compare the scanned items to a central database of fixed assets and keep the auditor informed of any remaining assets within each area of the company that have not yet been scanned.

Electronic data interchange (EDI) is another tool for collecting data. Since it has more functions than simple data collection, it is covered in a later section of this chapter. Its main contribution to data collection is that accounting transactions arriving from business partners, such as invoices from suppliers, are in a standard electronic format that can be sent directly into the accounting database without any manual intervention. This usually requires the creation of a custom interface that will reformat the incoming transaction into a format that is readable by the accounting software.

A point-of-sale (POS) system can also be used for data collection. This is an advanced form of cash register that records the precise type of sale made to a customer, and automatically sends a transaction to a central computer that records the sale as well as a reduction in the inventory balance for whatever item was just sold. A POS system may also operate in a batch mode, whereby an individual station will store transaction data until such time as a central computer polls it and downloads new information.

28-8   DATA STORAGE TOOLS

The accountant finds most of his or data stored within the accounting software package's file structure. However, there are several alternatives available for data storage that are worthy of consideration.

One data storage tool is the data warehouse. This is a central repository of information that contains not only accounting information, but also operational information that is pulled in from all parts of the company. This information is usually obtained through the use of customized interfaces that periodically access outlying databases, extract the information needed, and pull it back in for storage. By doing so, anyone in the company who has authorized access to it can plumb the database for a wide range of information. It is commonly used by managers as the source of information for executive information systems, which summarize key operational and financial information in the exact formats needed by managers to inform them of all aspects of company performance. However, the data warehouse is quite expensive and time-consuming to build, given its large number of interfaces and ongoing maintenance requirements. A less expensive form of the data warehouse can be created by adding extra accounts to the general ledger that can store non-accounting information, and then populating them with any desired data. This avoids the construction of a customized data warehouse, but still calls for interfaces into the general ledger, or else the manual entry of data from other sources. This option tends to be much less comprehensive than a full-blown data warehouse, since it is restricted by the structure of the accounting database.

Another data storage tool is provided by the company bank. Rather than receiving a packet of cleared checks along with the latest monthly bank statement, it is now possible to request this information on a compact disk. With this tool, the images of all cleared checks can be loaded into the corporate computer system and made available to anyone with access to a computer terminal. This approach also allows one to retain control over the image file in a central location, and have multiple people review the same information at the same time, while never having to worry about information that may be out of order (as is commonly the case with paper-based checks, after employees have thumbed through them a few times). Finally, the software that accompanies the compact disk allows one to search for checks using several different indexes, such as the check number, check date, and check amount. The only downside to this approach is that the bank charges a small extra fee for this service.

A document imaging system can be installed that will eliminate much of the paperwork that normally clutters the accounting department. This involves the acquisition of a document scanning, storage, and retrieval system such as the one noted in Exhibit 28-1. One typically inputs documents into the system by running them through a scanner, which creates a digitized image of each item. As the exhibit shows, it is also possible to create images from documents that are sent into the system from computers that create on-line document images, as well as from outlying sources that are accessed through a modem. Once digitized, each document record is assigned one or more index numbers that are used by the accounting staff to retrieve the image. Examples of indexes are the invoice number, purchase order number, name of the trading partner on the document, and the date when the document was created. The system will store the indexes in a separate server that contains a high-speed disk drive, so that the index file can be searched rapidly by users who are querying it. Since the scanned document records require a great deal of storage space, they are stored separately in a compact disk "jukebox," which is a device containing a large number of the high-capacity CDs. When anyone wants to access a digitized document, they request it through the index, which in turn locates the correct digital image and presents it on the computer terminal screen of the person who asked for the information. As noted in the exhibit, the image can also be sent straight to a printer to create a hard copy, or outside the company through a modem connection.

The great advantage of the document imaging system is that it eliminates the clerical tasks of manually storing and retrieving documents. This allows anyone to access any document within seconds, while also never having to worry about re-filing documents (which could have been filed in the wrong place). In addition, multiple people can review the same document at the same time, while the original image is kept secure in the CD jukebox. Some of the more advanced accounting systems will work with an imaging system for such applications as expense approvals; the image of the document is sent to an authorized approver, who can review the document, attach an approval code to it, and send it straight back to the accounts payable staff, all electronically.

Exhibit 28-1 Layout of a Document Imaging System

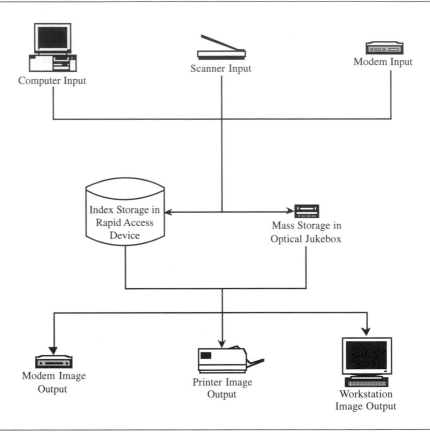

The chief problem with the document imaging system is cost. Though an inexpensive system can be cobbled together for as little as $10,000, a high-speed scanning system with large storage capacity and the best software is a six-figure investment, while large corporations can expect to spend well over $1 million. Also, there is a significant clerical cost associated with the initial scanning of large quantities of documents into the system, in order to create a base of digital images that goes back to the beginning of the current accounting year.

28-9 INTEGRATION OF ACCOUNTING SOFTWARE WITH OTHER SYSTEMS

The accounting system can be a strictly defined, stand-alone system that only encompasses billings, cash receipts, accounts payable, payroll, fixed assets, and the reporting of financial statements through the general ledger. However, such a view of the accounting system does not reveal the much greater level of effectiveness that can be wrung from the system if it is combined with other systems.

One system that greatly enhances the accounting system is material requirements planning (MRP). A more advanced version of this system that also encompasses labor and capacity planning is called manufacturing resources planning (MRP II). Both of these systems focus on the precise marshaling of the resources needed to manufacture goods in accordance with a production schedule. From the perspective of the accounting department, this means that the inventory records will be extremely accurate, since the MRP and MRP II systems require at least a 95% level of inventory accuracy in order to operate properly. Consequently, the accounting records related to inventory accuracy will be much more accurate. To be most effective, the accounting database should be linked to the inventory file of either of these systems, so that it can directly access these accurate inventory records.

Another benefit of both the MRP and MRP II systems is that they both require the use of bills of material for each product manufactured, and require a minimum accuracy level of 98%. This is of great assistance to the accounting staff, because it can use the bills to easily and accurately determine the cost of any product, as well as place accurate valuations on the work-in-process and finished goods inventories. For these reasons, the accounting staff should be given access to the bills of material, at least on a read-only basis.

The MRP II system also maintains labor routing records, which track the precise quantities and types of labor at each workstation in the production process that is required to create each product. Once again, the accounting staff can use this information to determine the cost of partially completed products within the manufacturing process. The best system is when both the bill of material and labor routing files are directly linked to the accounting system, so that the accounting programs can automatically create standard cost inventory valuations from them.

Both the MRP and MRP II systems use production schedules, which the accountant can use as a back-up system for ensuring that all invoices to customers have been generated. For example, if the shipping department fails to send shipping documentation to the accounting department, no associated invoice will be sent to the customer. However, if the accounting staff can periodically compare its invoice records to the production schedule in the MRP or MRP II systems, any product that was scheduled for completion and shipment, but that was never invoiced, will be flagged for further review.

An additional benefit of both systems is that they provide for such a detailed level of materials planning that it becomes a simple matter for the accounting staff to determine the timing of accounts payable payments that are related to the cost of goods sold. By itemizing the exact days (and even time of day) when materials are needed for the production process and generating purchase orders based on this information, the accounting staff can extrapolate payment dates from the delivery dates listed on the purchase orders, and the cost of the items listed on the purchase orders. This is a boon for the development of accurate cash forecasts. The MRP II system can be used to take this concept a step further, by also estimating the amount of direct labor needed to complete the production schedule in the future; the accounting staff can use this information to determine the cash flow associated with the direct labor portion of the payroll.

In its most advanced form, all of the preceding information can be used to create a reasonably accurate set of financial statements for a company for as far into the future as its production schedule goes. This information will be less accurate several months out, since this time frame is where the production planners are most likely to be juggling the status of customer orders. However, in the near term, where the status of the production schedule is usually locked in, a very accurate projected financial statement can be devised.

The accounting system will require significant alterations in order to work in conjunction with a just-in-time (JIT) manufacturing system. A JIT system relies upon fast equipment setups, small batch sizes (preferably of just one unit), and frequent supplier deliveries of small size to achieve the production of only those items needed right away by customers. There are several problems with this system from an accountant's perspective, which must be remedied through adjustments to the accounting system. One issue is that there are many more supplier deliveries than is normally the case, each of which involves a separate supplier invoice that must be verified before payment. Rather than hire more accounting personnel to handle this increased transaction volume, it is better to either pay each supplier once a month (which reduces the number of checks cut, but does nothing to reduce the labor of verifying deliveries) or to have the receiving staff match receipts against purchase orders through a computer terminal at the receiving dock. Suppliers are automatically paid based on the quantities received and the per-unit prices itemized in the purchase order, without any need to compare these items to a supplier invoice. A more advanced way to deal with this problem is to determine production volumes periodically, determine the amount of each component that was required to achieve that level of production, and pay the supplier based on this calculated volume; this last approach is only recommended if there is no receiving staff to review incoming deliveries, since it requires extremely accurate production and scrap reporting systems to ensure that suppliers are paid the correct amounts.

The cost allocation system will also be impacted by a JIT system, because it tends to focus on the consolidation of overhead costs into cost pools for later allocation, whereas a JIT system tends to focus costs on machine cells for allocation to the items produced within those cells. To accommodate this change, accounts should be added to the chart of accounts that can be used to accumulate costs by machine cell, while cost allocations from these accounts must be based on activity measures that are unique to each machine cell.

Under the JIT system, the direct labor staff tends to become involved in activities that are usually considered to be related to overhead, such as the maintenance, setup, and breakdown of equipment within their machine cells. Consequently, direct labor costs can be shifted to the overhead cost pools for each machine cell. This means that there is no need to track direct labor costs through the accounting system, nor the variety of labor variances that are commonly produced to track the efficiency of these employees.

A clear benefit for the accounting staff is that a JIT system is partially targeted at the reduction and eventual elimination of inventory, not only raw materials through the use of just-in-time deliveries, but also work-in-process inventory through the use of small batch sizes. The end result of this focus is that there may be so little inventory left on hand that the accounting staff no longer has to concern itself with inventory cutoff procedures, cycle counting, period-end physical counts, or inventory valuation.

Any of the three manufacturing systems just noted will have a profound impact on the way in which the accounting system operates. Rather than attempt to integrate an existing accounting system with these manufacturing systems, one can purchase some fully-integrated manufacturing systems that include accounting software. These packages have the advantage of seamless interfaces between all company functions. However, most such packages started out as manufacturing systems, with accounting functions being added at a later date, so one should expect the overall functionality and ease of use of the accounting portion of these packages to be less than what is found in the offerings of software providers who focus strictly on accounting software.

28-10 ELECTRONIC DATA INTERCHANGE

The accountant should be aware of how EDI works, as well as how it can be used to greatly improve the efficiency of the accounting department. The idea behind EDI is to create a standardized format that can be used to wrap around a typical accounting transaction, and send it electronically to one's trading partners, where they can unwrap the message, using the same transaction format. This approach results in the instantaneous transfer of information between companies, eliminates the risk of loss through the postal service, and also presents the opportunity to enter EDI transactions directly into one's accounting system with no manual keypunching.

There are over 100 standard EDI transaction formats, as designed and approved by a committee of the American National Standards Institute. The typical transaction includes three types of data: header information, detailed information, and summary information. For example, these would correspond on an invoice to the header information that contains bill-to and ship-to information, the detailed information that lists each line item being billed, and the summary information that lists the total amount billed. Once converted to the EDI format, the transaction may be electronically sent directly to a trading partner, where a computer will accept and store the information. However, because this can cause logjams if there are many transactions flowing in and out, and because the modem speeds should match at both ends of a transaction, it is more common to send one's EDI transactions to a value added network (VAN), which acts as a central repository for these transactions. Each participant is issued a mailbox, in which transactions are stored. It can then poll its mailbox periodically and extract transactions at that time. This process is shown in Exhibit 28-2, where we see that a company can send its transactions not only through a VAN, but also through direct modem linkages, in case there are very few trading partners who use EDI, or if there is a need for immediate updating of EDI transactions (as opposed to the slower polling process used with a VAN). The exhibit also shows that a trading partner may use a different VAN, so there are also linkages between VANs that transfer transactions.

A key item also noted in the exhibit is that transactions can travel from a VAN to a central transaction processor at a company location, where they are converted into the format needed by the internal accounting system, and then stored directly into that system—without any manual re-keying of the transaction. This approach also works in reverse, for the accounting system can just as easily create EDI transactions and issue them to trading partners with no manual labor requirement. This interface is of crucial importance to the accountant, for a fully configured and integrated EDI system can eliminate much of the clerical work required of a traditional accounting system, with computers now acting as translators between incoming and outgoing transactions.

Though a few of the more advanced accounting systems contain EDI linkages, most require a customized interface in order to create a seamless connection between the accounting system and EDI transactions. It may well be worth the effort to construct such an interface, but one must compare the cost of creating it to the benefit to be gained through reduced manual labor.

Exhibit 28-2   The Electronic Data Interchange Process Flow

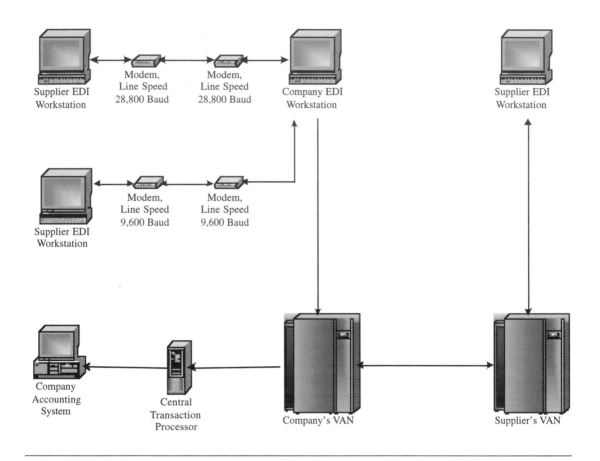

28-11 OUTSOURCING MANAGEMENT INFORMATION SYSTEMS

It is possible that the management team does not wish to deal with the management information system at all. There could be several reasons for this, such as the continuing incompetence of the managers running this function, the cost of creating and maintaining sufficiently advanced levels of technology, or the fact that management does not perceive MIS to be enough of a key strategic factor that it should concern itself with it. Whatever the reason, an alternative is to shift the function, either in part or in total, to a supplier through an outsourcing relationship.

A strong advantage that results from making this move is that a company can avoid further capital investments in expensive computer hardware and software, and might even be able to sell some of its equipment to the supplier who will be managing the function. The supplier can also field a strong team of managers who will ensure that the computer systems are properly installed and maintained. The supplier can also ensure that software upgrades are made in a timely manner, that application development is properly managed, and that the help desk is manned—possibly by supplier personnel who are already thoroughly experienced with a company's software, since they have already gained experience in maintaining these applications from working with other clients of the supplier.

Despite these advantages, there are also a number of problems with outsourcing one's management information systems. For example, the supplier of the company's packaged accounting software may not allow the company to transfer its software license over to the supplier, on the grounds that the supplier may already have such a license, and so will pay fewer maintenance fees to it when the supplier shifts company personnel over to its existing license. Another problem is that it will certainly cost more to have new applications written by the supplier's programmers than was the case when the same work was done internally, on the grounds that the supplier must add a profit percentage to all its costs. The only situation in which this may not occur is when the supplier has arranged for less-expensive offshore programming services, such as in India or Russia, which will result in lower programming fees.

Another problem is that the supplier may have a slower response time to computer system problems than was the case when this work was handled internally, on the grounds that the supplier may be handling crises at other clients at the same time, and so has too few resources to address the company's issues. This concern can be dealt with to some extent by inserting penalty clauses in the contract that are invoked when response times become slower than a minimum standard level. A reverse problem will arise with the supplier's sales personnel, who now have complete access to information about company operations, and will use this knowledge to attempt to sell yet more services to the company. Though this can be irritating, it is also a service of sorts, since the company will be presented with a series of possible solutions to problems that it has never addressed.

A final and very significant concern is the potential loss of in-house programming staff when this function is outsourced. Programmers may leave simply because they do not want to work for the supplier. They may also go to work for the supplier, and then be shifted away to other clients by the supplier. This latter case can be prevented in the short term by including a programmer retention clause in the supplier contract that specifies a minimum time period during which the existing staff will be kept working on company-specific tasks.

If any of these problems appear to be "show stoppers" that will not allow a company to proceed with outsourcing, then it may be more acceptable to divide the management information systems area into smaller pieces, and only outsource those activities that will most clearly result in the greatest benefit to the company. For example, some suppliers specialize in help desk support, while others only provide network management, others operate data centers, and still others specialize in hardware repairs. If this approach is taken and a company later decides to outsource additional functions, then it can assign the overall supplier management task to a single lead supplier, thereby reducing the amount of supplier management that it must handle by itself.

If a company elects to proceed with outsourcing, the following issues should be addressed when negotiating a contract with the supplier:

* *Change in ownership.* A company may have some difficulty in selling itself if the buyer must honor a large multi-year contract with the supplier. Accordingly, the contract should allow a new owner of the business to cancel the contract if more than a 50% change in ownership occurs.

- *Contract termination based on a change in technology.* If the supplier is engaged in servicing the company's hardware and software, the contract should allow the company to terminate the contract if it switches to some new form of technology. For example, the supplier may be greatly skilled in the maintenance of non-networked personal computers, but have no idea how to maintain "dumb" terminals attached to a central computer that may replace the personal computers.

- *Definition of ongoing maintenance.* The supplier will want to reduce the definition of maintenance activities to the absolute minimum, so that all remaining activities can be classified as new application development work (which commands an add-on price). To avoid this, the contract should include a detailed list of maintenance activities.

- *Disaster recovery planning.* A company's computer systems can be destroyed by an act of nature, such as a flood or earthquake, no matter who is operating them. To mitigate this problem, the contract should require the supplier to maintain a disaster recovery plan that calls for off-site backup data storage, maximum amounts of downtime, and periodic testing of conversion to a backup location.

- *Guaranteed system availability.* The supplier must have an incentive to keep the system fully operational during the company's business hours, rather than taking it down for maintenance during the peak period of activity. This can be accomplished by including in the contract a "carrot and stick" approach of charging penalties if downtime during business hours exceeds a certain percentage, while also providing for bonus payments if downtime is reduced to some negligible amount.

- *Ownership and marketing of custom applications.* If the company pays the supplier to produce new software applications, the contract should state who owns the rights to the software, in the event that it can be sold to other organizations. If there is joint ownership, then the contract should also note how the applications are to be jointly marketed, and how any resulting profits will be divided between the parties.

- *Severance payments to transferred employees.* If the company switches its management information personnel over to the supplier as part of an outsourcing arrangement, it may care enough about its former employees to require the supplier to issue severance pay to them in the event of their being laid off. If this clause is used, the supplier will insist on a maximum date within which it can occur, so that it is not held liable for severance payments for many years into the future.

- *Transfer of employees.* When employees are shifted to a supplier, the company should ensure that key former employees continue to work on the company's systems for some period of time, rather than being shifted to other clients by the supplier. The contract can provide for a maximum time period during which transfers are not allowed, or the concurrence of the company for transfers within that maximum time period.

Once the contract has been negotiated, the company needs to transfer its management information systems to the supplier. The first step in this process is to appoint a transition coordinator, who in turn will likely require a full-time staff to assist him in managing the process. This team must work with the supplier to coordinate the following activities:

- *Complete a confidentiality agreement.* The contract between the two parties might still fall apart at any time, resulting in a former supplier knowing a great deal about company operations, so the first step is to sign a mutual confidentiality agreement that will restrict the spread of knowledge about either company.

- *Obtain third-party consents.* There is no point in shifting a company's software licenses to a supplier if the software developer from whom it was purchased will not agree to the transfer. Since the supplier may have considerably more experience with this issue, the supplier can contact the developer on the company's behalf for this discussion.

- *Accumulate an employee skills database.* The supplier will need to know how many of its personnel to assign to the company for ongoing activities. To assist in this effort, it will need a list of the skills of all company employees who will either be shifted to it as part of the outsourcing agreement, or who will still be on hand to assist it, but will continue to work for the company. This list should itemize the formal education, continuing professional education, experience level, and current job responsibilities for every person working in the department.

- *Transfer operational documents to supplier.* The company will presumably have built up a lengthy list of procedures, help files, disaster recovery plans, and so on that the supplier will need to run the department. Before handing them over, be sure to make copies of all documents; this step gives a company the option of canceling the outsourcing agreement at any time, since it will still have all the operational information needed to run the department.

- *Train the supplier's personnel.* Though the intention in an outsourcing agreement is usually to hand over one's staff to the supplier, there will still be some supplier personnel who will be brought in to assist in operating the department. These people will require extensive training to ensure that they know about all facets of the department. To ensure that their training is sufficiently in-depth, it is useful to pay bonuses to some of the most senior departmental personnel at the end of the training, which gives them an incentive to stay with the company long enough to transfer their knowledge to someone else.

- *Transfer hardware and software to supplier.* If the supplier is going to take the company's systems off-site to its own data center, then there will be a formal transfer of equipment and software to the outside location. If downtime is a concern, then this must be a closely coordinated event, with plenty of detailed disaster recovery planning.

- *Transfer database to supplier.* As was the case for operational documents, the company should make copies of its electronic files prior to sending them to the supplier. Though these files will rapidly become outdated as new information is added to the files that are now under the supplier's control, the company will still have an option to restart its operations internally with these old files, in case there is a falling out with the supplier.

- *Transfer staff to supplier.* The most touchy step in the transfer process is shifting company personnel over to the supplier. This should be handled through a formal meeting with all staff, with representatives from both the company and supplier on hand. Employment and benefits forms should be prepared in advanced for each employee by the supplier, and the meeting should take as long as employees have questions about the transfer that need to be answered. Since there is always a chance of employees leaving as a result of being shifted to a new company, it is advisable to consider the compensation arrangement for the most crucial employees, and improvement in their pay or benefit levels as part of the transfer, in order to reduce their likelihood of departing.

Once the transfer process is completed, the transition coordinator should be retained, though his or her job will change to that of monitoring the supplier's performance and representing the company, and requesting system changes. Part of this person's task should include regularly scheduled meetings with the supplier, during which the performance measurements of the supplier are reviewed, and improvements to them are discussed. Further, the coordinator should be responsible for handing out bonuses or penalty charges to the supplier as a result of its performance measures. The coordinator should also keep a log of all changes to computer systems that are requested by company employees, and schedule their implementation in concert with the supplier. This person should authorize any changes that will result in additional fees by the supplier.

The in-house coordinator should make the greatest possible use of measurement systems to ensure that the supplier is matching or exceeding performance levels that were set in the outsourcing contract. The difficulty is that the supplier has control over much of the measurement process, especially if it is operating a company's computer systems from its own off-site data center. Nonetheless, one can have the company's internal auditors conduct spot checks of the measurement systems created by the supplier.

The types of measurements used should cover each key aspect of those management information systems that have been shifted to a supplier. For example, it is a simple matter to determine from published information when a software supplier has issued its latest software release, and then add up the days until the supplier updates the software with this upgrade. Another measurement is the average response time for first-time callers to the help desk, or the number of calls required to resolve a problem. Another measure is the average screen response time for those computer functions that are defined as mission-critical, or the amount of system downtime during regular business hours for these same functions. Downtime can also be measured across all functions (as opposed to just the mission-critical ones), especially during working hours, and can be measured in terms of percentage, duration, or number of instances of downtime.

Programming services can also be measured. One possibility is the cost per line of software code generated, though this can result in large quantities of inefficient code. Better measures relate to the supplier's ability to complete contracted programming work within specified deadlines, or to meet intervening milestones (as measured by tracking the number of days of cumulative variance from milestones).

The outsourcing of all or part of a company's management information systems is becoming increasingly common, and the preceding discussion should provide valuable guidelines for making the outsourcing decision and managing the supplier's activities. However, this can be a very expensive proposition that will affect a company's cash flow for many years to come (since a large number of outsourcing deals extend for up to a decade); thus, the entire management team should be consulted before making the outsourcing decision, while the services of a lawyer experienced in handling outsourcing contracts should be retained to assist with the initial contract negotiations with the supplier.

28-12 SUMMARY

This chapter has given the reader an overview of those key aspects of management information systems that the accountant is likely to encounter. Though the quantity of information presented here will give one a reasonable framework within which to plan for the selection, installation, and ongoing use of management information systems, this is a highly complex area that requires the services of a dedicated professional to ensure that it operates properly. Consequently, the accountant is well advised to either call upon the services of the in-house computer services staff or to hire experienced consultants to assist in making key decisions in this area.

CHAPTER 29

Records Management

29-1 INTRODUCTION

The accountant is put in charge of records management in most companies, except those organizations that are so large that this function can be shifted to a full-time staff. The accountant must keep several counter-balancing goals in mind when setting up a records management system. One issue is to minimize the cost of record keeping; however, this goal will conflict with the opposing goals of having ready access to necessary information, as well as of retaining documents for periods much longer than is economically the most efficient. Consequently, this is an area that should be governed by a strict set of policies and procedures that are carefully designed to balance the conflicting goals of the function. The accountant's optimum solution then becomes following those policies and procedures in the most effective and efficient manner possible.

In this chapter, we will itemize the various costs that are incurred by a record keeping system, so that the significant costs associated with this function are clearly understood. We will then proceed to a discussion of the policies and procedures that are necessary for record keeping, and finish with a short discussion of computerized records management systems.

29-2 RECORD KEEPING COSTS

The costs associated with record keeping are much higher than most people realize. Not only are there the clearly quantifiable costs of storage, but also the subjective ones related to lawsuits that are lost for lack of proper record keeping, as well as any forensic accounting needed to reconstruct lost information. Particularly in the case of lost lawsuits, the potential cost of record keeping can be startlingly high. Consequently, a clear understanding of these costs is necessary in order to point out the need for top-notch records management systems, as are described in the following sections.

The following bullet points note the most common quantifiable costs of record storage, as well as how they should be calculated:

- *Space rental.* Any space taken up by filing cabinets or boxes represents either a direct lease cost or else an opportunity cost for space that could more profitably be put to use for other activities. This is a particularly high cost if records are kept on site, as opposed to a lower-cost warehousing facility. To determine this cost, summarize not only the space directly taken up by stored records, but also the width of all walkways around them that cannot otherwise be used due to the potential for reduced access to the records. If the facility is entirely company-owned and there is no clear-cut way to sell off the storage space, then the cost of storage can be calculated by determining the costs that would not be incurred if other facilities could be consolidated into the storage space.

- *Storage equipment.* Storage equipment may be as minimal as cardboard boxes, or extend to the use of fireproof safes, storage cabinets, or forklifts. The expense associated with these investments should be added to the overall cost of storage. Be sure to tie the depreciation rate on capital items to their actual usage period (subject to standard depreciation period restrictions).

- *Fire suppression systems.* The local fire warden may require special fire suppression systems for storage areas, which may extend to the use of expensive sprinkler or halon systems. The cost of these items should also include the periodic cost of system inspections, testing, and maintenance.

- *Transportation.* If files are stored in other facilities, it will be necessary to move them back to the company's premises whenever needed. This cost of transport should be easy to calculate if movement is done by a third party, since there will be a billing for each move. If the transport function is kept within the company, then some portion of the moving staff's wages should be charged to this activity.

- *Insurance.* A modest amount of insurance is required to protect a company from loss of its records. However, there may be additional insurance required that protects the company from the increased fire hazard represented by stored records.

- *Clerical costs.* There is a significant cost associated with the personnel who are engaged in filing documents, retrieving them, shifting them to off-site locations, and bringing them back from time to time. If there is a great deal of "churn" in the amount of paperwork that is moved in and out of storage, this can be the largest cost associated with record storage.

- *Computer systems.* Those companies that have shifted over to electronic storage must account for the capital cost of computer acquisitions, as well as ongoing equipment replacement and maintenance costs. This cost should include an apportionment of the time required by the computer services staff to maintain the system.

By summarizing all of the preceding costs, many accountants will find that the cost of record management is very high. Consequently, there is a positive cost-benefit associated with the formalized record keeping systems noted in the following sections, so that the cost of this activity is minimized.

29-3 RECORD KEEPING POLICIES AND PROCEDURES

There are an enormous number of document types that flow through a corporation every year, many of which will be reviewed repeatedly for a number of years thereafter. Without a proper record keeping system, a company will incur substantially higher costs in the areas noted in the preceding section. The best way to ensure that these costs are minimized is to set up and follow a system of policies and procedures. The following policies should serve as the groundwork for a complete set of related procedures:

- *Document retention policy.* All too often, there is no criterion for how long a record is to be retained, and so documents will tend to pile up in a disorderly manner. To avoid this trouble, there should be a policy that carefully itemizes the number of years that each type of document will be stored before it is destroyed. The number of years for which various types of documents must be retained will, to some extent, be determined by local or federal government regulations. For a detailed listing of recommended storage intervals for documents, one can consult the "Guide to Record Retention Requirements," which is published by the U.S. Government Printing Office. If there is some expectation or history of lawsuits in certain areas of company operations, it may also be necessary to retain selected documents to serve as a possible future legal defense, in which case the statue of limitations will serve as the proper guideline for the date of document destruction. Accordingly, the legal staff should be consulted when this schedule is constructed. If there are contractual agreements with other entities that might result in audits of company records, then the retention period for any related documents should be tied to the termination dates of the contracts; for example, a cost-plus government construction job may require a company to retain all job costing records for a period of three years after the completion date of the contract. The records most likely to fall into this category are those related to billings, fixed assets, inventory, and manufacturing costs. There will also be a number of documents that should be kept for as long as the company is in existence. These documents include blueprints, formulas, copyrights, patents, trademarks, leases, the certificate of incorporation, bylaws and constitution, and the Board minute book. If there are other documents for which there are no governmental or legal reasons for retention, then the basis for determining a retention period should be the time period after which there is no reasonable expectation that they will be used. An example of a policy that incorporates these guidelines is shown in Exhibit 29-1. The time periods noted in the table are examples only, and should not be used for an actual document retention policy without first being reviewed by legal counsel. Any ongoing changes to this table should be authorized by legal counsel as well as the chief accounting position in the company.

- *Storage area policy.* Most records storage areas are located in spare rooms for which no other use can currently be found. No consideration is given to the safety or future condition of the records that will result from such storage. To avoid this problem, there should be a policy that specifies the condition of the designated storage area. This should include criteria for fireproofing, flood proofing, allowable minimum and maximum temperatures and humidity levels, and records fumigation.

Exhibit 29-1 Document Retention Table

Type of Record	Retention Period (years)
Advertising, original artwork	10
Advertising, research reports	2
Advertising, tear sheets and proofs	Permanent
Articles of incorporation	Permanent
Audit report, external	Permanent
Audit report, internal	10
Audit workpapers, internal	4
Bank reconciliation	6
Bank statement	6
Bond, fidelity	10
Budget	5
Check, dividend (canceled)	6
Check, payable (canceled)	6
Check, payroll (canceled)	3
Collection notes	While customer is active
Contract document	5 years after termination
Copyright application	Permanent
Cost estimates	5
Credit application, customer	While customer is active
Customs paperwork	5
Debit/credit memo	5
Deposit slip	6
Expense reports	5
Financial statements	Permanent
Forecasts	5
Franchise record	5 years after termination
Guarantees	5
Insurance claim, other than employee	3 years after completion
Insurance claim, workers' compensation	3 years after completion
Inventory, cost record	3
Inventory, count sheet	3
Invoice, company	5
Invoice, supplier	5
Journal entry	10
Lease document	5 years after termination
Ledger, general	Permanent
Ledger, subsidiary	Permanent
License, business	10

(continued)

Exhibit 29-1   Document Retention Table *(cont'd.)*

Type of Record	Retention Period (years)
Litigation record	5 years after termination
Minute book	Permanent
Mortgage	5 years after termination
Note payable	5 years after termination
Note receivable	5 years after termination
Overhead allocation calculations	5
Patent application	Permanent
Plan, annual	5
Plan, long-range	5
Proxy	6
Purchase order	5
Receiving record	5
Report, to shareholders	Permanent
Royalty record	10
Security registration	Review after 5 years
Shareholder list	6
Trademark application	Permanent

Reprinted with permission: Willson et al., *Controllership,* John Wiley & Sons, 1999, p. 1309.

- *Responsibility for record keeping policy.* The preceding policies involve tasks that will cut across the responsibilities of virtually all major company departments, which makes them very difficult policies to administer. Accordingly, a policy should be created that concentrates responsibility for these policies, as well as all attendant procedures, in a specific job position. The policy should describe the position's responsibilities in general terms, as well as its reporting relationship.

With these three policies in place, we now know which documents to retain, how long to do so, where to store them, and who will manage the process. However, this still leaves a number of unanswered questions at a more detailed level, such as how documents are to be identified, indexed, retrieved, and destroyed. The following procedures should be created so that guidelines will be available for these tasks:

- *Box indexing procedure.* A procedure is needed that will use a standard indexing system to identify each box of records. One possibility is to start an index number with the year to which the records pertain, and then add a sequential number that identifies the specific box for that year. For example, the thirteenth box of records for the year 2001 would be "2001-13." An indexing file could then be compiled that itemizes each document stored within each of these box numbers. However, a problem with this method is that when the time arrives to destroy records, the entire box may be destroyed, even though some of the records within the box may be scheduled for earlier or later destruction. One way around this problem is to separate documents that are to be kept in a permanent file, and store them elsewhere (given their nature, these documents should be stored in the highest security environment, and so deserve special handling in any case). Another possibility is to use the same indexing system just noted, but to use the year of document *destruction* as part of the index, rather than the year of document *creation*. This makes it much less likely that documents will be destroyed at the wrong time.

- *Box identification procedure.* In those instances where documents are kept in storage boxes, there should be a procedure that establishes a standardized type of identification, as well as common storage of similarly identified boxes. For example, the procedure should clarify the exact spot on the box where an identifying index number will be recorded, which should be the end of the box that will be readily apparent to the casual observer if the boxes are palletized, with only one side showing. Otherwise, labels attached to other sides of a box will not be visible, requiring the dismantlement of an entire pallet to ascertain the index number of each box. Another procedural issue is how the index number is to be marked on the box. If a label is used, it may fall off over time. A better approach is to mark the box with indelible ink, even if this means that the box will not be usable for some other purpose at a later date.

- *Confidential document storage procedure.* When most records are filed away for storage, they are kept in open areas that are readily accessible to many employees. However, if the records are of a sensitive nature, such as payroll or legal documents, then a procedure is needed that will segregate these records at once and ensure that they are stored in the most secure location. The procedure should specify, in detail, the documents or document categories that are to be handled in this manner. If there are many documents from a specific area, such as human resources, that will fall into the confidential category, then it may be easier for the procedure to state that all documents from this area will be confidential, unless specifically stated otherwise. The procedure should also note the minimum levels of security and document handling that will be required, as well as who is responsible for their safety. For example, the procedure may require off-site storage in containers that are protected against fire damage up to a specific temperature and for a specified time period, with access requiring the approval of people in stated company positions.

- *Document destruction procedure.* The destruction of documents requires special controls, for a company may have to defend this practice in court if there is an appearance of unscheduled destruction of documents whose use in court might otherwise be damaging to the company. Consequently, a procedure should require the use of a document destruction certificate, which specifies which documents are to be destroyed, a cross-reference to the company policy that itemizes the duration of document retention prior to destruction, approval signatures, and the signature of at least one person who witnesses the actual document destruction.

- *Document retrieval procedure.* If the corporate staff is allowed full access to all on-site records, it is very likely that the quality of record keeping will decline in short order, for only a trained clerk who is responsible for the records will have any reason to preserve order as documents are pulled and returned, and boxes are shifted about. Consequently, a procedure should specify how documents are to be requested from an authorized clerical staff, which will in turn retrieve the requested records, log them out, and turn them over to requesting employees. This procedure should include the use of a request form, a logout form, and a report that itemizes all withdrawn documents.

- *Document transfer-to-storage procedure.* Documents tend to be sent to long-term record storage by dumping them into storage boxes at the end of the fiscal year and carting them off. This makes it more likely that different types of documents with different storage requirements will be lumped together, which leads to the risk of their being destroyed after incorrect time periods. To avoid this problem, a procedure should identify how current documents should be segregated and reviewed before they are to be sent to long-term storage. This should include a formal sign-off on the contents of each shipping carton.

- *Storage area layout procedure.* The storage area should not become a large pile of disorganized boxes. Instead, a procedure should be created that outlines how different types of records are to be stored within the area. This may include separate storage for permanent files and confidential documents, separate storage by the year of document creation, the most recently filed documents in the most accessible area, or some other variations. The procedure may also make some provision for the labeling scheme to be used to identify aisles and bins in a logical manner.

The creation of the policies and procedures outlined in this section should be partially based on a cost-benefit analysis. This analysis should compare the expected risk that documents will be needed at some future date to the cost of retaining them. The result of this review may well be a reduction in the storage requirements or locations for some types of records, so that only the most critical documents are retained for long periods in the safest and most secure environment. This cost-benefit review should be conducted periodically, and especially as the nature of the business changes, to see if the perceived risk level for document retention has changed, and with it the need for changes in records management policies and procedures.

29-4 REQUIRED TAX RECORDS

Because of the propensity of various government entities to hand out penalties and interest charges when tax filings are incorrect or late, it behooves the accountant to maintain an especially high level of control over all tax records. Of particular importance is a calendar that itemizes all of the dates when tax forms are due for filing, when payments must be made, and when tax auditors are scheduled to arrive. An example of a tax calendar is shown in Exhibit 29-2.

A more advanced format for the tax calendar is to store it in a central database, so that the information contained within it can be readily updated and reviewed by all users who are involved with tax information. With such a system, it may also be possible to have the computer automatically issue e-mails to targeted employees, warning them of upcoming due dates.

Record keeping must also be maintained in great detail for all taxes for which a company must file a return. Failure to do so on the dates required can result in significant penalties and interest charges. In a few cases, a missing tax form can even lead to the suspension of a company's legal right to do business. Consequently, a tax summary table, such as the one shown in Exhibit 29-3, should be constructed. This table should include

Exhibit 29-2 Tax Calendar

Federal (consolidated)	Jan	Feb	Mar	Apr	May	Jun	Jul	Aug	Sep	Oct	Nov	Dec
Estimated payments for calendar year 2002				15		15			15			15
Tax return for year end 2002			15*			15*			15 (Final)			
Mail tax packages to subsidiaries and divisions for year end 2002	15											
Preliminary analysis of liability account for financial statements	31											
Discuss retirement, 5500 etc. package to be completed		28										
Final analysis of liability account for year end 2002										X		
Form 599-1099**		28										
Federal use tax—highway vehicles***							31					
Federal use tax—commercial aircraft***							31					
Federal excise quarterly return	31			30			31			31		
Federal excise monthly prepayment (2nd)	31	28	31	30	31	30	31	31	30	31	30	31
Federal excise monthly prepayment (1st)	15	15	15	15	15	15	15	15	15	15	15	15

Reprinted with permission: Willson et al., *Controllership*, John Wiley & Sons, 1999, p. 1309.

* May extend—not extension of time to pay total tax liability, only extension of time to file final return.

** Tax organization will file federal, New York, Massachusetts, Washington, D.C., and North Dakota.

*** Whenever applicable during tax year.

Exhibit 29-3   Tax Summary Table

Required Information	Colorado Personal Property Tax
Locations for which reporting required	Facilities in Centennial, Englewood, and Lone Tree
Tax form addressee	Douglas County Tax Assessor's Office, Colorado
Form name/number	Personal Property Declaration Form (92A)
Form due date	2/28/xx
Data sources for form completion	Fixed asset and asset addition/disposal records
General ledger source account	xx-1400 through xx-1650
Storage index location	Tax permanent file #12

summary-level information about each type of tax form that a company must complete, including the company locations for which reporting is required, the type of form needed, filing due dates, data sources, and related file storage locations. It may also be useful to note the size of potential tax penalties if a form is not filed in a timely manner, so that the tax preparation staff can categorize tax form preparations based on which ones could cost the company the most money. As a result, when the tax calendar shown in Exhibit 29-2 reveals that a form must be filed in the near future, someone on the tax staff can access the tax summary table for the specified tax, and have ready access to all of the key information needed to prepare the form.

The summary-level information associated with tax forms is by no means stable, so a company should assign someone the task of periodically updating these forms with the most recent information. If there is no staff time available for this, the tasks can also be outsourced to a competent tax review organization, which will send form updates to the company as tax-related changes arise.

Record keeping also extends to the working papers created during the process of completing tax forms. Since these documents may be called upon if taxing authorities question a company's submitted tax forms, there should be a system for organizing these workpapers. At a minimum, each set of working papers should include a copy of the completed tax form, as well as reference notes on the copy that refer back to those portions of the working papers that were used to compile the tax form. If tax research was conducted as part of the tax form preparation, then a copy of the research notes, containing lists of all referenced authorities, should be included in the working papers. If there is any related correspondence with taxing authorities, these letters should also be included in the file. The complete set of documentation should also be numbered sequentially and indexed, so that it will be obvious if any of the pages are subsequently removed from the file. Once each file of working papers is complete, it should be referenced in a master taxation index and stored in a secure location. Since there is some chance of paying additional taxes if a company's tax position is challenged and it cannot produce the underlying working papers to defend itself, the level of storage security provided must be of the highest order.

A final record keeping issue related to taxes is the proper structure of the chart of accounts (COA). If the COA is not properly designed to accumulate information that will feed into specific line items in various tax forms, the taxation staff must spend an inordinate amount of time in separately compiling the required information. Such information may be incorrect, since it is manually compiled, and is likely to contain errors. It is also difficult to re-compile if lost, which makes record keeping for it a particularly difficult task. A better alternative is to construct the COA with the advice of the tax staff, so that it can be properly structured to assist in accumulating tax-related information.

29-5 COMPUTER-BASED RECORD KEEPING

One can avoid most manual record keeping problems by digitizing the images of paper-based documents into computer storage. In brief, the system required to do this is a compact disk "jukebox" that has a very high storage capacity (necessary for the thousands or millions of document images that it will store), a high-speed scanner for digitizing images into the jukebox, and a separate computer server with high-speed magnetic disk access, on which an index to all of the documents is stored. A commercial software package is also needed for managing the storage and accessing of these records. Once this system is in place, users can access records from anywhere in the company that has a network connection to the document management system.

This system has the unique advantages of allowing for nearly instantaneous access to digitized documents, the complete absence of lost documents (since they are never moved from their storage locations on the CD jukebox), and access by multiple personnel to the same image at the same time. However, these advantages come at a high price. Specifically, a single digitized image will require at least 100,000 bytes of storage space, and may exceed one million, depending upon the denseness of the image. When multiplied by thousands of documents, this will require a very large amount of expensive storage capacity. Also, if there are many potential users, computer access must be arranged for all of them, while an expensive site license must be purchased that will encompass all potential users. Furthermore, it will be necessary to pay clerical help to input all new paper documents into the system on an ongoing basis. Thus, the clear advantages of this system must be offset against a potentially high cost.

It is also possible that it will never be cost-effective to store some types of documents in the document management system. For example, some documents may be so old or so rarely used that even the modest cost of scanning them into the system will not be justified. Also, some documents, such as title to any sort of property, must be maintained in its paper form for legal purposes. For these reasons, even a highly digitized corporation will still find that there are a small number of documents for which it must maintain an adequate manual record keeping system.

Another way to implement computer-based record keeping is to not print out documents at all, but rather to maintain as many of them as possible within a company's computerized accounting systems. If anyone needs to locate a record, it can be done more easily through the computer system than through a manual records management system. However, there are a few issues that may make this a less-than-effective solution. One is that many computer systems will automatically delete all records that are more than a preset number of years old. Though it is possible to override this limitation, the result may be either a massive increase in the amount of required storage capacity, or else a slowing down of the computer access speed, because the accounting database must search through a very large set of documents. Another issue is that many corporate documents may fall outside of the accounting system; for example, the purchasing department creates purchase orders, the receiving staff piles up receiver documents, and the shipping staff writes bills of lading. To ensure that these documents are also included in the on-line database, the accounting computer system should be expanded to become an enterprise resources planning (ERP) system, which encompasses virtually all company operations, as well as the paperwork that they generate. However, this is a very expensive proposition.

Another issue involving computer-based record keeping is how to store records that arrive electronically through electronic data interchange transactions. These are typically retrieved from a third-party electronic mailbox and transferred directly into the corporate accounting system, without any printout of the arriving transactions ever occurring. In most cases a company will simply store the electronic transaction in the computer system and print it out only when needed. Another alternative is to rely upon the sender of the transaction to also keep a copy of the transaction. It may even be possible to ask the third party that administers the electronic mailbox to keep an electronic copy of every transaction, which could be arranged for an additional fee. However, relying upon another party to store one's records is not normally a good option, since a company has minimal control over the storage process. The best alternative by far is to maintain a multi-layered off-site data backup facility, so that the risk of losing electronic data interchange transactions is kept to a minimum.

29-6 SUMMARY

Records management is a task that is frequently assigned to the accounting staff. To accomplish this task, the accounting staff must work with legal counsel to determine the best records retention policy that offsets the cost of record storage against the risk that documents will be needed at some point in the future. The resulting policy can then be used to set up procedures for a records management system. In its most technologically advanced form, this system can be replaced by an electronic storage system that features rapid document access and minimal physical storage costs, though at the price of an expensive computerized document management system.

Part Six

FINANCIAL MANAGEMENT

CHAPTER 30

Customer Credit

30-1 INTRODUCTION

A company may have many customers—perhaps thousands of them. It must decide, for each one, how much credit it will extend, the time period before which each payment is due, and the size and nature of any discounts given. This can be a monumental task, and must be done properly, or else the organization may suffer from bad debts so large that its cash reserves are drained. Alternatively, an excessively restrictive credit policy can result in lost sales that interfere with corporate growth. Given the critical nature of customer credit, we will review in this chapter the types of credit and credit terms most commonly used, how to conduct a credit evaluation of a customer, and how to collect overdue funds. We will see that a proper credit policy, when combined with credit extension and collection systems, can add to a company's profitability.

30-2 TYPES OF CREDIT

There are a wide array of credit types that can be extended to a customer, though merchandise credit and letters of credit tend to be used in all but a few situations. Accordingly, we will concentrate on these two categories of credit.

     Merchandise credit is used when products are sold to a customer against a promise by the customer of future payment, in accordance with a predetermined set of payment terms. Though merchandise credit can be extended on an order-by-order basis, it is more common to set up a customer with a pre-determined maximum amount of credit, beyond which shipments will not be made until the existing amount of unpaid invoices has been reduced. The decision to grant merchandise credit to a customer is usually made by the credit department, which is part of the treasurer's staff. In a smaller company, this chore will fall within the purview of the accounting department. The techniques used to derive the amount of credit are described in the "Credit Examination" section of this chapter.

If merchandise credit is not available, or if there is difficulty in collecting on such credit, a company can work with its customer to create a promissory note, under which the customer agrees to pay the company a fixed amount, at a fixed or variable interest rate, and in accordance with a fixed schedule of payments. Promissory notes can usually be sold to a third party, and so are a reasonably liquid form of repayment. However, it can take a great deal of time to negotiate one.

A simpler variation on the promissory note is to factor one's accounts receivable through a third party, which generates immediate cash at the price of a transaction fee. It is also common for the factoring organization to have recourse against the company if it cannot collect on an account receivable, so the risk of bad debt loss is still with the company. Though this is an expensive form of credit, it can dramatically accelerate a company's cash flow.

The letter of credit (LOC) is used almost entirely for international sales, since it gives the seller assurance that a shipment to another country will be paid for in full, without any credit problems arising. It is a major tool for the ongoing development of international trade, and so its terms are well-protected by many court cases that consistently rule in its favor.

The LOC is a document under which an entity can draw upon the credit of the bank that has issued the LOC for a specific amount, subject to a set of detailed performance conditions noted in the LOC. For example, Alpha Company wishes to purchase goods from Beta Company, which is located in a different country. Beta insists that the transaction be handled through an LOC. To do so, Alpha goes to its local bank and requests an LOC. The bank shifts money from Alpha's bank account into an escrow account, where it will be held until drawn down by Beta. Alpha's bank then sends the LOC document to its correspondent bank in Beta's country. When Beta has shipped the goods itemized on the LOC to Alpha, it takes its proof of delivery to the correspondent bank. Alpha's bank then sends the money to its correspondent bank, which pays Beta. In essence, this is an elaborate form of cash payment at the time of shipment, and can be construed as cash in advance, since many banks would require Alpha Company to hand over the full amount of cash listed on the LOC prior to their sending the documentation to the correspondent bank. Given the high level of probability that cash will be paid if the terms of the LOC are met, the LOC is sometimes used domestically.

An LOC is called "irrevocable" if the bank issuing it cannot cancel it until its stated expiration date. If the LOC is called "confirmed," then both the originating and correspondent banks have guaranteed its payment. These are standard features.

A modification on most types of credit is to have the parent company of a customer or an individual within it guarantee payment of any credit issued. By doing so, the company has two sources from which it can demand repayment. Customers will not normally agree to this provision, but can be forced to do so if their credit options are limited or if the company is the sole source of a particular service or product.

Another credit option is to sell on consignment, so that the goods sent to a customer are still the legal property of the company, and therefore can be taken back if the customer does not pay for them subsequent to their sale. However, the usual terms of such an agreement are that the company cannot expect payment until the point of sale by the customer, which may mean that it is funding a large amount of finished goods inventory for a long period of time.

The type of credit granted will be highly dependent upon the type of credit strategy adopted by a company. If its goal is to keep bad debt losses to an absolute minimum, then it will keep credit levels low, or only accept cash payments. However, if company managers want to greatly increase the rate of corporate growth, one approach is to offer credit to many more customers, and in larger quantities. By doing so, it can steal business away from competitors who have more restrictive credit policies, though at the cost of a higher level of bad debt. It may also want to loosen credit terms if it wishes to clear out an excessive amount of on-hand inventory, or to shut down a product line entirely. If the gross margin on a product sale is very high, then the associated credit terms can be loosened considerably, since the company stands to lose very little of its costs if the customer reneges on its payment. Whatever the mix of selling terms may be, the most appropriate level of credit granted to customers is the point at which increased margins from the sale of merchandise on relaxed credit terms is exactly offset by the increased cost of delayed payments and bad debts.

30-3 SELLING TERMS

There are a number of selling terms that can be used, as well as formats in which they are presented. The key factors in a set of selling terms are the time to maturity and the cash discount. The time to maturity is the number of days from the date of the invoice to the day when payment is required. For example, if the invoice date is March 1 and the terms are "net 30," then it is due for payment on March 30. The cash discount is the percentage that a customer can deduct from a payment if it pays before a pre-set date, which is useful for accelerating cash flows. The cash discount is not normally of much use for collections from customers with a history of payment delinquency, since they may not have enough cash on hand to take advantage of the discounts. An example of a cash discount is "2%/10," which means that the customer can take a 2% discount if it pays within 10 days of the invoice date. When the time to maturity and cash discount terms are combined from the previous examples, they would appear on an invoice as "2%/10 Net 30" or "2/10 N 30."

Some customers will take a cash discount even when they are not paying early (and may pay quite late). If so, the customer has abrogated the payment terms, so it is reasonable to charge back the customer for the amount of the discount taken. At a minimum, the general ledger should be arranged so that all discounts taken are stored in a separate account, with a notation regarding the name of the customer and whether or not it was incorrectly taken. By collecting this information, the accountant can inform the purchasing staff of problem customers, which they can use to increase prices to a point that will compensate for the improper discounts.

A much less common form of selling term is to specify the number of days after month-end when the payment is due. For example, the terms could be "10 EOM" or "Net 10 PROX," which means that the payment is due 10 days after the end of the month (hence the "EOM," for "end of month"). The PROX is an abbreviation for proximo, which is an old commercial term that refers to the next month. This selling term was more commonly used when computer systems were not available, since collection employees would not have to keep track of a wide range of invoice due dates, but instead knew that all invoices were due on the same day of each month, and could conduct collection activities in accordance with that information. This selling term assumes that some customers will be required to pay a little late, and others a little early, so that the average receivable period should be the same as under any other selling terms methodology; however, slow-paying customers who are invoiced near the end of the month will still pay late, which results in a net days' receivable figure that is somewhat longer under this system.

Seasonal dating can also be included in the selling terms. This is used when a company wants to sell goods that are out-of-season, both in order to clear out its warehouse and also to record some revenue during the slow part of the selling season. To do so, it guarantees its customers that they will not have to pay invoices until a specific date has been reached (usually well into the main part of the selling season), no matter when they took delivery. An example of such terms is "5 days, April 1ˢᵗ," or "5 April 1," which means that the invoice is due five days after April 1ˢᵗ.

There may also be a trade discount listed on an invoice, which is a discount given in exchange for either an especially large-volume order, or because the customer has agreed to purchase goods outside of the normal selling season. This discount is typically listed separately from the time to maturity and cash discount percentage.

An invoice may also state that an interest rate will be charged for payments that exceed a certain late date. Any notation regarding interest rates is typically added as a footnote to the bottom of the invoice. The upper range of this interest rate is bounded by each state's interest rate cap laws. Commonly, the interest rate will begin to apply after a grace period of at least 10 days has passed after the maturity date of the invoice. The interest rate is calculated automatically by the accounting software, and will generate invoices containing the interest rate at the end of each month. The accountant should be prepared to write off the majority of these interest rate charges, since most customers will refuse to pay them. Nonetheless, it can be an effective tool for reminding customers to pay on time.

In situations where customers have a poor credit history, or if the company has an immediate need for cash, its terms will be cash on delivery (COD). Under this arrangement, the company retains title to the shipped goods until payment is made by the customer to the delivery company at the point of shipment delivery. However, this form of selling terms is expensive, since the delivery company charges a fee for collecting the funds, while the company is also liable for the freight on any returned goods if the customer decides not to pay.

The COD concept can be accelerated even more to include either cash in advance for an entire order, or progress payments that are doled out by the customer as its order reaches various milestones of completion at the company. These terms are typically used when the product being ordered is a custom one that the company cannot otherwise sell if the customer cancels its order, or if the completion date is so far in the future that the company needs cash in advance in order to have sufficient working capital to complete the order.

30-4 CREDIT EXAMINATION

It can be quite difficult to determine an appropriate credit level for a customer, since the amount of investigation required to develop an accurate picture of a potential customer's financial situation may exceed the time available to the credit department. Accordingly, there are a number of shortcuts discussed in this section that yield good results while requiring less investigative effort. If the amount of credit contemplated is quite high, however, a full and detailed credit review is necessary. The contents of that review are also noted here.

If the amount of credit needed by a customer is quite low, then the credit department can authorize it by default, with no further investigation. However, in order to counterbalance this credit with the risk of loss, the amount given is usually very small. In order to authorize a larger amount of credit, the customer should be asked to fill out a credit form, on which is itemized the contact name of the customer's banker, as well as at least three of its trade references. If these references are acceptable, then the level of credit granted can be increased to a modest level. However, it is a simple matter for a customer in difficult financial straits to influence the credit "picture" that it is presenting to the company, by making sure that all of its trade references are paid on time, even at the expense of its other suppliers, who are paid quite late.

To avoid this difficulty, the credit department can invest in a credit report from one of the credit reporting agencies, such as Dun & Bradstreet. The price can vary from $20 to $70 per report, depending upon the type of information requested and the number of reports ordered (the credit services strongly encourage prepayment in exchange for volume discounts). These services collect payment information from many companies, as well as loan information from public records, financial information from a variety of sources, and on-site visits. The resulting reports give a more balanced view of a customer than its more sanitized trade references list.

Part of the credit report itemizes the average credit granted to the customer by its other trading partners. By averaging this figure, one can arrive at a reasonable credit level for the company to grant it, too. The report will also itemize the average days that it takes the customer to pay its bills. If this period is excessively long, then the credit department can reduce the average credit level granted by some factor, in accordance with the average number of days over which the customer pays its bills. For example, if the average outstanding credit is $1,000, and the customer has a record of paying its bills 10 days late, then the credit department can use the average credit of $1,000 as its basis, and then reduce it by 5% for every day over which its payments are delayed. This would result in the company granting credit of $500 to the customer.

However, credit reports can be manipulated by customers, resulting in misleading or missing information. For example, a privately-held firm can withhold information about its financial situation from the credit reporting agency. Also, if it knows that there are some poor payment records listed in its credit report, it can pay the credit agency to contact a specific set of additional suppliers (presumably with a better payment history from the customer), whose results will then be included in the credit report. Also, the information in the average credit report may not be updated very frequently, so the company purchasing the information may be looking at information that is so dated that it no longer relates to the customer's current financial situation.

If the amount of credit requested is much higher than a company is comfortable with granting based on a credit report, then it should ask for audited financial statements from the customer on an annual basis, and subject them to a review that includes the following key items:

• *Age of receivables.* If a customer has trouble receiving its invoices, then it will have less cash available to pay its suppliers. To determine receivables turnover, divide annualized net sales by the average balance of accounts receivable. In order to convert this into the number of days of receivables outstanding, multiply the average accounts receivable figure by 360 and divide the result by annualized net sales.

- *Size and proportion of the allowance for doubtful accounts.* If the customer is reserving an appropriate amount for its expected bad debts, then by comparing the amount of the allowance for doubtful accounts to the total receivable balance, one can see if the customer has over-committed itself on credit arrangements with its own customers. However, many organizations will not admit (even to themselves) the extent of their bad debt problems, so this figure may be underestimated.

- *Inventory turnover.* A major drain on a company's cash is its inventory. By calculating a customer's inventory turnover (annualized cost of goods sold divided by the average inventory), one can see if it has invested in an excessive quantity of inventory, which may impair its ability to pay its bills.

- *Current and quick ratios.* By comparing the total of all current assets to the total of current liabilities, one can see if a customer has the ability to pay for its debts with currently available resources. If this ratio is below 1:1, then it can be considered a credit risk, though this may be a faulty conclusion if the customer has a large, untapped credit line that it can use to pay off its obligations. A more accurate measure is the quick ratio (cash plus accounts receivable, divided by current liabilities). This ratio does not include inventory, which is not always so easily liquidated, and so provides a better picture of corporate liquidity. Of particular concern when reviewing these ratios is *over-trading.* This is a situation in which the current ratio is poor and debt levels are high, which indicates that the customer is operating with a minimum level of cash reserves, and so is likely to fail in short order. This type of customer tends to have a good payment history up until the point where it completely runs out of available debt to fund its operations, and abruptly goes bankrupt.

- *Ratio of depreciation to fixed assets.* If a customer has little available cash, it tends not to replace aging fixed assets. The evidence of this condition lies on the balance sheet, where the proportion of accumulated depreciation to total fixed assets will be very high.

- *Age of payables.* If a customer has little cash, its accounts payable balance will be quite high. To test this, compare the total accounts payable on the balance sheet to total non-payroll expenses and the cost of goods sold to see if more than one month of expenses is stored in the payables balance.

- *Short-term debt payments.* If a customer cannot pay for its short-term debt requirements, then it certainly cannot pay its suppliers. To check on the level of debt repayment, go to the audited financial statements and review the itemization of minimum debt payments located in the footnotes. This should be compared to the cash flow report to see if there is enough cash to pay for upcoming debt requirements.

- *Amount of equity.* If the amount of equity is negative, then warning bells should be ringing. The customer is essentially operating from debt and supplier credit at this point, and should not be considered a candidate for any credit without the presence of a guarantee or security.

- *Debt/equity ratio.* If investors are unwilling to put in more money as equity, then a customer must fund itself through debt, which requires fixed payments that may interfere with its cash flow. If the proportion of debt to equity is greater than 1:1, then calculate the times interest earned, which is a proportion of the interest expense to cash flow, to see if the company is at risk of defaulting on payments.

- *Gross margin and net profit percentage.* Compare both the gross margin and net profit percentages to industry averages to see if the company is operating within normal profit ranges. The net profit figure can be modified by the customer through the innovative use of standard accounting rules, and so can be somewhat misleading.

- *Cash flow.* If the customer has a negative cash flow from operations, then it is in serious trouble. If, on the other hand, it is on a growth spurt and has negative cash flow because of its investments in working capital and facilities, and has sufficient available cash to fund this growth, then the presence of a strong cash outflow is not necessarily a problem.

The key factor to consider when using any of the preceding credit review items is that the information presented is only a snapshot of the customer's condition at a single point in time. For a better understanding of the situation, the credit department should maintain a trend line of the key financial information for all customers to whom large lines of credit have been extended, so that any deleterious changes will be obvious.

If the financial statements are based on one time of year when the seasonality of sales may be affecting the reported accuracy of a company's financial condition, it may be better to request copies of statements from different periods of the year. For example, the calendar year-to-date June financial statements for a company with large Christmas sales will reveal very large inventory and minimal revenue, which does not accurately reflect its full-year condition.

The presence of potential credit problems will typically appear in just one or two areas, since the customer may be trying to hide the evidence from its suppliers. Fortunately, other sources of information can be used to confirm any suspicions aroused by a review of a customer's financial statements. For example, the sales staff can be asked for an opinion about the visible condition of the customer; if it appears run down, this is strong evidence that there is not enough money available to keep up its appearance.

Also, if the customer is a publicly held entity, a great deal of information is available about it through EDGAR On-line, which carries the last few years' worth of mandatory filings by the customer to the Securities and Exchange Commission. This information can be used to supplement and compare any information provided directly to the company by the customer.

It is critical that the financial information provided by a customer for review is fully audited, and not the result of a review or compilation. These lesser reviews do not ensure that the customer's books have been thoroughly reviewed and approved by an independent auditor, and so may potentially contain incorrect information that could mislead the credit department into issuing too much credit to the customer.

30-5 COLLECTION TECHNIQUES

The collection of overdue accounts receivable can be a messy and prolonged affair that results in irate customers and poor collection results. However, when properly organized, it can result in better customer relations, greatly improved cash flow, and fewer bad debts. To achieve this condition, the underlying collection methodology must be changed, as well as the methods used for contacting and dealing with customers.

The first step in improving the collection function is to re-organize the system that tracks overdue accounts. One approach is to purchase a collections software package that can be custom-designed to link to the existing accounting system. These packages contain a number of features that are most useful for the collections person, such as assigning certain overdue accounts to specific collections employees, so that they only see the accounts of customers assigned to them. The software also tracks contact information, stores notes about the most recent conversations with customers, and issues automatic reminders on the dates when customers should be called (even prioritized by time zone, so that calls will only be made during a customer's business hours). These systems can automatically issue dunning letters by fax or e-mail. The end result is a much more organized approach to collections than is normally the case.

If a company cannot afford to invest in such an automated system, it is still possible to create a simplified paper-based system that provides some of the same functionality, though not with the same degree of efficiency. For example, customers can be allocated to specific collections personnel and the accounts receivable aging report sorted in accordance with that allocation, so that subsets of the report are given to each collections person. Also, many aging reports include information about the contact name and phone number for each customer, so these reports can be used as the basis for collection calls. In order to create a history of contact information, each collections person can maintain a binder that includes for each customer a list of alternate contact names throughout their organizations, as well as the resolution of preceding collection problems.

Here are some of the techniques one can use to contact and deal with customers that can greatly improve the amount of money collected, as well as the speed with which it arrives:

- *Approve credit levels in advance.* Before the sales staff makes a sales call, they should first contact the credit department to see what level of credit will be granted. By doing so, the credit department's staff is not placed in the uncomfortable position of approving credit after an order has been received. However, this approach is not of much use if there is limited customer information available, or if the dollar volume of each sale is so small that there would not be much risk of exceeding the credit level.

- *Show respect.* Overriding all collection actions taken, it is critical to treat customers with the proper degree of respect. In the vast majority of cases, customers are not trying to actively defraud a company, but rather are trying to work through a short-term cash shortfall or perhaps have mislaid the payment paperwork. In these cases, shouting at a customer in order to obtain payment will probably have the reverse effect of being paid later in retaliation for the poor treatment.

- *Increase the level of contact.* In keeping with the first point, the level and intensity of contact should gradually increase as the delinquency period extends. For example, the accounting system can automatically send out a reminder e-mail or fax just prior to the due date on an invoice, which may be sufficient for someone at the customer to verify that the paperwork is in order and ready for payment. Then, if a payment is slightly overdue, a collections person can send a polite, non-confrontational fax to the customer. The next level of contact would be a friendly reminder call that follows up on the information in the fax. If subsequent calls do not rapidly result in resolution, then the level of contact increases by shifting to the manager of the accounts payable staff or some higher accounting position, possibly extending up to the owner or president. Only after these attempts have failed should the intensity of contact become more stern, progressing through more strident dunning letters, shifting to a letter from the corporate attorney, and finally being moved to a collection agency. By taking this approach, the vast majority of all contacts are made in a low-key and non-confrontational manner, which sets the stage for good long-term collection relations with a customer.

- *Involve the sales staff.* The salesperson who initially sold the product to a customer will have different contacts within that organization than those used by the collections person. By asking the salesperson to assist in collecting funds, a larger number of people can be brought into the payment decision at the customer location. This is particularly effective when salesperson commissions are tied to cash received, rather than invoices issued. Also, if the sales staff is aware of credit problems, they will be less inclined to exacerbate the situation by selling more products to the customer.

- *Contact in advance for large amounts.* If a company has extended a large amount of credit to a customer for a specific order, it makes sense to contact the customer prior to the due date of the invoice, just to make sure that all related paperwork in the accounts payable area is in order, thereby ensuring that the invoice will be paid on time.

- *Document all contacts.* If there is no record of whom a collections person talked to, or when the discussion took place, then it is very difficult to follow up with the correct person after the previously agreed-upon number of days, which results in very inefficient collections work. Instead, each collections person must diligently maintain a log of all activities. If possible, the accounting system should also generate a trend line of payments, so that a collections person can see if there are any developing cash flow problems at a customer.

- *Agree to and enforce a payment plan if necessary.* If a customer simply has no cash available with which to pay off an account receivable, it is reasonable to accept a payment plan under which portions are paid off over time, though one should attempt to obtain payment for the cost of the product as early as possible, so that only the profit margin is delayed. This keeps a company's own cash position from deteriorating, so that it can continue to pay its own bills. If a payment plan is used, the collections person should send a letter by overnight mail to the customer, confirming the terms of the agreement, and then contact the customer immediately if a scheduled payment is late by even one day, so that there is no question in the customer's mind that the company takes the collection process seriously, and will hold it to the terms of the agreement.

- *Obtain return of goods if cannot pay.* There will be a few instances in which the customer has no ability to pay the company at all. When this happens, try to persuade the customer to return the products to the company, even agreeing to pay for return freight if necessary. By doing so, the company can resell the goods and earn its profits elsewhere. This concept does not apply if the goods were custom-made, if freight costs are excessive, if the selling season is over, or if the goods may have sustained some damage.

- *Alter credit terms for problem customers.* If it is apparent that a customer is having ongoing trouble in paying for invoices, then its credit terms must be restricted. This can range from a minor reduction in the dollar total allowed it, or can extend to the use of cash on delivery or even cash in advance terms. This is also an effective collection tool, for the imposition of onerous terms can make a customer more likely to pay for outstanding invoices, if there is the prospect of easier terms once the invoices are paid.

- *Block shipments to problem customers.* If a customer has additional orders in process within the company, the collections person should be able to block their shipment until payments have been received on existing invoices. This action is made easier in some enterprise resources planning (ERP) systems, where one can freeze customer orders in the computer system by resetting a flag field in the accounting database.

The preceding recommendations will still allow some bad debts to occur, but the frequency of their incidence and their size will be reduced through the continuing attention to problem accounts that have been outlined here.

30-6   SUMMARY

This chapter has shown that there is a variety of ways in which a company can creatively extend credit to its customers, as well as different terms under which that credit can be paid back. A variety of analytical tools can also be used to determine the most appropriate level of credit that should be granted to a customer, while the collections function can be organized in such a way that bad debt losses are kept to a minimum. The key factor running through all of these tasks is that the customer credit function requires constant vigilance and careful management to ensure that credit losses are reduced, consistent with corporate credit policies.

CHAPTER 31

Financing

31-1 INTRODUCTION

A business of any size is likely to require extra funding at some point during its history that exceeds the amount of cash flow that is generated from ongoing operations. This may be caused by a sudden growth spurt that requires a large amount of working capital, an expansion in capacity that calls for the addition of fixed assets, a sudden downturn in the business that requires for extra cash to cover overhead costs, or perhaps a seasonal business that calls extra cash during the off-season. Different types of cash shortages will call for different types of funding, of which this chapter will show that there are many types. In the following sections, we will briefly describe each type of financing and the circumstances under which each one can be used, as well as the management of financing issues and bank relations.

31-2 MANAGEMENT OF FINANCING ISSUES

The procurement of financing should never be conducted in an unanticipated rush, with the management team running around town begging for cash to meet its next cash need. A reasonable degree of planning will make it much easier to not only tell *when* additional cash will be needed, but also *how much,* and what means can be used to obtain it.

To achieve this level of organization, the first step is to construct a cash forecast, which is covered in detail in Chapter 32, Cash Management. With this information in hand, one can determine the approximate amounts of financing that will be needed, as well as the duration of that need. This information is of great value in structuring the correct financing deal. For example, if the company is expanding into a new region and needs working capital for the sales season in that area, then it can plan to apply for a short-term loan, perhaps one that is secured by the accounts receivable and inventory purchased for the store in that region. Alternatively, if the company is planning to expand its production capacity through the purchase of a major new fixed asset, it may do better to negotiate a capital lease for its purchase, thereby only using the new equipment as collateral and leaving all other assets available to serve as collateral for future financing arrangements.

Besides this advanced level of cash flow planning, a company can engage in all of the following activities in order to more properly control its cash requirements and sources of potential financing:

- *Maximize the amount of loans using the borrowing base.* Loans that use a company's assets as collateral will offer lower interest rates, since the risk to the lender is much reduced. The accountant should be very careful about allowing a lender to attach all company assets, especially for a relatively small loan, since this leaves no collateral for use by other lenders. A better approach is to persuade a lender to accept the smallest possible amount of collateral, preferably involving specific assets rather than entire asset categories. The effectiveness of this strategy can be tracked by calculating the percentage of the available borrowing base that has been committed to existing lenders. Also, if the borrowing base has not yet been completely used as collateral, then a useful measurement is to determine the date on which it is likely to be fully collateralized, so that the planning for additional financing after that point will include a likely increase in interest costs.

- *Line up investors and lenders in advance.* Even if the level of cash planning is sufficient for spotting shortages months in advance, it may take that long to find lenders willing to advance funds. Accordingly, the accountant should engage in a search for lenders or investors as early as possible. If this task is not handled early on, then a company may find itself accepting less favorable terms at the last minute. The effectiveness of this strategy can be quantified by tracking the average interest rate for all forms of financing.

- *Minimize working capital requirements.* The best form of financing is to eliminate the need for funds internally, so that the financing is never needed. This is best done through the reduction of working capital, as is described later in the sections devoted to accounts receivable, accounts payable, and inventory reduction in this chapter.

- *Sweep cash accounts.* If a company has multiple locations and at least one bank account for each location, then it is possible that a considerable amount of money is lingering unused in those accounts. By working with its bank, a company can automatically sweep the contents of those accounts into a single account every day, thereby making the best use of all on-hand cash and keeping financing requirements to a minimum.

31-3 BANK RELATIONS

Part of the process of obtaining financing involves the proper care and feeding of one's banking officer. Since one of the main sources of financing is the bank with which one does business, it is exceedingly important to keep one's assigned banking officer fully informed of company activities and ongoing financial results. This should involve issuing at least quarterly financial information to the banking officer, as well as a follow-up call to discuss the results, even if the company is not currently borrowing any funds from the bank. The reasoning behind this approach is that the banking officer needs to become comfortable with the business's officers and also gain an understanding of how the company functions.

Besides establishing this personal relationship with the banking officer, it is also important to centralize as many banking functions as possible with the bank, such as checking, payroll, and savings accounts, sweep accounts, zero balance accounts, and all related services, such as lockboxes and on-line banking. By doing so, the bank officer will realize that the company is paying the bank a respectable amount of money in fees, and so is deserving of attention when it asks for assistance with its financing problems.

Company managers should also be aware of the types of performance measurements that bankers will see when they conduct a loan review, so that they can work on improving these measurements in advance. For example, the lender will likely review a company's quick and current ratios, debt/equity ratio, profitability, net working capital, and number of days on hand of accounts receivable, accounts payable, and inventory. The banking officer may be willing to advise a company in advance on what types of measurements the bank will examine, as well as the preferred minimum amounts of each one. For example, it may require a current ratio of 2:1, a debt/equity ratio of no worse than .40:1, and days of inventory of no worse than 70. By obtaining this information, a company can restructure itself prior to a loan application in order to ensure that its application will be approved.

Even by taking all of these steps to ensure the approval of financing, company management needs to be aware that the lender may impose a number of restrictions on the company, such as the ongoing maintenance of minimum performance ratios, the halting of all dividends until the loan is paid off, restrictions on stock buybacks and investments in other entities, and (in particular) the establishment of the lender in a senior position for all company collateral. By being aware of these issues in advance, it is sometimes possible to negotiate with the lender to reduce the amount or duration of some of the restrictions.

In short, a company's banking relationships are extremely important, and must be cultivated with great care. However, this is a two-way street that requires the presence of an understanding banking officer at the lending institution. If the current banking officer is not receptive, then it is quite acceptable to request a new one, or to switch banks in order to establish a better relationship.

The remaining sections describe different types of financing that a company can potentially obtain, including the reduction of working capital in order to avoid the need for financing.

31-4 ACCOUNTS PAYABLE PAYMENT DELAY

Though not considered a standard financing technique, since it involves internal processes, one can deliberately lengthen the time periods over which accounts payable are paid. For example, if a payables balance of $1,000,000 is delayed for an extra month, then the company has just obtained a rolling, interest-free loan for that amount, financed by its suppliers.

Though this approach may initially appear to result in free debt, it has a number of serious repercussions. One is that suppliers will catch on to the delayed payments in short order, and begin to require cash in advance or on delivery for all future payments, which will forcibly tell the company when it has stretched its payments too far. Even if it can stay just inside of the time period when these payment conditions will be imposed, suppliers will begin to accord the company a lesser degree of priority in shipments, given its payment treatment of them, and may also increase their prices to it in order to offset the cost of the funds that they are informally extending to the company. Also, if suppliers are reporting payment information to a credit reporting bureau, the late payments will be posted for all to see, which may give new company suppliers reason to cut back on any open credit that they would otherwise grant it.

A further consideration that argues against this practice is that suppliers who are not paid will send the company copies of invoices that are overdue. These invoices may very well find their way into the payment process and be paid alongside the original invoice copies (unless there are controls in place that watch for duplicate invoice numbers or amounts). As a result, the company will pay multiple times for the same invoice, thereby incurring an extra cost.

The only situation in which this approach is a valid one is when the purchasing staff contacts suppliers and negotiates longer payment terms, perhaps in exchange for higher prices or larger purchasing volumes. If this can be done, then the other problems just noted will no longer be issues.

Thus, unless payment delays are formally negotiated with suppliers, the best use of this financing option is for those organizations with no valid financing alternatives, that essentially are reduced to the option of irritating their suppliers or going out of business.

31-5 ACCOUNTS RECEIVABLE COLLECTION ACCELERATION

A great deal of corporate cash can be tied up in accounts receivable, for a variety of reasons. A company may have injudiciously expanded its revenues by reducing its credit restrictions on new customers, or it may have extended too much credit to an existing customer that it has no way of repaying in the short term, or it may have sold products during the off-season by promising customers lengthy payment terms, or perhaps it is in an industry where the customary repayment period is quite long. Given the extent of the problem, a company can rapidly find itself in need of extra financing in order to support the amount of unpaid receivables.

This problem can be dealt with in a number of ways. One approach is to offer customers a credit card payment option, which accelerates payments down to just a few days. Another alternative is to review the financing cost and increased bad debt levels associated with the extension of credit to high-risk customers, and eliminate those customers who are not worth the trouble. A third alternative is to increase the intensity with which the collections function is operated, using automated dunning letter (and fax) generation software, collections software that interacts with the accounts receivable files, and ensuring that enough personnel are assigned to the collections task. Finally, it may be possible to reduce the number of days in the standard payment terms, though this can be a problem for existing customers who are used to longer payment terms.

The reduction of accounts receivable should be considered one of the best forms of financing available, since it requires the acquisition of no debt from an outside source.

31-6 CREDIT CARDS

A large company certainly cannot rely upon credit cards as a source of long-term financing, since they are liable to be canceled by the issuing bank at any time, nor are they inexpensive, because credit card rates consistently approach the legal interest limits in each state. Furthermore, they may require someone's personal guarantee. Nonetheless, the business literature occasionally describes accounts by small business owners who have used a large number of credit cards to finance the beginnings of their businesses, sometimes using cash advances from one card to pay off the minimum required payment amounts on other cards. Given the cost of these cards and the small amount of financing typically available through them, this is not a financing method that is recommended for any but the most risk-tolerant and cash-hungry businesses.

31-7 EMPLOYEE TRADEOFFS

In rare cases, it is possible to trade off employee pay cuts in exchange for grants of stock or a share in company profits. However, a company in severe financial straits is unlikely to be able to convince employees to switch from the certainty of a paycheck to the uncertainty of capital gains or a share in profits from a company that is not performing well. If this type of change is forced upon employees, then it is much more likely that the best employees will leave the organization in search of higher compensation elsewhere. Another shortfall of this approach is that a significant distribution of stock to employees may result in employees (or their representatives) sitting on the Board of Directors.

In short, this option is not recommended as a viable form of financing.

31-8 FACTORING

Under a factoring arrangement, a finance company agrees to take over a company's accounts receivable collections and keep the money from those collections in exchange for an immediate cash payment to the company. This process typically involves having customers mail their payments to a lockbox that appears to be operated by the company, but which is actually controlled by the finance company. Under a true factoring arrangement, the finance company takes over the risk of loss on any bad debts, though it will have the right to pick which types of receivables it will accept in order to reduce its risk of loss. A finance company is more interested in this type of deal when the size of each receivable is fairly large, since this reduces its per-transaction cost of collection. If each receivable is quite small, the finance company may still be interested in a factoring arrangement, but it will charge the company extra for its increased processing work. The lender will charge an interest rate, as well as a transaction fee for processing each invoice as it is received. There may also be a minimum total fee charged, in order to cover the origination fee for the factoring arrangement in the event that few receivables are actually handed to the lender. A company working under this arrangement can be paid by the factor at once, or can wait until the invoice due date before payment is sent. The latter arrangement reduces the interest expense that a company would have to pay the factor, but tends to go against the reason why the factoring arrangement was established, which is to get money back to the company as rapidly as possible.

A similar arrangement is accounts receivable financing, under which a lender uses the accounts receivable as collateral for a loan, and takes direct receipt of payments from customers, rather than waiting for periodic loan payments from the company. A lender will typically only loan a maximum of 80% of the accounts receivable balance to a company, and only against those accounts that are less than 90 days old. Also, if an invoice against which a loan has been made is not paid within the required 90-day time period, then the lender will require the company to pay back the loan associated with that invoice.

Though both variations on the factoring concept will accelerate a company's cash flow dramatically, it is an expensive financing option, and so is not considered a viable long-term approach to funding a company's operations. It is better for short-term growth situations where money is in short supply to fund a sudden need for working capital. Also, a company's business partners may look askance at such an arrangement, since it is an approach associated with organizations that have severe cash flow problems.

31-9 FIELD WAREHOUSE FINANCING

Under a field warehousing arrangement, a finance company (usually one that specializes in this type of arrangement) will segregate a portion of a company's warehouse area with a fence. All inventory within it is collateral for a loan from the finance company to the company. The finance company will pay for more raw materials as they are needed, and is paid back directly from accounts receivable as soon as customer payments are received. If a strict inventory control system is in place, the finance company will also employ someone who will record all additions to and withdrawals from the secured warehouse. If not, then the company will be required to frequently count all items within the secure area and report this information back to the finance company. If the level of inventory drops below the amount of the loan, then the company must pay back the finance company the difference between the outstanding loan amount and the total inventory valuation. The company is also required under state lien laws to post signs around the secured area, stating that a lien is in place on its contents.

Field warehousing is highly transaction intensive, especially when the finance company employs an on-site warehouse clerk, and so is a very expensive way to obtain funds. This approach is only recommended for those companies that have exhausted all other less-expensive forms of financing.

31-10 FLOOR PLANNING

Some lenders will directly pay for large assets that are being procured by a distributor or retailer (such as kitchen appliances or automobiles) and be paid back when the assets are sold to a consumer. In order to protect itself, the lender may require that the price of all assets sold be no lower than the price the lender originally paid for them on behalf of the distributor or retailer. Since the lender's basis for lending is strictly on the underlying collateral (as opposed to its faith in a business plan or general corporate cash flows), it will undertake very frequent re-counts of the assets, and compare them to its list of assets originally purchased for the distributor or retailer. If there is a shortfall in the expected number of assets, the lender will require payment for the missing items. The lender may also require liquidation of the loan after a specific time period, especially if the underlying assets run the risk of becoming outdated in the near term.

This financing option is a good one for smaller or under-funded distributors or retailers, since the interest rate is not excessive (due to the presence of collateral).

31-11 INVENTORY REDUCTION

A terrific drain on cash is the amount of inventory kept on hand. The best way to reduce it, and therefore shrink the amount of financing needed, is to install a manufacturing planning system, for which many software packages are available. The most basic is the material requirements planning system (MRP), which multiplies the quantities planned for future production by the individual components required for each product to be created, resulting in a schedule of material quantities to be purchased. In its most advanced form, MRP can schedule component deliveries from suppliers down to a time frame of just a few hours on specific dates. If its shop floor planning component is installed, it can also control the flow of materials through the work-in-process area, which reduces work-in-process inventory levels by avoiding the accumulation of partially completed products at bottleneck operations. Understandably, such a system can make great inroads into a company's existing inventory stocks. A more advanced system, called manufacturing resources planning (MRP II), adds the capabilities of capacity and labor planning, but does not have a direct impact on inventory levels.

The just-in-time (JIT) manufacturing system blends a number of requirements to nearly eliminate inventory. It focuses on short equipment set-up times, which therefore justifies the use of very short production runs, which in turn keeps excessive amounts of inventory from being created through the use of *long* production runs. In addition, the system requires that suppliers make small and frequent deliveries of raw materials, preferably bypassing the receiving area and taking them straight to the production workstations where they are needed. Furthermore, the production floor is re-arranged into work cells, so that a single worker can walk a single unit of production through several production steps, which not only prevents work-in-process from building up between workstations, but also ensures that quality levels are higher, thereby cutting the cost of scrapped products. The key result of this system is a manufacturing process with very high inventory turnover levels.

The use of inventory planning systems to reduce inventory levels and hence financing requirements is an excellent choice for those organizations already suffering from a large investment in inventory, and that have the money and the time to install such systems. The use of MRP, MRP II, and JIT will not be of much help in alleviating short-term cash flow problems, since they can require the better part of a year to implement, and several more years to fine tune.

31-12 LEASE

A lease covers the purchase of a specific asset, which is usually paid for by the lease provider on the company's behalf. In exchange, the company pays a fixed rate, which includes interest and principal, to the leasing company. It may also be charged for personal property taxes on the asset purchased. The lease may be defined as an operating lease, under the terms of which the lessor carries the asset on its books and records a depreciation expense, while the lessee records the lease payments as an expense on its books. This type of lease typically does not cover the full life of the asset, nor does the buyer have a small-dollar buyout option at the end of the lease. The reverse situation arises for a capital lease, where the lessee records it as an asset and is entitled to record all related depreciation as an expense. In this latter case, the lease payments are split into their interest and principal portions, and recorded on the lessee's books as such.

The cost of a lease can be reduced by clumping together the purchases of multiple items under one lease, which greatly reduces the paperwork cost of the lender. If there are multiple leases currently in existence, they can be paid off and re-leased through a larger single lease, thereby obtaining a lower financing cost.

The leasing option is most useful for those companies that only want to establish collateral agreements for specific assets, thereby leaving their remaining assets available as a borrowing base for other loans. Leases can be arranged for all but the most financially shaky companies, since lenders can always use the underlying assets as collateral. However, unscrupulous lenders can hide or obscure the interest rate charged on leases, so that less financially knowledgeable companies will pay exorbitant rates.

31-13 LINE OF CREDIT

A line of credit is a commitment from a lender to pay a company whenever it needs cash, up to a pre-set maximum level. It is generally secured by company assets, and for that reason bears an interest rate not far above the prime rate. The bank will typically charge an annual maintenance fee, irrespective of the amount of funds drawn down on the loan, on the grounds that it has invested in the completion of paperwork for the loan. The bank will also likely require an annual audit of key accounts and asset balances to verify that the company's financial situation is in line with the bank's assumptions. One problem with a line of credit is that the bank can cancel the line or refuse to allow extra funds to be drawn down from it if the bank feels that the company is no longer a good credit risk.

The line of credit is most useful for situations in which there may be only short-term cash shortfalls or seasonal needs that result in the line being drawn down to zero at some point during the year. If one's cash requirements are expected to be longer term, then a term note or bond is a more appropriate form of financing.

31-14 LOAN, ASSET BASED

A loan that uses fixed assets or inventory as its collateral is a common form of financing by banks. The bank will use the resale value of fixed assets (as determined through an annual appraisal) and/or inventory to determine the maximum amount of available funds for a loan. If inventory is used as the basis for the loan, a prudent lender will typically not lend more than 50% of the value of the raw materials and 80% of the value of the finished goods, on the grounds that it may have to sell the inventory in the event of a foreclosure, and may not obtain full prices at the time of sale. Lenders will be much less likely to accept inventory as collateral if it has a short shelf life, is so seasonal that its value drops significantly at certain times of the year, or is subject to rapid obsolescence.

Given the presence of collateral, this type of loan tends to involve a lower interest rate. However, the cost of an annual appraisal of fixed assets or annual audit by the bank (which will be charged to the company) should be factored into the total cost of this form of financing.

31-15 LOAN, BOND

A bond is a fixed obligation to pay, usually at a stated rate of $1,000 per bond, that is issued by a corporation to investors. It may be a *registered bond*, in which case the company maintains a list of owners of each bond. The company then periodically sends interest payments, as well as the final principal payment, to the investor of record. It may also be a *coupon bond,* for which the company does not maintain a standard list of bond holders. Instead, each bond contains interest coupons that the bond holders clip and send to the company on the dates when interest payments arc due. The coupon bond is more easily transferable between investors, but the ease of transferability makes them more susceptible to loss.

A bond is generally issued with a fixed interest rate. However, if the rate is excessively low in the current market, then investors will pay less for the face value of the bond, thereby driving up the net interest rate paid by the company. Similarly, if the rate is too high, then investors will pay extra for the bond, thereby driving down the net interest rate paid.

A number of features may be added to a bond in order to make it more attractive for investors. For example, its terms may include a requirement by the company to set up a sinking fund into which it contributes funds periodically, thereby ensuring that there will be enough cash on hand at the termination date of the bond to pay off all bond holders. There may also be a conversion feature that allows a bond holder to turn in his or her bonds in exchange for stock; this feature usually sets the conversion ratio of bonds to stock at a level that will keep an investor from making the conversion until the stock price has changed from its level at the time of bond issuance, in order to avoid watering down the ownership percentages of existing shareholders. A bond offering can also be backed by any real estate owned by the company (called a real property mortgage bond), by company-owned equipment (called an equipment bond), or by all assets (called a general mortgage bond). In rare instances, bonds may even be backed by personal guarantees or by a corporate parent.

There are also features that bond holders may be less pleased about. For example, a bond may contain a call feature that allows the company to buy back bonds at a set price within certain future time frames. This feature may limit the amount of money that a bond holder would otherwise be able to earn by holding the bond. The company may also impose a staggered buyback feature, under which it can buy back some fixed proportion of all bonds at regular intervals. When this feature is activated, investors will be paid back much sooner than the stated payback date listed on the bond, thereby requiring them to find a new home for their cash, possibly at a time when interest rates are much lower than what they would otherwise have earned by retaining the bond. The bond holder may also be positioned last among all creditors for repayment in the event of a liquidation (called a subordinated debenture), which allows the company to use its assets as collateral for other forms of debt; however, it may have to pay a higher interest rate to investors in order to offset their perceived higher degree of risk. The typical bond offering will contain a mix of these features that impact investors from both a positive and negative perspective, depending upon its perceived level of difficulty in attracting investors, its expected future cash flows, and its need to reserve assets as collateral for other types of debt.

Bonds are highly recommended for those organizations large enough to attract a group of investors willing to purchase them, since the bonds can be structured to precisely fit a company's financing needs. Bonds are also issued directly to investors, so there are no financial intermediaries, such as banks, to whom transactional fees must be paid. Also, a company can issue long-maturity bonds at times of low interest rates, thereby locking in modest financing costs for a longer period than would normally be possible with other forms of financing. Consequently, bonds can be one of the lowest-cost forms of financing.

31-16 LOAN, BRIDGE

A bridge loan is a form of short-term loan that is granted by a lending institution on the understanding that the company will obtain longer-term financing shortly that will pay off the bridge loan. This option is commonly used when a company is seeking to replace a construction loan with a long-term note that it expects to gradually pay down over many years. This type of loan is usually secured by facilities or fixtures in order to obtain a modest interest rate.

31-17 LOAN, ECONOMIC DEVELOPMENT AUTHORITY

Various agencies of state governments are empowered to guarantee bank loans to organizations that need funds in geographic areas where it is perceived that social improvement goals can be attained. For example, projects that will result in increased employment or the employment of minorities in specific areas may warrant an application for this type of loan. It is usually extended to finance a company's immediate working capital needs. Given these restrictions, an economic development authority loan is only applicable in special situations.

31-18 LOAN, LONG-TERM

There are several forms of long-term debt. One is a long-term loan issued by a lending institution. These loans tend to be made to smaller companies that do not have the means to issue bonds or commercial paper. To reduce the risk to the lender, these loans typically require the company to grant the lender senior status over all other creditors in the event of liquidation. This is a standard requirement, because the lender is at much greater risk of default over the multi-year term of the loan, when business conditions may change dramatically. If there is no way for a lender to take a senior position on collateral, then the company should expect to pay a much higher interest rate in exchange for dropping the lender into a junior position in comparison to other creditors. If the lender also wants to protect itself from changes in long-term interest rates, it may attempt to impose a variable interest rate on the company. However, if the lender simply creates the loan and then sells it to a third party, it may be less concerned with future changes in the interest rate.

A long-term loan nearly always involves the use of fixed payments on a fixed repayment schedule, which will involve either the gradual repayment of principal, or else the gradual repayment of interest, with the bulk of the principal being due at the end of the loan as a balloon payment. In the latter case, a company may have no intention of paying back the principal, but instead will roll over the debt into a new loan and carry it forward once again. If this is the case, the company treasurer may review the trend of interest rates and choose to roll over the debt to a new loan instrument at an earlier date than the scheduled loan termination date, when interest rates are at their lowest possible levels.

Commercial paper is debt that is issued directly by a company, typically in denominations of $25,000. It is generally unsecured, and can be sold in a public market, since it is not registered to a specific buyer. Commercial paper is not an option for smaller companies, since the cost of placing the paper, as well as its level of acceptance in the public markets, will limit its use to only the largest organizations.

In summary, long-term debt is a highly desirable form of financing, since a company can lock in a favorable interest rate for a long time, which keeps it from having to repeatedly apply for shorter-term loans during the intervening years, when business conditions may result in less favorable debt terms.

31-19 LOAN, SMALL BUSINESS ADMINISTRATION

The Small Business Administration (SBA) provides guarantees on small loans to small businesses. These loans tend to carry reasonable interest rates, because of the back-up guarantee. However, the loans are issued by local lending institutions and must still pass their standard loan approval processes, so it is not that easy to obtain SBA loans if a company is in severe financial straits. The SBA tends to give guarantees to loans originating in economically depressed areas or where unemployment is high. For these reasons, SBA loans will only be available in a minority of situations, and not in sufficiently large amounts to cover many business needs.

31-20 LOAN, SHORT-TERM

The most common type of business loan extended by banks is the short-term loan. It is intended to be repaid within one year. The short time frame reduces the risk to the bank, which can be reasonably certain that the business's fortunes will not decline so far within such a short time period that it cannot repay the loan, while the bank will also be protected from long-term variations in the interest rate.

The short-term loan is intended to cover seasonal business needs, so that the cash is used to finance inventory and accounts receivable build-up through the main selling season, and is then repaid immediately after sales levels drop off and accounts receivable are collected. It can also be used for short-term projects, such as for the financing of the production requirements for a customer project that will be repaid as soon as the customer pays for the completed work. For these reasons, the timing of repayment on the loan should be right after the related business activity has been completed.

In some cases, a company may obtain such a loan if it really needs a long-term loan, but feels that it will obtain lower interest rates on long-term debt if it waits for interest rates to come down. However, this strategy can backfire if interest rates are on an upward trend, since a company will be at risk of large changes in interest rates every time that it pays off a short-term debt instrument and rolls the funds over into a new short-term loan.

31-21 PREFERRED STOCK

Preferred stock contains elements of both equity and debt, since it generally pays interest on the amount of funding paid in. However, the interest may be withheld on a cumulative basis by order of the Board of Directors, the shares do not have to be repaid, and they may be convertible to common stock. Also, the interest on preferred stock is considered a dividend under the tax laws, and so is not tax-deductible. As a result, the cost of preferred stock tends to be higher than other forms of debt, and, if the stock is convertible, shareholders may find that their ownership has been diluted by the preferred shareholders who have converted their shares to common stock.

Preferred stock is a good solution for those organizations that are looking for a long-term source of funds without a requirement to make fixed interest payments on *specific* dates (since preferred stock dividends can be deferred). It is also useful for companies that are being forced by their lending institutions to improve their debt/equity ratios, but that do not want to reduce the ownership percentages of their existing common stockholders through the infusion of new equity (only an option if the preferred shares are not convertible to common stock).

31-22 SALE AND LEASEBACK

Under this arrangement, a company sells one of its assets to a lender and then immediately leases it back for a guaranteed minimum time period. By doing so, the company obtains cash from the sale of the asset that it may be able to more profitably use elsewhere, while the leasing company handling the deal obtains a guaranteed lessee for a time period that will allow it to turn a profit on the financing arrangement. A sale and leaseback is most commonly used for the sale of a corporate building, but can also be arranged for other large assets, such as production machinery.

A sale and leaseback is useful for companies in any type of financial condition, for a financially healthy organization can use the resulting cash to buy back shares and prop up its stock price, while a faltering organization can use the cash to fund operations. Obviously, it is only an option for those organizations that have substantial assets available for sale.

31-23 SUMMARY

The previous discussion shows that there is a large array of approaches available to solve the problem of obtaining financing. The best ones by far involve the reduction of a company's working capital needs through internal management and process-oriented streamlining techniques, thereby reducing or eliminating the need for any financing. Once this approach has been maximized, a company that properly forecasts its cash needs and then makes long-range plans for the procurement of financing in the required amounts will be in a much better position to obtain the lowest-cost financing, as opposed to those organizations that must scramble for funding at the last minute.

CHAPTER 32

Cash Management

32-1 INTRODUCTION

Cash management is absolutely crucial to the operation of any but the most wealthy organizations. If there is ever a cash shortfall, payroll cannot be met, suppliers are not paid, scheduled loan payments will not be made, and investors will not receive dividend checks. Any one of these factors can either bring down a business or ensure a change in its management in short order.

In order to avoid these problems, this chapter covers how to construct a cash forecast and automate the creation of some of the information contained within it, as well as how to create a feedback loop for gradually increasing the accuracy of the forecast. We also describe a number of methods for controlling cash flows in order to avoid any shortfalls, as well as how to invest excess funds.

32-2 THE CASH FORECASTING MODEL

The core of any cash management system is the cash forecast. It is imperative for the management team to be fully apprised of any cash problems with as much lead time as possible. The sample model shown in Exhibit 32-1 is a good way to provide this information.

The cash forecast in the exhibit lists all cash activity on a weekly basis for the next nine weeks, which is approximately two months. These are followed by a partial month, which is needed in case the month that falls after the first nine weeks is also contained within the nine weeks. In the exhibit, the first week of May is listed, so the remaining three weeks of that month are described within a partial month column. There are also two more full months listed in the last two columns. By using this columnar format, the reader can see the expected cash flows for the next one-third of a year. The final two months on the forecast will tend to be much less accurate than the first two, but are still useful for making estimates about likely cash positions.

Exhibit 32-1 Sample Cash Forecast

Date Last Updated	3/9/01

Cash Forecast

For the Week Beginning on

	3/9/01	3/16/01	3/23/01	3/30/01	4/6/01	4/13/01	4/20/01	4/27/01	5/4/01	May-01 (partial)	Jun-01	Jul-01
Beginning Cash Balance	**$1,037,191**	$1,034,369	$968,336	$967,918	$918,082	$932,850	$918,747	$829,959	$834,924	$754,124	$808,592	$798,554
Receipts from Sales Projections:												
Coal Bed Drilling Corp.								$12,965		$16,937		$174,525
Oil Patch Kids Corp.										$48,521		$28,775
Overfault & Sons Inc.									$2,500		$129,000	
Platte River Drillers									$3,000	$53,000		
Powder River Supplies Inc.									$8,700		$18,500	$14,500
Submersible Drillers Ltd.										$2,500	$16,250	$16,250
Commercial, Various											$25,000	$25,000
Uncollected Invoices:												
Canadian Drillers Ltd.			$9,975									
Coastal Mudlogging Co.			$6,686									
Dept. of the Interior	$1,823			$11,629		$2,897				$18,510		
Drill Tip Repair Corp.				$5,575								
Overfault & Sons Inc.			$9,229									
Submersible Drillers Ltd.												
U.S. Forest Service		$2,967	$812	$4,245								
Cash, Minor Invoices	$2,355	—	$3,668	$8,715	$21,768							
Total Cash In	$4,178	$2,967	$30,370	$30,164	$21,768	$2,897	—	$12,965	$14,200	$139,468	$188,750	$259,050
Cash Out:												
Payroll + Payroll Taxes		$62,000		$65,000			$68,000		$71,000	$71,000	$138,000	$138,000
Commissions				$7,000					$7,000		$8,000	$9,000
Rent			$10,788				$10,788			$10,788	$10,788	$10,788
Capital Purchases			$10,000			$10,000			$10,000		$10,000	$10,000
Other Expenses	$7,000	$7,000	$10,000	$8,000	$7,000	$7,000	$10,000	$8,000	$7,000	$14,000	$32,000	$32,000
Total Cash Out:	$7,000	$69,000	$30,788	$80,000	$7,000	$17,000	$88,788	$8,000	$95,000	$85,000	$198,788	$199,788
Net Change in Cash	$(2,822)	$(66,033)	$(418)	$(49,836)	$14,768	$(14,103)	$(88,788)	$4,965	$(80,800)	$54,468	$(10,038)	$59,262
Ending Cash:	$1,034,369	$968,336	$967,918	$918,082	$932,850	$918,747	$829,959	$834,924	$754,124	$808,592	$798,554	$857,816
Budgeted Cash Balance:				897,636				833,352		800,439	815,040	857,113

445

The top row on the report in the exhibit lists the date when the cash report was last updated. This is crucial information, for some companies will update this report every day, and the management team does not want to confuse itself with information on old reports. The next row contains the beginning cash balance. The left most cell in the row is encircled by heavy lines, indicating that the person responsible for the report should update this cell with the actual cash balance as of the first day of the report. The remaining cells in the row are updated from the ending cash balance for each period that is listed at the bottom of the preceding column. The next block of rows contains the expected receipt dates for sales that have not yet occurred. It is useful to break these down by specific customer and type of sale, rather than summarizing it into a single row, so that the sales staff can be held responsible for this information. The sales staff should review this information regularly to see if the timing and amount of each expected cash receipt is still correct.

The next block of rows in the exhibit shows the specific weeks within which accounts receivable are expected to be collected. This section can become quite large and difficult to maintain if there are many accounts receivable, so it is better to only list the largest items by customer, and then lump all others into a minor invoices row, as is the case in the exhibit. The input of the collections staff should be sought when updating these rows, since they will have the best insights into collection problems. The sum of all the rows thus far described is then listed in the "Total Cash In" row.

The next block of rows in the exhibit shows the various uses for cash. A service company is being used in this forecast, so the largest single use of cash is payroll, rather than the cost of goods sold, as would be the case in a manufacturing company. Other key cash outflows, such as monthly commission and rental payments, as well as capital purchases, are shown in the following rows. Being a service business, there are few other expenses, so they are lumped together in an "other expenses" row. In this case, cash payments have a slight tendency to be toward the beginning of the month, so the cash flows are adjusted accordingly. If the cost of goods sold had been a major component of the forecast, then it would have either been listed in aggregate and based on a percentage of total sales, or else split into a different cash outflow for each product line. The latter case is more useful when the gross margin is significantly different for each product line, and when the sales by product line vary considerably over time.

There are a few other rows that could be added to the model, depending upon the type of payments that a company makes. For example, there could be an annual dividend payment, quarterly income tax payment, or monthly principal and interest payments to lenders. These and other items can be added to enhance the basic model, if needed. However, the model requires considerable effort to update, so one should carefully consider the extra workload needed before adding more information requirements to it.

The bottom of the exhibit summarizes the end-of-period cash position, while also comparing it to the budgeted cash balance for the end of each month. The comparison is important, for it tells management if actual results are departing significantly from expectations.

The exhibit assumes a high degree of manual data entry, rather than automation, but it is certainly possible to use additional formulas in the model in order to reduce the work required to update it. For example, an aggregate assumption can be made regarding the days of receivables that are generally outstanding, and have the model determine the total amount of cash receipts from existing invoices based on that assumption. However, if the total amount of accounts receivable is skewed in favor of a few large invoices, any changes in the timing of cash receipts for those few invoices can significantly alter the aggregate assumption for the number of days outstanding. Similarly, a days of inventory assumption is generally acceptable for deriving a cash usage figure for inventory purchases, but this is highly dependent upon the ability of the production department to manufacture exactly in accordance with the production schedule, so that actual inventory levels stay near their planned levels, while the purchasing staff only buys components in the quantities itemized by the manufacturing planning system.

32-3 MEASURING CASH FORECAST ACCURACY

A cash forecast is useless unless it can be relied upon to yield accurate forecasts. There are a number of ways to improve the forecast, all involving the continuing comparison of past forecasts to actual results and correcting the system to ensure that better information is provided for future forecasts.

A key area in which the cash forecast can be wildly incorrect is in receipts from sales forecasts. A detailed review of this area will reveal that some salespersons do not want to forecast any sales, because then they will be held accountable for their predictions. This problem requires constant feedback with the sales staff to correct, and may require reinforcement by including the sales forecasting function in the annual review and compensation plan for them.

Another problem is in the accounts payable area, where actual cash outflows will typically exceed forecast cash outflows. This imbalance is caused by a faulty accounts payable data entry process, whereby invoices are initially mailed by suppliers to people outside of the accounts payable department, or because invoices are sent out for approval before they are logged into the accounting system, thereby resulting in their late appearance in the forecast, usually just before they need to be paid. These problems can be solved by asking suppliers to send invoices straight to the accounting department, and by entering all invoices into the accounting system before sending them out for approval. It is also possible to review open purchase orders to see if there are any missing invoices that are supposed to be currently payable, thereby proactively starting a search for the missing invoices.

A major cash flow variance will arise if a fixed asset is suddenly purchased that was not included in the cash forecast. This problem is best resolved by giving the accounting staff complete access to the capital budgeting process, so that it can tell what capital requests are in queue for approval, and when they are likely to require cash payments to obtain.

In short, the accuracy of the cash forecast requires great attention to processes that provide its source data. The accounting staff should regularly compare forecasted to actual results, and work their way back through the underlying systems to determine what issues caused the error—and then correct them.

32-4 CASH FORECASTING AUTOMATION

The steps just noted to create a cash forecast can be quite cumbersome to accumulate, especially if there are multiple departments or subsidiaries spread out across many locations. When the cash forecast is generated on a regular basis, the required workload can be extraordinarily high. Automation can be used to avoid some of the most time-consuming steps.

Many off-the-shelf accounting software packages contain standard reports that itemize the daily or weekly time buckets in which payments are scheduled to be made, based on each supplier invoice date and the number of days before they are due for payment, including any requirements for early payment in order to take advantage of early payment discounts. The cash flow information provided by this report is quite reliable, but tends to be less accurate for the time period several weeks into the future, because of delays in the entry of supplier invoice information into the accounting system. This delay is usually caused by the divergence of incoming invoices to managers for approval. By first entering the invoice information and *then* sending the invoices out for approval, this time delay can be avoided, thereby improving the accuracy of the automated accounts payable payment timing report.

If there is a well-managed purchase order system in place that is stored in a purchasing database, then the accounts payable report format can be stretched further into the future with some accuracy. Since purchase orders may be issued for some months into the future, and involve specific delivery dates, this information can be compiled into a report that reveals when the payments to suppliers based on these purchase orders will be sent out. It is also useful for the purchase of fixed assets, since these orders are so large that suppliers will not normally process an order in the absence of a signed purchase order. However, a large asset purchase may require an up-front payment that will not become apparent until the purchase order is entered into the accounting system, which will result in the sudden appearance of a large cash requirement on the report in the near future.

There are some instances in which invoice payments can be predicted for well into the future even in the absence of a purchase order. These are typically recurring payments in a constant amount, such as facility lease payments or maintenance payments that are pre-specified under a long-term contract. If these payments are listed in the accounts payable system as recurring invoices, then the accounts payable payment timing report will include them.

The same report is available in many accounting software packages for accounts receivable, itemizing the day or week buckets in which invoice payments are scheduled to be received, based on their original issuance dates and the number of days before customers are required to pay for them. However, this report tends to be much less accurate, for any overdue invoice payments are scheduled for immediate payment in the current period, when in fact there may be collection problems that will delay receipt for quite some time. Also, the report does not account for the average delay in payments that varies by each customer, in accordance with each one's timeliness in making payments. Consequently, this report should be manually modified, especially for the largest outstanding invoices, to reflect the accounting staff's best estimates of when payments will actually be received.

In a few cases, software packages will also extend current payroll payments into the future, by assuming that the existing salaries for current employees will continue at the same rates, and that hourly employees will be paid for a regular workweek for all future reporting periods. This is not a viable option for those companies that outsource their payroll, since the in-house software will not have any way to predict cash flows if it does not contain any information about payroll.

The preceding discussion shows that there are numerous ways in which elements of the cash forecast can be automated. However, there are so many variables, such as uncertain receipt dates for accounts receivable, changes in payroll levels, and the sudden purchase of fixed assets, that any automatically generated reports should be adjusted by the accounting staff's knowledge of special situations that will throw off the results of the reports. Also, the basis for automated reports is primarily very short-term accounts receivable and payable information that will rapidly become inaccurate for periods much greater than a month, so manual adjustments to the cash forecast will become increasingly necessary for later time periods.

32-5 CASH MANAGEMENT CONTROLS

Once a cash forecasting system is in place, one can tell if there will be cash flow difficulties coming up in the short term, and take steps to ensure that the problems are minimized. In this section, we look at a variety of methods for controlling the flow of cash, which involve not only a speeding up of the cash handling process, but also an increased focus on reducing a company's cash requirements in all operational areas. The specific items are:

- *Avoid early payments.* Though it seems obvious, the accounts payable department will pay suppliers early from time to time. This can occur because the accounting staff has already input a default payment interval into the accounting computer, and is not regularly reviewing supplier invoices to see if the payment terms have changed. It is also possible that only a few check runs are being printed per month, which results in some invoices being paid slightly early, simply because the next check run is not scheduled for some time; this can be avoided through the use of either more check runs or the implementation of a policy to only pay on or after the payment due date, thereby shifting these checks to a later check run.

- *Avoid engineering design changes.* If minor modifications are allowed to be made to products currently in production, this probably means that some parts that were included in the old design will no longer fit in the new design. Unless great care is taken to use up all of the old parts prior to switching to the modified product, there will be a gradual buildup of parts in the warehouse that can no longer be used, thereby increasing the company's investment in raw materials inventory. For this reason, the value received from design changes must be clearly proven to outweigh their added inventory cost.

- *Avoid stuffing the distribution pipeline.* One way to manufacture abnormally high sales is to offer especially good deals to one's customers, thereby dumping on them an excessive quantity of goods. However, doing so will eventually backfire on the company, since customers will not need to purchase from the company again for some time, resulting in reduced future sales. For the purposes of this discussion, the issue is particularly important if the deal offered to customers is delayed payment in exchange for their accepting goods immediately. By doing so, a company greatly increases the amount of cash that is needed to fund a much larger accounts receivable balance.

- *Conduct a prompt bank reconciliation.* The management team can find itself scrambling for cash if the bank's and the company's cash records diverge significantly, due to delays in completing a bank reconciliation. To avoid this, it is possible to conduct a bank reconciliation every day through an on-line connection to the bank's database, or at least by immediately completing the reconciliation as soon as the report is received from the bank.

- *Eliminate excess checking accounts.* Most checking accounts do not earn interest on the funds stored within them, so the presence of more than one account means that an excess volume of cash is being spread out in too many accounts. By evaluating the need for each checking account and consolidating as many as possible, one can reduce the amount of unused cash in the system. For a further refinement to this approach, see the later comment in this section about zero balance accounts.

- *Eliminate invoicing errors.* An invoicing error of any type can result in a greatly delayed customer payment, while the problem is identified and corrected. To avoid this problem, the accounting department should keep a log of all errors encountered, and assign a task force to the chore of altering the invoicing process in order to eliminate the errors in the future.

- *Improve sales forecast accuracy.* If the forecasts upon which the production schedule is based are inaccurate, then there is a strong chance that there will be some production overages, which will result in excess inventory that must be funded for a long time, until the inventory can be sold off. This forecasting error can be improved upon by obtaining direct access to the forecasts of the company's customers, so that the production scheduling staff can see exactly what the demand levels are likely to be. It is also possible to switch to a just-in-time manufacturing system, where the focus is on producing to order, rather than to a forecast (though by no means always achievable). At a minimum, one should compare sales forecasts to historical sales records at both the customer and product level to see if the forecasts have any basis in historical fact, and investigate those with the greatest variances.

- *Install lockboxes.* Most banks offer the service of opening one's mail, extracting customer payments, and depositing them directly into one's account, which can shave anywhere from one to three days off the transit time required to move cash into one's account. The savings is especially great if lockboxes are distributed throughout the country, so that customers are directed to send their payments to those lockboxes located nearest to them. This requires the company to contact all customers and request them to shift their payments to the lockbox address, which will be a post office box number. In exchange for this service, the bank will charge a small monthly service fee, plus a fee for each check processed. During the processing of cash, the bank will photocopy each incoming check and mail it to the company, so that the accounts receivable staff can record the cash receipt in the accounting computer system.

- *Install zero balance accounts.* The concentration of all available cash can be heightened not only through the use of lockboxes, but also by keeping the resulting cash in investment accounts and then shifting the cash automatically to the checking accounts only when checks are drawn against them. This type of checking account is called a zero balance account. It can also be used for a payroll account.

- *Lengthen supplier payment terms.* If a few key suppliers have required the company to pay on very short terms, then this can greatly reduce the amount of cash that a company has available. The purchasing staff should be asked to negotiate with these suppliers to lengthen terms, perhaps at the cost of committing to larger purchasing volumes or slightly higher prices. When this change takes place, the purchasing staff must notify the accounting department, or else it will continue to pay on the original shorter terms, which are already listed in the accounts payable system, and will automatically be used for all future payments unless manually changed.

- *Outsource cash-intensive functions.* Some activities, such as computer services, require considerable investments in capital equipment. To avoid this expenditure, those departments can be outsourced to a supplier, thereby not only avoiding additional asset investments, but also allowing the company to sell off any existing assets, perhaps to the supplier that takes over the function. This tends to be a longer-term solution, since shifting any function outside a company requires a great deal of transitional planning.

- *Reduce purchasing overages.* An overly efficient purchasing department can buy greater quantities of items than are strictly needed in the short term, on the grounds that it does not want to issue a number of purchase orders for small quantities when a single order would have sufficed, thereby saving it a great deal of personnel time. These large purchases can lead to a considerable excess use of cash. A good way to avoid this problem is to invest in a materials management system, such as material requirements planning (MRP), under which the system specifies exactly what materials to buy, and can even issue the required purchase orders. The purchasing staff can also be evaluated based on the number of raw material inventory turns, which will focus them away from making unnecessarily large purchases.

- *Sell fixed assets.* The accounting department should regularly review the complete list of fixed assets to see if there are any that are no longer in use, and so can be sold. Though this task should be left up to the department managers, cash conservation is not one of their primary tasks, and so they tend to ignore old assets. One way around this performance problem is to measure department managers based on their return on assets; by doing so, they will constantly work to reduce the asset base for which they are responsible, which will lead to the increased conversion of old assets into cash.

- *Sell obsolete inventory.* The accounting staff should create a report that shows which inventory items have not been used recently, or which items are in such excessive quantities that they will not be drawn down for a long time. With this information, the purchasing department can contact suppliers to sell back the inventory or obtain credits against future purchases. If neither approach will work, the company may still be able to obtain a tax deduction by donating the inventory to a non-profit organization.

- *Tighten customer credit.* If the accounts receivable balance appears to be disproportionately high or if the proportion of overdue accounts receivable is excessive, then reduce the amount of credit extended to selected customers. However, this can interfere with the corporate growth rate if the strategy involves increasing sales through the use of easy credit.

- *Tighten the process flow that results in cash.* The entire process of taking a customer order, building the product, delivering it, sending an invoice, and receiving payment can be an extraordinarily involved and lengthy one. If it is handled improperly, the inflow of cash once a customer order has been received will be greatly delayed. In order to avoid this problem, one should periodically re-examine the entire process with the objective of minimizing the time required to receive cash at the end of the process. For example, one can avoid queue times when orders are waiting in the "in" boxes of employees by concentrating as many steps in the hands of one employee as possible (called process centering). Another possibility is to replace portions of the existing system with new technology, such as the use of lockboxes to accelerate the receipt of cash, or the use of a centralized ordering database that tracks the flow of orders through the system. For information about tightening the process, please refer to Bragg, *Just-in-Time Accounting,* Second edition, John Wiley & Sons, 2001.

- *Use a manufacturing planning system.* Any production planning system will greatly streamline the flow of materials through a manufacturing facility. Accordingly, any company engaged in production should invest in a material requirements planning (MRP), manufacturing resources planning (MRP II), or just-in-time (JIT) system. Though all have different underlying concepts and methods of operation, they will all result in reduced inventory levels. When properly installed, the JIT system is particularly effective in achieving this result.

- *Verify times when cash discounts are applicable.* Though it is standard practice to always take discounts in exchange for early payments to suppliers whenever they are offered, one should verify that the discounts taken are worth their cost. As noted in Exhibit 32-2, there are situations in which it does not make sense to take the discount. For example, the second column of the exhibit shows that an invoice paid on regular terms of 30 days, rather than at a discount of 1% after 10 days have passed, will have a net annualized interest cost to the company of 18.5%. We derive the 18% figure from the 1% interest cost that the company is incurring to wait an extra 20 days to make a payment; since there are roughly 18 20-day periods in a year, the annualized interest rate is about 18 times 1%, or 18%. To take the example a step further, if cash is in such short supply that the company cannot pay for the early discount, and in fact can only pay after 40 days have passed, its cost of funds will have dropped to 12.3%, which may be quite close to its existing cost of funds, and so may appear to be a reasonable alternative to paying early.

A key issue in the preceding bullet points is that the opportunity to manage cash lies in all areas of a company, for the points covered include the finance, accounting, production, sales, distribution, and engineering departments. Thus, the management of cash should not be considered the sole responsibility of the finance and accounting departments.

Exhibit 32-2   Annual Interest Cost of Not Taking a Cash Discount

If Paid On:	1/10, N 30	2/10, N 30
Day 10	0%	0%
Day 20	36.9%	73.8%
Day 30	18.5%	36.9%
Day 40	12.3%	24.6%

Reprinted with permission: Burton and Bragg, *Accounting and Finance for Your Small Business,* John Wiley & Sons, 2000, p. 123.

32-6 INVESTING FUNDS

Though the focus in this chapter has been on the use of cash forecasting to avoid or properly deal with cash shortages, there will also be situations in which there will be more cash on hand than is needed to fund ongoing operations. Though this money can be left in the corporate checking account, it is better to earn some interest income by investing it elsewhere.

When considering various forms of cash investment, one should first consider the safety of the principal being invested. It would not do to invest company funds in a risky investment in order to earn extraordinarily high returns if there is a chance that any portion of the principal will be lost. Accordingly, a company policy should be approved by the Board of Directors that limits investments to a specific set of low-risk investment types. Also, some consideration should be given to the maturity and marketability of an investment. For example, if an investment in a block of apartment houses appears to generate a reasonably risk-free return and a good rate of return, it is still a poor investment from a cash management perspective, because the investment probably cannot be converted to cash on short notice. Accordingly, it is best to only make investments where there is a robust market available for their immediate resale. The final consideration when making an investment is its yield—and this is truly the last consideration after the previous items have already been reviewed. Within the boundaries of appropriate levels of risk, maturity, and marketability, one can then pick the investment with the highest yield. Since these criteria tend to limit one to very low-risk investments, the yield will be quite low. Nonetheless, it is still a better investment than leaving the cash in a checking account.

Within the investment boundaries just noted, there are a number of available investment options available. Here are the most common ones that have low risk levels, short maturity dates, and high levels of marketability:

- *Bonds near maturity dates.* A corporate bond may not mature for many years, but one can always purchase a bond that is close to its maturity date. There tends to be a minimal risk of loss (or gain) on the principal amount of this investment, since there is a low risk that interest rates will change so much in the short time period left before the maturity date of the bond that it will impact its value. A variation on this type of investment is the municipal bond, for which there is no tax on the interest income; however, in consideration of this reduced liability, its yield also tends to be somewhat lower than on other types of bonds.

- *Certificate of deposit.* Banks issue these certificates, usually in small-dollar amounts such as $1,000. A CD requires a minimum investment period, and carries a rate slightly higher than what is found in a money market account. A CD does not allow one to write checks against it.

- *Commercial paper.* Larger corporations issue short-term notes that carry higher yields than those on government debt issuances. There is also an active secondary market for them, so there is usually no problem with liquidity. As long as one stays with the commercial paper issued by "blue chip" organizations, there is also little risk of default.

- *Money market fund.* This is a package of government instruments, usually comprised of treasury bills, notes, and bonds, that is assembled by a fund management company. The investment is highly liquid, with many investors putting in funds for as little as a day. It is possible to write checks against a money market account, though the number may be limited by the fund operator in order to keep a company from using the fund as its main checking account.

- *Repurchase agreement.* This is a package of securities that an investor buys from a financial institution, under the agreement that the institution will buy it back at a specific price on a specific date. It is most commonly used for the overnight investment of excess cash from one's checking account, which can be automatically handled by one's bank. The typical interest rate earned on this investment is equal to or less than the money market rate, since the financial institution takes a transaction fee that cuts into the rate earned.

- *U.S. Treasury issuances.* The United States government issues a variety of notes with maturity dates that range from less than a year (U.S. Treasury certificates) through several years (notes) to more than five years (bonds). The wide range of maturity dates gives one a broad range of investment options. Also, there is a strong secondary market for these issuances, so they can be liquidated in short order. U.S. government debts of all types are considered to be risk-free, and so have somewhat lower yields than other forms of investment.

32-7 SUMMARY

The cash management function is an important one that deserves the utmost attention from the accountant, since a cash shortfall can bring a company's operations to an abrupt halt in short order. The cash management process is based upon a foundation of detailed and ongoing cash forecasting, which should be regularly compared to actual results in order to review and improve the accuracy of the overall process. Only by doing so can a company predict the amount and timing of cash problems, and work to correct them in a timely manner.

CHAPTER 33

Risk Management[1]

33-1 INTRODUCTION

Some well-managed companies have fallen because they did not pay attention to risk. For example, it is difficult to recover from a fire that destroys a data center or production facility, or from the theft of all one's securities and cash. Though rare, these occurrences can be so catastrophic that it is not possible to recover. An otherwise healthy organization is destroyed, throwing many people out of work and eliminating the equity stake of the owners.

On a lesser scale and much more common are the lawsuits that nearly every company must face from time to time. These may relate to employee injuries, customer or supplier claims regarding contracts, or perhaps sexual harassment or some form of discrimination. These lawsuits do not normally end a company's existence, but they can cripple it if awards are excessive or the company is not in a solid financial position to begin with.

This chapter covers the risk management policies and procedures that keep a company from being seriously injured by these and other types of risk-related problems. In addition, it notes the role of the risk manager in mitigating a company's risk by modifying internal systems as well as by purchasing insurance. The types of insurance that a company can buy are also discussed, as well as how to select a broker or underwriter to help service a company's needs. The chapter concludes with coverage of how to administer insurance claims, and how to write a risk management report that clearly identifies a company's risks and how they are being addressed.

---

[1]This chapter is reprinted with permission from Willson, Roehl-Anderson, and Bragg, *Controllership*, (John Wiley & Sons, 1999), pp. 1316–1326.

33-2 RISK MANAGEMENT POLICIES

A company must determine the amount of risk that it is willing to undertake. When the Board of Directors attempts to quantify this, it frequently finds that it is uncomfortable with the level of risk that it currently has, and mandates more action, through new policies, that reduce the level of risk. The policies can include a number of risk management issues, such as the financial limits for risk assumption or retention, self-insurance parameters, the financial condition of insurance providers, and captive insurance companies. The policies do not have to cover some issues that are already required by law, such as workers' compensation insurance. An example of a comprehensive insurance policy is noted in Exhibit 33-1.

Exhibit 33-1   A Comprehensive Policy for Risk Management

1. ABC Company will obtain insurance only from companies with an A.M. Best rating of at least B++.
2. All self-insurance plans will be covered by an umbrella policy that covers all losses exceeding $50,000.
3. No insurance may be obtained from captive insurance companies.
4. The company must always have current insurance for the following categories, and in the stated amounts:
   - Director's and officer's insurance, $5 million.
   - General liability insurance, $10 million.
   - Commercial property insurance that matches the replacement cost of all structures and inventory.
   - Business interruption insurance, sufficient for four months of operations.

There are several key points to consider in the exhibit. First, a company may be tempted to purchase very inexpensive insurance, which typically comes from an insurance provider that is in poor financial condition. If the company subsequently files a claim on this insurance, it may find that the provider is not in a position to pay it. Consequently, the first policy item defines the minimum financial rating that an insurance provider must attain before the company will purchase insurance from it. Another is that a company wants to put a cap on the maximum amount of all risks that it is willing to tolerate, so that it cannot be blindsided by a large loss that is not covered by insurance. The second policy point, which requires a cap on self-insured risks, covers this problem. Finally, the Board may feel more comfortable defining the precise amount of insurance coverage needed in specific areas. Though the policy shows a few specific insurance amounts, it is usually better to define a formula for calculating the appropriate amount of insurance, such as commercial property insurance, that will cover the replacement cost of structures and inventory. This keeps the amount defined on the policy from becoming outdated due to changing business conditions. These are some of the most important insurance issues that a risk management policy should cover.

33-3 MANAGER OF RISK MANAGEMENT

In most large companies, the risk management function is assigned to a manager, who reports to the chief financial officer, treasurer, or controller. This executive is charged with the responsibility of implementing procedures consistent with the corporate risk management policy (as noted in Exhibit 33-1). This person works closely with other functional areas, such as engineering, safety and health, personnel and industrial relations, production, plant security, legal, and accounting. It is important that this person have a thorough knowledge of the company's operations, products, and services, as well as its risk history, so that he or she can evaluate risks and exposure properly. Within these constraints, the job description of the typical risk manager is:

- Ascertain and appraise all corporate risks.
- Estimate the probability of loss due to these risks.
- Ensure compliance with state, federal, and local requirements regarding insurance.
- Select the optimum method for protecting against losses, such as changes to internal procedures or by acquiring insurance.
- Work with insurance agents, brokers, consultants, and insurance company representatives.
- Supervise a loss prevention program, including planning to minimize losses from anticipated crises.
- Maintain appropriate records for all aspects of insurance administration.
- Continually evaluate and keep abreast of all changes in company operations.
- Stay current on new techniques being developed in the risk management field.
- Conduct a periodic audit of the risk management program to ensure that all risks have been identified and covered.

33-4 RISK MANAGEMENT PROCEDURES

Once the risk management policies have been defined, it is necessary to determine a number of underlying procedures to support them. These guide the actions of the risk manager in ensuring that a company has taken sufficient steps to ensure that risks are kept at a minimum. The procedures follow a logical sequence of exploring the extent of risk issues, finding ways to mitigate those risk internally, and then using insurance to cover any risks that cannot otherwise be reduced. In more detail, the five procedures are:

1. *Locate risk areas.* Determine all hazards to which the company is subject by performing a complete review of all properties and operations. This should include a review of not only the physical plant but also of contractual obligations, leasehold requirements, and government regulations. The review can be completed with insurable hazard checklists that are provided by most insurance companies, with the aid of a consultant, or by reviewing historical loss data provided by the company's current insurance firm. However, the person conducting this review must guard against the FUD Principle (Fear, Uncertainty, and Doubt) that is cheerfully practiced by all insurance companies. That is, they tend to hone in on every conceivable risk and amplify the chance of its occurrence, so that a company will purchase lots of unnecessary insurance. The best way to avoid this problem is to employ an extremely experienced risk manager who knows which potential risks can be safely ignored. The following areas, at a minimum, should be reviewed:

- *Buildings and equipment.* The risk manager should list the type of construction, location, and hazards to which each item is exposed. Each structure and major piece of equipment should be listed separately. The current condition of each item should be determined and its replacement cost evaluated.

- *Business interruption.* The risk manager should determine the amount of lost profits and continuing expenses resulting from a business shutdown as the result of a specific hazard.

- *Liabilities to other parties.* The risk manager should determine the risk of loss or damage to other parties by reason of company products, services, operations, or the acts of employees. This analysis should include a review of all contracts, sales orders, purchase orders, leases, and applicable laws to determine what commitments have been undertaken and what exposures exist.

- *Other assets.* The risk manager should review cash, inventory, and accounts receivable to determine the possible exposure to losses by fire, flood, theft, or other hazards.

2. *Determine the risk reduction method.* Match each risk area with a method for dealing with it. The possible options for each risk area include avoidance, reduction of the hazard, retaining the hazard (that is, self insurance), or transferring the risk to an insurance company. Note that only the last option in this list includes the purchase of insurance, for there are many procedures that a company can implement to reduce a risk without resorting to insurance. The selection of a best option is based on a cost-benefit analysis that offsets the cost of each hazard against the cost of avoiding it, factoring in the probability of the hazard's occurrence. The general categories of risk reduction are:

   - *Duplicate.* A company can retain multiple copies of records to guard against the destruction of critical information. In addition, key systems such as local area networks, telephone systems, and voice mail storage can be replicated at off-site locations to avoid a shutdown caused by damage to the primary site. For example, airlines maintain elaborate backup systems for their seat reservation databases.

   - *Prevent.* A company can institute programs to reduce the likelihood and severity of losses. For example, some companies invite the Occupational Safety and Health Administration (OSHA) to inspect their premises and report on unsafe conditions; the companies then correct the issues to reduce their risk of loss. If a company requires employees to wear hardhats in construction areas, then a falling brick may still cause an accident, but the hardhat will reduce the incident's severity. Examples of prevention techniques include improving lighting, installing protective devices on machinery, and enforcing safety rules.

   - *Segregate.* A company can split up key assets such as inventory and distribute it to multiple locations (for example, warehouses). For example, the military maintains alternate command centers in case of war.

3. *Implement internal changes to reduce risks.* Once the types of risk avoidance have been determined, it is time to implement them. This usually involves new procedures or installations, such as fire suppression systems in the computer processing

facility, or altered cash tracking procedures that will discourage an employee from stealing money. Changes to procedures can be a lengthy process, for they include working with the staff of each functional area to create a new procedure that is acceptable to all users, as well as following up with periodic audits to ensure that the procedures are still being followed.

4. *Select a broker.* Every company will require some insurance, unless it takes the hazardous approach of self-insuring virtually every risk. It is necessary to select a broker who can assist the company in procuring the best possible insurance. The right broker can be of great help in this process, not just in picking the least expensive insurance, but also in selecting the correct types of coverage, determining the financial strength of insurers, post-loss service, and general knowledge of the company's business and of the types of risk that are most likely to occur in that environment. Unfortunately, many companies look for new brokers every few years on the principle that a long-term broker will eventually raise prices and gouge the company. In reality, a long-term relationship should be encouraged, since the broker will gain a greater knowledge of the company's risks as problems occur and claims are received, giving it a valuable insight into company operations that a new broker does not have.

5. *Determine the types of insurance to be purchased.* Once the broker has been selected, the risk manager can show the preliminary results of the insurance review to the broker, and they can then mutually determine the types of insurance that are needed to supplement the actions already taken internally to mitigate risk. The types of insurance include the following:

   • *Boiler and machinery.* Covers damage to the boilers and machinery, as well as payments for injuries caused by the equipment. Providers of this insurance also review the company's equipment and issue a report recommending safety improvements.

   • *Business interruption.* Allows a company to pay for its continuing expenses and in some cases will pay for all or part of its anticipated profits.

   • *Commercial property.* The minimum "basic form" of this insurance covers losses from fires, explosions, wind storms, hail, vandalism, and other perils. The "broad form," which is an expanded version, covers everything in the basic form plus damage from falling objects, the weight of snow, water damage, and some causes of building collapse. Optional coverage includes an inflation escalator clause, replacement of destroyed structures at the actual replacement cost, and coverage of finished goods at their selling price (instead of at their cost).

   • *Comprehensive auto liability.* This coverage is usually mandatory and requires a minimum level of coverage for bodily injury and property damage.

   • *Comprehensive crime.* Covers property theft, robbery, safe and premises burglary, and employee dishonesty; in the case of employee dishonesty, the company purchases a fidelity bond, which can cover a named individual, a specific position, or all employees. Some policies will also cover ransom payments.

   • *Directors and officers.* Provides liability coverage to corporate managers for actions taken while acting as an officer or director of the corporation.

- *General liability.* Covers claims involving accidents on company premises, as well as by its products, services, agents, or contractors. An umbrella policy usually applies to liability insurance and provides extra coverage after the primary coverage is exhausted. An umbrella policy has few exclusions.

- *Group life, health, and disability.* There are several types of life insurance, *split-dollar life insurance* covers an employee, and its cost is split between the company and the employee, *key person insurance* covers the financial loss to the company in case an employee dies, and a *cross-purchase plan* allows the co-owners of a business to buy out the share of an owner who dies. *Health insurance* typically covers the areas of hospital, medical, surgical, and dental expenses. Disability insurance provides income to an individual who cannot work due to an injury or illness. The disability insurance category is subdivided into *short-term disability* (payments made while someone is recovering his or her health following an injury or illness) and *long-term disability* (continuing payments with no anticipation of a return to work).

- *Inland marine.* Covers company property that is being transported. Examples of covered items include trade show displays and finished goods being shipped.

- *Ocean marine and air cargo.* Covers the transporting vehicle (including loss of income due to loss of the vehicle), liability claims against the vehicle's owner or operator, and the cargo.

- *Workers' compensation.* Provides medical and disability coverage to workers who are injured while performing duties related to their jobs. The insurance is mandatory, the employer pays all costs, and no legal recourse is permitted against the employer. There are wide variations in each state's coverage of workers' compensation, including levels of compensation, types of occupations that are not considered, and the allowability of negligence lawsuits.

These steps allow a risk manager to determine the types and potential severity of a company's risks, as well as how to reduce those risks, either through internal changes or by purchasing various types of insurance coverage.

33-5 TYPES OF INSURANCE COMPANIES

There are several types of insurance companies. Each one may serve a company's insurance needs very well, but there are significant differences between them that a company should be aware of before purchasing an insurance contract. The types of insurance companies include:

- *Captive insurance company.* This is a stock insurance company that is formed to underwrite the risks of its parent company or in some cases a sponsoring group or association.

- *Lloyds of London.* This is an underwriter operating under the special authority of the English Parliament. It may write insurance coverage of a nature that other insurance companies will not underwrite, usually because of high risks or special needs not covered by a standard insurance form. It also provides the usual types of insurance coverage.

- *Mutual.* This is a company in which each policyholder is an owner, and where earnings are distributed as dividends. If a net loss results, policyholders may be subject to extra assessments. In most cases, however, nonassessable policies are issued.

- *Reciprocal organization.* This is an association of insured companies that is independently operated by a manager. Advance deposits are made, against which are charged the proportionate costs of operations.

- *Stock company.* This is an insurance company that behaves like a normal corporation—earnings not retained in the business are distributed to shareholders as dividends and not to policyholders.

Another way to categorize insurance companies is by the type of service offered. For example, a *monoline* company provides only one type of insurance coverage, while a *multiple line* company provides more than one kind of insurance. A *financial services company* provides not only insurance but also financial services to customers.

A company can also use *self-insurance* when it deliberately plans to cover losses from its own resources rather than through those of an insurer. It can be appropriate in any of the following cases:

- When the administrative loss of using an insurer exceeds the amount of the loss.

- When a company has sufficient excess resources available to cover even the largest claim.

- When excessive premium payments are the only alternative.

- When insurance is not available at any price.

A form of partial self-insurance is to use large deductibles on insurance policies, so that a company pays for all but the very largest claims. Finally, a company can create a *captive insurer* that provides insurance to the parent company. Captive insurers can provide coverage that is tailored to the parent organization, and can provide less dependence on the vagaries of the commercial insurance market. A variation on the captive insurer concept is a *fronting program,* in which a parent company buys insurance from an independent insurance company, which then reinsures the exposure with a captive of the parent company. This technique is used to avoid licensing the captive insurer in every state where the parent company does business, though the captive insurer must still be authorized to accept reinsurance. Fronting also allows the parent company to obtain local service from the independent insurance company while shifting the exposure to the captive company. No matter what form the self-insurance may take, the risk manager should work with the controller to determine the amount of loss reserves to set aside to pay for claims as they arise.

In some states, a company can become a self-insurer for workers' compensation. To do this, a company must qualify under state law as a self-insurer, purchase umbrella coverage to guard against catastrophic claims, post a surety bond, and create a claims administration department to handle claims. The advantages of doing this are lower costs (by eliminating the insurer's profit) and better cash flow (because there are no up-front insurance payments). The disadvantages of this approach are extra administrative costs as well as the cost of qualifying the company in each state in which the company operates.

These are some of the variations that a company can consider when purchasing insurance, either through a third party or a controlled subsidiary, or by providing its own coverage.

33-6 CLAIMS ADMINISTRATION

Some insurance companies take an extremely long time to respond to claims, and may reject them if they are not reported in a specific format. To avoid these problems, thereby receiving the full amount of claims as quickly as possible, the risk manager must implement a strict claims administration process, as described in this section.

The risk manager should assemble a summary of information to review whenever a claim is filed. By having this information in one place, the risk manager avoids missing any steps that might interfere with the prompt settlement of a claim. The summary should include:

- *Instructions for itemizing damaged items.* Be sure to compile a complete list of all damaged items, including their inventory values, estimates, appraisals, and replacement costs. This assists the claims adjusters in determining the price they will pay to compensate for any claims.

- *Claims representatives.* There should be a list of the names, addresses, and phone numbers of the claims adjusters who handle each line of insurance. This usually requires a fair amount of updating, since there may be a number of changes to this information every year, especially if a company uses a large number of insurance companies for its various types of risk coverage.

- *Key internal personnel.* Company policy may require that the risk manager notify internal personnel if claims have been filed or payments received on those claims. For example, the accountant may want to know if payment for a large claim has been received, so that an entry can be made in the accounting records.

- *Underlying problems.* The risk manager should have a standard group of follow-up steps to review whenever a claim occurs, so that there is a clear understanding of why a claim occurred, as well as how the underlying problem that caused the claim can be avoided in the future. Without these instructions, it is possible that a company will repeat the problem over and over again, resulting in many claims and a vastly increased insurance premium.

- *Instructions for safeguarding damaged items.* If material has been damaged, it is the responsibility of the company to ensure that it is not damaged further, which would result in a larger claim. For example, a company must protect the materials in a warehouse from further damage as soon as it discovers that the roof has leaked and destroyed some items. If it does not take this action, the insurer can rightly claim that it will only pay for the damage that occurred up to the point when the company could have taken corrective action.

The above information is necessary for the filing of every insurance claim. In addition, there are two steps related to claims administration that the risk manager should attend to on an ongoing basis:

1. *Accounting techniques.* The risk manager should work with the accountant to develop a standard set of accounting entries that are used for insurance claims as well as to summarize the cost of risk management. These relate to accumulating cost information for each claim, so that the risk manager can easily summarize the appropriate information related to each claim and use it to file for reimbursement. This information should include the costs of claims preparation, security and property protection, cleanup, repair costs, property identification, and storage costs.

2. *Audit program.* No matter how good the procedures may be for the claims administration process, it is common for the claims administration staff to forget or sidestep some procedures. This is especially common when there is frequent employee turnover in this area, with poor training of the replacement staff. To identify procedural problems, it is useful to conduct a periodic review of the claims administration process. To ensure consistency in this audit, there should be a standard audit program that forms the minimum set of audit instructions (to be expanded upon as needed) for use in conducting each audit.

It can be cost effective to have some claims administered by outside service companies, quite often by the insurance carrier itself. Usually high-volume, low-cost-per-unit items such as medical claims are in this category. When outside services are used, the accountant must establish with the provider the controls to be followed and the reports to be prepared. Periodic audits of the outside claims processing operation should be made by the company to ensure that claims are being handled in a controlled and effective manner.

33-7 INSURANCE FILES

Insurance record keeping is vital to ascertain that adequate insurance coverage has been obtained and is being administered properly. The primary risks that this record keeping avoids are inadvertently dropping insurance through lack of renewal and having inadequate insurance given a company's actual claims record. The layout of insurance records described in this section helps a company to avoid these problems.

There are several main categories of insurance records. The first section identifies each policy. The next section is a tickler file that lists key due dates for each policy. This is useful for ensuring that all policy payments are made on time, so that they do not lapse. The next section is the activity file, which describes the claim history and open claims for each policy. Finally, there is the value file, which itemizes the insurable values covered by each policy. The activity and value files are needed to determine the size of claims or the value being covered, so the risk manager can see if each policy provides a sufficient amount of coverage. When properly maintained, these files give the risk manager a basis for sound management of his or her function. The contents of each type of file are:

- *Identification file.* Lists key information on each policy:
  - Abstract of coverage, showing exclusions
  - Broker
  - Effective dates

- Insurer
- Policy number
- Rates, premiums, and refunds
- Type of insurance coverage

- *Tickler file.* Lists key dates for each policy:
  - Inspection dates
  - Policy expiration date
  - Premium payment dates
  - Reporting dates

- *Activity file.* Describes the claim history and open claims for each policy:
  - Historical comparison of premiums to losses
  - History file on closed claims
  - Reserves established
  - Status of each claim
  - Support and documentation of each claim

- *Value file.* Itemizes the insurable values covered by each policy:
  - Detail of actual cash value of each item covered by a policy
  - Detail of replacement cost of each item covered by a policy
  - Summary of insurable values listed on each policy

33-8 ANNUAL RISK MANAGEMENT REPORT

The risk manager should issue a risk management report to the Board of Directors every year. This document reviews all perceived risks to which a company is subject, and then describes the steps taken to mitigate those risks. It is of great value to the Board, because it needs to know the extent of potential risks and how they can impact company operations. Unfortunately, not many controllers or chief financial officers are aware of what should go into the annual risk management report. This presents a problem if the Board asks either of these managers, to whom the risk manager usually reports, about the contents of this document. To avoid this problem, the contents of a typical risk management report are described in this section, including an example based on an organization that provides training in high-risk outdoor activities.

The risk management report contains four sections. The first is an overview that describes the contents of the report, the timing of when it is issued, and to whom it is delivered. The second section itemizes all risks that are perceived to be significant. If every possible risk were to be listed, the document might be too voluminous for easy reading. These risks should be grouped with subheadings, rather than appearing as an enormous list that is difficult for the reader to digest. The third section notes the ways to cover those risks, excluding insurance (which is addressed in the fourth section). These are operational changes such as altered procedures or processes, or additional training. Finally, the fourth section notes the insurance that has been purchased to provide additional coverage to those risk areas that cannot be adequately covered by internal changes. These four sections give the Board an adequate knowledge of a company's efforts in the risk management area.

The example in Exhibit 33-2 presents an extract from the risk management report of an organization that provides outdoor training classes. The example skips the overview section and proceeds straight to the enumeration of risks, how they are covered, and what types of insurance are also needed. This is a good example of the format that an accountant should look for in a risk management report.

Exhibit 33-2   Example of a Risk Management Report

Section II: Review of Risks

- *Risk related to education:*

    1. Risk of school equipment failing

    2. Risk of accidents due to improper instruction

Section III: Ways to Cover Risks

- *Risk of school equipment failing.* School equipment is reviewed and replaced by the school governing committees on a regular basis. Instructors are also authorized to immediately remove equipment from use if they spot unusual damage that may result in equipment failure.

- *Risk of accidents due to improper supervision.* School instructors must first serve as assistant instructors under the supervision of a more experienced instructor, who evaluates their skills and recommends advancement to full instructor status. The typical instructor has previously completed all prerequisite courses, and has considerable outdoor experience. All instructors must have taken a mountain-oriented first aid class within the last year.

Section IV: Supplemental Insurance Coverage

- *Risk of school equipment failing.* The general liability policy covers this risk for the first $500,000 of payments to a claimant. The umbrella policy covers this risk for an additional $5 million after the coverage provided by the general liability policy is exhausted.

- *Risk of accidents due to improper instruction.* Same insurance coverage as for the risk of school equipment failing.

33-9 SUMMARY

In a larger company, there is usually a risk manager who identifies and finds ways to mitigate risk, either through internal changes or by purchasing insurance. Because this manager frequently reports to either the controller or CFO, it is important for these people to have an overall knowledge of how risk management works. This chapter answered the need by describing the policies and procedures used by a risk manager, and that person's job description. The types of insurance companies, the paperwork handled by the risk manager, and the annual risk management report were also described.

Part Seven

OTHER ACCOUNTING TOPICS

CHAPTER 34

Mergers and Acquisitions

34-1 INTRODUCTION

The chief interest that an accountant has in his or her company's merger and acquisition activities is how to account for the transactions. The chief method used is the purchase method, which is described in the next section. An alternative is the pooling of interests method, which is also described in this section; however, the FASB is continually reviewing the need for this method, and was close to eliminating it as of the publication date of this book. Nonetheless, the highly restrictive rules under which it is allowed, and the basic transactions required to record it are included here.

There are also many situations in which a company merely makes a small investment in another company, rather than making an outright purchase. This requires three possible types of accounting, depending upon the size of the investment and the degree of control attained over the subject company—all three methods, which are the cost, equity, and consolidation methods, are described here.

We also delve into special topics associated with mergers and acquisitions, including contingent payments, push down accounting, leveraged buyouts, spin-off and inter-company transactions, and the proper treatment of goodwill.

When reading this text, one should keep in mind that the terms "merger" and "acquisition" are not the same thing. An *acquisition* is a transaction in which both the acquiring and acquired company are still left standing as separate entities at the end of the transaction. A *merger* results in the legal dissolution of one of the companies, and a *consolidation* dissolves both of the parties and creates a new one, into which the previous entities are merged.

34-2 THE PURCHASE METHOD

In brief, this approach to accounting for a business combination assumes that the acquiring company spreads the acquisition price over the assets being bought at their fair market value, with any remaining portion of the acquisition price being recorded in a goodwill account. The company being purchased can be bought with any form of consideration, such as stock, cash, or property.

There are three primary steps involved in accounting for a purchase transaction. The first is to determine the purchase price, the second is to allocate this price among the various assets of the company being purchased, and the third is to account for the first-year partial results of the purchased entity on the buyer's financial statements. The issue with the first step is that the purchase price is based on the fair market value of the consideration given to the seller. For example, if the purchase is made with stock, the stock must be valued at its fair market value. If treasury stock is used as part of the consideration, then this must also be valued at its fair market value. If the buyer's stock is thinly traded or closely held, then it may be necessary to obtain the services of an investment banker or appraiser, who can use various valuation models and industry surveys to derive a price per share.

The second step in the purchase method is to allocate the purchase price among the acquired company's assets and liabilities, which are then recorded in the buyer's accounting records. The method of valuation varies by line item on the acquired company's balance sheet. Here are the key valuation rules:

- *Accounts receivable.* Record this asset at its present value, less the allowance for bad debts. Given the exceedingly short time frame over which this asset is outstanding, there is generally no need to discount this valuation, unless there are receivables with very long collection terms. Also, since the acquisition transaction is generally not completed until several months after the acquisition date (given the effort required to make the accounting entry), the amount of the allowance for bad debts can be very precisely determined as of the acquisition date.

- *Marketable securities.* These assets should be recorded at their fair market value. This is an opportunity for the buyer to mark up a security to its fair market value (if such is the case), since GAAP normally only allows for the recognition of reductions in market value. For this reason, this is an area in which there is some opportunity to allocate an additional portion of the purchase price beyond the original cost of the asset. However, since most companies only invest in short-term, highly liquid securities, it is unlikely that there will be a large amount of potential appreciation in the securities.

- *Inventory—raw materials.* These assets should be recorded at their replacement cost. This can be a problem if the acquiree is in an industry, such as computer hardware, where inventory costs drop at a rapid pace as new products rapidly come into the marketplace. Consequently, the buyer may find itself with a significantly lower inventory valuation as a result of the purchase transaction than originally appeared on the accounting records of the acquiree.

- *Inventory—finished goods.* These assets should be recorded at their selling prices, less their average profit margin and disposition costs. This can be a difficult calculation to make if the finished goods have variable prices depending upon where or in what quantities they are sold; in such cases, the determination of selling price should be based on a history of the most common sales transactions. For example, if 80% of all units sold are in purchase quantities that result in a per-unit price of $1.50, then this is the most appropriate price to use. This rule can be avoided, however, if the acquiree has firm sales contracts as of the date of the acquisition with specific customers that can be used to clearly determine the prices at which the finished goods will actually be sold.

If the acquirer had been using a last-in, first out (LIFO) inventory valuation system, then the newly derived valuation for the finished goods inventory shall be used as the LIFO base layer for all inventory obtained through the purchase transaction.

- *Inventory—work-in-process.* These assets receive the same valuation treatment as finished goods, except that the cost of conversion into finished goods must also be subtracted from their eventual sale price.

- *Property, plant, and equipment (PP&E).* These assets should be recorded at their replacement cost. This can be a difficult task that lengthens the interval before the acquisition journal entry is completed, because some assets may be so old that there is no equivalent product currently on the market, or equipment may be so specialized that it is difficult to find a reasonable alternative on the market. This valuation step frequently calls for the services of an appraiser.

- *Property, plant, and equipment (PP&E) to be sold.* If the buyer intends to sell off assets as of the acquisition date, then these assets should be recorded at their fair market value. This most accurately reflects their disposal value as of the acquisition date.

- *Capital leases.* If the acquiree possesses assets that were purchased with capital leases, then the accountant should value the asset at its fair market value, while valuing the associated lease at its net present value.

- *Research and development (R&D) assets.* If any assets associated with specific R&D projects are part of the acquiree, the accountant should charge these assets off to expense if there is no expectation that they will have an alternative future use once the current R&D project has been completed. The precise allocation of assets to expense or asset accounts can be difficult, since the existing projects may be expected to last well into the future, or the future use of the assets may not be easy to determine. Consequently, one should carefully document the reasons for the treatment of R&D assets.

- *Intangible assets.* These assets are to be recorded at their appraised values. If the buyer cannot reasonably assign a cost to them or identify them, then no cost should be assigned.

- *Accounts and notes payable.* Accounts payable can typically be recorded at their current amounts as listed on the books of the acquiree. However, if the accounts payable are not to be paid for some time, then they should be recorded at their discounted present values. The same logic applies to notes payable; since all but the shortest-lived notes will have a significantly different present value, they should be discounted and recorded as such. This treatment is used on the assumption that the buyer would otherwise be purchasing these liabilities on the date of the acquisition, not on a variety of dates stretching out into the future, and so must be discounted to show their value on the acquisition date.

- *Accruals.* These liabilities are typically very short-term ones that will be reversed shortly after the current accounting period. Accordingly, they are to be valued at their present value; discounting is rarely necessary.

- *Pension liability.* If there is an unfunded pension liability, even if not recognized on the books of the acquiree, it must be recognized by the buyer as part of the purchase transaction.

- *Stock option plan.* If the buyer decides to take over an existing stock option plan of the acquiree, then it must allocate part of the purchase price to the incremental difference between the price at which shares may be purchased under the plan and the market price for the stock as of the date of the acquisition. However, if the buyer forced the acquiree to settle all claims under the option plan prior to the acquisition, then this becomes a compensation expense that is recorded on the books of the acquiree.

If the acquiring company (Charleston Corporation) buys the acquiree's (Denton Corporation) stock with $500,000 of cash, the entry on Charleston's books would be:

	Debit	*Credit*
Investment in Denton Corporation	$500,000	
Cash		$500,000

Alternatively, if Charleston were to make the purchase using a mix of 20% cash and 80% for a note, the entry would be:

	Debit	*Credit*
Investment in Denton Corporation	$500,000	
Cash		$100,000
Note payable		400,000

Another approach would be to exchange 5,000 shares of Charleston's $1 par value stock for that of Denton as a form of payment. Under this method, the entry would be:

	Debit	*Credit*
Investment in Denton Corporation	$500,000	
Common stock—par value		$ 5,000
Common stock—additional paid-in capital		495,000

The result of all the preceding valuation rules is shown in Exhibit 34-1, where we show the calculation that would be required to adjust the books of an acquiree in order to then consolidate it with the results of the acquiring company. The exhibit shows the initial book cost of each account on the acquiree's balance sheet, followed by a listing of the required valuation of each account under the purchase method, the adjustment required, and the new account valuation. The new account valuation on the right side of the table can then be combined directly into the records of the acquiring company. Under the "Purchase Method Valuation" column, a designation of "NPV" means that the net present value of the line item is shown, a designation of "FMV" means that the fair market value is shown (less any costs required to sell the item, if applicable), "RC" designates the use of replacement cost, "SLM" designates the use of sale price less the gross margin, and "AV" designates an asset's appraised value.

In the exhibit, debits and credits are specified for each adjusting entry listed in the "Required Adjustment" column. The amount of goodwill shown in the "Required Adjustment" column is derived by subtracting the purchase price of $15,000 from the total of

Exhibit 34-1   Adjustments to the Acquiree's Books for a Purchase Consolidation

Account	Acquiree Records	Purchase Method Valuation	Required Adjustment	Adjusted Acquiree Records
Assets				
Cash	$ 1,413	$ 1,413	$ 0	$1,413
Receivables	4,000	4,000	0	4,000
Receivables, long term	1,072	(NPV) 808	(CR) 264	808
Marketable securities	503	(FMV) 490	(CR) 13	490
Inventory—raw materials	921	(RC) 918	(CR) 3	918
Inventory—WIP	395	(SLM) 429	(DB) 34	429
Inventory—finished goods	871	(SLM) 950	(DB) 79	950
Property, plant, & equipment	6,005	(RC) 7,495	(DB) 1,490	7,495
Equipment for sale	803	(FMV) 745	(CR) 58	745
Capital lease assets	462	(FMV) 500	(DB) 38	500
Goodwill	0	0	(DB) 4,677	4,677
Investment in acquiree	0	0	(CR) 14,600	−15,000
Intangibles	593	(AV) 650	(DB) 57	650
Total assets	$17,038	$18,398	(CR) $8,563	$8,075
Liabilities				
Accounts payable	$ 3,992	$ 3,992	$ 0	$3,992
Notes payable, long term	3,300	(NPV) 2,950	(DB) 350	2,950
Accrued liabilities	325	325	0	325
Capital lease liabilities	450	(NPV) 400	(DB) 50	400
Pension liability	408	408	0	408
Total liabilities	$ 8,475	$ 8,075	(DB) $ 400	$8,075
Shareholder's Equity				
Common Stock	4,586	—	(DB) 4,586	$0
Paid-in capital	100	—	(DB) 100	0
Retained earnings	3,877	—	(DB) 3,877	0
Total equity	$ 8,563	—	(DB) $8,563	$0
Total liabilities & equity	$17,038	—	(DB) $8,963	$8,075

all fair market and other valuations shown in the "Purchase Method Valuation" column. In this case, we have a fair market valuation of $18,398 for all assets, less a fair market valuation of $8,075 for all liabilities, which yields a net fair market value for the acquiree of $10,323. When this fair market value is subtracted from the purchase price of $15,000, we end up with a residual of $4,677, which is listed in the goodwill account. Please note that the "Adjusted Acquiree Records" column on the right side of the exhibit still must be added to the acquirer's records to arrive at a consolidated financial statement for the combined entities.

The third step in the acquisition process is to account for the first year partial results of the acquired company on its books. Only the income of the acquiree that falls within its current fiscal year, but after the date of the acquisition, should be added to the buyer's accounting records. In addition, the buyer must charge all costs associated with the acquisition to current expense—they *cannot* be capitalized. These acquisition costs should be almost entirely for outside services, since any internal costs charged to the acquisition would likely have been incurred anyway, even in the absence of the acquisition. The only variation from this rule is the costs associated with issuing equity to pay for the acquisition; these costs can be recorded as an offset to the additional paid-in capital account. An additional item is that a liability should be recognized at the time of the acquisition for any plant closings or losses on the dispositions of assets that are planned as of that date; this is not an expense that is recognized at a later date, since we assume that the buyer was aware at the purchase date that some asset dispositions would be required.

If the acquirer chooses to report its financial results for multiple years prior to the acquisition, it does *not* report the combined results of the two entities for years prior to the acquisition.

A *reverse acquisition* is one in which the company issuing its shares or other payment is actually the acquiree, because the acquiring company's shareholders do not own a majority of the stock after the acquisition is completed. Though rare, this approach is sometimes used when a shell company with available funding buys an operating company, or when a publicly held shell company is used to buy a non-public company, thereby avoiding the need to go through an initial public offering (IPO) by the non-public company. In this case, the assets and liabilities of the shell corporation are revalued to their fair market value and then recorded on the books of the company being bought.

34-3 THE POOLING OF INTERESTS METHOD

In brief, this approach to accounting for a business combination assumes that neither party to the combination is really purchasing the other, and that they are instead merely combining operations; based on this assumption, the accounting records of the two entities are essentially merged, or pooled. From a practical perspective, this usually means that the buying company's legal entity survives the merger, while the acquiree's legal entity is dissolved. It is also possible to dissolve both entities and merge them into a new one.

Under a pooling arrangement, the buying company exchanges its shares for the shares of the acquiree in some proportion that reflects the selling price of the acquiree. For example, if the acquiree is being sold at a price of $30.00 per share, and the shares of the buyer have a market price of $10.00, then shareholders of the acquiree will exchange one of their shares for three shares in the buying company.

There are two primary reasons why companies use the pooling of interests method whenever possible. One is that no goodwill is created as a result of the transaction. Goodwill must be written off over time, and so creates a drag on reported earnings for many years into the future. The other reason is that it is generally a tax-free combination. When the acquiree's shareholders accept shares, instead of cash, for their ownership interests in the acquiree, they have simply exchanged their basis in the acquiree's stock for a basis in the buyer's stock. Thus, they have not realized a gain or loss on the transaction that would be subject to taxation.

However, companies must carefully structure merger transactions in order to ensure that they will be acceptable under GAAP. The following rules must be met in order to use the pooling method; they are largely based on the principles of ensuring the independence of the merging parties prior to the transaction, and of an equitable merging of ownership interests among the various shareholders.

- *Complete purchase.* The acquiring company must issue common voting stock for at least 90% of the acquiree's voting common stock. This rule is based on the underlying assumption that the two parties to a merger are completely consolidating their operations, rather than allowing for the intrusion of minority interests. It is also not allowable to have an *accidental pooling,* such as would arise when a variety of compensation forms are offered for the shares of one company, and everyone happens to take common stock—in this case, the intent was not to have a pooling of interests, and so it must be accounted for as a purchase instead. However, if the acquiring company is also buying convertible securities of the acquiree, these may be acquired for some form of consideration besides stock, on the grounds that they do not represent an ownership interest, which is the primary target of the rule.

- *Equivalent shares.* The shares issued to the shareholders of the acquiree must have exactly the same rights as those of the same type of stock held by shareholders of the acquiring company, on the theory that there is to be an equitable merging of interests between the two groups of shareholders, which can only be accomplished with the use of shares with equivalent rights. If the rights associated with the issued shares are actually better than those they are replacing, the pooling method can still be used. If there are several classes of common stock at the acquiring company against which the shares of the acquired company can be matched, the key issue is that they match the rights of those shares that represent the controlling interest in the acquiring company. The shares issued to the shareholders of the acquiree can also be designated as a different class of stock, as long as their rights are equivalent to the controlling shares of the acquirer.

- *Equivalent ownership rights.* Each shareholder shall possess the same ownership proportion of the combined entity as was the case before the transaction occurred.

- *Equivalent voting rights.* There shall be no reduction in the equivalent voting rights of any shareholders as a result of the merger transaction.

- *Independence.* Both parties to the merger have not been subsidiaries of any other companies for at least the preceding two years. In addition, they must be independent of each other at the time of merger (as defined by having no more than 10% of each other's stock). This rule prevents a larger company from spinning off a subsidiary through a merger with another company, and avoiding tax liabilities from the resulting transaction. This rule is waived for companies that have not yet been in existence for two years at the time of the merger, as well as for companies that are required by government order to divest a subsidiary, with no other alternative than to divest.

- *No beneficial arrangements.* There cannot be a preferential payment or issuance of additional shares to any shareholders involved in the transaction, since this would not represent an equitable return to all shareholders. It is also not allowable to have an agreement with selected shareholders to buy back their stock, since this might involve a preferential and guaranteed return to them.

- *No carry-over provisions.* The merger agreement cannot contain any provisions that cannot be settled within one year of the merger date. The reason for this rule is that some shareholders may attempt to gain preferential treatment through the use of side agreements that give them extra consideration for their shares at a time much later than the effective merger date.

- *No changes in equity interests near the merger date.* Neither party to a merger can alter the amount of voting common stock held by its shareholders either in expectation of the merger, or within two years thereafter. This applies in particular to unusual stock distributions that would increase the ownership interests of specific shareholders, and which may be distributed in any form—such as stock, options, or warrants. This is not a problem if some employees or outside service providers have consulting or compensation agreements that pay them in stock, as long as the amounts paid do not appear to be disproportionately large; this can be evaluated in terms of previous payments to the same individuals, or to payments made to others who have performed similar services.

  If either participant in the merger has an existing option plan at the time of the merger, and chooses to issue options under its terms within two years of the merger, then this is assumed to be a change in equity interests, unless the management team can prove that the grants are reasonable, either in relation to a history of grants within the company, or in comparison to plans used by other companies. The same issue applies if a new option plan is created within two years of the merger date. If the terms of an existing option plan are altered, so that vesting or option exercise dates are accelerated, then this is assumed to be a change in equity interests.

  A change in the type of legal entity used by the merged entity at any point within two years of the merger date does not create a problem with this rule, as long as the equity interests of the shareholders are not altered as a result of the change in entity.

  A company may have a standstill agreement with one or more of its shareholders, under the terms of which they agree not to acquire additional shares of the company for a specified period of time. Such an agreement is not construed as impacting the change in equity interests rule unless the agreement is created as part of the merger transaction, and is concluded with a shareholder who controls at least 10% of the company's stock.

  If the merged entity issues a stock split or dividend at any time, this is not considered to be in conflict with the rule, unless the issuance is only to a restricted group of shareholders. An issuance of new or treasury stock within two years of the merger date is acceptable, as long as the company can present a reasonable business case for needing the resulting funds.

- *No post-merger stock buy-back plans.* The acquiring entity cannot have plans to buy back shares after the merger has been completed, and as part of the merger transaction, since this would effectively give selected shareholders a guaranteed return on their stock after the merger, and to the exclusion of other shareholders whose shares are not bought back by the company.

- *No spin-off provisions.* There can be no expectation of selling off company assets or divisions after the merger has been completed, with the exception of sales required to eliminate either duplicate assets or excess capacity. It is also allowable to have a spin-off if this is required by government mandate, as would be the case if the government will only allow a merger to occur if certain divisions are spun off that might otherwise result in a monopoly situation.

- *Previous ownership.* Neither party to the transaction can own more than 10% of each other's stock as of the date of the merger. This rule is used to ensure that mergers only take place between truly independent companies, rather than between closely-linked entities that may only be performing a merger in order to avoid taxes.

- *Rapid consummation.* The merger transaction must be completed in no more than one year, though this rule does not apply if the two entities are waiting for regulatory or legal approval (since they have no control over the time period that may be required). The reason for this rule is to ensure that no additional payments of any type are made to subsets of the shareholder group at some later date, thereby giving them a preferential return as part of the merger (albeit at a later date).

- *Share acquisition.* Neither the acquirer nor the acquiree shall acquire more than a normal number of their own shares, from the date when the merger talks begin and until the merger deal is finalized. An acceptable arrangement would be one where an ongoing and pre-announced share repurchase deal continues to buy a pre-set number of shares. An unacceptable arrangement would be one in which the company agrees to buy back shares from a shareholder at a preferential price that exceeds the return that the shareholder could expect to attain through the merger transaction.

If two companies can meet all of the restrictions and complete a merger, they still have some accounting rules to consider when accounting for the transaction. First, the purchase price of the merger is to be based on the fair market value of the stock issued by the acquirer on the legal date of the transaction. Second, and varying from the purchase method described earlier, the accountant is required to report the partial-year income of the merged entities *prior to* the date of the merger; this is because we assume that the two companies have simply combined their operations. If the accountant is issuing multi-year historical reports, then the results of both companies should be reported in each of the preceding years.

Another accounting issue is that all legal, registration, proxy solicitation, and consulting costs that are associated with the merger must be expensed at the time of the transaction. This also includes the cost of combining operations, which may include loss reserves for employee terminations, plant closures, and losses on assets sold. If there are gains or losses caused by the sale of assets that are duplicative or resulting from excess capacity, they may be recorded in operating income. However, if there are gains or losses from the sale of assets that are being disposed of for some other reason, then they must be recorded as income from an extraordinary item.

It is quite common to find that either party to a pooling transaction uses different accounting methods, such as one using FIFO inventory valuation and the other using LIFO, or straight-line depreciation at one entity and declining balance at the other. It may be necessary for reporting purposes to change the accounting methods at one of the companies to conform to those of the other. When this occurs, it will not cause a violation of any of the preceding rules, and is therefore allowable under a pooling transaction.

An example of the pooling of interests method when consolidating the results of the two entities for reporting purposes is shown in Exhibit 34-2. In this example, we have used most of the same initial acquiree accounts that were previously described in Exhibit 34-1 for the purchase method of accounting. In addition, we have listed in the "Required Adjustment" column the elimination of the investment in the acquiree by the acquirer, which we assume to be $3,000 (listed as $3,000 in the "Investment in Acquiree" account, as well as $100 in the par value account and $2,900 in the paid-in capital account).

Exhibit 34-2   Adjustments to the Acquiree's Books for a Pooling Consolidation

Account	Acquirer Records	Acquiree Records	Required Adjustment	Merged Records
Assets				
Cash	$ 2,250	$ 1,413		$ 3,663
Receivables	5,632	4,000		9,632
Receivables, long term	0	1,072		1,072
Marketable securities	200	503		703
Inventory—raw materials	450	921		1,371
Inventory—WIP	239	395		634
Inventory—finished goods	621	871		1,492
Property, plant, & equipment	8,000	6,808		14,808
Capital lease assets	0	462		462
Investment in acquiree	3,000	0	−$3,000	0
Intangibles	0	593		593
Total Assets	$20,392	$17,038	−$3,000	$34,430
Liabilities				
Accounts payable	$ 505	$ 3,992		$ 4,497
Notes payable, long term	4,005	3,300		7,305
Accrued liabilities	207	325		532
Capital lease liabilities	0	450		450
Pension liability	375	408		783
Total liabilities	$ 5,092	$ 8,475		$13,567
Shareholder's Equity				
Common stock, par value	1,000	4,586	−$ 100	$ 5,486
Paid-in capital	9,067	100	− 2,900	6,267
Retained earnings	5,233	3,877		9,110
Total equity	$15,300	$ 8,563	−$3,000	$20,863
Total liabilities & equity	$20,392	$17,038	−$3,000	$34,430

34-4 THE COST METHOD

The cost method is used to account for the purchase of another company's stock when the buyer obtains less than 20% of the other company's shares, and when it does not have management control over it. The buyer does not have control if it cannot obtain financial results from the other company that it needs to create entries under the equity method (see next section), or if it fails to obtain representation on the Board of Directors, is forced to relinquish significant shareholder rights, or the concentration of voting power is clearly in evidence among a different group of shareholders.

Under this method, the investing company records the initial investment at cost on its books. It then recognizes as income any dividends distributed by the investee after the investment date.

34-5 THE EQUITY METHOD

The equity method of accounting for an investment in another company is used when the investor owns more than 20% of the investee's stock, or less than 20% but with evidence of some degree of management control over the investee, such as control over some portion of the investee's Board of Directors, involvement in its management activities, or the exchange of management personnel between companies. The method is only used when the investee is a corporation, partnership, or joint venture, and when both organizations remain separate legal entities.

Under the equity method, the acquirer records its initial investment in the investee at cost. For example, if the initial investment in Company ABC were $1,000,000 in exchange for ownership of 40% of its common stock, then the entry on the books of the investor would be:

	Debit	Credit
Investment in Company ABC	$1,000,000	
Cash		$1,000,000

After the initial entry, the investor records its proportional share of the investee's income against current income. For example, if the investee has a gain of $120,000, the investor can recognize its 40% share of this income, which is $48,000. The entry would be:

	Debit	Credit
Investment in Company ABC	$48,000	
Investment income		$48,000

The credit in the last journal entry can more precisely be made to an undistributed investment income account, since the funds from the investee's income have not actually been distributed to the investor.

The investor should also record a deferred income tax expense based on any income attributed to the investee. To continue with the preceding example, if the incremental tax rate for the investor is 38%, then it would record the following entry that is based on its $48,000 of Company ABC's income:

	Debit	Credit
Income tax expense	$18,240	
Deferred taxes		$18,240

If the investee issues dividends, then these are recorded as an offset to the investment account and a debit to cash. Dividends are not recorded as income, since income was already accounted for as a portion of the investee's income, even though it may not have been received. For example, if dividends of $25,000 are received from Company ABC, the entry would be:

	Debit	Credit
Cash	$25,000	
Investment in Company ABC		$25,000

If the market price of the investor's shares in the investee drops below its investment cost, there are not normally any grounds for reducing the amount of the investment. However, if the loss in market value appears to be permanent, then a loss can be recognized and charged against current earnings. Evidence of a permanent loss in market value would be a long-term drop in market value that is substantially below the investment cost, or repeated and substantial reported losses by the investee, with no prospects for an improvement in reported earnings. For example, if the market price of the stock in Company ABC necessitated a downward adjustment in the investor's valuation, the entry would be:

	Debit	Credit
Loss on Investments	$50,000	
Investment in Company ABC		$50,000

If, after making a downward adjustment in its investment, the investor finds that the market price has subsequently increased, it cannot return the carrying amount of the investment to its original level. The new basis for the investment is the amount to which it has been written down. This will increase the size of any gain that is eventually recognized upon sale of the investment.

If the investee experiences an extraordinary gain or loss, the investor should record its proportional share of this amount as well. However, it is recorded separately from the usual investment accounts. For example, if Company ABC were to experience an extraordinary loss of $15,000, the entry would be:

	Debit	Credit
Undistributed Extraordinary Loss	$15,000	
Investment in Company ABC		$15,000

If the investee experiences such large losses that the investor's investment is reduced to zero, the investor should stop recording any transactions related to the investment, in order to avoid recording a negative investment. If the investee eventually records a sufficient amount of income to offset the intervening losses, then the investor can resume use of the equity method in reporting its investment.

If the investor loses control over the investee, then it should switch to the cost method of reporting its investment. When it does this, its cost basis should be the amount in the investment account as of the date of change. However, the same rule does not apply if the investor switches from the cost method to the equity method—in this case, the investor must restate its investment account to reflect the equity method of accounting from the date on which it made its initial investment in the investee.

When reporting the results of its investment in another company under the equity method, the investor should list the investment in a single investment in subsidiary line item on its balance sheet, and in an investment income line item on its income statement.

34-6 THE CONSOLIDATION METHOD

When a company buys more than 50% of the voting stock of another company, but allows it to remain as a separate legal entity, then the financial results of both companies should be combined in a consolidated set of financial statements. However, if the companies are involved in entirely different lines of business, it may still be appropriate to use the equity method; otherwise, the combined results of the two enterprises could lead to misleading financial results. For example, if a software company with 90% gross margins combines with a steel rolling facility whose gross margins are in the 25% range (both being typical margins for their industries), the blended gross margin presents a misleading view of the gross margins of both entities.

Another case in which a 50%+ level of ownership might not result in the use of a consolidation is when the investing company only expects to have temporary control over the acquiree (perhaps because it is reselling the acquiree) or if the buyer does not have control over the acquiree (perhaps because control is exercised through a small amount of restricted voting stock). In either case, the equity method should be used.

When constructing consolidated financial statements, the pre-acquisition results of the acquiree should be excluded from the financial statements. If there is a year of divestiture, the financial results of the acquiree in that year should only be consolidated up until the date of divestiture.

34-7 INTER-COMPANY TRANSACTIONS

When the acquirer elects to report consolidated financial information, it must first eliminate all inter-company transactions. By doing so, it eliminates any transactions that represent the transfer of assets and liabilities between what are now essentially different parts of the same company. The transactions that should be eliminated are:

- *Inter-company sales, accounts receivable and payable.* The most common inter-company transaction is the account receivable or payable associated with the transfer of goods between divisions of the parent company. From the perspective of someone outside the consolidated company, these accounting transactions have not really occurred, since the associated goods or services are merely being moved around within the company, and are not caused by a business transaction with an outside entity. Accordingly, for consolidation purposes, all inter-company accounts receivable, accounts payable, and sales are eliminated.

- *Inter-company bad debts.* A bad debt from another division of the same company cannot be recognized, since the associated sale and account receivable transaction must also be eliminated as part of the consolidation process. In short, if the sale never occurred, then there cannot be a bad debt associated with it.

- *Inter-company dividend payments.* This is merely a transfer of cash between different divisions of the corporate parent, and so should be invisible on the consolidated statement.

- *Inter-company loans and any associated discounts, premiums, and interest payments.* Though there are good reasons for using inter-company loans, such as the provision of funds to risky subsidiaries that might not be able to obtain funds by other means, this is still just a transfer of money within the company, as was the case for inter-company dividend payments. Thus, it must be removed from the consolidated financial statements.

- *Inter-company rent payments.* This is a form of inter-company payable, and so is not allowed.

- *Fixed asset sale transactions.* When fixed assets are sold from one subsidiary to another, the selling company will eliminate the associated accumulated depreciation from its books, as well as recognize a gain or loss on the transaction. These entries must be reversed, since the fixed asset has not left the consolidated organization.

- *Inter-company profits.* A common issue for vertically integrated companies is that multiple subsidiaries recognize profits on component parts that are shipped to other subsidiaries for further work. On a consolidated basis, all of these inter-company profits must be eliminated, since the only profit gained from the consolidated perspective is when the completed product is finally sold by the last subsidiary in the production process to an outside entity.

- *Inter-company investments.* The corporate parent's investment in any subsidiaries is removed from the consolidation. For example, if a corporate parent created a subsidiary and invested a certain amount of equity in it, this investment would appear on the books of both the parent (as an investment) and the subsidiary (as equity). In a consolidation, both entries are removed.

All inter-company eliminations are recorded on a separate consolidation worksheet. They are not recorded on the books of any of the subsidiaries, or of the parent company. In essence, these transactions are invisible to all but the accountant who is responsible for the consolidation reporting.

34-8 CONTINGENT PAYMENTS

A contingent payment is one that is made subsequent to the conclusion of a merger or acquisition, where the buying party may be obligated to make additional payments to the selling party, based on future events. For example, if the sold company produces profits that meet a certain benchmark, then the buyer must pay the seller an additional amount.

These types of transactions cause problems for the accountant, because they cannot be firmly determined as of the date on which the merger or acquisition occurs. Accordingly, one should only record the firm price associated with the transaction at the time of purchase. The accountant can recognize the payments associated with any contingencies as soon as they appear to be highly likely. When this entry is made, the accountant should use the current risk-free interest rate to discount the expected contingent payment down to its net present value, and record this reduced amount as the payment amount.

Since there may be a potentially large contingent payment hanging over the buying company, it is important to mention its existence in the footnotes attached to the buying company's financial statements, so that readers will at least be aware of the potential need to make additional payments.

The buying company may guarantee to the selling company a minimum price for the stock that it gives to the seller as part of the initial sale transaction. If the price does drop below this point, the buyer will hand over additional shares of stock to make up the difference. In this case, the contingent payment can be easily calculated by the accountant, simply by comparing the stock's market price to the minimum required price. Accordingly, this difference can be incrementally accrued in each accounting period up until the date on which the additional payment of stock must be made, rather than waiting until the payment date to record any additional liability. Also, if the payment is made in stock, then the accountant should record its full value as a liability, rather than its discounted value.

The offsetting account to which contingent payments should be charged is the goodwill account. Any additions to this account should be amortized over the same period as the original goodwill that was created as part of the same purchase transaction. However, if there is reasonable evidence that the contingent payment will only be made if specific employees are required to continue working for the company, then it can be reasonably construed to actually be a compensation expense; if so, a compensation expense should be recognized in the current period for the full amount of the contingent payment, instead of recording an increase in the goodwill account.

34-9 PUSH-DOWN ACCOUNTING

Push-down accounting is the inclusion of acquisition accounting adjustments in the books of the acquired company. These may be recorded separately in a worksheet that is used to create financial statements, or directly in the accounting records of the acquiree. The use of worksheet adjustments, rather than direct changes to the acquiree's accounting records, is preferable when the historical records are needed either for tax reporting purposes or to determine the amount of a minority interest share in the acquiree.

When push-down accounting is used, the acquiree can alter the valuation of all of its assets and liabilities to reflect those made by its corporate parent as part of the purchase method of accounting used to account for the consolidation. This will also result in a change in depreciation expense to reflect any changed fixed asset valuations (and possible changes in the expected useful lives of some assets). There may also be goodwill amortization to reflect the gradual reduction of a goodwill asset recognized as part of the purchase transaction.

There are several objections to push-down accounting. One is that it eliminates the use of the historical basis of accounting for transactions, which is one of the foundations of accounting theory. Another problem is that, in cases where an acquirer gradually buys an acquiree through a series of stock purchases, the use of push down accounting would result in a series of revaluations that would create multiple changes in the financial statements of the acquiree. Given that the AICPA has not given authoritative guidance on this issue, *privately* held companies may use it or not, as they so choose.

Push-down accounting is strongly favored by the SEC for *publicly* held companies that have concluded acquisitions under the purchase method of accounting that result in wholly-owned subsidiaries. The SEC requires that the subsidiary also include in its financial statements the cost of any debt used by the acquirer to purchase it if the acquiree guarantees the debt or plans a debt or equity offering to retire the existing debt, or if there are plans for the subsidiary to assume the debt.

If there are minority interests in the acquiree or if there is outstanding public debt or preferred stock issued by the subsidiary, then the SEC does not insist on the use of push-down accounting.

34-10 LEVERAGED BUYOUTS

A leveraged buyout occurs when funding, which is largely based on debt that is secured by the assets of the acquiree, is used to buy the acquiree. In such cases, it is useful to form a holding company, which buys the stock of the acquiree and becomes its corporate parent. A holding company is particularly useful if the acquiree is publicly held, since it can become the repository for any shares tendered by shareholders of the acquiree in the event of a tender offer.

The acquiree's management team is frequently part of the leveraged buyout, either because it has initiated the buyout itself, or because the investors buying the acquiree realize the importance of keeping the management team in place, and offer it either shares or stock options as an incentive to stay. If the management team already owns stock in the acquiree, it can avoid taxes by exchanging this stock for the stock of the holding company that is conducting the buyout.

Of particular concern to whoever is initiating a leveraged buyout is the type of accounting basis that it will be allowed to use when recording the transaction. If there is a change in voting control (which is governed by exceedingly complex rules), then the buyout must be recorded under the purchase method of accounting (see earlier section); this approach results in the recording of all acquiree assets and liabilities at their fair market values, with any remaining unallocated purchase price being recorded as goodwill, which must then be gradually written off. If there is a lesser degree of change in the amount of voting control (common enough when the management team is simply increasing its level of ownership), the buyout is considered to be a financial restructuring; in this case, there is no change in the accounting basis. The latter case has the advantage of resulting in no goodwill amortization over many future years, as would be the case under the purchase method, and so yields better financial results in later years.

34-11 SPIN-OFF TRANSACTIONS

A company may find it necessary to transfer an operating division directly to company shareholders as a separate entity. If so, it should be transferred at the book values of all assets and liabilities related to the division as of the date of transfer. If the net amount of all assets and liabilities to be transferred is a positive book value, then this amount is to be offset against the company's retained earnings account. Alternatively, if the division being transferred has a negative book value, then the offset (which will be an increase) is to the additional paid-in capital account; the change in account is based on the assumption that investors have essentially paid the company to take the negative net worth division off the company's hands, so they are contributing capital to the company for this privilege.

If the company only owns a small minority interest in the division, then the transaction should be considered a property dividend. Under this concept, the company's share in the division must be transferred at its fair market value, rather than its book value.

Another consideration is that the corporate parent must continue to track the financial results of the division being spun off up until the date of spin-off, and record the results of the division's operations through that date on its books.

34-12 THE TREATMENT OF GOODWILL

Goodwill is a by-product of the purchase method of accounting, in which any portion of the purchase price that cannot be allocated to assets is set aside in a separate account and gradually written off through amortization.

The chief area of interest to the accountant is the number of years over which goodwill shall be amortized, since this can have a major impact on the reported level of profitability for many years to come. The basic rule is that goodwill shall be amortized on a straight-line basis for the lesser of either 40 years or the number of periods expected to be benefited. The management team usually wants to use 40 years as the amortization period, since this spreads the recognition of amortization over the longest possible period of time. However, if it can be proven that there are contractual, regulatory, obsolescence, competitive, or other reasons why no benefit will continue from the acquisition for the next 40 years, then a shorter period must be used. The use of a shorter period can be a difficult one to prove. Examples would be the expected termination of a government patent granted to an acquiree for the use of a valuable invention, which was the primary reason why the acquiree was purchased; if intense competition is expected to arise as soon as the patent expires, then a good case could be made for amortizing goodwill over this shorter period.

It is also possible to have negative goodwill if the total value assigned to assets of the acquiree exceeds the purchase price. When this occurs, leave the valuation of all current assets (as well as the valuation of all long-term marketable securities) alone, and proportionally reduce the value of all long-term assets until the total corporate valuation matches the purchase price. If the recorded value of all long-term assets is driven to zero without reaching the point where the total value assigned to all assets equals the purchase price, then the accountant should record the difference as negative goodwill and amortize it.

The only exception to the reduction of asset values for the calculation of negative goodwill is when the acquirer plans to sell some fixed assets after the acquisition; valuing these items at below their fair market value would result in the recognition of a large gain at the point of sale, and would inflate the reported earnings of the acquirer. Accordingly, these assets must still be recorded at their fair market value, net of selling costs.

34-13 SUMMARY

There are two areas in this chapter that are the focus of ongoing attention by the Financial Accounting Standards Board. These are the use of the pooling of interests method of accounting, and the use of push-down accounting for subsidiaries. These are areas in which the accounting rules are in flux, and for which the information presented here is only accurate through the date of publication; consequently, one should consult with a mergers and acquisitions expert in regard to these matters before recording an accounting transaction.

CHAPTER 35

Taxation

35-1 INTRODUCTION

The issue of taxation is one that confronts the accountant on a regular basis, and in relation to a wide array of issues. This may include the proper treatment of overpayments to employees, the correct handling of personal property tax reporting, the tax impact of consignment revenue, and a broad array of other, highly specific items. The tax laws related to many of these issues change regularly, and so require the most up-to-date information. This chapter provides information that is current as of its publication date, but one should consult a taxation professional if there is any indication that the tax laws may have changed since that time.

The approach that a company should take to taxation issues is based upon its taxation strategy, which is noted in the first section. The remainder of the chapter lists nearly

50 taxation topics in alphabetical order, from the Accumulated Earnings Tax to the recognition of warranty expenses. If the reader does not see a specific topic in a section header, please refer to the index, since it may be included within another section or under a different section title. Also, given the large number of sections, the title of each one is noted below for easy reference:

35-2 THE STRATEGY OF TAX PLANNING

The obvious objective of tax planning is to minimize the amount of cash paid out for taxes. However, this directly conflicts with the general desire to report as much income as possible to shareholders. Only in the case of privately owned firms do these conflicting problems go away, since the owners have no need to impress anyone with their reported level of earnings, and would simply prefer to retain as much cash in the company as possible by avoiding the payment of taxes.

For those organizations that are intent on reducing their tax burdens, there are four primary goals to include in their tax strategies, all of which involve increasing the number of differences between the book and tax records, so that reportable income for tax purposes is reduced. The four items are:

1. *Accelerate deductions.* By recognizing expenses sooner, one can force expenses into the current reporting year that would otherwise be deferred. The primary

deduction acceleration involves deprecation, for which a company typically uses MACRS (an accelerated depreciation methodology acceptable for tax reporting purposes), and straight-line depreciation, which results in a higher level of reported earnings for other purposes.

2. *Take all available tax credits.* A credit results in a permanent reduction in taxes, and so is highly desirable. Unfortunately, credits are increasingly difficult to find, though one might qualify for the research and experimental tax credit (see later section). There are more tax credits available at the local level, where they are offered to those businesses willing to operate in economic development zones, or as part of specialized relocation deals (normally only available to larger companies).

3. *Avoid non-allowable expenses.* There are a few expenses, most notably meals and entertainment, that are completely or at least partially not allowed for purposes of computing taxable income. A key company strategy is to reduce these types of expenses to the bare minimum, thereby avoiding any lost benefits from non-allowable expenses.

4. *Increase tax deferrals.* There are a number of situations in which taxes can be shifted into the future, such as payments in stock for acquisitions, or the deferral of revenue received until all related services have been performed. This can shift a large part of the tax liability into the future, where the time value of money results in a smaller present value of the tax liability than would otherwise be the case.

One should refer back to these four basic tax goals when reading through the various tax issues noted in the following sections, in order to see how they fit into a company's overall tax strategy.

35-3 ACCUMULATED EARNINGS TAX

There is a double tax associated with a company's payment of dividends to investors, because it must first pay an income tax from which dividends *cannot* be deducted as an expense, and then investors must pay income tax on the dividends received. Understandably, closely held companies prefer not to issue dividends in order to avoid the double taxation issue. However, this can result in a large amount of capital accumulating within a company. The IRS addresses this issue by imposing an accumulated earnings tax on what it considers to be an excessive amount of earnings that have not been distributed to shareholders.

The IRS considers accumulated earnings of less than $150,000 to be sufficient for the working needs of service businesses, such as accounting, engineering, architecture, and consulting firms. It considers accumulations of anything under $250,000 to be sufficient for most other types of businesses. A company can argue that it needs a substantially larger amount of accumulated earnings if it can prove that it has specific, definite, and feasible plans that will require the use of the funds within the business. Another valid argument is that a company needs a sufficient amount of accumulated earnings to buy back the company's stock that is held by a deceased shareholder's estate.

If these conditions are not apparent, then the IRS will declare the accumulated earnings to be taxable at a rate of 39.6%. Also, interest payments to the IRS will be due from the date when the corporation's annual return was originally due. The severity of this tax is designed to encourage organizations to issue dividends on a regular basis to their shareholders, so that the IRS can tax the shareholders for this form of income.

35-4 ALTERNATIVE MINIMUM TAX

The Alternative Minimum Tax (AMT) is a separate tax system that is designed to ensure that one does not completely avoid the payment of taxes through a variety of income tax shelters. The AMT must be calculated alongside the usual income tax forms. If the amount payable under the AMT calculation is higher than under the regular tax calculation, then the AMT amount must be paid. The AMT does not apply to any company that is reporting its first tax year in existence, or if its average annual gross receipts for the preceding three years did not exceed $7.5 million. The AMT must be calculated for all other business entities.

The IRS form for the AMT is Form 4626, which is shown in Exhibit 35-1. The revenue figure reported on line one of the form is essentially the same one reported on a company's standard Form 1120. The differences from the typical tax system lie in the adjustments (generally reductions in reported expenses) and preferences (generally increases in reported revenue), which are itemized in a number of sub-categories under line two, the most commonly used being:

- *Depreciation.* The depreciation expense must be recalculated under AMT, which stipulates that any depreciation that had been calculated using the 200% declining balance method must now be calculated using the 150% declining balance method, switching to the straight-line method in the first year in which this yields a larger deduction. The period over which depreciation is calculated is not changed under the AMT calculation.

- *Long-term contracts.* The percentage of completion method must be used for AMT to calculate the taxable income from any long-term contract (with the exception of home construction contracts).

- *Installment sales.* The installment sale method cannot be used for AMT calculation purposes for any non-dealer property dispositions.

- *Passive activities.* All passive activity gains or losses for a closely held or personal service company must take into account the corporation's AMT adjustments, preferences, and AMT prior year unallowed losses.

- *Depletion.* Depletion deductions for mines, wells, and other natural deposits are limited to the property's adjusted basis at the end of the year, unless the corporation is an independent producer or royalty owner claiming percentage depletion for oil and gas wells.

The sum of these adjustments is carried forward to line three in Form 4626. We now switch to the Adjusted Current Earnings Worksheet, which is shown in Exhibit 35-2. This worksheet is used to reduce the differences between taxable and reported income under generally accepted accounting principles (GAAP). In general, any temporary timing difference between taxable and GAAP income must be added back to this worksheet. Typical areas in which temporary tax differences are voided are for intangible drilling costs, circulation expenditures, organization expenditures, LIFO inventory adjustments, and recognition of losses on the exchange of any pool of debt obligations. Only permanent differences between the two are not included in the worksheet.

Exhibit 35-1   Alternative Minimum Tax Form 4626

Form **4626**	**Alternative Minimum Tax—Corporations**	OMB No. 1545-0175
Department of the Treasury Internal Revenue Service	▶ See separate instructions. ▶ Attach to the corporation's tax return.	20**00**

Name	Employer identification number

1	Taxable income or (loss) before net operating loss deduction	**1**

2 **Adjustments and preferences:**

a	Depreciation of post-1986 property	**2a**
b	Amortization of certified pollution control facilities	**2b**
c	Amortization of mining exploration and development costs	**2c**
d	Amortization of circulation expenditures (personal holding companies only) . .	**2d**
e	Adjusted gain or loss	**2e**
f	Long-term contracts	**2f**
g	Installment sales	**2g**
h	Merchant marine capital construction funds	**2h**
i	Section 833(b) deduction (Blue Cross, Blue Shield, and similar type organizations only)	**2i**
j	Tax shelter farm activities (personal service corporations only)	**2j**
k	Passive activities (closely held corporations and personal service corporations only)	**2k**
l	Loss limitations	**2l**
m	Depletion	**2m**
n	Tax-exempt interest from specified private activity bonds	**2n**
o	Intangible drilling costs	**2o**
p	Accelerated depreciation of real property (pre-1987)	**2p**
q	Accelerated depreciation of leased personal property (pre-1987) (personal holding companies only)	**2q**
r	Other adjustments	**2r**
s	Combine lines 2a through 2r	**2s**

3	Preadjustment alternative minimum taxable income (AMTI). Combine lines 1 and 2s	**3**

4 **Adjusted current earnings (ACE) adjustment:**

a	Enter the corporation's ACE from line 10 of the worksheet on page 11 of the instructions	**4a**
b	Subtract line 3 from line 4a. If line 3 exceeds line 4a, enter the difference as a negative amount (see examples on page 6 of the instructions)	**4b**
c	Multiply line 4b by 75% (.75). Enter the result as a positive amount . . .	**4c**
d	Enter the excess, if any, of the corporation's total increases in AMTI from prior year ACE adjustments over its total reductions in AMTI from prior year ACE adjustments (see page 6 of the instructions). **Note:** *You* **must** *enter an amount on line 4d (even if line 4b is positive)*	**4d**

e	ACE adjustment:
	
	   If you entered a positive number or zero on line 4b, enter the amount from line 4c here as a positive amount.
	
	   If you entered a negative number on line 4b, enter the smaller of line 4c or line 4d here as a negative amount.
		4e

5	Combine lines 3 and 4e. If zero or less, stop here; the corporation does not owe alternative minimum tax	**5**
6	Alternative tax net operating loss deduction (see page 7 of the instructions)	**6**
7	**Alternative minimum taxable income.** Subtract line 6 from line 5. If the corporation held a residual interest in a REMIC, see page 7 of the instructions	**7**

For Paperwork Reduction Act Notice, see page 10 of separate instructions.   Cat. No. 12955I   Form **4626** (2000)

(continued)

Exhibit 35-1   Alternative Minimum Tax Form 4626 (*cont'd.*)

Form 4626 (2000)   Page **2**

8	Enter the amount from line 7 (alternative minimum taxable income)	**8**
9	**Exemption phase-out computation** (if line 8 is $310,000 or more, skip lines 9a and 9b and enter -0- on line 9c):	
a	Subtract $150,000 from line 8 (if you are completing this line for a member of a controlled group, see page 7 of the instructions). If zero or less, enter -0- . . **9a**	
b	Multiply line 9a by 25% (.25). **9b**	
c	Exemption. Subtract line 9b from $40,000 (if you are completing this line for a member of a controlled group, see page 7 of the instructions). If zero or less, enter -0-	**9c**
10	Subtract line 9c from line 8. If zero or less, enter -0-	**10**
11	Multiply line 10 by 20% (.20).	**11**
12	Alternative minimum tax foreign tax credit. See page 7 of the instructions	**12**
13	Tentative minimum tax. Subtract line 12 from line 11.	**13**
14	Regular tax liability before all credits except the foreign tax credit and possessions tax credit . . .	**14**
15	**Alternative minimum tax.** Subtract line 14 from line 13. If zero or less, enter -0-. Enter here and on Form 1120, Schedule J, line 4, or the appropriate line of the corporation's income tax return . . .	**15**

Form **4626** (2000)

Line six of Form 4626 is for the AMT net operating loss deduction. This is the combination of the AMT net operating loss carrybacks and carryforwards. This is the excess of the deductions allowed in figuring AMT income over the income included in AMT income. The net operating loss calculated under AMT rules is restricted to 90% of AMT income, which means that there will still be some taxable income under AMT, no matter how large the net operating loss might be. Any portion of the AMT net operating loss that is not used in the current year to offset income can be carried back or forward to other tax years.

The alternative minimum tax is listed on line seven of Form 4626 (at the bottom), and is the result of the preceding calculations. A credit of $40,000 can then be deducted from the AMT, but this deduction is gradually reduced if the amount of the AMT is at least $150,000, and entirely negated if the AMT reaches or exceeds $310,000. The remaining taxable amount is multiplied by 20%, which is the AMT tax rate. This tax can be further reduced by a foreign tax credit, as listed on line twelve in Form 4626. Once this has been netted out, the remaining alternative minimum tax is compared to the corporate tax that is due as per Form 1120. The company is liable for whichever tax is greater.

The preceding description of the various AMT line items is only the briefest overview of the required calculations. In practice, the AMT is one of the most difficult tax calculations to accurately complete, and requires the services of an experienced tax expert. Also, separate records should be kept for the AMT for a number of years, since some of the net operating losses and related deductions may be applicable to the tax returns filed in later years.

Exhibit 35-2   Adjusted Current Earnings Worksheet

Adjusted Current Earnings Worksheet
▶ See ACE Worksheet Instructions (which begin on page 8).

1 Pre-adjustment AMTI. Enter the amount from line 3 of Form 4626	**1**	
2 ACE depreciation adjustment:		
a AMT depreciation.	**2a**	
b ACE depreciation:		
(1) Post-1993 property	**2b(1)**	
(2) Post-1989, pre-1994 property	**2b(2)**	
(3) Pre-1990 MACRS property	**2b(3)**	
(4) Pre-1990 original ACRS property	**2b(4)**	
(5) Property described in sections 168(f)(1) through (4)	**2b(5)**	
(6) Other property	**2b(6)**	
(7) Total ACE depreciation. Add lines 2b(1) through 2b(6)	**2b(7)**	
c ACE depreciation adjustment. Subtract line 2b(7) from line 2a	**2c**	
3 Inclusion in ACE of items included in earnings and profits (E&P):		
a Tax-exempt interest income	**3a**	
b Death benefits from life insurance contracts	**3b**	
c All other distributions from life insurance contracts (including surrenders)	**3c**	
d Inside buildup of undistributed income in life insurance contracts	**3d**	
e Other items (see Regulations sections 1.56(g)-1(c)(6)(iii) through (ix) for a partial list)	**3e**	
f Total increase to ACE from inclusion in ACE of items included in E&P. Add lines 3a through 3e	**3f**	
4 Disallowance of items not deductible from E&P:		
a Certain dividends received	**4a**	
b Dividends paid on certain preferred stock of public utilities that are deductible under section 247	**4b**	
c Dividends paid to an ESOP that are deductible under section 404(k)	**4c**	
d Nonpatronage dividends that are paid and deductible under section 1382(c)	**4d**	
e Other items (see Regulations sections 1.56(g)-1(d)(3)(i) and (ii) for a partial list)	**4e**	
f Total increase to ACE because of disallowance of items not deductible from E&P. Add lines 4a through 4e	**4f**	
5 Other adjustments based on rules for figuring E&P:		
a Intangible drilling costs	**5a**	
b Circulation expenditures	**5b**	
c Organizational expenditures	**5c**	
d LIFO inventory adjustments	**5d**	
e Installment sales	**5e**	
f Total other E&P adjustments. Combine lines 5a through 5e	**5f**	
6 Disallowance of loss on exchange of debt pools	**6**	
7 Acquisition expenses of life insurance companies for qualified foreign contracts	**7**	
8 Depletion	**8**	
9 Basis adjustments in determining gain or loss from sale or exchange of pre-1994 property	**9**	
10 **Adjusted current earnings.** Combine lines 1, 2c, 3f, 4f, and 5f through 9. Enter the result here and on line 4a of Form 4626	**10**	

35-5 BANKRUPTCY TAX ISSUES

When a partnership or corporation declares bankruptcy, the court will appoint a trustee that is responsible for filing the regular income tax returns. The trustee may file for relief from filing a return with the IRS district director; this relief will likely be granted if the organization has ceased operations and has neither assets nor income remaining.

Of key concern is a company's liability for various types of taxes, which in most cases is not discharged as a result of a bankruptcy filing. Most pre-petition tax debts are classified as *eighth priority taxes*. They are:

- Income taxes for years prior to the bankruptcy.
- Income taxes assessed within 240 days prior to the bankruptcy filing.
- Income taxes not assessed, but assessable as of the petition date.
- Withholding taxes for which the company is liable.
- The employer's share of employment taxes on wages.
- Excise taxes on any transactions occurring prior to the bankruptcy date.

Any taxes that arise during the period when a company is in bankruptcy are considered to be ongoing administrative expenses, and so will be paid at once.

If a company files for liquidation under Chapter 7 of the bankruptcy law, then these eighth priority taxes will be paid out of whatever company assets are left, once the claims of creditors with a higher priority have been fulfilled. If the entity is under Chapter 11 bankruptcy protection, then it can pay these taxes to the IRS over six years; this will include an interest assessment.

If a company is late in paying the state unemployment tax, it is normally restricted to making a 90% deduction of the amount paid into the federal unemployment fund against the state tax. However, this penalty is waived in the case of a bankrupt company, so that the full amount of the federal unemployment payment can still be taken against the state unemployment tax.

In some cases, the amount of debt canceled while in bankruptcy is considered to be taxable income to the bankrupt entity. If so, the amount of the debt reduction can be used to reduce the basis of any depreciable property (but not more than the total basis of property held, less total liabilities held directly after the debt cancellation). As an alternative, it can be used to (1) offset any net operating loss for the year in which the debt cancellation took place, (2) offset any carryovers of amounts normally used to calculate the general business credit, (3) offset any minimum tax credit, (4) offset any net capital loss and any capital loss carryover, and then (5) offset any passive activity losses. These offsets can be dollar-for-dollar for canceled debt, except for the reduction of *credit* carryovers, which can be reduced at the rate of $33\frac{1}{3}$ cents for every dollar of canceled debt.

If a partnership has entered bankruptcy and obtained a debt cancelation, then the amount of this cancellation must be apportioned among the partners and reported on their individual tax returns as income.

35-6 BARTER

Barter occurs when a company receives goods or services in exchange for its own goods and services; cash is not exchanged as part of the transaction. When barter occurs, one must recognize income for the incremental gain in the fair market value of the products or services received over one's cost basis in the products or services given up.

The tax treatment of a barter transaction is more difficult if personal services are involved. For example, if an electrician performs services on a doctor's house in exchange for medical services from the doctor, both parties are providing services that have no cost basis, and so must be recorded at their full fair market value by both parties.

The tax treatment is somewhat different in the case of barter exchanges. A barter exchange occurs when a third party encourages the use of barter transactions by partially converting individual transactions into a form of money, giving each party a credit in exchange for its services that can then be used to "buy" the services of some other entity that is also listed on the exchange. The barter exchange must report to the IRS the fair market value of all transactions passing through it. There are certain instances when backup withholding on transactions conducted through a barter exchange will be required by the IRS.

35-7 BONUSES AND AWARDS

If a company gives its employees bonuses or cash awards of any type, these are taxable income and must be recorded on employee W-2 forms. If a non-cash award is given, then the fair market value of this award must also be recorded on the W-2 form as taxable income.

If an award is given that is based on achievement, such as a safety or length of service achievement, then the cumulative cost to the employer of up to $400 can be excluded from employee pay during the course of each calendar year. If these awards are given under a written award program, then the annual amount excluded per employee is increased to $1,600. This type of award cannot be a disguised pay supplement: to ensure that these payments are truly rewards for unique achievements, the IRS has imposed safeguard rules that disallow length of service awards if they are awarded for fewer than five years of service. Similarly, safety awards are considered taxable income to the recipient if they are given to a supervisor or other professional employee, or if more than 10% of all qualified employees receive such awards during the year. Finally, all such awards must be awarded as part of a meaningful presentation.

In addition to being excluded from the receiving employee's taxable income, any employee achievement awards that fall within the preceding guidelines are also excludable for employment tax purposes as well as from the social security benefit base.

35-8 CASH METHOD OF ACCOUNTING

The normal method for reporting a company's financial results is the accrual basis of accounting, under which expenses are matched to revenues within a reporting period. However, for tax purposes, it is sometimes possible to report income under the cash method of accounting. Under this approach, revenue is not recognized until payment for invoices is received, while expenses are not recognized until paid.

The cash basis of accounting can result in a great deal of manipulation from the perspective of the IRS, which discourages its use, but does not prohibit it. As an example of income manipulation, a company may realize that it will have a large amount of income to report in the current year, and will probably have less in the following year. Accordingly, it prepays a number of supplier invoices at the end of the year, so that it recognizes them at once under the cash method of accounting as expenses in the current year. The IRS prohibits this type of behavior under the rule that cash payments recognized in the current period can only relate to current-year expenses. Nonetheless, it is a difficult issue for the IRS to police. The same degree of manipulation can be applied to the recognition of revenue, simply by delaying billings to customers near the end of the tax year. Also, in situations where there is a sudden surge of business at the end of the tax year, possibly due to seasonality, the cash method of accounting will not reveal the sales until the following year, since payment on the invoices from customers will not arrive until the next year. Consequently, the cash method tends to under-report taxable income.

In order to limit the use of this method, the IRS prohibits it if a company has any inventories on hand at the end of the year. The reason for this is that expenditures for inventory can be so large and subject to manipulation at year-end that a company could theoretically alter its reported level of taxable income to an enormous extent. The cash basis is also not allowable for any "C" corporation, partnership that has a "C" corporation for a partner, or a tax shelter. However, within these restrictions, it is allowable for an entity with average annual gross receipts of $5 million or less for the three tax years ending with the prior tax year, as well as for any personal service corporation that provides at least 95% of its activities in the services arena.

The IRS imposes some accrual accounting concepts on a cash-basis organization in order to avoid some of the more blatant forms of income avoidance. For example, if a cash-basis company receives a check at the end of its tax year, it may be tempted not to cash the check until the beginning of the next tax year, since this would push the revenue associated with that check into the next year. To avoid this problem, the IRS uses the concept of *constructive receipt,* which requires one to record the receipt when it is made available to one without restriction (whether or not it is actually recorded on the company's books at that time). Besides the just-noted example, this would also require a company to record the interest on a bond that comes due prior to the end of the tax year, even if the associated coupon is not sent to the issuer until the next year.

There are some differences between the financial statements that a company reports under the accrual and cash methods. For instance, there are no accounts receivable or payable listed on the books of a cash-method business, which can be disconcerting for one who is attempting to determine the extent of an organization's true assets and liabilities. Also, there are no period-end accruals, such as would normally be found for salaries and wages, taxes, royalties, commissions, and other expenses. Furthermore, the receipt of property or services must be accounted for at their fair market value when reporting taxable income. Consequently, the use of the cash method of accounting for a company's other financial reporting needs is considered unsatisfactory from a purely informational perspective, thereby forcing a company to either maintain two sets of books, or to maintain just one using either basis of accounting, and then make adjustments to determine its results under the alternative basis of accounting.

35-9 CHANGE OF ACCOUNTING METHOD

It is acceptable to choose any permitted accounting method when a company files its first tax return. However, once the company elects to change its method of accounting, the IRS's approval must be obtained. The reason for this is that switching methods can result in a timing difference in the recognition of taxable income for a company; the IRS must see evidence that there is a non-tax reason for changing accounting methods before it will approve such a change. The application for a change of accounting method is Form 3115, the first half of which is shown in Exhibit 35-3.

Exhibit 35-3   Application for Change in Accounting Method, Form 3115

Form **3115**		
(Rev. May 1999)	**Application for Change in Accounting Method**	OMB No. 1545-0152
Department of the Treasury Internal Revenue Service	► **See page 1 of the instructions for the Automatic Change Procedures.**	

Name of applicant (If a joint return is filed, also give spouse's name.)	Identification number (See page 3 of the instructions.)
Number, street, and room or suite no. (If a P.O. box, see page 3 of the instructions.)	Tax year of change begins (mo., day, yr.) and ends (mo., day, yr.)
City or town, state, and ZIP code	District director's office having jurisdiction
Name of person to contact (If not the applicant, a power of attorney must be submitted.)	Contact person's telephone number/Fax number ( ) / ( )

Check the appropriate box to indicate who is filing this form.

☐ Individual
☐ Corporation
☐ Cooperative (Sec. 1381)
☐ Qualified Personal Service Corporation (Sec. 448(d)(2))
☐ Exempt organization. Enter code section ►

☐ Partnership
☐ S Corporation
☐ Insurance Co. (Sec. 816(a))
☐ Insurance Co. (Sec. 831)
☐ Other (specify) ► ....
....

Check the appropriate box to indicate the type of accounting method change being requested. (See page 3 of the instructions.)

☐ Depreciation or Amortization
☐ Financial Products and/or Financial Activities of Financial Institutions
☐ Other (specify) ►

Part I   **Eligibility To Request Change** (All applicants complete Parts I through IV.) (See page 2 of the instructions.)

		Yes	No
1	Is the applicant changing its method of accounting under a revenue procedure or other published guidance that provides for an automatic change? (See page 1 of the instructions.)		
	If "Yes," enter the citation of the revenue procedure or other published guidance ► _____		
2	Is the applicant changing its method of accounting under sections 263A, 447, 448, 460, or 585(c) for the first tax year the applicant is required to change?		
	If "Yes," the applicant is required to make the change in accounting method under the automatic change procedures set forth in the applicable regulations.		
3a	Does the applicant have any Federal income tax returns under examination by the IRS? See section 3.07 of Rev. Proc. 97-27, 1997-1 C.B. 680		
	If "Yes," complete line 3b.		
b	Is the method of accounting the applicant is requesting to change: (i) an issue under consideration or (ii) an issue placed in suspense by the examining agent(s)? See sections 3.08(1) and 6.01 of Rev. Proc. 97-27.		
	If "Yes," the applicant is not eligible to request the change in accounting method. If ™No, complete lines 3c through 3e.		
c	Indicate the "window period" the applicant is filing under or state if the change is being requested with the consent of the district director. ►_____ See section 6.01 of Rev. Proc. 97-27.		
d	Has a copy of this Form 3115 been provided to the examining agent(s) for all examinations that are in process? See section 6.01 of Rev. Proc. 97-27.		
e	Enter the name(s) and telephone number(s) of the examining agent(s). ►_____ See section 6.01 of Rev. Proc. 97-27.		
4a	Is the applicant before an appeals office with respect to any Federal income tax return issue?		
	If "Yes," complete line 4b.		
b	Is the method of accounting the applicant is requesting to change an issue under consideration by the appeals office? See sections 3.08(2) and 6.02 of Rev. Proc. 97-27		
	If "Yes," the applicant is not eligible to request the change in accounting method. If "No," complete lines 4c and 4d.		
c	Has a copy of this Form 3115 been provided to the appeals officer? See section 6.02 of Rev. Proc. 97-27		
d	Enter the name and telephone number of the appeals officer. ►_____ See section 6.02 of Rev. Proc. 97-27.		

Signature–All Applicants *(See page 3 of the instructions.)*

Under penalties of perjury, I declare that I have examined this application, including accompanying documents, and, to the best of my knowledge and belief, the application contains all the relevant facts relating to the application, and such facts are true, correct, and complete. Declaration of preparer (other than applicant) is based on all information of which preparer has any knowledge.

Applicant	**Parent corporation (if applicable)**
----------------------------------	----------------------------------
Officer's signature and date	Parent officer's signature and date
----------------------------------	----------------------------------
Name and title (print or type)	Name and title (print or type)
----------------------------------	----------------------------------
Signature(s) of individual or firm preparing the application and date	Name of firm preparing the application

For Privacy Act and Paperwork Reduction Act Notice, see page 1 of the instructions.   Cat. No. 19280E   Form **3115** (Rev. 5-99)

(continued)

Exhibit 35-3   Application for Change in Accounting Method, Form 3115 (*cont'd.*)

Form 3115 (Rev. 5-99)   Page **2**

Part I	**Eligibility To Request Change** (continued)	Yes	No

5a Is the applicant before a Federal court with respect to any Federal income tax issue?. . . . .
If "Yes," complete line 5b.

  b Is the method of accounting the applicant is requesting to change an issue under consideration by the Federal court?
See sections 3.08(3) and 6.03 of Rev. Proc. 97-27 .
If "Yes," the applicant is not eligible to request the change in accounting method. If "No," complete lines 5c and 5d.

  c Has a copy of this Form 3115 been provided to the counsel for the government? See section 6.03 of Rev. Proc. 97-27.

  d Enter the name and telephone number of the counsel for the government. ▶ _____
See section 6.03 of Rev. Proc. 97-27.

6a Is the applicant a member of an affiliated group filing a consolidated return for the year of change? . . . . . .

  b If "Yes," attach a statement listing the parent corporation's (1) name, (2) identification number, (3) address, and (4) tax year.

  c Has the applicant ever been a member of a consolidated group other than the current group?. . . . .
If "Yes," complete line 6b for each group of which the applicant was formerly a member.

  d If the applicant is (or was formerly) a member of a consolidated group, is any consolidated group under examination, before an appeals office, or before a Federal court for a tax year(s) that the applicant was a member of the group? See sections 3.07(1) and 4.02(5) of Rev. Proc. 97-27 . . . .
If "Yes," complete lines 3b through 3e, 4b through 4d, or 5b through 5d (whichever are applicable).

7 If the applicant is an entity (including a limited liability company) treated as a partnership or an S corporation for Federal income tax purposes, is the method of accounting the applicant is requesting to change an issue under consideration in an examination of a partner, member, or shareholder's Federal income tax return or an issue under consideration by an appeals office or by a Federal court with respect to a partner, member, or shareholder's Federal income tax return? See sections 3.08 and 4.02(6) of Rev. Proc. 97-27 . . . .
If "Yes," the applicant is not eligible to request the change in accounting method.

Part II	**Description of Change**

8 Is the applicant requesting to change its **overall** method of accounting? . . . .
If "Yes," check the appropriate boxes below to indicate the applicant's present and proposed methods of accounting. Also complete Schedule A on page 4 of the form.

  Present method: ☐ Cash   ☐ Accrual   ☐ Hybrid (attach description)
  Proposed method: ☐ Cash   ☐ Accrual   ☐ Hybrid (attach description)

9 If the applicant is **not** changing its overall method of accounting, attach a description of each of the following:
  a The item being changed.
  b The applicant's present method for the item being changed.
  c The applicant's proposed method for the item being changed.
  d The applicant's present overall method of accounting (cash, accrual, or hybrid).

10 Attach an explanation of the legal basis supporting the proposed method for the item being changed. Include all authority (statutes, regulations, published rulings, court cases, etc.) supporting the proposed method. The applicant is encouraged to include a discussion of any authorities that may be contrary to the proposed method.

11 Attach a description of the applicant's trade or business, including the goods and services it provides and any other types of activities it engages in that generate gross income.

12 Attach a copy of all documents directly related to the proposed change. (See page 3 of the instructions.)

13 Attach a statement of the applicant's reasons for the proposed change.

14a Attach an explanation of whether the proposed method of accounting will be used for the taxpayer's books and records and financial statements. (Insurance companies, see page 3 of the instructions.)

  b Attach an explanation of whether the proposed method of accounting conforms to generally accepted accounting principles (GAAP) and to the best accounting practice in the applicant's trade or business.

15a Does the applicant have more than one trade or business as defined in Regulations section 1.446-1(d)?. . . . . .

  b If "Yes," is each trade or business accounted for separately? . . . .
If "Yes," for each trade or business, attach a description of the type of business, the overall method of accounting, whether the business has changed any accounting method in the past 4 years, and whether the business is changing any accounting method as part of this application or as a separate application.

16 If the applicant is a member of an affiliated group filing a consolidated return for the year of change, do all other members of the consolidated group use the proposed method of accounting for the item being changed? . . . . .
If "No," attach an explanation.

17 If the applicant is changing to the cash method, or to the inventory price index computation (IPIC) method under Regulations section 1.472-8(e)(3), or is changing its method of accounting under sections 263A, 448, or 460, enter the gross receipts for the 4 tax years preceding the year of change. (See page 3 of the instructions.)

1st preceding year ended: mo. yr.	2nd preceding year ended: mo. yr.	3rd preceding year ended: mo. yr.	4th preceding year ended: mo. yr.
$ $	$		$

Exhibit 35-3   Application for Change in Accounting Method, Form 3115 (*cont'd.*)

Form 3115 (Rev. 5-99)   Page **3**

Part II   **Description of Change** (continued)

18   Attach a statement addressing whether the applicant has entered (or is considering entering) into a transaction to which section 381(c)(4) or (c)(5) applies (e.g., a reorganization or merger) during the tax year of change determined without regard to any (potential) closing of the year under section 381(b)(1). Also include in the statement an explanation of any changes in method of accounting that resulted (or will result) from the transaction(s).

Part III   **Section 481(a) Adjustment**

		Yes	No
19	Enter the net section 481(a) adjustment for the year of change. Indicate whether the adjustment is an increase (+) or a decrease (-) in income. ▶ $ _____		
20	Has the section 481(a) adjustment been reduced by a pre-1954 amount?.		
21a	If the section 481(a) adjustment is less than $25,000 (positive or negative), does the applicant elect to take the entire amount of the adjustment into account in the year of change?		
b	If "No," (or if the applicant declines to elect to take the entire amount of the adjustment into account in the year of change), enter the applicable period over which the applicant proposes to take the adjustment into account. ▶ _____		
22	Is any part of the section 481(a) adjustment attributable to transactions between members of an affiliated group, a controlled group, or other related parties?. . . . . If "Yes," attach an explanation.		

Part IV   **Additional Information**

		Yes	No
23	Has the applicant, its predecessor, or a related party requested or made (under either an automatic change procedure or a procedure requiring advance consent) a change in accounting method or accounting period in the past 4 years? If "Yes," attach a description of each change and the year of change. If the application was withdrawn, not perfected, or denied, or if a Consent Agreement was sent to the taxpayer but was not signed and returned to the IRS, or if the change was not made, include an explanation.		
24	Does the applicant, its predecessor, or a related party currently have pending any request for a private letter ruling, a request for change in accounting method or accounting period, or a request for technical advice? . . . . . . If "Yes," for each request, indicate the name(s) of the taxpayer, the type of request (private letter ruling, request for change in accounting method or accounting period, or request for technical advice), and the specific issue in the request.		
25	Has the applicant attached **Form 2848,** Power of Attorney and Declaration of Representative? (See the instructions for line 25 and "Person To Contact" on page 3 of the instructions.).		
26	Does the applicant request a **conference of right** at the IRS National Office if the IRS proposes an adverse response?.		
27	Enter the amount of **user fee** attached to this application. ▶ $ _____ (See page 2 of the instructions.)		
28	If the applicant qualifies for a reduced user fee for identical accounting method changes, has the information required by section 15.07 of Rev. Proc. 99-1, 1999-1 I.R.B. 6, been attached?.		

As noted in Part II of the form, any requested changes that are not already identified in the form will require the attachment of a note that itemizes the reason for the requested change, an explanation for its legal basis (including applicable statutes, references, published rulings, and court cases, as well as a thorough description of the company's main line of business). Lines 15 and 16 of Part II are of particular interest to the IRS, because the applicant must note if there is a common tax filing that involves more than one business. If so, the IRS will investigate whether the proposed change will impact the consolidated return. It is useful not to make a regular habit of requesting changes in accounting methods, since the IRS will determine if there is a history of changes (as noted in Line 23 of Part IV of the form) that has a pattern of reducing a company's tax liability. Also, when one perceives that there may be difficulty in obtaining approval of the change listed in a Form 3115, a request for a conference can be filed along with the form, which will be arranged before the IRS formally replies to the change in accounting method.

It is necessary to obtain IRS approval if there is a change from the cash method to the accrual method, or vice versa, or a change in the method used to value inventory (which requires a considerable amount of reporting on Schedule B of Form 3115, Parts I,

II, and III), or a change in the methodology for calculating depreciation expense. It also requires a complete explanation of any changes in the accounting for long-term contracts, as noted in Part I of Schedule C of Form 3115. One must also itemize any changes in the allocation methods for cost pools and the manner in which they are applied to inventory. Sections B and C of Schedule C of Form 3115 itemize the exact cost components that must be allocated, as well as other costs that are not required to be allocated. The form also mandates an explanation for any change in the calculation of revenues stemming from advance payments under service contracts. Given the detailed nature of these information requests, all schedules attached to Form 3115 are shown in Exhibit 35-4 for more in-depth review by the reader.

Any calculation errors, even if their correction results in a change in a company's reported level of taxable earnings, do not require IRS approval to fix.

Exhibit 35-4   Additional Schedules for Form 3115

Form 3115 (Rev. 5-99)   Page **4**

Schedule A–Change in Overall Method of Accounting (If Schedule A applies, Part I below must be completed.)

Attach copies of the profit and loss statement (Schedule F (Form 1040) for farmers) and the balance sheet, if applicable, as of the close of the tax year preceding the year of change. On a separate sheet, state the accounting method used when preparing the balance sheet. If books of account are not kept, attach a copy of the business schedules submitted with the Federal income tax return or other return (e.g., tax-exempt organization returns) for that period. If the amounts in Part I, lines 1a through 1g, do not agree with those shown on both the profit and loss statement and the balance sheet, explain the differences on a separate sheet.

| **Part I** | **Change in Overall Method** (See page 3 of the instructions.) |

1   Enter the following amounts as of the close of the tax year preceding the year of change. If none, state ™None.ĺAlso attach a statement providing a breakdown of the amounts entered on lines 1a through 1g.

		Amount
a	Income accrued but not received	$
b	Income received or reported before it was earned. Attach a description of the income and the legal basis for the proposed method. (See page 3 of the instructions.)	
c	Expenses accrued but not paid.	
d	Prepaid expense previously deducted.	
e	Supplies on hand previously deducted	
f	Inventory on hand previously deducted. Complete Schedule C, Part II	
g	Other amounts (specify) ▶	
h	**Net section 481(a) adjustment** (Add lines 1a±1g.) (See page 3 of the instructions.)	$

2   Is the applicant also requesting the recurring item exception (section 461(h))? (See page 4 of the instructions.)   ☐ Yes   ☐ No

| **Part II** | **Change to the Cash Method** (See page 4 of the instructions.) |

Applicants requesting a change to the cash method must attach the following information.

1   A description of the applicant's investment in capital items and leased equipment used in the trade or business, and the relationship between these items and the services performed by the business.

2   A description of inventory items (items that produce income when sold) and materials and supplies used in carrying out the business.

3   The number of employees, shareholders, partners, associates, etc., and a description of their duties in carrying out the applicant's business.

4   A schedule showing the age of receivables for each of the 4 tax years preceding the year of change.

5   A schedule showing the applicant's taxable income (loss) for each of the 4 tax years preceding the year of change.

6   A profit and loss statement showing the taxable income (loss) based on the cash method for each of the 4 tax years preceding the year of change.

Exhibit 35-4 Additional Schedules for Form 3115 (*cont'd.*)

Form 3115 (Rev. 5-99) Page **5**

Schedule B—Changes Within the LIFO Inventory Method (See page 4 of the instructions.)

Part I   General LIFO Information

Complete this section if the requested change involves changes within the LIFO inventory method. Also, attach a copy of all **Forms 970,** Application To Use LIFO Inventory Method, filed to adopt or expand the use of the LIFO method.

1   Attach a description of the applicant's present and proposed LIFO methods and submethods for each of the following items.

a   Valuing inventory (e.g., unit method or dollar-value method).

b   Pooling (e.g., by line or type or class of goods, natural business unit, multiple pools, raw material content, simplified dollar-value method, pooling method authorized under inventory price index computation (IPIC) method, etc.).

c   Pricing dollar-value pools (e.g., double-extension, index, link-chain, link-chain index, IPIC method, etc.).

d   Figuring the cost of goods in the closing inventory over the cost of goods in the opening inventory (e.g., most recent purchases, earliest acquisitions during the year, average cost of purchases during the year, etc.).

2   If any present method or submethod used by the applicant is not the same as indicated on Form(s) 970 filed to adopt or expand the use of the method, attach an explanation.

3   If the proposed change is not requested for all the LIFO inventory, specify the inventory to which the change is and is not applicable.

4   If the proposed change is not requested for all of the LIFO pools, specify the LIFO pool(s) to which the change is applicable.

5   Attach a statement addressing whether the applicant values any of its LIFO inventory on a method other than cost. For example, if the applicant values some of its LIFO inventory at retail and the remainder at cost, the applicant should identify which inventory items are valued under each method.

Part II   Change in Pooling Inventories

1   If the applicant is proposing to change its pooling method or the number of pools, attach a description of the contents of, and state the base year for, each dollar-value pool the applicant presently uses and proposes to use.

2   If the applicant is proposing to use natural business unit (NBU) pools or requesting to change the number of NBU pools, attach the following information (to the extent not already provided) in sufficient detail to show that each proposed NBU was determined under Regulations section 1.472-8(b)(1) and (2):

a   A description of the types of products produced by the applicant. If possible, attach a brochure.

b   A description of the types of processes and raw materials used to produce the products in each proposed pool.

c   If all of the products to be included in the proposed NBU pool(s) are not produced at one facility, the applicant should explain the reasons for the separate facilities, indicate the location of each facility, and provide a description of the products each facility produces.

d   A description of the natural business divisions adopted by the taxpayer. State whether separate cost centers are maintained and if separate profit and loss statements are prepared.

e   A statement addressing whether the applicant has inventories of items purchased and held for resale that are not further processed by the applicant, including whether such items, if any, will be included in any proposed NBU pool.

f   A statement addressing whether all items including raw materials, goods-in-process, and finished goods entering into the entire inventory investment for each proposed NBU pool are presently valued under the LIFO method. Describe any items that are not presently valued under the LIFO method that are to be included in each proposed pool.

g   A statement addressing whether, within the proposed NBU pool(s), there are items sold to others and transferred to a different unit of the applicant to be used as a component part of another product prior to final processing.

3   If the applicant is engaged in manufacturing and is proposing to use the multiple pooling method or raw material content pools, attach information to show that each proposed pool will consist of a group of items that are substantially similar. See Regulations section 1.472-8(b)(3).

4   If the applicant is engaged in the wholesaling or retailing of goods and is requesting to change the number of pools used, attach information to show that each of the proposed pools is based on customary business classifications of the applicant's trade or business. See Regulations section 1.472-8(c).

Part III   Change to Inventory Price Index Computation (IPIC) Method (See page 4 of the instructions.)

If changing to the IPIC method, attach the following items.

1   A completed Form 970.

2   A statement indicating which indexes, tables, and categories the applicant proposes to use.

(continued)

Exhibit 35-4 Additional Schedules for Form 3115 (*cont'd.*)

Form 3115 (Rev. 5-99)   Page **6**

Schedule C—Change in the Treatment of Long-Term Contracts, Inventories, or Other Section 263A Assets

Part I   Change in Reporting Income From Long-Term Contracts (Complete Part I and Part III below. See page 4 of the instructions.)

1   To the extent not already provided, attach a description of the applicant's present and proposed methods for reporting income from long-term contracts. If the applicant is a construction contractor, include a description of its construction activities.

2a Are the applicant's contracts long-term contracts as defined in section 460(f)(1)? (See page 4 of the instructions.) ☐ **Yes**   ☐ **No**

b   If "Yes," do all the contracts qualify for the exception under section 460(e)? (See page 4 of the instructions.)   ☐ **Yes**   ☐ **No**
        If line 2b is "No," attach an explanation.

3a Does the applicant have long-term manufacturing contracts as defined in section 460(f)(2)? . . . . ☐ **Yes**   ☐ **No**

b   If "Yes," explain the applicant's present and proposed method(s) of accounting for long-term manufacturing contracts.

c   If any of the manufacturing goods are sold or distributed without installation, attach an explanation.

4   If the applicant is requesting to use the percentage of completion method under section 460(b) for reporting its long-term contract income, indicate whether the applicant is electing to determine the completion factor for each long-term contract under the simplified cost-to-cost method. (See page 4 of the instructions.)

5   Does the applicant want to change the accounting method for all long-term contracts that were outstanding at the beginning of the year of change? . . . . ☐ **Yes**   ☐ **No**
        If "No," attach an explanation.

6   Attach a statement indicating whether any of the applicant's contracts are either cost-plus long-term contracts or Federal long-term contracts.

Part II   Change in Valuing Inventories (Complete Part III if applicable. See page 4 of the instructions.)

1   Attach a description of the inventory goods being changed.

2   Attach a description of the inventory goods (if any) NOT being changed.

3   Is the applicant's present inventory valuation method in compliance with section 263A? (See page 4 of the instructions.) . . . . ☐ **Yes**   ☐ **No**

4a Check the appropriate boxes below that identify the present and proposed inventory identification methods and valuation methods being changed and the present inventory identification methods and valuation methods not being changed.

	Inventory Being Changed		Inventory Not Being Changed
	Present method	Proposed method	Present method
Identification methods:			
Specific identification			
FIFO			
LIFO			
Valuation methods:			
Cost			
Cost or market, whichever is lower			
Retail cost			
Retail, lower of cost or market			
Other (attach explanation)			

b   Enter the value at the end of the tax year preceding the year of change . . . . |

5   Attach the computation used to determine the section 481(a) adjustment. If the section 481(a) adjustment is based on more than one component, show the computation for each component.

6   If the applicant is changing from the LIFO inventory method to a non-LIFO method, attach the following information. (See page 4 of the instructions.)

a   Copies of Form(s) 970 filed to adopt or expand the use of the method.

b   A statement describing how the proposed method is consistent with the requirements of Regulations section 1.472-6.

Part III   Method of Cost Allocation (See page 4 of the instructions.)

Complete this part if the requested change involves either property subject to section 263A or long-term contracts subject to section 460. Check the appropriate boxes in Sections B and C showing which costs, under both the present and proposed methods, are fully included, to the extent required, in the cost of property produced or acquired for resale under section 263A or allocated to long-term contracts under section 460. If a box is not checked, it is assumed that those costs are not fully included to the extent required. If a cost is not fully included, attach an explanation. Mark "N/A" in a box if those costs are not incurred by the applicant with respect to its production, resale, or long-term contract activities.

Exhibit 35-4 Additional Schedules for Form 3115 (*cont'd.*)

Form 3115 (Rev. 5-99) Page **7**

Section A—Allocation and Capitalization Methods (Schedule C, Part III continued.) (See page 4 of the instructions.)

Attach a description (including sample computations) of the present and proposed method(s) the applicant uses to capitalize direct and indirect costs properly allocable to property produced or acquired for resale. Include a description of the method(s) used for allocating indirect costs to intermediate cost objectives such as departments or activities prior to the allocation of such costs to property produced or acquired for resale. The description must include the following information.

1 The method of allocating direct and indirect costs (i.e., specific identification method, burden rate method, standard cost method, or other reasonable allocation method).

2 The method of allocating mixed service costs (i.e., direct reallocation method, step-allocation method, simplified service cost method using the labor-based allocation ratio, or the simplified service cost method using the production cost allocation ratio).

3 The method of capitalizing additional section 263A costs (i.e., simplified production method with or without the historic absorption ratio election, simplified resale method with or without the historic absorption ratio election including permissible variations, or the U.S. ratio method).

Section B—Direct and Indirect Costs Required To Be Allocated (See Regulations under sections 263A and 451.)

		Present method	Proposed method
1	Direct material		
2	Direct labor		
3	Indirect labor		
4	Officers' compensation (not including selling activities)		
5	Pension and other related costs		
6	Employee benefits		
7	Indirect materials and supplies		
8	Purchasing costs		
9	Handling, processing, assembly, and repackaging costs		
10	Offsite storage and warehousing costs		
11	Depreciation, amortization, and cost recovery allowance for equipment and facilities placed in service and not temporarily idle		
12	Depletion		
13	Rent		
14	Taxes other than state, local, and foreign income taxes		
15	Insurance		
16	Utilities		
17	Maintenance and repairs that relate to a production, resale, or long-term contract activity		
18	Engineering and design costs (not including section 174 research and experimental expenses)		
19	Rework labor, scrap, and spoilage		
20	Tools and equipment		
21	Quality control and inspection		
22	Bidding expenses incurred in the solicitation of contracts awarded to the applicant		
23	Licensing and franchise costs		
24	Capitalizable service costs (including mixed service costs)		
25	Administrative costs (not including any costs of selling or any return on capital)		
26	Research and experimental expenses attributable to long-term contracts		
27	Interest		
28	Other costs (Attach a list of these costs.)		

Section C—Other Costs Not Required To Be Allocated

1	Marketing, selling, advertising, and distribution expenses		
2	Research and experimental expenses not included on line 26 above		
3	Bidding expenses not included on line 22 above		
4	General and administrative costs not included in Section B above		
5	Income taxes		
6	Cost of strikes		
7	Warranty and product liability costs		
8	Section 179 costs		
9	On-site storage		
10	Depreciation, amortization, and cost recovery allowance not included on line 11 above		
11	Other costs (Attach a list of these costs.)		

(continued)

Exhibit 35-4   Additional Schedules for Form 3115 (*cont'd.*)

Schedule D—Change in Reporting Advance Payments and Depreciation/Amortization

Part I   **Change in Reporting Advance Payments** (See page 4 of the instructions.)

1   If the applicant is requesting to defer advance payment for services under Rev. Proc. 71-21, 1971-2 C.B. 549, attach the following information.

a   Sample copies of all service agreements used by the applicant that are subject to the requested change in accounting method. Indicate the particular parts of the service agreement that require the taxpayer to perform services.

b   If any parts or materials are provided, explain how the parts or materials relate to the services provided and provide the cost of such parts or materials as an absolute number and a percentage of the contract price.

c   If the change relates to contingent service contracts, explain how the contracts relate to merchandise that is sold, leased, installed, or constructed by the applicant and whether the applicant offers to sell, lease, install, or construct without the service agreement.

d   A description of the method the applicant will use to determine the amount of income earned each year on contingent contracts and why that method clearly reflects income earned and related expenses in each year.

2   If the applicant is requesting a deferral of advance payments for goods under Regulations section 1.451-5, attach the following information.

a   Sample copies of all agreements for goods or items requiring advance payments used by the applicant that are subject to the requested change in accounting method. Indicate the particular parts of the agreement that require the applicant to provide goods or items.

b   A statement providing that the entire advance payment is for goods or items. If not entirely for goods or items, a statement that an amount equal to 95% of the total contract price is properly allocable to the obligation to provide activities described in Regulations section 1.451-5(a)(1)(i) or (ii) (including services as an integral part of those activities).

Part II   **Change in Depreciation or Amortization** (See page 4 of the instructions.)

Applicants requesting approval to change their method of accounting for depreciation or amortization complete this section. Applicants must provide this information for each item or class of property for which a change is requested.

Note: *If the property has been disposed of before the beginning of the year of change, a method change is not permitted for that property. See **Automatic Change Procedures** on page 1 of the instructions for information regarding automatic changes under sections 167, 168, and 197. Also see **When Not To File Form 3115** on page 4 of the instructions for information concerning retroactive elections and election revocations.*

1   Is depreciation for the property figured under Regulations section 1.167(a)-11 (CLADR)?   . . . . ☐ **Yes**   ☐ **No**
If "Yes," the only changes permitted are under Regulations section 1.167(a)-11(c)(1)(iii).

2   Is any of the depreciation or amortization required to be capitalized under any Code section (e.g., section 263A)? ☐ **Yes**   ☐ **No**
If "Yes," enter the applicable section ▶ ....

3   Has a depreciation or amortization election been made for the property (e.g., the election under section 168(f)(1))? ☐ **Yes**   ☐ **No**
If "Yes," state the election made ▶ ....

4a   To the extent not already provided, attach a statement describing the property being changed. Include in the description the type of property, the year the property was placed in service, and the property's use in the applicant's trade or business or income-producing activity.

b   If the property is residential rental property, did the applicant live in the property before renting it?   . . . . . ☐ **Yes**   ☐ **No**
c   Is the property public utility property?   . . . . ☐ **Yes**   ☐ **No**

5   To the extent not already provided in the applicant's description of its present method, explain how the property is treated under the applicant's present method (e.g., depreciable property, inventory property, supplies under Regulations section 1.162-3, nondepreciable section 263(a) property, property deductible as a current expense, etc.).

6   If the property is not currently treated as depreciable or amortizable property, provide the facts supporting the proposed change to depreciate or amortize the property.

7   If the property is currently treated and/or will be treated as depreciable or amortizable property, provide the following information under both the present (if applicable) and proposed methods.

a   The Code section under which the property is depreciated or amortized (e.g., section 168(g)).

b   If the property is depreciated under section 168, identify the applicable asset class in Rev. Proc. 87-56, 1987-2 C.B. 674. (If none, state so and explain why.) Also provide the facts supporting the asset class under the proposed method.

c   The depreciation or amortization method of the property, including the applicable Code section (e.g., 200% declining balance method under section 168(b)(1)).

d   The useful life, recovery period, or amortization period of the property.

e   The applicable convention of the property.

35-10 CHANGE OF TAX YEAR

It may be necessary to change to a different tax year from the one that a business entity originally used when it was created. A good reason is that the nature of the business results in a great deal of transactional volume at the same time that the company is attempting to close its books for the year, which can be quite difficult to do. For example, many retailers prefer to have a fiscal year that terminates at the end of January, so that they will have processed all of the sales associated with the Christmas holiday and will now have minimal inventories left to count for their year ends.

To apply to the IRS for a change in the tax year, use Form 1128, which is available on-line at the IRS Web site. The form requires one to itemize the current overall method of accounting (that is, cash basis, accrual basis, or a hybrid method), and also to describe the general nature of the business. The IRS will also want to know if you have requested a change in the tax year at any time in the past three years, as well as the amount of the taxable gain or loss in those years, plus an estimate of the gain or loss during the short year that will be a by-product of the changeover to a new year.

The form will also require information about the business organization's relationship to any special types of organizations, such as a controlled foreign corporation, a passive foreign investment company, a foreign sales corporation, an "S" corporation, or a partnership, or if it is the beneficiary of an estate.

One must also attach a written explanation of the reason for the request to change the tax year. If this explanation is not included, then the request will automatically be denied. If the requesting organization is an "S" corporation or a partnership and already has a tax year that is not a fiscal year, then one must explain how permission for this change was obtained (since the IRS requires a calendar year for these entities, unless special permission has been granted). Finally, if a foreign-controlled corporation is requesting the change, a complete list of all shareholders in it, as well as their addresses and ownership shares, must be provided.

35-11 CLUB DUES

The IRS does not recognize as a valid business expense any payments to clubs, including initiation fees or dues, that provide entertainment activities to its members or guests. This ban includes country clubs, airline clubs, and athletic clubs. If an employee submits an expense report to a company that contains these non-deductible expenses and the company chooses to reimburse the employee for them, then these are to be considered income to the employee, and must be included in his or her W-2 form.

This restriction does not apply to any expenses incurred to attend a trade association or professional association meeting, or to initiate or maintain one's membership in such organizations, though the meetings must be related to the industry in which one does business, or one's professional area of interest.

35-12 CONSIGNMENT REVENUE

A company should not report shipments to dealers or distributors under consignment sales as taxable revenue (or as reportable revenue under generally accepted accounting principles). The sale should not be recognized until a sale of the goods has been made by the consignee. Even if title to the goods has transferred to the buyer, it should still be considered a consignment sale if the buyer has the right to return the product and the buyer does not have to pay until the buyer resells the product, or the seller must repurchase the goods at the buyer's request (which includes the cost of the buyer's storage).

35-13 DEFERRED COMPENSATION

There are a variety of deferred compensation plans used by employers who attempt to lock in their employees as far into the future as possible. Under any of these plans, an employee's tax objective is to only pay a tax when the compensation is actually received, while the employer wants to receive a full expense deduction for any amounts paid—and the sooner, the better.

If a plan meets enough criteria to be classified as an *exempt trust* or *qualified plan,* then a company can immediately recognize the expense of payments made into it, even though the employees being compensated will not be paid until some future tax year. Also, the value of funds or stock in the trust can grow on a tax-deferred basis, while participants in the plan will not be taxed until they are paid from it. In addition, the funds paid from such a plan may be eligible for rollover into an IRA, which results in an additional delay in the recognition of taxable income. While the funds are held in trust, they are also beyond the reach of any company creditors.

In order to become a qualified plan, it must meet a number of IRS requirements, such as a minimum level of coverage across the company-wide pool of employees, the prohibition of benefits under the plan for highly compensated employees to the exclusion of other employees, and restrictions on the amount of benefits that can be issued under the plan. Since many employers are only interested in creating deferred compensation plans in order to retain a small number of key employees, they will instead turn to a *nonqualified plan,* which avoids the requirement of having to offer the plan to a large number of employees.

If the plan is nonqualified, then the employer can only record the compensation expense at the same time that the employees are compensated. A company that only wants to extend deferred compensation agreements to a few select employees will tend to use this type of plan, since it does not require payments to a large number of employees, and it allows the company to increase the amount of per-person compensation well beyond the restricted levels required under a qualified plan.

A useful variation on the nonqualified plan concept is the *rabbi trust,* which is an irrevocable trust that is used to fund deferred compensation for key employees. Under this approach, a company contributes stock to a third party trustee, such as a bank or trust company, with the stock being designated for eventual payment to a few key employees. Employee vesting can take seven years or even longer in a few instances, which gives companies an excellent tool to lock in key employees over long periods of time with such plans. Employees can be paid from the trust either in stock or cash, and will recognize income at the time of receipt. The company can recognize an expense at the same time that the employee recognizes income; however, if the employee gradually vests in the plan, the expense can be proportionally recognized by the company at the time of vesting. If the payments made into the trust are in the form of company stock, then the company must only record as an expense the value of the stock at the time of grant, and can ignore any subsequent changes in the stock's value. A company that uses a rabbi trust does not have to make extensive reports to the government under ERISA rules; instead, it is only necessary to make a one-time disclosure of the plan within four months of its inception. It is also necessary to initiate the plan prior to the start of any services to which the payments apply, or at least include in the plan a forfeiture clause that is active throughout the term of the deferred compensation agreement.

The terms of a rabbi trust must also state that a key employee's benefits from the plan cannot be shifted to a third party. It must also state that the trust be an unfunded one for the purposes of both taxes and Title I of ERISA. Further, the plan must define the timing of future payments, or the events that will trigger payments, as well as the amount of payments to be made to recipients.

A key consideration for any company contemplating the creation of a rabbi trust is that the plan assets must be unsecured, and cannot unconditionally vest in the employees who are beneficiaries of the plan. This requirement is founded on the economic benefit doctrine, which holds that the avoidance of taxation can only occur if the receipt of funds is subject to a substantial risk of forfeiture. To this end, the plan document must state that plan participants are classed with general unsecured creditors in terms of their right to receive funds from the plan. The contractual obligation to pay employees from the plan cannot be secured by any type of note, since this defeats the purpose of having the assets be available to general creditors. However, just because the funds can be claimed by general creditors does not mean that they are available for other company uses — payment obligations to targeted employees must be made before any funds may be extracted for other company uses.

The unsecured status of a rabbi trust can be a cause of great concern for the employees who are being paid under its terms. Not only are the funds contributed to the trust at risk of being claimed by general creditors, but so too are all salary deferrals made by the targeted employees into the trust. This is a particular problem in the event of corporate bankruptcy, since secured creditors will be paid in full before the key employees can claim any remaining funds from the trust, which may result in a small payment or none at all. When a bankruptcy occurs or seems likely, the company is required to notify the trustee, which must halt all subsequent scheduled payments to plan participants and hold all remaining funds for distribution to secured creditors. Further, a change in control may result in a new management team that is not inclined to honor the terms of a deferred compensation agreement that require additional payments into the trust, in which case the recipients under the plan may sue the company for the missing benefits. There is some protection for key employees in this case, however, because the terms of the deferred compensation agreement will require the third party trustee to make payments to employees as they become due; the main problem is that the funds for these payments will only continue to be available if the company pays funds into the trust.

If the perceived risk to plan participants outweighs the advantages of having a rabbi trust, it is also possible to create a *secular trust.* Under this approach, plan participants will have their assets protected in the event of corporate insolvency, but the reduced level of risk is offset by current taxation of the deferred compensation, which defeats the purpose of having the plan. A combined version of the two plans, called a *rabbicular trust,* starts as a rabbi trust, but then converts to a secular trust if the company funding the plan approaches bankruptcy. However, this approach will still result in the immediate recognition of all income at the time of conversion to a secular trust.

Though the rabbi trust concept can result in substantial benefits to both an employer and key employees, it is not allowed in some states, or only in a modified form. Also, rabbicular trusts must be carefully written to comply with all deferred compensation laws at both the state and federal levels. Consequently, the assistance of a qualified taxation professional should be obtained before setting up either type of deferred compensation plan.

35-14 DEPRECIATION

The depreciation calculation that the IRS allows for the calculation of taxable income requires the use of the Modified Accelerated Cost Recovery System (MACRS) in nearly all cases. MACRS consists of two depreciation systems, one being the General Depreciation System (GDS) and the other being the Alternative Depreciation System (ADS).

The ADS depreciation system uses straight-line depreciation calculations and a longer recovery period than is required for GDS. One must use ADS for tangible property that is used mostly outside of the United States, as well as any tax-exempt use property,

Exhibit 35-5   Percentage of Depreciable Basis by Tax Year and Property Class

Year of Recovery	200% Declining Balance				150% Declining Balance	
	3-Year Class	5-Year Class	7-Year Class	10-Year Class	15-Year Class	20-Year Class
1	33.33	20.00	14.29	10.00	5.00	3.750
2	44.45	32.00	24.49	18.00	9.50	7.219
3	14.81	19.20	17.49	14.40	8.55	6.677
4	7.41	11.52	12.49	11.52	7.70	6.177
5		11.52	8.93	9.22	6.93	5.713
6		5.76	8.92	7.37	6.23	5.285
7			8.93	6.55	5.90	4.888
8			4.46	6.55	5.90	4.522
9				6.56	5.91	4.462
10				6.55	5.90	4.461
11				3.28	5.91	4.462
12					5.90	4.461
13					5.91	4.462
14					5.90	4.461
15					5.91	4.462
16					2.95	4.461
17						4.462
18						4.461
19						4.462
20						4.461
21						2.231

or tax-exempt bond-financed property. These are rare cases, so many businesses will never run an ADS calculation, though they can elect to use ADS instead of GDS. Given the reduced amount of up-front depreciation that is recognized under this approach, few companies choose to do so.

The much more common depreciation method is GDS, which uses the declining balance method for depreciation calculations and has a shorter recovery period. Under GDS, property can be placed into eight property classes, each of which has a different recovery period. The six main property classes (3-year, 5-year, 7-year, 10-year, 15-year, and 20-year) are shown in Exhibit 35-5, where the percentage of original depreciable basis that can be taken in each successive taxable year is shown. The remaining two property classes that are not shown are for nonresidential real property and residential rental property.

The cumulative total amount of depreciation for each of the property classes is shown in Exhibit 35-6, rather than the annual depreciation percentage that was shown in the last exhibit.

Exhibit 35-6   Cumulative Depreciation Percent by Tax Year and Property Class

Year of Recovery	200% Declining Balance				150% Declining Balance	
	3-Year Class	5-Year Class	7-Year Class	10-Year Class	15-Year Class	20-Year Class
1	33.33	20.00	14.29	10.00	5.00	3.75
2	77.78	52.00	38.78	28.00	14.50	10.97
3	92.59	71.20	56.27	42.40	23.05	17.65
4	100.00	82.72	68.76	53.92	30.75	23.82
5		94.24	77.69	63.14	37.68	29.54
6		100.00	86.61	70.51	43.91	34.82
7			95.54	77.06	49.81	39.71
8			100.00	83.61	55.71	44.23
9				90.17	61.62	48.69
10				96.72	67.52	53.15
11				100.00	73.43	57.62
12					79.33	62.08
13					85.24	66.54
14					91.14	71.00
15					97.05	75.46
16					100.00	79.92
17						84.39
18						88.85
19						93.31
20						97.77
21						100.00

The most common types of property allowed under the 5-year GDS category are computers, office equipment, automobiles and light trucks, appliances, and carpets. If ADS were to be used, the depreciation period would lengthen to six years for office equipment and nine years for appliances and carpets. The types of assets that fall into the 7-year GDS category are office furniture, as well as any property that has not been designated as falling into a different category. For ADS calculation purposes, office furniture is depreciated over 10 years, while default assets are depreciated over 12 years. The type of assets that fall into the 15-year GDS category are fences, roads, and shrubbery (all of which are depreciated over 20 years under ADS).

When calculating depreciation under the GDS system, different conventions are used for the amount of depreciation recognition allowed in the first year. Generally, the IRS prefers to see a half-year convention used, under which property purchased at any point during the first year receives as much depreciation expense as if it had been purchased at the mid-point of the year. A mid-month convention is also used for all nonresidential real property (which is land or improvements to land) and residential rental property. A mid-quarter convention is also sometimes used if the dollar amount of the property placed in service during the last three months of the tax year comprises more than 40% of the total base of all property placed in service for the entire year; this calculation does not include the cost of property that was bought and sold within the same year.

There are a few cases where MACRS cannot be used. Specifically, it cannot be used to depreciate intangible property, motion picture film or videotape, or sound recordings.

It is allowable in some situations to use a different depreciation method besides MACRS, as long as it is not based on the number of years that have elapsed. For example, the units of production method depreciates a fixed asset based upon the number of units of production that have passed through it. If it is estimated that a total of 500,000 units of production can be completed by a machine, and 124,500 units were actually produced in a year, then 124,500/500,000, or 24.9% of the total cost of the machine can be depreciated in that year.

A small amount of asset purchases in each year can be charged off to expense at once under IRS rules, rather than depreciating them, thereby reducing the amount of taxable income reported. This situation is described under Section 179 of the Internal Revenue Code. The maximum Section 179 deduction allowed for the few tax years is:

- Maximum deduction in 2000 is $20,000
- Maximum deduction in 2001 is $24,000
- Maximum deduction in 2002 is $24,000
- Maximum deduction in 2003 is $25,000

The Section 179 deduction is allowable for any tangible personal property (such as machinery and equipment), other tangible property used as an integral part of a manufacturing or extraction (mining) operation, or for use by utilities. There is also a special application for property used in the production or distribution of petroleum products. It is allowable to use the deduction if the acquired property is used at least 50% for business purposes; if there is some proportion of usage that is less than 100%, one can arrive at the correct deduction by multiplying the item's cost by the percentage of business usage. Also, if an asset is partially purchased with cash and partially with some other asset as a trade-in, then only the cash portion of the payment can be deducted under Section 179.

There are also a few instances where no Section 179 deduction can be made. It cannot be used if assets are acquired from a related party, or if acquired by one member of a controlled group (that is, subsidiary) from another member of the same controlled group.

Section 179 deductions cannot be used to create a taxable loss for a business, though they can be used to offset other sources of business income to arrive at a reduced level of reported taxable income. Given these restrictions, the Section 179 deduction is of minor interest to large corporations, but can be a useful way to delay tax payments for smaller businesses with modest amounts of reported taxable income.

35-15 DISTRIBUTIONS

This section describes a variety of distributions to the shareholders or partners in "C" and "S" corporations, as well as partnerships, and their varying treatment under the tax laws.

A return of capital to shareholders in a "C" corporation is first offset against the shareholders' basis in their stock, resulting in no taxable gain. If the return of capital exceeds the shareholders' basis, then the excess amount is taxed as a capital gain. If the distribution is part of a corporate liquidation, and the amount returned is less than the shareholders' basis, then the difference can be claimed as a capital loss.

If a corporation issues a dividend to its shareholders, it must be recorded as ordinary income by the shareholders, on the grounds that it is the result of earnings within the short-term, and so has no reason to be considered a long-term capital gain. If the company also has a dividend reinvestment plan available under which shareholders can purchase more shares with their dividends, then any discount on the purchase of additional dividends must be reported as ordinary taxable income in the current period.

If an entity sells stock prior to the payment date of a dividend but after the date when it was declared, then the entity to whom the dividend check is addressed must include the amount of dividend in its taxable income.

A company may distribute a stock dividend to its shareholders. If so, there is no immediate taxable income to the recipient. However, the shareholder must allocate his or her basis in the existing stock between it and the newly acquired stock dividend in direct proportion to the fair market value of each one on the date when the stock dividend was issued.

If an "S" corporation distributes its current or retained earnings to shareholders, it is treated as a nontaxable reduction in one's basis in the stock. Distributions in excess of one's basis are treated as a gain. All current-year income or loss experienced by an "S" corporation is passed directly through to its shareholders, and must be reported by them in proportion to their ownership shares in the business. One's current-year share of income in an "S" corporation will increase one's basis in the corporation.

Mutual funds and real estate investment trusts are allowed to make capital gain distributions to their shareholders, which will be taxed under the reduced long-term capital gains tax.

If a distribution is made to a partner in a partnership in the form of marketable securities, the partner need only recognize taxable income to the extent that the current market value of the securities on the day of the distribution exceeds the basis of the partner's interest (which is the money and adjusted basis of any property that the partner originally contributed to the partnership).

35-16 ESTIMATED TAXES

Corporations are required to pay to the IRS an estimated quarterly income tax. It is clearly not to a company's advantage to estimate too high and have the government hold its money until its final Form 1120 has been completed, so one should be aware of the rules regarding minimum estimated tax payments.

The IRS cannot levy a penalty for under-payment of estimated taxes if the full-year corporate tax is estimated to be less than $500. The same rule applies if a company remits four equal estimated payments that total at least 100% of the prior year corporate tax liability, except in cases where the company did not file a return in the previous year (since the estimated tax would always be zero), if there was no tax liability in the previous year, or if the prior tax year was less than 12 months (which happens when a company switches to a new tax year). A different rule applies to corporations with at least $1 million of taxable income in any one of the immediately preceding three tax years; they can use the prior year tax liability as the basis for the first quarterly estimated tax payment of the new tax year, but must then use an estimate of current year results to make payments for the final three quarters of the year.

If a company has a tax year that matches the calendar year, then its estimated tax payments are due on April 15th, June 15th, September 15th, and December 15th. If the tax year covers any other time period, then the four payments are sequentially due on the 15th day of the fourth, sixth, ninth, and twelfth months of the tax year. If any of these days fall on a weekend or legal holiday, then payments remitted on the following day will still be counted as being paid on time.

In the event that an estimated tax payment was higher than the actual result, a corporation can file for a quick refund, using Form 4466, which is the Corporation Application for Quick Refund of Overpayment of Estimated Tax. The form must be filed after a corporation's tax year end and before the 16th day of the third month after the tax year, but in advance of its filing its annual income tax return. The quick refund is only available to those corporations having made estimated payments that exceed their expected liability by at least 10% and by at least $500.

35-17 FINANCIAL REPORTING OF TAX LIABILITIES

The proper reporting of tax liabilities is covered by statement number 109 of the Financial Account Standards Board (FASB). In it, the FASB outlines the proper reporting standards for the effects of income taxes resulting from a company's activities. The primary objectives of these standards are to recognize not only the amount of taxes payable for the current reporting year, but also any deferred tax liabilities and assets for the future tax consequences of events that have already been reported on in the company's financial statements or tax returns.

The standards set forth in FASB 109 are based on a few key principles. First, a current asset or liability account is recognized to the extent that there are current year taxes payable or refundable. Second, a company must recognize a deferred tax liability or asset in the amount of any estimated future taxes that can be reasonably attributed to temporary tax differences or carryforwards. Third, the recognition of any deferred tax assets is to be reduced by any tax assets that are not reasonably expected to be realized.

If there is a difference between the amount of recognized income or loss in a given year that is allowed by tax laws, as opposed to financial reporting standards, then these temporary differences must be recognized on the financial statements as deferred tax assets or liabilities. These accounts will be gradually drawn down over time as the deferred impact of the reporting differences are gradually recognized. For example, revenue may be recognized in the current year under generally accepted accounting principles (GAAP), but deferred under applicable tax laws, which will result in a deferment in the recognition of taxable income to later years; in this case, a tax liability will be created in the amount of the applicable tax that has been deferred. On the other hand, an increase in the deferred asset account for taxes will occur if the tax laws require a company to defer the recognition of expenses that have already been recognized under GAAP, since these can be used at a later date to reduce the amount of taxable income.

There are also differences between taxable and GAAP reporting that are permanent differences—that is, the differences between the two reporting methods will never be reconciled. An example is the interest income on municipal bonds, which is recognized in the financial records, but is permanently excluded from reportable income on the tax records. When permanent differences are involved, no asset or liability is recorded on the financial records, since there is no prospect of the differences ever being recognized.

The first step in calculating deferred tax assets and liabilities is to itemize the nature and amount of each type of loss and tax credit carryforward, as well as the remaining time period over which each carryforward is expected to extend. Next, we separately summarize the total deferred tax liability for all temporary differences and the total deferred asset related to all carryforwards. The final step is to ascertain the amount (if any) of a valuation allowance needed to offset the deferred tax asset. This allowance can be necessary if there is evidence that some proportion of the deferred tax asset may not be recognized. For example, there may be an expectation that the full amount of a credit carryforward cannot be offset against a sufficient amount of income during the upcoming time period during which the tax laws allow a company to use the credit. The estimates used to create the allowance will require a great deal of judgment, so the FASB has added some guidelines that take away some of the uncertainty. It requires one to review several sources of likely future income against which the carryforwards can be offset, which are the (1) future reversal of temporary tax differences, (2) future taxable income that will arise, exclusive of the reversal of any temporary tax differences, (3) tax planning strategies, and (4) existing taxable income for which carrybacks are permitted. If there is a reasonable basis for a taxable source of revenue income from any one or a combination of these four items, then there is no need for a valuation allowance.

Also, all reasonable forms of evidence regarding future expectations for taxable income should be included in the review. It is also possible to take into account during the review the presence of any tax strategies that a prudent company would consider in order to take advantage of and use any tax assets in the future. As a result of the review, a valuation allowance should be set up if it is more likely than not that there will not be sufficient taxable income in the future to offset any tax assets. However, it is not allowable to set up a valuation allowance when there is no clear need for one.

When these calculations are completed, it is necessary to separately report the deferred liability, deferred asset, and valuation allowance for the deferred asset on the balance sheet. In the first year when this entry is made, a company can include the entire adjustment in net income as of the beginning of the year of adoption of the FASB 109 rules, or it can restate the financial results of prior years to include the changes, which yields a better year-to-year comparison of financial results.

After the correct entries are booked, the accountant's job is still not complete, for the entries may require periodic updates to reflect changes in the tax rates that apply to the company. The tax rate at which a tax liability or asset is computed for financial statement reporting purposes is either the maximum tax rate to which the business is generally subject (assuming that its income is always so high that it exceeds any graduated rates) or else an average rate for the general range of tax rates within which its taxable income usually carries it. If there is a change in the tax laws that results in a different income tax rate structure, then the journal entries used to record the tax liabilities and assets must be altered to more appropriately reflect the new tax rates. For example, if a company has a tax asset, an increase in the tax rate will result in an increase in the recorded asset. This change to the financial records should take place as of the day when the new tax rates take effect. The entire effect of a change in tax rates on the reporting of deferred tax assets or liabilities is recorded in the period when the tax rate change occurs.

35-18 FOREIGN EARNED INCOME

The foreign earned income (FEI) tax is only applicable to individuals, not to a corporation. Nonetheless, it is mentioned here because it applies to any employee posted outside of the United States.

Under FEI, employees living abroad can exclude up to $76,000 of their foreign earned income from taxation in 2000. This exclusion rose to $78,000 in 2001, and then $80,000 in 2002. The only type of revenue that can be excluded with this exemption is that which is earned from personal services (which includes one's salary, bonuses, commissions, housing and automobile allowance, and cost of living allowance); it does not include dividends, capital gains, interest, and income from rental properties.

If a person is only out of the country for part of the tax year, then the amount of the exclusion must be prorated to cover only that portion of his or her time that was spent outside of the country.

An individual qualifies for this exclusion if he or she has a tax home in a foreign country, is a United States citizen, and either has been outside of the country for 330 days within a consecutive 12-month period, or passes a foreign residency test that is based on the permanence of the foreign dwelling occupied, the type and duration of the visa under which one is working within the foreign country, and the status of any dwelling being maintained within the United States at the same time.

35-19 GIFTS

The IRS imposes a maximum deduction of just $25 for every gift that a company gives directly or indirectly to another person. For example, if a company gives a $25 gift to each of ten people, then $250 is deductible. However, if a company gives 10 $25 gifts to one person, then only $25 is deductible. This restriction does not include any incidental costs, such as the shipping and handling associated with the shipment of gifts.

The limitation does not apply to any gift that costs $4 or less, has the company name clearly imprinted on it, and is part of a mass distribution of the gift (such as an imprinted company pen or calendar). Under this variation, a company could give any number of gifts to a person, and could deduct the cost of all the gifts handed out.

There is some flexibility in categorizing a cost as a gift or an entertainment expense, depending upon one's participation in the gift. For example, if the company has tickets to a sporting event, and an employee takes a customer to the game, then the cost of the tickets can be expensed as either a gift (which is subject to the $25 limitation) or an entertainment expense. However, if the tickets are simply given to the customer and no employee accompanies the person to the game, then the tickets are categorized as a gift.

35-20 GOODWILL AND OTHER INTANGIBLES

The tax treatment of intangible expenses falls under the category of Section 197 of the IRS regulations. Expenses can only be included in this category if they are related to a significant change in the ownership or use of a company, such as a startup or the acquisition of another business or a substantial part of its assets. Goodwill is the excess of the purchase price of an acquisition over the cost of the assets acquired. Any expenses that fall into this category will be amortized on a straight-line basis over 15 years. The following expenses can be amortized under Section 197:

- *Workforce in place.* This includes the cost of buying out an existing employee contract as part of an acquisition, or workforce-related costs that are strictly based upon the circumstances of an acquisition.

- *Business books and records.* This includes the cost of customer lists, subscription lists, and lists of advertisers and clients, as well as the intangible value of technical and training manuals that are being acquired.

- *Customer-based intangibles.* This includes that portion of an acquisition purchase price that relates to a customer or circulation base or any customer relationship resulting in the provision of future goods and services.

- *Government licensing cost.* This includes the cost to apply for any government-granted license, such as a liquor license.

- *Patents, copyrights, franchises, and trademarks.* This includes the purchase price of any acquired legal rights, as well as the legal cost of applying for patents, copyrights, and trademarks. It also includes the purchase price of a franchise (though not of a sports franchise).

- *Supplier-based intangible.* This includes that portion of an acquisition purchase price that relates to favorable supply contracts or relations with distributors.

To keep companies from claiming a loss on an intangible expense that has been capitalized under Section 197 (if it has become worthless), one must allocate the remaining unamortized expense among all other types of intangibles acquired through the same transaction, thereby continuing to amortize the expense.

To keep companies from using Section 197 to an excessive degree, there are anti-churning rules in place that prevent amortization from being used in cases where a change of ownership is really caused by the shifting of property among related parties. The rules governing anti-churning are quite lengthy, but essentially state that churning cannot take place when property passes between family members, between companies that are owned by the same parent organization, or if there is any provable degree of common control over both entities involved in a transfer of property.

35-21 HYBRID METHODS OF ACCOUNTING

The IRS allows a combination of cash, accrual, and special methods of accounting as long as the resulting system clearly shows taxable income, and if the system is used consistently. However, hybrid systems must factor in the following systemic requirements:

- *Accrual method.* If the accrual method of accounting is used to record expenses, then it must also be used to record revenue.

- *Cash method usage.* If the cash method of accounting is used to record revenue, then it must also be used consistently for the recording of all expense items.

- *Inventory.* If inventory is present, then the accrual method must be used for recording purchases and sales, though the cash method can be used for recording other items appearing on the income statement.

Though these restrictions may appear to severely hamper the use of any hybrid system, it is still possible to create one where the accrual method is only used to record revenue, or where the cash method is only used to record expenses.

35-22 IMPUTED INTEREST EXPENSE

The amount of interest income that a company receives is considered by the IRS to be fully taxable ordinary income, which falls into the highest tax bracket. For that reason, the IRS uses the imputed interest concept to make sure that all interest income is recognized. Under this concept, a company must record interest income (or expense, if it is paying for the associated debt) at the current market rate at the time a debt instrument is initiated. If not, the IRS will assume (or impute) a higher interest rate that is 110% of the interest rate paid on whatever type of Treasury debt has approximately the same number of years to maturity as the debt instrument in question. This higher rate is called the *Applicable Federal Rate.*

This rule also applies to installment sales, so the interest portion of these payments must also be broken out if the total amount of a series of installment payments exceeds $3,000. The general rule to see if an installment sale requires the calculation of imputed interest if the total of all payments due more than six months after the date when the sale occurred is greater than the present value of the payments, plus the present value of any interest charges noted in the installment sale contract.

Another variation on the imputed interest concept is the *Original Issue Discount* (OID). This applies to situations when an investor buys a bond, note, or other long-term debt instrument at a price that is lower than its eventual redemption price. The difference between its purchase price and the final redemption price at maturity is the OID. The IRS requires the investor to recognize the income from the OID as it accrues over time, irrespective of the presence of any interest income actually received from the issuer of the debt.

35-23 INSTALLMENT SALES

Under an installment sale, the sale of an asset becomes an installment sale if the contract states that at least one payment is made in a tax year later than the one in which the sale took place. When this happens, many entities that are on the accrual basis of accounting are allowed to use what is essentially an income recognition method under the cash basis of accounting to recognize the gross profit from the sale over the years in which payments are made.

Under the installment sale rules, such a sale is essentially an exchange of the seller's property for the buyer's promise to pay at some later time through the use of a debt instrument, which becomes an exchange of assets rather than the payment of cash for the seller's asset. Under the normal tax rules for an exchange of property, the increase in value over the fair market value of the item sold is to be recognized at once as income, but the installment sale rule varies from this approach in assuming that income is not considered to have been received until the cash associated with the buyer's debt instrument is received. In essence, tax recognition under an installment sale is designed to let a seller pay taxes only when the cash is available with which to pay the taxes.

The installment sales method cannot be used to report a gain from the sale of stock or securities traded on an established securities market, nor does it apply to those businesses that regularly sell the same type of property on an installment plan (such as a car dealership). It also cannot be used if the installment sale results in a loss. In this case, it can only be deducted in the tax year in which the transfer of property occurs.

In order to calculate the amount of gain to recognize in each year, it is necessary to split the payments received into their interest income component (see the "Imputed Interest" section), a gain on sale of the property, and a return on the taxpayer's adjusted basis in the property (which is increased by any associated selling expenses). The portion of each payment that is ascribed to interest income will be taxed as ordinary income, while the gain may be taxed as a long-term capital gain (depending on the circumstances), and the return on the taxpayer's adjusted basis will be tax-free. This means that the taxpayer will be taxed on that portion of the gross profit recognized each year, which spreads out the amount of the total tax payment over the full term of the installment sale agreement.

If the total selling price is reduced prior to the completion of all payments on an installment sale, the gross profit on the sale will also change, and therefore the amount of tax due. One must then recalculate the gross profit percentage for the remaining payments with the reduced sale price and then subtract the gain already reported in previous tax years. The remaining gain can be spread over the remaining future installment payments.

Form 6252, which is used to report installment sales to the IRS, is shown in Exhibit 35-7. This form should not be filed by an accrual basis taxpayer who "elects out" of using the installment method, recognizes the entire gain from a sale of property, and pays the associated tax at once. Any entity that chooses to use the installment method by filing Form 6252 does not have the option to switch back to a full and immediate recognition of income under the accrual basis of accounting, unless an amended return is filed no more than six months after the due date of the return, excluding extensions.

Exhibit 35-7 Installment Sale Income Form 6252

Form **6252** | **Installment Sale Income** | OMB No. 1545-0228

▶See separate instructions. ▶ Attach to your tax return.
▶Use a separate form for each sale or other disposition of property on the installment method.

Department of the Treasury
Internal Revenue Service

2000
Attachment
Sequence No. **79**

Name(s) shown on return | Identifying number

1 Description of property ▶ ....

2a Date acquired (month, day, year) ▶ [/ /] **b** Date sold (month, day, year) ▶ [/ /]

3 Was the property sold to a related party after May 14, 1980? See instructions. If "No," skip line 4 . . . ☐ Yes ☐ No

4 Was the property you sold to a related party a marketable security? If "Yes," complete Part III. If "No," complete Part III for the year of sale and the 2 years after the year of sale . . . . ☐ Yes ☐ No

Part I **Gross Profit and Contract Price.** Complete this part for the year of sale only.

5 Selling price including mortgages and other debts. **Do not** include interest whether stated or unstated | 5

6 Mortgages and other debts the buyer assumed or took the property subject to, but not new mortgages the buyer got from a bank or other source . | 6

7 Subtract line 6 from line 5 . . . . | 7

8 Cost or other basis of property sold . . . . | 8

9 Depreciation allowed or allowable . . . . | 9

10 Adjusted basis. Subtract line 9 from line 8 . . . . | 10

11 Commissions and other expenses of sale . . . . | 11

12 Income recapture from Form 4797, Part III. See instructions . . | 12

13 Add lines 10, 11, and 12 . . . . | 13

14 Subtract line 13 from line 5. If zero or less, **stop here. Do not** complete the rest of this form . | 14

15 If the property described on line 1 above was your main home, enter the amount of your excluded gain. Otherwise, enter -0-. See instructions . . . . | 15

16 **Gross profit.** Subtract line 15 from line 14 . . . . | 16

17 Subtract line 13 from line 6. If zero or less, enter -0- . . . . | 17

18 **Contract price.** Add line 7 and line 17 . . . . | 18

Part II **Installment Sale Income.** Complete this part for the year of sale **and** any year you receive a payment or have certain debts you must treat as a payment on installment obligations.

19 Gross profit percentage. Divide line 16 by line 18. For years after the year of sale, see instructions | 19

20 **For year of sale only:** Enter amount from line 17 above; otherwise, enter -0- . . . . . . | 20

21 Payments received during year. See instructions. **Do not** include interest, whether stated or unstated | 21

22 Add lines 20 and 21 . . . . | 22

23 Payments received in prior years. See instructions. **Do not** include interest, whether stated or unstated . . . . | 23

24 **Installment sale income.** Multiply line 22 by line 19 . . . . | 24

25 Part of line 24 that is ordinary income under recapture rules. See instructions . . . . . . | 25

26 Subtract line 25 from line 24. Enter here and on Schedule D or Form 4797. See instructions . | 26

Part III **Related Party Installment Sale Income. Do not** complete if you received the final payment this tax year.

27 Name, address, and taxpayer identifying number of related party ....

....

28 Did the related party resell or dispose of the property ("second disposition") during this tax year? . . . ☐ Yes ☐ No

29 **If the answer to question 28 is "Yes," complete lines 30 through 37 below unless one of the following conditions is met. Check the box that applies.**

a ☐ The second disposition was more than 2 years after the first disposition (other than dispositions of marketable securities). If this box is checked, enter the date of disposition (month, day, year) ▶ [/ /]

b ☐ The first disposition was a sale or exchange of stock to the issuing corporation.

c ☐ The second disposition was an involuntary conversion and the threat of conversion occurred after the first disposition.

d ☐ The second disposition occurred after the death of the original seller or buyer.

e ☐ It can be established to the satisfaction of the Internal Revenue Service that tax avoidance was not a principal purpose for either of the dispositions. If this box is checked, attach an explanation. See instructions.

30 Selling price of property sold by related party . . . . | 30

31 Enter contract price from line 18 for year of first sale . . . . | 31

32 Enter the **smaller** of line 30 or line 31 . . . . | 32

33 Total payments received by the end of your 2000 tax year. See instructions . . . . . . | 33

34 Subtract line 33 from line 32. If zero or less, enter -0- . . . . | 34

35 Multiply line 34 by the gross profit percentage on line 19 for year of first sale . . . . . | 35

36 Part of line 35 that is ordinary income under recapture rules. See instructions . . . . . | 36

37 Subtract line 36 from line 35. Enter here and on Schedule D or Form 4797. See instructions . | 37

For Paperwork Reduction Act Notice, see back of form. Cat. No. 13601R Form **6252** (2000)

Most of the installment sale tax rules were repealed in 1999, requiring accrual-basis entities to include in income currently all gain realized (or to be realized) from the sale of property, even in cases where the taxable entity would receive some or all of the proceeds in a future tax year. This caused a considerable burden on taxpayers, since they were required to pay taxes on gains that had not yet been earned, thereby placing them in a cash crunch. It was estimated that this decreased the value of more than 250,000 small businesses by as much as 20%, because their owners were less likely to accept installment payments for sale of their businesses. Given the outcry, this 1999 ruling (which was located in IRC Section 453(a)(2)) was retroactively repealed in 2000.

35-24 INVENTORY VALUATION

When inventory is used to support the sale of goods, the type of accounting method used to determine what is included in inventory and how its cost is established is crucial to the development of an accurate amount of reported taxable income.

From the perspective of the IRS, the types of items that should be included in a company's inventory are the same as those authorized under generally accepted accounting principles — that is, raw materials, work-in-process, finished goods, and supplies that are integrated into the finished product. A company that wants to avoid tax payments will likely attempt to narrowly define what is included in inventory, so that all items falling outside that definition will be charged to expense, thereby reducing the level of taxable income.

The area in which large shifts in the level of inventory are most likely to occur is in the definition and recognition of the point at which a company obtains title to inventory, and when this title is transferred to another entity. For example, once a company pays for raw materials or merchandise, that inventory should be recorded on the company's books, even though it may very well be still in transit to the company. At the other end of the sales cycle, goods should no longer be included in inventory once they have been handed over to a third party freight company for delivery to a customer, except for the case in which the shipping terms specify that the company retains title to the goods until they reach the customer's receiving dock. This latter instance is similar to a cash on delivery (COD) arrangement, where the company should continue to record an item as being in stock until it is paid for by the customer at the time of delivery. If goods have been sent to a distributor under a consignment agreement, then the company retains title to the products until sold, and so those items must continue to be recorded in inventory. If the company is the distributor, and is receiving consigned goods, then of course the reverse situation applies, and it should not record the inventory as its own asset. Additionally, any inventory used for marketing purposes, such as display items, should also be recorded in inventory.

Once the quantity of inventory on hand has been firmly established, the next issue is to properly determine its cost in a manner that is acceptable to the IRS. The most approved method for doing so is the *specific identification method*, under which a company tracks the exact cost of each item in stock. This is easiest to do if each unit of stock is clearly identifiable, but in most cases this is not practical, especially when there are large quantities of each item running through the warehouse. In this latter case, the IRS prefers that either the FIFO or LIFO method be used.

Under the FIFO method, the assumption is that the first product purchased will also be the first one to be used, and so the earliest cost at which a product was purchased will be the first one applied to the sale of a product. This tends to result in a higher level of ending inventory dollars, on the assumption that inventory costs are constantly rising (as is generally the case in an inflationary economy). The opposite philosophy is true under the LIFO assumption, which assumes that the last item purchased will be the first one used. This method tends to result in a lower ending inventory valuation, since the most recent (and higher) costs will have been charged to the cost of goods sold. Companies that are trying to avoid paying income taxes will have a preference for the LIFO method, since it yields a lower level of reported earnings.

A company can convert to the LIFO method by filing Form 970, Application to Use LIFO Inventory Method, with the IRS.

It is also possible to use the *retail method* for valuing inventory for tax purposes. This method is most commonly applied to the inventories of retailers or distributors, who have nothing but finished goods in stock. To derive costs under the retail method, the total selling price of goods in stock is reduced by the average markup originally applied to the inventory, thereby yielding a close approximation to the original cost. The first step in this process is to determine the markup percentage. To do so, add together the total retail price of all goods in the beginning inventory and the total retail price of all items purchased subsequently. Then subtract the total cost of goods sold contained within the beginning inventory and the cost of all items subsequently purchased from the total price just calculated. Finally, divide the result, which is the total markup dollars, by the total selling price that was initially calculated. With the markup percentage in hand, we can now multiply it by the total retail price of the ending inventory, which results in the total markup dollars in the ending inventory. By subtracting this amount from the total retail price of the ending inventory, we arrive at the cost of the ending inventory. Since there may be different markup percentages for different classes of product, it is more accurate to cluster together products with similar markup percentages into groups, and calculate the cost of each inventory group separately.

If a company uses the retail method in conjunction with the LIFO valuation method, then it must adjust its ending retail selling prices so that they factor in the impact of price markdowns and markups. If the retail method is used without the LIFO valuation method, then the ending retail selling prices can only be adjusted for markups, not markdowns.

It is not acceptable under IRS rules to apply the direct costing method to inventory. Under this practice, all costs not directly associated with a product (such as most overhead costs) are charged directly to the cost of goods sold during the current period, rather than being allocated to ending inventory. If this method were allowable, a company could charge off a larger part of its costs in the current period, thereby reducing the amount of taxable income.

No matter which method (specific identification method, FIFO, LIFO, or retail method) is used, there is still the issue of what costs to allocate to the cost of each inventory item. For example, if a company buys raw materials under a volume purchasing discount, it cannot charge to inventory the list price, but rather only the price paid, which is net of the volume discount. On the other hand, the amount of any cash discount taken in exchange does not have to be factored into the inventory valuation (but whatever method chosen must be used consistently).

A company should not artificially inflate the value of any inventory on hand, so one should periodically reduce the inventory valuation by comparing the current market price that can be obtained for each inventory item to its cost, and adjust its recorded cost down to the lower of cost or market. This is also in accordance with generally accepted accounting principles. This rule does not apply for tax purposes if the inventory being reviewed is to be sold to a customer under a firm fixed price contract, nor does it apply to any inventory that is accounted for under the LIFO valuation method.

There will also be cases in which a company has second-hand or damaged goods in stock that it cannot sell at full price. Though it may be tempting to write off the total value of these items, thereby increasing the cost of goods sold and reducing the level of reported income, the IRS prefers that a company never value them at less than their scrap value, and preferably at their estimated sale price (less the cost of disposition); by requiring this higher valuation, the IRS ensures that the amount of taxable income reported will be higher than if the value of these items were simply eliminated from the inventory valuation.

It is allowable to value a company's inventory using one method for book purposes and another for tax purposes, except in the case of the LIFO inventory valuation method. In this case, the tax advantages to be gained from the use of LIFO are so significant that the IRS requires a user to employ it for both book and tax purposes. Furthermore, if LIFO is used in any one of a group of financially related companies, the entire group is assumed to be a single entity for tax reporting purposes, which means that they must all use the LIFO valuation approach for both book and tax reporting. This rule was engendered in order to stop the practice of having LIFO-valuation companies roll their results into a parent company that used some other method of reporting, thereby giving astute companies high levels of reportable income and lower levels of taxable income at the same time.

35-25 LIFE INSURANCE

It is common practice for a company to provide group term life insurance to its employees as part of a standard benefit package. This requires some extra reporting from a tax perspective, however. If the amount of the life insurance benefit exceeds $50,000, the company must report the incremental cost of the life insurance over $50,000 (to the extent that the employee is not paying for the additional insurance) on the employee's W-2 form as taxable income. In the less common case where the company provides life insurance that results in some amount of cash surrender value, then the cost of this permanent benefit to the employee must also be included in the employee's W-2 form. The only case in which these costs are not included on an employee's W-2 form is when the company is the beneficiary of the policy, rather than the employee. The opposite situation arises if the company is providing life insurance only to a few key employees, rather than to all employees; in this case, the entire cost of the insurance must be reported on the employee's W-2 form as taxable income.

35-26 LIKE-KIND EXCHANGES

Under Section 1031, if one exchanges business or investment property solely for business or investment property of a like kind, then no gain or loss is recognized on the transaction. To be acceptable to the IRS, the assets exchanged must be of a similar nature (such as an office building for an office building), and the owner must use both assets for the same purpose. If other types of property or payment are received as part of the transaction, then these other items are recognized as a taxable gain on the transaction, though the rest of the transaction still qualifies as a like-kind exchange. The like-kind exchange rule does not apply to exchanges of inventory, securities, or partnership interests, nor does it apply to exchanges of real property located inside the United States for property located outside the United States.

It is also possible to have a deferred exchange even when there is a delay in the time when one asset is sold and another is bought. It is typically called a *1031 tax deferred exchange,* or a *Starker,* which is named after the first person to be challenged by the IRS over this transaction. For this exchange to qualify as a like-kind exchange, the replacement property must be identified within 45 days of the transfer of the asset given up and the earlier of the receipt of the replacement property (no later than 180 days after the date of transfer) or the due date of the tax return for the year of initial asset transfer. In the interim, a third party, such as a title company, holds the proceeds from the first sale in escrow, and then purchases the new property on the behalf of the original seller and transfers it to that entity.

35-27 LOSSES

A net operating loss (NOL) may be carried back and applied against profits recorded in the two preceding years, with any remaining amount being carried forward for the next 20 years, when it can be offset against any reported income. If there is still an NOL left after the 20 years have expired, then the remaining amount can no longer be used. One can also irrevocably choose to ignore the carryback option and only use it for carryforward purposes. The standard procedure is to apply all of the NOL against the income reported in the earliest year, with the remainder carrying forward to each subsequent year in succession until the remaining NOL has been exhausted.

The number of carryback years can be extended to three years from the standard two years if the NOL was caused by a casualty or theft, or if it was attributable to a disaster, as declared by the president, and the company is a qualified small business (which is a sole proprietorship or partnership that has average annual revenue of $5 million or less during the three-year period ending with the tax year of the NOL). A farming business is allowed to use a five-year carryback.

If an NOL has been incurred in each of multiple years, then the NOLs should be applied against reported income (in either prior or later years) in order of the first NOL incurred. This rule is used because of the 20-year limitation on an NOL, so that an NOL incurred in an earlier year can be used before it expires.

The quickest way to receive cash back as a result of an NOL carryback is to file a Form 1045 (Application for Tentative Refund), but there is a shorter time period available in which to file it. It must be filed on or after the date when the tax return identifying the NOL is filed, but no later than one year after the NOL year.

The NOL is a valuable asset, since it can be used for many years to offset future earnings. A company buying another entity that has an NOL will certainly place a high value on the NOL, and may even buy the entity strictly in order to use its NOL. To curtail this type of behavior, the IRS has created the Section 382 limitation, under which there is a limitation on its used if there is at least a 50% change in the ownership of an entity that has an unused NOL. The limitation is derived through a complex formula that essentially multiplies the acquired corporation's stock times the long-term tax exempt bond rate. The Section 382 rules can also limit the NOL recognition of a company that has not changed its ownership, simply because of the manner in which a change in ownership is defined under the Section. To avoid these problems, a company with an unused NOL that is seeking to expand its equity should consider issuing straight preferred stock (no voting rights, no conversion privileges, and no participation in future earnings) in order to avoid any chance that the extra equity will be construed as a change in ownership.

If a company has incurred an NOL in a short tax year, it must deduct the NOL over a period of six years, starting with the first tax year after the short tax year. This limitation does not apply if the NOL is for $10,000 or less, or if the NOL is the result of a short tax year that is at least nine months long, and is less than the NOL for a full 12-month tax year beginning with the first day of the short tax year. This special NOL rule was designed to keep companies from deliberately changing their tax years in order to create an NOL within a short tax year. This situation is quite possible in a seasonal business where there are losses in all but a few months. Under such a scenario, a company would otherwise be able to declare an NOL during its short tax year, carry back the NOL to apply it against the previous two years of operations, and receive a rebate from the IRS.

35-28 MILEAGE AND PARKING REIMBURSEMENT

The standard rate of reimbursement that the IRS recommends companies pay to their employees for the use of their vehicles on company business is 32.5 cents per mile. If a company pays an employee less than this amount, then the employee can deduct the difference from his or her income tax return as a deduction when determining taxable income. If the amount reimbursed is higher than the federal rate per mile, then the difference must be included on employees' W-2 forms at year-end.

If the company provides free parking to its employees in lieu of other forms of compensation, then the company must report the fair market value of this parking as income to the employee, if the amount exceeds $175 per month. This amount is indexed based on the rate of inflation, starting in 1997, and so will increase over time.

35-29 MERGERS AND ACQUISITIONS

A key factor to consider in corporate acquisitions is the determination of what size taxable gain will be incurred by the seller (if any), as well as how the buyer can reduce the tax impact of the transaction in current and future years. In this section, we will briefly discuss the various types of transactions involved in an acquisition, the tax implications of each transaction, and whose interests are best served by the use of each one.

There are two ways in which an acquisition can be made, each with different tax implications. First, one can purchases the acquiree's stock, which may trigger a taxable gain to the seller. Second, one can purchase the acquiree's assets, which triggers a gain on sale of the assets, as well as another tax to the shareholders of the selling company, who must recognize a gain when the proceeds from liquidation of the business are distributed to them. Because of the additional taxation, a seller will generally want to sell a corporation's stock, rather than its assets.

When stock is sold to the buyer in exchange for cash or property, the buyer establishes a tax basis in the stock that equals the amount of the cash or fair market value of the property transferred to the seller. Meanwhile, the seller recognizes a gain or loss on the eventual sale of the stock that is based on its original tax basis in the stock, which is subtracted from the ultimate sale price of the stock.

It is also possible for the seller to recognize no taxable gain on the sale of a business if it takes some of the acquiring company's stock as full compensation for the sale. However, there will be no tax only if *continuity of interest* in the business can be proven by giving the sellers a sufficient amount of the buyer's stock to prove that they have a continuing financial interest in the buying company. A variation on this approach is to make an acquisition over a period of months, using nothing but voting stock as compensation to the seller's shareholders, but for which a clear plan of ultimate control over the acquiree can be proven. Another variation is to purchase at least 80% of the fair market value of the acquiree's assets solely in exchange for stock.

When only the assets are sold to the buyer, the buyer can apportion the total price among the assets purchased, up to their fair market value (with any excess portion of the price being apportioned to goodwill). This is highly favorable from a taxation perspective, since the buyer has now adjusted its basis in the assets substantially higher; it can now claim a much larger accelerated depreciation expense in the upcoming years, thereby reducing its reported level of taxable income and reducing its tax burden. From the seller's perspective, the sale price is allocated to each asset sold for the purposes of determining a gain or loss; as much of this as possible should be characterized as a capital gain (since the related tax is lower) or as an ordinary loss (since it can offset ordinary income, which has a higher tax rate).

The structuring of an acquisition transaction so that no income taxes are paid must have a reasonable business purpose besides the avoidance of taxes. Otherwise, the IRS has been known to require tax payments on the grounds that the structure of the transaction has no reasonable business purpose besides tax avoidance. Its review of the substance of a transaction over its form leads the accountant to consider such transactions in the same manner, and to restructure acquisition deals accordingly.

There is a specialized tax reduction available for the holders of stock in a small business, on which they experience a gain when the business is sold. Specifically, they are entitled to a 50% reduction in their reportable gain on sale of that stock, though it is limited to the greater of a $10 million gain or 10 times the stockholder's basis in the stock. This exclusion is reserved for "C" corporations, and only applies to stock that was acquired at its original issuance. There are a number of other exclusions, such as its inapplicability to personal service corporations, real estate investment trusts, domestic international sales corporations, and mutual funds. This type of stock is called *qualified small business stock*. The unique set of conditions surrounding this stock make it clear that it is intended to be a tax break specifically for the owners of small businesses.

A key reason for completing an acquisition used to be the purchase of net operating loss carryforwards held by the acquiree. The IRS has severely restricted the benefit to be derived from this practice. For more information about this issue, please refer to the "Losses" section in this chapter.

The tax issues presented here for acquisitions are only a brief overview of a highly complex area. Expert tax advice is highly recommended before any tax-related actions are taken in this area. For more detailed information about mergers and acquisitions in general, please refer to Chapter 34, Mergers and Acquisitions.

35-30 NEXUS

A company may have to complete many more tax forms than it would like, as well as remit taxes to more government entities, if it can be established that it has nexus within a government's area of jurisdiction. Consequently, it is very important to understand how nexus is established.

The rules vary by state, but nexus is generally considered to have occurred if a company maintains a facility of any kind within a state, or if it pays the wages of someone within that state. In some locales, the definition is expanded to include the transport of goods to customers within the state on company-owned vehicles (though nexus is not considered to have occurred if the shipment is made by a third-party freight carrier). A more liberal interpretation of the nexus rule is that a company has nexus if it sends sales personnel into the state on sales calls or training personnel there to educate customers, even though they are not permanently based there. To gain a precise understanding of how the nexus rules are interpreted by each state, it is best to contact the department of revenue of each state government.

A recent issue that is still being debated in the courts is that Internet sales may be considered to have occurred within a state if the server used to process orders or store data is kept within that state, even if the server is only rented from an Internet hosting service.

If nexus has been established, a company must file to do business within the state, which requires a small fee and a re-filing once every few years. In addition, it must withhold sales taxes on all sales within the state. This is the most laborious issue related to nexus, since sales taxes may be different for every city and county within each state, necessitating a company to keep track of potentially thousands of different sales tax rates. Also, some states may require the remittance of sales taxes every month, though this can be reduced to as little as once a year if the company predicts that it will have minimal sales taxes to remit, as noted on its initial application for a sales tax license.

Some states or local governments will also subject a company to property or personal property taxes on all assets based within their jurisdictions, which necessitates even more paperwork.

Though the amount of additional taxes paid may not be that great, the key issue related to the nexus concept is that the additional time required to track tax liabilities and file forms with the various governments may very well require additional personnel in the accounting department. This can be a major problem for those organizations in multiple states, and should be a key planning issue when determining the capacity of the accounting department to process tax-related transactions. Some organizations with a number of subsidiaries will avoid a portion of the tax filing work by only accepting the nexus concept for those subsidiaries that are clearly established within each governmental jurisdiction, thereby avoiding the tax filing problems for all other legal entities controlled by the parent corporation.

35-31 ORGANIZATIONAL EXPENSES

When setting up a business, some costs can be capitalized and then amortized over at least 60 months. These organizational costs fall into the following three categories:

1. *Business start-up costs.* A cost falls into this category if it is incurred prior to the first day of business, or if it is incurred in order to operate an existing business.

Examples of this type of cost are market surveys, fees for such professionals as accountants and lawyers who are working on the incorporation of the business, travel costs to set up business arrangements with suppliers and customers, the salaries of employees while they are being trained to perform services for the company, and advertisements related to the initial startup of the business. However, costs incurred in order to research and purchase a specific business entity cannot be amortized as organization expenses.

2. *Corporation organization costs.* A cost falls into this category if it is incurred within a corporation's first tax year, and includes organizational meetings for directors and shareholders, incorporation fees, and accounting and legal fees related to the startup (such as the creation of a corporate charter, bylaws, minutes of meetings, and the formulation of the terms to be included on original stock certificates). Costs incurred to create or issue stock certificates cannot be amortized as organizational costs, nor can the cost of transferring assets to the corporation.

3. *Partnership organization costs.* The same costs can be included in this category as for corporate organization costs. The cost of admitting or removing partners is not included, nor are the costs of syndication fees for marketing or issuing interests in the partnership.

The amortization period begins during the first month in which business operations are started. Any remaining costs yet to be amortized at the point when a business is sold can be deducted at the time of sale.

35-32 PARTNERSHIP TAXATION

A group of two or more people carrying on any sort of business without becoming incorporated is considered to be a partnership. An entity with these characteristics cannot be termed a partnership if it is an insurance company, a real estate investment trust, or a tax-exempt organization, or is owned by a local or regional government.

If the partnership takes the form of a *general partnership,* in which all of the partners are active, then each partner is liable for the negligence of any and all other partners, as well as for the liabilities of the partnership. To get around this significant problem, it is possible to create a *limited partnership,* in which limited partners are only liable for the funds they have invested as capital in the business, while a general partner, who operates the partnership on their behalf, is liable for all activities and losses. A limited partnership is subject to the IRS regulations governing passive activities (see the "Passive Activity Losses" section), which keeps the partnership from recognizing passive losses that exceed the income derived from any passive activities. Also, if the partnership has losses so large that they exceed the capital contributions of the partners (for example, the amount they have at risk in the business), then IRS rules will prohibit the recognition of any losses that exceed the amount that the partners have at risk.

A variation on the partnership concept is a *limited liability company;* this is an entity that files articles of incorporation, and whose members are not personally liable for the organization's liabilities.

A partnership is governed by a partnership agreement, which specifies how the ownership percentages of the partnership are determined, and under what circumstances and payment plans partners can be bought out by the remaining partners. The partnership agreement can specify preferential returns for some of the partners. If the partnership agreement is not clear about how income is to be distributed, then it will be based on the partners' relative contributions to the partnership. If there are variations in the proportional share of each partner during the tax year, perhaps due to additional contributions to the partnership, then the average share of each partner must be calculated and used to determine the proportional distribution of income among the partners at the end of the tax year; however, alternative arrangements for preferential returns, if specified in the partnership agreement, will override this calculation.

Every partnership must file an information return on Form 1065 that specifies its taxable income at the end of the year, as well as the identity of each partner and the amount of the income that is attributable to each one. The partnership must issue Schedule K-1 of Form 1065 to all partners on a timely basis, or else a penalty will be charged against the partnership for each K-1 form not issued. The K-1 form is used by each partner as a source of income or loss from the business that is then included in his or her personal income tax return. If the partnership does not file a tax return in a timely manner, then it can be assessed a penalty of $50 per partner for each month in which the return is late, up to a maximum of five months.

Even if the profits from a partnership are not distributed to its partners, the profits are still taxable income to the partners. This generally results in a minimum distribution to the partners each year, which allows them to pay their taxes, and which also keeps large amounts of money from accumulating within the business. If any funds are retained in the business rather than being distributed, they increase the capital contribution of the partners for tax purposes.

If a partnership experiences a loss, the share distributed to each partner will only be allowable to the extent that it offsets the adjusted basis in each partner's partnership interest. If the amount of the loss exceeds the adjusted basis, then it cannot be deducted in that year, but may be carried forward for potential offsets against future increases in the interests of the partners. This principle is based on the concept that a partner cannot lose more than his or her total interest in the partnership.

Partners may have to make estimated tax payments during the course of the tax year as a result of income from a partnership. If so, the estimated tax must, at a minimum, be the smaller of 90% of the expected partnership income for the year, or 100% of the total tax paid in the preceding year. Also, partners are not counted as employees of a partnership, and so must pay a self-employment tax.

A partnership can make a number of elections regarding the reporting of income. For example, it can choose among the accounting, cash, and hybrid methods of accounting. It can also choose between two types of MACRS depreciation, various types of revenue recognition, and different approaches for recognizing organizational expenses. These issues are dealt with throughout this chapter. The main point is that the accounting methodology choices available to a partnership are the same as those available to a corporation.

If a partner contributes money to a partnership, followed by a distribution to the partner from the partnership, the two transactions will be netted and treated as a sale of property, especially if the contribution is contingent upon the later distribution, and if the partner's right to the distribution is not impacted by the success of partnership operations. However, if the contribution and later distribution occur more than two years apart, then it is presumed that the transactions are separate and unrelated.

Distributions can be made to partners up to the amount of their adjusted basis in the company. The partnership will not recognize any gain or loss as a result of a distribution to its partners, since this is a flow-through of accumulated capital to them. If a distribution of property is made to the partners, they will not recognize a gain or loss on the transaction until they later dispose of it.

35-33 PASSIVE ACTIVITY LOSSES

Many individuals and some businesses passively participate in business activities that result in income or losses. They can claim passive activity losses on their tax returns based on these financial results. Passive participation is defined as having a trade or business activity in which one does not materially participate during the tax year, or participating in a rental activity (even if there is evidence of a substantial level of activity in the venture). One is considered to be an active investor if any of the following tests is true:

- One annually expends more than 500 hours of participation in the activity.

- One's participation comprises essentially all of the activity for a business.

- More than 100 hours of annual participation, which was at least as much as that of any other participant in the business.

- Materially participated in the business in any five of the last 10 tax years.

- Materially participated in a personal service business for any three previous tax years.

A limited partner is generally not considered to be materially involved in a business. A closely held corporation or a personal service corporation is considered to materially participate in a business if shareholders owning more than 50% of the corporation's shares materially engage in the business. Also, an investing entity is considered to be materially engaged in a business if it has an interest in an oil or gas well that is held directly or through an entity that does not reduce its liability.

Passive activity losses can only be claimed by individuals, estates, trusts, personal service corporations, and closely held "C" corporations. Conversely, passive activity losses cannot be claimed by grantor trusts, partnerships, and "S" corporations.

If passive activity losses have occurred, they can only be offset against passive activity gains. Activities that are defined by the IRS as *not* passive are gains on the sale of property that has not been used in a passive activity, investment income, and personal services income. If there is an excess credit from a passive loss after all offsets have been made against passive income, then the credit can be carried forward to the next tax year for a later offset. However, all passive losses that are carried forward can be recognized at the time when the passive investor liquidates the investment.

The total amount of a passive loss will be limited to the total amount for which a passive investor is at risk. For example, if an entity invests $1,000 in a business venture, then it is only at risk for $1,000, and cannot deduct more than that amount under any circumstances as a passive loss.

35-34 PROPERTY TAXES

Local governments use property tax assessments as one of their primary forms of tax receipt. Personal property taxes are assessed based on a company's level of reported fixed assets in the preceding year, and typically are paid once a year. In order to minimize this tax, the accounting department should regularly review the fixed asset list to see which items can be disposed of, thereby shrinking the taxable base of assets. Also, by increasing the capitalization limit, fewer items will be classified as assets, and so will also not be taxed.

Local taxing authorities can also impose a tax based on any real property owned by a business. The buildings and land that fall into this category will be appraised by the local assessor, with the resulting assessment being multiplied by a tax rate that is determined by the local government. The assessment can be challenged. If a recent assessment change results in a significant boost in the reported value of a business's real property, it is certainly worthwhile to engage the services of a private assessor to see if the new valuation can be reduced.

If a business rents its property, the tax on real property can either be absorbed by the landlord or passed through to the business, depending upon the terms of the lease. If subleasing from another business, the property tax can either be absorbed by that entity or passed through to the business, again depending on the terms of the lease.

35-35 RESEARCH AND EXPERIMENTAL TAX CREDIT

A company can choose to write off the costs of research and experimentation, rather than capitalizing them for tax purposes. Costs that qualify for an immediate write-off are those that help eliminate uncertainty about the development or improvement of a product. Under this definition, a product can be a formula, invention, patent, pilot model, process, or technique. However, it does not include the cost of advertising, surveys, management studies, quality control testing, or the acquisition of someone else's patent, model, or process. The choice to write them off at once must be made during the first year in which they are incurred. Other choices for the tax treatment of research and experimental costs are to expense them on a straight-line basis over a 10 year period, or to amortize them over a period of at least five years.

It is also possible to take a tax credit for increasing one's research activities. This option is covered under IRS Form 6765, which is shown in Exhibit 35-8. The only type of expense that qualifies for this credit is that which is undertaken to discover information that is technical in nature, and its application must be intended for use in developing a new or improved business component for the taxpayer. Also, all of the research activities must be elements of a process of experimentation relating to a new or improved function, or that enhances the current level of performance, reliability, or quality. A credit cannot be taken for research conducted after the beginning of commercial production, for the customization of a product for a specific customer, for the duplication of an existing process or product, or for research required for some types of software to be used internally.

Exhibit 35-8   Credit for Increasing Research Activities, Form 6765

Form **6765**

Department of the Treasury
Internal Revenue Service

Credit for Increasing Research Activities

▶ See separate instructions.
▶ Attach to your return.

OMB No. 1545-0619

20**00**

Attachment
Sequence No. **81**

Name(s) shown on return

Identifying number

Part I   **Current Year Credit** (Members of controlled groups or businesses under common control, see instructions.)

Section A—Regular Credit. Skip this section and go to Section B if you are electing or previously elected the alternative incremental credit.

1	Basic research payments paid or incurred to qualified organizations (see instructions)	1	
2	Qualified organization base period amount	2	
3	Subtract line 2 from line 1. If zero or less, enter -0-	3	
4	Wages for qualified services (do not include wages used in figuring the work opportunity credit)	4	
5	Cost of supplies	5	
6	Rental or lease costs of computers (see instructions).	6	
7	Enter the applicable percentage of contract research expenses (see instructions)	7	
8	Total qualified research expenses. Add lines 4 through 7	8	
9	Enter fixed-base percentage, but not more than 16% (see instructions)	9	%
10	Enter average annual gross receipts (see instructions)	10	
11	Multiply line 10 by the percentage on line 9	11	
12	Subtract line 11 from line 8. If zero or less, enter -0-	12	
13	Multiply line 8 by 50% (.50)	13	
14	Enter the **smaller** of line 12 or line 13	14	
15	Add lines 3 and 14	15	
16	**Regular credit.** If you are not electing the reduced credit under section 280C(c), multiply line 15 by 20% (.20), enter the result, and see the instructions for the schedule that must be attached. If you are electing the reduced credit, multiply line 15 by 13% (.13) and enter the result. Also, write "Sec. 280C" on the dotted line to the left of the entry space. Go to Section C	16	

Section B—Alternative Incremental Credit. Skip this section if you completed Section A.

17	Basic research payments paid or incurred to qualified organizations (see the line 1 instructions)	17	
18	Qualified organization base period amount	18	
19	Subtract line 18 from line 17. If zero or less, enter -0-	19	
20	Multiply line 19 by 20% (.20)	20	
21	Wages for qualified services (do not include wages used in figuring the work opportunity credit)	21	
22	Cost of supplies	22	
23	Rental or lease costs of computers (see the line 6 instructions)	23	
24	Enter the applicable percentage of contract research expenses (see the line 7 instructions) . .	24	
25	Total qualified research expenses. Add lines 21 through 24.	25	
26	Enter average annual gross receipts (see the line 10 instructions)	26	
27	Multiply line 26 by 1% (.01)	27	
28	Subtract line 27 from line 25. If zero or less, enter -0-	28	
29	Multiply line 26 by 1.5% (.015)	29	
30	Subtract line 29 from line 25. If zero or less, enter -0-	30	
31	Subtract line 30 from line 28	31	
32	Multiply line 26 by 2% (.02)	32	
33	Subtract line 32 from line 25. If zero or less, enter -0-	33	
34	Subtract line 33 from line 30	34	
35	Multiply line 31 by 2.65% (.0265)	35	
36	Multiply line 34 by 3.2% (.032)	36	
37	Multiply line 33 by 3.75% (.0375)	37	
38	Add lines 20, 35, 36, and 37	38	
39	**Alternative incremental credit.** If you are not electing the reduced credit under section 280C(c), enter the amount from line 38, and see the line 16 instructions for the schedule that must be attached. If you are electing the reduced credit, multiply line 38 by 65% (.65) and enter the result. Also, write "Sec. 280C" on the dotted line to the left of the entry space	39	

Section C—Total Current Year Credit for Increasing Research Activities

40	Pass-through research credit(s) from a partnership, S corporation, estate, or trust	40	
41	**Total current year credit.** Add line 16 **or** line 39 to line 40, and **go to Part II** on the back . .	41	

For Paperwork Reduction Act Notice, see separate instructions.   Cat. No. 13700H   Form **6765** (2000)

Exhibit 35-8   Credit for Increasing Research Activities, Form 6765 (*cont'd*)

Form 6765 (2000)   Page **2**

Part II   Suspended and Allowable Current Year Credits

42	Enter the amount from line 41		**42**
43	Credit attributable to the first suspension period. Multiply line 42 by the applicable suspension percentage (see instructions)	**43**	
44	Credit attributable to the second suspension period. Multiply line 42 by the applicable suspension percentage (see instructions)	**44**	
45	Add lines 43 and 44		**45**
46	Subtract line 45 from line 42		**46**

Part III   Tax Liability Limit (See **Who Must File Form 3800** to find out if you complete Part III or file Form 3800.)

47 Regular tax before credits:
- Individuals. Enter the amount from Form 1040, line 40 . . . .
- Corporations. Enter the amount from Form 1120, Schedule J, line 3; Form 1120-A, Part I, line 1; or the amount from the applicable line of your return **47**
- Estates and trusts. Enter the sum of the amounts from Form 1041, Schedule G, lines 1a and 1b, or the applicable line of your return . . . .

48 Alternative minimum tax:
- Individuals. Enter the amount from Form 6251, line 28 . . . . . .
- Corporations. Enter the amount from Form 4626, line 15 . . . . **48**
- Estates and trusts. Enter the amount from Form 1041, Schedule I, line 39 .

49 Add lines 47 and 48 . . . . **49**

50a	Foreign tax credit	**50a**	
b	Credit for child and dependent care expenses (Form 2441, line 9) .	**50b**	
c	Credit for the elderly or the disabled (Schedule R (Form 1040), line 20)	**50c**	
d	Education credits (Form 8863, line 18)	**50d**	
e	Child tax credit (Form 1040, line 47)	**50e**	
f	Mortgage interest credit (Form 8396, line 11)	**50f**	
g	Adoption credit (Form 8839, line 14)	**50g**	
h	District of Columbia first-time homebuyer credit (Form 8859, line 11)	**50h**	
i	Possessions tax credit (Form 5735, line 17 or 27)	**50i**	
j	Credit for fuel from a nonconventional source	**50j**	
k	Qualified electric vehicle credit (Form 8834, line 19)	**50k**	

l Add lines 50a through 50k **50l**

51 Net income tax. Subtract line 50l from line 49 . . . . **51**

52 Tentative minimum tax (see instructions):
- Individuals. Enter the amount from Form 6251, line 26 . . . .
- Corporations. Enter the amount from Form 4626, line 13 . . . .
- Estates and trusts. Enter the amount from Form 1041, Schedule I, line 37 . . . .   **52**

53 Net regular tax. Subtract line 50l from line 47. If zero or less, enter -0-   **53**

54 Enter 25% (.25) of the excess, if any, of line 53 over $25,000 (see instructions) **54**

55	Enter the greater of line 52 or line 54		**55**
56	Subtract line 55 from line 51. If zero or less, enter -0-		**56**
57	**Total credit allowed for the current year. Individuals, estates, and trusts:** Enter the **smallest** of line 42, line 56, or the amount from the formula in the instructions for line 57. **Corporations:** Enter the **smaller** of line 42 or line 56.		**57**
58	**Suspended credit allowed for the current year.** Subtract line 46 from line 57. If zero or less, enter -0- (see instructions for when and how to claim)		**58**
59	**Credit for increasing research activities allowed on current year return.** Subtract line 58 from line 57. Enter here and on Form 1040, line 49; Form 1120, Schedule J, line 6d; Form 1120-A, Part I, line 4a; Form 1041, Schedule G, line 2c; or the applicable line of other returns		**59**

Form **6765** (2000)

As noted in line one of the form, it is also possible to obtain a credit for basic research if cash payments are made to a university or scientific research organization, and if the amount paid exceeds the base period amount paid over the preceding three years. If the amount paid does not exceed the expense incurred during the base period, then a reduced amount of 65% can still be claimed as contract research expenses (or 75%, if the payments are made to a tax-exempt organization that is operated primarily to conduct scientific research). If one cannot use the entire credit for the current tax return, it can be carried back one year and forward up to 20 years until the amount of the credit is exhausted.

35-36 RETIREMENT PLANS

There is an enormous variety of retirement plans available, each of which has a slightly different treatment under the tax laws, resulting in varying levels of investment risk to the employee or different levels of administrative activity. In this section, we will give a brief overview of each type of retirement plan.

A *qualified retirement plan* is one that is designed to observe all of the requirements of the Employee Retirement Income Security Act (ERISA), as well as all related IRS rulings. By observing these requirements, an employer can immediately deduct allowable contributions to the plan on behalf of plan participants. Also, income earned by the plan is not taxable to the plan. In addition, participants can exclude from taxable income any contributions they make to the plan, until such time as they choose to withdraw the funds from the plan. Finally, distributions to participants can, in some cases, be rolled over into an Individual Retirement Account (IRA), thereby prolonging the deferral of taxable income. The two types of qualified retirement plan are:

1. *Defined contribution plan.* This is a plan in which the employer is liable for a payment into the plan of a specific size, but not for the size of the resulting payments from the plan to participants. Thus, the participant bears the risk of the results of investment of the monies that have been deposited into the plan. The participant can mitigate or increase this risk by having control over a number of different investment options. The annual combined contribution to this type of plan by both the participant and employer is limited to the greater of $35,000 or one-quarter of a participant's compensation (though this is restricted in several cases—see the following specific plan types). Funds received by participants in a steady income stream are taxed at ordinary income tax rates, and cannot be rolled over into an IRA, whereas a lump sum payment can be rolled into an IRA. Some of the more common defined contribution plans are as follows:

   • *401(k) plan.* This is a plan set up by an employer, into which employees can contribute the lesser of $10,500 or 15% of their pay, which is excluded from taxation until such time as they remove the funds from the account. All earnings of the funds while held in the plan will also not be taxed until removed from the account. Employers can also match the funds contributed to the plan by employees, and also contribute the results of a profit sharing plan to the employees' 401(k) accounts. The plan typically allows employees to invest the funds in their accounts in a number of different investment options, ranging from conservative money market funds to more speculative small cap or international stock funds;

the employee holds the risk of how well or poorly an investment will perform—the employer has no liability for the performance of investments. Withdrawals from a 401(k) are intended to be upon retirement or the attainment of age 59½, but can also be distributed as a loan (if the specific plan document permits it), or in the event of disability or death.

- *403(b) plan.* This plan is similar to a 401(k) plan, except that it is designed specifically for charitable, religious, and educational organizations that fall under the tax-exempt status of 501(c)(3) regulations. It varies from a 401(k) plan in that participants can only invest in mutual funds and annuities, and also in that contributions can exceed the limit imposed under a 401(k) plan to the extent that participants can catch up on contributions that were below the maximum threshold in previous years.

- *Employee stock ownership plan (ESOP).* The bulk of the contributions made to this type of plan are in the stock of the employing company. The employer calculates the amount of its contribution to the plan based on a proportion of total employee compensation, and uses the result to buy an equivalent amount of stock and deposit it in the ESOP. When an employee leaves the company, he or she will receive either company stock or the cash equivalent of the stock in payment of his or her vested interest.

- *Money purchase plan.* The employer must make a payment into each employee's account in each year that is typically based on a percentage of total compensation paid to each participant. The payments must be made, irrespective of company profits (see next item).

- *Profit sharing plan.* Contributions to this type of plan are intended to be funded from company profits, which is an incentive for employees to extend their efforts to ensure that profits will occur. However, many employers will make contributions to the plan even in the absence of profits. This plan is frequently linked to a 401(k) plan, so that participants can also make contributions to the plan.

2. *Defined benefit plan.* This plan itemizes a specific dollar amount that participants will receive, based on a set of rules that typically combine the number of years of employment and wages paid over the time period when each employee worked for the company. An additional factor may be the age of the participant at the time of retirement. Funds received by participants in a steady income stream are taxed at ordinary income tax rates, and cannot be rolled over into an IRA, whereas a lump sum payment can be rolled into an IRA. This type of plan is not favorable to the company, which guarantees the fixed payments made to retirees, and so bears the risk of unfavorable investment returns that may require additional payments into the plan in order to meet the fixed payment obligations. Some of the more common defined benefit plans are:

- *Cash balance plan.* The employer contributes a *pay credit* (usually based on a proportion of that person's annual compensation) and an *interest credit* (usually linked to a publicly available interest rate index or well-known high-grade investment such as a U.S. government security) to each participant's account within the plan. Changes in plan value based on these credits do not impact the fixed benefit amounts to which participants are entitled.

- *Target benefit plan.* Under this approach, the employer makes annual contributions into the plan based on the actuarial assumption at that time regarding the amount of funding needed to achieve a targeted benefit level (hence the name of the plan). However, there is no guarantee that the amount of the actual benefit paid will match the estimate upon which the contributions were based, since the return on invested amounts in the plan may vary from the estimated level at the time when the contributions were made.

The preceding plans all fall under the category of qualified retirement plans. However, if a company does not choose to follow ERISA and IRS guidelines, it can create a *nonqualified retirement plan.* By doing so, it can discriminate in favor of paying key personnel more than other participants, or to the exclusion of other employees. All contributions to the plan and any earnings by the deposited funds will remain untaxed as long as they stay within the trust. However, the downside of this approach is that any contribution made to the plan by the company cannot be recorded as a taxable expense until the contribution is eventually paid out of the trust into which it was deposited and to the plan participant (which may be years in the future). Proceeds from the plan are taxable as ordinary income to the recipient, and cannot be rolled over into an IRA. For more information about nonqualified retirement plans, see the "Deferred Compensation" section in this chapter.

An example of a nonqualified retirement plan is the 457 plan, which allows participants to defer up to $8,500 of their wages per year. It is restricted to the use of government and tax-exempt entities. Distributions from the plan are usually at retirement, but can also be at the point of the employee's departure from the organization, or a withdrawal can be requested on an emergency basis. A key difference between the 457 plan and the qualified retirement plans is that the funds deposited in the trust by the employer can be claimed by creditors, unless the employer is a government entity.

A plan that can fall into either the defined contribution or defined benefit plan category is the Keogh plan. It is available to self-employed people, partnerships, and owners of unincorporated businesses. When created, a Keogh plan can be defined as either a defined contribution or defined benefit plan. Under either approach, the contribution level is restricted to the lesser of 25% of taxable annual compensation (or 20% for the owner) or $35,000. It is not allowable to issue loans against a Keogh plan, but distributions from it can be rolled over into an IRA. Premature withdrawal penalties are similar to those for an IRA.

An employer may want neither to deal with the complex reporting requirements of a qualified retirement plan, nor set up a nonqualified plan. A very simple alternative is the *personal retirement account* (PRA), of which the most common is the individual retirement arrangement. The primary types of PRAs are:

- *Individual retirement arrangement (IRA).* This is a savings account that is set up for the specific use of one person who is less than $70\frac{1}{2}$ years old. Contributions to an IRA are limited to the lesser of $2,000 per year or a person's total taxable compensation (which can be wages, tips, bonuses, commissions, and taxable alimony). There is no required minimum payment into an IRA. Contributions to an IRA are not tax deductible if the contributor also participates in an employer's qualified retirement plan, and his or her adjusted gross income is greater than $42,000 if single filer, $62,000 if filing a joint return, or $10,000 if married and filing a separate return. The deductible amount begins to decline at a point $10,000 lower than all of these values. If a working spouse is not covered by an employer's qualified retirement plan, then he or she may make a fully deductible contribution of up to $2,000 per year to the IRA, even if the other spouse has such coverage. However, this deduction is eliminated when a couple's adjusted gross income reaches $160,000, and begins to decline at $150,000. Earnings within the plan are shielded from taxation until distributed from it.

It is mandatory to begin withdrawals from an IRA as of age $70\frac{1}{2}$; if distributions do not occur, then a penalty of 50% will be charged against the amount that was not distributed. When funds are withdrawn from an IRA prior to age $59\frac{1}{2}$ they will be taxed at ordinary income tax rates, and will also be subject to a 10% excise tax. However, the excise tax will be waived if the participant dies, is disabled, is buying a home for the first time (to a maximum of $10,000), is paying for some types of higher education costs or medical insurance costs that exceed $7\frac{1}{2}$% of the participant's adjusted gross income (as well as any medical insurance premiums following at least one-quarter year of receiving unemployment benefits). The following list reveals the wide range of IRA accounts that can be set up:

- *Education IRA.* This type of IRA is established for the express purpose of providing advanced education to the beneficiary. Though contributions to this IRA are not exempt from taxable income, any earnings during the period when funds are stored in the IRA will be tax-free at the time when they are used to pay for the cost of advanced education. The annual contribution limit on this IRA is $500, and is limited to the time period prior to the beneficiary reaching the age of 18. The maximum contribution begins to decline at the point when joint household income reaches $150,000 (and is eliminated at $160,000), and $95,000 for a single tax filer (and is eliminated at $110,000). The amount in this IRA can be moved to a different family member if the new beneficiary is less than 30 years old. The amount in the IRA must be distributed once the beneficiary reaches the age of 30. If a distribution is not for the express purpose of offsetting education expenses, then the distribution is taxable as ordinary income, and will also be charged a 10% excise tax.

- *Group IRA.* Though the intent of an IRA is for it to be the sole possession of one person, it can also be set up and contributed to by another entity. In the case of a group IRA, an employer, union, or other entity can set up a cluster of IRAs for its members or employees and make contributions into each of the accounts.

- *Individual retirement annuity.* This is an IRA that is comprised of an annuity that is managed through and paid out by a life insurance company.

- *Inherited IRA.* This is either a Roth or traditional IRA that has been inherited from its deceased owner, with the recipient not being the deceased owner's spouse. After the owner's death, no more than five years can pass before the beneficiary receives a distribution, or an annuity can be arranged that empties the IRA no later than the beneficiary's life expectancy. This IRA is not intended to be a vehicle for ongoing contributions from the new beneficiary, so tax deductions are not allowed for any contributions made into it. Also, the funds in this IRA cannot be shifted into a rollover IRA, since this action would circumvent the preceding requirement to distribute the funds within five years.

- *Rollover IRA.* This is an IRA that an individual sets up for the express purpose of receiving funds from a qualified retirement plan. There are no annual contribution limits for this type of IRA, since its purpose is to transfer a pre-existing block of funds that could be quite large. Funds deposited in this account, as well as any earnings accumulating in the accounts, are exempt from taxation until removed from it. Rollover funds can also be transferred (tax-free) into another qualified retirement plan. A common use of the rollover account is to "park" funds from the qualified plan of a former employer until the individual qualifies for participation in the plan of a new employer, at which point the funds are transferred into the new employer's plan.

- *Roth IRA.* Under this IRA, there are offsetting costs and benefits. On the one hand, any contribution to the IRA is not deductible; however, withdrawals from the account (including earnings) are not taxable at all, as long as the recipient is at least $59\frac{1}{2}$ years old, is disabled, uses the funds to buy a first-time home, or is made a beneficiary following the death of the IRA participant. Contributions are limited to $2,000 per year, and can be continued indefinitely, irrespective of the participant's age. However, no contribution is allowed once the participant's adjusted gross income reaches $160,000 for a joint filer, or $110,000 for a single filer, and will gradually decline beginning at $150,000 and $95,000, respectively.

    There are special rules for transferring funds into a Roth IRA from any other type of IRA. Transfer is only allowed if the adjusted gross income of the transferring party is $100,000 or less in the year of transfer (the same limitation applies to both single and joint filers). Distributions from the Roth IRA that come from these rolled over funds will not be taxable, but only if they have been held in the Roth IRA for at least five years following the date of transfer.

- *Savings incentive match plan for employees* (SIMPLE). Under this IRA format, an employer with no other retirement plan and who employs fewer than 100 employees can set up IRA accounts for its employees, into which employees can contribute up to $6,500 per year. The employee commits to make a matching contribution of up to 3% of the employee's pay, depending upon how much the employee has chosen to contribute. The combined employee/employer contribution to the plan cannot exceed $13,000 per year. The employer also has the option of reducing its contribution percentage in two years out of every five consecutive years, or can commit to a standard 2% contribution for all eligible employees, even if they choose not to contribute to the plan. Vesting in the plan is immediate. The downside to this plan from an employee's perspective is that the excise tax assessment for a withdrawal within the first two years of participation is 25%, rather than the usual 10% that is assessed for other types of IRA accounts.

- *Spousal IRA.* This is an IRA that is funded by one spouse on behalf of the other, but only if the spouse being funded has less than $2,000 in annual taxable income. This contribution is only valid if the couple files a joint tax return for the year in which the contribution took place.

- *Simplified employee pension.* This plan is available primarily for self-employed persons and partnerships, but is available to all types of business entities. It can only be established if no qualified retirement plan is already in use. The maximum contribution that an employer can make is the lesser of 15% of an employee's compensation, or $30,000. The amount paid is up to the discretion of the employer. The contribution is sent at once to an IRA that has been set up in the name of each employee, and that is owned by the employee. Once the money arrives in the IRA, it falls under all of the previously noted rules for an IRA.

35-37 S CORPORATIONS

An "S" corporation has unique taxation and legal protection aspects that make it an ideal way to structure a business if there are a small number of shareholders. Specifically, it can only be created if there are no more than 75 shareholders, if only one class of stock is issued, and if all shareholders agree to the "S" corporation status. All of its shareholders must be either citizens or residents of the United States. Shareholders are also limited to individuals, estates, and some types of trusts and charities. Conversely, this means that "C" corporations and partnerships cannot be shareholders in an "S" corporation. The requirement for a single class of stock may prevent some organizations from organizing in this manner, for it does not allow for preferential returns or special voting rights by some shareholders.

The "S" corporation generally does not pay taxes. Instead, it passes reported earnings through to its shareholders, who report the income on their tax returns. This avoids the double taxation that arises in a "C" corporation, where a company's income is taxed, and then the dividends it issues to its shareholders are taxed as income to them a second time. An "S" corporation's reported income is passed through to shareholders on Schedule K-1 of Form 1120S. The amount of income is allocated to each shareholder on a simple per-share basis. If a shareholder has held stock in the corporation for less than a full year, then the allocation is on a per-share, per-day basis. The per-day part of this calculation assumes that a shareholder still holds the stock through and including the day when the stock is disposed of, while a deceased shareholder will be assumed to retain ownership through and including the day when he or she dies.

An "S" corporation is required to file a tax return, no matter how small its reported profit or loss may be, until it is completely dissolved. The required filing date is the 15th day of the month following the close of an "S" corporation's tax year, though it can be extended for an additional six months. If a tax payment is late (in the few instances where an "S" corporation owes a tax), then a late filing penalty equal to 5% of the tax owed per month may be imposed, up to a limit of 25%. There is also a penalty of $50 per shareholder if the "S" corporation fails to provide K-1 forms to the shareholders, which they need to report their proportional share of the corporation's income.

There are a few cases where an "S" corporation can owe taxes. For example, it can be taxed if it has accumulated earnings and profits from an earlier existence as a "C" corporation and its passive income (see the "Passive Activity Losses" section) is more than 25% of total gross receipts. It can also be liable for taxes on a few types of capital gains, recapture of the old investment tax credit, and LIFO recapture. If any of these taxes applies, then the "S" corporation must make quarterly estimated income tax payments. On the other hand, an "S" corporation is not subject to the alternative minimum tax.

If the management team of an "S" corporation wants to terminate its "S" status, the written consent of more than 50% of the shareholders is required, as well as a statement from the corporation to that effect. If the corporation wants to become an "S" corporation at a later date, there is a five-year waiting period from the last time before it can do so again, unless it obtains special permission from the IRS.

35-38 SALES AND USE TAXES

Sales taxes are imposed at the state, county, and city level—frequently by all three at once. It is also possible for a special tax to be added to the sales tax and applied to a unique region, such as for the construction of a baseball stadium or to support a regional mass transit system. The sales tax is multiplied by the price paid on goods and services on transactions occurring within the taxing area. However, the definition of goods and services that are required to be taxed will vary by state (not usually at the county or city level), and so must be researched at the local level to determine the precise basis of calculation. For example, some states do not tax food sales, on the grounds that this is a necessity whose cost should be reduced as much as possible, while other states include it in their required list of items to be taxed.

A company is required to charge sales taxes to its customers and remit the resulting receipts to the local state government, which will split out the portions due to the local county and city governments and remit these taxes on the company's behalf to those entities. If the company does not charge its customers for these taxes, it is still liable for them, and must pay the unbilled amounts to the state government, though it has the right to attempt to bill its customers after the fact for the missing sales taxes. This can be a difficult collection chore, especially if sales are primarily over the counter, where there are few transaction records that identify the customer. Also, a company is obligated to keep abreast of all changes in sales tax rates and charge its customers for the correct amount; if it does not do so, then it is liable to the government for the difference between what it actually charged and the statutory rate. If a company overcharges its customers, the excess must also be remitted to the government.

The state in which a company is collecting sales taxes can decide how frequently it wants the company to remit taxes. If there are only modest sales, the state may decide that the cost of paperwork exceeds the value of the remittances, and will only require an annual remittance. It is more common to have quarterly or monthly remittances. The state will review the dollar amount of remittances from time to time, and adjust the required remittance frequency based on this information.

All government entities have the right to audit a company's books to see if the proper sales taxes are being charged, and so a company can theoretically be subject to three sales tax audits per year—one each from the city, county, and state revenue departments. Also, since these audits can come from any taxing jurisdiction in which a company does business, there could literally be thousands of potential audits.

The obligation to collect sales taxes is based on the concept of *nexus,* which is covered in another section of this chapter. If nexus exists, then sales taxes must be collected by the seller. If not, the recipient of purchased goods instead has an obligation to compile a list of items purchased, and remit a use tax to the appropriate authority. The use tax is in the same amount as the sales tax. The only difference is that the remitting party is the buyer instead of the seller. Use taxes are also subject to audits by all taxing jurisdictions.

If the buyer of a company's products is including them in its own products for resale to another entity, then the buyer does not have to pay a sales tax to the seller. Instead, the buyer will charge a sales tax to the buyer of *its* final product. This approach is used under the theory that a sales tax should only be charged one time on the sale of a product. However, it can be a difficult chore to explain the lack of sales tax billings during an audit, so sales taxes should only be halted if a buyer sends a sales tax exemption form to the company, which should then be kept on file. The sales tax exemption certificate can be named a resale certificate instead, depending upon the issuing authority. It can also be issued to government entities, which are generally exempt from sales and use taxes. As a general rule, sales taxes should always be charged unless there is a sales tax exemption certificate on file—otherwise, the company will still be liable for the remittance of sales taxes in the event of an audit.

35-39 SALES RETURNS/BAD DEBTS

A company can reduce the amount of its gross revenue for tax reporting purposes based on the amount of returned goods from customers at the point when it has accepted liability for the returned goods. This means that any items that are still in dispute with customers at the end of the tax year cannot yet be removed from gross revenue.

There are two ways to reduce gross revenue by the amount of bad debts. The first is called the *specific charge-off method,* and is the most commonly used approach for tax purposes. Under this method, a company can deduct that portion of a specific bad debt that is uncollectible. The proof of uncollectibility is that the company must have taken reasonable steps to collect the debt or receivable. Good evidence of a bad debt is the bankruptcy of the debtor, though in this case the amount of the debt must be reduced by the amount of any asset distribution from the bankruptcy proceedings. Also, if a debtor has paid for part of its debt by transferring property to the company, then the amount of the debt should be reduced by the fair market value of the received property as of the date when the property was received (not the date when the property was later converted to cash).

Under the specific charge-off method, a company is limited in its deduction to that portion of a bad debt that the company also wrote off on its financial records during the tax year, which prevents a company from manipulating its tax records to achieve a lower tax liability than is indicated by its financial results. If the IRS audits a company's books and disallows a partial deduction for a bad debt, and the bad debt becomes fully worthless in a later year, then the company can still deduct the full amount in the tax year when it became fully worthless. A bad debt cannot be deducted in a year after the one in which it became worthless and was recorded as such in the company's financial records. Instead, a company must file for a refund by the later of seven years after the date when the original return was due, or two years from the date when it paid the tax for the year when the bad debt became worthless. If the refund is for a partially worthless debt, then the time frame in which to file for a refund drops to the later of three years from the date when an original return was due or two years from the date when the tax was paid.

The *nonaccrual experience method* can also be used to recognize bad debts for tax purposes, but only if a company uses the accrual method of accounting, and if the bad debt is related to the performance of services, and does not involve a debt on which interest or a penalty is charged for late payment. Under this method, a company does not accrue income that it expects to be uncollectible, thereby avoiding the need for a specific charge-off of bad debts.

If a company uses the cash method of accounting, it is not possible to ever take any bad debt deduction, since the related revenue is only recognized at the time of cash receipt, which never occurs if the billing is a bad debt.

35-40 SOCIAL SECURITY TAX

As of 1990, the standard tax rate that is not only withheld from employee pay, but also matched by employers, is 6.20% of gross pay. For a self-employed person, the rate is 12.40%. The maximum amount of wages and tips subject to the social security tax is $76,200; this figure is increased regularly, so be sure to review it each year.

35-41 STOCK APPRECIATION RIGHTS

A Stock Appreciate Right (SAR) is a form of compensation that rewards an employee if there is an increase in the value of a company's stock, without actually owning the stock. For example, an employee is given 1,000 SARs at the company's current stock price. When the stock price later increases, the employee exercises the SARs at his or her option, resulting in a cash payment by the company to the employee for the net amount of the increase. No stock actually changes hands.

The employee recognizes no income and the company no expense at the time the SARs are granted. Tax recognition only occurs for both parties once the employee chooses to exercise the SARs and the company issues a payment for them. The company will treat this cost as a salary or bonus expense.

35-42 STOCK OPTIONS

A stock option gives an employee the right to buy stock at a specific price within a specific time period. Stock options come in two varieties: the *incentive stock option* (ISO) and the *nonqualified stock option* (NSO).

Incentive stock options are taxable to the employee neither at the time they are granted, nor at the time when the employee eventually exercises the option to buy stock. If the employee does not dispose of the stock within two years of the date of the option grant or within one year of the date when the option is exercised, then any resulting gain will be taxed as a long-term capital gain. However, if the employee sells the stock within one year of the exercise date, then any gain is taxed as ordinary income. An ISO plan typically requires an employee to exercise any vested stock options within 90 days of that person's voluntary or involuntary termination of employment.

The reduced tax impact associated with waiting until two years have passed from the date of option grant presents a risk to the employee that the value of the related stock will decline in the interim, thereby offsetting the reduced long-term capital gain tax rate achieved at the end of this period. To mitigate the potential loss in stock value, one can make a Section 83(b) election to recognize taxable income on the purchase price of the stock within 30 days following the date when an option is exercised, and withhold taxes at the ordinary income tax rate at that time. The employee will not recognize any additional income with respect to the purchased shares until they are sold or otherwise transferred in a taxable transaction, and the additional gain recognized at that time will be taxed at the long-term capital gains rate. It is reasonable to make the Section 83(b) election if the amount of income reported at the time of the election is small and the potential price growth of the stock is significant. On the other hand, it is not reasonable to take the election if there is a combination of high reportable income at the time of election (resulting in a large tax payment) and a minimal chance of growth in the stock price, or if the company can forfeit the options. The Section 83(b) election is not available to holders of options under an NSO plan.

The alternative minimum tax (AMT) must also be considered when dealing with an ISO plan. In essence, the AMT requires that an employee pay tax on the difference between the exercise price and the stock price at the time when an option is exercised, even if the stock is not sold at that time. This can result in a severe cash shortfall for the employee, who may only be able to pay the related taxes by selling the stock. This is a particular problem if the value of the shares subsequently drops, since there is now no source of high-priced stock that can be converted into cash in order to pay the required taxes. This problem arises frequently in cases where a company has just gone public, but employees are restricted from selling their shares for some time after the IPO date, and run the risk of losing stock value during that interval. Establishing the amount of the gain reportable under AMT rules is especially difficult if a company's stock is not publicly held, since there is no clear consensus on the value of the stock. In this case, the IRS will use the value of the per-share price at which the last round of funding was concluded. When the stock is eventually sold, an AMT credit can be charged against the reported gain, but there can be a significant cash shortfall in the meantime. In order to avoid this situation, a employee could choose to exercise options at the point when the estimated value of company shares is quite low, thereby reducing the AMT payment; however, the employee must now find the cash to pay for the stock that he or she has just purchased, and also runs the risk that the shares will not increase in value and may become worthless.

An ISO plan is only valid if it follows these rules:

* Incentive stock options can only be issued to employees. A person must have been working for the employer at all times during the period that begins on the date of grant and ends on the day three months before the date when the option is exercised.

* The option term cannot exceed 10 years from the date of grant. The option term is only five years in the case of an option granted to an employee who, at the time the option is granted, owns stock that has more than 10% of the total combined voting power of all classes of stock of the employer.

* The option price at the time it is granted is not less than the fair market value of the stock. However, it must be 110% of the fair market value in the case of an option granted to an employee who, at the time the option is granted, owns stock that has more than 10% of the total combined voting power of all classes of stock of the employer.

* The total value of all options that can be exercised by any one employee in one year is limited to $100,000. Any amounts exercised that exceed $100,000 will be treated as a nonqualified stock option (to be covered shortly).

* The option cannot be transferred by the employee and can only be exercised during the employee's lifetime.

If the options granted do not include these provisions, or are granted to individuals who are not employees under the preceding definition, then the options must be characterized as nonqualified stock options.

A *nonqualified stock option* is not given any favorable tax treatment under the Internal Revenue Code (hence the name). It is also referred to as a *nonstatutory stock option*. The recipient of an NSO does not owe any tax on the date when options are granted, unless the options are traded on a public exchange. In that case, the options can be traded at once for value, and so tax will be recognized on the fair market value of the options on the public exchange as of the grant date. An NSO option will be taxed when it is exercised, based on the difference between the option price and the fair market value of the stock on that day. The resulting gain will be taxed as ordinary income. If the stock appreciates in value after the exercise date, then the incremental gain is taxable at the capital gains rate.

There are no rules governing an NSO, so the option price can be lower than the fair market value of the stock on the grant date. The option price can also be set substantially higher than the current fair market value at the grant date, which is called a *premium grant*. It is also possible to issue *escalating price options,* which use a sliding scale for the option price that changes in concert with a peer group index, thereby stripping away the impact of broad changes in the stock market and forcing the company to outperform the stock market in order to achieve any profit from granted stock options. Also, a *heavenly parachute* stock option can be created that allows a deceased option holder's estate up to three years in which to exercise his or her options.

Company management should be aware of the impact of both ISO and NSO plans on the company, not just employees. A company receives no tax deduction on a stock option transaction if it uses an ISO plan. However, if it uses an NSO plan, the company will receive a tax deduction equal to the amount of the income that the employee must recognize. If a company does not expect to have any taxable income during the stock option period, then it will receive no immediate value from having a tax deduction (though the deduction can be carried forward to offset income in future years), and so would be more inclined to use an ISO plan. This is a particularly common approach for companies that have not yet gone public. On the other hand, publicly held companies, which are generally more profitable and so must search for tax deductions, will be more inclined to sponsor an NSO plan. Research has shown that most employees who are granted either type of option will exercise it as soon as possible, which essentially converts the tax impact of the ISO plan into an NSO plan. For this reason also, many companies prefer to use NSO plans.

35-43 TAX RATE, CORPORATE

Exhibit 35-9 shows the tax rate schedule that should be used for determining a corporation's tax due on its 1120 form.

A qualified personal service corporation is taxed at a flat rate of 35% on taxable income. This situation arises when a corporation performs substantially all of its work on personal services, and at least 95% of the corporation's stock is owned by its employees, retired employees, or the estate of a deceased employee.

Exhibit 35-9   IRS Corporate Tax Rate Schedule

Over	But not Over	The Tax Is (Base Amount)		Percentage	Of the Amount Over:
$0	$50,000	—		15%	$0
50,000	75,000	$7,500	+	25%	50,000
75,000	100,000	13,750	+	34%	75,000
100,000	335,000	22,250	+	39%	100,000
335,000	10,000,000	113,900	+	34%	335,000
10,000,000	15,000,000	3,400,000	+	35%	10,000,000
15,000,000	18,333,333	5,150,000	+	38%	15,000,000
18,333,333	—	—		35%	0

35-44 TAX YEAR

A company reports its taxable income to the IRS based on a tax year, which is determined at the time a company files its first tax return. This determination must be made by the due date when an entity's tax return is due following the end of the tax year. For a "C" corporation or "S" corporation, the due date is the 15th day of the third month following the end of the tax year, while the due date for individuals, participants in a partnership, and shareholders in an "S" corporation is the 15th day of the fourth month after the end of the tax year.

The default period to use for a tax year is the calendar year, which is January 1 through December 31. Unless special permission is given, the calendar year must be used as the tax year for a sole proprietor, a shareholder in an "S" corporation, or a personal service corporation. A personal service corporation is a "C" corporation, primarily performs personal services (as defined by compensation costs for personal services activities being at least 50% of all compensation costs), and the owners are primarily owners who not only perform much of the services work, but who also own more than 10% of the company's stock. Personal services include activities in the areas of consulting, the performing arts, actuarial work, accounting, architecture, health and veterinary services, law, and engineering.

The rule for setting the tax year of a partnership is more complex; if one or multiple partners having the same tax year own a majority interest in the partnership, then the partnership must use their tax year; if there is no single tax year used by the majority partners, then the partnership must use the tax year of all its principal partners (those with a stake of at least 5%); if the partners do not share the same tax year, then the tax year used must be the one that results in the smallest amount of deferred partner income. This is calculated by determining the number of months remaining in each partner's tax year (using as the basis of calculation the earliest tax year-end among the partners), and multiplying this amount by the percentage share in partnership earnings for each partner. Then add up this calculation for all partners, and determine the tax year-end that will result in the smallest possible number. The result will generally be the earliest tax year-end among the partners that follows the existing partnership year-end.

The use of the calendar year as the tax year is also required if one does not keep sufficiently accurate tax-related records, use an annual accounting period, or if one's present tax year does not qualify as a fiscal year (which the IRS defines as 12 consecutive months ending on the last day of any month except December).

It is also possible to file for a 52-to-53 week tax year, as long as the fiscal year is maintained on the same basis. The 52-to-53 week year always ends on the same day of the week, which one can select. This can result in tax years that end on days other than the last day of the month. In order to file for this type of tax year with the IRS, one should include a statement with the first annual tax return that notes the month and day of the week on which its tax year will always end, and the date on which the tax year ends. It is possible to change to a 52-to-53 week tax year without IRS approval, as long as the new tax year still falls within the same month under which an entity currently has its tax year end, and a statement announcing the change is attached to the tax return for the year in which the change takes place.

The 52-to-53 week tax year presents a problem for the IRS, since it is more difficult to determine the exact date on which changes to its tax rules will apply to any entity that uses it. To standardize the date of the tax year-end for these entities, the IRS assumes that a 52-to-53 week tax year begins on the first day of the calendar month closest to the first day of its tax year, and ends on the last day of the calendar month closest to the last day of its tax year.

A company can apply to the IRS to have its tax year changed if there is a valid business purpose for doing so. When reviewing an application for this change, the IRS is primarily concerned with any possible distortion of income that will have an impact on taxable income. For example, a cause for concern would be shifting revenues into the following tax year, as would be the case if a company switched to a tax year that ended just prior to the main part of its selling season, thereby shifting much of its revenue (and taxable income) to a future period. To use the same example, this might also cause a major net operating loss during the short tax year that would result from the change, since much of the revenue would be removed from the year. In cases such as this, the IRS would not be inclined to approve a change in the tax year. If the IRS sees that the change will result in a neutral or positive change in reported income, then it will more favorably review any business reasons for supporting the change, such as timing the year-end to correspond with the conclusion of most business activities for the year (such as the use of January as a year-end for many retailing firms). Thus, the prime consideration for the IRS when reviewing a proposed change of tax year will always be its potential impact on tax receipts.

The one case in which the IRS will automatically approve a change in the tax year is the 25% test. Under this test, a company calculates the proportion of total sales for the last two months of the proposed tax year as compared to total revenues for the entire year. If this proportion is 25% or greater for all of the last three years, then the IRS will grant a change in the tax year to the requested year-end date. If a company does not yet have at least 47 months of reportable revenues upon which to base the calculation, then it cannot use this approach to apply for a change in its tax year.

A tax year must fall under the rules just stated, or else it is considered to be improper, and must be changed with IRS approval. For example, if a company were founded on the 13th day of the month, and the owner assumes that the fiscal and tax year will end exactly one year from that point (on the 12th day of the same month in the next year), this is an improper tax year, because it does not end on the last day of the month, nor does it fall under the rules governing a 52-to-53 week year. In such cases, a company must file an amended income tax return that is based on the calendar year and then get IRS approval to change to a tax year other than the calendar year (if the calendar year is not considered appropriate for some reason).

When a company either changes to a new tax year or is just starting operations, it is quite likely that it will initially have a short tax year. If so, it must report taxable income for that short period beginning on the first day after the end of the old tax year (or the start date of the organization, if it is a new one) and ending on the day before the first day of the new tax year. The key issue when reporting taxable income for a short tax year is that the amount subject to tax is not the reported net income for the short year, but rather the annualized amount. The annualized figure is used because it may place the company in a higher tax bracket. For example, if the Hawser Company has a short tax year of six months and has taxable income for that period of $50,000, it must first annualize the $50,000, bringing full-year taxable income to $100,000. The tax percentage is higher on $100,000 than on $50,000, resulting in a tax of $22,500 on the annualized figure. The Hawser Company then pays only that portion of the tax that would have accrued during its short tax year, which is $\frac{1}{2}$ of the $22,500 annualized tax, or $11,250.

The tax calculation method for a short tax year can cause problems for those organizations that have highly seasonal revenue patterns, since they may have a very high level of income only during a few months of the year, and losses during the remaining months. If the short tax year falls into this high-revenue period, the company will find that by annualizing its income as per the tax rules, it will fall into a much higher tax bracket than would normally be the case, and pay considerably more taxes. This issue can be addressed in the following year by filing for a rebate. However, in case an uncomfortable cash shortfall occurs that may not be alleviated for some months, one should be aware of this problem in advance and attempt to plan the timing of the short tax year around it.

If a company wishes to change its tax year, it must obtain approval (with a few exceptions) from the IRS. To do so, complete and mail IRS Form 1128 by the 15th day of the second calendar month following the close of the short tax year. Do not actually change tax years until formal approval from the IRS has been received.

35-45 TRANSFER PRICING

Transfer pricing is a key tax consideration, because it can result in the permanent reduction of an organization's tax liability. The permanent reduction is caused by the recognition of income in different taxing jurisdictions that may have different tax rates.

The basic concept behind the use of transfer pricing to reduce one's overall taxes is that a company transfers its products to a division in another country at the lowest possible price if the income tax rate is lower in the other country, or at the highest possible price if the tax rate is higher. By selling to the division at a low price, the company will report a very high profit on the final sale of products in the other country, which is where that income will be taxed at a presumably lower income tax rate.

For example, Exhibit 35-10 shows a situation in which a company with a location in Countries Alpha and Beta has the choice of selling goods either in Alpha or transferring them to Beta and selling them there. The company is faced with a corporate income tax rate of 40% in Country Alpha. To permanently avoid some of this income tax, the company sells its products to another subsidiary in Country Beta, where the corporate

Exhibit 35-10 Income Tax Savings from Transfer Pricing

	Country Alpha Location	Country Beta Location
Sales to subsidiary:		
Revenue	$1,000,000	
Cost of goods sold	$ 850,000	
Profit	$ 150,000	
Profit percentage	15%	
Sales outside of company:		
Revenue		$1,500,000
Cost of goods sold		$1,000,000
Profit		$ 500,000
Profit percentage		33%
Income tax percentage	40%	25%
Income tax	$ 60,000	$ 125,000
Consolidated income tax	$ 185,000	
Consolidated income tax percentage	28%	

Reprinted with permission, Bragg, *Cost Accounting: A Comprehensive Guide,* John Wiley & Sons, 2001, p. 618.

income tax rate is only 25%. By doing so, the company still earns a profit ($60,000) in Country Alpha, but the bulk of the profit ($125,000) now appears in Country Beta. The net result is a consolidated income tax rate of just 28%.

The IRS is well aware of this tax avoidance strategy, and has developed tax rules that do not eliminate it, but that will reduce the leeway that an accountant has in altering reportable income. Under Section 482 of the IRS code, the IRS's preferred approach for developing transfer prices is to use the market rate as its basis. However, very few products can be reliably and consistently compared to the market rate, with the exception of commodities, because there are costing differences between them. Also, in many cases, products are so specialized (especially components that are custom-designed to fit into a larger product) that there is no market rate against which they can be compared. Even if there is some basis of comparison between a product and the average market prices for similar products, the accountant still has some leeway in which to alter transfer prices, because the IRS will allow one to add special charges that are based on the cost of transferring the products, or extra fees, such as royalty or licensing fees that are imposed for the subsidiary's use of the parent company's patents or trademarks, or for administrative charges related to the preparation of any documentation required to move products between countries. It is also possible to slightly alter the interest rates charged to subsidiaries (though not too far from market rates) for the use of funds sent to them from the parent organization.

If there is no basis upon which to create prices based on market rates, then the IRS's next most favored approach is to calculate the prices based upon the *work back method.* Under this approach, one begins at the end of the sales cycle by determining the price at which a product is sold to an outside customer, and then subtract the subsidiary's standard markup percentage and its added cost of materials, labor, and overhead, which results in the theoretical transfer price. The work back method can result in a wide array of transfer prices, since a number of different costs can be subtracted from the final sale price, such as standard costs, actual costs, overhead costs based on different allocation measures, and overhead costs based on cost pools that contain different types of costs.

If that approach does not work, then the IRS's third most favored approach is the cost plus method. As the name implies, this approach begins at the other end of the production process and compiles costs from a product's initiation point. After all costs are added before the point of transfer, one then adds a profit margin to the product, thereby arriving at a transfer cost that is acceptable by the IRS. However, once again, the costs that are included in a product are subject to the same points of variation that were noted for the work back method. In addition, the profit margin added should be the standard margin added for any other company customer, but can be quite difficult to determine if there are a multitude of volume discounts, seasonal discounts, and so on. Consequently, the profit margin added to a product's initial costs can be subject to a great deal of negotiation.

An overriding issue to consider, no matter what approach is used to derive transfer prices, is that taxing authorities can become highly irritated if a company continually pushes the outer limits of acceptable transfer pricing rules in order to maximize its tax savings. When this happens, a company can expect continual audits and penalties on disputed items, as well as less favorable judgments related to any taxation issues. Consequently, it makes a great deal of sense to consistently adopt pricing policies that result in reasonable tax savings, are fully justifiable to the taxing authorities of all involved countries, and do not push the boundaries of acceptable pricing behavior.

Another transfer pricing issue that can modify a company's pricing strategy is the presence of any restrictions on cash flows out of a country in which it has a subsidiary. In these instances, it may be necessary to report the minimum possible amount of taxable income at the subsidiary, irrespective of the local tax rate. The reason is that the only way for a company to retrieve funds from the country is through the medium of an account receivable, which must be maximized by billing the subsidiary the highest possible amount for transferred goods. In this case, tax planning takes a back seat to cash flow planning.

Yet another issue that may drive a company to set pricing levels that do not result in reduced income taxes is that a subsidiary may have to report high levels of income in order to qualify for a loan from a local credit institution. This is especially important if the country in which the subsidiary is located has restrictions on the movement of cash, so that the parent company would be unable to withdraw loans that it makes to the subsidiary. As was the case for the last item, cash flow planning is likely to be more important than income tax reduction.

A final transfer pricing issue to be aware of is that the method for calculating taxable income may vary in other countries. This may falsely lead one to believe that another country has a lower tax rate. A closer examination of how taxable income is calculated might reveal that some expenses are restricted or not allowed at all, resulting in an actual tax rate that is much higher than originally expected. Consultation with a tax expert for the country in question prior to setting up any transfer pricing arrangements is the best way to avoid this problem.

35-46 TRAVEL AND ENTERTAINMENT REIMBURSEMENT

If the IRS conducts an audit and finds that it cannot find adequate substantiation of amounts paid to employees for their travel costs, then it can make an assumption that the employees are receiving an indirect form of revenue—especially if the amounts paid to the employees for their travel appear to be unreasonably high. To avoid these problems, a company can use the Federal Travel Regulation (FTR), which is issued by the General Services Administration, and which is available both on the Internet (at *policyworks.gov*) and through the U.S. Government Printing Office. The FTR is a detailed list of reimbursement rates for travel to most major cities in the United States. For each location, there is a meals and incidental expenses rate, which is $30 per day in most parts of the country, but which can be substantially higher in such high-cost locations as New York City. It also contains a lodging rate that can vary substantially not only by location, but also by time of year (since some prime tourist locations have major price increases during their high seasons). The reimbursement rate is designed for the expense reports of government employees and any government contractors who intend to bill their travel costs to the government. The rates are updated frequently, and so can be considered a reasonable estimate of costs for employee travel that can be used as the basis for per diem reimbursements. An example of these rates is shown in Exhibit 35-11, which is an extract of the actual federal reimbursement rates for several cities within Nevada on January 1, 2000. Notice that Incline Village and Crystal Bay have different reimbursable occupancy rates, which are dependent upon the time of year.

If an employee is given a travel advance and then does not either account for the use of these funds on an expense report or return them following the trip, then the company should report this as income on the employee's W-2 form at year-end.

Exhibit 35-11   Federal Per Diem Rates for Nevada

Key City Location	Key County Location	Maximum Lodging Amount (Room Rate Only)	+	Meals & Incidental Expenses Rate	=	Maximum Per Diem Rate
Incline Village/ Crystal Bay	City limits of Incline Village and Crystal Bay					
(Jun. 1–Sep. 30)		94		38		132
(Oct. 1–May 31)		74		38		112
Las Vegas	Clark County, Nellis AFB	72		38		110
Reno	All locations in Washoe County, except Incline Village and Crystal Bay	55		30		85
Stateline	Douglas (see also South Lake Tahoe, CA)	108		42		150

35-47 UNEMPLOYMENT TAXES

Both the state and federal governments will charge a company a fixed percentage of its payroll each year for the expense of unemployment funds that are used to pay former employees who have been released from employment. The state governments administer the distribution of these funds and will compile an experience rating on each company, based on the number of employees it has laid off in the recent past. Based on this experience rating, it can require a company to submit larger or smaller amounts to the state unemployment fund in future years. This can become a considerable burden if a company has a long history of layoffs. Consequently, one should consider the use of temporary employees or outsourcing if this will give a firm the ability to retain a small number of key employees and avoid layoffs while still handling seasonal changes in workloads. Also, if a company is planning to acquire another entity, but plans to lay off a large number of the acquiree's staff once the acquisition is completed, it may make more sense to only acquire the acquiree's assets and selectively hire a few of its employees, thereby retaining a pristine unemployment experience rating with the local state government.

The federal unemployment tax is imposed on a company if it has paid employees at least $1,500 in any calendar quarter, or had at least one employee for some portion of a day within at least 20 weeks of the year. In short, nearly all companies will be required to remit federal unemployment taxes. For the 2001 calendar year, the tax rate was 6.2% of the first $7,000 paid to each employee; this tends to concentrate most federal unemployment tax remittances into the first quarter of the calendar year. In many states, one can take a credit against the federal unemployment tax for up to 5.4% of taxable wages, which results in a net federal unemployment tax of only .8%. This tax should be computed and remitted on a quarterly basis—if the quarterly total is $100 or less, it may be carried forward to the next quarter rather than be remitted.

If a company is shifting to a new legal entity, perhaps because of a shift from a partnership to a corporation, or from an "S" corporation to a "C" corporation, it will probably have to set itself up with a new unemployment tax identification number with the local state authorities. This is a problem if the organization being closed down had an unusually good experience rating, since the company will be assigned a poorer one until a new experience rating can be built up over time, which will result in higher unemployment taxes in the short term. To avoid this problem, one should contact the local unemployment taxation office to request that the old company's experience rating be shifted to the new one.

35-48 WARRANTY EXPENSES

An accountant may be tempted to reduce the amount of taxable income by increasing the reserve for warranty costs, or to manipulate the reserve over time in order to report "managed" income figures. The IRS has foreseen this issue by banning the recording of a warranty reserve for the purposes of calculating taxable income. Instead, warranty costs can only be recognized as they are incurred, thereby avoiding the temptation to manipulate taxable income in this area.

35-49 SUMMARY

The key goal when dealing with any of the preceding tax issues is to steer a course that minimizes or delays a company's tax liability, preferably without also reducing the level of income listed on its financial statements.

Using a questionable approach to reporting taxable income can result in fines and penalties so large that the savings one was trying to achieve are thoroughly reversed. It is therefore highly recommended that a company work with a professional tax accountant or lawyer to determine the best course of action when dealing with each of the tax issues noted in this chapter, in order to adopt a course of action that meets the company's tax goals while also staying within the intent of the tax law.

APPENDICES

APPENDIX A

The Chart of Accounts

This appendix describes the types of account numbering formats that can be used to construct a chart of accounts, and also lists sample charts of accounts that use each of the formats. All of the charts of accounts shown in this appendix follow the same general sequence of account coding, which itemizes the accounts in the balance sheet first, and the income statement second. That sequence looks like this:

Current assets

Fixed assets

Other assets

Current liabilities

Long-term liabilities

Equity accounts

Revenue

Cost of goods sold

Selling, general and administrative expenses

Income taxes

Extraordinary items

THREE-DIGIT ACCOUNT CODE STRUCTURE

A three-digit account code structure allows one to create a numerical sequence of accounts that contains up to 1,000 potential accounts. It is useful for small businesses that have no pre-defined departments or divisions that must be broken out separately. A sample chart of accounts using this format is shown below:

Account Number	Description
010	Cash
020	Petty cash
030	Accounts receivable
040	Reserve for bad debts
050	Marketable securities
060	Raw materials inventory
070	Work-in-process inventory
080	Finished goods inventory
090	Reserve for obsolete inventory
100	Fixed assets—Computer equipment
110	Fixed assets—Computer software
120	Fixed assets—Furniture and fixtures
130	Fixed assets—Leasehold improvements
140	Fixed assets—Machinery
150	Accumulated depreciation—Computer equipment
160	Accumulated depreciation—Computer software
170	Accumulated depreciation—Furniture and fixtures
180	Accumulated depreciation—Leasehold improvements
190	Accumulated depreciation—Machinery
200	Other assets
300	Accounts payable
310	Accrued payroll liability
320	Accrued vacation liability
330	Accrued expenses liability—Other
340	Unremitted sales taxes
350	Unremitted pension payments
360	Short-term notes payable
370	Other short-term liabilities
400	Long-term notes payable
500	Capital stock
510	Retained earnings
600	Revenue
700	Cost of goods sold—Materials
710	Cost of goods sold—Direct labor
720	Cost of goods sold—Manufacturing supplies
730	Cost of goods sold—Applied overhead
800	Bank charges
805	Benefits
810	Depreciation
815	Insurance
825	Office supplies
830	Salaries and wages
835	Telephones
840	Training

Account Number	Description
845	Travel and entertainment
850	Utilities
855	Other expenses
860	Interest expense
900	Extraordinary items

Notice how each clearly definable block of accounts begins with a different set of account numbers. For example, current liabilities begin with "300," revenues begin with "600," and cost of goods sold items begin with "700." This not only makes it easier to navigate through the chart of accounts, but is also mandated by many computerized accounting software packages.

FIVE-DIGIT ACCOUNT CODE STRUCTURE

A five-digit account code structure is designed for those organizations with clearly defined departments, each of which is tracked with a separate income statement. This format uses the same account codes for the balance sheet accounts that we just saw for three-digit account codes, but replicates at least the operating expenses for each department (and sometimes for the revenue accounts, too). An example of this format is as follows, using the engineering and sales departments to illustrate the duplication of accounts:

Account Number	Department	Description
00-010	xxx	Cash
00-020	xxx	Petty cash
00-030	xxx	Accounts receivable
00-040	xxx	Reserve for bad debts
00-050	xxx	Marketable securities
00-060	xxx	Raw materials inventory
00-070	xxx	Work-in-process inventory
00-080	xxx	Finished goods inventory
00-090	xxx	Reserve for obsolete inventory
00-100	xxx	Fixed assets—Computer equipment
00-110	xxx	Fixed assets—Computer software
00-120	xxx	Fixed assets—Furniture and fixtures
00-130	xxx	Fixed assets—Leasehold improvements
00-140	xxx	Fixed assets—Machinery
00-150	xxx	Accumulated depreciation—Computer equipment
00-160	xxx	Accumulated depreciation—Computer software
00-170	xxx	Accumulated depreciation—Furniture and fixtures
00-180	xxx	Accumulated depreciation—Leasehold improvements
00-190	xxx	Accumulated depreciation—Machinery
00-200	xxx	Other assets
00-300	xxx	Accounts payable

(continued)

Account Number	Department	Description
00-310	xxx	Accrued payroll liability
00-320	xxx	Accrued vacation liability
00-330	xxx	Accrued expenses liability—Other
00-340	xxx	Unremitted sales taxes
00-350	xxx	Unremitted pension payments
00-360	xxx	Short-term notes payable
00-370	xxx	Other short-term liabilities
00-400	xxx	Long-term notes payable
00-500	xxx	Capital stock
00-510	xxx	Retained earnings
00-600	xxx	Revenue
00-700	xxx	Cost of goods sold—Materials
00-710	xxx	Cost of goods sold—Direct labor
00-720	xxx	Cost of goods sold—Manufacturing supplies
00-730	xxx	Cost of goods sold—Applied overhead
10-800	Engineering	Bank charges
10-805	Engineering	Benefits
10-810	Engineering	Depreciation
10-815	Engineering	Insurance
10-825	Engineering	Office supplies
10-830	Engineering	Salaries and wages
10-835	Engineering	Telephones
10-840	Engineering	Training
10-845	Engineering	Travel and entertainment
10-850	Engineering	Utilities
10-855	Engineering	Other expenses
10-860	Engineering	Interest expense
20-800	Sales	Bank charges
20-805	Sales	Benefits
20-810	Sales	Depreciation
20-815	Sales	Insurance
20-825	Sales	Office supplies
20-830	Sales	Salaries and wages
20-835	Sales	Telephones
20-840	Sales	Training
20-845	Sales	Travel and entertainment
20-850	Sales	Utilities
20-855	Sales	Other expenses
20-860	Sales	Interest expense
00-900	xxx	Extraordinary items

In this example, all expense accounts are replicated for every department. This does not mean, however, that all accounts must be *used* for every department. For example, it is most unlikely that bank charges will be ascribed to either the engineering or sales departments. Accordingly, those accounts that are not to be used can be rendered inactive in the accounting system, so that they never appear in the general ledger.

SEVEN-DIGIT ACCOUNT CODE STRUCTURE

A seven digit account code structure is used by those companies that not only have multiple departments, but also multiple divisions or locations, for each of which the management team wants to record separate accounting information. This requires the same coding structure used for the five-digit system, except that two digits are placed in front of the code to signify a different company division. These new digits also apply to balance sheet accounts, since most organizations will want to track assets and liabilities by division. The following chart of accounts, which identifies accounts for divisions in Atlanta and Seattle, and which continues to use the engineering and sales departments, is an example of how the seven-digit account code structure is compiled.

Account No.	Division	Department	Description
10-00-010	Atlanta	xxx	Cash
10-00-020	Atlanta	xxx	Petty cash
10-00-030	Atlanta	xxx	Accounts receivable
10-00-040	Atlanta	xxx	Reserve for bad debts
10-00-050	Atlanta	xxx	Marketable securities
10-00-060	Atlanta	xxx	Raw materials inventory
10-00-070	Atlanta	xxx	Work-in-process inventory
10-00-080	Atlanta	xxx	Finished goods inventory
10-00-090	Atlanta	xxx	Reserve for obsolete inventory
10-00-100	Atlanta	xxx	Fixed assets—Computer equipment
10-00-110	Atlanta	xxx	Fixed assets—Computer software
10-00-120	Atlanta	xxx	Fixed assets—Furniture and fixtures
10-00-130	Atlanta	xxx	Fixed assets—Leasehold improvements
10-00-140	Atlanta	xxx	Fixed assets—Machinery
10-00-150	Atlanta	xxx	Accumulated depreciation—computer equipment
10-00-160	Atlanta	xxx	Accumulated depreciation—Computer software
10-00-170	Atlanta	xxx	Accumulated depreciation—Furniture and fixtures
10-00-180	Atlanta	xxx	Accumulated depreciation—Leasehold improvements
10-00-190	Atlanta	xxx	Accumulated depreciation—Machinery
10-00-200	Atlanta	xxx	Other assets
10-00-300	Atlanta	xxx	Accounts payable
10-00-310	Atlanta	xxx	Accrued payroll liability
10-00-320	Atlanta	xxx	Accrued vacation liability
10-00-330	Atlanta	xxx	Accrued expenses liability—other
10-00-340	Atlanta	xxx	Unremitted sales taxes
10-00-350	Atlanta	xxx	Unremitted pension payments
10-00-360	Atlanta	xxx	Short-term notes payable
10-00-370	Atlanta	xxx	Other short-term liabilities
10-00-400	Atlanta	xxx	Long-term notes payable

(continued)

Account No.	Division	Department	Description
10-00-500	Atlanta	xxx	Capital stock
10-00-510	Atlanta	xxx	Retained earnings
10-00-600	Atlanta	xxx	Revenue
10-00-700	Atlanta	xxx	Cost of goods sold—Materials
10-00-710	Atlanta	xxx	Cost of goods sold—Direct labor
10-00-720	Atlanta	xxx	Cost of goods sold—Manufacturing supplies
10-00-730	Atlanta	xxx	Cost of goods sold—Applied overhead
10-10-800	Atlanta	Engineering	Bank charges
10-10-805	Atlanta	Engineering	Benefits
10-10-810	Atlanta	Engineering	Depreciation
10-10-815	Atlanta	Engineering	Insurance
10-10-825	Atlanta	Engineering	Office supplies
10-10-830	Atlanta	Engineering	Salaries and wages
10-10-835	Atlanta	Engineering	Telephones
10-10-840	Atlanta	Engineering	Training
10-10-845	Atlanta	Engineering	Travel and entertainment
10-10-850	Atlanta	Engineering	Utilities
10-10-855	Atlanta	Engineering	Other expenses
10-10-860	Atlanta	Engineering	Interest expense
10-20-800	Atlanta	Sales	Bank charges
10-20-805	Atlanta	Sales	Benefits
10-20-810	Atlanta	Sales	Depreciation
10-20-815	Atlanta	Sales	Insurance
10-20-825	Atlanta	Sales	Office supplies
10-20-830	Atlanta	Sales	Salaries and wages
10-20-835	Atlanta	Sales	Telephones
10-20-840	Atlanta	Sales	Training
10-20-845	Atlanta	Sales	Travel and entertainment
10-20-850	Atlanta	Sales	Utilities
10-20-855	Atlanta	Sales	Other expenses
10-20-860	Atlanta	Sales	Interest expense
10-00-900	Atlanta	xxx	Extraordinary items
20-00-010	Seattle	xxx	Cash
20-00-020	Seattle	xxx	Petty cash
20-00-030	Seattle	xxx	Accounts receivable
20-00-040	Seattle	xxx	Reserve for bad debts
20-00-050	Seattle	xxx	Marketable securities
20-00-060	Seattle	xxx	Raw materials inventory
20-00-070	Seattle	xxx	Work-in-process inventory
20-00-080	Seattle	xxx	Finished goods inventory
20-00-090	Seattle	xxx	Reserve for obsolete inventory
20-00-100	Seattle	xxx	Fixed assets—Computer equipment
20-00-110	Seattle	xxx	Fixed assets—Computer software
20-00-120	Seattle	xxx	Fixed assets—Furniture and fixtures
20-00-130	Seattle	xxx	Fixed assets—Leasehold improvements

Account No.	Division	Department	Description
20-00-140	Seattle	xxx	Fixed assets—Machinery
20-00-150	Seattle	xxx	Accumulated depreciation—Computer equipment
20-00-160	Seattle	xxx	Accumulated depreciation—Computer software
20-00-170	Seattle	xxx	Accumulated depreciation—Furniture and fixtures
20-00-180	Seattle	xxx	Accumulated depreciation—Leasehold improvements
20-00-190	Seattle	xxx	Accumulated depreciation—Machinery
20-00-200	Seattle	xxx	Other assets
20-00-300	Seattle	xxx	Accounts payable
20-00-310	Seattle	xxx	Accrued payroll liability
20-00-320	Seattle	xxx	Accrued vacation liability
20-00-330	Seattle	xxx	Accrued expenses liability—other
20-00-340	Seattle	xxx	Unremitted sales taxes
20-00-350	Seattle	xxx	Unremitted pension payments
20-00-360	Seattle	xxx	Short-term notes payable
20-00-370	Seattle	xxx	Other short-term liabilities
20-00-400	Seattle	xxx	Long-term notes payable
20-00-500	Seattle	xxx	Capital stock
20-00-510	Seattle	xxx	Retained earnings
20-00-600	Seattle	xxx	Revenue
20-00-700	Seattle	xxx	Cost of goods sold—Materials
20-00-710	Seattle	xxx	Cost of goods sold—Direct labor
20-00-720	Seattle	xxx	Cost of goods sold—Manufacturing supplies
20-00-730	Seattle	xxx	Cost of goods sold—Applied overhead
20-10-800	Seattle	Engineering	Engineering—Bank charges
20-10-805	Seattle	Engineering	Engineering—Benefits
20-10-810	Seattle	Engineering	Engineering—Depreciation
20-10-815	Seattle	Engineering	Engineering—Insurance
20-10-825	Seattle	Engineering	Engineering—Office supplies
20-10-830	Seattle	Engineering	Engineering—Salaries and wages
20-10-835	Seattle	Engineering	Engineering—Telephones
20-10-840	Seattle	Engineering	Engineering—Training
20-10-845	Seattle	Engineering	Engineering—Travel and entertainment
20-10-850	Seattle	Engineering	Engineering—Utilities
20-10-855	Seattle	Engineering	Engineering—Other expenses
20-10-860	Seattle	Engineering	Engineering—Interest expense
20-20-800	Seattle	Sales	Sales—Bank charges
20-20-805	Seattle	Sales	Sales—Benefits
20-20-810	Seattle	Sales	Sales—Depreciation
20-20-815	Seattle	Sales	Sales—Insurance
20-20-825	Seattle	Sales	Sales—Office supplies

(continued)

Account No.	Division	Department	Description
20-20-830	Seattle	Sales	Sales—Salaries and wages
20-20-835	Seattle	Sales	Sales—Telephones
20-20-840	Seattle	Sales	Sales—Training
20-20-845	Seattle	Sales	Sales—Travel and entertainment
20-20-850	Seattle	Sales	Sales—Utilities
20-20-855	Seattle	Sales	Sales—Other expenses
20-20-860	Seattle	Sales	Sales—Interest expense
20-00-900	Seattle	xxx	Extraordinary items

APPENDIX B

Journal Entries

This appendix contains a list of the most common journal entries that an accountant is likely to deal with. There are a plethora of possible transactions that would require an immense tome to address, so the emphasis here is solely on the most common journal entries, not on those that will only crop up on rare occasions.

The journal entries are listed in alphabetical order, and include explanatory text. This text may be sufficient for one to copy into actual journal entry descriptions, with slight modifications. The text makes additional explanatory notations where necessary, but the main focus is on presenting a brief summarization of each entry.

A set of accounts are listed for each sample journal entry, which may vary somewhat from the titles of accounts used in one's company. If there are a wide range of possible entries to different accounts, then this is noted with an entry in brackets, such as "[Salaries—itemize by department]." A triple "x" is noted under the debit or credit heading for each entry, denoting the most likely entry that would be made. If there is a reasonable chance that either a debit or credit entry would be made, then this is noted in the description.

There are a few instances in which journal entries should be reversed in the following accounting period. When this is necessary, a warning note is attached to the bottom of the relevant journal entries.

Accounts Payable, Reversal: To reverse an account payable transaction that had previously been entered. There are a variety of possible accounts to which a reversal could be credited, so many possible accounts are noted in brackets.

	Debit	*Credit*
Accounts payable	xxx	
[Expense account]		xxx
[Asset account]		xxx
[Accrued liability account]		xxx

Accounts Payable, Void Company Check: To reverse a previous check payment to a supplier. This entry assumes that there is an additional charge from the bank for a stop payment on the check, as well as the reversal of an early payment discount on the original payment.

	Debit	Credit
Bank charges (stop payment)	xxx	
Early payment discount	xxx	
Cash	xxx	
[Expense or asset for which payment was made]		xxx

Accounts Receivable, Write Off: To cancel an account receivable by offsetting it against the reserve for bad debts located in the bad debt accrual account.

	Debit	Credit
Bad debt accrual	xxx	
Accounts receivable		xxx

Accrue Bad Debt Expense: To accrue for projected bad debts, based on historical experience.

	Debit	Credit
Bad debt expense	xxx	
Bad debt accrual		xxx

Accrue Benefits: To accrue for all employee benefit expenses incurred during the month, for which an associated accounting entry has not yet been made.

	Debit	Credit
Medical insurance expense	xxx	
Dental insurance expense	xxx	
Disability insurance expense	xxx	
Life insurance expense	xxx	
Accrued benefits		xxx

This entry should be *reversed* in the following accounting period.

Accrue Property Taxes: To accrue for the property tax liability incurred during the accounting period based on the known base of fixed assets.

	Debit	Credit
Property tax expense	xxx	
Accrued property taxes		xxx

This entry *should not be reversed* in the following accounting period, since the tax payment will not normally occur in the following period, but instead only a few times per year. Instead, the actual payment should be charged directly against the accrual account.

Accrue Salaries & Wages: To accrue for salaries and wages earned through the end of the accounting period, but not yet paid to employees as of the end of the accounting period.

	Debit	Credit
Direct labor expense	xxx	
[Salaries—itemize by department]	xxx	
Accrued salaries		xxx
Accrued payroll taxes		xxx

This entry should be *reversed* in the following accounting period.

Accrue Vacation Pay: To accrue vacation pay earned by employees, but not yet used by them, subject to the year-end maximum vacation carryforward limitation. The same entry can be used to record accrued sick time.

	Debit	Credit
Payroll taxes	xxx	
[Salaries—itemize by department]	xxx	
Accrued salaries		xxx
Accrued payroll taxes		xxx

This entry *should not be reversed* in the following accounting period, since the vacation time may not be used in the following period. Instead, the actual vacation-related payment should be charged directly against the accrual account.

Acquisition, Pooling Method: To record an acquisition using the book value of assets and liabilities. This should be essentially all balance sheet accounts currently in use.

	Debit	Credit
Accounts receivable	xxx	
Marketable securities	xxx	
Inventory	xxx	
Computer equipment	xxx	
Computer software	xxx	
Furniture & fixtures	xxx	
Manufacturing equipment	xxx	
Bad debt accrual		xxx
Obsolete inventory reserve		xxx
Accumulated depreciation		xxx
Accounts payable		xxx
Debt		xxx
Common stock		xxx
Additional paid-in capital		xxx

Acquisition, Purchase Method: To record an acquisition using the fair market value of assets and liabilities, with an entry to goodwill that records the difference between this total and the price paid.

	Debit	Credit
Accounts receivable	xxx	
Marketable securities (current market value)	xxx	
Inventory (lower of cost or market)	xxx	
Computer equipment (appraised value)	xxx	
Computer software (appraised value)	xxx	
Furniture & fixtures (appraised value)	xxx	
Manufacturing equipment (appraised value)	xxx	
Goodwill	xxx	
Accounts payable		xxx
Debt (book value)		xxx
Common stock		xxx
Additional paid-in capital		xxx

Bank Reconciliation: To adjust the accounting records to reflect differences between the book and bank records. The cash entry is listed as a credit, on the assumption that bank-related expenses outweigh the interest income.

	Debit	Credit
Bank charges	xxx	
Credit card charges	xxx	
Interest income		xxx
Cash		xxx

Depreciation: To record the depreciation incurred during the month. The amortization account is used to write off goodwill.

	Debit	Credit
Depreciation, computer equipment	xxx	
Depreciation, computer software	xxx	
Depreciation, furniture & fixtures	xxx	
Depreciation, leasehold improvements	xxx	
Depreciation, manufacturing equipment	xxx	
Amortization expense	xxx	
Accum. depreciation, computer equipment		xxx
Accum. depreciation, computer software		xxx
Accum. depreciation, furniture & fixtures		xxx

	Debit	Credit
Accum. depreciation, leasehold improvements		xxx
Accum. depreciation, manufacturing equipment		xxx
Goodwill		xxx

Dividend Declaration: To separate the sum total of all declared dividends from retained earnings once dividends have been approved by the Board of Directors.

	Debit	Credit
Retained earnings	xxx	
Dividends payable		xxx

Dividend Payment: To issue payment to shareholders for dividends declared by the Board of Directors.

	Debit	Credit
Dividends payable	xxx	
Cash		xxx

Fixed Asset (Sale of): To record the cash received from the sale of an asset, as well as any gain or loss in its sale. This entry also eliminates all associated accumulated depreciation that has built up over the term of the company's ownership of the asset.

	Debit	Credit
Cash	xxx	
Accumulated depreciation	xxx	
Loss on sale of assets	xxx	
[various fixed asset accounts]		xxx
Gain on sale of assets		xxx

Fixed Asset (Write off): To record the unreimbursed disposal of an asset. This entry also eliminates all associated accumulated depreciation that has built up over the term of the company's ownership of the asset.

	Debit	Credit
Accumulated depreciation	xxx	
Loss on disposal of assets	xxx	
[various fixed asset accounts]		xxx

Foreign Currency Gain/Loss: To record in the *first entry* the loss expected to occur on foreign currency accounts payable at the end of the accounting period. To record in the *second entry* the income arising from a gain on foreign currency accounts payable at the end of the accounting period.

	Debit	Credit
Unrealized loss on currency fluctuations	xxx	
Accounts payable		xxx
Accounts payable	xxx	
Gain on currency fluctuations		xxx
Cash		xxx

Goodwill, Amortization: To record the periodic reduction in the amount of recorded goodwill. There are two methods available for making this entry. The *first entry* charges amortized goodwill directly to the goodwill asset account, while the *second entry* charges it to a contra account that is netted against the goodwill asset account.

	Debit	Credit
Goodwill amortization expense	xxx	
Goodwill (asset account)		xxx
Goodwill amortization expense	xxx	
Accumulated goodwill expense		xxx

Interest, Imputed: To reduce the balance of a note payable by the difference between the market interest rate and the interest rate itemized on the note (*first entry*), as well as to recognize the associated interest expense over time (*second entry*).

	Debit	Credit
Unamortized premium on notes payable	xxx	
Note payable		xxx
Interest expense	xxx	
Unamortized premium on notes payable		xxx

Inventory, Adjust to Physical Count: To adjust inventory balances, either up or down, as a result of changes in the inventory quantities that are noted during a physical count. The following entries assume that there are increases in inventory balances. If there are declines in the inventory balances, then the debits and credits are reversed.

	Debit	Credit
Raw materials inventory	xxx	
Work-in-process inventory	xxx	
Finished goods inventory	xxx	
Cost of goods sold		xxx

Inventory, Obsolescence: To charge an ongoing expense to the cost of goods sold that increases the balance in a reserve against which obsolete inventory can be charged (*first entry*). The *second entry* charges off specific inventory items against the reserve.

	Debit	Credit
Cost of goods sold	xxx	
Obsolescence reserve		xxx
Obsolescence reserve	xxx	
Raw materials inventory		xxx
Work-in-process inventory		xxx
Finished goods inventory		xxx

Investment (Equity Method), Record Share of Investee Income: To record the company's proportional share of the income reported by [name of company in which investment was made] (*first entry*), as well as the income tax associated with this income recognition (*second entry*).

	Debit	Credit
Investment in [company name]	xxx	
Income from equity share in investment		xxx
Income tax expense	xxx	
Income taxes payable		xxx

Investment (Equity Method): To record the company's cash or loan investment in another business entity.

	Debit	Credit
Investment in [company name]	xxx	
Cash		xxx
Notes payable		xxx

Lease, Capital (Initial Record by Lessee): To record the initial capitalization of a lease, including imputed interest that is associated with the transaction and both the short-term and long-term portions of the associated account payable. A *second entry* records the interest expense associated with each periodic payment on the capital lease. A *third entry* records the depreciation expense associated with the capital lease in each accounting period.

	Debit	Credit
Capital leases	xxx	
Unamortized discount on notes payable	xxx	
Short-term liabilities		xxx
Long-term liabilities		xxx
Interest expense	xxx	
Unamortized discount on notes payable		xxx

	Debit	Credit
Depreciation expense	xxx	
Accumulated depreciation—capital		xxx
leases		

Life Insurance Transactions: To record the net increase in the cash surrender value of officer's life insurance for which the company is the beneficiary, as well as that portion of the life insurance that is used in the current period and therefore charged to expense.

	Debit	Credit
Life insurance expense	xxx	
Cash surrender value of life insurance	xxx	
Accounts payable		xxx

Marketable Security (Acquisition): To record the acquisition of marketable securities. If the security purchased is one that cannot be liquidated in the short term, then the debit would instead be to the long-term asset account, listed here as "marketable securities, long term."

	Debit	Credit
Marketable securities, short-term	xxx	
Marketable securities, long-term	xxx	
Cash		xxx

Marketable Security (Adjust to Fair Market Rate): To charge to expense the amount of a reduction in the market value of a marketable security below its purchase price.

	Debit	Credit
Unrealized investment losses	xxx	
Reserve for losses on marketable securities		xxx

Marketable Security (Disposition): To record the sale of a marketable security, while also eliminating all earlier reserves for losses on its market value. The entry includes line items for the sale of both short-term and long-term marketable securities.

	Debit	Credit
Cash	xxx	
Reserve for losses on marketable securities	xxx	
Marketable securities, short-term		xxx
Marketable securities, long-term		xxx

Overhead, Allocation: To allocate the contents of all cost pools to cost objects, which are contained within the cost of goods sold and all inventory accounts. The raw materials account is included in this categorization, since this inventory can accumulate overhead costs associated with the purchasing, receiving, and materials handling activities.

	Debit	*Credit*
Cost of goods sold	xxx	
Raw materials inventory	xxx	
Work-in-process inventory	xxx	
Finished goods inventory	xxx	
[Overhead—itemize by overhead cost pool]		xxx

Overhead, Transfer to Cost Pools: To transfer manufacturing expenses into one or more overhead cost pools for later allocation to cost objects.

	Debit	*Credit*
[Overhead—itemize by overhead cost pool]	xxx	
Maintenance expenses		xxx
Manufacturing supplies		xxx
Rent, manufacturing related		xxx
Repairs, manufacturing related		xxx
Salaries, maintenance department		xxx
Salaries, materials handling department		xxx
Salaries, production control department		xxx
Salaries, purchasing department		xxx
Salaries, quality control department		xxx
Salaries, supervisory		xxx
Scrap, normal		xxx
Utilities		xxx
[Depreciation—various accounts]		xxx

Revenue (Installment Basis): To record installment sales as a liability, as noted in the *first entry.* As the revenue is earned over time, the *second entry* is used to recognize portions of the installment sales as current revenue.

	Debit	*Credit*
Accounts receivable	xxx	
Unearned installment revenue		xxx
Unearned installment revenue	xxx	
Revenue		xxx

Standard Costing, Labor Rate Variance: To record the difference between standard and actual direct labor rate costs. This entry assumes that the variance results in a write up of labor rates. If the result is a write down, then reverse all debits and credits.

	Debit	*Credit*
Work-in-process inventory	xxx	
Finished goods inventory	xxx	
Direct labor rate variance		xxx

Standard Costing, Price Variance: To record the difference between the standard and actual purchase price for materials. This entry assumes that the variance results in a write up of material prices. If the result is a write down, then reverse all debits and credits.

	Debit	*Credit*
Raw materials inventory	xxx	
Work-in-process inventory	xxx	
Finished goods inventory	xxx	
Materials price variance		xxx

Transfer to General Ledger from Disbursements Journal: To transfer the summary totals for all cash payments made through the disbursements journal to the general ledger for the current accounting period. If cash disbursements are made with ACH or wire transfers and there is a known bank charge for this service, then the associated bank charge can be recorded as an expense, as well.

	Debit	*Credit*
Accounts payable	xxx	
Bank charges	xxx	
Cash		xxx
Early payment discounts taken		xxx

Transfer to General Ledger from Payables Journal: To transfer the summary totals for all accounts payable recorded in the payables journal to the general ledger for the current accounting period.

	Debit	*Credit*
Raw materials inventory account	xxx	
[Various expense accounts]	xxx	
[Various fixed asset accounts]	xxx	
Accounts payable		xxx

Transfer to General Ledger from Payroll Journal: To transfer the summary totals for all payroll transactions recorded in the payroll journal to the general ledger for the current accounting period. It may also be necessary to credit various expense accounts if employees are paying back the company for any purchases they have made through it.

	Debit	*Credit*
Direct labor expense	xxx	
[Salaries—itemize by department]	xxx	
Cash		xxx
Federal withholding taxes payable		xxx
Social security withholding taxes payable		xxx
Medicare withholding taxes payable		xxx
Federal unemployment taxes payable		xxx
State withholding taxes payable		xxx
State unemployment taxes payable		xxx
Garnishments payable		xxx

Transfer to General Ledger from Receipts Journal: To transfer the summary totals for all cash receipts recorded in the receipts journal to the general ledger for the current accounting period.

	Debit	*Credit*
Cash	xxx	
Early payment discounts	xxx	
Accounts receivable		xxx

Transfer to General Ledger from Sales Journal: To transfer the summary totals for all sales transactions recorded in the sales journal to the general ledger for the current accounting period. The freight expense is credited if the company bills customers for freight charges incurred.

	Debit	*Credit*
Accounts receivable	xxx	
Sales taxes payable		xxx
GST taxes payable		xxx
Freight expense		xxx
[Various revenue accounts]		xxx

Treasury Stock, Purchase: To record the acquisition by the company of stock, which is paid for in cash.

	Debit	*Credit*
Treasury stock	xxx	
Cash		xxx

Treasury Stock, Sale: To record the sale of treasury stock to investors by the company, with payments in excess of treasury stock cost being credited to the additional paid-in capital account.

	Debit	*Credit*
Cash	xxx	
Treasury stock		xxx
Additional paid-in capital		xxx

APPENDIX C

Interest Tables

There are five tables in this appendix that relate to the most common calculations used for interest rate analyses. Each one uses a standard format that lists the interest rate, from 1% to 13%, across the top, and the number of years, from 1 to 30, down the left side. The underlying calculation for each one is noted below, as well as a brief example describing how to use each one.

SIMPLE INTEREST TABLE

The simple interest table in Exhibit C-1 is used to find the total interest expense on an investment or debt that is to be completed in some future period, without factoring in the impact of any compounding of interest. The calculation is:

$$(\text{interest rate} \times \text{number of years that interest accrues})$$

For example, to determine the total amount of an investment of $50,000 at the end of seven years, using an interest rate of 9%, go to the simple interest table. Then move down to the row that contains interest rate factors for seven years, and move across to find the cell for the 9% interest rate, which contains a factor of 1.63. Then multiply this by $50,000 to arrive at $81,500.

COMPOUND INTEREST (FUTURE AMOUNT OF 1 AT COMPOUND INTEREST DUE IN N PERIODS)

The table in Exhibit C-2 is used to find the total interest expense on an investment or debt that is to be completed in some future period, including the impact of any compounding of interest. The calculation is:

$$(1 + \text{interest rate})^{\text{number of years}}$$

For example, to determine the total amount of an investment of $50,000 at the end of 11 years, using an interest rate of 8%, go to the compound interest table for future amounts, move down to the row that contains interest rate factors for 11 years, and move across to find the cell for an 8% interest rate, which contains a factor of 2.3316. Then multiply this by $50,000 to arrive at $116,580.

COMPOUND INTEREST (PRESENT VALUE OF 1 DUE IN N PERIODS)

The table in Exhibit C-3 is used to determine the discounted current value of an investment that will be payable in a fixed amount at some point in the future. The calculation is:

$$\frac{1}{(1 + \text{interest rate})^{\text{number of years}}}$$

For example, to determine the discounted current value of a payment of $50,000 that will occur in 17 years, assuming a compounded rate of investment in the interim of 7%, go to the compound interest table for the present value of money due in future periods. Move down to the row that contains discounting factors for 17 years, and move across to find the cell for a 7% interest rate, which contains a factor of .3166. Then multiply this by $50,000 to arrive at $15,830.

PRESENT VALUE OF ORDINARY ANNUITY OF 1 PER PERIOD

The table in Exhibit C-4 is used to find the present value of a fixed number of payments in the future. The calculation is:

$$\frac{1 - \dfrac{1}{(1 + \text{interest rate})^{\text{number of years}}}}{\text{interest rate}}$$

For example, to determine the present value of a series of annual payments of $2,500 for the next 22 years at a discount rate of 13%, go to the table for the present value of an ordinary annuity of 1 per period. Move down to the row that contains discounting factors for 22 years, and move across to find the cell for a 13% interest rate, which contains a discount factor of 7.1695. Then multiply this by $2,500 to arrive at a present value of $17,923.75.

FUTURE AMOUNT OF ORDINARY ANNUITY OF 1 PER PERIOD

The table in Exhibit C-5 is used to determine the future value of a series of fixed payments. The calculation is:

$$\frac{(1 + \text{interest rate})^{\text{number of years}} - 1}{\text{interest rate}}$$

For example, to determine the future value of a series of 10 $5,000 annual payments at an interest rate of 5%, go to the table for the future amount of an ordinary annuity. Move down to the row that contains compounding factors for 10 years, and move across to find the cell for a 5% interest rate, which contains a discount factor of 12.5779. Then multiply this by $5,000 to arrive at a future value of $62,889.50.

Exhibit C-1 Simple Interest Table

Number of Years / *Interest Rate*

Number of Years	1%	2%	3%	4%	5%	6%	7%	8%	9%	10%	11%	12%	13%
1	1.01	1.02	1.03	1.04	1.05	1.06	1.07	1.08	1.09	1.10	1.11	1.12	1.13
2	1.02	1.04	1.06	1.08	1.10	1.12	1.14	1.16	1.18	1.20	1.22	1.24	1.26
3	1.03	1.06	1.09	1.12	1.15	1.18	1.21	1.24	1.27	1.30	1.33	1.36	1.39
4	1.04	1.08	1.12	1.16	1.20	1.24	1.28	1.32	1.36	1.40	1.44	1.48	1.52
5	1.05	1.10	1.15	1.20	1.25	1.30	1.35	1.40	1.45	1.50	1.55	1.60	1.65
6	1.06	1.12	1.18	1.24	1.30	1.36	1.42	1.48	1.54	1.60	1.66	1.72	1.78
7	1.07	1.14	1.21	1.28	1.35	1.42	1.49	1.56	1.63	1.70	1.77	1.84	1.91
8	1.08	1.16	1.24	1.32	1.40	1.48	1.56	1.64	1.72	1.80	1.88	1.96	2.04
9	1.09	1.18	1.27	1.36	1.45	1.54	1.63	1.72	1.81	1.90	1.99	2.08	2.17
10	1.10	1.20	1.30	1.40	1.50	1.60	1.70	1.80	1.90	2.00	2.10	2.20	2.30
11	1.11	1.22	1.33	1.44	1.55	1.66	1.77	1.88	1.99	2.10	2.21	2.32	2.43
12	1.12	1.24	1.36	1.48	1.60	1.72	1.84	1.96	2.08	2.20	2.32	2.44	2.56
13	1.13	1.26	1.39	1.52	1.65	1.78	1.91	2.04	2.17	2.30	2.43	2.56	2.69
14	1.14	1.28	1.42	1.56	1.70	1.84	1.98	2.12	2.26	2.40	2.54	2.68	2.82
15	1.15	1.30	1.45	1.60	1.75	1.90	2.05	2.20	2.35	2.50	2.65	2.80	2.95
16	1.16	1.32	1.48	1.64	1.80	1.96	2.12	2.28	2.44	2.60	2.76	2.92	3.08
17	1.17	1.34	1.51	1.68	1.85	2.02	2.19	2.36	2.53	2.70	2.87	3.04	3.21
18	1.18	1.36	1.54	1.72	1.90	2.08	2.26	2.44	2.62	2.80	2.98	3.16	3.34
19	1.19	1.38	1.57	1.76	1.95	2.14	2.33	2.52	2.71	2.90	3.09	3.28	3.47
20	1.20	1.40	1.60	1.80	2.00	2.20	2.40	2.60	2.80	3.00	3.10	3.40	3.60
21	1.21	1.42	1.63	1.84	2.05	2.26	2.47	2.68	2.89	3.10	3.31	3.52	3.73
22	1.22	1.44	1.66	1.88	2.10	2.32	2.54	2.76	2.98	3.20	3.42	3.64	3.86
23	1.23	1.46	1.69	1.92	2.15	2.38	2.61	2.84	3.07	3.30	3.53	3.76	3.99
24	1.24	1.48	1.72	1.96	2.20	2.44	2.68	2.92	3.16	3.40	3.64	3.88	4.12
25	1.25	1.50	1.75	2.00	2.25	2.50	2.75	3.00	3.25	3.50	3.75	4.00	4.25
26	1.26	1.52	1.78	2.04	2.30	2.56	2.82	3.08	3.34	3.60	3.86	4.12	4.38
27	1.27	1.54	1.81	2.08	2.35	2.62	2.89	3.16	3.43	3.70	3.97	4.24	4.51
28	1.28	1.56	1.84	2.12	2.40	2.68	2.96	3.24	3.52	3.80	4.08	4.36	4.64
29	1.29	1.58	1.87	2.16	2.45	2.74	3.03	3.32	3.61	3.90	4.19	4.48	4.77
30	1.30	1.60	1.90	2.20	2.50	2.80	3.10	3.40	3.70	4.00	4.30	4.60	4.90

Exhibit C-2 Compound Interest Table (Future Amount of 1 at Compound Interest Due in N Periods)

Number of Years							Interest Rate						
	1%	2%	3%	4%	5%	6%	7%	8%	9%	10%	11%	12%	13%
1	1.0100	1.0200	1.0300	1.0400	1.0500	1.0600	1.0700	1.0800	1.0900	1.1000	1.1100	1.1200	1.1300
2	1.0201	1.0404	1.0609	1.0816	1.1025	1.1236	1.1449	1.1664	1.1881	1.2100	1.2321	1.2544	1.2769
3	1.0303	1.0612	1.0927	1.1249	1.1576	1.1910	1.2250	1.2597	1.2950	1.3310	1.3676	1.4049	1.4429
4	1.0406	1.0824	1.1255	1.1699	1.2155	1.2625	1.3108	1.3605	1.4116	1.4641	1.5181	1.5735	1.6305
5	1.0510	1.1041	1.1593	1.2167	1.2763	1.3382	1.4026	1.4693	1.5386	1.6105	1.6851	1.7623	1.8424
6	1.0615	1.1262	1.1941	1.2653	1.3401	1.4185	1.5007	1.5869	1.6771	1.7716	1.8704	1.9738	2.0820
7	1.0721	1.1487	1.2299	1.3159	1.4071	1.5036	1.6058	1.7138	1.8280	1.9487	2.0762	2.2107	2.3526
8	1.0829	1.1717	1.2668	1.3686	1.4775	1.5938	1.7182	1.8509	1.9926	2.1436	2.3045	2.4760	2.6584
9	1.0937	1.1951	1.3048	1.4233	1.5513	1.6895	1.8385	1.9990	2.1719	2.3579	2.5580	2.7731	3.0040
10	1.1046	1.2190	1.3439	1.4802	1.6289	1.7908	1.9672	2.1589	2.3674	2.5937	2.8394	3.1058	3.3946
11	1.1157	1.2434	1.3842	1.5395	1.7103	1.8983	2.1049	2.3316	2.5804	2.8531	3.1518	3.4785	3.8359
12	1.1268	1.2682	1.4258	1.6010	1.7959	2.0122	2.2522	2.5182	2.8127	3.1384	3.4985	3.8960	4.3345
13	1.1381	1.2936	1.4685	1.6651	1.8856	2.1329	2.4098	2.7196	3.0658	3.4523	3.8833	4.3635	4.8980
14	1.1495	1.3195	1.5126	1.7317	1.9799	2.2609	2.5785	2.9372	3.3417	3.7975	4.3104	4.8871	5.5348
15	1.1610	1.3459	1.5580	1.8009	2.0789	2.3966	2.7590	3.1722	3.6425	4.1772	4.7846	5.4736	6.2543
16	1.1726	1.3728	1.6047	1.8730	2.1829	2.5404	2.9522	3.4259	3.9703	4.5950	5.3109	6.1304	7.0673
17	1.1843	1.4002	1.6528	1.9479	2.2920	2.6928	3.1588	3.7000	4.3276	5.0545	5.8951	6.8660	7.9861
18	1.1961	1.4282	1.7024	2.0258	2.4066	2.8543	3.3799	3.9960	4.7171	5.5599	6.5436	7.6900	9.0243
19	1.2081	1.4568	1.7535	2.1068	2.5270	3.0256	3.6165	4.3157	5.1417	6.1159	7.2633	8.6128	10.1974
20	1.2202	1.4859	1.8061	2.1911	2.6533	3.2071	3.8697	4.6610	5.6044	6.7275	8.0623	9.6463	11.5231
21	1.2324	1.5157	1.8603	2.2788	2.7860	3.3996	4.1406	5.0338	6.1088	7.4002	8.9492	10.8038	13.0211
22	1.2447	1.5460	1.9161	2.3699	2.9253	3.6035	4.4304	5.4365	6.6586	8.1403	9.9336	12.1003	14.7138
23	1.2572	1.5769	1.9736	2.4647	3.0715	3.8197	4.7405	5.8715	7.2579	8.9543	11.0263	13.5523	16.6266
24	1.2697	1.6084	2.0328	2.5633	3.2251	4.0489	5.0724	6.3412	7.9111	9.8497	12.2392	15.1786	18.7881
25	1.2824	1.6406	2.0938	2.6658	3.3864	4.2919	5.4274	6.8485	8.6231	10.8347	13.5855	17.0001	21.2305
26	1.2953	1.6734	2.1566	2.7725	3.5557	4.5494	5.8074	7.3964	9.3992	11.9182	15.0799	19.0401	23.9905
27	1.3082	1.7069	2.2213	2.8834	3.7335	4.8223	6.2139	7.9881	10.2451	13.1100	16.7386	21.3249	27.1093
28	1.3213	1.7410	2.2879	2.9987	3.9201	5.1117	6.6488	8.6271	11.1671	14.4210	18.5799	23.8839	30.6335
29	1.3345	1.7758	2.3566	3.1187	4.1161	5.4184	7.1143	9.3173	12.1722	15.8631	20.6237	26.7499	34.6158
30	1.3478	1.8114	2.4274	3.2434	4.3219	5.7435	7.6123	10.0627	13.2677	17.4494	22.8923	29.9599	39.1159

Exhibit C-3 Compound Interest Table (Present Value of 1 Due in N Periods)

Interest Rate

Number of Years	1%	2%	3%	4%	5%	6%	7%	8%	9%	10%	11%	12%	13%
1	0.9901	0.9804	0.9709	0.9615	0.9524	0.9434	0.9346	0.9259	0.9174	0.9091	0.9009	0.8929	0.8850
2	0.9803	0.9612	0.9426	0.9246	0.9070	0.8900	0.8734	0.8573	0.8417	0.8264	0.8116	0.7972	0.7831
3	0.9706	0.9423	0.9151	0.8890	0.8638	0.8396	0.8163	0.7938	0.7722	0.7513	0.7312	0.7118	0.6931
4	0.9610	0.9238	0.8885	0.8548	0.8227	0.7921	0.7629	0.7350	0.7084	0.6830	0.6587	0.6355	0.6133
5	0.9515	0.9057	0.8626	0.8219	0.7835	0.7473	0.7130	0.6806	0.6499	0.6209	0.5935	0.5674	0.5428
6	0.9420	0.8880	0.8375	0.7903	0.7462	0.7050	0.5663	0.6302	0.5963	0.5645	0.5346	0.5066	0.4803
7	0.9327	0.8706	0.8131	0.7599	0.7107	0.6651	0.6227	0.5835	0.5470	0.5132	0.4817	0.4523	0.4251
8	0.9235	0.8535	0.7894	0.7307	0.6768	0.6274	0.5820	0.5403	0.5019	0.4665	0.4339	0.4039	0.3762
9	0.9143	0.8368	0.7664	0.7026	0.6446	0.5919	0.5439	0.5002	0.4604	0.4241	0.3909	0.3606	0.3329
10	0.9053	0.8203	0.7441	0.6756	0.6139	0.5584	0.5083	0.4632	0.4224	0.3855	0.3522	0.3220	0.2946
11	0.8963	0.8043	0.7224	0.6496	0.5847	0.5268	0.4751	0.4289	0.3875	0.3505	0.3173	0.2875	0.2607
12	0.8874	0.7885	0.7014	0.6246	0.5568	0.4970	0.4440	0.3971	0.3555	0.3186	0.2858	0.2567	0.2307
13	0.8787	0.7730	0.6810	0.6006	0.5303	0.4688	0.4150	0.3677	0.3262	0.2897	0.2575	0.2292	0.2042
14	0.8700	0.7579	0.6611	0.5775	0.5051	0.4423	0.3878	0.3405	0.2992	0.2633	0.2320	0.2046	0.1807
15	0.8613	0.7430	0.6419	0.5553	0.4810	0.4173	0.3624	0.3152	0.2745	0.2394	0.2090	0.1827	0.1599
16	0.8528	0.7284	0.6232	0.5339	0.4581	0.3936	0.3387	0.2919	0.2519	0.2176	0.1883	0.1631	0.1415
17	0.8444	0.7142	0.6050	0.5134	0.4363	0.3714	0.3166	0.2703	0.2311	0.1978	0.1696	0.1456	0.1252
18	0.8360	0.7002	0.5874	0.4936	0.4155	0.3503	0.2959	0.2502	0.2120	0.1799	0.1528	0.1300	0.1108
19	0.8277	0.6864	0.5703	0.4746	0.3957	0.3305	0.2765	0.2317	0.1945	0.1635	0.1377	0.1161	0.0981
20	0.8195	0.6730	0.5537	0.4564	0.3769	0.3118	0.2584	0.2145	0.1784	0.1486	0.1240	0.1037	0.0868
21	0.8114	0.6598	0.5375	0.4388	0.3589	0.2942	0.2415	0.1987	0.1637	0.1351	0.1117	0.0926	0.0768
22	0.8034	0.6468	0.5219	0.4220	0.3418	0.2775	0.2257	0.1839	0.1502	0.1228	0.1007	0.0826	0.0680
23	0.7954	0.6342	0.5067	0.4057	0.3256	0.2618	0.2109	0.1703	0.1378	0.1117	0.0907	0.0738	0.0601
24	0.7876	0.6217	0.4919	0.3901	0.3101	0.2470	0.1971	0.1577	0.1264	0.1015	0.0817	0.0659	0.0532
25	0.7798	0.6095	0.4776	0.3751	0.2953	0.2330	0.1842	0.1460	0.1160	0.0923	0.0736	0.0588	0.0471
26	0.7720	0.5976	0.4637	0.3607	0.2812	0.2198	0.1722	0.1352	0.1064	0.0839	0.0663	0.0525	0.0417
27	0.7644	0.5859	0.4502	0.3468	0.2678	0.2074	0.1609	0.1252	0.0976	0.0763	0.0597	0.0469	0.0369
28	0.7568	0.5744	0.4371	0.3335	0.2551	0.1956	0.1504	0.1159	0.0895	0.0693	0.0538	0.0419	0.0326
29	0.7493	0.5631	0.4243	0.3207	0.2429	0.1846	0.1406	0.1073	0.0822	0.0630	0.0485	0.0374	0.0289
30	0.7419	0.5521	0.4120	0.3083	0.2314	0.1741	0.1314	0.0994	0.0754	0.0573	0.0437	0.0334	0.0256

Exhibit C-4 Present Value of Ordinary Annuity of 1 per Period

| | | | | | | Interest Rate | | | | | | | |
Number of Years	1%	2%	3%	4%	5%	6%	7%	8%	9%	10%	11%	12%	13%
1	0.9901	0.9804	0.9709	0.9615	0.9524	0.9434	0.9346	0.9259	0.9174	0.9091	0.9009	0.8929	0.8850
2	1.9704	1.9416	1.9135	1.8861	1.8594	1.8334	1.8080	1.7833	1.7591	1.7355	1.7125	1.6901	1.6681
3	2.9410	2.8839	2.8286	2.7751	2.7232	2.6730	2.6243	2.5771	2.5313	2.4869	2.4437	2.4018	2.3612
4	3.9020	3.8077	3.7171	3.6299	3.5460	3.4651	3.3872	3.3121	3.2397	3.1699	3.1024	3.0373	2.9745
5	4.8534	4.7135	4.5797	4.4518	4.3295	4.2124	4.1002	3.9927	3.8897	3.7908	3.6959	3.6048	3.5172
6	5.7955	5.6014	5.4172	5.2421	5.0757	4.9173	4.7665	4.6229	4.4859	4.3553	4.2305	4.1114	3.9975
7	6.7282	6.4720	6.2303	6.0021	5.7864	5.5824	5.3893	5.2064	5.0330	4.8684	4.7122	4.5638	4.4226
8	7.6517	7.3255	7.0197	6.7327	6.4632	6.2098	5.9713	5.7466	5.5348	5.3349	5.1461	4.9676	4.7988
9	8.5660	8.1622	7.7861	7.4353	7.1078	6.8017	6.5152	6.2469	5.9952	5.7590	5.5370	5.3282	5.1317
10	9.4713	8.9826	8.5302	8.1109	7.7217	7.3601	7.0236	6.7101	6.4177	6.1446	5.8892	5.6502	5.4262
11	10.3676	9.7868	9.2526	8.7605	8.3064	7.8869	7.4987	7.1390	6.8052	6.4951	6.2065	5.9377	5.6869
12	11.2551	10.5753	9.9540	9.3851	8.8633	8.3838	7.9427	7.5361	7.1607	6.8137	6.4924	6.1944	5.9176
13	12.1337	11.3484	10.6350	9.9856	9.3936	8.8527	8.3577	7.9038	7.4869	7.1034	6.7499	6.4235	6.1218
14	13.0037	12.1062	11.2961	10.5631	9.8986	9.2950	8.7455	8.2442	7.7862	7.3667	6.9819	6.6282	6.3025
15	13.8651	12.8493	11.9379	11.1184	10.3797	9.7122	9.1079	8.5595	8.0607	7.6061	7.1909	6.8109	6.4624
16	14.7179	13.5777	12.5611	11.6523	10.8378	10.1059	9.4466	8.8514	8.3126	7.8237	7.3792	6.9740	6.6039
17	15.5623	14.2919	13.1661	12.1657	11.2741	10.4773	9.7632	9.1216	8.5436	8.0216	7.5488	7.1196	6.7291
18	16.3983	14.9920	13.7535	12.6593	11.6896	10.8276	10.0591	9.3719	8.7556	8.2014	7.7016	7.2497	6.8399
19	17.2260	15.6785	14.3238	13.1339	12.0853	11.1581	10.3356	9.6036	8.9501	8.3649	7.8393	7.3658	6.9380
20	18.0456	16.3514	14.8775	13.5903	12.4622	11.4699	10.5940	9.8181	9.1285	8.5136	7.9633	7.4694	7.0248
21	18.8570	17.0112	15.4150	14.0292	12.8212	11.7641	10.8355	10.0168	9.2922	8.6487	8.0751	7.5620	7.1016
22	19.6604	17.6580	15.9369	14.4511	13.1630	12.0416	11.0612	10.2007	9.4424	8.7715	8.1757	7.6446	7.1695
23	20.4558	18.2922	16.4436	14.8568	13.4886	12.3034	11.2722	10.3711	9.5802	8.8832	8.2664	7.7184	7.2297
24	21.2434	18.9139	16.9355	15.2470	13.7986	12.5504	11.4693	10.5288	9.7066	8.9847	8.3481	7.7843	7.2829
25	22.0232	19.5235	17.4131	15.6221	14.0939	12.7834	11.6536	10.6748	9.8226	9.0770	8.4217	7.8431	7.3300
26	22.7952	20.1210	17.8768	15.9828	14.3752	13.0032	11.8258	10.8100	9.9290	9.1609	8.4881	7.8957	7.3717
27	23.5596	20.7069	18.3270	16.3296	14.6430	13.2105	11.9867	10.9352	10.0266	9.2372	8.5478	7.9426	7.4086
28	24.3164	21.2813	18.7641	16.6631	14.8981	13.4062	12.1371	11.0511	10.1161	9.3066	8.6016	7.9844	7.4412
29	25.0658	21.8444	19.1885	16.9837	15.1411	13.5907	12.2777	11.1584	10.1983	9.3696	8.6501	8.0218	7.4701
30	25.8077	22.3965	19.6004	17.2920	15.3725	13.7648	12.4090	11.2578	10.2737	9.4269	8.6938	8.0552	7.4957

Exhibit C-5 Future Amount of Ordinary Annuity of 1 per Period

Number

of Years	*Interest Rate*												
	1%	2%	3%	4%	5%	6%	7%	8%	9%	10%	11%	12%	13%
1	1.0000	1.0000	1.0000	1.0000	1.0000	1.0000	1.0000	1.0000	1.0000	1.0000	1.0000	1.0000	1.0000
2	2.0100	2.0200	2.0300	2.0400	2.0500	2.0600	2.0700	2.0800	2.0900	2.1000	2.1100	2.1200	2.1300
3	3.0301	3.0604	3.0909	3.1216	3.1525	3.1836	3.2149	3.2464	3.2781	3.3100	3.3421	3.3744	3.4069
4	4.0604	4.1216	4.1836	4.2465	4.3101	4.3746	4.4399	4.5061	4.5731	4.6410	4.7097	4.7793	4.8498
5	5.1010	5.2040	5.3091	5.4163	5.5256	5.6371	5.7507	5.8666	5.9847	6.1051	6.2278	6.3528	6.4803
6	6.1520	6.3081	6.4684	6.6330	6.8019	6.9753	7.1533	7.3359	7.5233	7.7156	7.9129	8.1152	8.3227
7	7.2135	7.4343	7.6625	7.8983	8.1420	8.3938	8.6540	8.9228	9.2004	9.4872	9.7833	10.0890	10.4047
8	8.2857	8.5830	8.8923	9.2142	9.5491	9.8975	10.2598	10.6366	11.0285	11.4359	11.8594	12.2997	12.7573
9	9.3685	9.7546	10.1591	10.5828	11.0266	11.4913	11.9780	12.4876	13.0210	13.5795	14.1640	14.7757	15.4157
10	10.4622	10.9497	11.4639	12.0061	12.5779	13.1808	13.8164	14.4866	15.1929	15.9374	16.7220	17.5487	18.4197
11	11.5668	12.1687	12.8078	13.4864	14.2068	14.9716	15.7836	16.6455	17.5603	18.5312	19.5614	20.6546	21.8143
12	12.6825	13.4121	14.1920	15.0258	15.9171	16.8699	17.8885	18.9771	20.1407	21.3843	22.7132	24.1331	25.6502
13	13.8093	14.6803	15.6178	16.6268	17.7130	18.8821	20.1406	21.4953	22.9534	24.5227	26.2116	28.0291	29.9847
14	14.9474	15.9739	17.0863	18.2919	19.5986	21.0151	22.5505	24.2149	26.0192	27.9750	30.0949	32.3926	34.8827
15	16.0969	17.2934	18.5989	20.0236	21.5786	23.2760	25.1290	27.1521	29.3609	31.7725	34.4054	37.2797	40.4175
16	17.2579	18.6393	20.1569	21.8245	23.6575	25.6725	27.8881	30.3243	33.0034	35.9497	39.1899	42.7533	46.717
17	18.4304	20.0121	21.7616	23.6975	25.8404	28.2129	30.8402	33.7502	36.9737	40.5447	44.5008	48.8837	53.7391
18	19.6147	21.4123	23.4144	25.6454	28.1324	30.9057	33.9990	37.4502	41.3013	45.5992	50.3959	55.7497	61.7251
19	20.8109	22.8406	25.1169	27.6712	30.5390	33.7600	37.3790	41.4463	46.0185	51.1591	56.9395	63.4397	70.7494
20	22.0190	24.2974	26.8704	29.7781	33.0660	36.7856	40.9955	45.7620	51.1601	57.2750	64.2028	72.0524	80.9468
21	23.2392	25.7833	28.6765	31.9692	35.7193	39.9927	44.3652	50.4229	56.7645	64.0025	72.2651	81.6987	92.4699
22	24.4716	27.2990	30.5368	34.2480	38.5052	43.3923	49.0057	55.4568	62.8733	71.4027	81.2143	92.5026	105.4910
23	25.7163	28.8450	32.4529	36.6179	41.4305	46.9958	53.4361	60.8933	69.5319	79.5430	91.1479	104.6029	120.2048
24	26.9735	30.4219	34.4265	39.0826	44.5020	50.8156	58.1767	66.7648	76.7898	88.4973	102.1742	118.1552	136.8315
25	28.2432	32.0303	36.4593	41.6459	47.7271	54.8645	63.2490	73.1059	84.7009	98.3471	114.4133	133.3339	155.6196
26	29.5256	33.6709	38.5530	44.3117	51.1135	59.1564	68.6765	79.9544	93.3240	109.1818	127.9988	150.3339	176.8501
27	30.8209	35.3443	40.7096	47.0842	54.6691	63.7058	74.4838	87.3508	102.7231	121.0999	143.0786	169.3740	200.8406
28	32.1291	37.0512	42.9309	49.9676	58.4026	68.5281	80.6977	95.3388	112.9682	134.2099	159.8173	190.6989	227.9499
29	33.4504	38.7922	45.2189	52.9663	62.3227	73.6398	87.3465	103.9659	124.1354	148.6309	178.3972	214.5828	258.5834
30	34.7849	40.5681	47.5754	56.0849	66.4388	79.0582	94.4608	113.2832	136.3075	164.4940	199.0209	241.3327	293.1992

579

APPENDIX D

Ratios

This appendix contains the formulas needed to calculate many of the most common accounting ratios, as well as brief explanations for each one. They are listed in alphabetical order.

- *Accounts payable days.* This formula is similar to the accounts payable turnover calculation, except that it converts the amount of outstanding payables into the average number of days of purchases that are currently unpaid. The formula is:

$$\frac{\text{Ending accounts payable}}{\text{Annual purchases} / 365}$$

- *Accounts payable turnover.* This formula reveals the speed with which a company is paying its accounts payable, and is a particularly effective way to determine company liquidity levels when tracked on a time line, so that changes in payment patterns are readily apparent. The formula is:

$$\frac{\text{Total purchases}}{\text{Average level of accounts payable}}$$

- *Accounts receivable days.* This formula is similar to the accounts receivable turnover calculation, except that it converts the amount of outstanding receivables into the average number of days it will take to collect them. The formula is:

$$\frac{(\text{Beginning accounts receivable} + \text{ending accounts receivable}) / 2}{\text{Annualized revenue} / 365}$$

- *Accounts receivable turnover.* This formula is used to determine the number of days over which the average account receivable is outstanding. It is best used when plotted on a trend line, in order to spot and act upon any unfavorable changes. The formula is:

$$\frac{\text{Annualized credit sales}}{(\text{Beginning accounts receivable} + \text{ending accounts receivable}) / 2}$$

* *Backlog to sales ratio.* This formula is a good way to determine if there will be trouble achieving sales goals in the near term, since a low proportion of backlog to sales reveals that only some last-minute orders will allow a company to reach its sales targets. However, the ratio can be misleading if sales are highly seasonal, since the backlog will drop significantly once the prime sales season is over. The formula is:

$$\frac{\text{Dollar total of all orders not yet in production}}{\text{Average monthly revenue}}$$

• *Backlog days ratio.* This formula is similar to the backlog to sales ratio, except that it converts the backlog amount into the number of days sales that they represent. The formula is:

$$\frac{\text{Total backlog}}{\text{Annualized revenue} / 365}$$

• *Bill of material accuracy.* This formula reveals the percentage of line items on a company's bills of material that contain accurate part numbers, quantities, and units of measure. Though this is not strictly an accounting measure, the accuracy of a company's bill of material records has a major impact on the accuracy of its finished goods and work-in-process inventory, and so is of concern to the accountant. The formula is:

$$\frac{\text{Number of accurate parts itemized on a bill of material}}{\text{Total number of parts itemized on a bill of material}}$$

• *Book value.* This formula results in a price per share that should theoretically be realized if a company were to liquidate, paying off all liabilities. It is strictly theoretical, for it presumes that the liquidation value of all assets and liabilities on the books exactly matches the amounts shown on the balance sheet. The formula is:

$$\frac{\text{Stockholder's equity}}{\text{Number of common shares outstanding}}$$

• *Breakeven plant capacity.* This formula reveals the manufacturing capacity level at which a company will break even. This formula must be used with some caution, for the fixed expense level used in its calculation is assumed to be constant through a wide range of capacity levels (which is not always true), while it also assumes that the current level of capacity usage is known (which may be difficult to determine). Consequently, the results may not be precise. The formula is:

$$\frac{\text{Fixed expenses} \times \text{current percent of plant usage}}{\text{Revenue} - \text{variable expenses}}$$

- *Breakeven point.* This formula is used to determine the minimum sales level at which a company or some smaller business unit will generate a profit of exactly zero. It is particularly useful when compared to production capacity, since it can reveal that a company may use nearly all of its capacity just to reach breakeven, and so has no chance to earn more than a small profit even at full capacity. The formula is:

$$\frac{\text{Total operating expenses}}{\text{Average gross margin}}$$

Total operatuing expenses are defined as all expenses related to the business unit that are not part of the cost of goods sold.

- *Capital employed ratio.* This formula is used to determine how efficiently capital is being used to generate sales. It subtracts all assets not directly associated with operations, such as investments, and divides the remainder into annual sales. The formula is:

$$\frac{\text{Annualized revenue}}{\text{(Capital)} - \text{(assets not directly related to operations)}}$$

- *Cash flow adequacy.* This formula is the most comprehensive one for determining if a company's cash flows are sufficient to meet all ongoing commitments outside of standard operations, such as asset purchases, dividend payouts, and debt payments. A ratio of more than one indicates a sufficient level of cash flow. The formula is:

$$\frac{\text{Cash flow from operations}}{\text{All budgeted payments for asset purchases, debt, and dividend payments}}$$

- *Cash ratio.* This formula is more restrictive than the quick ratio, because it compares only those assets that can be immediately converted to cash to any current liabilities (for example, it excludes accounts receivable from the calculation). This gives the best picture of extremely short-term liquidity for an organization. The formula is:

$$\frac{\text{Cash} + \text{Marketable securities}}{\text{Current liabilities}}$$

- *Cash turnover ratio.* This formula is used to determine the level of efficient use that management is making of its cash. Ideally, there should be only the minimum amount of cash on hand to deal with operating needs, while all other cash is shifted to investments. The formula is:

$$\frac{\text{Total sales}}{\text{Total period-end cash}}$$

- *Collection period.* This formula is used to determine the average number of days that invoices are outstanding. Any changes in the collection period over time are indicative of either changes in the level of collection effort, or in the credit policies being extended to customers. The formula is:

$$\frac{\text{Average annualized accounts receivable}}{\text{Average daily credit sales}}$$

- *Current ratio.* This is a simple means for determining a company's level of liquidity. If the ratio of current assets to current liabilities is substantially greater than one, then the company can be said to have good liquidity. However, since a component of this calculation is inventory (which may not be readily convertible to cash), it can be misleading. A better calculation for the purposes of determining liquidity is the quick ratio. The formula for the current ratio is:

$$\frac{\text{Cash + accounts receivable + marketable securities + inventory}}{\text{Accounts payable + other short-term liabilities}}$$

- *Debt/equity ratio.* This formula is used by lenders to determine the degree of leverage that a management team has created. Though this measure will vary widely by industry, a debt level that is higher than the amount of equity will generally be an indication of excessive leverage. The formula is:

$$\frac{\text{Long-term debt + short-term debt}}{\text{Total equity}}$$

- *Dividend payout ratio.* This formula is used to determine the proportion of cash flow that is being consumed by dividend payments. It is most useful when tracked on a time line, so that one can see if there is a trend that may result in a company's inability to pay dividends. The formula is:

$$\frac{\text{Total dividend payments}}{\text{Cash flow from operations}}$$

- *Economic value added.* This formula is used to determine if a company is earning a return on capital that is higher than its cost of capital, and is useful for tracking a company's ability to provide good returns on invested capital to its investors. The formula is:

$$(\text{Net investment}) \times (\text{actual return on assets—required minimum rate of return})$$

- *Fixed asset turnover.* This formula is used to determine the amount of fixed assets needed to obtain a specified sales level. It should not be relied upon for precise predictions of asset investments that will be needed to support increased sales levels, but can be a reasonable method for cross-checking the adequacy of budgeted capital purchases at various levels of sales activity. The formula is:

$$\frac{\text{Net sales}}{(\text{Beginning fixed assets} + \text{ending fixed assets})/2}$$

- *Fixed assets to total assets ratio.* This formula is used to determine the proportion of fixed assets that are likely to be required as other asset levels change. It is most often used as a cross-check when developing budgets, in order to verify if budgeted capital expenditure levels are in line with historical experience. The formula is:

$$\frac{\text{Total fixed assets prior to depreciation}}{\text{Total assets}}$$

- *Fixed assets to debt ratio.* This formula is of most use to a company's lenders, who may have collateralized their lending with its fixed assets. Lenders will have some assurance that they can offset unpaid debts with the sale of company assets if this ratio is less than one. However, the ratio uses the original book value of the fixed assets, rather than their current fair market value, so the ratio can be misleading. The formula is:

$$\frac{\text{Total fixed assets}}{\text{Total collateralized debt}}$$

- *Fringe benefits to direct labor ratio.* This formula is used to determine if a company's benefits expenditures are in line with those of its competitors. It can also be compared to the same ratio for specific departments of companies within other industries, in order to verify that benefit levels are sufficient for specific job categories, as well as industries. The formula is:

$$\frac{\text{Total fringe benefit expense}}{\text{Total labor salary and wage expense}}$$

- *General and administrative productivity.* This formula is used to compare the overhead costs in the selling, general and administrative expense categories to overall sales activity. It can be used for benchmarking purposes to see if a company's expenses in these areas are in line with those of similar companies. The formula is:

$$\frac{\text{Selling, general \& administrative expenses}}{\text{Annualized revenue}}$$

- *Indirect to direct labor ratio.* This formula is used to determine the level of efficiency a company has achieved in keeping its supporting staff of indirect labor personnel as small as possible. The formula is:

$$\frac{\text{Number of indirect labor full-time equivalents}}{\text{Number of direct labor full-time equivalents}}$$

- *Inventory accuracy.* This formula is used to determine the record accuracy within the inventory database. It requires one to compare a detailed list of booked inventory items to the inventory physically in the warehouse, and record as errors anything that has an inaccurate part or product description, location, quantity, or unit of measure. This information is critical to the accountant, who relies on accurate inventory records to create the financial statements. The formula is:

$$\frac{\text{Number of accurate inventory test items}}{\text{Total number of inventory items sampled}}$$

- *Inventory days on hand.* This formula is used to determine the number of days it would take to use up all of the inventory on hand, given an average level of sales to do so. The formula is:

$$365 \text{ days} \times \frac{\text{Ending inventory}}{\text{Annualized cost of goods sold}}$$

- *Inventory turnover ratio.* This formula is frequently used to compare the proportion of inventory on hand to the level of sales. It can be compared to industry averages to see if there is too much inventory in stock. However, it can be misleading if sales levels fluctuate considerably during the year, resulting in wide fluctuations in the measurement. The formula is:

$$\frac{\text{Annualized cost of goods sold}}{\text{Average inventory}}$$

- *Net income to capital ratio.* This formula is used to determine the return, free and clear of all expenses, that investors are receiving on their invested equity. Though this provides some information to investors, the gain or loss on an investor's equity is also influenced by the perception of the future value of the company, which may be quite unrelated to the net income figure used in the calculation of this ratio. The formula is:

$$\frac{\text{Net income}}{\text{Stockholders' equity}}$$

- *Number of times interest earned.* This formula is used to determine the amount of excess cash that a company has available to cover its debt payments. If there is barely enough cash available to do so, then the organization has reached the practical limit of its borrowing capacity. The formula is:

$$\frac{\text{Average interest expense}}{\text{Total excess cash flow before interest payments}}$$

- *Obsolete inventory percentage.* This formula is used to determine the proportion of inventory that may require an obsolescence reserve. It is a highly judgmental calculation, since the "no recent usage" part of the calculation can refer to any time period that one may choose. The formula is:

$$\frac{\text{Cost of inventory items with no recent usage}}{\text{Total inventory cost}}$$

- *Overhead to direct cost ratio.* This formula may be of interest when a company is deciding whether to use an activity-based costing (ABC) system. If this ratio is greater than one, then a strong case can be made to switch to ABC, because the company's cost structure leans so heavily toward overhead costs that it is necessary to take the greatest possible care in allocating it properly. The formula is:

$$\frac{\text{Total overhead costs}}{\text{Total direct material} + \text{total direct labor costs}}$$

- *Price-earnings ratio.* This formula is used by investors to compare the relative price of a company's stock in relation to that of other companies in the same industry. If the ratio is low relative to the industry, then it may be worth buying, on the grounds that the market price of the stock should eventually return to the mean by rising. Also, a high ratio shows that investors have high expectations for the company, and so have bid up its price. The formula is:

$$\frac{\text{Current market price per share}}{\text{Earnings per share}}$$

- *Purchase discounts proportion of total payments.* This formula is used to determine the percentage of accounts payable for which discounts are being taken, and is most useful when tracked on a time line, in order to see if there are changes in the percentage that are indicative of missed discounts. The formula is:

$$\frac{\text{Total number of purchase discounts taken}}{\text{Total number of supplier invoices paid}}$$

- *Operating cash flow.* This formula is used to strip away all impacts on reported cash flows that are caused by financing activities, so that one can see how much cash flow (if any) is being created by operations on an ongoing basis. The formula is:

$$\text{Profit} + \text{non-cash expenses} +/- \text{changes in working capital}$$

- *Quick ratio.* This formula is used to determine a company's liquidity. It is better than the current ratio, because it excludes the impact of inventory (which may not be easily liquidated). A quick ratio of greater than one is indicative of a reasonable level of liquidity. The formula is:

$$\frac{\text{Cash} + \text{accounts receivable} + \text{marketable securities}}{\text{Accounts payable} + \text{other short-term liabilities}}$$

- *Retained earnings to capital ratio.* This formula is useful for determining the proportion of a company's capital that is comprised of retained profits. A high ratio reveals that a company has not only brought in a large amount of funds through profits, but also that it has retained the funds, rather than paid them out through dividends. The formula is:

$$\frac{\text{Retained earnings}}{\text{Stockholders' equity}}$$

- *Return on assets.* This formula is used to determine if company assets are being efficiently utilized to create profits. It focuses attention on the amount of assets used within a company, and frequently leads to tighter management of the capital budgeting process. Be aware that the "total assets" part of the equation includes all assets, such as cash, accounts receivable, inventory, and fixed assets. A common misconception is to only include fixed assets in the calculation. The formula is:

$$\frac{\text{Net income}}{\text{Total assets}}$$

- *Sales per person.* This formula gives an indication of the efficiency of a company in generating sales and manufacturing products or services. It should be compared to industry averages, since this measure varies widely by industry. The formula is:

$$\frac{\text{Revenue}}{\text{Total number of full-time equivalent employees}}$$

- *Scrap percentage.* This formula tracks the proportion of scrap that is spun off by a production operation. It is most useful when calculated for specific production lines or machines, so that problem areas can be more quickly identified and corrected. The formula is:

$$\frac{\text{(Actual cost of goods sold)} - \text{(standard cost of goods sold)}}{\text{Standard cost of goods sold}}$$

- *Work-in-process turnover.* This formula is useful for determining the proportion of work-in-process inventory that is required to produce a specific amount of product. It is closely watched by those companies installing accelerated production systems, such as just-in-time, that should result in reduced inventory levels in this area. The formula is:

$$\frac{\text{Total work-in-process inventory}}{\text{Annual cost of goods sold}}$$

- *Working capital productivity.* This formula is used to determine changes in the proportion of working capital to sales; a reduction in the proportion of working capital is evidence of enhanced levels of operational improvement. The formula is:

$$\frac{\text{Annual net sales}}{\text{(Beginning working capital} + \text{ending working capital)}/2}$$

APPENDIX E

Dictionary of Accounting Terms

Absorption costing   A methodology under which all manufacturing costs are assigned to products, while all non-manufacturing costs are expensed in the current period.[1]

Accelerated depreciation   Any of several methods that recognize an increased amount of depreciation in the earliest years of asset usage. This results in increased tax benefits in the first few years of asset usage.[1]

Accounting change   An alteration in the accounting methodology or estimates used in the reporting of financial statements, usually requiring discussion in a footnote attached to the financial statements.

Accounting entity   A business for which a separate set of accounting records is being maintained.

Accounts payable   A current liability on the balance sheet, representing short-term obligations to pay suppliers.

Accounts receivable   A current asset on the balance sheet, representing short-term amounts due from customers who have purchased on account.

Accrual accounting   The recording of revenue when earned and expenses when incurred, irrespective of the dates on which the associated cash flows occur.

Accumulated depreciation   The sum total of all deprecation expense recognized to date on a depreciable fixed asset.

Activity-based costing (ABC)   A cost allocation system that compiles costs and assigns them to activities based on relevant activity drivers. The cost of these activities can then be charged to products or customers to arrive at a much more relevant allocation of costs than was previously the case.[1]

Actual cost   The actual expenditure made to acquire an asset, which includes the supplier-invoiced expense, plus the costs to deliver and set up the asset.[1]

---

[1]Reprinted with permission: Bragg, *Cost Accounting: A Comprehensive Guide,* John Wiley & Sons, 2001, Appendix B.

Additional paid-in capital   Any payment received from investors for stock that exceeds the par value of the stock.

Advance   A payment made by a customer to the company, or by the company to a supplier, in advance of the performance of any associated service or delivery of product.

Allocation   The process of storing costs in one account and shifting them to other accounts, based on some relevant measure of activity.[1]

Allowance for bad debts   An offset to the accounts receivable balance, against which bad debts are charged. The presence of this allowance allows one to avoid severe changes in the period-to-period bad debt expense by expensing a steady amount to the allowance account in every period, rather than writing off large bad debts to expense on an infrequent basis.

Amortization   The write-off of an asset over the period when the asset is used. This term is most commonly applied to the gradual write-down of intangible items, such as goodwill or organizational costs.

Annual report   A report issued to a company's shareholders, creditors, and regulatory organizations at the end of its fiscal year. It typically contains at least an income statement, balance sheet, statement of cash flows, and accompanying footnotes. It may also contain management comments, an audit report, and other supporting schedules that may be required by regulatory organizations.

Appreciation   An increase in the perceived or actual value of an asset.

Asset   A resource, recorded through a transaction, that is expected to yield a benefit to a company.

Average inventory   The beginning inventory for a period, plus the amount at the end of the period, divided by two. It is most commonly used in situations in which just using the period-end inventory yields highly variable results, due to constant and large changes in the inventory level.[1]

Bad debt   An account receivable that cannot be collected.

Balance sheet   A report that summarizes all assets, liabilities, and equity for a company for a given point in time.

Bank reconciliation   A comparison between the cash position recorded on a company's books and the position noted on the records of its bank, usually resulting in some changes to the book balance to account for transactions that are recorded on the bank's records but not the company's.

Batch cost   A cost that is incurred when a group of products or services are produced, and which cannot be identified to specific products or services within each group.[1]

Bill of materials   An itemization of the parts and subassemblies required to create a product, frequently including assumed scrap rates that will arise as part of the production process.[1]

Book inventory   The amount of money invested in inventory, as per a company's accounting records. It is comprised of the beginning inventory balance, plus the cost of any receipts, less the cost of sold or scrapped inventory. It may be significantly different from the actual on-hand inventory, if the two are not periodically reconciled.[1]

Book value   An asset's original cost, less any depreciation that has been subsequently incurred.[1]

Bottleneck   An operation in the midst of a manufacturing or service process in which the required production level matches or exceeds the actual capacity.[1]

Breakeven point   The sales level at which a company, division, or product line makes a profit of exactly zero, and is computed by dividing all fixed costs by the average gross margin percentage.[1]

Budget   A set of interlinked plans that quantitatively describe a company's projected future operations.

By-product   A product that is an ancillary part of the primary production process, having a minor resale value in comparison to the value of the primary product being manufactured. Any proceeds from the sale of a by-product are typically offset against the cost of the primary product, or recorded as miscellaneous revenue.[1]

Capital   The investment by a company's owners in a business, plus the impact of any accumulated gains or losses.

Capital asset   A fixed asset, something that is expected to have long-term usage within a company, and which exceeds a minimum dollar amount (known as the capitalization limit, or cap limit).

Capital budgeting   The series of steps one follows when justifying the decision to purchase an asset, usually including an analysis of costs and related benefits, which should include a discounted cash flow analysis of the stream of all future cash flows resulting from the purchase of the asset.[1]

Capital gain   The gain recognized on the sale of a capital item (fixed asset), calculated by subtracting its sale price from its original purchase price (less the impact of any associated depreciation).

Capital lease   A lease in which the lessee obtains some ownership rights over the asset involved in the transaction, resulting in the recording of the asset as company property on its general ledger.

Capitalize   A purchase that has been recorded on the company books as an asset. The grounds for capitalizing an item include a purchase price that is higher than a minimum limit (known as the capitalization limit) and an estimated lifetime for the item that will exceed one year.

Chart of accounts   A listing of all accounts used in the general ledger, usually sorted in order of account number.

Consolidation   A summarization of the financial statements of a parent company and those of its subsidiaries over which it has voting control of common stock.

Constant dollar accounting   A method for restating financial statements by reducing or increasing reported revenues and expenses by changes in the consumer price index, thereby achieving greater comparability between accounting periods.[1]

Contribution margin   The margin that results when variable production costs are subtracted from revenue. It is most useful for making incremental pricing decisions where a company must cover its variable costs, though perhaps not all of its fixed costs.[1]

Corporation   A legal entity, organized under state laws, whose investors purchase shares of stock as evidence of ownership in it. A corporation is a legal entity, which eliminates much of the liability for the corporation's actions from its investors.

Cost   The expense incurred to create and sell a product or service. If a product is not sold, then it is recorded as an asset, whereas the sale of a product or service will result in the recording of all related costs as an expense.[1]

Cost depletion   A method of expensing the cost of a resource consumed by first determining the total investment in the resource (such as the procurement of a coal mine), then determining the total amount of extractable resource (such as tons of available coal), and then assigning costs to each consumed unit of the resource, based on the proportion of the total available amount that has been used.[1]

Cost driver   A factor that directly impacts the incidence of a cost, and which is generally based on varying levels of activity.[1]

Cost object   An item for which a cost is compiled. For example, this can be a product, a service, a project, a customer, or an activity.[1]

Cost of capital   The blended cost of a company's currently outstanding debt instruments and equity, weighted by the comparative proportions of each one. During a capital budgeting review, the expected return from a capital purchase must exceed this cost of capital, or else a company will experience a net loss on the transaction.[1]

Cost of goods sold   The accumulated total of all costs used to create a product or service, which is then sold. These costs fall into the general sub-categories of direct labor, materials, and overhead.[1]

Cost pool   A cluster of cost items.[1]

Current asset   Typically the cash, accounts receivable, and inventory accounts on the balance sheet, or any other assets that are expected to be liquidated within a short time interval.

Current cost   Under target costing concepts, this is the cost that would be applied to a new product design if no additional steps were taken to reduce costs, such as through value engineering or kaizen costing. Under traditional costing concepts, this is the cost of manufacturing a product with work methods, materials, and specifications currently in use.[1]

Current liability   This is typically the accounts payable, short-term notes payable, and accrued expense accounts on the balance sheet, or any other liabilities that are expected to be liquidated within a short time interval.

Debt   Funds owed to another entity.

Default   The failure by a debtor to make a principal or interest payment in a timely manner.

Deficit   A negative balance in the retained earnings account that is caused by cumulative losses that exceed the amount of equity.

Depletion   The reduction in a natural resource, which equates to the cost of goods sold in a manufacturing organization.[1]

Depreciation   Both the decline in value of an asset over time, as well as the gradual expensing of an asset over time, roughly in accordance with its level of usage or decline in value through that period.

Direct cost   A cost that can be clearly associated with specific activities or products.[1]

Direct costing   A costing methodology that only assigns direct labor and material costs to a product, and which does not include any allocated indirect costs (which are all charged off to the current period).[1]

Direct labor   Labor that is specifically incurred to create a product.[1]

Direct materials cost   The cost of all materials used in a cost object, such as finished goods.[1]

Direct materials mix variance   The variance between the budgeted and actual mixes of direct materials costs, both using the actual total quantity used. This variance isolates the unit cost of each item, excluding all other variables.[1]

Director   A member of a company's Board of Directors.

Disclosure   Additional information attached to a company's financial statements, usually as explanation for activities whose related transactions have influenced the financial statements.

Discontinued operation   A business segment that has been or is planned to be closed or sold off.

Discounted cash flow   A technique that determines the present value of future cash flows by applying a rate to each periodic cash flow that is derived from the cost of capital. Multiplying this discount by each future cash flow results in an amount that is the present value of all the future cash flows.[1]

Dividend   A payment made to shareholders that is proportional to the number of shares owned. It is authorized by the Board of Directors.

Driver   A factor that has a direct impact on the incurring of a cost. For example, adding an employee results in new costs to purchase office equipment for that person; therefore, additions to headcount are cost driver for office expenses.[1]

Economic life   The period over which a company expects to be able to use an asset.

Entry   The act of recording an accounting transaction in the accounting books.

Equity   The difference between the total of all recorded assets and liabilities on the balance sheet.

Exit value   The value that an asset is expected to have at the time it is sold at a predetermined point in the future.

Expenditure   A payment or the incurrence of a liability by an entity.

Expense   The reduction in value of an asset as it is used for current company operations.

Extraordinary item   A transaction that rarely occurs, and which is unusual, such as expropriation of company property by a foreign government. It is reported as a separate line item on the income statement.

Factoring   The sale of accounts receivable to a third party, with the third party bearing the risk of loss if the accounts receivable cannot be collected.

Factory overhead   All the costs incurred during the manufacturing process, minus the costs of direct labor and materials.[1]

Fair market value   The price that an asset or service will fetch on the open market.

Finished goods inventory   Goods that have been completed by the manufacturing process, or purchased in a complete form, but which have not yet been sold to customers.[1]

First in, first-out costing method   A process costing methodology that assigns the earliest cost of production and materials to those units being sold, while the latest costs of production and materials are assigned to those units still retained in inventory.[1]

Fiscal year   A 12 month period over which a company reports on the activities that appear in its annual financial statements. The 12 month period may conform to the calendar year, or end on some other date that more closely conforms to a company's natural business cycle.

Fixed asset   An item with a longevity greater than one year, and which exceeds a company's minimum capitalization limit. It is not purchased with the intent of immediate resale, but rather for productive use within a company.[1]

Fixed cost   A cost that does not vary in the short run, irrespective of changes in any cost drivers. For example, the rent on a building will not change until the lease runs out or is re-negotiated, irrespective of the level of business activity within that building.[1]

Fixed overhead   That portion of total overhead costs which remains constant in size irrespective of changes in activity within a certain range.[1]

Freight in   The transportation cost associated with the delivery of goods from a supplier to a company.

Freight out   The transportation cost associated with the delivery of goods from a company to its customers.

Gain   The profit earned on the sale of an asset, computed by subtracting its book value from the revenue received from its sale.

General ledger   The master set of accounts that summarizes all transactions occurring within a company. There may be a subsidiary set of ledgers that summarizes into the general ledger.

Generally accepted accounting principles   The rules that accountants follow when processing accounting transactions and creating financial reports. The rules are primarily derived from regulations promulgated by the various branches of the AICPA Council.

Goodwill   The excess of the price paid to buy another company over the book value of its assets and the increase in cost of its fixed assets to fair market value.

Go public   The process of offering a company's shares for sale to the public through an initial public offering.

Gross margin   Revenues less the cost of goods sold.[1]

Gross sales   The total sales recorded prior to sales discounts and returns.

Historical cost   The original cost required to perform a service or purchase an asset.[1]

Hurdle rate   The minimum rate of return that a capital purchase proposal must pass before it can be authorized for acquisition. The hurdle rate should be no lower than a company's incremental cost of capital.

Income Net earnings after all expenses for an accounting period are subtracted from all revenues recognized during that period.

Income statement A financial report that summarizes a company's revenue, cost of goods sold, gross margin, other costs, income, and tax obligations.

Income tax A government tax on the income earned by an individual or corporation.

Incremental cost The difference in costs between alternative actions.[1]

Indirect cost A cost that is not directly associated with a single activity or event. Such costs are frequently clumped into an overhead pool and allocated to various activities, based on an allocation method that has a perceived or actual linkage between the indirect cost and the activity.[1]

Indirect labor The cost of any labor that supports the production process, but which is not directly involved in the active conversion of materials into finished products.[1]

Intangible asset A nonphysical asset with a life greater than one year. Examples are goodwill, patents, trademarks, and copyrights.

Interest The cost of funds loaned to an entity. It can also refer to the equity ownership of an investor in a business entity.

Internal rate of return The rate of return at which the present value of a series of future cash flows equals the present value of all associated costs. This measure is most commonly used in capital budgeting.[1]

Invoice A document submitted to a customer, identifying a transaction for which the customer owes payment to the issuer.

Job A distinctly identifiable batch of a product.[1]

Joint cost The cost of a production process that creates more than one product at the same time.[1]

Joint product A product that has the highest sales value from among a group of products that are the result of a joint production process.[1]

Journal entry The formal accounting entry used to identify a business transaction. The entry itemizes accounts that are debited and credited, and should include some description of the reason for the entry.

Just-in-time manufacturing The term for several manufacturing innovations that result in a "pull" method of production, in which each manufacturing workstation creates just enough product for the immediate needs of the next workstation in the production process.[1]

Kaizen costing The process of continual cost reduction that occurs after a product design has been completed and is now in production. Cost reduction techniques can include working with suppliers to reduce the costs in *their* processes, implementing less costly re-designs of the product, or reducing waste costs.[1]

Labor efficiency variance The difference between the amount of time that was budgeted to be used by the direct labor staff and the amount actually used, multiplied by the standard labor rate per hour.[1]

Labor rate variance The difference between the actual and standard direct labor rates actually paid to the direct labor staff, multiplied by the number of actual hours worked.[1]

Last-in, first-out   An inventory costing methodology that bases the recognized cost of sales on the most recent costs incurred, while the cost of ending inventory is based on the earliest costs incurred. The underlying reasoning for this costing system is the assumption that goods are sold in the reverse order of their manufacture.[1]

Leasehold improvement   This is any upgrade to leased property by a lessee that will be usable for more than one year, and which exceeds the lessee's capitalization limit. It is recorded as a fixed asset and depreciated over a period no longer than the life of the underlying lease.

Ledger   A book or database in which accounting transactions are stored and summarized.

Lessee   The entity that contracts to make rental payments to a lessor in exchange for the use of an asset.

Lessor   The entity that rents property that it owns to a second party in exchange for a periodic set of rental payments.

Leveraged buyout   The purchase of one business entity by another, largely using borrowed funds. The borrowings are typically paid off through the future cash flow of the purchased entity.

Liability   A dollar amount of obligation payable to another entity.

Liquidation   The process of selling off all the assets of a business entity, settling its liabilities, and closing it down as a legal entity.

Long-term debt   A debt for which payments will be required for a period of more than one year into the future.

Loss   An excess of expenses over revenues, either for a single business transaction or in reference to the sum of all transactions for an accounting period.

Loss carryback   The offsetting of a current year loss against the reported taxable income of previous years.

Loss carryforward   The offsetting of a current year loss against the reported taxable income for future years.

Lower of cost or market   An accounting valuation rule that is used to reduce the reported cost of inventory to its current resale value, if that cost is lower than its original cost of acquisition or manufacture.[1]

Manufacturing resource planning (MRP II)   An expansion of the material requirements planning concept, with additional computer-based capabilities in the areas of direct labor and machine capacity planning.[1]

Marginal cost   The incremental change in the unit cost of a product as a result of a change in the volume of its production.[1]

Marketable security   An easily traded investment, such as treasury bills, which is recorded as a current asset, since it is easily convertible into cash.

Market value   The price at which a product or service could be sold on the open market.

Markup   An increase in the cost of a product to arrive at its selling price.

Matching principle   The process of linking recognized revenue to any associated costs, thereby showing the net impact of all transactions related to the recognition of revenue.

Materiality   The proportional size of a financial misstatement. It can be construed as the net impact on reported profits, or the percentage or dollar change in a specific line item.

Material requirements planning (MRP)   A computer-driven production methodology that manufactures products based on an initial demand forecast. It tends to result in more inventory of all types than a just-in-time (JIT) production system.[1]

Materials price variance   The difference between the actual and budgeted cost to acquire materials, multiplied by the total number of units purchased.[1]

Materials quantity variance   The difference between the actual and budgeted quantities of material used in the production process, multiplied by the standard cost per unit.[1]

Merger   The combination of two or more entities into a single entity, usually with one of the original entities retaining control.

Moving average inventory method   An inventory costing methodology that calls for the re-calculation of the average cost of all parts in stock after every purchase. Therefore, the moving average is the cost of all units subsequent to the latest purchase, divided by their total cost.[1]

Negative goodwill   A term used to describe a situation in which a business combination results in the fair market value of all assets purchased being more than the purchase price.

Net income   The excess of revenues over expenses, including the impact of income taxes.

Net present value   A discounted cash flow methodology that uses a required rate of return (usually a firm's cost of capital) to determine the present value of a stream of future cash flows, resulting in a net positive or negative value.[1]

Net realizeable value   The expected revenue to be gained from the sale of an item or service, less the costs of the sale transaction.

Net sales   Total revenue, less the cost of sales returns, allowances, and discounts.

Obsolescence   The reduction in utility of an inventory item or fixed asset. If it is an inventory item, then a reserve is created to reduce the value of the inventory by the estimated amount of obsolescence. If it is a fixed asset, the depreciation method and timing will be set to approximate the rate and amount of obsolescence.

Operating expense   Any expense associated with the general, sales, and administrative functions of a business.

Operating income   The net income of a business, less the impact of any financial activity, such as interest expense or investment income, as well as taxes and extraordinary items.

Operating lease   The rental of an asset from a lessor, but not under terms that would qualify it as a capital lease.

Opportunity cost   Lost revenue that would otherwise have been realized if a different decision point had been selected.

Other assets   A cluster of accounts that are listed after fixed assets on the balance sheet, and which contain minor assets that cannot be reasonably fit into any of the other main asset categories.

Owners' equity   The total of all capital contributions and retained earnings on a business's balance sheet.

Paid-in capital   Any payment received from investors for stock that exceeds the par value of the stock.

Parent company   A company that retains control over one or more other companies.

Pareto analysis   The 80:20 ratio that states that 20% of the variables included in an analysis are responsible for 80% of the results. For example, 20% of all customers are responsible for 80% of all customer service activity, or 20% of all inventory items comprise 80% of the inventory value.[1]

Partnership   A form of business organization in which owners have unlimited personal liability for the actions of the business, though this problem has been mitigated through the use of the limited liability partnership.

Par value   The stated value of a stock, which is recorded in the capital stock account. Equity distributions cannot drop the value of stock below this minimum amount.

Payback method   A capital budgeting analysis method that calculates the amount of time it will take to recoup the investment in a capital asset, with no regard for the time cost of money.[1]

Pension plan   A formal agreement between an entity and its employees, whereby the entity agrees to provide some benefits to the employees upon their retirement.

Perpetual inventory   A system that continually tracks all additions to and deletions from inventory, resulting in more accurate inventory records and a running total for the cost of goods sold in each period.[1]

Pooling of interests   An method for accounting for a business combination. When used, the expenses of the combination are charged against income at once, and the net income of the acquired company is added to the full-year reported results of the acquiring company.

Preferred stock   A type of stock that usually pays a fixed dividend prior to any distributions to the holders of common stock. In the event of liquidation, it must be paid off before common stock. It can, but rarely does, have voting rights.

Prepaid expense   An expenditure that is paid for in one accounting period, but which will not be entirely consumed until a future period. Consequently, it is carried on the balance sheet as an asset until it is consumed.

Privately held   A company that is entirely owned by a small number of people; further, its shares are not publicly traded.

Process   A series of linked activities that result in a specific objective. For example, the payroll process requires the calculation of hours worked, multiplication by hourly rates, and the subtraction of taxes before the final objective is reached, which is the printing of the paycheck.[1]

Process costing   A costing methodology that arrives at an individual product cost through the calculation of average costs for large quantities of identical products.[1]

Product cost   The total of all costs assigned to a product, typically including direct labor, materials (with normal spoilage included), and overhead.[1]

Production yield variance The difference between the actual and budgeted proportions of product resulting from a production process, multiplied by the standard unit cost.[1]

Profit center An entity within a corporation against which both revenues and costs are recorded. This results in a separate financial statement for each such entity, which reveals a net profit or loss, as well as a return on any assets used by the entity.[1]

Pro forma A set of financial statements that incorporates some assumptions, usually regarding future events. For example, pro forma statements can be constructed that extend a company's financial statements through the end of its fiscal year, and which contain assumptions regarding the final few months of the year, which have not yet occurred.

Property, plant, and equipment This item is comprised of all types of fixed assets recorded on the balance sheet, and is intended to reveal the sum total of all tangible, long-term assets used to conduct business.

Proration The allocation of either under- or over-allocated overhead costs among the work-in-process, finished goods, and cost of goods sold accounts at the end of an accounting period.[1]

Public offering The sale of new securities to the investing public.

Purchase method An accounting method used to combine the financial statements of companies. This involves recording the acquired assets at fair market value, and the excess of the purchase price over this value as goodwill, which will be amortized over time.

Quick asset Any asset that can be converted into cash on short notice. This is a subset of a current asset, for it does not include inventory. Its most common components are the cash, marketable securities, and accounts receivable accounts.

Raw materials inventory The total cost of all component parts currently in stock that have not yet been used in work-in-process or finished goods production.[1]

Recognition The act of verifying the existence of a business transaction by recording it in the accounting records.

Replacement cost The cost that would be incurred to replace an existing asset with one having the same utility.[1]

Reporting period The time period for which transactions are compiled into a set of financial statements.

Retained earnings A company's accumulated earnings since its inception, less any distributions to shareholders.

Revenue An inflow of cash, accounts receivable, or barter from a customer in exchange for the provision of a service or product to that customer by a company.[1]

Rework Refers to a product that does not meet a company's minimum quality standards, but which is then repaired in order to meet those standards.[1]

Sales allowance A reduction in a price that is allowed by the seller, due to a problem with the sold product or service.

Sales discount A reduction in the price of a product or service that is offered by the seller in exchange for early payment by the buyer.

Sales value at split-off   A cost allocation methodology that allocates joint costs to joint products in proportion to their relative sales values at the split-off point.[1]

Salvage value   The expected revenue to be garnered from the sale of a fixed asset at the end of its useful life.

Scrap   The excess unusable material that is left over after a product has been manufactured.[1]

Security   Either the collateral on a loan, or some type of equity ownership or debt, such as a stock option or note payable.

Segment reporting   A portion of the financial statements that breaks out the results of specific business units.

Selling price variance   The difference between the actual and budgeted selling price for a product, multiplied by the actual number of units sold.[1]

Setup cost   The cluster of one-time costs incurred whenever a production batch is run, which includes the cost to configure a machine for new production and all batch-related paperwork.[1]

Share   The minimum unit of ownership in a corporation.

Shrinkage   The excess of inventory listed in the accounting books of record, but which no longer exists in the actual inventory. Its disappearance may be due to theft, damage, miscounting, or evaporation.[1]

Split-off point   The point in a production process when clearly identifiable joint costs can be identified within the process.[1]

Spoilage, abnormal   Spoilage arising from the production process that exceeds the normal or expected rate of spoilage. Since it is not a recurring or expected cost of ongoing production, it is expensed to the current period.[1]

Spoilage, normal   The amount of spoilage that naturally arises as part of a production process, no matter how efficient that process may be.[1]

Standard cost   A predetermined cost that is based on original engineering designs and production methodologies. It is frequently used to determine the degree of additional actual costs incurred above the standard rates.[1]

Statement of cash flows   Part of the financial statements; it summarizes an entity's cash inflows and outflows in relation to financing, operating, and investing activities.

Statement of retained earnings   An adjunct to the balance sheet, providing more detailed information about the beginning balance, changes, and ending balance in the retained earnings account during the reporting period.

Step cost   A cost that does not change steadily, but rather at discrete points. For example, a facility cost will remain steady until additional floor space is constructed, at which point the cost will increase to a new and higher level.[1]

Stock certificate   A document that identifies a stockholder's ownership share in a corporation.

Stockholder   A person or entity that owns shares in a corporation.

Stock option   A right to purchase a specific maximum number of shares at a specific price no later than a specific date. It is a commonly used form of incentive compensation.

Subsidiary account   An account that is kept within a subsidiary ledger, which in turn summarizes into the general ledger.

Subsidiary company   A company that is controlled by another company through ownership of the majority of its voting stock.

Transaction   A business event that has a monetary impact on an entity's financial statements, and is recorded as an entry in its accounting records.

Transfer price   The price at which one part of a company sells a product or service to another part of the same company.[1]

Transferred-in cost   The cost that a product accumulates during its tenure in another department that is earlier in the production process.[1]

Unearned revenue   A payment from a customer that cannot yet be recognized as earned revenue, because the offsetting service or product for which the money was paid has not yet been delivered.

Unissued stock   Stock that has been authorized for use, but which has not yet been released for sale to prospective shareholders.

Useful life   The estimated life span of a fixed asset, during which it can be expected to contribute to company operations.

Variable cost   A cost that changes in amount in relation to changes in a related activity.[1]

Variance   The difference between an actual measured result and a basis, such as a budgeted amount.[1]

Working capital   The amount of a company's current assets minus its current liabilities; it is considered to be a prime measure of its level of liquidity.

Work-in-process inventory   Inventory that has been partially converted through the production process, but for which additional work must be completed before it can be recorded as finished goods inventory.[1]

Write off   The transfer of some or all of the contents of an asset account into an expense account upon the realization that the asset no longer can be converted into cash, can be of no further use to the company, or has no market value.

INDEX